The Jewish Thought of
EMIL FACKENHEIM

Emil Fackenheim, 1986.

The Jewish Thought of
EMIL FACKENHEIM

•A READER•

Edited and Introduced by Michael L. Morgan

Selected in Collaboration with Emil Fackenheim

WAYNE STATE UNIVERSITY PRESS • DETROIT • 1987

Library of Congress Cataloging-in-Publication Data

Fackenheim, Emil L.
  The Jewish thought of Emil Fackenheim.

  "Bibliography of works by Emil Fackenheim": p.
  Includes bibliographical references and index.
    1. Judaism—20th century.   2. Judaism—Doctrines.
3. Holocaust, Jewish (1939–1945)   4. Holocaust
(Jewish theology)   I. Morgan, Michael L., 1944–
II. Title.
BM565.F33   1987   296   87-2116
ISBN 0-8143-1820-7
ISBN 0-8143-1821-5 (pbk.)

Frontispiece photo by Cynthia De Grand, Bloomington, Indiana.

Grateful acknowledgment is made to the Wayne State
University Press Board of Advisors Fund Account for financial
assistance in the publication of this volume.

Contents

Preface

This book is Michael Morgan's as much as it is mine. He not only wrote the introductions but also made the selections and gave structure to the whole. I have given advice and approved the final product, so that in this sense the book may be considered as "authorized." However, as a whole it bears the stamp of his understanding and his judgment. Since one is too close to one's own thought, it is better so, provided the editor has the necessary qualifications. This is certainly true of Professor Morgan. He is a prizewinning university teacher. And he belongs to that extremely small group that may be called Jewish philosophers. What is "Jewish philosophy," as distinct from the wider category "Jewish thought"? It comes to be only when, in search for truth in which all remnants of apologetics are cast aside, a specifically Jewish commitment becomes involved with philosophy at large; and when, out of the "perplexity" that such an involvement inevitably generates, a positive result emerges. The most authoritative work in Jewish philosophy is Maimonides' *Guide for the Perplexed*.

In history up to the present time, Jewish philosophy has come to be found only in two traditions, in the Jewish involvement with Greek philosophy that began with Philo and lasted to the end of the Middle Ages, and in the Jewish involvement with modern continental, mostly German, philosophy that began with Spinoza and has not yet ended. Modern Jewish philosophy reached a high point in the works of Hermann Cohen, Martin Buber, and Franz Rosenzweig. Where it must go after the cataclysmic events in recent Jewish history is for future Jewish philosophy to explore.

In view of the facts just stated, a Jewish philosopher today must be professionally competent not only in Jewish but also in either Greek or modern continental philosophy. My own competence lies in the latter, Professor Morgan's in the former. Nevertheless, he is fully competent to do an anthology of my Jewish writings, just as I would consider myself competent to do an anthology of a medieval Jewish philosopher's writings, provided, that is, I had become familiar with his works. No one is more familiar with my Jewish writings than Michael Morgan.

Only the first two items in this anthology are included at my own special request. Both are hitherto unpublished. In 1938 several rabbinical students at the Berlin *Hochschule für die Wissenschaft des Judentums* planned a book born of a shared commitment. Obviously we would have to leave Nazi Germany. We had

7

no idea where fate would carry us. (The possibility that our fate might be a gas chamber occurred to none of us, nor to anyone else.) Nevertheless, we were determined not to be just victims of fate. We would go wherever fate would take us with our Jewish commitment, and before leaving we would publish a book spelling out that commitment. Manfred Bräude was to write an article on Judaism and modern culture, Günther Friedländer on Jewish theology, Hanns Harf on the meaning of a congregation, Heinz Fischel on the meaning of the Bible, and I chose the subject of Halacha, the commandments of the Torah. I have long lost touch with Bräude and Friedländer. With Harf, long a rabbi in Buenos Aires, and Fischel, now Professor Emeritus at Indiana University, I have had life-long ties of friendship, and I do remember that both men completed their articles just as I completed mine. But then the Krystallnacht of November 9 made a brutal end to our project, and Harf, Fischel and I found ourselves fellow-victims in the concentration camp of Sachsenhausen, a shared experience which did much to cement our friendship. None of our essays was ever published.

When the present project was being prepared, I reread that essay of mine written nearly half a century ago, and so far as I remember, read for the first time since then. To my astonishment I discovered that, while no doubt I would today write it a little less obscurely and with more sophistication, I fully subscribe to its contents and would alter it, were I to write it today, only with respect to two radical events that had not yet occurred—the Holocaust and the establishment of the State of Israel. I have therefore asked Professor Morgan to include this essay, as a help to those who may wish to decide for themselves what has, and has not, changed in my Jewish thought these many years, and why. And since I also discovered—this too with some astonishment—that at one time I could write good German, I have also asked him to include the original in an appendix. I am not sure that my own 1985 translation does the 1938 text full justice.

The other item which I specifically asked to be included is "The Psychology of the Drum." This is one of a good many radio talks I gave between 1943 and 1948 in Hamilton, Canada, where I then served as a liberal rabbi. It is the only such talk that I remember having any special significance. The occasion was November 11, the day on which those are remembered who have laid down their lives for a noble cause. The year was 1945, ending a war in which the fallen of the Allied armies had laid down their lives for a cause of which none in history was more noble and more desperate: the defeat of Hitler's Germany. Without them and their sacrifice, Nazi Germany would now rule the world, and one shudders even now at the very thought. But one shudders, too, at another thought: that Hitler's soldiers—human beings like ourselves—were prepared to lay down their lives, and in my radio talk for November 11, 1945 I tried to grapple with that fact. At that time, I was quite unable to confront the Holocaust. But I did try to confront the eerie, somehow unreal, yet altogether mortal, threat that Naziism had posed for all humanity, and was filled then, as I am filled now, with gratitude toward all whose courage and sacrifice helped defeat it.

Emil L. Fackenheim
Written just prior to Simhat Torah 1985, the feast on which Jews rejoice because of the gift of the Torah.

Editor's Note

The present collection is intended as an introduction to Emil Fackenheim's Jewish thought as it has developed over a period of more than forty years and is presented in several books and dozens of articles. I have tried to set out in the general introduction my goals as an editor with some account of why the anthology is organized as it is. Briefly put, I have tried to weave together articles, chapters, and selections that reveal three things: (1) the development of Fackenheim's thought with the decisive turn occurring in the writings of the late 1960s; (2) the systematic nature of his work; (3) the rich diversity of themes that emerge as a result of his appreciation of the centrality of history in general, and of the Holocaust in particular, for contemporary Jewish thought.

Fackenheim is an attentive and powerful stylist; his essays and books show a keen awareness of the interconnections of form and content. For this reason, an editor should be reluctant to chop up articles and chapters, mutilating the shape of the work, and possibly distorting the content. I have been cautious about doing this, but I have done so, nonetheless. The reason is that I have wanted to expose a central line of thinking that is first introduced in the writings in Part Three, Section II, and is then adumbrated, revised, and deepened throughout the subsequent works. At the same time, central themes—like the "uniqueness" of the Holocaust—appear time and again in different contexts, and I have wanted to show what Fackenheim has thought, and come to think, on these themes and issues. Hence, to make all of this clear and to organize it in a way that is helpful and accessible, I have been forced to select from articles and books. When I have made such selections, I have edited the results minimally, to make them more easily understood and self-contained; I have renumbered footnotes and edited out phrases or brief passages that would divert the reader. The result, I hope, is a fair expression of what Fackenheim originally wrote. For those who want to continue their study of his work and thought, all the sources are provided, and I encourage a return to them and to the whole works from which I have excerpted.

The selections were made after careful consideration of all of Fackenheim's published work and a great deal of unpublished material. Essays were often selected because they best represent his thinking or because they express his thought in an especially memorable way. In only some cases, however, do I think

9

that no other piece would have sufficed; the original table of contents from which I chose was probably twice the size of the present one.

Three final comments. First, rather than try to sketch a brief biography in my introduction, I have added a final section that includes what amounts to intellectual memoirs. They, together with the reminiscence of Sachsenhausen, speak of some of the most central experiences that have influenced Fackenheim's thinking—his early years in Germany and the onset of Nazism, the period in Sachsenhausen, the flight to Aberdeen and then to Toronto, teaching in Canada, dialogue with Christian theologians and leaders, and finally *aliyah* to Jerusalem. These memoirs, plus the frequent sprinkling of personal reflections that occur throughout Fackenheim's more recent articles and books, should provide a more interesting portrait of him than I could give in a brief paragraph or two.

Secondly, there is a significant dimension of Fackenheim's Jewish thought that is only indirectly represented here—his encounters with great figures in the history of Jewish thought and philosophy. In the course of his career he has written fascinating articles and chapters on Martin Buber, Franz Rosenzweig, Leo Strauss, Baruch Spinoza, Hermann Cohen, Maimonides, and many others. The pieces we have included shed significant light on Fackenheim's own thinking; the others are listed in our bibliography and might be consulted by anyone interested in the intellectual heritage that has helped to shape Fackenheim's thinking.

Finally, the original plan for this book included an early section on philosophical foundations; it contained articles on Kant, Hegel, Heidegger, and on the examination of the relation between thought and life, philosophy and human existence. I was advised that my selections could not well represent the depth and extent of Fackenheim's philosophical work, nor could they easily aid the reader who wanted an introduction to his Jewish thought. The book ceased to be two books in one and became a single book, an effort to shed light on one dimension of Emil Fackenheim's thought. To be sure, his thought is a whole, and to segregate one aspect may not really be possible. Nonetheless, one can appreciate its philosophical character while focussing on its Jewishness, and that is what I have tried to do.

Two years ago Robert Mandel suggested this project to Emil Fackenheim and to me. In the interim he has encouraged, gently coaxed, and counseled so that the book would finally see the light of day. One could not have a more serious and devoted editor, and I know that both Professor Fackenheim and I believe that we have in him a friend of the greatest sensitivity.

Several people deserve my personal thanks. Rachel Jacobs-Miller helped with the early preparation of the manuscript; Jean Owen and Irene Bintz of Wayne State University Press, while bringing that manuscript into publishable form, taught me a good deal about what authors and editors take for granted. To Nancy Spencer of the Department of Philosophy at Indiana University I owe what orderliness my life has, and to Helen and Marty Schwartz a generous gift that facilitated the volume's publication. Graeme Nicholson and Louis Greenspan, editors of an upcoming volume on Emil Fackenheim's work, kindly allowed me to publish an adaptation of a complete bibliography that will appear in that volume.

My further debts go far back, but in the end there is one that is most profound and most important. Emil Fackenheim was my teacher and my intellectual hero long before we first met; he has continued to be those things of course, but in these twenty years or so he has become much more. This book is a small attempt to pay tribute to him—to his tremendous intellectual depth, his great humanity, and his intense sense of Jewish pride. It is, at the same time, an equally small tribute to Rose, to Michael, David, Suzie, Yossi, and all the Fackenheim felines through the years, for what they have shared with me and my family.

In the end, like all accomplishments that take time and effort, this one owes most not to the author as much as to his or her family. If there is something of value here, it is because of Emil Fackenheim, on the one hand, and because of Audrey, Debbie, Sara, Tammy, and Blaze, on the other. He has always been my intellectual, philosophical guide; they have been and done—and often have had to do—everything else. I cannot thank them; they mean more to me than mere thanks. But I can acknowledge their love and endurance.

M. L. M.

Introduction

Emil Fackenheim is fond of reminiscing about an incident that took place in 1924, when he was eight years old. Some 20 years earlier, his father had founded a Jewish sports club in Halle, their home town, and the club was celebrating its special anniversary when two Nazis appeared on the scene, ready to pick a fight. The elder Fackenheim, long time president of the club, confronted the pair and ended up punching one in the nose. Not temperamentally a militant or a violent person, Emil Fackenheim, nonetheless, recalls his father's rugged show of conviction—of Jewish fidelity—with pride. He recalls, too, the sequel: the embarrassed Nazis returned with a mob of cronies and the entire crowd of Jewish celebrants were herded into the building, leaving behind young Emil and his brother Wolfgang. The two boys stood at attention, for they had never been ordered to leave their posts.

This blend of Jewish fidelity and unflinching self-discipline are found everywhere in Fackenheim's Jewish thought. In the early period that saw him emerge as a philosophical expositor of German Idealism and a major Jewish thinker, these twin virtues express themselves in rigorously argued essays that try to understand and revive the commitment to faith and relevation as the core of Jewish existence. In later essays and books, they recur as the pillars of religiosity and secularity which support a resigned commitment to give history its due and to survive, to confront the darkest horror and live. From the disciplined, dialectical philosopher grappling with revelation, to the militant Zionist discerning the intermingling of the religious and the secular in post-Holocaust Jewish life, Fackenheim relives the old incident. The boy has become a man who is uniquely his own person, but he forever remains his father's son.

The present anthology collects writings of Emil Fackenheim from his earliest unpublished piece, written in 1938, to his most current work. It is an attempt to display his Jewish-philosophical journey—from Berlin to Toronto, and finally to Israel, and to do so through a carefully organized selection of his most important Jewish writings. In short, this anthology will hopefully provide the teacher and student of modern Jewish thought with a vehicle for viewing and critically examining the main lines of development and systematic character of Fackenheim's Jewish thought.

Fackenheim is the author of eight books and well over 100 articles. He has written at many levels for a variety of audiences but he has always written as a philosopher. Sometimes, to be sure, his work is highly technical, the product of a sensitive, deep philosophical mind, schooled in Berlin, Aberdeen, and Toronto, and deeply indebted for its style and method to the tradition of German Idealism and its existentialist progeny. These works—including, for example, *The Religious Dimension in Hegel's Thought* and *Metaphysics and Historicity*—are philosophically demanding even for the specialist and quite impenetrable for those without philosophical training. Yet Fackenheim's Jewish writings cannot be easily segregated from his philosophical corpus, and perhaps nothing has done more to qualify his influence than this interdependence of his Jewish thinking and his philosophical method, concepts, and argument. Even in Jewish writings that stem from public lectures, Fackenheim is a philosopher, a patient, probing, dialectical thinker who moves in the world of Midrash and current political affairs with the same intensity and rigor that inform his purely philosophical enterprises. But if this philosophical character of his thinking makes it difficult for the nonspecialist to understand his work, it also is what gives it its specific power and depth; in part, it is what makes his writings so well worth the effort of patient study.

Still, it may seem that a thinker so widely published does not need a new anthology to present his thought. This is not so. Because of the range and philosophical depth of his writings, Fackenheim does need such an anthology, a vehicle that isolates especially important discussions of crucial ideas, memorable uses of text and example, and the main lines of his thinking that tie together systematically what appears in diverse settings in dozens of articles and his several books. For this thought is a whole, albeit a fragmentary, recalcitrant whole, that winds its way between its twin poles, philosophy and history.

Further reasons recommend such an anthology. One such reason is that Fackenheim's essays, especially those composed after 1967, are generally topical, written for special occasions against the background of a rapidly changing political situation and incorporating new insights into the interplay between a basic argument—rooted in the thinking of 1967–68—and the special circumstances of the moment. Because some things need to be repeated in order to make anything clear but also because not everything can be said all at once, these essays—when presented as a collection[1]—have the obvious deficiencies of being both repetitive on the one hand and compressed and oblique on the other. To read Fackenheim correctly is to read him as a whole, but this strategy is too demanding or unreasonable for some, while too repetitive for others. The current collection, by organizing pieces thematically and by editing out repetitions, tries to lay bare the systematic connections among the themes addressed, while at the same time showing how the work of the 1970s and 1980s develops a line of thinking as old as the Six Day War and indeed cannot be properly understood independently of it.

A further reason is associated with the present one. Fackenheim's most widely read book is *God's Presence in History*, and its prominence is not surprising. The book's length and terseness, its time of publication, its power, its dramatic use of Midrash, its statement of the Holocaust's unprecedented character, and its derivation of the 614th commandment as the orienting norm for post–Holocaust Jewish life are all features which indicate clearly why it has been and continues to be so popular. At the same time, however, *God's Presence in History* does not emerge from a vacuum, and more importantly it is not Fackenheim's final word on most—if not all—the issues it addresses. To treat a twenty-year-old work as representative of the "essence" of Fackenheim's contribution to Jewish thought is an error. One of the goals of this reader is to place *God's Presence in History*—among the other essays that appear around 1967–68, and the themes that these works address—within the context of Fackenheim's earlier theological work and of his later books and essays.

But there is another reason for our collection, and it concerns not just *God Presence in History* but all the articles of that period dealing with the Holocaus and the exposure of Jewish thought, and indeed *all* thought, to that event. T line of thinking, the philosophical core, expressed in this work is not well-und stood, even when it is identified. Part Three, the heart of this anthology, inclu three sections that set out the three main steps in Fackenheim's thinking of that crucial period. To be sure, the steps were taken at different times and often retraced in different ways, but our readings try to show what they are and how at each step his thinking deepened as time went on. The first step concerns the Holocaust itself and the perception of it as an unprecedented explosion of the most radical evil; the second concerns the line of thinking that initially exposes thought to the event, recoils after failure, and finally—not immediately but after several carefully defined movements—results in a multifaceted set of imperatives for future Jewish life and much else; the third is the outcome of deepening that thinking, finally employing the concept of *tikkun olam* (mending the world) as an articulation of what shape post-Holocaust resistance should take.

This line of thinking, however, is not easy to discern in Fackenheim's writings, for they are the work of an outstanding stylist, whose powerful, crafted, rhetorically moving prose can overwhelm the unsuspecting student. Reading Fackenheim, one can be swept along, excited by a surprising turn of phrase or a memorable formulation, latching onto bits of phrases or even whole sentences like life rafts, exuberant at the thrill of the ride and fragmentary insight but overwhelmed by the experience as a whole, with the final outcome that much about the river and its scenery has simply escaped us, unnoticed. More often than not, what has slipped by in a reading of Fackenheim is what is really centrally important—the cumulative evidence for the Holocaust's "uniqueness" and what that embattled adjective means, the rigor of his thinking, and the justification or ground for the 614th commandment, among much else.

Finally, although Fackenheim's work continues and his thinking still develops, *To Mend the World* surely marks an apex, a peak. But in many ways this attempt to set "foundations for future Jewish thought" is a very internal book; more than any other of his books, *To Mend the World* is the record of a self-conversation, of a private dialogue in which Fackenheim rethinks the old line of thinking in as deep and thoroughgoing a way as he knows how, so that in the end he can go on to the future.[2] For this reason Fackenheim avoids no issue no matter how philosophically subtle and evasive and deep; he rethinks the work of Spinoza, Rosenzweig, Hegel, and Heidegger—his "masters"—and confronts each with thinking of increasing complexity and difficulty about Auschwitz. What does he hope to gain by these encounters? He hopes to find the categories and the ground for understanding how life and thought can continue thereafter. This task yields no easy results—either easy to write or easy to read and understand. One can imagine Fackenheim, upon completion of the book, like a gymnast after an intense series of moves on the high bar, relieved but exhausted; even the student who cannot follow Fackenheim's every move but does manage a close reading of the encounters with Auschwitz[3] must surely feel this same expenditure, this exhaustion. Watching the mind try to cope with a "whole of horror" can hardly leave one unsettled. If we want to understand Fackenheim at his deepest, then, we have to understand something of *To Mend the World*. But this is no mean task. In a sense, this anthology is a preparation for and perhaps even an introdution to it. We have selected passages from *To Mend the World* that can be studied on their own and as part of the portrait we outline of Fackenheim's thinking. With this reading as a guide, then, one can go on to grapple with *To Mend the World* as a whole and win greater success at understanding its important but difficult message.

I hope we can rest assured that there is every reason for an anthology such as this one. It is not a repetition of what can be found elsewhere, nor is it a mere selection of interesting, topical, or well-written articles and chapters. It is instead a kind of map or, better yet, a travel guide. It gives samples of sights one ought to visit and study; at the same time, it organizes these samples in such a way that the whole gives an overall representation of what the territory is like, what makes it a unity.

As a kind of guide, this reader has two main goals—to show the *development* of Fackenheim's Jewish thinking and to display its *systematic* nature. We have already said something about development; one should note that not only is the entire anthology organized to exhibit that development but also selections within chapters and sections are generally placed with the same goal in mind. In addition, *system* is a central goal. For Fackenheim, Jewish philosophy must be systematic; it must move from point to point and theme to theme with rigorous attention to the connectedness of thought. No leaps; no arbitrary transitions; no uncontested gaps; nothing without support or a reflective understanding of why none is needed. Behind Fackenheim's work—from the patiently argued account of selfhood in *Metaphysics and Historicity* to the moving reflection on the relation between kibbutz Yad Mordekhai and the heroic death of Mordecai Anielewicz in the Warsaw Ghetto—is a "systematic impulse," a discipline of thought that never flags and never is absent. All this the guide shows, or tries to show, not by saying it is so but rather by letting Fackenheim himself show this systematic connectedness in his own way.

If it is clear why this anthology is desirable, is it also clear why the present time is appropriate for its publication? Emil Fackenheim is surely one of the great Jewish thinkers of this century. In the post-Holocaust period, he is preeminent. Yet preeminent among whom? At doing what? The present moment finds no plethora of Jewish thinkers, certainly of Jewish philosophers. There is no consensus about the nature of Jewish thought or Jewish philosophy, either in Israel or in the Diaspora. There is no accepted model or models for performing these tasks, nor are there standard styles of Jewish thinking that attract widespread allegiance. In short, Jewish thinking and Jewish philosophy are in total disarray.

Who can be certain that what some perceive as disorder and chaos is in fact not really liberating, opening the doors of Jewish theology or Jewish thinking to a new, as yet uncharted future? Whether or not one is optimistic, however, the scene is the same. Some contrive fanciful if moving accounts of Judaism out of retooled Aggadic or Halachic categories. Others blend contemporary analytic philosophy with medieval Jewish philosophy or other strains of Jewish thought. Some use sociological or hermeneutical categories to analyze Jewish existence, while others examine Jewish thinkers past and present in the hopes of finding some guidance. There is little if any agreement about method and subject matter, about beginnings or goals, about what is being sought, why, and by whom. And the situation is hardly different for secular or religious Jews.

Marked by such diversity and apparent disorder, Jewish thought can hardly afford to ignore an intensely reflective, profoundly insightful, powerfully philosophical thinker in its midst. And if Jewish life and Christian theology, as well as Jewish thought, are in need of a rich and powerful conception of Jewish existence today, neither can he be ignored by Jews and Christians everywhere. At a time such as this, one must seek out the great contemporary thinkers and encounter them, and Fackenheim is surely one to be encountered honestly and seriously and not to be ignored.

In so doing, one may of course come with questions: is Fackenheim a model for how Jewish thought, philosophical and religious, should be done? Is it necessary or desirable for genuine Jewish thought to be philosophical? If so, how? Is Fackenheim the "last" of the German Jewish philosophers and not wholly relevant to American Jewish experience? Is the tradition of continental philosophy, which has so significantly shaped Fackenheim's thinking, inaccessible to American Jewish experience? Does it somehow fail to articulate its shape and character? Are the Holocaust and the rebirth of the Jewish state focal points for contemporary Jewish thought and life? Is Fackenheim right about the unavoidability of history? The radical and unprecedented character of the Holocaust? The paradigmatic role of Israel?

In *To Mend the World* Fackenheim tries to find a way to ground his own future as a Jewish thinker, and of course his way is not a private one, nor are his hopes for the results of his work. He achieves his goal by turning to Spinoza and Rosenzweig, Hegel and Heidegger—and to Leo Strauss, a special inspiration to him. Minimally, perhaps there is guidance in his strategy. The hope of Jewish thought may be to retrace the steps of Jewish life and thought back to Sinai in order to hear the Voice once again and then, with a new attentiveness, to articulate what we have heard and what it now means to us. To be sure, to listen is no easy task, nor is it an uncontested one, but it may be premature to worry much about it. For that retracing of steps will be a long process that must surely begin today, with our own situation and our own thinkers. At some point we shall study again Buber and Rosenzweig, Cohen and Mendelssohn, Maimonides and Halevi, Akiba and Yochanan ben Zakkai, and on and on. But to begin we must look closer to home. There we may find, as our primary figure, the son of a German lawyer who once founded a Jewish sports club, still confronting the evil of Nazism and the hopes for the Jewish future with indignant self-discipline and with the image of his father's Jewish fidelity ever before his eyes.

Notes

1. The charge of repetitiveness has been leveled specifically against *The Jewish Return into History* and generally against all of Fackenheim's work subsequent to *God's Presence in History*.

2. In this regard *To Mend the World* (*TMW*, 1970) is in some ways like Rosenzweig's *Star of*

Redemption, trans. William Hallo (New York: Holt, Rinehart and Winston, 1970, 1971). The introduction to *TMW* is something like the essay "The New Thinking," in *Franz Rosenzweig: His Life and Thought*, ed. N. Glatzer, New York: Schocken Books, 1953).

    3. *TMW*, 181–89, 206–15, 241–47.

1

Intimations: From 1938 to 1945

1 *Our Position toward Halacha*

It is characteristic of the man of today to approach religion from without, i.e., to judge it in terms of standards he already brings to it, and to relate himself to it accordingly. Its teachings are examined with a view to their relevance to human society, or, as the case may be, with a view to the appeal they have to the individual's emotional needs. Whether the standard is rationalist or irrationalist, whether the appeal is to society or the individual, in common is the fact that religion is measured by the nature of the one who does the judging.

In this situation the gravest offense is given by the sum total of customs that confronts us as Halacha. To understand this offense aright, it is first of all necessary to protect that original claim of Halacha against two attempts to mitigate it, to make it less offensive. One consists of the attempt to integrate Halacha into the general history of religion: just as in every religion customs evolve at a certain point, so it is with Halacha in Judaism. Several conclusions may be drawn from this process of the "normalization" of Halacha, but these differ from each other only in degree and not in principle: whether we nowadays can dispense with such "customs and ceremonies," having transcended the need for them, or whether they have relevance even now—say, a moral significance or a more specifically "religious one" in that they arouse religious feelings or fill religious "needs." Radically at odds with this whole approach may be the attempt to interpret Halacha as national rather than religious customs even though, in this case, the demand may actually be to rejuvenate customs long abandoned, in the context of an attempt to rejuvenate the Jewish nation. Yet this attempt only appears to be *radically* at odds

Written in German in 1938, when the author was a student at the *Hochschule für die Wissenschaft des Judentums,* for a projected volume of essays on Judaism. The themes of the essay, revelation and Jewish law, are developed in several essays included in Part Two (below). The German original is included in the Appendix.

This, the Ethical and Demanding, is forever revolutionary, demanding absolutely, ever disturbing nature, driving onward, and putting what-is into question. Only our age has unjustly degraded this element to a mere part of the order of existence as-it-is. Thus for example the demand for absolute justice has been reduced to a demand for mere order of human society within the context of what-is. The Absolute, that for this reason ever disturbs the natural course of things, has been reduced to something relative, i.e., a servant of nature-as-it-is and society-as-it-is.

It is at Sinai that Israel experiences the absolutely Demanding with the most elemental power, such that from now on this people suffers a total loss of natural harmony, of being "natural-and-nothing-else," of unquestionableness. Whether this people wills it or not, "the mountain" is "placed on top of them" ever since. This is a seeming paradox. Here is a living, flesh-and-blood people, in living community both horizontally and vertically—i.e., with its contemporaries and its ancestors. Yet this flesh-and-blood people is at the same time "unnatural," without natural harmony, ever called into question.

Now this people has always made the attempt to answer to this demand, to understand it and to fulfil it. It has always attempted *not to say it to itself but to let itself be addressed*. Hence Halacha in its present form, committed as it is to writing, stands before us as the testimony of the effort of countless generations to let themselves be addressed, by that which cannot exhaustively be expressed by the pre-Sinaitic Ethical which, indeed, is in principle not exhaustively expressible. And thus it came to pass that, born of a will endowed with metaphysical seriousness to do justice to the elemental demand with a strength that is only human, monumental thought-structures were erected on the foundations of the simple Biblical Word, and heavy tomes were filled with laws and prescriptions, too numerous to be counted. We stand before that work in astonishment. Here is an energy that, filled in total inwardness with the fact that the Commandment transcends human power, drove intensity and depth, as it were, into breadth: the striving to subject human life to the Commandment right into its minute details.

We can still understand the certainty of faith that made it possible for our forefathers to carry out prescriptions precisely circumscribed down to the smallest detail, and yet to know that they did not say it to themselves but had let themselves be addressed. We cannot, however, share that certainty. For us the absolutely Demanding is no longer, as for them it was, in the very midst of life. For us it is only at the border of existence, and for that reason darker, more inexpressible and less accessible, and for that reason also less capable of being fulfilled through practice. We are able to believe that *their* acting and their life was a genuine response to the demand coming from Sinai, that it was a genuine fulfillment, that genuine acceptance of the Torah which at all times is alone the last fulfilling response of the compulsion that has placed the mountain on top of Israel. We are unable to believe, however, that that system of detailed prescription which, as reflection of *their* response, is before us, systematically ordered, committed to print, clearly expressed, and do-able for everyone—that this is the Commandment and that nothing more is necessary than to just do it.

What prevents us from any such response is more than mere modern scholarship—the knowledge that, in fact and considered detail, we have in the tradition much that originally *was* mere folk custom, often even influenced by other cultures, and that in this sense later generations really laid down prescriptions in the name of earlier ones that were never dreamt of by the latter. Far more important is the insight that, through such a reaction, the Inexpressible would for the first time be made expressible, that in this way the Infinite would be reduced to finitude. Hence the Shulchan Aruch is for us the *form* in which fulfillment once took place, and for that reason we study it with reverence. We can even grant that, in our days still, fulfillment is possible in many quarters and to a considerable degree. What we cannot grant is that the Shulchan Aruch is identical with the Demanding, the Inexpressible: God is mysterious, and so, in the last analysis, is his Commandment.

With this conclusion, however, we may seem to find ourselves in a situation bordering on despair. How can every one of us let himself be addressed when "it" is not being said to him? And how shall the Inexpressible, Mysterious, nevertheless be expressed and fulfilled by us—fulfilled above all? To these two questions we must now give definite answers, and on these depends the fate of Halacha in our time.

The individual as individual is not intended, never has been intended. The call from Sinai addresses the *K'lal Yisrael*, the bond of contemporaries in its own bond with the chain of generations. As for the contemporaries today, these have lost the certainty of the faith of their ancestors. What they have not lost, however, is openness to faith. The task of the present generation is to be ready for faith, i.e., *ready to let the Other as Demanding enter into its very midst.* Toward this end, the House of Israel today must seek to recover a bond with its ancestors, in order thus to be able, as it were, to stand at Sinai itself, i.e., in order thus genuinely to become K'lal Yisrael not only horizontally but vertically as well.

Whether or not our doing will answer to the Demanding we cannot know. All we can do is be ready, and in this readiness *attempt to do even as we remain questioners.* If we place ourselves into the chain of generations, this, while not identical with fulfillment, will bring us a bit closer, closer to Sinai. Hence it will surely be necessary, in practice and in detail, to begin with some of the doing of our ancestors. This, to be sure, will be of no use at all if we "take it over" merely as "custom" or if we do no more than try to find a "moral meaning" in it, i.e., if we "say it to ourselves." However, if we approach the heritage coming from our ancestors with the readiness to let ourselves be addressed, commanded; to allow the Infinite to enter into the finite, Mystery into the manifest, the more-than-Natural into the natural; in short, if we *act* in the readiness-to-faith, then that is done which in our time lies within Israel's power.

If we approach our heritage in this way, then it may well become evident that in a deeper sense there is truth in the ancient belief that Rashi merely explains what Moses means; that both—that all generations—stand at *the same* Sinai; that, to be sure, everyone hears and fulfills the Commandment in a different form, but that the "Word to Israel" itself is always one and the same. Perhaps it is possible even for us, despite all modern academic scholarship, to hear that Word, and to know that what is heard and fulfilled by us is what Moses wrote in the Torah and Rashi expounded.

We can have no certainty of faith but only readiness to faith. This has also the necessary consequence that it will hardly be possible for us to possess Halacha as a fixed order of our lives. To be sure, Halacha is to be practiced in the whole of life, but it cannot be for us an unquestionable reality, which at bottom it never quite ought to be. For perpetually to stand under God's Command is to lead a life in nature and yet not in nature: it is to live in a paradox. And yet we see—and this is as if it were a promise to ourselves—that our ancestors were nevertheless able to *live*. And life, after all, requires also being-without-questions, i.e., a vitality which is natural.

Hence, as Israel today goes forward in readiness to faith and realization, it carries along a promise and a hope—that the realization of the Infinite in the finite, of Mystery in the manifest which, so it would seem, is Israel's task can nevertheless also be a life: "life" in the whole fulness of meaning that attaches to this keyword of Creation.

2 *The Psychology of the Drum*

On this day, the 11th of November, our thoughts go back to that day 27 years ago when, after 4 years of mortal battle, the guns became silent. And as the drums of memory are beaten softly, a feeling of reverent remembrance comes over us turning our thoughts to those who then laid down their lives to make the silence of the guns possible in a world safe for democracy.

But as our thoughts wander into the past, shadows enter our minds, frightening ghosts which will not be turned away. We cannot dispel them, for they come to us saying: "If you honor the memory of those who fell in sacrifice for a noble cause, you cannot evade us; you must face us and battle with us, to exorcise us for all time."

In silent memory of the 11th of November 1918 the drums beat softly. But a discord has entered, the sound of another drum, and the memory of another date: November 9th, 1923, the date of the first attempt of Nazism at power. Only a small discord as yet, like the sound of a distant thunder, but already disturbing the harmony of the other drum, and chilling the warmth of the dream of a world safe for democracy. And ever noisier becomes the sound of that drum, the drum of the oppressor, ever louder the sound of the goose step, until the soft drum of memory is almost completely drowned, until we are shocked out of our dream of a drum beaten for peace and brotherhood, and a march undertaken for justice and happiness of all humanity. We are now chilled to the marrow by the demonic laughter of the ghosts now entering the soul. For another date has arrived: November 10th, 1938, the date of the first mass atrocities against Jews; the date when the oppressor throws off his mask of peace and shows to the world his readiness to wipe out

An address given over station CKOC, Hamilton, Ontario, November 11, 1945, by Dr. Emil L. Fackenheim, Rabbi, Anshe Sholom Synagogue.

the memory of 1918, and to assault the world with his drum of war and the noise of his goose step.—

The ghosts will not be turned away, no, not even now, in 1945, the year of victory. The demons say to us: You will exorcise us only if you know our secret and conquer us.

What is it, this dreadful secret which created hordes of barbarians destroying all that 1918 attempted to create? We must know it, not only in order to explain what happened, but also to make safe the achievement of 1945.

The secret lies in the uncanny power of the drum, in the demonic spell which marching can exercise over the souls of men. We all know of the drum in its rightful role, as a faithful tool in the noble efforts of men. It does its work when there is need for men to leave their homes and to rally in defense of the freedom of the nation. When men must march together in unity, subordinating their aims to a common aim, the drum arouses them to noble effort. What we usually do not perceive clearly enough is that the drum has the power to overthrow the mastery of the noble purpose to which it is subordinated and to become an uncanny demon; that the marching of the masses can become an evil frenzy destroying the humanity in man and forging them into a brutal machine of cruelty and destruction.

How can we explain what happened in Germany between November 1918 and November 1938? Certain factors we know well enough: economic insecurity and oppression; political coercion; the militaristic tradition and a set of historical circumstances. But this leaves the most important question still unanswered: how is it that any dictatorship however oppressive, economic pressure however severe, and a tradition however strong could wield millions into a brutal, inhuman machine shrinking back from no crime, a machine run by robots giving themselves fully, and to the last breath, to the vicious ends to which they had sworn loyalty? It is futile to pile up explanations concerned with the external situation; we must look inside the people, we must see what happened to their souls.

This is what happened: cynicism, materialism, and a general inward emptiness had pervaded large segments of the German people after the last war. While the difficulties of livelihood provided concern to many thousands, the inability to find a meaning to their lives was an even deeper worry; a concern pervading not only the economically insecure, but every stratum of society. To be sure, this inward emptiness was often unnoticed, and the lack of a true faith, the incapacity for devotion to a true ideal often provided no conscious concern, but it needed only the psychological cunning of a Hitler to transform this apathy and emptiness into a violent frenzy willing to embrace everything, arousing the emotions however false, willing to give whole-hearted devotion to anything however perverse, if only it was the sort of thing that commanded such whole-hearted devotion.

Slowly, slowly, the beating of the drum began to be heard, and the goose-stepping of the first storm troopers. A careful, cunning experiment: would it work, to beat the drum not to men living by ideals to arouse them to sacrifice for them, but before the ears of men devoid of faith and with emptiness in their hearts? A drum beaten not for the sake of a higher end, but as an end in itself? A drum bidding not awareness of inner resources, but intellectual suicide and an escape into blind obedience. A drum bidding men to march not for the sake of a noble end, but to march for its own sake.

It worked. The result is there to be beheld by a shuddering mankind. The great march began which was a march of crime because its cause was not an ideal anchored in the breasts of men, but the frenzied desire to drown the emptied self in a march in which the end did not matter: the march of nihilism. The drum sounded: arouse yourselves and march onward; do not mark the aim of this march, mark the heels of the robot in front of you. Know that the meaning of this march lies in the intensity with which you march, not in its aim. March with but one aim: to march, to trample underfoot whatever resists this march which is the law of your life.

This ghastly march, where is it to lead? It leads to whatever infamous depths those who beat the drum desire. Nay, it must lead to the depth of infamy, for even he who beats the drum is no longer free; he is driven by the fetishistic frenzy of those who march behind him saying: lead wherever you wish, but lead! Let this march never stop, lest we awaken from this frenzy and be annihilated by the emptiness from which we must escape. Let the drum become ever louder, the goose step ever noisier. Let him who leads continue to lead even after his death, let his myth and memory continue to beat the drum in which the life of the machine pulses. Until the hour when death ends the march for the individual who even then is under the demonic spell, deceiving himself into believing that his end is that of a hero.

These are the ghosts emerging before our eyes saying: will you be our match? This is indeed the question: will we be able to exorcise the demons which with utter destructiveness have gained hold of the souls of men? To join battle with the demons of barbarism is a duty for us far greater than that of placing stones of memorial to honor the memory of those whose death these demons caused to be vain, and of those whose sacrifice they made necessary.

There is need for both defensive and offensive action. On the defensive, we must be ever wary lest the demons of the drum enslave us. In rightful respect for the role the drum plays in arousing loyalty to the ideal, we must be on guard that its role should never be perverted, that it should never become an end in itself. Lest it deprive us of the true standards of morality and faith whereby every beating of the drum and every call to march must be measured. Lest we cease to measure him who beats the drum by the righteousness of his leadership and have left as the only measure its efficiency. Lest we become robots. And you are a robot when you accept unconditionally the call of the drum, when you march for the sake of the march itself.

But from the defensive we must proceed to the offensive. We must feed the souls of men with faith. Overcome cynicism and inward emptiness, and establish in the hearts of men the true meaning of life: to do justly, to love mercy and to walk humbly with God. For these are truths beyond all cynicism and superseding all inward emptiness. Be it known once more to this generation that to give justice to every man however poor, to every nation however weak is the true standard governing our lives; that the qualities of mercy and love are those wherein our souls can find happy fulfillment; that, and let us probe the recesses of our souls to establish it, a Redeemer liveth ready to resolve all despair and perplexity of those who put their trust in Him.

To supplant the inner emptiness which dwells in so many hearts with this faith is not a task which can be accomplished by the beating of the drum, or by causing the people to march in masses. One can bring justice into the world only by being just; one can teach mercy only by being merciful; one can bring God into the world only by allowing Him to enter one's soul. Unlike the work of destruction, it cannot be done to people in masses, but to each person slowly and quietly. But such is the work of the Lord.

In the measure to which we remove emptiness within and create inward loyalty to what is good we shall exorcise the demons of destruction. In the measure to which the people of this generation will make the law of God the meaning of their lives, will they succeed in making permanent a true peace and a better world.

2

The Early Stage: From 1945 to 1967

Introduction

The following seven selections are intended as a sample of Fackenheim's Jewish writings during an early twenty-year period. Arguably it was the most philosophically productive and rich period of his life. In addition to four books, he published dozens of articles. Included among these works are a series of articles on Kant and Schelling, the monograph *Metaphysics and Historicity*—his most sustained systematic work in metaphysics, and his masterful study of Hegel, *The Religious Dimension in Hegel's Thought*.[1] It was during these years that the newly transplanted German student became an accomplished philosophical interpreter of German Idealism and at the same time a central figure in the post-war revival of Jewish theology.

Even though Fackenheim later speaks of this period as one in which the philosopher and the Jewish thinker were kept apart,[2] this retrospective judgment is not meant to exaggerate the dichotomy. Viewed against the conscious, cautious attempt to bring philosophy and Jewish thought together—in *Encounters Between Judaism and Modern Philosophy* (1973) and *To Mend the World* (1982)—the early period does seem a stark contrast. But in many ways, the separation is even there mitigated by interdependence. In the 1950s and 1960s the Jewish essays are decidedly philosophical in style and mode of thinking, even if the Jewish commitment is ever present and the posture of philosophical criticism is set aside in favor of the posture of faith. Similarly, Fackenheim's philosophical work, while conducted in a rigorously philosophical manner, nonetheless bears the stamp of his Jewish commitment. This commitment expresses itself most clearly in his subjects—first Maimonides and selected Arabic philosophers on creation, then the existential turn in Schelling's later philosophy, radical evil in Kant's moral thought, Kant's conception of history, and finally religion in Hegel's thought. Fackenheim's method of thinking is philosophically precise and dialectical, both here and in the Jewish works, but the philosophical questions he asks are often determined by a deep uncertainty about the nature of Jewish thinking and Jewish philosophy that is harnessed to an equally deep commitment to both philosophy, on the one hand, and Judaism, on the other.

The nature and possibility of a genuine Jewish philosophy in the modern world are themes that run through the present selections. These themes are explicitly addressed in the introduction to the essay on Kantian ethics and Jewish morality.

But they are already present in the reviews of Buber and Rosenzweig. In the former piece, a review of Buber's *Israel and Palestine,* Fackenheim notices how Buber's Zionist thought is a case of genuine Jewish religious thought because it aspires to grasp a set of timeless truths and values but only as they are expressed in a particular history, the history of the Jewish people and its reflections on the role of Zion in Jewish destiny. Fackenheim argues that Buber's thinking is able to recover these truths from this particular history only because the past is not dead and surpassed. Rather the Jewish past is a past enriched by a spiritual reality that is still alive today, and that "spiritual reality" is the encounter between God and man in history. The truths and values of history and nation can be recovered from a particular past because the reality that infuses that past is still alive today. The Divine Presence that shaped that history is still available to shape the contemporary life and understanding which we call Zionism.

The review of Buber raises two serious questions for Fackenheim. First, the review shows one way in which genuine Jewish thought must be both philosophical and historical. But is this the primary or only way that Jewish thought must be philosophical, i.e., by needing the guidance of timeless truths and values provided by philosophy? Secondly, why should a contemporary Jew—living in a secular world inspired by the modern critique of revelation—still believe in its possibility? Why think that the old reality is still alive today?

With remarkable economy Fackenheim responds to both questions with a single, Napoleonic strategy, and that strategy includes a recovery and defense of the Buber-Rosenzweig concept of revelation. Before we consider the content of that recovery and how it is justified, we must digress to ask why Fackenheim in these years followed Buber in thinking that the "spiritual reality" that infuses Jewish history and self-understanding is the reality of divine-human encounter.

The answer to this central question is complex. Here we can only itemize and not examine Fackenheim's reasons for advocating a "believing openness" to the Divine Presence. One reason is surely that for Fackenheim "God's existence is man's existential *a priori*,"[3] for human existence and religious thought can endure neither a flight from the world nor a total immersion in it. Naturalism, or empiricism, however conceived, is an expression of a faith alternative to that of Judaism, so that when viewed historically and philosophically, either appears as an attack *ab extra* that can win the hearts of Jews not by genuine argument but only by its anaesthetic power.[4]

Secondly, Fackenheim recognizes that the modern world has indeed generated a wholesale assault on our knowledge of the existence of God and on the possibility of religious experience, i.e., revelation. Fackenheim's ability to meet that challenge—to confront and dispense with Feuerbach, Marx, Freud, and others—spurs his conviction that faith—an immediacy after reflection, to use Kierkegaard's phrase[5]—is the center of Jewish existence.

Thirdly, Fackenheim appreciates that naturalism, endorsed but not definitively demonstrated by someone as imposing as Spinoza, does not reach its modern form until the 19th century and later. The great philosophers of the modern period—Kant, Schelling, Hegel, Kierkegaard, Nietzsche—do not rule God out from the beginning. In the course of their thinking, they confront the divine and take it with utter seriousness, either by accepting it, overcoming it, or rejecting it, but never simply by dispensing with it from the outset. None of them allow their initial presuppositions to dispose of revelation or divine existence *ab initio,* as is the case, for example, with so much of 20th century analytic philosophy. If the existential religious thought of Kierkegaard, Buber, and Rosenzweig, then, can be shown to be more acceptable than the "old thinking" of Kant and Hegel, one result is that the divine need not be either rejected or overcome but rather can be allowed to remain in its own right, a reality to be confronted as part of the human situation. For Fackenheim, the Divine Presence is not successfully "idealized" by Hegel or Kant, by Schleiermacher or Cohen; what remains is a divine reality that can be confronted in history and neither transformed into an idea nor superseded by infinite spirit.

Finally, persuaded by all of this that Jewish experience is open to the encounter between God and man, Fackenheim finds this reality, revelation, expressed everywhere in that genre of Rabbinic writing which is "the greatest theological writing ever produced within Judaism,"[6] Midrash. Later we shall say a word or two about Fackenheim's conception of Midrash and how he thinks it is the earliest expression of the fundamental experiences of Judaism. For the moment it is sufficient to notice that here he finds in Midrash expressed again and again the divine-human encounter, the paradoxical interplay of the finite and the infinite, of Divine Power and human freedom, of transcendence and immanence.[7]

We can now return to Fackenheim's early attempt to show how Jewish thought must be philosophical and, at the same time, to question why the past reality of revelation is still alive today. The former problem is beautifully put in Rosenzweig's *The Star of Redemption.* In that momentous, but difficult, work, Rosenzweig engages in the "new thinking," a mode of thinking that emerges out of the thinker's personal situation and from his own point of view, one that moves historically—like a conversation or dialogue—from point to point. Part II of *The Star* is a map of the "new" or personal thinker's understanding of God's relation to nature, i.e., Creation, of his own relation to God in the world, i.e., Revelation, and of his relation to others in response to his relation to God, i.e., Redemption. But the thinker, while moving in thought in such a way that his personal standpoint and the temporality of his thinking are both crucial, still purports to be a philosophical thinker. Only later, in Part III, do the Jew and the Christian enter the drama as particular agents and thinkers. Against this background, Rosenzweig asks his important question, one which Fackenheim explores deeply in his review: "Is this science?" i.e., how can this personal, existential religious thinking still yield objective, philosophical results? Rosenzweig's answer, which Fackenheim explains and in subsequent articles appropriates,[8] is that the bridge between radical subjectivity and objective validity is the concept of revelation.[9] The philosophical defense of the modern conception of revelation—against Feuerbach, Marx, Freud, and its other despisers—is what makes the otherwise subjective thinking objective. Genuine existential religious thought cannot ignore the philosophical need to defend—by argument and reason—the respectability of revelation. The result is two-fold: a Jewish thought that is and must be philosophical and a demonstration of why a spiritual reality that infuses the past is still alive today.

We need not say too much here about what that concept is. Fackenheim explores it critically in his study of Buber's concept of revelation (see below), and the account of revelation is noticed and sometimes developed in a variety of pa-

erating in a situation—biological, cultural, and so on—this does not preclude the possibility of philosophical "transcendence," i.e., of a kind of thinking that grasps timeless truths. At least until the late 1960s, Fackenheim remains firmly committed to this possibility—that there are some philosophical truths that nothing empirical or historical can refute. Partially Fackenheim thinks that the denial of this view—historicism—is a form of relativism and that such thinking is self-refuting. The historicist cannot be a thoroughgoing historicist without jeopardizing his own commitment to the truth of historicism. In a letter to Reinhold Neibuhr, he says that "unless philosophical reason can transcend, at least in principle, the existential corruption of self-interest, it cannot avoid a self-refuting relativism."[13] Eventually, he will deepen this criticism, especially in confrontation with Heidegger's far more subtle historicism, which it does not touch,[14] but he still abjures it philosophically. At the same time, as the Niebuhr letter shows, Fackenheim's concern with historicism is a moral one; it is corrupting, and in the extreme, as our selection from the beginning of *Metaphysics and Historicity* shows, can become "ideological fanaticism." Ultimately of course it can become even more diabolical.

Repelled by the radical historicity of thought, Fackenheim resisted it in Jewish, as he had in philosophical, thought. There is no more unequivocal formulation of this resistance than the following statement in "On the Eclipse of God": "religious faith can be, and is, empirically verifiable; but nothing empirical can refute it." Yet, while he is repelled by historicism in this early period, he is not blind to its profound attractions. We have already seen them arise in his account of revelation. These attractions emerge again in the account of the existential individual as a self-constituting process set in the biological, cultural, historical situation. In time they will arise once more—when it will be agonizing to call them "attractions," perhaps "necessities" would be a more appropriate word—as his thought—and indeed *all* thought—becomes thoroughly exposed to Auschwitz and the reality of radical evil.

Note on Readings

As a supplement to our selections, one might read "Jewish Existence and the Living God" (*QPF*, ch. 7) and "The Dilemma of Liberal Judaism" (*QPF*, ch. 8). Of Fackenheim's strictly philosophical writings, the most important—but also the most demanding—are *Metaphysics and Historicity, The Religious Dimension of Hegel's Thought,* (*RDH,* 1970), and the article "The Transcendence and Historicity of Philosophical Truth." The article "Kant and Radical Evil" is important for understanding Fackenheim's later thought, as is "Schelling's Conception of Positive Philosophy."

Notes

1. In addition to the two books, the most important articles include "Schelling's Philosophy of Religion" (1952), "Schelling's Conception of a Positive Philosophy" (1954), "Kant and Radical Evil" (1954), "Kant's Concept of History" (1957), and "The Transcendence and Historicity of Philosophical Truth" (1967). The recently published "Immanuel Kant" (1985) was also written during this period.

2. Fackenheim is not unaware of the interdependence, although he focuses on the separation, e.g., in the preface to *Quest for Past and Future,* (*QPF,* 1970). He says, "It is fitting that *Quest for Past*

and Future should appear in the same year, and with the same publishers, as my *The Religious Dimension in Hegel's Thought*. The two works (which have occupied me during the same years) are related in their very difference. In the philosophical work all religious commitment is suspended by reflection; in the theological work all philosophical thinking is geared to a commitment." A similar sentiment is expressed in the acknowledgments to *Encounters between Judaism and Modern Philosophy* (*EJM*, 1980).

3. "Self-Realization and the Search for God," *QPF*, 37.

4. See *EJM*, ch. 1.

5. "On the Eclipse of God," *QPF*, 243

6. *QPF*, 16.

7. Notice the extensive use of Midrash in two papers reprinted here, "Self-Realization and the Search for God" (1970) and "The Revealed Morality of Judaism and Modern Thought" (1978).

8. In "Martin Buber's Concept of Revelation" (1967), he develops an interpretation of how Buber's concept can be articulated and defended against the modern critique; in "On the Eclipse of God" (1966), and in chapter 2 of *God's Presence in History* (*GPH*, 1968), he appropriates the critique for himself. Cf. *EJM* ch. 3, and *TMW*, ch. 3.

9. Review of N. Glatzer, *Franz Rosenzweig: His Life and Thought* (1953).

10. See *QPF*, chapters 4, 6, 8, and 14.

11. *QPF*, 327n. 22.

12. See *QPF*, 80, 141–47; Franz Rosenzweig, *On Jewish Learning*, ed. and trans. N. Glatzer (New York: Schocken Books, 1955).

13. The unpublished letter of Niebuhr to Fackenheim is dated 1956. In addition see *Metaphysics and Historicity*, 77–79n. 44 together with Leo Strauss's unpublished letter to Fackenheim dated 1961.

14. In "The Transcendence and Historicity of Philosophical Truth" (1967), Fackenheim continues the argument with Heidegger.

3 Modern Man and the Predicament of History

History is a predicament for man who must live in it. In order to act in history he must seek to rise above it. He needs perspectives in terms of which to understand his situation, and timeless truths and values in terms of which to act in it. Yet the perspectives which he finds often merely reflect his age; and what he accepts as timelessly true and valid is apt to be merely the opinion which is in fashion. Thus while man must always try to rise above his historical situation he succeeds at best only precariously.

This predicament, always part of the human condition, is felt by contemporary Western man more keenly than by man in any previous age. This is in part because of the breath-taking swiftness of contemporary events. Never have men had so much cause to seek a transcending wisdom in terms of which to understand and influence the course of events, and yet to fear that such a wisdom is beyond their reach. For never has yesterday's wisdom become stale so quickly, and hence has present counsel been regarded with so much doubt.

This effect of contemporary events is reinforced by an intellectual development which, in the West, began in the nineteenth century. For a century and a half, Western man has developed an ever increasing historical self-consciousness. And this has not been without grave spiritual effects. In earlier ages, most men could simply accept religious beliefs or moral principles, as unquestionably true. In this historically self-conscious age, few men can ever forget that what seems unquestionably true to one age or civilization differs from what seems unquestionably true to others. And from historical self-consciousness there is but one step—albeit a long and fateful one—to a wholesale historical scepticism: to the despairing view that history discloses a variety of conflicting *Weltanschauungen,*

Reprinted, with changes, from *Metaphysics and Historicity* (Milwaukee: Marquette University Press, 1961), 1–8, by permission of the publisher.

with no criterion for choice between them anywhere in sight. But when events move as they do today this step is easily taken.[1]

Just how commonly it is in fact taken may be illustrated by a review of three typically contemporary attitudes. The first is what may be called *sceptical paralysis*. Here historical self-consciousness has led to two results: to the insight that wherever there has been a great purpose there has been a great faith; and to the loss of capacity for commitment to such a faith. Hence there is paralysis which recognizes itself as paralysis and preaches doom.[2]

Then there is what may be called *pragmatic make-believe*. Here man, caught in scepticism, seeks escape from its paralyzing consequences. Unable to believe and yet seeking a purpose, he falls to pretending to believe, hoping that a pretended might do the work of an actual faith. But it cannot. For a pretended faith is no faith at all. Pragmatic make-believe collapses in self-contradiction.[3]

When men truly suffer from this contradiction they may seek escape in the most ominous form of modern spiritual life: *ideological fanaticism*. Unlike pragmatic make-believe and like faith, ideology asserts itself absolutely. But unlike faith and like pragmatic make-believe, it is shot through with historical scepticism. For it knows itself to be not truth, but merely one specific product of history.

Hence unlike faith, ideology must by its very nature become fanatical. When challenged by a conflicting faith, faith may withdraw on its certainty of *being* true. Because it knows itself to be but one product of history, ideology can achieve certainty only by *making* itself true; and this it can do absolutely only be re-creating all history in its own image. When challenged, therefore, ideology cannot withdraw on itself; it must seek to destroy the challenger. That is, in order to resolve its internal conflict between absolute assertion and historical scepticism, it must engage in a total war from which it hopes to emerge as the only ideology left on earth.[4]

Notes

1. For the development of modern Western historical consciousness, cf. especially F. Meinecke, *Die Entstehung des Historismus* (Munich: Oldenbourg, 1936).

Gerhard Krueger describes the predicament of history as follows: "We are able to inquire into history only while being part of it. We seek permanent truths about history; yet we ourselves, our whole thinking included, are nothing permanent. This is the predicament of history, radically stated: that we are so changeable and yet are in such need of the permanent." *Grundfragen der Philosophie* (Frankfurt: Vittorio Klostermann, 1958), p. 49. Krueger describes the development of Western awareness of this predicament as follows. The Greeks had not yet discovered it. Thinkers such as St. Augustine coped with it in terms of the Christian doctrine of Providence. The Enlightenment dealt with it in terms of the belief in progress. Because it was first to abandon the belief in the superiority of the present over the past, Romanticism was first to discover the predicament of history; but both Romanticism and German Idealism sought to resolve it by rising above history into timelessness. Because the belief in the possibility of such a rise is no longer acceptable in the present age, this age is "an age of total historicity," one of "mutually incompatible standpoints." Ibid., p. 8. This lecture will make clear that we do not wholly agree with Krueger's account; we have summarized it here because it is profoundly challenging.

2. The first great warning against the possible ill-effects of a strongly developed historical self-consciousness was given in 1874, in Nietzsche's *Use and Abuse of History*. The most famous literary document which illustrates these effects is Oswald Spengler's *The Decline of the West* (London: Allen and Unwin, 1926–28).

3. Contemporary manifestations of pragmatic make-believe are so common as to leave one at

a loss which to cite as an example. As apt as any is the current North American search for a purpose, when what is wanted is not a truth which commands dedication, but merely an effective tool in the struggle against neurosis, juvenile delinquency or cold war foes. Such a tool, if it is merely a tool, is foredoomed to ineffectiveness.

Commenting on pragmatic make-believe in its religious application, Erich Frank writes: "If we believe in . . . God not because He is the truth, but assume His truth only because we believe in Him, then there are as many gods and as many truths and values as there are beliefs. In that case, pluralism is the inescapable consequence, and it remains for the individual and his liking to choose his own truth and his own God. . . . This subjective concept of belief is a contradiction in itself. A belief that believes only in itself is no longer a belief. For true belief transcends itself; it is a belief in something—in a truth which is not determined by faith but which, on the contrary, determines faith." *Philosophical Understanding and Religious Truth* (London-New York-Toronto: Oxford University Press, 1945), pp. 42–43.

The pragmatic is by no means to be confused with the existentialist concept of religious truth. The latter does not assert that commitment *makes* a belief true. It asserts that only in commitment can a person discover whether a belief *is* true, and hence—since commitment is "subjective" whereas the truth to which it commits itself is "objective" (if it is truth at all)—that all religious commitment is shot through with risk. Thus Abraham's predicament, as expounded in Kierkegaard's *Fear and Trembling* (Garden City, N.Y.: Doubleday, 1954), is that *if* God commands him to sacrifice Isaac, then this commandment is "objective," i.e., valid quite independently of Abraham's belief or lack of belief; but that, at the same time, Abraham has no standards other than his own "subjective" belief in terms of which to decide whether the commandment is objective and divine, or the mere product of his own imagination.

4. So long as "belief which believes only in itself" (cf. note 3) still believes in *one* thing beyond itself—democratic tolerance—it will tolerate a pluralism of beliefs. It is when the overwhelming need for certainty and absoluteness destroys this one remaining belief that "belief which believes only in itself" turns into ideological fanaticism. On the connection between scepticism and fanaticism, cf. Karl Jaspers, *Philosophie* (Berlin: Springer-Verlag, 1948), p. 208. On the most demonic form of contemporary ideological fanaticism, cf. Hermann Rauschning, *The Revolution of Nihilism* (New York: Longmans, Green and Company, 1939).

Perhaps the most arresting account of totalitarianism is Hannah Arendt's *The Origins of Totalitarianism* (New York: Meridian Books, 1958). Among the countless insights offered in this brilliant work is the close and indeed inseparable connection, in totalitarianism, between nihilism, ideology, fanaticism and the perpetuity of "movement." It was an essential part of Nazism to assert "the futility of everything that is an end in itself" (ibid., p. 323); for only then could the deified "movement of history" be absolute and all-embracing. Yet this "movement" was itself devoid of definable ends toward which it was directed; for only thus could the "Fuehrer's" authority have the kind of absoluteness which included the defining and arbitrary redefining of every "program" as whim dictated. It was therefore not at all out of character that men such as Hitler and Goebbels should, in the end, have expressed ghoulish satisfaction at the prospect that their downfall might carry in train the doom, not only—or even at all—of their enemies, but of the "master-race."

4 Self-Realization and the Search for God

A Critique of Modern Humanism and a Defence of Jewish Supernaturalism

Therefore shall a man first take upon himself the yoke
of the Kingdom of Heaven, and then take upon himself
the yoke of the commandments.

M. Berakot 2.2

I

∗ Man will at all times seek ultimate integration. It is intolerable to him that his life as a whole should not have a unity through which he can assess meaning to all its aspects.

It is significant that the criterion governing most modern attempts at such a synthesis can be expressed by the term "self-realization." Idealists and romanticists mean by this term the realization of an ideal self slumbering within every person; pragmatists and naturalists refer rather to the whole realm of human living, physical as well as spiritual. They agree that to give ultimate meaning to his life man must turn on himself, arousing those powers in himself which represent his highest opportunity.

Underlying this view is the faith that what is contradictory and evil in human nature is merely a lack of something; that it is "unreal" or "unnatural"; and that the individual can master it and aspire to perfection by realizing what is positive, his "real" or "natural" self. Thus, "self-realization" means to the idealist the realization or approximation of an envisaged ideal self. And it is taken for granted, first, that the individual is able to form the right conception of his ideal self, and secondly, that to realize or approximate it is a task which is obstructed by no basic obstacle. In the naturalist frame of reference, the prime criterion of self-realization is health. Evil is "the unnatural," which health automatically eliminates. Health produces social harmony because it balances pleasure and duty—a healthy egoism and a healthy altruism; it produces inner harmony because the healthy man concentrates on such of his problems as are solvable, ignoring those which are not. Health also gives freedom to the individual's creative powers while providing harmless outlets for his destructive urges—and creativity is fulness of life. Harmony eliminates evil; creativity eliminates emptiness.

Reprinted from *Quest for Past and Future* (Bloomington: Indiana University Press, 1968), 27–51, 319–22.

Religion also is interpreted in terms of self-realization. The fact that many modern definitions of religion do not even include God indicates what has happened: religion has been transformed from a total integration of life through relation to a supernatural God into total integration through self-realization. The convictions leading to this transformation are again the same: all meaning that the individual can find in his life is inherent in his own nature; and any meaning that he cannot find in himself is both unattainable and practically irrelevant, therefore properly to be ignored.

Other interpretations of religion do include God. But, again, in many of these, He appears as an *idea* only, His *existence* being acknowledged with embarrassment if acknowledged at all. Afterlife, salvation, eternal judgment are here meaningless words; nature and history are interpreted in terms of science. An existing God, if affirmed at all, is at best permitted to retain the function of a First Cause, required perhaps for cosmological interpretation but of little if any significance for the life of the individual. *Ideas* of God, however, are here regarded as of utmost importance for the individual's life. For the kind of idea he has of God will determine his scale of values and, thus, indirectly, the kind of life he is motivated to live. Individual life, as well as human history, can become

> a battle for the pure idea of God and man, which is not to end until the principle of divine holiness has done away with every form of life that tends to degrade and disunite mankind, and until Israel's Only One has become the unifying power and the highest ideal of all humanity.[1]

Here man undoubtedly creates God in his own image, ideas of God deriving not from an existing God who reveals Himself, but from human conception and evaluation. Again, the actual faith behind this religion is a faith in the "true" or "real" self which enables man both to form adequate ideas of God and to live without basic difficulty in *imitatio Dei.*

What becomes of prayer when God is understood as an idea only? Where every trace of even unconscious belief in the being of God is lost, prayer is no longer an appeal to the Other for help and guidance; it is an activity designed to arouse and inspire the better, the true self. The individual no longer seeks help from God, but from himself.

Whatever may be the lasting value of this ideal of self-realization or the partial truth in it, as a principle of ultimate integration it is totally inadequate. The reason for its inadequacy is the error of the faith on which it is based. If an ultimate self, harmonious, perfect, and unambiguous, were realizable, "self-realization" could perhaps serve as the principle of ultimate integration. A man's ideals might not, then, be absolute, but they would be the best he could know or be expected to know. As to his realization of the ideals, he might be far from complacent; but he could be confident at least that the degree of perfection he would achieve would depend only on his knowledge of the ideals and on the energy he was ready to devote to their realization. He would definitely not need the guidance or mercy of an existing God. His unconcern with his own ultimate destiny could be understood as the heroic attitude of a good soldier who is concerned to do his duty, but gives no thought to his own fate.

But this kind of self-confidence and heroic self-sufficiency rest on a tragic illusion. [There is no such thing as a single, unambiguous, perfect self, the source and end of ultimate integration.] On the contrary, the more deeply the individual searches his soul, the more clearly does he come to understand the irreducible tensions which lie in his nature. Biological necessity and spiritual freedom are not merely mutually irreducible, which would still make possible a division of authority, as it were, between these two parts of human nature; they are also inextricably intertwined. Face these tensions in their sharpness and profundity, and you at once recognize that the one potential self is an illusion; you can no longer discover the unambiguous self you can and ought to be—and to give it adjectives such as "ideal," "creative," "natural," or "healthy," is no help at all.

The unprejudiced man soon senses that there is something wrong with self-realization as the principle of ultimate integration. If he attempts self-realization in the naturalist terms of health, he himself transcends this attempt sufficiently to feel that health does not exhaust his ultimate obligation. Health, with all its happy implications, seems to be merely what makes him fit to face that obligation. At times, it even seems necessary to sacrifice health in the service of ultimate responsibility. Health comes to seem something like an ultimate criterion only when sickness renders him unable to be genuinely responsible.[2] If he attempts self-realization in idealist terms, setting up an ideal and striving to reach it, he transcends this attempt sufficiently to marvel at his presumptuousness. Knowing his ideal to stem from himself, he suspects it of being tainted with hidden self-interest. And even while striving to reach that ideal, he knows his effort to be vitiated by motives which are anything but pure. Nor can he ever free himself entirely from the fetters of this impurity. For every effort designed to achieve that effect has its own admixture of impure motives.

That these misgivings are not empty scruples, the twentieth century illustrates with abundant clarity. It demonstrates the fact that destructiveness is not merely something "unnatural," the product of sickness, and it demonstrates that an idealistic attitude is not in itself a sufficient guarantee of moral goodness. "Normal" men beyond suspicion of sickness, morbidity, and frustration "express themselves" in war, destruction, and wholesale murder. "Idealistic" youths serve evil tyrants in noble devotion, committing nameless crimes out of a sincere sense of duty, and sacrificing their lives to the kingdom of evil. [This is the stark fact: when health becomes the ultimate law, the "blond beast" is set free for breaking the fetters of morality; when the spirit is its own unqualified measure, Satan, the perverted spirit, is free also, transforming a mere urge for security into a metaphysical lust for power, a mere desire for survival and perpetuation into a mystic yearning for eternal glory gained through terror and destruction.]

To recoil from these criminal manifestations is not to free oneself of the roots of the evil. Who does not know the ruthlessness and hardness of heart that sometimes go with health, or the difficulty of controlling the destructive urges stemming from vitality? And as for man's spiritual life, what of envy masquerading as righteousness, cruelty as justice, selfishness called freedom, avarice called equality? Happily, in most cases, such perversions only partly corrupt the ideal into which they enter; but, tragically, the perversion is only partly conscious, and only partly corrigible. The individual who understands this situation and still has the courage to attempt the realization of a pure and ideal self will do so in profound humility. But this humility, too, if conceived in terms of self-realization, becomes tainted with self-righteousness.

✱ [Ultimate integration is inaccessible through self-realization: it is equally inaccessible through religion defined in terms of self-realization.] As a historical and psychological phenomenon, religion may, and perhaps even must, be defined in terms of self-realization; but as a way of life claiming to be a *valid* synthesis, it cannot be defined in these terms. Characteristically, liberalism sees no need to distinguish radically between religion considered from the standpoint of history or psychology, and religion considered from the standpoint of its validity. For its whole faith rests on the hypothesis of one normative self, progressively revealed in personal and human history. But once this illusion is destroyed, a religion defined in terms of self-realization is revealed as pure nihilism.

The weakness inherent in a religion defined in terms of self-realization cannot be overcome by merely choosing another aspect or activity of the self as the source of certainty. In Schleiermacher's celebrated definition, religion is held to be, "a feeling of unqualified dependence."[3] But "feeling," too, is a kind of self-realization, and a religion defined in such terms suffers from the same weakness. Thus, if "feeling of unqualified dependence" refers to such feelings as are actual, religion will include sacrificial devotion to dictators and charlatans, and blind obedience to nation or race exalted as the manifestation of the Absolute.[4] If, on the other hand, we mean by this "feeling" an emotion men *ought* to have, we either set up arbitrarily someone's actual feeling as absolute standard, or we seek this standard through the conception of an ideal feeling. But then religion—the actual feeling of unqualified dependence—becomes secondary to the philosophy defining that ideal feeling, and dependent on its fate. Religion is no longer the ultimate source of total integration.

No religion, of course, can dispense with ideas man forms of God. What we are discussing here is the view that holds God to be an idea *only*, or else to be known and relevant only as such. Such God-ideas serve here as an ultimate principle of integration by making an absolute claim on man's allegiance. Now, it is plain that God-ideas have undergone a vast development in the history of civilization, and the claim of the liberal era that this development has the form of inevitable progress toward one fixed aim can hardly be sustained. On what basis, then, does a man give *absolute* allegiance to an idea which is relative to his civilization and to the caprices of his own nature? But let us suppose we could assume that the God-idea is steadily progressing toward absolute purity. If we believe that our God-idea is not altogether pure yet, by what standards do we know how high we have risen in the scale of purity? And by what right do we give *absolute* allegiance to an idea whose degree of relativity we do not know? If, on the other hand, we claim to have reached the final degree of purity in our idea of God, will not a later age smile at our presumptuousness? And again, by what standards do we measure its finality?

But the main objection to the religion of self-realization is not relativism; quite possibly an adequate philosophy of religion could overcome it. Let us assume, therefore, that we could conceive a God-idea sufficiently free from relative admixture to claim our absolute allegiance. This God, who is an idea only, can perhaps persuade and inspire; but He surely cannot succor, love, and forgive. To speak of the succor, love, and forgiveness of a God who is an idea only is to employ a misleading metaphor. There are, of course, those who find their lives totally integrated through divine commandment and inspiration, and who calmly do without succor and forgiveness. But these are people who are caught in the idealist illusion about their nature and power which we have already analyzed. To know of the inextricable togetherness of freedom and bondage which is our state, is to know that no total unity comes from a God-idea "enthroned on high," but unable to "look down low" (Ps. 113:5–6). While the Absolute Ideal may perhaps inspire to imitation, it at the same time paralyzes because of its very absoluteness. A God, then, who is an idea only, or relevant only as such, still fails to integrate our lives; and *this* failure is more critical than any we have yet considered. Indeed, it is the crucial failure of the religion of self-realization.

If life is to find total integration, we must seek it in a Reality transcending our contradictory self and the ideals and standards relative to it.

II

Though he may perceive the futility of attempting ultimate integration through self-realization, modern man feels that somehow he cannot escape that futility. Religious tradition once believed that it had found access to a Reality transcending the relativity of the self through divine *revelation* or else through *rational proof* of God's existence. Modern man seems to find both these paths closed to him.

Modern man has no reason to doubt the sincerity of those who have taken their own experience or the experience of others to be divine revelation. But his own intellectual conscience compels him to interpret "revelation" in terms of "experience-of-revelation." To him the authority of revelation depends on the authority of human experience.[5] This is still a form of self-realization, afflicted with all the weakness inherent in it. Thus, modern man feels himself confronted with the dilemma between a flight to a supernatural revealed authority which he can no longer accept, on the one hand, and a flight to an authoritativeness of human experience as little acceptable to him, on the other. Morally, this seems to be a dilemma between the sins of intellectual dishonesty and spiritual pride.

Nor does modern man find himself any better off when he tries to establish God's existence by rational proof. He may presuppose that his reason is equipped for the task and that, though it is part of mere relative man, its axioms and laws are those which govern ultimate reality. If so, he presupposes rather than proves the existence of a God who gave him reason so that he might know Him. This kind of faith appears to be implied in the traditional proofs of God. If modern man refuses to make that *apriori* assumption, the certainty of God becomes dependent on the capricious and relative "certainties" acquired by a relative reason; for by these God is to be proven. Such a God is never really certain; He is always a mere hypothesis, living in dependence on precarious certainties. Nor is He really God. It has often been pointed out that a God who is proved without being presupposed in this proof is both too "far" and too "near" to be God: He is too "far" because there is something nearer and more certain by which He is proved; He is too "near" because man's finite reason can pass judgment on Him. Again man is faced with a dilemma. To ascertain God's existence by rational proof he must presuppose either a God who fashioned his reason, or the capacity of his reason to prove a God whom he has not fashioned. To attempt rational proof of God in awareness of this situation seems either self-deception or outright insolence.

III

An iron logic, it seems, has led man from a synthesis found in God, to a synthesis found in an autonomous self, to the surrender of all aspiration toward ultimate standards and ultimate meaning. A self revealed as caught in relativity cannot be the source of ultimate integration, nor does it seem able to recover any access to an absolute God. But we should be reluctant to accept this development as inexorable. This would be to dismiss lightly and *in toto* what seemed unquestionable reality to so many religious generations. We must, then, probe a little more deeply into man's ultimate situation. To make this difficult task somewhat easier, let us first try to understand the meaning of God and of life with God as reflected in biblical and rabbinic tradition. For modernity has unconsciously tended to misinterpret these, in accordance with its own very different ideas.[6]

The biblical and rabbinic tradition is pervaded by the conviction that it is impossible to doubt or deny the existence of God.

The modern mind will at once attribute this conviction to philosophical naiveté and the inability to deal critically with evidence. But this notion hardly goes beyond the surface. It is true, of course, that the evidence presented for divine revelation is not examined as critically as it might be. Nature is too simply taken as evidence of a God who guides it. History is too naively assumed to prove divine retribution. The certainty stemming from personal experience is not subjected to adequate criticism. But, this kind of naive acceptance of evidence is only incidental to the certainty of the existence of God. For it is realized that the evidence frequently fails. Nature harbors evil as well as good. Human nature appears afflicted with shortcomings such as cannot be attributed to man's own fault. History, above all, shows conditions which impel a Jeremiah to contend: "Wherefore doth the way of the wicked prosper? Wherefore are all they secure that deal very treacherously?" (Jer. 12:1), and a rabbi must admit: "It is not in our power to explain either the prosperity of the wicked or the afflictions of the righteous."[7] "Times of wrath" occur, when "all people cry and weep, but their voice is not heard, even though they decree fast-days, roll themselves in dust, cover themselves with sackcloth and shed tears."[8] And often man finds no evidence in his heart of the presence of God.

But while the evidence can become doubtful, God cannot. If nature reveals evil, then God "form[s] light and create[s] darkness, make[s] peace and create[s] evil" (Isa. 45:7). The fact that men cannot see divine purpose evidenced in history merely proves that: "My thoughts are not your thoughts, neither are My ways your ways" (Isa. 55:8). If inner experience is dead, it is because God "hides his face" (Ps. 13:2; 44:35; 69:18), "stands off" (Ps. 10:1), "forgets" (Ps. 13:2), "forsakes" (Ps. 22:2), or "sleeps" (Ps. 44:24); but the failure of inner evidence never suggests that God does not exist. Even the great skeptic of the Bible, Kohelet, who regards life as a whole as vanity, concludes from this conviction: "This is the end of the matter, all having been heard: fear God, and keep His commandments; for this is the whole man" (Eccl. 12:13). No objective evidence to the contrary, and no feeling of being deserted, can affect the certainty of God. As Job puts it: "Though He slay me, yet will I trust in Him" (Job 13:15).

We cannot fairly dismiss this absolute and fact-defying certainty of God as the mental habit of a religious civilization. How then can we understand it? We shall be totally unable to do so unless we rid ourselves of the modern prejudice that all religious life is an evolution of religious *feelings* or *ideas*. In accordance with this prejudice, man forms notions of God with the assistance of external and internal evidence, and the more he becomes conscious of this activity of his, the more thoroughly does he arrive at a state of objective detachment in which he judges the merits of the God-idea, and weighs the evidence for the existence of God. However, when in Jewish tradition God's existence is nowhere doubted nor made dependent on evidence, this is not because man is here at too primitive a level to have reached the stage of objective and critical detachment; it is because of a profound certainty that such a detachment is impossible. *God's existence is man's existential apriori.*

> Whither shall I go from Thy spirit? Or whither shall I flee from Thy presence?
> If I ascend up into heaven, Thou art there;
> If I make my bed in the netherworld, behold, Thou art there.
> If I take the wings of the morning,
> And dwell in the uttermost parts of the sea;
> Even there would Thy hand lead me,
> And Thy right hand would hold me (Ps. 139:7–10).[9]

This is not a rather primitive and unscientific statement of a universal God-idea. From a God-idea one could "flee" at least to the extent of viewing it in an attitude of objective detachment. The God of the Bible is not an ultimate object; He is *the* Subject, each man's living, personal God. Any attempt to subject God's existence to critical judgment is, therefore, held to be insolence, because it means to judge the Judge. To deny His existence is more than insolence: it is "folly" (Ps. 14:1; 53:2), since it is the rejection by man of his own "light and salvation" (Ps. 27:1); it is rebellion, since it is the attempt to replace God's authority by man's (Ps. 10:4; also Ezek. 28:9). The denial of God is self-destruction or rebellion; it is never merely an erroneous objective statement. In his ultimate relation to Reality, man must be *participant*; he cannot remain *spectator*.

Attempts to describe the nature of this God in biblical and rabbinic tradition must be understood as part of this fundamental situation. The avowed task here is not to describe consistently and adequately an infinite God as He is in Himself, a task that could be undertaken only by an objective spectator. The task is to describe the living relation between this infinite God and finite man, and to do so as an inevitable participant.

God is infinite and yet directly related to each finite person. This is the inexplicable, yet indubitable, basic fact about God. He is "enthroned on high and looketh down low" (Ps. 113:5–6). He is both "far and near":

> God is far, for is He not in the heaven of heavens? And yet He is near, . . . for a
> man enters a synagogue, and stands behind a pillar, and prays in a whisper, and God

hears his prayer, and so it is with all His creatures. He is as near to His creatures as the ear to the mouth.[10]

The direct relation between the infinite God and the finite human person is by its very nature paradoxical. If this relation were one-sided, it would destroy itself; for then the infinite God would devour the finite person's freedom and his very identity. It is a mutual relation. "Everything is in the hands of Heaven except the fear of Heaven,"[11] is the word of a rabbi to whom human freedom is real yet limited by Divided Presence. But if this relation is a mutual one, then paradoxically the free actions and reactions of finite men make a difference to the infinite God. Biblical and rabbinic tradition express the reality of this paradoxical relation in a well-nigh infinite variety of metaphors. These metaphors, which are mostly anthropomorphisms, cannot be regarded as "impure" philosophical notions; they are *symbolic* terms designed to describe a relation which cannot be grasped in any terms other than symbolic. Occasionally the rabbis are fully conscious of this, especially when in their stress on human responsibility they even make the omnipotent God dependent on impotent man.

> *Ye are My witnesses, saith the Lord, and I am God* (Isa. 43:12). That is, when ye are My witnesses, I am God, and when ye are not My witnesses, I am, as it were, not God.[12]
>
> When the Israelites do God's will, they add to the power of God on high. When the Israelites do not do God's will, they, as it were, weaken the great power of God.[13]

The paradox in these statements is fully intended, and the term *"as it were"* has the full rank of a technical term in rabbinic theology, indicating the symbolic character of the statement it qualifies.[14]

God's nature, as revealed in His relation to man, reflects the paradox inherent in this relation. In rabbinic theology, the concepts of divine *justice* and divine *mercy* are striking in their prominence.[15] Philosophically, absolute justice and absolute mercy are mutually exclusive; but in rabbinic theology, they remain mutually irreducible. God's mercy, to the exclusion of His justice, would wipe out the difference between the righteous and the wicked. His justice, without His mercy, would destroy all men; and even if it be conceived that God tempers His justice to finite man, "demanding according to man's power," infinite divine retribution would still be totally incommensurable with finite human sin.

> *The Lord made heaven and earth.* This may be compared to a king who had some empty glasses. Said the king: "If I pour hot water into them, they will burst; if cold, they will contract and snap." What then did the king do? He mixed hot and cold water and poured it into them, and so they remained unbroken. Even so, said the Holy One, blessed be He: "If I create the world on the basis of mercy alone, its sins will be great; on the basis of justice alone, the world cannot exist. Hence I will create it on the basis of justice and mercy, and may it then stand."[16]

This togetherness of justice and mercy is not a harmonious compromise. In a mutual limitation through compromise, both justice and mercy would lose their meaning. Thus R. Akiba insists on the absolute and unqualified justice of God's judgment,[17] and in the Midrash God is made to say:

> All I do, I do in justice. If I sought to pass beyond justice but once, the world could not endure.[18]

Consequently, men are warned not to make light of their responsibility before the bar of divine justice:

> He who says, God is indulgent, his life shall be outlawed.[19]
> If the evil inclination says to you, "Sin, and God will forgive you," believe it not.[20]

But on the other hand, divine mercy is likewise absolute and unqualified. For whatever their relative merits, before God all men need mercy absolutely. Even Moses and David asked that their sins be forgiven, by reason not of their merits, but of God's grace.[21] Nor did they pray thus only because of their humility.

> All men need grace, including Abraham, for whose sake grace came plenteously into the world.[22]

The Midrash expresses the principle of mercy:

> He said, 'I owe no creature anything, but I give to them gratuitously.'[23]

Justice and mercy coexist:

> If we have merit, and if we possess good deeds, He gives us of what is ours; if not, then He acts charitably and lovingly toward us from what is His.[24]

But do not then both justice and mercy become meaningless? They may become so in philosophical theory, but not in the religious life. The ultimate unity of mercy and justice in God is indeed an ineffable mystery.[25] Man not only can, but must live in the double certainty of his responsibility before the bar of divine justice and of his security in divine mercy. For radically speaking, man can, and cannot, do the will of God. Insofar as he can do His will, it is only by reason of God's help;[26] yet insofar as he cannot do it, his contrition is a spontaneous and acceptable offering.[27] Man must pray, not only for forgiveness of sins already committed, but also for divine help against future temptations.[28] Yet a man who acts has full freedom, and no sin is preordained.[29]

The sins of the past, of which no man is free, do not destroy the freedom of present and future. For man is at all times free to repent, whatever the sins of the past.[30] In contrast with the gates of prayer which, tragically, are often closed, the gates of repentance are always open.[31] But again, even for the ability to repent man must pray for divine assistance.[32]

Thus the religious life is a tension between two certainties: responsibility before God, and safety in Him. There is no *apriori* limitation to either of these.

> The Israelites say to God, "Lord of the world, Thou knowest how hard is the strength of the evil inclination." God says, "Remove it a little in this world, and I will rid you of it altogether in the world-to-come."[33]

How much is "a little"? That cannot be known. That is why man must both tremble and rejoice: he trembles because, before the throne of divine justice, what he does is nothing compared with what he ought to do; he rejoices because, nevertheless, it is something, and because through the mercy of God it is everything. Therefore it has been said: "Love and fear God; tremble and rejoice when you perform the commandments."[34]

IV

Guided by the insights of biblical and rabbinic tradition, we may penetrate the problem of man's ultimate integration sufficiently to grasp this basic fact: the way in which modern man has arrived at the situation we have tried to describe is not, as he has habitually assumed, necessary and unquestionable; on the contrary, it is rather founded on subjective and dubious assumptions. Modern man has dogmatically assumed the same approach in his search for ultimate integration as he has adopted in his scientific inquiries—an attitude of objective, critical detachment.

This attitude is quite proper in the case of scientific inquiry, because scientific inquiry deals with the realm of *objects*. We know objects by detaching ourselves from involvement in them, and by simultaneously subjecting them to our critical judgment. The exercise of autonomous judgment is possible because man is, in principle, able to view the world as object. It is necessary because he requires objectivity to plan both his biological and his moral life.

However, if modern man claims objective detachment and the autonomy of his critical judgment to be basic to the problem of his ultimate integration, he commits a plain fallacy. For man's *existence* cannot become an object for him, neither can he assume toward it an attitude of objectivity, detachment, and autonomy. While he thinks in "detachment," he is in fact involved in existence. Thus, an attitude of objective detachment and objective judgment toward the problem of ultimate integration is a form of self-deception, due to our inability to free ourselves from the habits we form in relation to the world of objects. Or it is a hidden dogma, a subjective decision taken in relation to his own existence. In the very act of assuming an attitude of detachment, and of subjecting it to his autonomous judgment, man is already deciding to be his own judge and the master of his own life. Little wonder that the results at which he arrives on this basis confirm the hidden initial dogma.

In the same manner, we must consider the question of God's existence. If there is a God, and if He is *God*, He embraces man's existence with such totality as to make objective detachment altogether impossible. If a man can pass judgment on God and His existence, it is not God on whom he passes judgment. A God who can be an *object* is not God. Because a God who is subjected to man's objective judgment is not God, *God can neither be proven nor disproven.* If God is God, He is not an object, but *the* Subject. He is man's absolute existential *apriori*.

Insight into the impossibility of assuming an attitude of detachment and autonomous judgment would, in itself, lead merely to an infinite suspension of judgment. But if man becomes fully aware of his position, he realizes too that he must go further. For he cannot remain neutral here. Thought can be suspended, but not existence. Suspension of judgment itself is here an impermissible judgment. Man exists by compulsion; he is therefore compelled to make a *decision.* For to refuse to make a decision is also to decide.

Thus, because man cannot detach himself from his existence, he is compelled to meet it with decision. And if he is in search of ultimate integration, he must seek it in ultimate decision. Ultimate decision must be made in the perspective constituting his existence: the togetherness of, and conflict between, dependence and transcendence, and the inherent necessity to integrate these into ultimate unity.

What, basically, are the choices possible in this situation?

Man can make an effort to recover the blissful pagan ignorance which he has lost. He can tell himself that his transcendence is reducible to his dependence or his dependence to his transcendence; that his responsibility is merely the function of his needs, or that it can easily rule them. But as we have seen, history sooner or later shocks man out of such ignorance or self-deception.

Man can face his conflict but belittle the need for its ultimate integration. He may claim to be satisfied with transforming his one problem into many problems, and with solving these merely pragmatically. But he transcends the relativity of his life sufficiently to remain profoundly disturbed by a wholly relative existence.

Man can face his conflict and accept it as inexorable fate, realizing that ultimate integration cannot come through himself, and deciding to live in that knowledge. This is tragic existence. For if he lives his unreconciled conflict absolutely, his vitality and his search for happiness become tragic futility, his responsibility and sacrifice become tragic quixotism.

Man can, and in this situation often will, rise in rebellion. Aware of the inexorability of the conflict, he may yet strive to transcend it and to become his own measure. But this is the counsel of despair; it makes man say:

> I shall persist in utter metaphysical defiance, infinitely lonely, supported only by my moral insight. I shall offer absolute resistance to the ultimate principle and shall despise it.[35]

Were man's weakness only biological, he might well take this heroic attitude. He might despise pain, unhappiness, and death because of the autonomy of his moral insight. But his weakness is not only biological; it is also spiritual, because it is spiritually that he is sinful. Therefore, this attempt at self-redemption amounts to rebellion, and is tragically futile.

But man can make yet another decision, the decision of faith. He can submit to God as his existential *apriori;* he can accept the "yoke of the Kingdom of Heaven."

V

The decision of faith differs from other decisions as radically as these do from objective detachment. Decision stems from the insight that existence is inescapable. The decision of faith stems from the insight that God is inescapable. Man surrenders his neutrality in the realization that he cannot be neutral; he surrenders authority over his existence in the realization that he cannot be his own authority. In the state of existential decision, he knows that he cannot refute God;

in the decision of faith, he knows that he cannot reject or escape Him. He knows that whatever he decides, he is under the authority of God: Nebuchadnezzar does the will of God as fully as do Moses or David. Indeed, the very agony in which man tries to reject God, testifies to Him. And in rebellion, man harms not God, but himself.

We must understand clearly the specific nature of the decision of faith. A modern writer properly warns:

> If we believe in . . . a . . . God not because He is the truth, but assume His truth only because we believe in Him, then there are as many gods and as many truths and values as there are beliefs.[36]

If the decision of faith is on the same level as other possible decisions, man makes God's sovereignty or even His existence depend on his belief in, or acceptance of, Him. This is the final heresy. The distinctive nature of the decision of faith is that it is at the same time no decision at all, because in accepting God's sovereignty man realizes that he accepts that to which he is subject regardless of his decision.

We are here at the crucial point in man's religious situation. *Before* he makes the decision of faith, he is free not to make it. He may thereby lose all hope of ultimate integration; he may live a life of self-contradiction; he may arrive at self-destruction: all the same, he is free not to accept the "yoke of the Kingdom of Heaven." *After* the decision of faith, there is no freedom to reject God; there is merely freedom to rebel against Him. But in rebellion as well as in submission, man now testifies to God. Even the non-believer testifies to Him, through his tragic ignorance.

Here, then, we have the fundamental tension in the religious life: the decision of faith in which man expresses the irrelevance of all his deciding to the sovereignty of God is, nevertheless, the greatest of all decisions. Total submission to God is not only the ultimate in humility; it is also the extreme in self-confidence: "Everything is in the hands of Heaven except the fear of Heaven."[37] If God exists, He is the *absolute existential apriori*; yet man dares to leap from a position in which he is free not to accept Him to total acceptance of His sovereignty. Whence this momentous audacity?

Man finds the grounds for both his humility and his self-confidence in himself. He is in a state of dependence; yet he transcends it in that he knows it. It is because he knows of his sin that he cannot escape his obligation. Sin would not be sin if man could not know of it. Knowing it, he must face the responsibility to combat it. What is man's ultimate attitude to be? If humility leads him to surrender his obligation, he escapes from what he knows to be his responsibility. If awareness of his responsibility leads him to battle his weakness entirely by himself, he becomes involved in sinful pride.

From this contradictory situation the decision of faith derives both its audacity and its humility, which become an ineffable unity. Realizing the audacity implied in the decision of faith, man knows that to let his humility destroy *this* audacity is to escape from his responsibility. If there is a God, he does not wipe out man's responsibility; He makes it inescapable. He is each man's own personal God—"near," not "far."

But, all the same, man could not venture the decision of faith were it not for the fact that this daring is at the same time no daring at all, and that therefore man's supreme self-confidence is at the same time his supreme humility. For if there is a God, man's total dependence on Him includes both his dependence and his transcendence, both his acceptance and his rejection of Him. Man's faith, his own *decision*, is then at the same time *given*. Revelation, which becomes revelation only through man's decision to accept it as such, is then at the same time absolutely given, because God's sovereignty includes man's decision. For if there is a God, He is the sovereign of each man's personal destiny—"near," not "far."

The decision of faith, then, is the only decision which man can make without qualification. To accept the yoke of the Kingdom of Heaven is the only ultimate integration man can realize, because here it is not he alone who realizes it. But this ultimate integration does not imply an infallible security. On the contrary, because it transcends all evidence, proofs, and refutations, faith is the greatest of all risks. Even the ancients, who felt so secure in their faith, sensed this. "Even though He slay me, yet will I trust in Him," are the words of Job. The Mishnah says: " 'Thou shalt love the Lord thy God with . . . all thy soul' (Deut. 6:5),—that is to say, even if He takes thy soul from thee."[38]

Modern man knows that the risk is vastly greater even than this. For he understands what the ancients in their faith were not always conscious of: the position of man before the decision of faith. In a paradoxical paraphrase of the passage of the Mishnah, modern man might tell himself: " 'Thou shalt love the Lord thy God with . . . all thy soul'—that is to say: thou shalt love absolutely Him of whom thou hast certainty only by reason of thy love. And thou shalt rejoice in this thy unique opportunity for absolute love."

VI

"A man must first take upon himself the yoke of the Kingdom of Heaven, and then take upon himself the yoke of the commandments."[39] To accept direct and absolute responsibility is to the man facing God—the decision of faith having been made—not only a possibility, but a necessity.

Before God, man becomes free. For at last, he is redeemed from his tragic dilemma. No longer must he accept his responsibility with an implicit claim to moral autonomy—obvious presumptuousness, in the light of his confused insight and sinful actions—or live in an action-paralyzing humility which betrays his responsibility. To accept total responsibility is now no longer an act vitiated by hidden pride or self-assertion: it is a glorification of God. For it is God who "gave the Law," and along with it "all the implements by which it is carried out."[40] It is His grace which makes Him "demand according to *our* power"[41]—a power which stems from Him. The self-confidence required for the assumption of responsibility is here identical with total humility. Of course, there is still, as there always is, danger of self-perversion through sinful pride; but man may risk this danger now for the sake of God.

Man's *decision for* responsibility is here redeemed from its inherent enigma; his *life in* responsibility is freed from the stifling influence of human failure. Environment, which often reveals individuals and their consciences as products rather than agents, bedevils their sense of responsibility. Tantalizing evidence of so-called "inexorable" "waves of the future" saps the strength of conscience. But such spells have no power over the man who lives before God. For he knows that, fundamentally, he finds his law not in looking forward, but in looking upward. And he knows: "It is not given in thy hand to complete the work, but thou art not free to desist from it."[42]

Even more dangerous to life in responsibility is the failure of the individual himself. Nothing ordinarily threatens a man's sense of responsibility more than the seeming inevitability of failure and defeat. But upon the individual living before God the effect is very different. For the tension between ideal responsibility and actual sinfulness becomes a source of ever-renewed spiritual energy, drawn from the certainty that through the mercy of God the discrepancy is not after all catastrophic.

To the man who lives before God the *possibility* of taking upon himself the "yoke of the commandments" is a *necessity*. God is man's own, personal God: he cannot elude or escape Him; he is personally responsible to Him; he cannot evade the directness of this claim by seeking shelter in "circumstances"—at least in principle he is always responsible. Nor can he escape it through referring to his own past habits: the doors of repentance are always open.

But how can man know the commandments of God so that he may do them? What is it that he is to do? The man who lives under the "yoke of the Kingdom of Heaven" need never be in a state of total ignorance. His knowledge of himself before God involves solid principles of social conduct. If men are directly responsible, then they possess a dignity requiring that they never treat one another "as means only."[43] If God makes men responsible, this requirement is the law of God.

But man can never hope to possess the law of God in a set of general norms to which he need only subordinate his individuality. Even in the realm of social conduct, the need for its application involves a leap from the security of the general norm into hazardous individual decision. And the individual's responsibility before God is not confined to the realm of social conduct. How then is man to gain knowledge? Is he to determine the law of God in his heart? Is not "the heart . . . deceitful above all things, and exceedingly weak" (Jer. 17:9)? In this conflict man turns to God, calling upon Him to be his God *here and now*, even as he himself must be His servant here and now. His general fate and freedom are given to him by God in His "farness"; he now calls upon God's "nearness" to give him specific guidance. "Give me understanding that I may keep Thy law" (Ps. 119:34). "Teach me Thy statutes" (Ps. 119:26). Sometimes, his plea is answered. Sometimes, he can say: "Thy word is a lamp unto my feet, and a light unto my path" (Ps. 119:105). But sometimes, too, he learns the law of God only in his affliction, and at other times no answer comes at all. For God hides His face and answers not.

This is tragic affliction: man's life as a whole is in God's hands, but he does not know its meaning here and now; he has accepted the "yoke of the commandments," but he is not told the unique laws which pertain to his unique situation. Yet even this affliction need not be catastrophic. If God is not "near," He is at least "far." Where God fails to speak, man both can and must dare attempt to fathom His law. He *must* do so because of his responsibility before God's judgment. He *can* do so because of the ultimate security of all he does and plans in God's mercy.

VII

"Do His will as if it were thy will, and He will do thy will as if it were His will."[44] Man cannot ultimately make himself the measure of his life. "Self-realization" cannot be his standard of ultimate integration; rather must he surrender his self to the "yoke of the Kingdom of God" and to the "yoke of His commandments." But strangely, he who thus loses his self gains it; he who surrenders the aim of self-realization to God arrives at the fulness of self-realization.

To accept the law of God is to accept the limitations of human existence. For this law is given to *men*; it is given neither to angels, who have no natural urges, nor to animals, who do not possess the direct responsibility of freedom. Therefore, to accept the law of God is neither to mortify vitality nor to stupefy moral responsibility; it is to find redemptive reconciliation between the joy of living and the burden of responsibility.

Once, when he had caught a glimpse of the radical contradictions inherent in his condition, man's vitality was paralyzed. The joy of his every breath was withered by an inescapable sense of guilt. For while he enjoyed even a single breath of life, he knew that others were crying to heaven in mortal pain. To give his joy precarious survival, he had to try to escape from his moral self. But now it is different. Having surrendered to God's commandment his self-assertive joy of living, he receives it back as a gift from God. Accepting humbly God's law to men, he accepts as part of it the life of nature. What was before egoistic self-assertion set up against duty is now glorification of God through acceptance of the human lot. At least in principle, man's vital and moral selves have found reconciliation.

In the last analysis, to attempt ultimate integration through self-realization is to attempt to escape human nature. In seeking unity in himself in spite of the contradictions inherent within him, man cannot but strive to become either an angel or a beast. Both of these attempts end in a hopeless loss of self. Man finds his self only when he surrenders himself to God, because thus only does he come to accept the contradictions of his state. He no longer runs away from, but lives, his human existence. He can live thus, and do so serenely, because of his confidence that ultimately all contradictions rest in the mercy and justice of God.

Man continues to live in pain and anguish. He continues to be troubled by the question of where the expression of his vitality begins to conflict with his moral responsibility. But after his humble and serene acceptance of his human lot as a whole, this question is no longer paralyzing, this conflict no longer catastrophic. And even his pain and anguish are now a praise of God.[45]

Notes

1. Kaufmann Kohler, *Jewish Theology* (New York, 1918), p. 15.

2. Psychologists may argue that all men are sick. But if this is true to an extent rendering all human responsibility relative, then men can neither heal themselves or each other, and no one can lay down standards of health and sickness.

3. F.D.E. Schleiermacher, *Dogmatik*, §36; cf. also *Ueber die Religion* (Leipzig, 1880), p. 75; *Psychologie* (Berlin, 1862), p. 461.

4. That Schleiermacher actually came close to such a position is shown by Reinhold Niebuhr, *The Nature and Destiny of Man*, vol. i (New York, 1945), pp. 86ff.

5. We are here concerned only with the naive, uncritical acceptance of revelation and its critical dissolution into humanism. We are, of course, very far from holding that revelation must ulti-

mately be interpreted in terms of experience-of-revelation, and that humanism, rather than supernaturalism, has the last word.

6. In these paragraphs, we do not, of course, attempt to give a complete picture of biblical and rabbinic views on the subject. Our task here is rather to select such aspects as will clarify the perspective in which biblical and rabbinic views must be understood. For thorough interpretations, see G. F. Moore, *Judaism*, vol. i (Cambridge, 1927), pp. 357ff.; also S. Schechter, *Some Aspects of Rabbinic Theology* (London, 1909), pp. 21ff.

7. M. Abot 4.19. We follow the interpretation of J. Hertz, *Pirke Aboth* (New York, 1945), p. 77. The sentiment here expressed is, of course, unusual in rabbinic theology.

8. Tosefta Derek Eretz, Perek Haminim, 31 (*The Treatise Derek Eretz*, ed. by M. Higger [New York, 1935], text pp. 293ff., translation pp. 110ff.).

9. For biblical literature, cf. especially the Book of Jonah; for rabbinic literature, passages quoted by Newman-Spitzer, *The Talmudic Anthology* (New York, 1945), pp. 163ff.

10. J. Berak. ix.1, 13a, line 17. In this and many other subsequent quotations, I have followed the translation of Montefiore and Loewe, *A Rabbinic Anthology* (London, 1938).

11. B. Berak. 33b.

12. Midr. Ps. on Ps. 123:1.

13. Lam. R. I, 33, on Lam. 1:6.

14. This is expressed with particular clarity in this passage: "R. Simeon b. Yohai said: . . . 'Only when Israel does God's will is His heavenly palace secure' . . . Nevertheless, R. Simeon b. Yohai also quoted, 'This is my Lord and I will praise Him' (Ex. 15:2), and he said: 'When I praise Him, He is glorified, and when I do not praise Him, He is, *as it were,* glorified in Himself' " (Sifre Deut., Berakah, 346, 144a).

15. It is, of course, well known that the rabbis interpreted the biblical *Elohim* as referring to the divine attribute of justice, and *YHWH* to that of mercy; cf., e.g., Pesikta (ed. Buber), 164a.

16. Gen. R. XII, 15. Cf., among numerous similar passages, the following: "Abraham said unto God, 'If thou desirest to maintain the world, strict justice is impossible; and if thou desirest strict justice, the world cannot be maintained. . . . Thou desirest the world and thou desirest justice. Take one or the other. Unless thou art a little indulgent, the world cannot endure' " (Gen. R. XXXIX, 6); cf. also Lev. R. X, 1.

17. Tanhuma (ed. Buber), Wayera, 49a.

18. Tanhuma (ed. Buber), Mishpatim, 41b.

19. B. Baba K. 50a; cf. also J. Shek. v. 2, 48d, line 35.

20. B. Hag. 16a.

21. Sifre Deut., Waethanan, 26, 70b. The whole of Israel is represented as making the same request (Midr. Ps. on Ps. 71:2).

22. Gen. R., Hayye Sarah, LX, 2.

23. Tanhuma B., Deut., Waethanan, 5a.

24. Midr. Ps. on Ps. 72:1.

25. This is indicated in Midr. Ps. on Ps. 72:1.

26. Cf., e.g., Deut. R., Nitztzabim, VIII, 6: "The law and all the implements by which it is carried out have been given, namely, modesty, beneficence, uprightness, and reward."

27. Cf., e.g., Pes. K. 158b: "If a mortal man uses broken vessels, it is a disgrace, but with God it is otherwise, for all His servants are broken vessels, as it is said, 'The Lord is nigh unto the brokenhearted and the contrite in spirit he will save' (Ps. 34:18)."

28. Cf. Raba's prayer: "O Lord! Before I was formed, I was without worth; and even now, having been formed, I am as if I had not been formed. Dust I am in my life; how much more in my death! Behold, I am before Thee a vessel of shame and disgrace. May it be Thy will, O Lord my God, that I do not sin; but the sins which I have already committed before Thee, wash them away with Thy great mercy, but not through tribulations and diseases" (B. Berak. 17a); cf. also B. Yoma 87b.

29. In Lev. R. Metzora, XVIII, 1, God is represented as demanding of man that he return his soul to God in the same state of purity in which it was given to him.

30. "If your sins are as high as heaven, even unto the seventh heaven, and even unto the throne of glory, and you repent, I will receive you" (Pes. R. 185a); cf. also Pes. K. 163b; Midr. Ps. on Ps. 120:7.

31. Lam. R., III, 60, on Lam. 3:43.

32. Cf. J. Berak. vi. 2, 7d, line 46: "May it be Thy will, O Lord our God and God of our fathers, that Thou put it into our hearts to perform a perfect repentance before Thee . . ."

33. Num. R., Behaaloteka, XV, 16.

34. Ab. R.N. (vers. I), XLI, 67a.

35. One of Dostoevsky's formulations of the nihilistic point of view, quoted by E. Frank, *Philosophical Understanding and Religious Faith* (New York, 1945), p. 38.

36. Frank, op. cit., p. 42.

37. B. Berak. 33b.

38. M. Berak. 9.5.

39. M. Berak. 2.2.

40. Deut. R., Nitztzabim, VIII, 6.

41. Num. R., Pinehas, XXI, 22.

42. M. Abot 2:21.

43. Cf. Immanuel Kant's celebrated dictum.

44. M. Abot 2.4.

45. M. Berak. 9.5.

5 *Franz Rosenzweig and the New Thinking*

The dust-jacket of this book,[1] with a humility not often found on dust-jackets, informs us that it is not intended as an analysis or interpretation of Franz Rosenzweig's work. Professor Glatzer seeks as much as possible to disappear behind his subject, and to present Rosenzweig in his own words. His attitude recalls Rosenzweig's own remark about Jewish tradition, to the effect that ten lines of translation are better than all "about."

Glatzer's modesty should not blind us to the fact that American Judaism owes him a considerable debt of gratitude. Rosenzweig may well be the most important Jewish thinker of our time; he is certainly the most difficult to transplant to America. To make him intelligible to American Jews without distorting or mutilating his thought was a task not for a slapdash compiler, but a serious scholar. Glatzer, a close student of both Rosenzweig and the contemporary Jewish scene in America, has succeeded most admirably.

Despite his rebellion against it, Rosenzweig is profoundly influenced by the great German idealistic tradition, in his problems, method and even his language. This is the main fact accounting for the difficulties in transplanting him. Because Kierkegaard's thought developed in the struggle with Hegel, the reader ignorant of Hegel is frequently unable to understand him. The same holds for Rosenzweig, except that in his case the influence of Schelling is even more marked. But who nowadays knows Hegel, let alone Schelling?[2]

But if Rosenzweig were a philosopher's philosopher, like Hegel and Schelling, it would be neither possible nor necessary to present him in a manner intelligible to the American Jewish layman. His central problem, however, is not a theoretical one, important and intelligible only to school philosophers. It is: how can and should the Jew live before God? Technical philosophy is important to him only in

Reprinted from *Judaism*, Vol. 2 (October, 1953): 367–72.

order to justify this question, and to help answer it. But this is a question which concerns, not the philosopher, but every Jew. And Rosenzweig's answer (or answers) to this question must, at least in principle, be intelligible to every Jew.

The present volume is addressed to Rosenzweig's fellow-Jews rather than his fellow-philosophers. This imposes the task on the compiler to omit, as far as possible, technical philosophical matter while concentrating on what we might call the existential. In employing this principle of selection, Glatzer is justified not merely by practical considerations, but by Rosenzweig himself. In Rosenzweig's later years, he observed that, in order to live and think as a Jew before God, he no longer required the *Stern der Erloesung*. That work—his "system of philosophy" (cf. *Zweistromland* p. 241)—had been a mere stage on his road back to Judaism.

The omission of technical philosophy from this volume, then, is not only justified but inevitable. Nevertheless, it involves certain dangers. There is already a widespread opinion that the so-called existential philosophy and theology are anti-scientific and irrationalist; indeed, not thought at all but autobiography posing as a system. The omission of Rosenzweig's technical thought, necessary though it is, may serve to strengthen this opinion. Glatzer tries his best to guard against this misunderstanding. But it is nevertheless to be feared that some of our critics will see in Rosenzweig just another one of those who could reenter the doors of a "medieval" synagogue only by leaving their reason outside.

This danger is, paradoxically, still further increased by the fact that Rosenzweig's was an impressive life. The story of his early religious and Jewish indifference, of his dramatic conversion to Judaism, of the heroic martyrdom of his seven years' illness is by now well-known. But it comes to life only in his letters, a remarkable, if not unique, document in Jewish spiritual autobiography. It was essential that Glatzer should have devoted fully as much space to Rosenzweig's life as to his thought. But precisely because he lived so impressively what he thought, some may feel that his thought is merely the reflection of his life, and thus, of no universal significance. And this would be a serious misunderstanding, and an injustice to Rosenzweig's intention.

What troubles us is the possibility that Rosenzweig's "new thinking" will be seriously misunderstood. Professor Glatzer, alive to the importance of the topic and the danger of the misunderstanding, gives this heading to his first group of selections. But fully to understand what the "new thinking" means, one must study, not only the *Stern der Erloesung* and the essay *Das neue Denken*, but some Hegel and Schelling as well. Those who lack the means of doing so may well regard this thinking, just because it is in some sense "personal," "subjective," "existential," as lacking all rationality and system. To help guard against this misunderstanding, we shall attempt to give some indication as to Rosenzweig's meaning.

According to Rosenzweig, the "new" thinking differs from the "old" in that in it the person of the philosopher is essential to his philosophy. After Hegel, he asserts, such a "personal" philosophy is the only one still possible, and he points to such men as Schopenhauer, Nietzsche and Kierkegaard to illustrate his contention.

But what is "personal" thinking? We may conveniently explain it by contrasting Greek with Biblical thought. The God of Greek philosophy is timeless, unchanging, and indifferent toward all but Himself. Man can relate himself to Him only by means of thought. This thought, if true, is timelessly true; and it is a truth indifferent toward the thinker's individuality. Indeed, in Aristotle the thinker, *qua* thinker, ceases to be an individual and becomes pure thought.

The Biblical God, too, may be timeless. But He is known only through His revelation; and that is *not* timeless. It is addressed not to man as such, but to *this* man, or *this* people, here and now. Moreover, the content of this revelation does not consist of timelessly true propositions; whether it is God's commandment, His promise, or God Himself, it is not abstractable from the moment to which it belongs, nor from those to whom it is addressed. Clearly then, Biblical man's thinking about God cannot be detached from his person. He must ask: what is God's command, or promise, to *me*. A person who commits such a detachment commits, in the eye of Biblical man, a grave error, no matter how loudly he may proclaim his "monotheism"; he to whom God is merely a "cosmic force," "first cause" or "source of value" is, no less than the *rasha* of the Haggadah, a *kofer b'ikkar*.

Now, this "personal standpoint" is, of course, not new at all in religion. On the contrary, every religious believer (at least every Jewish and Christian religious believer) shares it. But it *is* new in philosophy. The crucial question arises whether it is compatible with the objective which, in philosophy, is indispensable. At first sight it seems that it is not. If so, the "new thinking" will be neither new nor thinking.

Our question is answered if we consider what positions objective thought may adopt toward the personal standpoint of the believer. The first, and most obvious, position is to regard the objective standpoint of thought as superior to and more comprehensive than the personal standpoint of the believer. This is the position of Hegel, and the challenge which Rosenzweig faced. To Hegel, religion at its highest is that truth which is not in the form of truth. It is a true experience, but in an incomplete form. It regards God and man, while related, as yet truly separate; whereas in truth this separateness is but appearance. Absolute truth is reached, not in the faith and commitment of the religious believer, but in pure thought alone. The twentieth century American (who is not concerned with Hegel) finds a similar challenge in the psychologizing or sociologizing philosophies of our day. The believer speaks of God, His promise and His law; the "philosopher of religion" speaks of religious experience, its modes and laws: God has disappeared. Differ though they may in everything else, Hegel and modern "philosophy of religion" have this in common: the standpoint of objective thought is regarded not only as different from, but also as superior to, the personal commitment of the believer, and if this is true, then the authenticity of the God-man-relation has disappeared. Religious experience there may be, and it may be regarded as having all kinds of value; but God does not really speak to the believer who seems to hear His voice. Hegel forthrightly admitted this implication, whereas our "philosophers of religion" are more squeamish about admitting it; but the conclusion is, for all that, no less obvious.

Now let us consider the other alternative. Objective thought looks at the personal standpoint of faith and decides that it is authentic and true. God really speaks; and if and when He does His voice can be heard only from the personal standpoint. This implies at once that objective thought about the God-man-relation is less, not more than the actual relation; and that the philosopher cannot hear the voice of God *qua* philosopher, but only by making the leap into faith—*qua under.*[3]

This is an inversion of the Hegelian relationship between the personal and the objective standpoints. But this inversion does not necessarily reduce objectivity to shambles. True, the actual relation of man to God escapes philosophy. How could it be otherwise? But that relation has metaphysical presuppositions, which it is the business of thought and philosophy to clarify and defend. Among these are the doctrines argued in the *Stern der Erloesung:* the real separateness of God, man, world (argued against Hegel); the conception of history as a developing God-man-encounter (rather than the mere evolution of religious experience)—and many others. We do not here wish to consider whether the arguments by which Rosenzweig supports these doctrines are adequate. The point is that they *are* arguments: that the "new thinking" is—thinking.

In view of the importance of this matter and the prevailing misconceptions, let us consider it once more, from a slightly different angle. After having stressed the inevitability of the "personal standpoint," Rosenzweig asks: "is this still science?" (*Stern der Erloesung,* 1st edition, p. 135). He means: can the personal standpoint claim objective validity? He answers his own question as follows: "the bridge from the most subjective to the most objective is built by the theological concept of revelation." (*ibid.*) Let us analyze this statement. When the prophet proclaims "thus saith the Lord," he is not making a statement which is empirically verifiable. All that is verifiable is that he has had a certain religious experience. But he asserts, over and above the "subjective" fact of his experience, the "objective" fact that God has spoken. But what guarantee can he have that God has *really* spoken, and that "God" and "revelation" are not mere projections of his own mind? Here we must make a distinction on which everything depends. If we ignore this distinction (as many contemporary writers do), we shall be devoured either by the Scylla of an obscurantist and indiscriminate supernaturalism, or the Charybdis of a wholesale positivistic scepticism. The distinction is between an *actual* revelation, and the general *concept* of revelation. That God has actually spoken to me, here and now, is an assertion for which, in the end, I can never have any rational guarantee. Here is commitment pure and simple; and for that reason the prophet must always speak in fear and trembling. One need only read what the Bible has to say on false prophets, in order to understand that there may be some negative criteria; but that there is an ultimate point where all that remains is the personal bearing witness of the prophet himself. But it is quite another thing to consider the general concept of revelation. (Note that Rosenzweig, in the passage quoted, speaks of this. He is speaking as a philosopher-theologian, not as a prophet). Here we do not ask: was this the voice of God, or the projection of my mind? We ask: is revelation in principle reducible to mental projection? Or is the human situation such that the principle of revelation is defensible, or even unavoidable? If we seek to answer this question, one way or the other, we do so, not by appealing to a personal and private experience or commitment, but by means of theory, argument, system. Rosenzweig seeks to justify the principle of revelation. Again we forebear to ask whether his arguments are adequate; for again our point is merely the fact that they *are* arguments. Neither Rosenzweig nor any other respectable existentialist thinker misuses his personal commitments in order to escape the rigours of logic and system, wide-spread misconceptions to the contrary notwithstanding.

The foregoing may suffice as an account of Rosenzweig's "personal thinking." The thoughtful reader will be prepared to grant that Rosenzweig, while stressing the uniqueness and authenticity of the individual's commitment before God, does not destroy the significance of the universal categories of philosophy and theology. What is as yet wholly unclear is how Rosenzweig arrives at Judaism. Yet the main (or at any rate, best-known) part of the *Stern* is devoted to the exposition of the covenant of God with Israel; and the remainder of Rosenzweig's life was devoted to the endeavour to live in this covenant. Hence, we must give some space to making his theological method and position in this matter intelligible.

The problem we face is this. Thus far, we have some understanding of the position in Rosenzweig's thinking of abstract thought, which is radically universal, and personal commitment, which is radically individual. But Judaism—the covenant of God with the flesh-and-blood *community* of Israel—fits into neither. And, therefore, it seems, thus far, that Rosenzweig's foundation of Judaism is a wholly arbitrary dogma.

Glatzer shows good judgment in offering, almost in its entirety, the section from the *Stern* in which Rosenzweig describes the religious life of Israel. It is one of the best descriptions of Jewish life ever written; and it is profoundly meaningful to any reader, no matter what his theological position. But what cannot become clear in the selection here offered is the fact that the method of description here used by Rosenzweig serves a very definite and subtle methodological purpose. As it stands, the significance of this description of Jewish life, as a whole, cannot but remain ambiguous. A description, after all, is factual; and the fact in this case is not the covenant between God and Israel, but merely that Jews have believed in the existence of such a covenant and lived by it. A description of Jewish life cannot show that what it is about is true. Could not an agnostic historian give exactly the same account? Can history ever amount to a theology?

A mere empirical history, of course, cannot. But Rosenzweig's "absolute empiricism," as Glatzer recognizes (p. 207), is Schelling's, not Hume's. It is not, in principle, opposed to metaphysical construction; rather, it is a leaping-to-fact to which a priori construction itself leads, by reaching its limits. Rosenzweig thus begins with metaphysical construction. But this yields only abstract categories—God, man, world. At least in the case of two of these (God and man), the abstractness consists, in part, in the fact that part of the essence is freedom. To know what God and man *can* do is not to know what they actually *will* do: for that we must turn to brute, "empirical" fact. In other words, we must turn to history. But the history to which we turn is not "empirical" in the ordinary sense. It already presupposes metaphysical categories, which, in this case, have established history, not as human, but as human-divine (Schelling's term); an infinitely free God, and a finitely free man, whose essential historicity lies in his relation to God. It is within this frame of reference that Rosenzweig "narrates" Jewish history: as one of the three possibilities by which man may be related to God.

Once again, then, we arrive at the conclusion that Rosenzweig's position is arrived at not without argument. The argument here is *a posteriori*, though *a posteriori* in a specific sense. Again we must refrain from inquiring into the adequacy of the argument, and content ourselves with the fact that there *is* argument.

In the foregoing two paragraphs we have moved far beyond the limits of what is ordinarily contained in a book review. Our reason for doing so was the fear that some readers might read the selections offered by Glatzer with the conviction that Rosenzweig is not fully intellectually respectable. We hope that something has been done to counteract this conviction. But we have no wish to overemphasize the importance of philosophy and theology for Rosenzweig. They served merely the purpose of making possible what he tried to do in the latter years of his life: living as a Jew before God, and "learning" in the traditional Jewish sense—that is to say, learning in the sight of God. Glatzer rightly devotes the bulk of his material to this learning. It is to be hoped that there are readers, not too corroded by intellectual indecision, to share at least some of his "learning" with Rosenzweig; and that there are others, who still live the unbroken tradition of Jewish learning. To these two groups of readers, above all, the volume is addressed.

Notes

1. The review is of *Franz Rosenzweig: His Life and Thought*. Presented by Nahum N. Glatzer. A Schocken Book published with Farrar, Straus and Young, 1953.

2. In this reviewer's opinion, Schelling's *Weltalter* is the philosophical work which influenced the *Stern der Erloesung* most. (Cf. Rosenzweig's *Briefe*, pp. 208, 298, 399, 711ff., for a significant disagreement with Schelling, cf. p. 718.) Schelling's work is now available in English (*The Ages of the World*, tr. Bolman), and the interested reader can form his own judgment about the difficulties of transplanting this type of German thought to America.

3. This phrase is often misunderstood and hence ridiculed. It has at least three different (though not unconnected) meanings. (1) The first implies a metaphysics according to which man can find, and *live before*, God only in crisis. This crisis is here life's deepest meaning; self-assertion and love of God are in necessary conflict; the leaping into the latter cannot be transcended. (2) The second meaning of the term refers to His sight; if we wish, to an act of conversion. When used in this sense, the term does not imply that, after the leap, man might not live, and live harmoniously, in His sight. (3) The third meaning of the term is strictly logical. It refers to the logical gap between objective knowledge and the "personal standpoint" of the believer. It is in this last sense that we here use the term.

6 *Martin Buber on Israel and Palestine*

This book traces the history of an idea,[1] the idea of the relation between Israel and the land of Israel. It seeks to show that this idea has a genuine history, i. e., both continuity and development. Its development is shown through Bible and rabbinic literature, medieval philosophy and mysticism, finally issuing into modern Zionist thought.

But although this book may be regarded as a history of Zionist thought, it would be a mistake—a pedantic mistake—to judge its merits in terms of the completeness and objectivity which it accords to its subject. For its method is frankly selective, and the principle of selection is not that of the "objective" historian. For this book is not, after all, primarily a contribution to the historiography of Zionism. It is rather a distinguished contribution to Zionist thinking itself. And it assumes the form of a history only because the author's Zionism—unlike many other Zionisms—is deeply and consciously rooted in Jewish tradition. On every page it is implied that Zionism has a more or less unbroken tradition, and that there is an intimate relation between what is essential in the Jewish past, and what ought to be essential for Zionist present and future. Hence Buber offers here, in inseparable unity, a history and a philosophy. He does not seek to give a detached account of the past, for its own sake, but to discover what is valid for today and tomorrow. Yet to make that discovery, he finds it necessary to turn to the past.

That historical understanding and philosophical outlook must be intimately related is the basic underlying conception of Buber's present work, determining its scope, method and conclusions. We must therefore ask precisely what the nature of this relation is. And it is, at first sight, not easy to find a satisfactory answer. On the one hand, the history is determined by the philosophy. Refusing to report

Reprinted from *The Jewish Quarterly Review* 45,2 (October, 1954), 170–74.

indiscriminately the profound and the trite, the living and the dead, Buber tries to fix attention on the essential. And what is essential depends on the standards provided by the philosophy. Yet on the other hand, the philosophy is determined by the history. For, Jewishly speaking, it is the history alone which saves the philosophy from arbitrariness. Without living contact with the former, there might be an indefinite number of "Jewish" or "Zionist" philosophies; and all of them would appropriate either of these adjectives without justification. Indeed, if Buber did not believe his philosophy to be rooted in Jewish history, it is difficult to see why he should have been concerned to write a history of Zionist thought at all.

Now, this position involves a logical circle from which an escape may well seem impossible. For if the history depends on the philosophy, then it does not reach the past *per se*, but the past as it looks from the adopted standpoint; and (if the position makes any sense) we cannot then penetrate from this past to a truer past, by adopting a different standpoint, or no standpoint at all. Yet on the other hand, if the philosophy is in turn to arise from the history, this must be the result of an immersion into the past apart from the standpoint, the past *per se*. Yet such an immersion, it is implied, is both undesirable and impossible. Can there be an escape from this circle?

We may begin by observing that if Buber's book involves this difficulty, it is a difficulty which it shares with all Zionist thought seeking to ground itself in history; and indeed, with all Jewish thought save the orthodox. For all such thought is faced with essentially the same dilemma. It cannot, on the one hand, seek to establish what is true and valid by independent philosophical or scientific criteria. For why should such thought be called Jewish? Contemporary Jewish and Zionist literature abounds with writings which attempt to erect philosophies on the basis of Jewishly independent criteria, be they taken from metaphysics, political philosophy, psychology, or anthropology. Yet despite being prettily decorated with random quotations from Bible and Talmud, their claim to Jewishness rests on wholly mysterious grounds. On the other hand, it is equally impossible for modern Jewish and Zionist thought to abandon Jewishly independent criteria and principles and, in an attempt to achieve Jewish validation, simply to immerse itself in the Jewish past. This is, indeed, possible for orthodox Jewish thought, for it finds in revelation an authoritative past, precisely defined in content and extent. But any non-orthodox thought which attempted to immerse itself in the Jewish past (even granting that such an immersion were possible) would simply arrive at declaring the whole past, indiscriminately, valid for the future. On what basis could it distinguish between the essential and the unessential, the profound and the trite, the living and the dead?

In view of the universality of the problem, we ask with renewed insistence: is Buber able to break the circle, in which a method of thinking is involved which tries at once to be philosophical, and rooted in history? Although Buber does not discuss this problem explicitly in this book, this reviewer seems to detect his perpetual awareness of it. More, the entire book would seem to illustrate his solution.

Buber's book illustrates his faith that we can escape the dilemma of either seeking truth and value *de novo*, apart from the Jewish historical tradition, or else, abandoning the search for truth and value, becoming mere narrators of a dead Jewish past. On the very first page Buber states the assumption which alone makes such an escape possible. This is that the Jewish past is not dead at all; it is a spiritual reality still living and present (cf. p. vii).

Perhaps we should qualify. If the Jewish spiritual past were *simply* alive in the modern Jew, then the thought of the latter would be Jewish simply by virtue of his living in the Jewish spiritual reality; and no conscious historical orientation on his part would be necessary. The Jewish spiritual past, we must rather say, is dormant and capable of being revived. Such a revival is not possible by abstract speculation on universal truths, nor by mere detached objective historical study. The revival must be (if we may use the much–abused and much misunderstood term) existential. This term may, for the present context, be defined by three characteristics. (i) The thinking in question must not, like, e. g., ordinary history, be detached and non-committal. It must be a committing search for truth and value. (ii) Unlike philosophical thinking, it must not be abstract and universally human. It must arise from the concrete situation of the Jew and be concerned with his existence as a Jew. (iii) It must, in its search for present and future, encounter and recollect the past. And the past can be encountered or recollected only if it is still dormantly alive. It is obvious that it is this last characteristic which is crucial; which distinguishes Buber's prescription for the authentic Jew and Zionist from a prescription such as J. P. Sartre's. We have said that the assumption that the Jewish past is alive, or capable of revival, alone can validate Buber's entire approach. We may go further and say that *Israel and Palestine* is but an attempt to contribute to such a revival. As such it deserves the closest attention not only of Zionist thinkers but of Jewish thinkers in general. For it is not too much to say that whether the basic assumption of this book is true or not is *the* question on which the future of Jewish thought depends. If that assumption is false, then the future may still produce scholarly works concerned with Jewish subjects; and it may produce philosophical thought whose authors happen to be Jews with vague Jewish loyalties. But genuinely Jewish thought, i. e., thought at once concerned with truth and value for today and tomorrow, and rooted in Jewish tradition, will disappear.

We have devoted much space to considering the foundations of Buber's work because without these the significance of the work as a whole cannot be understood. We are therefore compelled to deal very briefly with its content. This is the tracing of a single idea, of its life through Jewish history, accompanied by the implicit claim that it either is still alive or else capable of revival. What is this idea? In rabbinic language, we might say that God, Israel and the land of Israel are one. Or, as Buber puts it in more modern language, "whenever the action of nature as well as spirit is perceived as a gift, Revelation takes place." (p. 26)

In his treatment of this trinity, Buber tends to emphasize nature (or the land of Israel), and this is with polemic intent. Much of Buber's thought was formed in a polemic against idealism and conventional liberalism, and this tendency continues to be evident in the present volume, particularly in the treatment of the Bible. Idealism had argued that in the process of history, nature was superseded by spirit, and natural religion by spiritual religion. Within Judaism, idealism inspired the sort of liberalism which sought to "purify" Jewish tradition of its naturalistic elements. A more "spiritual" Judaism, it used to be argued, needed neither the attachment to nature nor to specific natural conditions, such as the land of Israel. And the dispersion of Israel, far from being *Galuth*, could be regarded as a providential act of history which, by depriving Israel of its "narrow" nationalistic basis, raised it to a higher and more universal spiritual level. It is easy to see why the circles believing in this philosophy should have been vigorously anti-Zionist, and, indeed, should have shown lack of comprehension of Zionism. It is also easy to see why Buber, a life-long Zionist never willing to sell his spiritual birthright for a mess of nationalistic pottage, should have waged a life-long war against that philosophy.

The idea of Israel *and* Palestine is essentially the idea that spiritual existence requires roots; that spirit requires nature and is a mere empty abstraction without it. Further, nature is not a mere servant of spirit but an equal partner. And it is "Israel and Palestine" rather than "Spirit (or History) and Nature" because the conjunction of the latter two is still abstract, a mere philosophical proposition. But "Israel and Palestine" is a search for and encounter with God, by a concrete people in a concrete land; or, if not that, it is at least the concrete longing for such an existence.

There can be no doubt that Buber describes a true idea, and a true reality; and also that he is correct in his protest against conventional liberalism. The only question is whether, in this age of naturalism, nationalism and pragmatic hardheadedness, his emphasis should not have been otherwise. For in our age, the danger that only "spirit" to the exclusion of "nature" should be "perceived as a gift" seems remote indeed. The present danger seems to be that the modern Jew in America and (unless we are mistaken) in Israel is either unprepared to perceive anything as a "gift" at all; or else that this gift is nature to the exclusion of spirit. Judaism may be endangered by rootless spirituality. It is certainly no less endangered by the idolatry of the roots.

Yet one cannot fairly accuse Buber of underestimating the latter danger. This very book testifies to his awareness, inasmuch as its claim is the revival of an idea. An idea, any idea, belongs to the spirit, even the idea of the land. The Jew living in the land of Israel requires both the land (which is nature) and the idea of the land (which is of the spirit).

We have asserted that Buber describes a true idea and a true reality; that is to say, an idea and a reality by which the Jew once lived. But are the idea and the reality capable of revival? This the present-day Jew cannot know. He can only work, believe and wait.

Notes

1. *Israel and Palestine: The History of an Idea.* By Martin Buber. East and West Library, London—New York, 1952.

7 *The Revealed Morality of Judaism and Modern Thought*
A Confrontation with Kant

Preface: On Jewish Philosophy Today

This preface is in the nature of an afterthought, written after the essay itself. Its purpose is to state the method which the essay itself uses, and to clarify the reasons for the use of this method, a clarification which will show that this essay means to fall into the discipline of modern Jewish philosophy.

First, while the essay is throughout concerned with the revealed morality of Judaism, it nowhere categorically affirms the reality of revelation. This is not because I am not prepared to make such an affirmation but rather because, in my view, to do so would transcend the scope of philosophy, Jewish philosophy included. For I hold the affirmation of revelation to presuppose a commitment, which in turn permeates the religious thinking which springs from it. Philosophical thinking, however, both presupposes, and stays with, objective detachment, which is why both a religious commitment and the religious thinking flowing from it are, as such, extraphilosophical. I hasten to add that they are not for that reason antiphilosophical.

This is enough to indicate that the very concept of a Jewish philosophy is gravely problematical. How can thinking be at once truly philosophical and yet essentially Jewish? To say that it must be *essentially* Jewish is to dismiss, as deserving no further thought, that a philosophy might become Jewish by virtue of the accidental Jewish origin of its author. How then can it at once have the objectivity and universality which is required of it as philosophy, and yet be essentially committed to a content which has Jewish particularity? To judge by many contemporary samples of Jewish philosophizing, it must sacrifice either one or the other. If it is a rational endorsement of "values" found in Jewish history and literature, the very endorsement—which, being rational, is universal—makes these values essen-

Reprinted from *Quest for Past and Future* (Bloomington: Indiana University Press, 1968), 204–28, 327–29.

tially human, because universally valid, thus reducing their Jewishness to a historical accident. But if it remains bound to specifically Jewish goals, such as the survival of Jewish life, this limitation deprives it of the radical detachment and the radical universality required of philosophy. This is not to say, incidentally, that either of these pursuits is useless or illegitimate.

Can there be a Jewish philosophy, then, which is at once genuinely philosophical and yet essentially Jewish? This was possible at least under the special intellectual conditions which prevailed in the Jewish Middle Ages. Jewish philosophy then was the *confrontation between philosophy and Judaism.* This confrontation presupposed that philosophy and Judaism were different from each other and irreducible to each other; that it was necessary to confront them; and that it was possible to confront them in a manner which would compromise neither.

In the Middle Ages, all these conditions were accepted by those who engaged in Jewish philosophy. They accepted, first, the existence of two independent sources of truth, of which one was human reason, and the other a divine revelation embodied in the sacred Jewish Scriptures. On the basis of this fundamental assumption, they accepted these additional ones: that reason and revelation cover at least in part the same ground; that there is at least some apparent conflict between them; and that the conflict is apparent only—that it can be resolved without violence to either reason or Judaism. Without the first and third of these additional assumptions, there would have been no possibility of a Jewish philosophy, and without the second, no necessity for it.

It is noteworthy that, although there was a continuous tradition of Jewish philosophy in the Middle Ages, Jewish philosophy has appeared only sporadically in the modern age, and then unsure of its status. This is no accident. First, it has not been easy—to put it mildly—for modern philosophers to accept revelation as a source of truth, over and above reason itself. Reason, in the modern world, is apt to take itself as autonomous and all-encompassing. It is evident that, on such an assumption, philosophy cannot *confront* Judaism. If taking note of Judaism at all, it can only *absorb* it. Judaism then turns out to be, essentially, a "religion of reason," which is Jewish only by accident.

But even when philosophic reason does not make such radical claims a modern philosophic confrontation with Judaism is beset with difficulties unknown in the Middle Ages. At that time, it was assumed that there was at least one common basis for argument, in principle acceptable to both philosophers and religious believers. Revelation at Sinai—or revelation anywhere else—if actual, was an objective historical fact exactly like any other historical fact. If its acceptance as fact depended on the acceptance of authorities, this was true of *any* historical fact. Judah Halevi could argue, *both* as a philosopher and a believing Jew, that the testimony of the six hundred thousand present at Mt. Sinai could not have been mistaken.

But this view concerning revelation and authority is no longer acceptable either to modern philosophers or to thoughtful modern believers. Modern analysis has disclosed that it is not authority which is the source of faith but rather faith which is the source of acceptance—if any—of authority. An agnostic, had he been present at Mt. Sinai, would have heard only the thunder and no voice of God. Revelation, as an objective event of communication, is hearable only to those already listening; and the listening is a listening in faith. This is a view accepted alike by modern philosophers and the best of modern religious thinkers. At any rate, it is my view.

It is on this view that the question arises whether, under modern circumstances, there can be a Jewish philosophy at all. For if that view is correct, then religious thinking—at least Jewish religious thinking vis-à-vis revelation—is from beginning to end *committed* thinking, which stands in dialogical relation to the God of Israel. But, as has been said, philosophical thinking must be from beginning to end *detached* thinking. It may thus seem that there is now no basis for meeting, as there was under medieval assumptions, since revelation is accessible, if at all, only to a commitment which is *ipso facto* non-philosophical. At best there could be only an attempt to show the compatibility of modern reason with a modern acceptance of revelation; and even such an attempt, unlike its medieval precursors, would be more concerned with keeping the two apart than with binding them together.

It is in this precarious situation that the following essay seeks, nevertheless, to contribute to a revival of Jewish philosophy. Although insisting both on the detachment of philosophic thought and on commitment as the condition of the accessibility of revelation, I nevertheless assume that revelation is not *wholly* inaccessible to philosophic reason. Under what conditions can this be possible?

As has already been said, this requires, in the first place, that the philosopher, *qua* philosopher, should suspend judgment as to the actuality of revelation. The essay which follows confronts the revealed morality of Judaism with certain modern philosophical standards of morality. It does not commit itself to the actuality of a revealed morality.

But how, without such a commitment, can there be a philosophical understanding of the *nature* of a revealed morality? The essay undertakes such an understanding through what may be called a *sympathetic phenomenological re-enactment.* This remains bound to the limits of philosophical detachment, while at the same time seeking a sympathetic understanding of truths accepted only on the basis of a commitment. Such an understanding will obviously have certain limits. One cannot, for example, remain a detached philosopher and yet ask—let alone find an answer to—the authentic Jewish question, "What does the God of Israel demand of *me?*" At the same time, it would seem that to deny in principle the possibility that detached thinking might understand some of the meaning of committed faith is impossible, for it is to be led to absurd consequences, such as that unless one shares the faith of a religious literature it must be wholly unintelligible; or that a leap from detachment to commitment, if and when it occurs, must be wholly blind. It would also be to imply that a Jewish philosophy is impossible in the present age.

The argument for the possibility of such a philosophy, as presented in this preface, is obviously fragmentary. It is hoped that the reader may find less fragmentary the example of Jewish philosophizing given in the following pages.

I

Can a law be at once moral and the will of God? Can one accept it as at the same time a moral duty and divinely revealed? Or is, perhaps, a revealed morality, radically considered, nothing less than a contradiction in terms?

At one time, such questions would have seemed preposterous to uncritical religious believers, and even critically minded philosophers would have seen no need to ask them. Today, they have become part of the fabric even of popular religious thought. This is due, more than to anything else, to the influence of one single philosopher. Present-day academic moral philosophy may not pay much attention to Kant; most popular moral or religious tracts may not so much as mention his name. But on the topic of revealed morality, moral and religious thought at both levels is still much influenced—consciously or unconsciously—by Kant's moral philosophy.

A Jewish philosopher concerned with that topic does not therefore engage in a mere antiquarian academic exercise if he seeks a confrontation of Kant and Judaism; that is if, investigating this topic, he takes Judaism as his example of a revealed morality, and Kant as his main guide in moral philosophy. This is the undertaking of the present essay which, under double guidance, asks whether the moral characteristics of a religious law or commandment must clash with the way in which it is revealed. We say: "must clash." For that a clash is *possible* must be taken for granted, and one need not be either modern or a philosopher to know it. Rabbinic teachers, for example, knew well enough that human behavior falls short of true morality if it is motivated solely by fear of heavenly punishment or the hope of divine reward.[1]

II

Philosophy has always questioned revelation in general and revealed morality in particular. But no philosopher prior to Kant found it necessary to question all revealed morality as being less than truly moral simply by virtue of being revealed. The question whether all revealed morality might be a contradiction in terms is a question which was not asked.

This may be shown by a brief review of the most radical objection to revealed morality made by pre-Kantian philosophy on grounds of morality alone. Theologians often claim that revelation is the sole source of our knowledge of moral law. Philosophy has almost always been forced to reject this claim. For to be obligated to any law, a man must be able to know that law; and to qualify as moral, a law must be universally obligatory. But, on the admission of theologians themselves, revealed moral law is accessible only to those who possess the revealed Scriptures.

It will be noted that this objection by no means amounts to a rejection of revealed morality. It is merely a threat of rejection, unless a certain demand is met. The demand is for an independent, universally human access to moral law, in addition to revelation.

Can Judaism meet this philosophical demand? One's first resort would be to the general Noachidic revelation which, unlike the revelation at Mount Sinai, is given to all men. But this can satisfy the philosopher only if he can exact a further concession. The Noachidic "revelation"—if one chooses to retain this term—must be accessible without a Scripture: for the Noachides have no Scripture. It must be, that is, a universal human capacity; in short, just what the philosopher has called reason all along.

Traditional Judaism may have misgivings about this concession. If pressed, however, it will nevertheless concede. For it must then, itself, distinguish between *moral* revealed laws which, "had they not been written by God, would have had to be written by men," and *non-moral* revealed laws, "to which Satan and the Gentiles object."[2] But if, except for divine action, men would have *had* to write moral law, they must be *able* to write it. And if the Gentiles—who object to non-moral revealed law—do *not* object to moral revealed law they must, in fact, have written or be able to write at least some of it.

This clarifies sufficiently for the present purpose the relation between Jewish revealed morality and philosophical rational morality, as set forth prior to Kant. However loudly and lengthily the two moralities may quarrel about the *content* of moral law, they have no necessary quarrel concerning its *foundations.* The philosopher has no moral reason for objecting in principle to a morality resting on revelation. And the Jewish theologian has no religious reason for objecting in principle to a morality resting on reason. What is more, this mutual tolerance concerning the foundations of morality produces opportunities for settling conflicts concerning its content as well. This is attested to by a long line of Jewish rationalists who believed that, since the same God was the creator of human reason and the giver of the Sinaitic revelation, the discoveries of reason and the teachings of Judaism could be in no genuine conflict.

III

This peaceful coexistence was upset by a thesis advanced by Immanuel Kant, first prominently stated in his *Fundamental Principles of the Metaphysics of Morals* (1785). Kant himself recognized that his thesis was both crucial and revolutionary; he held that previous moral philosophy did not contain it, and that, because of this failure, it had failed as a whole. Kant also recognized the revolutionary implications of his thesis for revealed morality. Indeed, this is a theme to which he kept returning, as if unable to leave it alone.

In a passage exemplary for our purpose Kant writes:

> [If the will is moral] it is not merely subject to law, but subject in such a way that it must also be regarded as imposing the law on itself, and subject to it for that reason only. . . . All past efforts to identify the principle of morality have failed without exception. For while it was seen that man is bound by his duty to laws, it was not seen that he is subject only to his own, albeit at the same time universal legislation, and obligated to act only according to his own, albeit universally legislating will. So long as one thought of man as merely subject to a law, whatever its content, without this law originating in his own will, one had to think of him as impelled to action by something other than himself. The law had to carry with it some interest which induced or impelled him to action. But in this way all labour to discover the supreme ground of duty was lost beyond recovery. For one could thus never arrive at duty, but merely at the necessity of acting for some interest.[3]

But this, Kant concludes, is at best only an impure morality. An externally compelling or cajoling law must necessarily by heteronomous or impure so far as moral motivation is concerned. To be pure, a moral law must be autonomous, or self-imposed.

We must be sure to grasp the essence of the Kantian thesis. It is by no means the mere assertion—as we have seen, far from new—that in order to be morally obligatory, a law must have a universality enabling all men to know it. Kant would have thought this condition satisfied by those ancient moralists who identified the moral law with the law of the universe, or by their present-day heirs who identify it with the laws of mental health. The essence of the Kantian thesis is that neither of these laws, however universal, can by itself *obligate* a man to obedience; they can do no more than promise happiness or mental health as the reward of obedience, and threaten unhappiness or neurosis as the punishment of defiance. This is because both laws confront man only from without. They are not imposed on man by man himself. A law which cannot unconditionally obligate may be prudent, wise, or beneficial. It cannot be moral.

According to Kant, then, there may be much that can induce us or force us to obey. But no law in heaven or on earth can obligate us to obey unless we *accept ourselves* as obligated to obey. And unless we can accept ourselves as obligated we cannot *be* obligated. Once clearly identified, the Kantian thesis seems very nearly irresistible.

It poses, however, an unprecedented challenge to every revealed morality, regardless of content, and simply by virtue of its being revealed. *If in order to be moral a law must be self-imposed, not imposed from without, then how can a law given or imposed by God have genuine moral qualities?* Pre-Kantian moral philosophy, as was seen, could accept revealed morality conditionally. Kant's moral philosophy threatens it radically. It does so because revelation is either a gift to man from without—the gift of a God *other* than man—or else it is not revelation at all.

IV

According to one widely popular interpretation of Kant's thesis, the will, in imposing moral law on itself, *creates* that law. Moral law is the collective creation of the human spirit; and only because it is such a creation is it moral at all. In rising to the life of morality, man actively transforms his own being in the light of ideals which are themselves a creative human product. All true morality is creative simply by virtue of being truly moral. And all passive submission, no matter to whom or what, is less than truly moral simply *because* it is passive submission.

Philosophers who accept this version of the Kantian thesis must reject in principle all revealed morality, radically, unequivocally, and immediately. To them, such a morality must be at worst a mere passive submission to the whims of an alien Deity. Even at best, it is just a creative morality which fails to recognize itself for what it is, for it mistakes its own creation for a passively received gift. And by virtue of this mistake it still falls short in some measure of the ideal morality.

But it is a matter of great importance that this version of the Kantian thesis is decidedly not Kant's own.[4] Kant does not assert that the human spirit creates moral law; he emphatically denies it. And his denial dramatizes his conviction—often stated by Kant himself but frequently overlooked by his interpreters—that in order to impose moral law on himself, man need be neither its individual nor collective creator. He need be capable only of *appropriating* a law, which in fact he has *not* created, *as though* he had created it. The attacks of "creative morality" philosophies on revealed morality, whatever their merits, we may thus ignore.

Unlike these, Kant's own doctrine does not rule out revealed morality from the start. For if the moral will need only appropriate, and not create, moral law, why might it not be *prima facie* possible for it to appropriate a law given by God? This, however, seems possible only *prima facie;* while not ruling out revealed morality from the start, Kant's doctrine deeply threatens it in the end. Indeed, this threat may be described as far more dangerous than that of "creative morality" philosophies. These latter—which reject revealed morality on the basis of criteria external to it—invite a like treatment from the defenders of revealed morality. This is not true of Kant, who takes revealed morality in its own right with a considerable degree of seriousness before he questions it radically.

Kant does not rule out revealed morality from the start; his moral will does not create moral law. Yet he threatens that morality in the end: for his moral will must act as though it were the creator of moral law. This Kantian assertion confronts the believer in a revealed morality with a grave dilemma: *Either he concedes that the will can and must impose the God-given law upon itself; but then its God-givenness becomes irrelevant in the process of self-imposition and appropriation; or else he insists that the God-givenness of the law does not and cannot at any point become irrelevant; but then the will cannot impose the law on itself—it can only submit to it for such non-moral reasons as trust in divine promises or fear of divine threats.*[5]

Kant himself perceives this dilemma with the utmost clarity; only for him it is not a dilemma. In his view, the religious man must choose between what Kant terms, respectively, "theological morality" and "moral theology." But to choose moral theology is to gain everything and to lose nothing.

The religious man chooses theological morality when he accepts laws as moral because they are the will of God. In so doing he not only submits to an alien law, but he submits to it because it is alien. Hence he cannot impose that law upon himself; and he can obey it—if he does obey it—because of its external sanctions only.[6] "Theological morality" is, and must be, heteronomous morality.

The religious man can rise above this only if he embraces "moral theology." He must not accept laws as moral because they are the will of God, but he must ascribe laws to God because they are intrinsically moral, and known to be so, quite apart from the will of God. It is because the will is capable of recognizing their intrinsic morality that it can impose laws upon itself, thus achieving moral autonomy. But this achievement is bought at a price. In imposing moral laws on itself, the will need not and, indeed, cannot pay heed to their God-givenness. The same act which appropriates the God-given moral law reduces its God-givenness to irrelevance.

One might therefore well ask why Kant's religious man, when achieving moral autonomy, should still *be* a religious man. Why should he end up with "moral theology" rather than with morality pure and simple? What necessity is there for ascribing the moral law to divine authorship, and what is the function of this ascription? This is a question of some complexity. But so long as we move in a purely moral context—asking ourselves what our duty is and why we should do it—the question does not arise at all. In that context, the question of the authorship of the moral law may be, or possibly even must be, left open. Kant writes:

> The veiled goddess before whom we bend our knees is the moral law within us . . .
> To be sure, we hear her voice and clearly understand her commandments, but are, in

hearing them, in doubt as to who is speaking: whether man, in the self-sufficient power of his own reason, or Another, whose nature is unknown, and who speaks to man through the medium of his reason. Perhaps we would do better to refrain even from inquiring. For such a question is merely speculative, and our duty remains the same, whatever the source from which it issues.[7]

V

Such, then, is the challenge of Kant to revealed morality. The student who in its light considers the revealed morality of Judaism makes two extraordinary discoveries. One is that this morality cannot be classified as either autonomous or heteronomous in the Kantian sense. The other is that, in the nearly two hundred years since the Kantian doctrine first appeared to challenge them, Jewish religious thinkers have noticed this fact but rarely, and, when they have noticed it, only dimly.

Apologetic tendencies have marred at least all the standard Jewish responses to the Kantian challenge. Thus, orthodox thinkers can certainly never have forgotten that, according to a central traditional Jewish doctrine, the commandments are not truly performed until they are performed for their own sake. Yet when faced with the Kantian challenge they have tended to behave as though they had indeed forgotten that Jewish doctrine. Rightly concerned to rescue the divine Law-giver from irrelevance, they have been prone to argue that, but for the divine sanctions behind the commandments, the latter would remain universally and necessarily unperformed. They should have insisted that the revealed morality of Judaism is not heteronomous. What they did insist all too often was that all human morality must be so. But thereby they not only put forward a false doctrine but pleaded Judaism guilty to a mistaken charge.

Liberal responses to Kant have suffered even more gravely from apologetic bias. While orthodox thinkers argued that the morality of Judaism is revealed but heteronomous, their liberal colleagues have often acted as though it were autonomous but not revealed. They would have prophets and rabbis speak with the Kantian voice of self-legislating reason.

This can be done in one of two ways; but both are foredoomed to failure. One can say that prophets and rabbis taught an autonomous morality, as it were, unconsciously: for they still gave conscious fealty to a revealing God. But then their morality stood, after all, still in need of liberal purification which finally eliminated the revealing God. Or one can picture prophets and rabbis teaching an autonomous morality for what it is—but this picture is a scandalous distortion of historical fact.

Because of the haste with which they resorted to apologetics, both these standard reactions to Kant failed to bring to light the authentic revealed morality of Judaism, which takes it out of the realm of both autonomous and heteronomous morality. One group of apologists saw that the revealed morality of Judaism is not autonomous, because it stands in an essential relation to a commanding God. The other saw that it is not heteronomous because, bidding man to perform the commandments both for their own sake and for the sake of God, it rises above all blandishments and threats. But neither group was able to perceive the essential togetherness of these two elements. And yet the source and life of the revealed morality of Judaism lies precisely in that togetherness; a divine commanding Presence which never dissipates itself into irrelevance, and a human response which freely appropriates what it receives. The Jewish thinker does not respond adequately to the Kantian challenge until he brings this togetherness to philosophical self-consciousness, in order to ask a question which Kant literally forces upon him: *How can man appropriate a God-given law or commandment, accepting and performing it as though it were his own, while yet remaining, in the very act of appropriation, essentially and receptively related to its divine Giver? How can man* morally *obey a law which yet is, and never ceases to be,* essentially revealed? According to Kant, this is clearly impossible. Puzzlement and wonder arise for the Jewish philosopher because—if he is to believe the testimony of both Jewish life and Jewish thought—what Kant thought impossible is real.

VI

We must take care above all lest what is essential in this remarkable togetherness slip from notice. This would happen if one were to attend now to the divine commanding Presence in its otherness, and then to the human response in its power of free appropriation, but not to the two together. This togetherness is essential. In displaying it, we shall find that it exists in Judaism from its beginnings and throughout its history. Only in periods of spiritual decay can the one element seem capable of existence without the other. And this *is* the decay. With the exception of such periods, there is no age in the spiritual history of Judaism so "primitive" as to manifest—in the style of "theological morality"—only a divine commanding Presence but "not yet" an act of human appropriation. Nor is there an age "advanced" enough to manifest—in the style of "moral theology"—only a free human appropriation but "no longer" a commanding God who can be present in all His otherness.

At no moment in the spiritual history of Judaism is the otherness of the divine commanding Presence so starkly disclosed as in that pristine one in which the Divine, first reaching out to the human, calls him to His service. For in that moment there are as yet no specified commandments but only a still unspecified divine commanding Presence. Abraham is commanded to go to another country without being told of the country, nor of the purpose which his migration is to serve. Prophets are called as messengers, without as yet being given a specific message. Israel as a whole is challenged, knowing as yet no more of the challenge than that it is divine. In the pristine moment, the divine commanding Presence does not communicate a finite content which the human recipient might appraise and appropriate in the light of familiar standards. On the contrary, it calls into question all familiar content, and, indeed, all standards. Whatever may be true of subsequent history, there can be, at any rate, no mistaking this initial voice for one already familiar, such as conscience, reason, or "spiritual creativity."[8]

It may therefore seem that, whatever the nature of the human response to this pristine challenge, it cannot, at any rate, be free appropriation. There can certainly be no appropriation of specific commandments in the light of commensurate human standards; for there are as yet no such commandments. And how could there be an appropriation of the unspecified divine commanding Presence itself, when in the pristine moment it discloses itself as wholly other than human? It may thus seem that, if there is human freedom at all in the pristine moment, it can at most be only heteronomous freedom; the kind, that is, which is conditioned by fear or hope.

And yet a freedom of this sort could not survive the touch of the divine Presence. Such freedom might survive, perhaps, in moments of divine distance which, giving rise only to finite fear or hope, could leave room, as it were, for a freedom conditioned by them. But a fear or hope produced by the touch of divine Presence would of necessity be an absolute Fear or Hope; and as such it would of necessity overwhelm the freedom conditioned by them. If in relation to God man is capable of heteronomous freedom only, then the event of divine Presence would reduce him, while that event lasts, to a will-less tool of a blind fate.

Such a reduction is indeed the primordial experience of some religions. But it is not the primordial experience of Judaism. For here the Divine manifests Itself as *commanding,* and in order to do so it requires real human freedom. And since the Divine is *Presence* as well as commanding, the required human freedom cannot be merely conditional; it must be unconditional and absolute. Finally, this unconditional and absolute freedom must be more even than the freedom to accept or reject, for their own sake and on their own merit, specific commandments: there are as yet no such commandments. The freedom required in the pristine moment of the divine commanding Presence, then, is nothing less than *the freedom to accept or reject the divine commanding Presence as a whole, and for its own sake— that is, for no other reason than that it* is *that Presence.* It is such freedom that the prophet displays when he responds, "Here I am, send me"; or the people as a whole, when they respond, "we shall do and hearken."[9]

This pristine human freedom of choice is not autonomous. Without the Other, man might have the self-sufficient power for all kinds of choice, but the power of choice to accept or reject the divine commanding Presence he would not have. How could he accept God, unless God had become present to him, for him to accept? How could he reject Him, unless He had become present to him, for him to reject? The divine commanding Presence, then, may be said to *give* man choosing power. It may even be said to *force* the actual choice upon him. For in being present, It *singles out;* and in singling out It rules out every escape from the choice into some spurious third alternative.

And yet this pristine choice most decidedly *is* a choice. The divine commanding Presence may force the choice on singled-out man. It does not force him to choose God, and the choice itself (as was seen) is not heteronomous; for it accepts or rejects the divine commanding Presence for no other reason than that it *is* that Presence. But this entails the momentous consequence that, *if and when a man chooses to accept the divine commanding Presence, he does nothing less than accept the divine Will as his own.*

But how is this humanly possible? We have already asked this question, in a general form. But it may now be given a sharper form which states in full clarity what is at stake: *How can man, in the very moment which starkly discloses the gap between him and God, presume to bridge that gap, by accepting God's will simply because it is God's, thus making it his own? How can man presume to act out of love for the sake of God?* It is perhaps no wonder that a philosopher, when first coming upon this decisive question, should shrink from it in thought. Even prophets shrank from it, when first confronted with it in life.[10]

VII

It may therefore seem prudent for a philosopher to suspend if not to avoid that question, by turning from the pristine moment which initiates the revealed morality of Judaism, to the developed life of that morality itself. Here revelation has become a system of specified laws and commandments; and at least insofar as those are moral in nature they possess in Judaism undoubted permanence and undoubted intrinsic value.[11] A Jeremiah may believe that whereas in one situation God demands resistance to the enemy, in another He demands submission.[12] But one cannot conceive of him as saying that concerning justice or love and injustice or hatred. Just how moral law can assume permanence and intrinsic value within the framework of a revealed morality is indeed a deep and weighty question, which requires treatment in its own right.[13] The fact of its doing so, in Judaism at any rate, can be in no serious doubt.

This may suggest to the philosopher that, once permanent law of intrinsic value has made its appearance in Judaism, the divine commanding Presence of the pristine moment has vanished into an irrelevant past. What could be the function of His Presence? If it contradicted moral standards already in human possession, its voice would surely have to be rejected, as a voice of temptation. And if it confirmed these standards, it would only tell what is already known. In short, once revelation has become specified as a system of laws, new and revealing immediacy is either false or superfluous.[14]

If this were the full truth of the matter, then revealed moral law in Judaism would allow of only two human responses: One obeys it for its own sake, by recognizing and appropriating its intrinsic value. Then, however, one obeys it for its own sake *only*, and the divine Giver of the law becomes irrelevant in the process of appropriation, and so does the revealed quality of the law itself. Or one obeys it *because* it is revealed. But then one could not obey it either for God's sake or for its own; not the former because the Divine, having lost commanding presence—immediacy—after the rise of law, would have reduced itself to the mere external sanction behind the law; and not the latter, because the law would then need such sanctions. In short, one would be driven back to the Kantian alternative between a "moral theology" which is essentially unrevealed, and a "theological morality" which is less than fully moral.

But must the divine Presence pass into irrelevance once revealed moral law has appeared? To ask this question is to recognize that the Kantian alternative contains a hidden premise. This premise, to be sure, is hard to reject, but Judaism implicitly rejects it. According to the testimony of Jewish life and teaching, the divine commanding Presence does *not* pass into irrelevance once moral law has assumed permanence and intrinsic value. The Torah is given whenever men are ready to receive it,[15] and the act of receiving Torah culminates in the confrontation with its Giver. The prophet, to be sure, has a specific message; yet the words "thus saith the Lord" are not an empty preamble but an essential part of the message itself. Kant holds that, mediating between man and God, moral law rules out or renders irrelevant an immediate divine commanding Presence. Judaism affirms that, despite the mediating function of the revealed moral law, the Divine is still present in commanding immediacy. The Kantian presence is that moral law is a *bar* between man and its divine Giver. The premise of Judaism is that it is a *bridge*.

How can the law be a bridge? Only by making a most startling demand. For Kant, all morality, including religious morality, demands a two-term relationship between man and his human neighbor. The revealed morality of Judaism demands a three-term relationship, nothing less than a relationship involving man, his human neighbor, and God Himself. If it demanded a human relationship only, then the God in Whose name it was demanded would indeed reduce Himself to mere external sanction behind the demand. The startling claim of the revealed morality of Judaism is, however, that God Himself enters into the relationship. He confronts man with the demand to turn to his human neighbor, and in doing so, turn back to God Himself. Micah's celebrated summary of the commandments does more than list three commandments which exist side by side. It states an internally related whole. For there is no humble walking before God unless it manifests itself in justice and mercy to the human neighbor. And there can be only fragmentary justice and mercy unless they culminate in humility before God. Here lies the heart and core of Jewish morality.[16]

What human response is adequate to this divine demand? The response remains fragmentary until the commandments are performed, on the one hand, for *their* sake, and on the other for *God's* sake. And each of these must point to the other.

Moral commandments, to be moral, must be performed for *their* sake. For unless so performed they do not realize a three-term relationship which takes the human neighbor in his own right seriously; they function merely within an attempted two-term relation between man and God. We say "attempted." For such a relationship is rejected by God Himself. It is God Himself Who bids man to take his neighbor in his own right seriously. To obey God, man accepts both his neighbor, and the commandment concerning him, as possessing intrinsic value. He performs the commandment for its own sake.

And yet the commandment remains fragmentary if performed for its own sake *alone*. For if such performance discloses the human neighbor, and ourselves, too, as beings of intrinsic value, it is ultimately *because the divine commanding Presence so discloses them*. This is why, even if beginning with the acceptance of the disclosure only, a man is finally led to confront the divine Discloser; why performance of the commandment for *its* sake points to its performance for *God's* sake. Both are certainly part of Jewish teaching. And they exist not contingently side by side, but in an internal and necessary relation. God is not barred from direct human access by the intrinsic value of man, or by the intrinsic value of the commandment which relates to man. On the contrary, *He discloses Himself through all intrinsic value, as its ultimate Source.* And the man who accepts this disclosure acts for the sake of God. In the hour of his martyrdom, Rabbi Akiba knew that the love of God is not one commandment side by side to others. It is the life of all.[17]

Thus, the territory in which we have sought philosophic refuge from the decisive but bewildering question raised by the pristine moment of divine commanding Presence, while no doubt safer, is by no means absolutely safe, if by "safety" is meant the comfortable distance, and hence the irrelevance, of the Divine. We first saw that in the pristine moment of divine commanding Presence there is already the possibility of free human appropriation, and we have now seen that, once human freedom can appropriate specific laws and commandments endowed with permanence and intrinsic value, the divine commanding Presence will still confront it. Divine commanding Presence and appropriating human freedom still point to each other. And the philosophical question raised by their togetherness can no longer be suspended or avoided. In the light of the foregoing, we may reformulate that question, to read as follows: *how can man presume to participate in a three-term relationship which involves not only his human neighbor but also God Himself? How can he—as he must, in order to participate in such a relationship—act out of love for the sake of God, when God is God while man is only man?* In Kantian language, what is the condition of the possibility of such action?

VIII

It is a testimony to Kant's genius as a religious thinker that he should not have wholly ignored this question. He even supplied it with an answer. But Kant's answer is not and cannot be the Jewish answer. Instead, we come to a final parting of ways.

Kant writes:

> The virtuous man fears God without being afraid of Him. This is because he is not worried lest he himself might wish to resist Him or His commandments. God is awe-inspiring to him because such resistance, while unthinkable in his own case, is not in itself impossible.[18]

For Kant's virtuous man, it is "unthinkable" that he might not will the will of God. For a prophet when first singled out, it is unthinkable how he *could* will it. To fear God at all, Kant's virtuous man must imagine himself as willing what he is in fact incapable of willing. The rabbis need no such strategy in order to stand in fear of God. Their impossible possibility is not the fear but rather the love of God.[19] For Kant, the oneness of the human with the divine will is automatic once virtue is achieved. For prophets and rabbis, such oneness is very far from automatic even for the virtuous man, and, in a sense, for him least of all. For prophets and rabbis, there is a radical gulf between God, Who is God, and man, who is only human. How then is a oneness of wills possible at all?

It is possible if God Himself has made it possible. Man can appropriate divine commandments if they are handed over for human appropriation. He can live by the Torah in the love and for the sake of God, if the Torah itself is a gift of divine love, making such a life a human possibility. He can participate in a three-term relationship which involves God Himself if God, Who in His power does not need man, in His love nevertheless chooses to need him.

The belief in the reality of such a divine love is as pervasive in Judaism as is the belief in revealed law itself. For here divine commandment and divine love are not only coeval, they are inseparable. The Torah manifests love in the very act of manifesting commandment; for in commanding *humans* rather than angels, it accepts these humans in their humanity.[20] Hence in accepting the Torah, man can at the same time accept himself as accepted by God in his humanity. This is why to attempt to perform the commandments, and to do so both for their sake and for the sake of God, is not to attempt the humanly impossible. At least in principle, the commandments *can* be performed in joy.[21]

This belief in divine love manifest in the divine commandment is present in Judaism from its pristine beginnings and throughout its history. From its beginnings: having first shrunk from the divine commanding Presence, the prophet ends up accepting it because he has experienced the divine love which makes acceptance possible.[22] Throughout its history: our daily prayer renders thanks for the divine love in which God has given the commandments.

If this faith permeates Jewish life so universally and so obviously, one may well ask why Jewish thought, when confronted with the Kantian challenge, should have failed to bring it clearly to philosophical self-consciousness. Had it done so, it would not have accepted so meekly the terms of the Kantian dilemma, between a morality which, because genuinely moral, cannot be essentially revealed, and a morality which, because essentially revealed, must be less than truly moral. It would have repudiated this dilemma, recognizing—and clearly stating—that, if divine love is manifest in the revealed commandments, the dilemma does not arise.

Perhaps it is not far-fetched to identify as the cause of failure, in the case of non-Jewish philosophers like Kant, an ancient prejudice against Judaism bolstered by ignorance of Judaism; and, in the case of Jewish philosophers, uncritically assimilated reliance on non-Jewish modes of philosophical thought.

An ancient prejudice contrasts Jewish law with Christian love; and this is only slightly modified by the concession that love "evolves" in later stages of Judaism as well. Against this prejudice, it is by no means enough to insist that divine love is as ancient in Judaism as is divine commandment. For such love might still be confined, in Pelagian style, to the remission of sins which strict justice would condemn; and this would still leave law itself prior to love, and in itself loveless. In Judaism the primordial manifestation of divine love is not subsequent to but *in* the commandments; primordial human joy is not in a future subsequent to the life of the commandments but in that life itself.

Now it is precisely this teaching which Paul either could not comprehend or could not accept. Paul did not merely assert that the commandments cannot be performed wholly, which to the rabbis was not new. He asserted that they cannot be performed at all. This was because, while accepting one aspect of Jewish teaching he did not accept the other. He saw man commanded to act for God's sake, by a God incommensurate with all things human. But he did not see, or was personally unable to experience, the divine love which, handing the commandments over for human appropriation, makes their performance a human possibility. Hence he thought man was obligated to do the humanly impossible.

Kant's moral philosophy may be regarded, among many other things, as a protest against this Pauline conclusion. It rightly insisted that man can be morally obligated to do only what he is able to do, and hence that, if an unbridged gap exists between the human and the Divine, divine commandments cannot be moral commandments. It also properly refused to divorce the Divine from the moral. But this compelled it to deny the gap between the Divine and the human. And the result was that the divine will became a moral redundancy.[23] In all this, Kant's anti-Pauline protest shares one assumption with Paul's own position; the denial of divine love manifest in the God-given commandment. From the standpoint of the revealed morality of Judaism, Kant may therefore be viewed as the nemesis of a tradition which begins with Paul.

IX

Throughout our essay, the term "Judaism" has meant classical Judaism which finds literary expression in the Hebrew Bible and in rabbinic literature. Re-enacting this Judaism in thought, we have rejected the Kantian dilemma between a morality which, if autonomous, is not essentially revealed, and, if essentially revealed, must necessarily be heteronomous.

But can the Jewish philosopher of today do more than give a phenomenological re-enactment of the classical faith? Can he accept it himself? It is all too obvious that faith in a divine love manifest in revealed commandments, always under much pressure in life, is subject to pressures of the gravest kind not only in modern life but in the realm of modern thought as well.

This is a question for separate inquiry, the results of which one cannot anticipate. One can only be certain that the Jewish philosopher who conducts it must not, at any rate, surrender quickly to modern pressures. For if there is anything that makes him a *Jewish* philosopher, it is precisely the duty to confront, and take seriously, his own Jewish tradition. He would fail in his duty if he were ever to forget that his ancestors could often live by the belief that "when the Torah came into the world, freedom came into the world."[24]

Notes

1. Cf., e.g., the famous passage in *Pirke Abot*, I 3.

2. *Bab. Talmud, Yoma*, 67 b.

3. *Fundamental Principles of the Metaphysics of Ethics*, translated by Abbott (London, 1926), pp. 59, 61. I have revised Abbott's translation. When possible, readily available English translations of Kant are quoted; otherwise, the Prussian Academy edition, 23 vols., 1900–56, is the source, and the translation is my own.

4. The "creative morality" interpretation of Kant, given by thinkers from Fichte to Hermann Cohen, has affected quite un-Kantian philosophies, such as those of Nietzsche and Dewey, as well as much popular moral and psychological thinking. Instead of documenting the view that it is not Kantian, which I intend to do elsewhere, I refer only to G. Krüger, *Philosophie und Moral in der Kantischen Kritik* (Tübingen, 1931).

5. A remarkable nineteenth century Jewish thinker neatly illustrates this dilemma. Samuel Hirsch subscribed to Kantian autonomous morality. Yet he also believed quite literally in revelation. Aware of the possibility of conflict, he sought to resolve it by interpreting revelation (following Lessing) as divine education toward moral autonomy. Hirsch's ingenuity in developing this doctrine does not save it from ultimate failure. Revelation here is a divine guidance the sole purpose of which is to emancipate man from the need for guidance, and hence from revelation itself. Cf. my article "Samuel Hirsch and Hegel" in *Studies in Nineteenth-Century Jewish Intellectual History*, ed. A. Altmann (Cambridge, Mass., 1964), pp. 171–201.

6. Kant returns to this theme on countless occasions. We confine ourselves to quoting one representative passage: "so far as practical reason has the right to guide us, we shall not regard actions as obligatory because they are divine commandments. We shall regard them as divine commandments because we are inwardly obligated to them" *Critique of Pure Reason*, b. 847.

7. Prussian Academy edition, VIII, 405.

8. Cf., e.g., Gen. 12:1ff.; Exod. 3:4ff., and 19:5ff.; Isa. 6:1ff.; Jer. 1:1ff. When bidden to become a holy nation (Exod. 19:5–6), Israel is, of course, already in possession of *some* commandments in

terms of which the content of holiness may be specified. Still, it is of the greatest importance that the bulk of revealed commandments are yet to come.

9. Isa. 6:8; Exod. 24:7. We follow the traditional interpretation of the last passage.

10. Cf., e.g., Isa. 6:4; Jer. 1:6.

11. Whether or not *all* the 613 commandments of traditional Judaism may be regarded as having permanence and intrinsic value is a large question, and one transcending the scope of this essay.

12. Jer., 27.

13. Our brief remarks on this topic are not, of course, meant to be an adequate treatment of this subject.

14. It is interesting to note that Kant and Kierkegaard use the same Biblical tale—Abraham's sacrifice of Isaac—for opposite purposes: Kant to argue that, since we must judge the claims of supposed divine voices in the light of our moral standards, such voices must be *a priori* either false or superfluous (Prussian Academy edition. VIII, 63ff.; *Religion within the Limits of Reason Alone*, translated by Greene and Hudson [New York, 1960], p. 175); Kierkegaard to argue that, if revelation is to be a present possibility, there must be, in an extreme situation, the possibility of a teleological suspension of the ethical (*Fear and Trembling* [New York, 1954]). Any Jewish interpreter of the Abraham story will surely be dissatisfied with both the Kantian and the Kierkegaardian accounts. But one must face the fact that if, as Kant argues, a revealed morality is necessarily heteronomous, there is no third possibility.

15. Cf., e.g., *Midrash Tanhuma*, Yitro, and many other passages, in hasidic as well as rabbinic literature.

16. Mic. 6:8. The point made in this section is perfectly expressed in a Midrash in which God is made to say, "Would that they had deserted Me, and kept My Torah; for if they had occupied themselves with the Torah, the leaven which is in it would have brought them back to Me" (*Pesikta Kahana*, XV). Liberal writers are fond of quoting the first half of this Midrash only, thereby perverting a profound statement of the morality of Judaism into a humanistic platitude.

17. *Bab. Talmud, Berakhot* 61b.

18. *Critique of Judgment*, tr. Meredith (Oxford, 1952), p. 110. The translation is mine.

19. According to one Midrash (*Tanhuma, Hukkat*), the righteous do not cease to fear God even though they have received His assurance. According to another (*Sifre Deut., Wa'ethanan*, No. 32), while everywhere else love drives out fear, this is not true of the love and fear of God.

20. In *Tanhuma, Behukkotai*, God is made to reject the offer of the angels to observe the Torah, on the ground that the Torah is appropriate only for human observance.

21. Cf., e.g., *Bab. Talmud, Berakhot* 31a, *Shabbat* 30b.

22. Isa. 6:6-7; Jer.1:7-8.

23. As already indicated (*supra*, section IV), for reasons which are beyond the scope of this essay, Kant does not regard the divine will as an *absolute redundancy*. He does, however, regard it as redundant within a purely moral context.

24. *Midrash Genesis Rabba, Wayyera* LIII 7.

8 Martin Buber's Concept of Revelation

I

The core of both the Jewish and the Christian faiths is the belief that a God who is other than the world nevertheless enters into the world; that He enters into the world because He enters into the life of man. The Jewish and Christian God descends to meet man, and "a man does not pass, from the moment of supreme meeting, the same being as he entered into it."[1] Judaism and Christianity, or groups within either faith, may differ as to what, more specifically, revelation is; they may also differ as to when it has taken place, when it takes place, or when it will take place. But they agree that God *can* reveal Himself and that, in the entire history of man, He has done so at least once.

This core of religious belief persisted unimpaired until the Age of Enlightenment. But since that time it has become the object of ever more formidable criticism. There may be no conflict between modern thought and Biblical "monotheism," taken by itself, or between modern thought and Biblical "ethics," taken by itself. But there does seem to be a necessary conflict between modern thought and the Biblical belief in revelation. All claims to revelation, modern science and philosophy seem agreed, must be repudiated, as mere relics of superstitious ages. But Biblical "monotheism" is the monotheism of a self-revealing God, and Biblical "ethics" is an aspect of His revelation. Neither the monotheism nor the ethics can, without distortion, be taken by itself. The conflict between modern thought and the Biblical faith is therefore radical.

This fact did not become fully clear until the nineteenth century. Until that time, most modern thinkers were prepared to exempt spheres of reality from critical inquiry, provided they were protected by the walls of a sacred authority, and

Reprinted from *The Philosophy of Martin Buber*, Library of Living Philosophers, Vol. 12, eds. Paul A. Schilpp and Maurice Friedman, by permission of Open Court Publishing Company, La Salle, Illinois. Copyright© 1967 by The Library of Living Philosophers, Inc.

the "supernatural" was permitted to live behind such walls. But the nineteenth century—the age of critical history, Biblical criticism, and, last but not least, critical psychology—did away with all authorities, sacred or otherwise, and the moment this happened the modern assault on revelation exhibited itself as unqualified and radical.

The modern attack was directed not merely on a particular claim on behalf of an actual revelation, or even on all such claims. It was directed on the very *possibility* of revelation; and this was because it seemed radically incompatible not merely with this or that modern principle, but with the one principle basic to all modern thought, namely, the supreme principle of rational inquiry. This asserted that knowledge consisted in the discovery of uniformities, and that to hit upon the non-uniform was not to discover an exception to uniformity, but merely to become aware of one's ignorance. There were no lawless or causeless events; there were merely events whose laws or causes were not, or not yet, known.

It followed from this principle that there could be no revelations, that is, events not wholly due to natural laws or causes. There could only be a belief in revelations; and this was possible only because of partial or total ignorance of the laws or causes actually responsible for the events in question. To refute the belief in revelation, it was not necessary to discover the particular natural laws or causes of particular "revelations"; it was enough to know that all events must have such laws or causes: and to know *that* was to understand that revelation is in principle impossible.

Despite his rationalism, a mediaeval metaphysician such as Maimonides could allow miraculous interruptions of the order of nature, of which revelation was the most important instance.[2] A modern metaphysician could not allow such interruptions. To him, all miracles were only apparent miracles, and all revelations only apparent revelations. God, if admitted at all, was either a power beyond the universe or a force within it. The Biblical God—who is beyond the universe yet enters into it—was a mere myth of bygone ages.

The same conclusion was reached by those who, scorning metaphysical speculation, confined themselves to the analysis of human experience. A mediaeval empiricist such as Judah Hallevi[3] could argue for revelation by pointing to the authority of the six hundred thousand Israelites who had been present at Mount Sinai. A modern empiricist would reject this argument even if the dubious appeal to authority could be eliminated, that is, if he could project himself into the past so as to be personally present at Mount Sinai. To be sure, he might, in such a situation, hear not merely the thunder but also the voice of God. But his subsequent analysis would quickly eliminate the latter. He had heard the thunder because there had been thunder to be heard. But whatever the causes of his hearing of a voice of God, among them had not been an actual voice of God. For such a voice was not, on the one hand, a physical or psychical event, nor could it, on the other, interrupt the orderly sequence of such events. Hence the hearing of the voice of God had merely been an imagined hearing, mistaken for real hearing only by the ignorant.

How could the modern Jew or Christian meet this attack on revelation? He could, of course, simply refuse to meet it at all. But this could perhaps satisfy his heart but hardly his mind. Or he could seek shelter behind ancient authorities. But these no longer provided shelter. For a time it seemed that there was only one thing that could honestly be done, and that was to give in by "modernizing" the ancient faiths. A modernized faith was a faith without revelation. God became—as in Deism past and present—a reality external to the world unable to enter into human experience; or He became—as in religious idealism past and present[4]—a force immanent in human experience which could not exist, or could exist only incompletely, apart from human experience.[5] All these modernized versions of the ancient faiths had this in common: God could not reveal Himself, that is, be present to man. The God of religious idealism is at most present *in* man, never present *to* man; and the God of Deism cannot be present at all.

But since the middle of the nineteenth century, it has become gradually clear that retreat was not the only way in which to meet the modern attack on revelation. It was possible to counter-attack. But this had to be done in rather a special way. One could not meet the attack on revelation by simply attacking, in turn, the principle on which the attack was based. To reject, or arbitrarily limit, the principle of modern rational inquiry was merely to fall prey, wittingly or unwittingly, to obscurantism. But it was possible that that principle, while unlimited in application, nevertheless applied only within a sphere which was itself limited, and that revelation fell outside that sphere.

This possibility first became obvious through the work of Immanuel Kant, who argued that the law- or cause-discovering kind of knowledge discloses only a phenomenal world. But Kant's argument neither sprang from a wish to defend revelation, nor did it issue, in Kant himself, in a defense of revelation. This latter task was undertaken by religious existentialism. If the law- or cause-discovering kind of knowledge is phenomenal, existentialism argues, it is because it presupposes the detachment of a knower who makes the world his object. So long as he perseveres in this standpoint he discovers laws upon laws or causes upon causes. But what he discovers in this way is, as a whole, not reality, but merely reality made into an object or objectified. Reality ceases to be an object if we cease to view it as an object; that is, if instead of viewing it in detachment we become engaged with it in personal commitment. In such a personal commitment there is knowing access to the transphenomenal, an access which consists not in the discovery of laws or causes, but in a direct encounter. And the most important fact that can be encountered is divine revelation.

This argument, first stated by Schelling and Kierkegaard in the mid-nineteenth century, has found its most profound spokesman in our time in Martin Buber. To examine his argument is the task of the present essay. Such an examination must necessarily subordinate all its efforts to answering a single question: is Buber's counter-attack on the modern attack on revelation successful? Does he make it possible at the same time to accept without compromise the modern principle of rational inquiry and yet to embrace the ancient faith in a self-revealing God?

II

This question cannot even be raised, let alone be answered, by a biographical account, that is, the kind of account which explains an author's teachings in terms of his personal experience. The more perceptive of the modern critics of revelation are quite prepared to admit that there is experience-of-revelation; but they deny that there is revelation. They grant that there are those who sincerely believe themselves in dialogue with God; but they assert that all such dialogues are but disguised monologues.[6] If Buber has a reply to this criticism, it cannot consist in his personal experience; and the interpreter who looks for such a reply cannot look for it in that experience. For the question is not whether, from the standpoint of religious experience, there appears to be revelation. The question is whether there is, or at least can be, revelation; that is, whether the religious standpoint which accepts the category of revelation is justified.

The faults of the biographical approach are not remedied by an emphasis on Buber's life-long encounter with traditional sources, notably Hasidism and the Hebrew Bible. There is no doubt that Buber's historical studies are closely related to his own views, particularly as regards revelation. Indeed, his chief merit as a Bible interpreter may well be seen in his insistence that the Bible be understood in Biblical ("dialogue between God and man") rather than in modern ("religious experience," "evolution of ideas" and the like) categories. But by itself this insistence only means that Buber has understood the Biblical belief in revelation; it does not mean that he has justified his own acceptance of it.

This last point is nicely illustrated by the fact that Buber did not always accept the belief in revelation. In 1911 he wrote:

> the spiritual process of Judaism is . . . the striving for the ever more perfect realization of three internally connected ideas: the idea of unity, the idea of action and the idea of the future; these ideas . . . are not abstract tendencies, but natural tendencies of folk character.[7]

Had Buber retained the standpoint indicated in this passage he could without doubt have mustered, as a historian, the imagination necessary in order to understand the Biblical belief in revelation; but he would have at the same time asserted, as a philosopher, that what was to Biblical man a dialogue with God was in fact a form of human self-realization and nothing else; that is, a disguised monologue.

The conclusion, then, is clear. Our approach to Buber's work must be systematic, not biographic. Only a systematic account can answer the questions which must be answered if Buber's stature as a thinker who is modern and yet affirms revelation is to be fairly appraised. The questions are: does Buber offer a doctrine intended to meet the modern critique of revelation? And if so, does his doctrine in fact meet that critique?

III

The first of these two questions can be answered at once in the affirmative. Buber does offer a doctrine of revelation intended, among other things, to meet the modern critique of revelation. This is an extension of a wider doctrine which must first be considered briefly. We refer to the celebrated doctrine of the "*I*" and the "*Thou.*"

There are, Buber teaches, two types of relation I may establish with another, namely, an *I-It* and an *I-Thou* relation. I have an *I-It* relation when I use the other, or when I know the other in an attitude of objective detachment. These relations are one-sided, for the other is for me while I am not for the other. When I use or observe the other, my person remains unengaged. The other cannot *do* anything to me; that is, even if the other happens to be a person, I am not open to him as a person but treat him as a mere object.

The *I-It* relation is abstract. Users and objective observers, on the one hand, objects of use or observation, on the other, are interchangeable. In using an object, I never intend the unique object but merely a *kind* of object; and in observing it my inevitable aim is to bring it under general laws of which it is a mere instance. The unique individuality of the other does not enter into the *I-It* relation.

Nor does the unique individuality of the *I*. Qua user, I am only a *kind* of user; and the supreme condition of all objective observation is that anyone who would take my place would observe the same. In the *I-It* relation anyone else *could* take my place.

The *I-It* relation contrasts in every respect with the *I-Thou* relation. This relation is, above all, mutual. The other is for me, but I am also for the other. I do something to the other, but the other also does something to me. This happens in the relation of dialogue, which is a relation of address and response-to-address. The other addresses me and responds to my address; that is, even if the other happens to be a lifeless and speechless object, it is treated as one treats a person.

It would, to be sure, be gross anthropomorphizing to assert that the lifeless object *is* a person; that a tree or a stone can be an *I* to themselves and I a *Thou* to them. But it is not anthropomorphic to assert that I can be an *I* to myself, and the tree or stone a *Thou* to me. From the standpoint of one partner at least, the human partner, *I-Thou* relations are possible, not only with other human beings, but with anything whatever. This is not to say that such relations are easy, or possible to anyone, or possible at any time. It is merely to say that there are no a priori limitations to the possible partners I may have in an *I-Thou* relationship.

While the *I-It* relationship is necessarily abstract, the *I-Thou* relationship cannot be abstract. The partners communicate not this or that, but themselves; that is, they must *be in* the communication. Further—since the relation of dialogue is mutual—they must be in a state of openness to the other, that is, to *this* other at *this* time and in *this* place. Hence both the *I* and the *Thou* of every genuine dialogue are irreplaceable. Every dialogue is unique.

All this is possible only because the *I* is not a complete, self-sufficient substance. In the *I-Thou* relation I *become* an I by virtue of the relationship to a *Thou*. My whole being enters into the meeting, to emerge from it other than it was. And what is essential between an *I* and a *Thou*—such as love and friendship—is not in the mind of either the *I* or the *Thou*, or even in the minds of both; it is *between* an *I* and a *Thou*, who would both be essentially different if the relation did not exist. To be sure, there are relations in which there is nothing between the *I* and the other, and which do not alter the substance of the *I*; but these, far from being original relations with another, are merely the kind of derivative relations in which "reflexion" or "withdrawal"[8] has corrupted the immediacy of openness: in other words, *I-It* relations. Only from the standpoint of this corrupt state—into which we all perforce often fall—does the dialogue with a *Thou* appear as an unessential act on the part of a self-complete and self-sufficient *I*. In truth it is what constitutes both the *I* and the *Thou*, to the extent to which they are constituted at all. And in the actual dialogue this is known to both.[9]

It is not necessary, for our present purpose, to describe Buber's doctrine of the *I* and *Thou* in further detail. But it is necessary to ask: is it a doctrine at all, that is, a body of metaphysical and epistemological assertions? Or is it a pure homily, that is, the kind of teaching intended solely for spiritual guidance?

This question is of crucial importance. It will be seen that Buber's teaching concerning revelation is an application of his teaching concerning the *I* and *Thou*. If the latter were a pure homily the same would necessarily be true of the former. But whatever the undoubted religious merits of a homily on revelation, it could only ignore, but not come to grips with, the modern critique of revelation. This latter, as we have seen, readily admits that there may be experience-of-revelation yet stoutly denies that there can be revelation. If this criticism is to be met rather than ignored, there is need, in addition and indeed logically prior to appeals which might make men spiritually receptive to revelation, for a doctrine which argues, against the modern critique, that the category of revelation in terms of which the religious standpoint understands itself is the category in terms of which it must be understood.

But Buber's teaching concerning the *I* and *Thou* is not a pure homily; it is a doctrine as well. Indeed, it is the latter rather than the former that distinguishes his work from that of many others. Literature abounds with poems which describe, and sermons which exalt, the wealth of interpersonal relationships. *Buber's distinctive teaching lies in his interpretation of the* I-Thou *relation, as such, and as contrasted with the* I-It *relation, as such.*

An illustration will serve to show, both that Buber's teaching is a doctrine, and what the doctrine is. Consider a scientific psychologist who also, it happens, has near-perfect *I-Thou* relations with his wife, his children and close friends. His professional business is to understand people as cases falling under laws; but his private life is such as to enable him to understand those close to him in living dialogue. But would such a person grant that both kinds of knowledge *are* knowledge? If his outlook were typical, he would assert that only the former kind of knowledge has any chance of getting at the truth about human nature, for it alone is objective; the latter kind of "knowledge" cannot be regarded as knowledge at all precisely because it is engaged; it is the sort of "biased" opinion which has a right to persist only because it is indispensable in life.

Now if Buber has a quarrel with this hypothetical psychologist, it is clearly neither with his psychology nor with his way of life. As for his psychology, it must be, like all science, a form of *I-It* knowledge. And as for his way of life, it is *ex hypothesi* such as to find Buber's complete approval. It follows that if Buber's teaching were a pure homily, there would be no quarrel at all. Yet a quarrel there certainly is. It concerns the epistemological status of *I-Thou* and *I-It* knowledge, and the metaphysical status of *Thou* and *It*, respectively. The hypothetical psychologist has one doctrine in this matter, and Buber can quarrel with it only because he too has a doctrine.

But Buber's doctrine is diametrically opposite. It asserts that *in the committed* I-Thou *relation there is knowing access to a reality which is inaccessible otherwise; that uncommitted "objective" knowledge which observes as an* It *what may also be encountered as a* Thou *is a lesser kind of knowledge, and that the most profound mistake in all philosophy is the epistemological reduction of* I-Thou *to* I-It *knowledge, and the metaphysical reduction of* Thou *to* It.

We must subsequently ask whether, and if so how, Buber defends this most basic of all his doctrines. For the moment it is enough to observe that, if adequately defended, it can be the basis for a counter-attack on the modern attack on revelation. For, first, it implies complete acceptance of the modern principle of rational inquiry; secondly, it yet limits the sphere to which that principle applies; thirdly, it points beyond this sphere to quite another sphere in which it is at least not impossible that revelation could be found.

Buber accepts the modern principle of rational inquiry because he finds a legitimate place for *I-It* knowledge. His acceptance of the principle is complete because there is no attempt on his part to limit arbitrarily the range of *I-It* knowledge. Science has the world as its object, and this world—which includes the psychological world—displays itself to rational inquiry as a unity shattered by no irrational incursions of God. The doctrine of the *I* and *Thou* is not at war either with specific conclusions of science or with the assumptions which underlie science as a whole.

It is at war, however, with all metaphysics which regard reality as an *It* or a system of *Its*, and with all epistemologies which reduce all knowledge to *I-It* knowledge. It is also at war, therefore, with the kind of philosophy which identifies reality as understood by science with reality as it ultimately is, and scientific with metaphysical knowledge. For the doctrine of the *I* and *Thou*, every *It*, including the *It* of science, is something less than the fullness of reality, whether an "objectification," "abstraction" or "logical construct"; and all *I-It* knowledge, including scientific knowledge, falls short of being metaphysical knowledge, that is, of grasping reality in its fullness. Rational inquiry ties *It* to *It* but remains itself tied to the world of *It*. Thus Buber limits the sphere to which the principle of rational inquiry applies.

This sphere is transcended not when the *I* comes upon an *It* supposedly escaping rational inquiry, but when the *I* abandons the detachment of the *I-It* relation for the engagement of the *I-Thou* relation. If the *Thou* escapes rational inquiry, it is not because the latter is rational but because it presupposes detachment.[10] And the shortcomings of rational inquiry are epistemological and metaphysical only because the engaged *I-Thou* dialogue is itself a form of knowledge; indeed, it is the form of knowledge in which the fullness of reality is encountered.

It follows, as we have said, that the doctrine of the *I* and *Thou* can be a basis for a counter-attack on the modern attack on revelation. For while the system of laws or causes is never shattered from the standpoint of *I-It* detachment it is always shattered from the standpoint of *I-Thou* engagement. If the doctrine of the *I* and *Thou* is true, there is no need for special doctrinal provisions for the reconciliation of the category of revelation with the principle of rational inquiry.

But the doctrine of the *I* and *Thou* is no more than a mere basis for a modern doctrine of revelation. By itself, it justifies not the positive assertion of the possibility of revelation, but merely the bare empty denial of its impossibility; and it justifies even that only on the assumption that it is part of an *I-Thou* rather than of an *I-It* relation. To justify more positive assertions, it is necessary that the general doctrine of the *I* and *Thou* be extended into a doctrine of revelation. This latter must accomplish three tasks. It must show that religion is an *I-Thou* rather than an *I-It* relation; it must identify the criteria which distinguish it from all other *I-Thou* relations; and it must locate revelation within it.

IV

We may begin with Buber's critique of the widely held view that religion is feeling. For Buber, all genuine religion is an *I-Thou* relation with God, rather than merely subjective feeling.

> Feelings are a mere accompaniment to the metaphysical and metapsychical fact of the relation which is fulfilled not in the soul but *between* the *I* and *Thou*.[11]

A "religion" whose essence is feeling is either the mere solitary disport of the soul with itself, cut off from God; or, if not cut off from God, not a relation; or, if a relation, not immediate. But the first—subjective feeling by itself—is not religion but merely the pseudo-religion of a degenerate age.[12] The second—God found in and identified with religious feeling—is mysticism, and mysticism is only a grandiose illusion. The third—God inferred from religious feeling—is at once pseudo-religion and bad philosophy.

Buber's argument in support of these assertions is the doctrine of the *I* and *Thou*. In every *I-Thou* relation the *I* is open to a *Thou*, not absorbed with images of a *Thou*; the latter state is not original, but the mere product of the corruption of "withdrawal."[13] Absorption with God-images too is a mere corruption; and this corruption is by no means overcome by an attempt to proceed by inference from the God-image to God Himself. For the God-image is a mere part of the self, and the inferred God a mere *It*.[14] If there is genuine religion at all, it can only consist of the direct dialogical meeting of the human *I* with a divine *Thou*.

This is why mysticism, too, is a form of pseudo-religion. For it denies either the reality of all meeting, or else at least that the supreme moment is a moment of meeting.[15] In the supreme moment of mysticism the *I*, rather than meet a *Thou*, dissolves into the Ineffable. But "all real living is meeting."[16] Mysticism, far from being a way into reality, is on the contrary a flight from it.

If there is such a thing as genuine religion it involves, on the human side, the kind of committed openness which is ready to address God and to be addressed by Him. But it also involves, on the divine side, a God who at least *can* be the partner in such a dialogical relationship. To be sure, it is not necessary that God should always be available for partnership, and genuine religion may consist, for long periods of time, of the mere human address which listens in vain for a reply. But all such addressing and listening would be wholly vain if God could not, by His very nature, be addressed or listened to. If religion is to be—as it must be—*between* God and man, revelation must at least be possible. Thus, the "modernized" religions without revelation are not merely religions which Buber happens to disagree with; they are not geniune religions at all. *Merely by virtue of being an* I-Thou *relation*, all *genuine religion involves at least the possibility of revelation.*

Further, merely by virtue of being part of an *I-Thou* relation, revelation must have certain characteristics. Above all, it must be the address of a *Thou* who *is in* what He communicates. Consequently, revelation cannot be either a system of dogmas[17] or a system of laws.[18] For both would cut the communication off from Him who communicates, thus perverting the living *I-Thou* dialogue into the fixity of the *I-It*. It will be seen, to be sure, that revelation must translate itself into human statement, and that an essential part of the statement is commandment.[19]

But a genuine translation must spring from, and reflect, the pregnancy of the event of divine presence; and the commandment must give Him who commands along with the commandment. A *system* of dogmas is not the reflection of His presence, but a statement made about Him in His absence; and to obey a *system* of laws—independent in its validity of the Giver and of the hour for which He gives it—is not to respond to revelation but on the contrary to flee from it.

All this is true because the Giver who is present in the given is not a timeless Presence. The God of dialogue, like any Thou of any dialogue, speaks to a unique partner in a unique situation, disclosing Himself according to the unique exigencies of each situation. "If we name the speaker of this speech God, then it is always the God of a moment, a moment God."[20] If He has a general name at all, it is "I shall be who I shall be,"[21] that is, He who cannot be comprehended as He may be in His timeless essence, but can only be encountered in each here and now, as He may show Himself in each here and now.

These above implications for revelation may be derived from Buber's assertion that all genuine religion is an *I-Thou* relationship. But we must now ask what distinguishes religion from every other *I-Thou* relation, the divine *Thou* from every other *Thou*, and revelation from every other address. Such a quest for distinguishing criteria is clearly necessary. For in their total absence the very words "religion," "divine" and "revelation" would be meaningless to those not—or not yet—participating in a human-divine dialogue; and Buber would have to persuade them to decide to participate in such a dialogue, in total blindness not only as to whether it exists but even as to what it means. In short, Buber's doctrine of the *I* and *Thou* would turn into a pure homily at the precise point at which an attempt is made to extend it into a doctrine of revelation. And as we have already seen, such a homily on revelation, whatever its religious merits, could not come to grips with the modern critique of revelation. Why, even if he granted that there are all sorts of *I-Thou* relationships, should anyone grant that among them is a divine-human relationship, if the very word "divine" is meaningless to all except those who stand in such a relationship?

But would that word be meaningful even to those who *do* stand in such a relationship? To be sure, Buber tells us that the self-revealing God must be a *moment-God*, that is, a God whose self-disclosure cannot be anticipated by means of universal criteria. But he also tells us that the moment-God is a *God*, and that "out of the moment-Gods there arises for us with a single identity the Lord of the voice, the One."[22] But if all criteria of identification were totally lacking, how could the moment-Gods merge into the One God? Indeed, how could the moment-Gods be, and be recognized to be, Gods at all?

It is clearly necessary, then, to seek criteria in terms of which *concepts* of God, religion and revelations may be framed. But we must not seek the wrong kind of criterion and the wrong kind of concept. A concept of revelation which contained, even only implicitly, the whole content of revelation would be a contradiction in terms. For revelation is the reception of the wholly new, but the concept would deny that it is wholly new; revelation demands committed openness which the concept would make impossible. The kind of concept required is the same that may be given of a *Thou* as such, or of a human *Thou* as such. The former may be defined as the kind of other who can be in dialogue with me, and the latter, as the kind of other who can be in human dialogue with me, that is, the kind of dialogue carried on through words and gestures. Both definitions, far from denying the uniqueness of every *Thou* and of every address, explicitly contain this element.

God, Buber asserts, is the *Thou* "that by its nature cannot become an *It*."[23] All genuine religion, therefore, is an *I-Thou* relationship with the *Thou* that cannot become an *It*; and every revelation reveals the *Thou* that cannot become an *It*. Here we have Buber's criterion of distinction.

But it is one thing to state the criterion, another to understand it. How can revelation be tied to the moment of encounter, revealing only a God of the moment, and yet reveal a God who cannot be an *It* at *any* moment? How can the God of the moment at the same time be recognized as infinite[24] and eternal?[25] And yet if He is not so recognized, it now seems, He is not recognized as God at all. Does this not mean that expressions such as "moment God" and "divine *Thou*" *are nothing less than contradictions in terms?*

The answer to all these questions is this, that *in the moment of revelation no* It *retains its independence.*[26] In that moment, every *It* becomes either a symbol through which God speaks, or the partner to whom He speaks. But the former is not an independent *It* and the latter is not an *It* at all. In making transparent every *It*, in the moment of His presence, God discloses that no *It* can remain opaque to His presence; that there can be both an independent *It* and a present God, but not both at the same time. In revealing Himself as "I shall be who I shall be," God does not disclose when or how He will be present. But He does disclose that He will be present as an *I*, if present at all.

Thus if God is known as eternal and infinite, it is not by thought which rises above the encounter to speculate on His essence; it is known *in* the encounter. God is infinite, because in the moment of encounter there is no *It* which can limit Him; He is eternal, because it is known in the here and now that He cannot turn into an *It* in any here and now.

This, then, is the minimum content of all revelation. But why is the minimum content not also the maximum content? Why does the God who reveals Himself as God nevertheless speak differently in every situation? This is because, while in the presence of the divine *Thou* no independent *It* remains, an independent human *I* remains; indeed, it must remain if the divine *Thou* is to be a *Thou* at all. But while the divine *Thou* is infinite and eternal the human *I* is finite and temporal. The divine *Thou* speaks *into* the situation to a human *I* who can respond only out of the situation. But what He says into each situation transcends all conceptual anticipation.

Can there be conceptual anticipation of the human response to the divine address? Not, to be sure, of the particular response appropriate to each particular situation. But just as every revelation reveals the divine *Thou* every human response must be *to* the divine *Thou*. And this lends it a characteristic which distinguishes this response from every other kind.

Any response to any *Thou* requires, ideally, total commitment. But committed *I-Thou* relations in general can, and always do, degenerate into uncommitted *I-It* relations. Commitment, therefore, admits of degrees; and perhaps total commitment is an ideal which may be approximated but not wholly attained. But all this is impossible in the case of the human response to revelation. For revelation reveals the divine *Thou* who cannot become an *It*. The kind of *I-Thou* relation which it initiates cannot, therefore, degenerate into an *I-It* relation; and commitment cannot here admit of degrees. This relation is the absolute relation,[27] that is, the relation which exists either absolutely or not at all.

We have given an account of the divine address and of the human response. We must now turn to their relation. The central question here is this: is revelation independent of the response? Or does it not become revelation unless and until there is response? Buber would appear to lean at times toward both alternatives, but to end up rejecting both.

Revelation is an address to a *Thou*. It is not revelation unless it has its *Thou*. This implies that, if revelation is independent of human response, being-a-*Thou* is, in this case, not a matter of human response but a product of revelation.

> He is the infinite *I* that *makes* every It His *Thou*.[28]

> In order to speak to man, God must become a person; but in order to speak to him, He must *make him* too a person.[29]

In addressing us God forces us to listen; and having been forced to listen we give our free response.

But this conclusion is difficult. For according to Buber, the essence of human response to revelation is the committed turning to God; and this committed turning is involved, not only in whatever we do subsequently to hearing, but in the hearing as well. For unless we listen in commitment we do not hear at all.

Must we conclude, then, that revelation is not revelation until we respond? That it is not, at any rate, an address to *us* until we decide to listen? This would appear to be implied in Buber's suggestion that God speaks at all times,[30] for revelation manifestly does *not* occur at all times. Our committed listening would translate, in that case, what is in itself only potential revelation into actuality.

But this alternative, too, is in the end rejected, if only because there are times in which God is silent. To be sure, an eclipse of God may be due to our failure to listen to what there is to be heard; but it may also be due to a divine silence which persists no matter how devoutly we listen.[31]

Buber's final conclusion is that the relation between divine address and human response is an antimony which thought cannot resolve.[32] In speaking to *me* the Infinite *Thou* makes me His listening *I*; yet unless I make myself His listening *I* neither shall I be His *Thou* nor He mine.

> I know that 'I am given over for disposal' and know at the same time that 'It depends on myself'. . . . I am compelled to take both to myself, to be lived together, and in being lived they are one.[33]

This conclusion has important implications concerning the content of revelation. The philosophical task here is not the identification of a particular content, for this can be done only, primarily by the person who lives in the revealing situation, secondarily, by the historian who relives it in his mind. The task is to define the status of the content of revelation, namely, the extent to which it is divine and the extent to which it is human. But the attempt at definition ends in an antimony.

It was seen that the core of revelation is not the communication of content but the event of God's presence. Nevertheless, revelation must assume content. For it is an address which calls for a response; and the response called for is not some universal response, but the unique response appropriate to the situation. Speaking *into* the situation, "into my very life,"[34] revelation assumes the most concrete content there can be. But does revelation assume this content independently of our response or only by virtue of our response? Both alternatives are impossible.

Revelation is "hearable" content only in relation to committed listening. If it is to be nevertheless independent of our response, revelation must force us into committed listening. But this, we have already seen, is impossible. Hence there cannot be a divinely-handed-down content, passively received; all content is the result of committed appropriation, and thus "a statement which is human in its meaning and form."[35]

> I experience what God desires of me for this hour . . . not earlier than in this hour. But even then it is not given me to experience it except by answering before God for this hour as my hour.[36]

Is revelation, then, wholly without content apart from my answering? This too is impossible. Revelation would, in that case, not be an address at all, let alone an address to *me*. And the "statement which is human in its meaning and its form" would be, not a translation of revelation into human speech, but the product of self-sufficient human spontaneity. Yet it *is* a translation,[37] and the listener knows it to be a translation, that is, a human product "stimulated"[38] by God.

Once more Buber admits frankly the antinomy at which he has arrived.

> It is not man's own power that works here, nor is it God's pure effective passage, but it is a mixture of the divine and the human.[39]

> In my answering I am given into the power of His grace, but I cannot measure Heaven's share in it.[40]

With this last point Buber's concept of revelation is complete. Whatever goes beyond it is concerned with the actuality of particular revelations, and this transcends the limits of the present essay.[41]

But if Buber's counter-attack on the modern attack on revelation is to be wholly successful there is one task he must still accomplish. We have suggested that if Buber's doctrine of the *I* and *Thou* is true, and if it can be extended into a doctrine of revelation, the latter constitutes an effective answer to the modern critique of revelation. The question remains *whether* the former doctrine is true, and hence whether the latter is acceptable; or—to put it more modestly—whether the grounds on which both are advanced lend them an impressive claim to truth.

V

But in a search for such grounds one fundamental point must be borne in mind with the utmost clarity. Buber's doctrine—which asserts that in the committed *I-Thou* relation there is knowing access to a reality which escapes *I-It* knowledge—cannot itself be an instance of, or be based on, *I-It* knowledge. For the latter, which either ignores the *Thou* or else treats it as an *It*—can neither understand its own limitations *as I-It* knowledge, nor can it recognize *I-Thou* knowledge *as* knowledge.

Thus a psychologist who examined *I-Thou* relations would use *I-It* knowledge, not furnish a critique of it; and he would arrive, not at the doctrine of the *I* and *Thou*, but at laws of interhuman relationships. In his studies of religion, he would not be the committed partner in a dialogue with God, but only the detached observer of other people's dialogue with God. But for this detached standpoint there could not be an address of God, but only other people's *feeling*-of-being addressed-by-God; in short, "psychic phenomena." The investigation would be carried on within a system of categories which is merely "a temporary construction which is useful for psychological orientation."[42]

Must Buber's doctrine, then, be classified, without qualification, within *I-Thou* knowledge? This conclusion is inescapable if *I-Thou* and *I-It* knowledge constitute exhaustive alternatives, and this Buber in at least one essay[43] clearly implies. Conceivably there could be a third kind of knowledge which is unlike *I-It* knowledge in that it understands, and at least to that extent transcends, the limitations of *I-It* knowledge; but which is unlike *I-Thou* knowledge in that it is detached rather than committed. Such a knowledge would have to be classified as philosophical. But philosophy, Buber asserts in the essay referred to, is *I-It* knowledge pure and simple.[44]

But can the doctrine of the *I* and *Thou* really be classified, without qualification, within *I-Thou* knowledge? Let us begin our consideration of this question by turning once more to the hypothetical psychologist to whom we have already had recourse for illustrative purposes.[45] We have argued above that Buber would find fault with neither his science nor his way of life, but rather with a third thing, namely, his interpretation, respectively, of *I-Thou* and *I-It* knowledge. But if this interpretation is to be classified, without qualification, within *I-Thou* knowledge, how can it be a third thing? Would it not follow that the psychologist, if in possession of the knowledge of but a single *Thou*, would *ipso facto* possess knowledge also of the true nature of *I-Thou* and *I-It* knowledge? Would Buber not be driven to the unpalatable conclusion of having to cast aspersions on the way of life lived by wrong-headed philosophers?

But perhaps this conclusion need not follow. For surely even if the doctrine of the *I* and *Thou* is to be classified wholly within *I-Thou* knowledge, a distinction must still be made between the immediate dialogical knowledge of a *Thou* and the knowledge of the *doctrine* of the *I* and *Thou*. The latter could not be identical with, but at most only be somehow implicit in the former. And it would be the philosopher's task to show how it is implicit, and to make the implicit explicit. It would follow that the hypothetical psychologist's mistake was, after all, not due to a lack of *I-Thou* relations, but merely to a failure to recognize their metaphysical and epistemological implications, or else to a tendency to forget them whenever he turned to his professional job.

Such a view may seem plausible enough in the case of interhuman *I-Thou* relations. After all, in the case of these even the most fanatical devotee of *I-It* knowledge must make two admissions: first, that there is an actual address by another, secondly, that this address is never *wholly* understood in terms of *I-It* knowledge. (Of these two admissions, the first is primary; for unless it is made the question of understanding the address *as* address does not arise.) In the case of these relations, therefore, it is not difficult to be persuaded that the doctrine that the *I-Thou* relation yields a unique knowledge of another should be implicit in the actual dialogical knowledge of the other. But it is not easy to be persuaded of this in the case of *I-Thou* relations in which the *Thou* is not human, whether it be a stone or a tree or God. For here one does not have to be a fanatical devotee of *I-It* knowledge in order to doubt that there is an actual—rather than merely an apparent—address by another; indeed, one should be lacking in intellectual responsibility if one did *not* doubt it, demanding an argument for the removal of the doubt. But the crucial difficulty is that, if the doctrine of the *I* and *Thou* is wholly derived from the dialogue with the *Thou*, such an argument must be in principle unavailable. The doctrine of the *I* and *Thou*, far from being able to argue that there is actual rather than merely apparent dialogue, would on the contrary wholly flow from the belief that there is the former rather than the latter. Buber could do nothing to argue that the category of revelation in terms of which the religious standpoint understands itself is the category in terms of which it must be understood; for his doctrine of revelation would, in the end, wholly spring from the religious standpoint, that is, from a dialogue with God whose actuality is accepted simply on faith.

Such a conclusion, we hasten to emphasize, would not be as irrational as it may at first sight appear. For Buber's body of doctrine, even if wholly derived from committed *I-Thou* knowledge, would still be a body of doctrine. It would contain a critique of *I-It* knowledge and an interpretation of the status of *I-Thou* knowledge; it would identify revelation as part of a kind of *I-Thou* knowledge and refute those who assert that revelation is impossible. It would, to be sure, in all its doctrinal assertions be unconvincing to those who stubbornly remain on the *I-It* standpoint; but it would at least show that the objections raised from the *I-It* standpoint have no force for those who adopt the *I-Thou* standpoint. It may be said that this is all that may be asked of a body of doctrine, particularly of a body of religious doctrine into which faith must presumably at some point enter.

But the fact would still remain—at least in the case of all but interhuman *I-Thou* relations—that Buber's entire thought would spring from, rather than be able to argue for, the reality of dialogue; that is, it would have to presuppose that there *is* a reality of dialogue. But is it possible for the modern-minded to grant this presupposition? An ancient prophet could take it for granted that the voice of God may be heard by the committed listener; a modern man can hardly take this for granted, though he may very well be led to accept it. But he will surely accept it only if he is offered some kind of argument, cogent to the *I-It* standpoint, which points to the *I-Thou* standpoint as being, in the case of divine-human as well as interhuman relationships, a standpoint of truth. But if the whole doctrine of the *I* and *Thou* derives from *I-Thou* knowledge such an argument cannot be given.

But perhaps Buber's doctrine does not derive wholly from *I-Thou* knowledge, after all. To the present writer at least it appears that while Buber characterizes philosophy as *I-It* knowledge,[46] the pure philosophizing which he himself does is a *critique* of *I-It* knowledge. It is pure philosophizing because it is detached rather than committed, but it nevertheless transcends the realm of *I-It* in that it recognizes its limitations and, in recognizing them, points beyond them to the realm of the *I and Thou*.

Consider the following very remarkable passage.

The philosopher, if he were really to wish to turn his back on that God [i.e., the *It*-God of the philosophers], would be compelled to renounce the attempt to include God in his system in any conceptual form. Instead of including God as one theme among others, that is, as the highest theme of all, his philosophy both wholly and in part would be compelled to point toward God, without actually dealing with Him. This means that the philosopher would be compelled to recognize and admit the fact that his idea of the Absolute was dissolving at the point where the Absolute *lives;* that it was dissolving at the point where the Absolute is loved; because at that point the Absolute is no longer the 'Absolute' about which one may philosophize, but God.[47]

How is philosophy to "point toward God without actually dealing with Him?" If the division into *I-Thou* and *I-It* knowledge is exhaustive this must be impossible. For the latter knows nothing of the *Thou*-God and hence cannot point to Him, whereas the former not merely points to, but deals with Him; moreover, being committed it is not philosophy. The passage quoted clearly implies that the division into *I-Thou* and *I-It* knowledge is not exhaustive; that philosophy, at least at its profoundest point, is not *I-It* knowledge but the dialectic of *I-It* knowledge. As such it mediates between *I-It* and *I-Thou* knowledge; for, being a detached critique of detached knowledge, it points beyond detached knowledge and thus beyond itself; and what it points to is the commitment of the *I-Thou* standpoint. This is the kind of philosophizing which Buber, at least on important occasions, would appear to be doing. And it is, at least in the opinion of this writer, the only kind of philosophizing which properly belongs, not only with Buber's doctrine of the *I* and *Thou*, but with any kind of existential thought. Indeed, a study of post-Kantian and more particularly post-Hegelian thought would show that it is in connection with this kind of philosophizing that existential philosophy has emerged as a philosophy.[48]

But while there are many samples of such philosophizing to be found in Buber's writings,[49] it must be said that they do not add up to a systematic body of thought. Possibly this is because Buber has chosen, throughout his life, to concentrate on the kind of thinking which flows out of the reality of the dialogue, leaving it to others to supply the propaedeutic, namely, the thinking which argues for the reality of the dialogue. But it is possible that Buber's ultimate stand is that philosophy is only *I-It* knowledge, after all. This would mean that not only the critique of *I-It* knowledge but Buber's doctrine as a whole would derive from *I-Thou* knowledge and nothing else. It would also mean that it is not, strictly speaking, philosophical. Such detached criticizing of detached knowledge as Buber may be doing would have to be regarded, in that case, as a mere series of lapses, due possibly to Kantian or post-Kantian influence.

If this interpretation should be correct, Buber would emerge, in the ultimate analysis, not as a philosopher but as a Hebrew sage in modern garb. He would be in modern garb because, taking note of the modern attack on revelation, he develops a body of doctrine wholly capable of repulsing that attack; but he would be a sage rather than a philosopher because the ultimate basis of his doctrine is an unargued commitment to the dialogue with the ancient God of Israel, a commitment which the reader is called upon to share. Buber's own commitment, and the commitment he asks of his reader, would simply rest on the ancient and irrefutable faith that God can speak even though He may be silent; that He can speak at least to those who listen to His voice with all their hearts.

Notes

1. Martin Buber, *I and Thou* (Edinburgh, 1957), p. 109.

2. Cf. E. L. Fackenheim, "The Possibility of the Universe in Al-Farabi, Ibn Sina and Maimonides," *Proceedings of the American Academy for Jewish Research*, 16 (New York, 1947), 39–70.

3. While Judah Hallevi is hardly an empiricist in any precise sense of the term, there is some justification in applying this term to a thinker who frowned on efforts to support the Jewish religion through metaphysical speculation, pointing instead to the testimony of those who had been present at Mount Sinai.

4. Buber recognizes with the utmost clarity that Jung's "religion of pure psychic immanence," for example, is nothing but a "translation of post-Kantian idealism into psychology," *Eclipse of God* (Harper's Torchbook Edition), pp. 78ff. We might add that the translation is rather less impressive than the original product, cf. E. L. Fackenheim, "Schelling's Philosophy of Religion," *University of Toronto Quarterly*, 22 (Toronto, 1952), 1ff.

5. For the transcendental kind of idealism there is an idea of God but not an existing God, while for the ontological kind the existing God becomes fully real only in human experience. Kant and Hegel do not wholly fit into either of these classes.

6. Buber clearly recognizes the criticism which asserts that "religion has never been anything but an intra-psychic process whose products are 'projected' on a plane in itself fictitious but vested with reality by the soul"; and that, therefore, "every alleged colloquy with the divine was only a soliloquy, or rather a conversation between various strata of the self." *Eclipse of God*, p. 13. In recognizing the criticism, he also recognizes the task confronting those who would answer it.

7. *Drei Reden Ueber Das Judentum* (Frankfurt, 1920), p. 71. For a full account of Buber's early thought, cf., Maurice S. Friedman, *Martin Buber: The Life of Dialogue*, pp. 27–53.

8. Cf. *Between Man and Man* (Boston, 1955), pp. 22ff., and *I and Thou*, pp. 115ff.

9. It is obvious that some of the above remarks apply only in the case of relations which are *I-Thou* relations from the standpoint of both partners, such as inter-human relations.

10. This is why Buber can call *I-Thou* knowledge "higher than reason" (*ueber-vernuenftig*) rather than irrational, *I and Thou*, p. 49. The implications of Buber's term are too many to be considered here.

11. *I and Thou*, p. 81, my italics. Cf. also *Eclipse of God*, pp. 3, 123.

12. *Eclipse of God*, p. 13.

13. Cf. *supra*, note 8.

14. *I and Thou*, pp. 80ff.

15. *Ibid.*, p. 84. Cf. also *Israel and the World* (New York, 1948), p. 22: "He who imagines that He knows and holds the mystery fast can no longer face it as his *Thou*."

16. *I and Thou*, p. 11.

17. *Eclipse of God*, p. 135; *Between Man and Man*, p. 18.

18. *Moses* (Oxford and London, 1946), p. 188, and a letter to Franz Rosenzweig published in: Franz Rosenzweig, *On Jewish Learning* (New York, 1955), pp. 111ff.

19. *Israel and the World*, p. 209. Perhaps Buber's most explicit statement on the Torah is found in *Two Types of Faith* (London, 1951), p. 93.

20. *Between Man and Man*, p. 15.

21. *Exodus 3:14*. Cf. Buber's commentaries, *Israel and the World*, p. 23, *Moses*, pp. 52ff., *The Prophetic Faith* (New York, 1949), pp. 28ff.

22. *Between Man and Man*, p. 15.

23. *I and Thou*, pp. 75, 112.

24. *Ibid.*, p. 80.

25. *Ibid.*, p. 75.

26. This point is most clearly brought out in Buber's comments on Biblical miracles, cf., e.g., *Moses*, p. 77: "The real miracle means that in the astonishing experience of the event the current system of cause and effect becomes, as it were, transparent and permits a glimpse of the sphere in which

the sole power, not restricted by any other, is at work." Cf. also *The Prophetic Faith*, p. 46, and *Israel and Palestine* (London, 1952), p. 26: "wherever the action of nature as well as spirit is perceived as a gift, revelation takes place."

27. *I and Thou*, p. 81.

28. *Between Man and Man*, p. 56, my italics.

29. *The Prophetic Faith*, pp. 164ff., my italics.

30. Cf. *I and Thou*, esp. p. 119.

31. Cf. *Two Types of Faith*, p. 168 and many other passages. But it would appear that Buber has not wholly decided his stand on this last, and in an age of manifest "eclipse of God" most troubling, question, cf., e.g., *At the Turning* (New York: 1952), pp. 61ff.

32. *I and Thou*, p. 95.

33. *Ibid.*, p. 96.

34. *Between Man and Man*, p. 12.

35. *Eclipse of God*, p. 135.

36. *Between Man and Man*, p. 68.

37. *The Prophetic Faith*, p. 164.

38. *Eclipse of God*, p. 135.

39. *I and Thou*, p. 117.

40. *Between Man and Man*, p. 69.

41. Our reasons for omitting this aspect of Buber's thought—which includes his interpretation of Judaism—are first, as indicated, that this transcends the mere abstract *concept* of revelation; secondly, the fact that it is treated by other contributors to the present volume. We by no means suggest that the aspects of Buber's thought here treated are more important than those omitted.

42. *Israel and the World*, p. 98. Cf. also Buber's incisive criticism of the thought of C. G. Jung, *Eclipse of God*, pp. 78–92, 133–137.

43. "Religion and Philosophy," *Eclipse of God*, pp. 27–46.

44. "*I-It* finds its highest concentration and illumination in philosophical knowledge," *Eclipse of God*, p. 45. Consequently, Buber argues in this essay, philosophy deals in abstractions in which existential reality is lost. Its objects are mere "constructions" and "objectifications." Presumably philosophy is unaware of these limitations. For it either fails to discover God among its objects or else mistakes Him for a mere object. Could it look for Him among objects, or mistake Him for an object, if it *knew* that objects are only "constructions" or "objectifications"? Cf. *infra*, pp. 98ff.

45. Cf. *supra*, pp. 90ff.

46. Cf. *supra*, note 44.

47. *Eclipse of God*, p. 50.

48. The philosopher most instructive on this fundamental problem is Schelling who, in his *Philosophie der Mythologie und Offenbarung, Werke* 11–14 (Stuttgart und Augsburg, 1856–61), distinguishes between a "positive" philosophy which is based on a commitment, and a "negative" philosophy which is a dialectical argument for this commitment. Cf. E. L. Fackenheim, "Schelling's Conception of Positive Philosophy," *The Review of Metaphysics*, 7, no. 4 (1954) 563–582.

49. We confine ourselves to a single but crucially important example. Buber asserts that revelation is "the inexpressible confirmation of meaning. Meaning is assured. Nothing can any longer be meaningless. The question about the meaning of life is no longer there. But were it there, it would not have to be answered," *I and Thou*, p. 110. Buber clearly teaches that the question about the meaning of life *is* there prior to the meeting with the divine *Thou*. He also clearly teaches that it cannot be answered—or rather removed—by anything but the meeting with the divine *Thou*. For, every other *I-Thou* relation being incomplete (*I and Thou*, p. 99), man's "sense of *Thou* cannot be satiated till he finds the endless *Thou*," (*I and Thou*, p. 80). All this implies that, prior to the commitment to the dialogue with God, it is possible to point to the commitment to this dialogue, indicating at least something of what it would mean should such a dialogue take place. It follows that the concepts of religion, revelation, and the divine *Thou* are at least not *wholly* derived from the actuality of the divine-human dialogue.

9 *On the Eclipse of God*

In one of his writings, Martin Heidegger quotes with approval, as applying to the present, these words of the early 19th-century German poet Hölderlin: "Alas, our generation walks in night, dwells as in Hades, without the Divine." When Hölderlin wrote these words, there cannot have been many people who agreed with him, for it was an age which thought of itself as about to reach the very summit of religious enlightenment. In our own age, by contrast—an age which is acquainted with catastrophe and stands in fear of even greater catastrophes to come—hardly anyone can think of himself as walking in anything but night. And while it is not immediately clear whether this means that we must dwell "without the Divine"—indeed, that is the question to which these reflections are addressed—it is at any rate perfectly clear that we are undergoing an unprecedented crisis of religious faith.

According to a widespread view, it is the very catastrophes of the 20th century which have brought the crisis about. The ancient belief that the Divine is with us—that God lives and cares—cannot, it is said, be sustained in the face of these catastrophes, for to sustain it requires smugness and blindness to tragedy. Yet the fact is that this view reflects a complete lack of understanding of the nature of religious faith in general and Biblical faith in particular. Biblical faith—and I mean both Jewish and Christian—is never destroyed by tragedy but only tested by it; and in the test it both clarifies its own meaning and conquers tragedy. Here, precisely, lies the secret of its strength.

Consider a few representative examples. The prophet Jeremiah lives to see the destruction of the Temple, of Jerusalem, of the whole national existence of Judah. He does not deny the tragedy or seek to explain it away. But neither does it occur to him that God's existence has now been refuted, or that He can no longer be con-

Reprinted from *Quest for Past and Future* (Bloomington: Indiana University Press, 1968), 229–43.

ceived as just, or as loving His people, Israel. To Jeremiah the destruction of the Temple *is* a manifestation of divine justice. And it does not mark the end of divine love: "There is hope for the future."

The case of Job is still more extreme because Job is struck by tragedies which are explicitly said to be beyond the bounds of any conceivable divine justice. Yet Job never denies the existence of God; nor does he follow his wife's suggestion that he curse God and die. His faith is reduced to utter unintelligibility, yet he persists in it.

Let me give a final example which, at least in one respect, is still more extreme—the example of the Psalmist. Even in the midst of unintelligible tragedy, Job never wholly loses his sense of the presence of God. The Psalmist *in extremis*, however, does, when He complains that God has "hidden His face." God is not—at least not now—present. Unlike Job, the Psalmist does not ask that God's ways be made intelligible to him. He does not ask that the valley of the shadows or the netherworld be made to vanish; he asks only that God be present while he walks through them, as God was present to him before. Yet even in this most extreme of all crisis situations—God having "hidden His face"—the Psalmist never loses his faith. He never says that God does not, after all, exist; nor that, though existing, He has finally ceased to care. (In practice the two assertions would amount to the same thing.) What he does say is that, unaccountably, God has hidden His face; that He has hidden it for only a while; and that He will turn His face back to man again.

Put radically, this means that there is no experience, either without or within, that can possibly destroy religious faith. Good fortune without reveals the hand of God; bad fortune, if it is not a matter of just punishment, teaches that God's ways are unintelligible, not that there *are* no ways of God. A full heart within indicates the Divine Presence; an empty heart bespeaks not the non-existence or unconcern of God, but merely His temporary absence. *Religious faith can be, and is, empirically verifiable; but nothing empirical can possibly refute it.*[1]

Philosophers of science rightly assert that such an attitude toward the empirical is in principle illegitimate in the sciences. It is, however, hardly surprising that it should be of the essence of religious faith. Science is forever hypothetical. But what could one make of a religious faith which was forever hypothetical, wavering between belief in good times and unbelief in bad? Since, as we have seen, the characteristic of genuine faith is not only to survive in tragic times but to survive in them most triumphant, it is no accident that adherents of Biblical faith should always have regarded times of external or internal darkness not as evidence against God, but rather—to use Martin Buber's expression—as evidence of an "eclipse of God." To follow Buber's metaphor, an eclipse of the sun is something that occurs, not to or in the sun, but between the sun and the eye; moreover, this occurrence is temporary. Hence the catastrophes of our time, however great, cannot by themselves account for the contemporary crisis of religious belief; or rather, they can be regarded as having produced this crisis only on the assumption that religious belief was already undermined. What, then, undermined it?

Most people would say: modern science. The story begins with Copernicus, who shows that the earth is but one of many stars; it is carried forward by Darwin, who shows that man is but a higher animal; and it culminates with Freud, who shows that the one indubitably distinctive human characteristic—rationality—is neither very significant nor even very distinctive. Once at the center of the universe, man has been moved to the periphery. Once the crown of creation, man has become a fleck of dust.

Another and related aspect is perhaps still more important. The pre-modern universe was shot through with value: there was a hierarchy of purposes into which man with his human purposes could fit and feel at home. By contrast, the universe of modern science is a universe of fact without purpose; and because man cannot live without purpose, there arises a dichotomy between "fact" and "value." Values are now human *only:* man finds that he and his values have no counterpart in the world of sheer fact around him—he is radically alone. When Aristotle gazed at the stars, he could regard them as manifesting purposes somehow akin to human purposes. When the Stranger of Albert Camus's novel gazes at the stars, he must regard them as neutral. Thus it seems that man is not only a marginal being within the universe of modern science, but also that his purposes and values, inextricably bound up with any conceivable religion, lack the kind of "objective" warrant which could be given them by some Archimedean point outside himself. How, then, can he still look upon himself as being under the special care of a cosmic God?

But this whole argument, however plausible on the surface, is utterly invalid. Since Biblical belief is empirically irrefutable, scientific evidence can no more affect it than the evidence of historical tragedy or the evidence of an empty heart. The Biblical God, to be sure, has always revealed Himself. But He has always concealed Himself as well. At most, therefore, modern science should have had no greater effect on Biblical belief than to show that its God was even more inscrutable than had hitherto been thought, and His revelations even more ambiguous and intermittent.

Perhaps, however, it would be rash to dismiss the threat of modern science to Biblical faith on such general grounds alone. Conceivably there is a special affinity between that faith and the *Weltanschauung* of the pre-modern world, and conceivably the very different *Weltanschauung* that goes with modern science is radically in conflict with Biblical faith. Science may be unable to refute faith, yet it may be that one cannot really live by both.

But is it true that pre-modern science and Biblical faith are temperamentally compatible, while modern science and Biblical faith are mutually hostile? A. N. Whitehead argues, and argues plausibly, that the opposite is the case. According to Whitehead, pre-modern and modern science differ not only in their conclusions about nature but also in their approach to nature. Pre-modern science did not experiment with—"torture"—nature: who would wish to torture something divine, or shot through with divinity? It was because they regarded nature as divine that the Greeks thought only of contemplating it and not of putting it to human use. Thus, though they developed so much else, they never systematically developed experimentation. To the Protestant mind, schooled in the Bible, nature is not divine, but the *work* of God; and God created it for human use. It was this belief—still according to Whitehead—that made modern experimental science possible. Hence one might well conclude that in some ways modern science is closer in spirit to Biblical faith than its pre-modern predecessor. Is there not rivalry between a science which finds gods in nature and a faith whose God is beyond nature? And is not a science for which nature is at any rate un-divine free from conflict with a faith which, however different in all other aspects, agrees at least on this one point?

Nevertheless, it might still remain true that this un-divine nature of modern science threatens, if it does not rule out, any religious recourse to a Divinity beyond nature. If man is a mere fleck of dust in a blind universe, can he plausibly resort to such a God—a God, furthermore, essentially concerned with *him?* But closer inspection reveals that this is, and has been since the rise of modern science, only half the story. As the *object* of scientific investigation, man may be infinitely small. As the *subject* undertaking the investigation, however, he is infinitely large, if only because he knows that he is infinitely small. Man, growing ever smaller in stature as modern science progressed, at the same time grew ever larger as well; for whereas all else in the universe was only part of a whole, it was man who *knew* the whole and his own position within it. And so far as we can tell even today, man is unique in this respect. What makes him unique, moreover, is not a mere capacity for abstract theory which is relevant to a few thinkers alone; it is the power this capacity gives him to transform nature, as well as to transform the whole human condition. Because of technology man can be more fully controlled than ever before; he becomes the object of physical and social engineering. But the engineer is himself human.

I hope it is clear that my purpose is not to exalt human greatness in an attempt—like those of earlier times—to struggle by means of faith in man toward faith in God. Rather what I want to stress is man's dialectical condition: that he is at once small and large, part of the universe and yet not reducible to a mere part—in short, and for better or worse, a terror, wonder, and mystery to himself. Now in this regard, modern man is not really so far from the Psalmist who writes: "What is man that Thou art mindful of him, and the son of man that Thou shouldst think of him? Yet has Thou made him but little lower than the angels, and crowned him with honor and glory." It is, to be sure, a decisive difference that the Psalmist feels at once small and large *before God.* His feeling and ours, however, have much in common.

If, then, the historical catastrophes of our time cannot explain the crisis of contemporary religious belief, neither can modern science and all its works. Indeed, one might go so far as to say that the whole battle between science and religion rests on nothing but gigantic misunderstandings on both sides. It was because faith had *already* been undermined by the time this battle was joined in the 19th century, that religion had to resort either to a fundamentalism hostile to all science, or else to a modernism seeking props for its own weakness in a science which would not and could not provide them.

Our question concerning the cause of the modern crisis of faith thus remains unanswered. In seeking the answer, we do well to keep a firm grasp on the essence of Biblical faith, which is the *believer's certainty of standing in relation to an unprovable and irrefutable God.* What could have undermined such a certainty? The process was extremely complex, but let us for the sake of better understanding try to describe it as though it took place in three clearly distinct stages.

First came what may be called the discovery of the circle of authority and faith. A pre-modern man, asked about the grounds of his religious certainty, would presumably have pointed to an authority—a prophet, a sacred scripture, a church, even the voice of his own heart. This, however, involves a circle. If Moses beheld the Presence of God in the burning bush, it was because he was already open to that Presence; a modern agnostic, beholding the same bush, would perceive only a chemical phenomenon. No conceivable datum—neither a natural fact, nor an inner experience, nor an existing scripture—can serve as an authority authenticating a religious truth except for those already prepared to accept that truth on faith. Faith may base itself on authority; but the authority *is* an authority only where faith can be presupposed.

The discovery of this circle is not by itself fatal to faith, as can be seen from the fact that pre-modern thinkers were by no means wholly unaware of it. (Saint Thomas Aquinas knew, for example, that he could not argue with a nonbeliever on the basis of the revealed Scriptures, since the issue between them was precisely whether the Scriptures *were* revealed.) Nevertheless, the discovery, by focusing attention on faith instead of on authority, leads the modern critic to a second and more decisive step. To the believer, faith is the *immediate relation* between himself and God. To the critic, faith is merely the *feeling* of standing in such a relation, plus an *inference* from that feeling to an actual God.

The step just described may seem a matter of mere philosophical subtlety; yet everything centers around it. For once this second step is taken, the third—and it is the *coup de grâce*—quickly follows: the elimination, with the help of Ockham's razor, of the inferred God. Ockham asserted the rational necessity of eliminating unnecessary assumptions, as one shaves off an unwanted beard. And it is all too clear that God, as an assumption made to account for the feeling of His Presence, is indeed both unwanted and unnecessary.

In the first place, a God inferred to explain religious feelings would at most be a probable inference, capable of refutation and never really certain. And in the second place, anyone in agreement with Kant (and with a good many other philosophers as well) would regard such an inference—moving from a natural effect to a supernatural cause—as in principle illegitimate.

Thus modern criticism, operating through three stages, explains faith as an inference from religious feeling, and eliminates the inference as a redundancy. To complete the destruction of faith, it remains only to explain how the inference should ever have been mistaken for an immediate relationship. *That* is achieved by defining God as in fact an unconscious projection, and faith as in fact a solitary disport with religious feelings (however these, in turn, are to be explained).

The reason we can consider this whole process—which may be termed subjectivist reductionism—as *the* cause of the modern religious crisis, is that it is not a mere intellectual argument carried on by abstract thinkers. Subjectivist reductionism has become a modern—perhaps *the* modern—way of life. Which came first—the argument or the way of life—we need not here inquire.

Much that passes for an independent assault on religion is actually a version, or an application, of the three-stage argument just presented. Consider, first, Biblical criticism, which, it is sometimes supposed, constitutes a refutation of the claim that the Scriptures are the revealed word of God. But in fact Biblical criticism either presupposes what it imagines itself to be proving, or else it leaves the issue open. For if the critic declares that what the Bible itself regards as the reflection of human dialogues with God is nothing more than an expression of the evolution of religious feelings and ideas, it is he who has brought such categories to the Bible, not the Bible which has yielded them to him. His criticism, in other words, already assumes a position of subjectivist reductionism.

Consider, next, humanism. Feuerbach, possibly the greatest of modern humanists, speaks for all: "What man is not, but wills to be or wishes to be, just that and only that, nothing else, is God." But to the religious believer, God is not what *he* wills to be; He is the other-than-human with Whom the believer stands in relation. How, then, does the humanist refute the believer? Only by a form of subjectivist reductionism. And what is true of Feuerbach is true of Marx and Freud as well. To unmask *some* gods as pseudo-gods, they can rely on specific empirical evidence in specific spheres. But to unmask all gods as pseudo-gods is in the end to rest one's case not on specific empirical evidence but on an *a priori* philosophical argument; and the argument is a form of subjectivist reductionism.

So pervasive is subjectivist reductionism in the modern world that it has enlisted friends of religion as well as foes in its ranks—although it must be said that this friendship is of the most dubious kind. Its nature may be illustrated by two examples, the one widespread and popular, the other more or less confined to academics. Pragmatism—and a good deal of popular psychology as well—is apt to assert that while religious beliefs are mere wish-or need-projections, they are useful, or even necessary, for comfortable survival in an uncomfortable world. The question thus arises as to how they can be preserved, and the answer would appear to be: by keeping their illusory character concealed. For who can live by a belief which he knows to be illusory? Yet such concealment is not only practically impossible in the modern world; the particular friends of religion presently under consideration do not even seem to desire it. Hence in many circles religion has become a collective make-believe: something which is good for most, accepted as true by others, rejected as false by oneself. Religion of this sort is not a bulwark against religious crisis; it is one of its gravest manifestations.

Much the same can be said of the other, more academic form of friendship for religion displayed by some of the linguistic philosophers who have now taken over from the logical positivists. Logical positivism was a clear foe of religious faith. It declared religious language to be emotive only, referring to no objective reality. Thus "God" really meant "three cheers for the world"; and a revivalist preacher, urging his congregation to give three cheers for God, was really saying "Let's give three cheers for three cheers for the world." Here was subjectivist reductionism accompanied by forthright hostility. The heirs of logical positivism, the linguistic philosophers, on the whole feel no such hostility. Science tells us about the world, they say, while religion reflects attitudes toward the world—and why should we not have attitudes? Indeed, how can we live without them? But if religion is acknowledged to be an attitude *only*, and the God toward whom religion is an attitude is excluded, then subjectivist reductionism has won the day. Defending the attitude *as* attitude does not protect religious faith: it helps bring about its doom.

Has subjectivist reductionism, then, won the day? It has not. For the Biblical faith has been restated in our time, both by Jews and Christians, with a purity perhaps unmatched in centuries; and this restatement has fully risen to the challenge posed by subjectivist reductionism.

Here are two quotations, one taken from Bertrand Russell's *My Philosophical Development*, the other from Buber's *Eclipse of God*. Russell writes:

> If A loves B the relation . . . consists in certain states of mind of A. Even an atheist must admit that a man can love God. It follows that love of God is a state of the man who feels it, and not properly a relational fact.

Contrast this with Buber:

> Great images of God fashioned by mankind are born, not of imagination, but of real encounters with Divine power and glory.

Russell here admirably states the subjectivist-reductionist view. Although he expressly speaks only of the love of God, what he says would apply equally well to faith. Just as an atheist can "admit that a man can love God," he can admit faith in another man. Faith would be a subjective state and God would become an inference made by the believer which the atheist would declare invalid.

Buber's statement, once contrasted with Russell's, is seen in its full significance and polemical power. Man does not have private feelings from which he infers the Divine. *If related to God at all, he is primordially open to Him; and his subjective feelings and the images of God he fashions are mere by-products of this primordial openness.* No doubt man can be imprisoned by images and feelings, and no doubt he can seek to escape from the prison of these images and feelings by inferring from them to a God beyond them. But such imprisonment is pseudo-religion, and the attempt to escape from it is futile. Or rather, the true escape is not to infer God from images and feelings, but to turn away from these to God Himself.

On Buber's thesis, an atheist can certainly "admit that a man can love God." But it is questionable whether an atheist can do something far more important—understand what the love of God *means*. For how can he distinguish between the pseudo-love which, being feeling *only*, is a disguised love of self, and the real love which obtains between God and man? And what holds of the distinction between love and pseudo-love also holds of the distinction between "great" images of God and trivial or superficial ones. Perhaps the atheist does not wholly lack the power to make these distinctions; but then, not everyone protesting atheism is a simple and unequivocal atheist.

Here we have, then, two assertions. How are we to judge between them? I will approach this decisive question through a perennial problem, though it can carry us only to the threshold of an answer. Philosophers often ask how one can know other minds. I can immediately know my own feelings; and I can immediately observe other people's behavior. But how can I know the feelings of others? Well, I can infer them from their behavior. But this inference would seem to presuppose that their behavior is like mine—that, for example, they behave when they feel pain as I do when I feel pain. This assumption may be perfectly plausible. But it *is* an assumption. Hence I can never know, and certainly never know *immediately*, that I am not radically alone.

I am persuaded that, while this line of reasoning has some value in bringing to light certain specific philosophical issues, it is altogether misguided. A self is primordially open to other selves; and unless it were thus open it would never become a self at all. A child *becomes* an "I" in a relation of openness to a "Thou"; indeed, he knows the meaning of "Thou" before he knows the meaning of "I." There is, to be sure, a problem involved in knowing other selves. But the problem is not whether they exist; it is who they are. And it arises, not because the self is to begin with in a subjectivist prison from which it must subsequently try to escape; it arises because, born free of prisons of this kind, the self is subsequently cast into them by the breakdown of communication. And when the breakdown is complete there is mental disease.

This much, at least, would seem arguable or even demonstrable: genuine love between humans does not consist of subjectivist solitudes externally related; it is *one* relation, although always impaired in its unity, often threatened by temporary eclipse and sometimes by total destruction. A demonstration of this proposition, however, would—as has already been said—take us only to the threshold of the question we have been struggling with. For it might well be the case that, whereas genuine love between humans consists of an immediate relation, the love of God consists of feeling *only*. Indeed, this is bound to be true if the faith which knows this God is itself nothing more than subjective feeling. What, in the light of the foregoing, are we to make of this possibility?

The first thing to say is that if it is true, there can be no genuine love of God at all, since there can be no openness to the other which even love between humans requires. The second thing is that pseudo-love of God is the legitimate object of destructive criticism, and that from a perspective like Buber's, one cheerfully supports the criticism. And the third and most important thing to say is that genuine love of God—if there be such love—escapes the grasp of the subjectivist critic. For genuine love of God, which is openness to the Divine, can be known only in actual openness, and this is precisely what the critic cannot or will not have. Hence he is left only with the images and feelings which are its by-product. How then can he judge them *as* by-products? How, indeed, can he safely distinguish between the pseudo-faith and pseudo-love which are merely feelings projected onto a pseudo-god, and the genuine faith and love which constitute a relation to God? It would seem, therefore, that the critic's reduction even of pseudo-faith must always remain ambiguous, and can never be final.

This does not prevent him, however, from *deciding* that religious images and feelings are *never* "born of real encounters," that they are *always* mere "imagination." Only in making this decision, he does not give a *demonstration*. Buber's response to the challenge of subjectivist reductionism has disclosed that it does not refute Biblical faith, but rather that it opposes one faith to another. Biblical faith stakes all on man's primordial openness to the Divine—an openness, to be sure, which is interrupted by eclipses of God. The reductionist "faith" stakes all on the thesis that man is primordially shut off from God, and that all supposed openness is mere self-delusion. But in the perspective of Buber's modern reaffirmation of the Biblical faith, reductionism itself appears as a self-delusion: it mistakes withdrawal from God for the natural and inevitable human condition.

In such manner does faith refute the refutation proposed by subjectivist reductionism. But this is not to say that faith can prove its own case against subjectivist reductionism. It cannot refute but only reject it; and it can testify against it. For the argument cuts both ways. The reductionist cannot use observable data—religious images and feelings—to demonstrate the subjectivity of faith. But neither can the believer use these same data to demonstrate the objectivity of faith. For not only is it the case that the reductionist critic cannot or will not enter into the actual relation of openness to God; it is also the case that for the believer himself the "knowledge" obtained is shot through with the gravest of risks. After all, does not disguised self-love, being disguised, mistake itself for love of God? Are not god-projections, being unconscious, mistaken for real gods by those who are prey to them?

Some part of this risk has always been understood by believers in the Biblical tradition, who realized that false prophets, no less than true, can be sincere. The full extent of the risk, however, has become obvious only to the modern believer. His ancestor rarely doubted that man was in principle open to the Divine; hence the risk of which he was aware extended for the most part only to deciding when and how such openness was truly manifest. The modern believer, by contrast, has glimpsed the possibility that *all* openness to the Divine may be pseudo-openness only—that man may be radically alone. He does not stand in immediate openness to the Divine. He seeks, in Kierkegaard's expression, an immediacy after reflection. The Psalmist *in extremis* experienced an eclipse of God. The extremity of faith in the modern age is uncertainty as to whether what is experienced *is* an eclipse of God, or the final exposure of an illusion.

Hence if the modern believer works and waits for an end to this eclipse, he must carry in his working and waiting a uniquely modern burden. The Psalmist *in extremis* could rest in the irrefutability of faith. The modern believer *in extremis* must endure the full impact of its being undemonstrable as well; he must suffer the knowledge that to the world around him the concealed God is a non-existent God, and that he himself can do no more than testify to the contrary.

Under these circumstances, it is natural that there should be those who wish to be told whether the present crisis of religious faith will lead to a renewal. But anyone who asks for a prediction does not understand what has been said. Pronouncements upon the future that is at stake here could not take the form of scientific or historical prediction, but only of indulgence in prophecy. And a rabbinic sage wisely observed that when Biblical times came to an end, prophecy was taken away from prophets and given over to fools and children.

Notes

1. Lest this controversial assertion be misunderstood, I should stress that it holds for the believer only. For the unbeliever or detached critic, what is verified, or immediately verified, is good fortune or "religious experience"—and nothing else.

3

The Holocaust and the 614th Commandment

Introduction

The jarring juxtaposition of the optimism and resiliance of faith with a horrifying reminiscence of Sachsenhausen is not accidental; nor is the circular movement that has this volume begin with a youthful piece, written but never published in 1938, only now to return, *via* memory, to events just subsequent to the writing of that early article that in part precluded its publicaton. "On the Eclipse of God" marks a crucial stage in Fackenheim's thought—as he often mentions[1]—for it expresses his belief that faith is impenetrable to historical falsification. Doubtless this belief was never an easy one to hold in this unqualified form, but hold it Fackenheim did—until events, among them the Six Day War, mandated a new attentiveness to memory. In 1967 Fackenheim had come to realize that one could advance into the future only by honestly exposing oneself, one's thought, and indeed all thought, to the past and its unspeakable, unimaginable horrors.[2]

In Fackenheim's own words, "philosophical and religious thought widely take themselves to be immune and indeed indifferent to the 'accidents' of 'mere' history. The conscious repudiation of this view, first in abstracto and subsequently in relation to the events of our age, is the major change in my thinking. . . . Thought, or at any rate Jewish thought, shows its strength precisely by making itself vulnerable."[3] Later Fackenheim will say that this admission is "the greatest doctrinal change" in his career and that its outcome is "the central question of all Jewish and indeed all 'post-Holocaust' thought."[4] It is the admission, *contra* Rosenzweig, that something radically new, albeit even something radically evil, can occur "in Jewish religious history between Sinai and the Messianic days,"[5] with the result that much, if not all, has thereby changed.

By 1967, then, Fackenheim had begun to ask what Judaism and life itself could be like once thought is made to confront openly and seriously the horrors of Auschwitz. It is a question that has without respite burdened his thinking ever since, and for that reason the sections of this chapter form the central core of our presentation of his work. The first section includes selections in which Fackenheim describes the Holocaust—its victims, its criminals, its special features—all in an attempt to recognize the event for what it was, an expression of radical, unprecedented evil. This effort—to describe and think through the horrors of Auschwitz in order to lay bare its "unprecedented" evil—is one to which Fackenheim has returned frequently throughout the years since 1967.[6]

113

Neither the depth nor the frequency of his analyses have prevented this task from being misunderstood. He is thought to have exaggerated or overemphasized the Holocaust, to have neglected equally horrible catastrophes, such as Hiroshima, Vietnam, Biafra, and Cambodia, to have dwelled on the particularity of this horror when the appropriate categories—genocide or the demonic—show the Holocaust to be nothing unique at all, its atrocities notwithstanding. We are not going to show how or why such criticisms are generally misguided and uncharitable; one sees this best when one reads Fackenheim himself. Our selections are intended to offer this opportunity by showing how his encounter with the event has deepened over the years and how open and sensitive is his cumulative response to the cruelties, the cunning, the agony of those years. To be sure, one may reject parts of his understanding of what in fact the Holocaust was—an intentional attempt to exterminate Judaism and Jews, whose very existence was considered a crime; neither a pragmatic project nor the "negative side of a positive religious or political fanaticism"; but rather "an end in itself," implemented not by "sadists or perverts" but by "ordinary jobholders" directed by "idealists" whose "ideals were torture and death."[7] But reject what one will, if the reader studies Fackenheim thoroughly, faithfully, and without an antecedent incredulity, he or she can hardly fail to share his "unknowing horror" at an event that surely had no recognizable precedent in human history.

All of the pieces in the first section were written after the three selections in the second, but this alteration of chronology in fact highlights the systematic nature of Fackenheim's thinking. First is the event, as it presents itself to the thinker who is also a survivor; then the response to it, the exposure of thought that first paralyzes and then revives thinking, only finally to come to rest in a fragmentary understanding of what shape post-Holocaust Jewish life should take.

The very precise line of reasoning that is first expressed in Fackenheim's contribution to the Symposium, "Jewish Values in a Post-Holocaust Future," has not been well-understood.[8] Developed in "Jewish Faith and the Holocaust" and again in Chapter 3 of God's Presence in History, this line of thinking is, however, the framework for virtually all Fackenheim's subsequent work. To fail to grasp it is to fail to understand Fackenheim. Surely all depends on how honestly the horror can be faced, but it also depends on what thought does as a result, when the depth and "uniqueness" of the evil is seen to stop thought in its tracks.

Let us follow Fackenheim's thinking, if only in a schematic way.[9] Auschwitz, "the scandal of evil for evil's sake,"[10] resists both rational and religious explanations. Up to a point we can explain why the event occurred—psychologically, economically, and politically—but only up to a point, and then the explanations fail, as does the attempt to understand the cruelty and destruction religiously, as a punishment for sin, a test, or an unrecognized and yet-to-be-redeemed "good." "No purpose, religious or non-religious, will ever be found in Auschwitz. The very attempt to find one is blasphemous."[11] If thought is paralyzed, however, life is not. ". . . seeking a purpose is one thing, but seeking a response quite another. The first is wholly out of the question. The second is inescapable." Although thought can find no way to place Auschwitz meaningfully within some general pattern, to comprehend it, nonetheless the event can carry some meaning, not purpose, to be sure, but meaning. It can be an object of our response, a reality to be addressed, opposed, a memorial to the most radical evil and the most noble humanity. But Fackenheim, who in his *Judaism* piece had formulated his imperative of opposition—the 614th Commandment—without adequate preparation, here moves more cautiously. He begins the thinking that will result in that imperative and its articulation with an insight that is both determinative and yet, in a sense, provisional.

> I confess that it took me twenty years until I was able to look at this scandal [i.e., the particularity of Auschwitz], but when at length I did, I made what to me was, and still is, a momentous discovery: that while religious thinkers were vainly struggling for a response to Auschwitz, Jews throughout the world—rich and poor, learned and ignorant, religious and nonreligious—had to some degree been responding all along. . . . In ordinary times [such] a commitment [to Jewish group survival] may be a mere mixture of nostalgia and vague loyalties not far removed from tribalism. . . . [But] in the age of Auschwitz a Jewish commitment to Jewish survival is in itself a monumental act of faithfulness, as well as a monumental, albeit as yet fragmentary, act of faith.[12]

Into these highly charged words is packed a very precise movement of thought. Systematic, explanatory thought, paralyzed by the event, seeks mediation, a way to respond. It finds that mediation in the ongoing Jewish commitment of those who continue to live Jewish lives. For their actions—doubtless performed with little if any conscious attention to the catastrophe so recently past—can be *understood by the thinker* as responsive, as acts of indignant opposition. And what, the thinker asks, is the ground of such uncompromising, unconditional opposition but an absolute, unconditional imperative, for the response is such that neither whim nor "nostalgia" nor some sense of "vague loyalty" can account for its weight and givenness.

Furthermore, in Judaism the only such imperatives are Divine Commands, human interpretations of the Divine Presence and its meaning for Jewish life. Hence, with uncertainty and a sense of despair, the Jewish thinker *concludes* that what makes the responsiveness of contemporary Jews intelligible is a Divine Commanding Presence, whose command is interpreted as an imperative to oppose Nazi purposes in every way, a 614th Commandment that supplements the existing corpus of tradition by giving it a new orientation, a new framework.[13] To be sure, there are both religious and secular "hearers" of this commandment. The agnostic authentic Jew may hear *only the commandment*; he may know at least that some gods are false and who the devil is.[14] The religious authentic Jew "can hardly hear more," although Fackenheim says that he does hear "the voice of the *metzaveh* [the commander] in the *mitzvah* [the commandment]."[15] And if the initial broad understanding of this commandment is not to give Hitler posthumous victories, the further elaboration includes a host of fragmentary imperatives, including the maintenance of the Jewish people, its faith, and the affirmation of human solidarity and dignity.[16]

In the next chapter and its several sections we offer selections that exhibit, among other things, the diverse ways that the 614th Commandment is further ramified by Fackenheim in a systematic, extensive, and rich way. Before we turn to these pieces, however, we must perform one more pressing task. Fackenheim, in his final *magnum opus*, *To Mend the World*, both explores and deepens the line of thinking we have been discussing. Glancing ahead at this work reveals how self-critical is Fackenheim's approach and how provisional is the work of the period 1967–68.

As presented in these early pieces, the line of thinking is fraught with gaps and presumptions and with deficiencies of caution and restraint. First, the radical character of the Holocaust, its "uniqueness" or "particularity," required more elaboration than it received in these works, and we have collected in Section 1 some but not all of his subsequent writings in which that elaboration is pursued. Of special importance is clarification of what it means to call the event "unique" and why the more historical word "unprecedented" is better suited to the task. Secondly, the demonstration of the "impotence of thought"—psychological, historical, religious—as it is exposed to Auschwitz needs enrichment. Thirdly, the introduction of God, although not wholly incautious, is still too facile; even the most committed Jew, after the mechanical incineration of innocent children, may be unable to hear the Voice—to acknowledge a Divine Presence that sponsors his opposition but did not save. But finally—and here most importantly—the movement from the paralysis of thought to a description and comprehension of the conduct of contemporary Jews as responsive and from there to the formulation of an imperative of opposition—all this seems groundless, arbitrary, without a justification commensurate with the ultimacy of the event itself. The moral necessity that impels subsequent life and thought needs a ground *in* the event, and that ground must itself be ultimate, with a defense that secures its ultimacy in every way.

To Mend the World may be one of the four or five most important works of Jewish thought in this century; it is certainly one of the most difficult. But although it is far from a perspicuous work or easy to read, one dimension of its achievement can be readily discerned. In a precise way Fackenheim attempts to define, defend, and ground both the undeniable "world of horror" that was the Holocaust Kingdom and the 614th Commandment that orients future life and thought in opposition to it. Thereby he engages the problems just itemized and sets out to complete the fragmentary character of his earlier line of thinking in order to provide genuine "foundations for future Jewish thought."[17]

There is no substitute after all for reading *To Mend the World* and following Fackenheim's thought as it moves from Spinoza and Rosenzweig to Hegel and the Hegelians and finally to Heidegger, each time grappling with a thinker in his own terms only to exhibit in the end his shortcomings when his thought is exposed to Auschwitz. We include selections that give some impression of two moments in this process—when thought comes to recognize the increasing depths of horror that characterize the Holocaust and when Jewish thought provides and then employs a category—*tikkum olam* [mending the world]—for articulating the shape that post-Holocaust resistance should take. But important as these are as moments in Fackenheim's thinking, they do not capture its drama and continuity; only a close reading of chapter IV of the book, especially sections 7–10, can do that.

We should state the basic line of Fackenheim's argument in *To Mend the World*, if only to place our selections within it. Heidegger is the most historically sensitive of modern philosophers; if anyone is capable of being honestly exposed to Auschwitz, it should be he. But both the man and his thought fail, and with that failure—and the failure of others like Martin Buber, Isaac Deutscher, and Paul Celan—thought itself reaches an impasse. Recalling Theodor Adorno's question, Fackenheim asks: has the metaphysical capacity itself been paralyzed?[18] But at this critical juncture, Fackenheim recognizes that while the event "paralyzes" thought contemporary with and subsequent to it, it does not paralyze the existence of those singled out by it. He proceeds to a description and definition of resistance during the event: "In an *Umwelt* whose sole ultimate self-expression is a system of humiliation, torture, and murder, the maintenance by the victims of a shred of humanity is not merely the basis of resistance but already part of it. In such a world . . . life does not need to be sanctified: it already is holy."[19]

This major step having been taken, Fackenheim makes another, even more momentous. Recognizing that such acts of resistance might be considered rare but explicable, not "ultimate" but rather reducible to well-known psychological and historical categories, he sets out to refute these criticisms and to defend the "ultimacy" of resistance—to establish the resistance of the victims as an "ontological category."[20] One of our selections contains a crucial stretch of that defense (*TMW*, 241–47), in which Fackenheim makes thought confront the criminals in order to arrive at its final "resisting stance." One thinks of the criminals as the victims did, trying to grasp their evil. In the end, one succeeds and fails at once; one grasps "the evil *as a whole*" not in an act of "comprehension" but with a "surprised acceptance and a horrified resistance."[21] And at that instant, when thought—confronting the evil only in the exact sense in which it was confronted by the resisting victims themselves[22]—can move no further, when, in its "horrified surprise," it is "forced to accept what is yet in all eternity unacceptable," it is compelled to "point beyond resistance within its own native sphere, to a resistance that is beyond the sphere of thought altogether, and in the sphere of life."[23] Philosophical thought, having defined and defended the category of resistance as ontological, is forced to become *deontological*—issuing in an imperative.

The interpretation of this imperative to resistance, its articulation—for Jewish life, Christianity, philosophy, and much else—requires the introduction of a new category (*tikkun olam*), drawn from the Jewish past and employed to shape, among other domains, the Jewish future. Our final selections from *To Mend the World* (Section 3) show both this recovery and its implementation.

Notes

1. For references, see note 3.

2. These adjectives allude to Hannah Arendt, *The Origins of Totalitarianism* (New York: Harcourt Brace Jovanovich, 1951), 359.

3. See *The Jewish Return into History* (*JRH*, 1978), Introduction, xi; for the first expression of this sentiment; see *Quest for Past and Future*, 17, on the openness of the Midrashic framework to history.

4. *TMW*, 13.

5. *JRH*, 44, 189.

6. In addition to our selections, see *GPH*, 69–71; the foreword to Yehuda Bauer, *The Jewish Emergence from Powerlessness* (1979), vii–ix; "Idolatry as a Modern Possibility," reprinted as chapter 4 of *EJM*; *JRH*, 89–94, 156–62, 222–23, 228–30; and *TMW*, 130–36.

7. *TMW*, 12; cf. the Preface to Bauer; Fackenheim's indebtedness to Arendt's *The Origins of Totalitarianism* is evident.

8. Even then Fackenheim was reluctant to confront the Holocaust and its implications for Jewish existence and Jewish thought. He has told me that his participation in the Symposium was the result of a moral pressure.

9. We include all three early versions of this line of thinking to enable the reader to follow and examine the development of Fackenheim's reasoning and then to assess it.

10. "Jewish Faith and the Holocaust," *JRH*, 29; cf. *QPF*, 17.

11. Ibid.

12. Ibid., 30–31; cf. *QPF*, 19.

13. Cf. *GPH*, 83.

14. Cf. *EJM*, ch. 3, 167.

15. *JRH*, 23; the reader should notice the Rosenzweigian motif, that the genuine Jew, appropriating traditional texts and conduct for himself, seeks to transform *Gesetz* [law] into *Gebot* [commandment], thereby enabling himself to draw close to the *metzaveh* [commander] through the *mitzvah* [commandment].

16. The only systematic elaboration of the 614th commandment is given in chapter 3 of *GPH*, 84–92.

17. This of course is the subtitle of *To Mend the World.*

18. *TMW*, 200.

19. Ibid., 225.

20. The term "ontological" is here being used in a quasi-Heideggerian sense. The category in question is the result of the self-reflective recognition of the reality of resistance in life performed by the resistors themselves. The case of which Fackenheim makes much use, that of Pelagia Lewinska, is cited by Terrence Des Pres in *The Survivor* (New York: Oxford University Press, 1976).

21. *TMW*, 247.

22. Ibid., 248.

23. Ibid., 247.

RADICAL EVIL AND AUSCHWITZ AS UNPRECENDENTED EVENT

10 *Sachsenhausen 1938: Groundwork for Auschwitz*

In this essay I shall argue three separate, but in this case interrelated, theses: (1) that, following the events of *Krystallnacht* in 1938, Sachsenhausen was a groundwork for the Holocaust; that is, whether the Nazis at that time already planned murder camps for Jews or made that terrible decision only later on, the 1938 concentration camp possessed certain features without which the murder camps of the war years would not have been possible;[1] (2) that a built-in feature of the system of 1938 was deception of the victims; for them to *recognize* the features I will outline was extraordinarily difficult if not totally impossible; (3) that for the reason just offered, certain hermeneutical rules normally accepted in historical research become questionable in the extreme case under discussion. It is normally assumed that, with all due allowance for bias of perception and memory, the eyewitness is the most reliable source of "what actually happened." When the eyewitness is caught in a scheme of things systematically calculated to deceive him, subsequent reflection is necessary if truth is to be given to his testimony.

The occasion of this paper was the study of a document entitled *Konzentrationslager Sachsenhausen* (1938), by Dr. K. J. Ball Kaduri, which is found in the Yad Vashem Archives. My method on this occasion is critical reflection upon what I, then a youth of twenty-two, remembered of the camp of which I myself had been an inmate, in the light of what I read about it more than thirty years later, in an account given by a man much older than myself, much more trained to observe and analyze—an account, moreover, that the author himself apparently did not compose until 1946. In order to *understand* what I myself had experienced, I had to *see* it, so to speak, *objectified on paper*, in a report written by someone more articulate than I was, or could have been, at the time. Hence I feel that my personal idiosyncrasies, while entering into the following account, play no im-

Reprinted from *The Jewish Return into History* (New York: Schocken Books, 1978), 58–67, by permission of the publisher.

119

portant role in my three theses. Everybody has *some* idiosyncrasies; and it was a built-in feature of the Nazi system to exploit them all.

I. Torture through Senseless System

As a rule those of us considered fit to work were sent every day to work in a tile factory several miles outside the camp. I begin with Ball's description of the customary march to and from that factory.

> The marching columns are formed in the camp in rows of four, and then the march begins through the gate to the *Klinkerwerke*. How refreshing such a march could be after the stay in the camp in the morning, or even after a day's hard labor at night! But what happens? The march is made into a hellish torture, through a diabolical system which produces perpetual chaos. Normally such a large column would be divided into groups, with a distance between them. Here, however, the unit is as large as 1000 men. . . . Suddenly the front is being slowed down, but no command is issued to this effect. Consequently, those behind are unaware of it and run into those in front of them. Whereupon those in front are ordered to run, to run as fast as possible, with the result that front and back fall apart again, and those behind are ordered to run even faster, until they barge into those before them once more.
>
> In this spurious march *the fiction is maintained* that each row must keep in step, that no one must fall behind. The moment disorder occurs, either when those in the back fall behind, or those in front are too far ahead, the stormtroopers hit the offenders with their rifle butts, and someone is an offender even if his heavy breathing shows that he finds it difficult to keep up. (Italics added)

The moment I read this passage I understood it. Then why, so far as I recall, had I *never once* understood the spuriousness of this "march" during the three months when, many times, I participated in it? True, I was twenty-two and athletic, while Dr. Kaduri was more than twenty years older, so that running never bothered me, and my friends were in the same position. However, none of us young ones were heartless or insensitive, and I recall many an occasion when two of us would take an older man between us and support him on his "march." Was I, then, too young and naive to understand *any part* of the "diabolical system"? Yet some of it we understood well enough. Our work at the *Klinkerwerke* was partly ordinary labor directed to a purpose. Partly, however, it was also so obviously senseless that the fact could escape no one. Thus, many a day we spent carrying sand—always on the double!—from place A to place B, only in order to be ordered the next day to carry it back from place B to place A. The senselessness of this labor was so obvious that everyone understood it. Moreover—this is the crux—understanding it, we formed inner defenses against it. With regard to the meaningful labor we too had our inner defenses. Like the British officer in *The Bridge on the River Kwai*, we were many times tempted by the meaningfulness of the labor to find meaning in it and perform it well, forgetting that it was labor for the enemy, but then we would recognize this and resort to small acts of sabotage. We never fooled ourselves into thinking that we did or could do any noticeable harm to the Nazis. Still, even small acts of sabotage maintained our morale.

In the case of the back-and-forth sandcarrying race (whose senselessness was obvious) we kept our morale through humor. We *knew* that this system had no purpose. Hence we also knew that its only purpose could be torture for torture's sake—to break us down. *And, aware of this purpose, we resisted it.* I recall an incident early in our imprisonment (when we were still quite naive) when a well-known Berlin rabbi and I lined up outside the medical barrack for treatment for a sore or infected leg (I forget which). After a while the Nazi medical officer came out, kicked us with his jackboots and shouted "Run, Jews!" As we were running, the rabbi turned to me and asked: "Are you still sick?"

In contrast with these two cases of obviously meaningful and obviously meaningless labor, the *Klinker*-march, as described by Dr. Kaduri, was *meaningless labor systematically endowed with a fictitious meaning.* This fooled me and, I am sure, almost everyone else. Moreover, it was clearly *designed* to fool us, so as to rob us of the means of inner defense. With the wisdom of hindsight—and with the truth objectified for me in Dr. Kaduri's perceptive account—I am certain that as early as 1938 the concentration camp had *one* purpose, i.e., slave labor, but also a *higher* purpose superseding slave labor and its benefits to the Nazi system, i.e., to rob its victims of their humanity if not yet of their lives. I am also certain that, as early as then, the Nazis recognized that in order to achieve the higher purpose (or at any rate in order to achieve it most effectively) it was not enough to have two labor systems of which one was obviously meaningful and the other obviously meaningless. They had to produce (and did produce) a Kafkaesque system in which there *appeared* to be meaning, *was* none, and in which this truth was either systematically *kept from* the victims, or in any case *the fiction was still maintained even when the secret was out.* Thus a clear line of development leads from the *Klinker*-march at Sachsenhausen in 1938 to the incredible and unprecedented legend on the gate to Auschwitz—*Arbeit macht frei.*

II. System of Supermen and Subhumans

I give my second quotation from Ball Kaduri's account:

> The first and most severe rule of the camp was that the slaves were absolutely forbidden to initiate a conversation with any member of the SS. Such an "address" was simply unthinkable. On the other hand, they were naturally required to answer any question addressed to them. Most of these questions were simple cases of chicanery, containing no order, and having the sole purpose of reacting to the prisoner's answers with insults or blows. Most of these questions concerned one's profession, and the only thing that mattered was a prompt answer. *Whether the answer was true or false did not matter in the slightest and was never investigated.* (Italics added)

Let me comment on the last part of this passage first. On our first day in Sachsenhausen, following a whole night of alternatively having to stand at attention and march about, there took place an "investigation" lasting several hours. An S.S. officer would stroll along, leisurely look at this or that person, and at length pick someone and ask him for his profession. And no matter what answer the person would give—"doctor," "lawyer," businessman," etc.—it was an occasion for insults and blows. "You have defiled German women!" "You have perverted German law!" "You have cheated your German customers!" and so forth.

The remarkable thing that first day was not the Nazi behavior but rather that of us Jews. As if by a silent compact we all felt that this day could be our last, and that we would not lower ourselves to the level of the Nazis by telling lies. One man was ordered to say that he had betrayed Germany, and although they beat him for a long time, he refused to say it. (I need hardly add that any form of physical resistance was out of the question. The S.S. man with the machine gun stood in readiness right behind the investigating officer.)

On the second day we changed our minds. It was, we began to feel, a rather foolish bit of heroics to tell the truth to these Nazis, particularly since it became clear that no one checked our answers, and that one could spare oneself insults and blows by telling believable but inoffensive lies. Thus, for example, we rabbinical students decided that "public school teacher" was a prudent answer, and experience proved we were right.

All this was clear. What was not clear to me until I read Ball's account was that *in resisting the Nazis as we did we fell into their trap.* In retrospect and in the light of hindsight knowledge, it is quite absurd to assume that their system of asking-all-questions-and-checking-no-answers was accidental. We *were meant* to tell our innocent lies, for in so doing, to be sure, we protected ourselves, but at the same time we also lost some of our dignity. *To them* Jews were subhumans whose answers did not matter, and *we,* considering ourselves pretty smart, fell into the trap. Of course, the trap was rather harmless at the time. It did not, however, remain so, for one begins compromising one's dignity on behalf of safety a little, then a little more, until finally a sliding scale is reached where it becomes more and more difficult to escape from the system.

This was one side of the trap. The other, as Ball puts it quite brilliantly, was that it was "unthinkable" for us to initiate a conversation with a stormtrooper. We didn't do so, of course. In fact, we wouldn't have dreamed of either wanting to speak to them or drawing attention to ourselves. What I did not realize until I read this account is that *this too was part of the system.* If the inmates were not only *considered* subhuman but lured into *accepting themselves as such,* the masters, unknown to us and not understood by us, were placed in a position of being superhuman. You not only *didn't* address them, but it was *unthinkable* that you should do so, not because of who they were but because of the black uniforms that they wore. Here in essence is the system that not only caught us but, for long years, the whole world. How well those of us old enough remember the surprise that filled us when we saw those pictures of the Nuremberg trials where the big Nazi leaders were finally shown as the little, contemptible men they were! Yet while the system lasted it was almost invincible. *And among the first to break it were the Jewish fighters of the Warsaw Ghetto.*

Note this remarkable statement by Itzhak Cukierman, one of the leaders of the Warsaw Ghetto uprising:

> On the second day our fortified division achieved new victories without having even one casualty. We were able, with great determination, to overcome the Germans. By following guerrilla warfare theory, we saved lives, added to our supply of arms and—most important—*proved to ourselves that the German was but flesh and blood, as any man.*
>
> *And prior to this we had not been aware of this amazing truth! If one lone Ger-*

man appeared in the Ghetto, the Jews would flee en masse, as would Poles on the Aryan side. Now it became clear that the armed Jew had the advantage over the German . . . something for which to fight. And now the German—once cocky and bent on murder and plunder—felt insecure, knowing that he might not emerge alive from a Jewish house or cellar; and he ceased harrassing Jews. (Italics added)[2]

In the situation in which it was acquired, with a desperate heroism that passes belief and understanding, this insight must be considered as nothing short of revelation. Yet with how little effort the evil Nazi system might have been wiped out a few years earlier—assuredly not by its inmates and victims, but by the outside world which chose either to look on or, more frequently, to look away! Except for good fortune—the Nazi loss of the war—the "Holocaust Kingdom," which had come close to running itself, might today run the world.

III. The Use of Christian Antisemitism by Nazi Antisemitism

The two above phenomena were general. My last example concerns what may well be confined to the special idiosyncrasies of a small minority. However, as I have said, this appears to me of no significance, since everyone has *some* idiosyncrasies, *and the Nazi system sought to exploit them all.* Quoting once again from Ball's document, I cite a "poem" which on one occasion he was forced to bellow again and again:

> Dear old Moses, come again,
> Lead our Jewish fellowmen
> Once more to their promised land.
> Split once more for them the sea,
> Two huge columns let it be
> Fixed as firmly as two walls.
> When the Jews are all inside
> On their pathway, long and wide,
> Shut the trap, Lord, do your best!
> Give the world its lasting rest!

I confess that, no matter how hard I have tried since I first read this utterly obscene "poem" more than a year ago, I cannot recall ever having heard it before, to this day. Yet I *must* have heard it for, as Ball reports, it was not the product of Nazi antisemitism, but rather a heritage from Stoecker's Christian antisemitism of the 1880s. In other words, my failure to remember is a textbook case of repression. The particular repression may be mine, but repression *as such* was inevitably a general phenomenon during the entire Nazi period—and the Nazis counted on it. It was simply humanly impossible, first for German Jews, then for European Jews, to recognize that the enemies were so many and so vicious. Hence, on the Jewish side, wishful thinking, and on the Nazi side, its systematic exploitation. Believe it or not, in the early period of the Nazi régime, Jews sometimes felt that maybe Göring wasn't so bad after all—after Goebbels had just made a particularly bloodcurdling speech. In Sachsenhausen itself it sometimes seemed that one *Sturmführer* was quite human—because another dwarfed him in viciousness. I no longer doubt that the "human" *Sturmführer* was deliberately planted. The abnormal situation shook all our normal standards—*and to shake them was part of the machine.*[3]

In my own case, why did I block the above "poem," i.e., the fact that Christian antisemitism was used by and built into Nazi antisemitism? Why did I live for months and years afterward by the comforting illusion that Nazism was equally opposed to Jews and Christians? Generally, because it was hard to recognize enemies on so many sides; specifically because I happened to know, and be friends with, a handful of stoutly anti-Nazi Christians, exactly *three* (sic!) of them (one a "non-Aryan") fellow inmates in Sachsenhausen itself. I then did not and could not face the fact that the vast majority of German Christians were Nazis, Nazi sympathizers, or at any rate passive accomplices. Far more true to the situation of the time than the testimony of the few anti-Nazi Christians was a telegram addressed to Hitler by a certain *Landesbischof* Wiedemann of the city of Bremen.[4] (If I had seen that telegram at the time, I would not have believed it.) Its text was as follows:

To: The *Führer* and *Reichskanzler* Adolf Hitler:
The three churches of gratitude in Bremen have been inaugurated. They bear your name, *mein Führer*, in gratitude to God for the miraculous redemption of our nation at your hands from the abyss of Jewish-materialistic bolshevism. I thank you for having enabled us to express in these new churches what is a deep confession for us who are fully conscious Christian National Socialists.

Heil, mein Führer!

This telegram is dated November 28, 1938—less than two weeks after the synagogues burned all over Germany, Jewish homes and stores were looted in the broad light of day, and Jews themselves disappeared one knew not where. It was this time that *Landesbischof* Wiedemann, and countless other Christians with him, chose to hand their churches over to Satan, without ever being able to say: "Lord, forgive us, for we knew not what we did."

Notes

1. The notorious Wannsee Conference did not take place until January 20, 1942.
2. Meyer Barkai, tr. and ed., *The Fighting Ghettos* (New York: Tower, 1962), pp. 26–27.
3. Dr. Ball Kaduri has seen the present article and agrees with the rest of it but disagrees with this particular point. He is of the opinion that the togetherness of relatively "human" with more vicious stormtroopers was not part of a plot but rather chance. This disagreement between us reflects a current disagreement in scholarship in which a "monolithic" view of Nazism as a thoroughgoing totalitarian system is attacked by another which stresses "the limits of Hitler's power," if indeed it does not go so far as to view Nazism as a "totalitarian anarchy." This is not the place to take sides in this debate, except to stress that the second school would become mendacious and apologetic if it failed to give full attention to the fact that, however "twisted" may have been the road that led the various Nazi fiefdoms to Auschwitz, it *did* lead there without *radical* opposition from *any* of them.
4. I am indebted to Professor Uriel Tal of Tel Aviv University for acquainting me with this document.

11 *"The Two Work Permits" and the Victims of Faith*

I

I have . . . acquired one religious certainty as great as any in this religiously uncertain age. Søren Kierkegaard once perceived his "knight of faith" as forever obliged to retrace Abraham's road to Mount Moriah, the place where he was to sacrifice Isaac. The Jewish believer and theological thinker today—as well as a century or a millennium hence—is obliged to retrace, again and again, the *via dolorosa* that led one-third of his people to the human sacrifice in the Nazi gas chambers. He is forbidden the cheap and often sacrilegious evasions that tempt him on every side: the "progressive" ideology that asserts that memory is unnecessary, that Auschwitz was an accidental "relapse into tribalism" (an insult to any tribe ever in existence); the "psychiatric" ideology that holds that memory is masochism even as Auschwitz itself was sadism, thus safely belittling both; the "liberal-universalist" ideology that asserts that memory is actually immoral, that because Jews must care about Vietnam, the Black ghetto, and Arab refugees, they are obliged to forget the greatest catastrophe suffered by their own people.

That last-named ideology is especially insidious, for good Jews are tempted by it. When I first called Auschwitz unique my assertion was at once taken to mean that a dead Jewish child at Auschwitz is a greater tragedy than a dead German child at Dresden. That was a misunderstanding possible only because of an antisemitism (conscious or unconscious) that distinguishes "universalistic" Jews concerned with others to the point of consenting to group suicide, and "particularistic" Jews who deserve this nasty epithet if they show any concern whatever for the fate of their own people. This ideology, I say, tempts many: witness the countless Jews today who risk much in behalf of Vietnam or the Black ghetto but will not utter a word against Polish or Soviet antisemitism. Hatred of

Reprinted, with changes, from "The People Israel Lives," in *The Jewish Return into History* (New York: Schocken Books, 1978), 44–48, by permission of the publisher.

Jews on the part of others has always produced self-hating Jews—never more so than when disguised as a moral ideology.

I call Auschwitz unique because it *is* unique. As my wife, Rose, put it in a letter to a minister, Auschwitz was

> overwhelming in its scope, shattering in its fury, inexplicable in its demonism. Unlike Hiroshima, it was no miscalculation of a government at war. It was minutely planned and executed over a twelve-year period, with the compliance of thousands of citizens, to the deafening silence of the world. Unlike slaughtered Russian villages, these were no chance victims of the fury of war. They were carefully chosen, named, listed, tabulated, and stamped. The Nazis went to incredible lengths to find even a single missing Jew. It did not help but hindered the war effort. For while antisemitism was in the beginning politically advantageous to the Nazis the actual crime of genocide had often to be carefully hidden from their own people. Troop trains were diverted from the Russian front in order to transport Jews to Auschwitz. Unique in all human history, the Holocaust was evil for evil's sake.

No wonder the mind seeks refuge in comparisons—some shallow, some obscene, all false—between Auschwitz and Hiroshima, or Vietnam, or the Black ghetto, or even the American campus. Indeed, the very words "Holocaust" and "six million" are evasive abstractions, empty universal substitutes for the countless particulars each of which is an inexhaustible mystery of sin and suffering. And when Jewish theologian Richard Rubenstein writes (in his essay in *The Religious Situation* [Beacon, 1968]) that "the facts are in" and that since "the theological options . . . will not magically increase with the passing of time" we may as well make our choice now, we must conclude that he does not know whereof he speaks.

Let me take just one of those particulars. In issuing "work permits" that were designed to separate "useless" Jews to be murdered at once from "useful" ones to be kept useful by diabolically contrived false hopes and murdered later, the Nazis customarily issued two such permits to an able-bodied Jewish man. One was untransferable, to be kept for himself; the other was to be given at his own discretion to his able-bodied mother, father, wife, or one child. The Nazis would not make the choice, even though to do so would have produced a more efficient labor force. Jewish sons, husbands, or fathers themselves were forced to decide who among their loved ones was—for the time being—to live, who to die at once.

I search the whole history of human depravity for comparisons. In vain. I would reject the comparisons cited above even if they compared the comparable: let each human evil be understood in its own terms. What makes the comparisons utterly odious is that in effect if not intention they abuse Auschwitz, deny that it ever happened, rob its victims even of memory. There is a qualitative distinction between evils—even gigantic ones—perpetuated for such "rational" ends as gain, victory, real or imagined self-interest, and evils perpetrated for evil's sake.

Moreover, there can be a difference even among evils for evil's sake. Theologians call these "the demonic," and I myself once found escape in this theological abstraction. I find it no more. In the history of demonic evil (which, incidentally, in this age of uncritical theological celebrations, someone should write) conceivably there are examples comparable to the Nazi custom of issuing the two work permits. But until such examples are found my religious life and theological thought must lack the comfort of comparisons as I retrace the *via dolorosa* that leads to Auschwitz, trying at the desperate utmost to match the solitude, the despair, the utter abandonment of every one of my brethren who walked that road. And I shall always fail.

II

If the crime of Auschwitz is unique, so is the threat to the faith of its victims. I search the history of religious suffering for comparisons. Once again, in vain. Other believers (Jewish and Christian) have been tortured and murdered for their faith, secure in the belief that God needs martyrs. Black Christians have been tortured and murdered for their race, finding strength in a faith not at issue. The children of Auschwitz were tortured and murdered, not because of their faith nor despite their faith nor for reasons unrelated to the Jewish faith. The Nazis, though racists, did not murder Jews for their "race" but for the Jewish faith of their great-grandparents. Had those great-grandparents failed to show the minimum commitment to the ancient covenant on the raising of Jewish children, their twentieth-century offspring might have been among the Nazi murderers; they would not have been among the Jewish victims. At some time in the mid-nineteenth century, European Jews, like Abraham of old, brought a child sacrifice; but unlike Abraham they did not know what they were doing—and there was no reprieve. It is as if Satan himself had plotted for four thousand years to destroy the covenant between God and Israel, and had at last found the way.[1]

For the desperate question for us after Auschwitz is this: nineteenth-century European Jews did not know—what if they *had* known? And what of us who *do* know? Dare we *morally* raise Jewish children, exposing our offspring to a possible second Auschwitz decades or centuries hence? And dare we *religiously not* raise Jewish children, completing Satan's work on his behalf?[2]

My soul is aghast at this impossible choice, unprecedented in the annals of faith anywhere. And I am filled with shame of mind as well as of soul when I consider that my earlier theology had ruled it out on neat a priori grounds, when it implied that nothing radically new could happen in Jewish religious history between Sinai and the messianic days. My intentions, I still think, were good, for I had sought to make the Jewish faith immune to "merely empirical" and "secular" history, irrefutable as well as unprovable. The result, however, was a betrayal, however unwitting, of the victims of Auschwitz—a betrayal committed even as they were suffering their unique martyrdom.

Moreover, I now think that my earlier theological aim lacked Jewish authenticity. To be sure, when the Romans destroyed the second Temple the talmudic rabbis refused to despair of God's covenant with Israel, but at the same time they let the catastrophe call it into question. Whether picturing God as in exile with Israel or as lamenting his own decision or even as engaged in bitter self-recrimination, they showed the courage to make their faith vulnerable to actual—i.e., empirical and "secular"—history. How shall we live with God after Auschwitz? How without him? Contend with God we must, as did Abraham, Jacob, Job. And we cannot let him go.

Notes

1. See "Jewish Faith and the Holocaust" and "From Bergen-Belsen to Jerusalem" in *Jewish Return*, pp. 30 and 136. I find myself compelled to keep returning to this fundamental point (and indeed to quote myself verbatim) since it would seem to be *the* shibboleth of post-Holocaust Jewish self-understanding, whether religious or secular.

2. This contradiction, unlike Kierkegaard's teleological suspension of the ethical, does not involve morality on one side only. Among the worst of the Spanish inquisitors were descendants of converted Jews, and Reinhard Heydrich is said to have had a Jewish ancestor. By choosing for our children not to be victims, may we be exposing them to the possibility, or the likelihood, that they will be murderers?

12 The "Crime" of Jewish Existence

To confront the Holocaust is to be overwhelmed by inevitable failure. And to persist in the effort is to face a dilemma: if one seeks to grasp the whole, its horror dissipates itself into such meaningless abstractions as "the six million" or "the symbol Auschwitz"; and if one seeks the truth of the horror in some one particular, one encourages reactions such as the paradigmatic one of a German woman who, having seen the Anne Frank movie, exclaimed: "At least this one should have been spared!"[1] One can avoid this dilemma only by taking hold of individual examples which, at the same time, cannot be rejected by the mind as exceptions, aberrations, mistakes or excesses because they manifest altogether unmistakably the horror of the whole.

So totally integrated was the whole in question (rightly called by names such as "Holocaust Kingdom" or "Planet Auschwitz") that to find the required examples is not, after all, very difficult. Raul Hilberg cites two secret German army lists reporting capital punishment meted out in occupied Russia:

Punishable Offences by Members of the Population

Report I

Espionage	1
Theft of Ammunition	1
Suspected Jews (*Judenverdacht*)	3

Reprinted, with changes, from "Midrashic Existence after the Holocaust," in *The Jewish Return into History* (New York: Schocken Books, 1978), 252–72, by permission of the publisher.

Moving about with Arms (*Freischärlerei*) 11
Theft 2
Jews 2[2]

The meaning of these lists is shocking but simple. All others had to *do* something in order to be subject to punishment; in contrast, to *be* a Jew—indeed, to be under *Judenverdacht*—was *in itself* and without further ado a punishable offense (*strafbare Handlung*).

One may object that the German war on Europe was one thing, the Nazi persecution of the Jews another; that while both reached a climax in Russia, they were only accidentally intermingled; and that to the end enemies of the *Reich* were punished for their deeds, whereas Jews, even when they were murdered, were not "punished." In short, the Holocaust, while quite possibly a whole-in-itself, was an accident—for historians a footnote—in the larger whole: the Nazi-German empire and its goals. Auschwitz, as it were, was a "mistake": not only Anne Frank, but all should have been spared.

Let those taking this view consider the following *Häftlings Personal Karte* (prisoner's identity card) which at this time of writing is on display at the Yad Vashem Museum in Jerusalem:

Name: Kreisler, Andor
Place: some town in Hungary
Religion: Mosaic
Date of imprisonment: 25.4.1944
Authority: Gestapo Vienna
Concentration Camp: Mauthausen
Reason: Hungarian Jew
Previous criminal record: none

Note, first, the archaic term "Mosaic" under the rubric "religion," a clear proof that (except in cases of Gentile converts to Judaism) religion, *as something one could freely accept or reject*, was of no interest to the authors of the form. Note, second, the utterly illogical but supremely revelatory sequence of these categories: " 'reason' for imprisonment" and "previous criminal record." The illogic is obvious. "Previous criminal record" is senseless unless preceded by the category "crime"; and any "reason" for imprisonment other than "crime"—analogous, say, to wartime internment of Germans in Britain or Japanese in the United States and Canada—is senselessly (and insultingly) followed by the category "previous criminal record." Yet precisely this illogic is revealing: the category "reason" *had* to be wide enough to include *for "punishment"* those who had *done* something as well as those for whom it was sufficient to *be* something. With the possible exception of the Gypsies, this latter group was Jews.

Yet a third point must be noted about the *Häftlings Personal Karte:* that it *was* a *Karte*, a form, carefully conceived, printed in countless copies, and used in who knows how many cases. This decisive fact demolishes any remnant of the idea that in the Nazi system the identification of Jewish existence with criminality was an accident.

However, we may still try to understand this identification as essential only to the murder-camp system, and not to the larger Nazi system of which it was a part. What gives us pause in this attempt is the fact that, though concealing the camps themselves, the Nazis made no attempt to hide the *beliefs* enacted in the camps. Indeed, years of propaganda concerning the "hereditary criminality" of the Jews had preceded a progression of actions which escalated until finally, so far as this crucial point is concerned, S.S. murder-camp forms and army lists of executed "criminals" can no longer be distinguished.

Disdaining to hide their beliefs from the populace outside the camps, the Nazis disdained even less concealment from the victims inside. At least as far back as 1938, concentration camp prisoners had their respective categories emblazoned on their uniforms in the form of triangles: red for "political," green for "professional criminal," brown for "unemployable," pink for "homosexual," and yellow for "Jew." Once again with the possible exception of the Gypsies (who were sometimes considered as *inherently* unemployable), everybody had to have *done* something in order to land in a concentration camp. Only Jews had simply to *be*. And, as if to underscore this distinction, when finally all Jews had conspired to do something—for such was the official theory about the assassination of Freiherr vom Rath by Herschel Grynszpan in November 1938—those Jewish members of the conspiracy who were incarcerated in concentration camps had *two* triangles on their uniform, neatly arranged into a Star of David: a red one for the political crime in which they had conspired, and a yellow one for "Jew." Significantly, Jews in the camps at the time seem to have had no adequate understanding of the explosive distinction of which they themselves were victims. The present writer, at any rate, did not have it. Indeed, on a visit to Yad Vashem just half a year ago he understood Andor Kreisler's *Häftlings Karte* sufficiently to copy it, but still not sufficiently to copy it in its entirety. This is why he cannot report the name of the town in Hungary which had once been Andor's home.

The distinction, then, between criminals-by-dint-of-actions and criminals-by-dint-of-birth was not only uniquely explosive but also applied with an insidiousness which even in hindsight staggers the mind. We must now face this insidiousness in its full scope. The late Leo Strauss has rightly observed that the Nazi regime was "the only German regime—the only regime ever anywhere—which had no other clear principle than murderous hatred of Jews, for 'Aryan' had no clear meaning other than 'non-Jewish.' "[3] If the "non-Aryan" was a criminal-by-dint-of-birth, then "man" no longer was, as once he had been, innocent-by-dint-of-birth. Each and every person was presumed to be guilty-by-dint-of-birth until he had proved his innocence, and this he could do only by proving his "Aryan" ancestry. So openly, yet insidiously, did the Nazi *Reich* implicate in its crime against the Jewish people, not only its direct agents and their accomplices, but each and every person proving, or even prepared to prove, his "Aryan" innocence. Indeed, even those surviving on the presumption of innocence of *Judenverdacht* are implicated. Only those rejecting outright the whole system of "non-Aryan" guilt and "Aryan" innocence are wholly pure, and those were sure to become honorary Jews, i.e., victims themselves.

We are thus forced to give up the comfortable conventional wisdom that the Nazi tyranny was much like all other tyrannies, except of course for the shocking murder camps; and that the Nazi murder camps were much like other murder camps, except of course for treating a whole people as a "race" of hereditary criminals. The uncomfortable truth is rather the reverse. The murder camp was no accident of the Nazi system but its inmost essence. And what made the murder camp into a kingdom not of this world—the Holocaust kingdom—was an unheard-of principle: that a whole people—Jews, half-Jews, quarter-Jews, honorary Jews—are guilty by dint not of actions but of existence itself. The process governed by this principle climaxed in an apocalypse. It began before the first Jew was ever "punished" for his "crime." Hilberg writes: "When in the early days of 1933 the first civil servant wrote the first definition of "non-Aryan" into a civil service ordinance, the fate of European Jewry was sealed."[4] So, one must add, was the moral fate of the twelve-year *Reich*—the twelve years equal to a thousand—which has no analogue in history but at most only in the imagination when it pictures hell.

Hell Surpassed

History provides many examples of the strong vanquishing the weak without scruple, and of ideologies, recently taking the form of "social Darwinism," that endorse such unscrupulousness. But neither in such struggles nor in the ideologies endorsing them is weakness ever considered a *crime*, or the conquest or even "extermination" of the weak a *punishment*.

Again, history shows no dearth of societies governed by unjust laws. Yet the "criminals" of such societies are always punished for something they have *done*, namely, the breaking of the unjust laws. Hence, even the most unjust society cannot but recognize the free will, responsibility, rationality and thus humanity of its purported criminals. It is this circumstance that caused Hegel to remark—controversially but intelligibly and even defensibly—that a bad state is better than no state at all.

The Nazi state was no mere quasi-Darwinian, quasi-natural state, recognizing no right other than might.[5] It was not merely an unjust state, forced to recognize, if nothing else, the responsibility and hence humanity of its victims.[6] The identification of existence itself with criminality, involving as it did *all* human existence, "Aryan" and "non-Aryan" alike, caused *this* state to be neither a subhuman quasi-state nor an imperfect human state but rather an *anti-state*, that is, a system *absolutely* perverting *all* things human. Indeed, since the perversion is surpassable not in quality but only in quantity, the Nazi state was *the* anti-state *par excellence*. Hegel would condemn it as worse than chaos. As we have said, it has an analogue, if anywhere, only in hell.

Yet as one ponders this possibility, one wonders whether even hell is adequate. The devil is insidious in the ways he tempts us but does not place us into a kingdom, onto a planet, of which insidiousness is a built-in feature. He punishes sinners beyond desert but cannot so much as touch the innocent. He may have an infinity of time. But he has only finite power. Perhaps this is why Roy Eckardt has said that sooner or later the devil becomes a bore.[7]

We ask: what will limit the power of the devil if existence itself is a crime? If he can and does touch the innocent—indeed, them above all? What of a hell in which the question of punishment according to, or beyond, desert no longer arises? What will *then* limit the innocent suffering of the purported criminals, or the criminal actions of the purported judges and law-enforcers?

There can be no limit, or would have been none, if, by good fortune, Planet Auschwitz had not been destroyed. Hence, a whole generation after, we still accept its possiblity only because of its brute facticity. We do not accept it because we understand it. Though the misbegotten creature of our civilization, Planet Auschwitz transcends the resources of our imagination, those pagan, on the one hand, those Jewish and Christian, on the other.

Wisest of the pagans, the Greek philosophers confronted the brute facticity of filth but could not conceive of an enthusiasm fired not by good but evil.[8] In contrast, biblically-inspired poets and theologians did indeed imagine such an evil, a fallen angel saying to evil, "be thou my Good!" But on their part, believing as they did in a divinely created world, they could not confront the facticity of filth.[9] One must therefore summon the resources of both our Western traditions to begin to grasp a kingdom which was *anus mundi* and hell in one; ruled in an eerie compact by "disgusting" pornographic Streichers and "fanatical National Socialist" idealists whose "cause" was "serious antisemitism";[10] and run by a wholly new species of human beings: men and women who performed by day their quite new "jobs," and yet by night continued to relax as men and women have always relaxed—playing with their dogs, listening to fine music, and celebrating Christmas.

Commemorating the twenty-fifth anniversary of the liberation of Bergen-Belsen in nearby Hannover, Norbert Wollheim, a leading spokesman of the survivors, referred in his memorial address to Hitler as Goethe had referred to the devil: "misbegotten creature of filth and fire." Perhaps only the wisest of Germans—close to Christianity and classical antiquity and yet identified with neither—was able, if not to predict, prophesy or imagine, so at least to find words adequate to describe, of all the Germans, the most depraved. It is not certain how long the world will be inspired and instructed by the wisest German. But we must live with the grim certainty that the shadow of the most depraved German will never cease to haunt it.[11]

Notes

1. Reinhard Baumgard, "Unmenschlichkeit beschrieben: Weltkrieg und Faschismus in der Literatur," in *Merkur* XIX (January 1965), no. 1, p. 46.

2. Raul Hilberg, *The Destruction of the European Jews* (New York: Quadrangle, 1961), p. 657.

3. "Preface to the English Edition of *Spinoza's Critique of Religion*," in *The Jewish Expression*, ed., Judah Goldin (New York: Bantam, 1970; New Haven: Yale University Press, 1976), p. 345.

4. Hilberg, *Destruction*, p. 669.

5. The presence of a social Darwinist element in Nazism and its antecedents is evident. (See e.g., H. G. Zmarzlik, "Social Darwinism in Germany," in *Republic to Reich*, ed., H. Holborn [New York: Vintage, 1973], pp. 436ff.) However, a quantum leap is necessary if the "right" or even "duty" of the strong to "exterminate" the weak is to become a criminal prosecution in which the weak suffer "extermination" as a just punishment. This difference was fully revealed in the *Götterdämmerung*, when Hitler declared that the mighty Russians had, after all, historical right on their side, even as he wrote a last will and testament obligating future generations to complete the "Final Solution"—the "extermination" of a people which, in his view, fully matched the Russians in might.

6. The present writer was able to observe in 1938 that S.S. men, too, could land in a concentra-

tion camp and that, if they did, they were punished as brutally as the other inmates. But their punishment was, of course, for acts of disobedience.

7. In his classic "The Devil and Yom Kippur" (*Midstream*, August–September 1974) Eckardt deals with the monotonous repetition by antisemites in ever new code words, of the same false accusations and mendacious arguments. However, he does not deal with Nazism in this article.

8. In Plato's *Republic, thymos* or the emotional part of the soul which is capable of enthusiasm, is merely chaotic, not a possibility of the demonic; and the worst state is not hell but merely a tyranny governed by cynicism.

9. Hell is related to purgatory. But filth does not purge. See Terrence Des Pres, *The Survivor*, chap. 3, "Excremental Assault" (New York: Oxford University Press, 1976).

10. See Rudolf Hoess, *Commandant of Auschwitz* (London: Pan, 1974), p. 145. In this autobiography, written in prison, the Auschwitz *Kommandant* writes: "I was opposed to *Der Stürmer*, Streicher's anti-Semitic weekly, because of the disgusting sensationalism with which it played on people's basest instincts. Then, too, there was its perpetual and often savagely pornographic emphasis on sex. This paper caused a lot of mischief and, far from serving serious anti-Semitism, it did a great deal of harm. It is small wonder that after the collapse it was learnt that a Jew edited the paper and that he also wrote the worst of the inflammatory articles it contained."

The last sentence is, of course, quite untrue, but all the more significant when it is remembered that Hoess was in *total* command of *all* the actions at Auschwitz, the Streicher-type included. In his introduction to the German edition of the Hoess memoirs, Martin Broszat rightly notes how, even after, Hoess fancied himself as a decent person deeply moved by the murder of children—as if he had not himself ordered the murders! Broszat can find no better adjective than the obviously inadequate "schizophrenic" to describe this consciousness. M. Broszat, ed., *Kommandant in Auschwitz* (Stuttgart: Deutsche Verlags-Anstalt, 1958), pp. 17–18.

11. The preceding account is in no way opposed to the numerous investigations to the effect that not all Germans were Nazis, not all Nazis S.S. men, not all S.S. men murderers, and that the whole *Reich* contained within itself different and even conflicting fiefdoms. However, the *Reich*—if anything ever—was a whole which was more than the sum of the parts. If historical investigators lose sight of this truth they lose the whole.

13 The Uniqueness of the Holocaust

The World War II Jewish genocide resembles most closely the World War I Armenian genocide. Both were (i) attempts to murder a whole people; (ii) carried out under cover of war; (iii) with maximum secrecy; (iv) after the deportation of the victims, with deliberate cruelty, to remote places; (v) all this provoking few countermeasures or even verbal protests on the part of the civilized world. Doubtless the Nazis both learned from and were encouraged by the Armenian precedent.

These are striking similarities. As striking, however, are the differences. The Armenian deportations from Istanbul were stopped after some time, whether because of political problems or the logistical difficulties posed by so large a city. "Combed" for Jews were Berlin, Vienna, Amsterdam, Warsaw. In this, greater Teutonic efficiency was secondary; primary was a *Weltanschauung*. Indian reservations exist in America. Jewish reservations in a victorious Nazi empire are inconceivable: already planned instead were museums for an "extinct race." For, unlike the Turks, the Nazis sought a *"final* solution" of a "problem"—final only if, minimally, Europe and, maximally, the world would be *judenrein*. In German this word has no counterpart such as *polenrein, russenrein, slavenrein*. In other languages it does not exist at all; for whereas Jordan and Saudi Arabia are in fact without Jews, missing is the *Weltanschauung*. The Holocaust, then, is but one case of the class "genocide." As a case of the class: "intended, planned, and largely successful *extermination*," it is without precedent and, thus far at least, without sequel. It is unique.

Equally unique are the means necessary to this end. These included (i) a scholastically precise definition of the victims; (ii) juridical procedures procuring their

Reprinted, with changes, from "The Holocaust and Philosophy," *The Journal of Philosophy* LXXXII, 10 (October, 1985): 506–9, 510–11.

rightlessness; (iii) a technical apparatus culminating in murder trains and gas chambers; and (iv), most importantly, a veritable army of murderers and also direct and indirect accomplices: clerks, newspapermen, lawyers, bank managers, doctors, soldiers, railwaymen, entrepreneurs, and an endless list of others.

The relation between direct and indirect accomplices is as important as the distinction. The German historian Karl Dietrich Bracher[1] understands Nazi Germany as a dual system. Its inner part was the "S.S. state"; its outer, the traditional establishment—civil service, army, schools, universities, churches. This latter system was allowed separate existence to the end, but was also increasingly penetrated, manipulated, perverted. *And since it resisted the process only sporadically and never radically, it enabled the S.S. state to do what it could never have done simply on its own.* Had the railwaymen engaged in strikes or sabotage or simply vanished there would have been no Auschwitz. Had the German army acted likewise there would have been neither Auschwitz nor World War II. U.S. President Ronald Reagan should not have gone to Bitburg even if no S.S. men had been buried there.

Such was the army required for the "how" of the Holocaust. Its "why" required an army of historians, philosophers, theologians. The historians rewrote history. The philosophers demonstrated that mankind is "Ayran" or "non-Aryan" before it is human. The theologians were divided into Christians who made Jesus into an "Aryan" and neo-pagans who rejected Chrisitianity itself as "non-Aryan"; their differences were slight compared to their shared commitments.

These were direct accomplices. But here too there was need for indirect accomplices as well. Without the prestige of philosophers like Martin Heidegger and theologians like Emanuel Hirsch, could the *National-Sozialistische Weltanschauung* have gained its power and respectability? Could it have won out at all? The Scottish-Catholic historian Malcolm Hay asks why what happened in Germany did not happen in France forty years earlier, during the Dreyfus affair. He replies that in France there were fifty righteous men.[2]

What *was* the "why" of the Holocaust? Astoundingly, significantly, even the archpractitioners rarely faced it. 'Archpractitioner' indisputably fits Treblinka Kommandant Franz Stangl. (Treblinka had the fewest survivors.) In a postwar interview Stangl was asked: "What did you think at the time was the reason for the extermination of the Jews?" Stangl replied—as if Jews had not long been robbed naked!—"they wanted their money."[3] Did Stangl *really* not know? Yet, though Treblinka itself was secret, its *raison d'être* had always been public. In the Nazi *Weltanschauung* Jews were vermin, and one does not execute vermin, murder it, spare its young or its old: one *exterminates* vermin—coldly, systematically, without feeling or a second thought. Is 'vermin' (or 'virus' or 'parasite') a "mere metaphor"? In a 1942 "table-talk," right after the Wannsee conference that finalized the "Final Solution," Hitler said:

> The discovery of the Jewish virus is one of the greatest revolutions . . . in the world. The struggle we are waging is of the same kind as that of Pasteur and Koch in the last century. How many diseases can be traced back to the Jewish virus! We shall regain our health only when we exterminate the Jews.[4]

For racism, "inferior races" are still human; even for Nazi racism there are merely too many Slavs. For Nazi antisemitism Jews are not human; they must not exist at all.

Stangl failed with his interviewer's first question. He failed with her second as well. "If they were going to kill them anyway," he was asked, "what was the point of all the humiliation, why all the cruelty?" He replied: "To condition those who actually had to carry out the policies. To make it possible for them to do what they did." The interviewer had doubted Stangl's first answer, but accepted his second as both honest and true. Honest it may have been; true it was not. The "cruelty" included horrendous medical nonexperiments on women, children, babies. The "humiliation" included making pious Jews spit on Torah scrolls and, when they ran out of spittle, supplying them with more by spitting into their mouths. Was all this easier on the operators than pulling triggers and pushing buttons? *Treblinka—the Holocaust—had two ultimate purposes: extermination* and also *maximum prior humiliation and torture.* This too—can Stangl have been unaware of it?—had been part of the public *Weltanschauung* all along. In 1936 Julius Streicher declared that "who fights the Jew fights the devil," and that "who masters the devil conquers heaven" (MW 188). And this basest, most pornographic Nazi only echoed what the most authoritative (and equally pornographic) Nazi had written many years earlier:

> With satanic joy in his face, the black-haired Jewish youth lurks in wait for the unsuspecting girl whom he defiles with his blood . . . By defending myself against the Jew, I am fighting for the work of the Lord.[5]

To "punish" the "Jewish devil" through humiliation and torture, then, was part of "Aryan" salvation. Perhaps it was all of it.

"Jewish devil" and Jewish "vermin" (or "bacillus," "parasite," "virus") existed side by side in the Nazi theory. For example, this single Hitler-passage of 1923:

> The Jews are undoubtedly a race, but they are not human. They cannot be human in the sense of being in the image of God, the Eternal. The Jews are the image of the devil. Jewry means the racial tuberculosis of the nations (cited by Fest, *op. cit.*).

Side by side in the theory, "devil" and "vermin" were synthesized in the Auschwitz *praxis*, and this was a *novum* without precedent in the realm of either the real or the possible. Even in the worst state, punishment is meted out for a *doing*—a fact explaining Hegel's statement, defensible once but no more, that any state is better than none. And, even in the hell of poetic and theological imagination, the innocent cannot be touched. The Auschwitz *praxis* was based on a new principle: *for one portion of mankind, existence itself is a crime, punishable by humiliation, torture, and death.* And the new world produced by this *praxis* included two kinds of inhabitants, those who were given the "punishment" and those who administered it.

Few have yet grasped the newness of that new world. Survivors have grasped it all along. Hence they refer to *all* the "punished" victims as *k'doshim* ("holy ones"); for even criminals among them were innocent of the "crime" for which they were "punished." Hence, too, they refer to the new world created by the victimizers as a "universe" other than ours, or a "planet" other than the one we inhabit. What historians and philosophers must face is that Auschwitz was a kingdom not of this world.

. . . . .

Allan Bullock stresses that Hitler's orginality lay not in ideas but in "the terrifying literal way in which he . . . translate[d] fantasy into reality, and his unequalled grasp of the means by which to do this."[6] One original product of this "translation" was the so-called *Muselmann.* If in the Gulag the dissident suffers torture-through-psychiatry, on the theory that in the workers' paradise such as he must be mad, then the Auschwitz *praxis* reduces the "non-Aryan" to a walking corpse covered with his own filth, on the theory that he must reveal himself as the disgusting creature that he has been, if disguisedly, since birth. To be sure, the *Muselmänner* included countless "Aryans" also. But, just as "the Nazis were racists because they were antisemites" is truer than the reverse, so it is truer that non-Jewish *Muselmänner* were Jews-by-association than that Jewish *Muselmänner* were a sub-species of "enemies of the *Reich.*"

The process was focused on Jews in particular. Its implications, however, concern the whole human condition, and, therefore, philosophers. Among these few would deny that to die one's own death is part of one's freedom; in Martin Heidegger's *Being and Time* this freedom is foundational. Yet, of the Auschwitz *Muselmann,* Primo Levi writes:

> Their life is short, but their number is endless; they, the Muselmänner, the drowned, form the backbone of the camp, an anonymous mass, continually renewed and always identical, of non-men who march and labor in silence, the divine spark dead within them, already too empty really to suffer. *One hesitates to call them living; one hesitates to call their death death.*[7]

To die one's own death has always been a freedom subject to loss by accident. On Planet Auschwitz, however, the loss of it was made essential, and its survival accidental. Hence Theodor Adorno writes:

> With the administrative murder of millions death has become something that never before was to be feared in this way. Death no longer enters into the experienced life of the individual, as somehow harmonizing with its course. It was no longer the individual that died in the camps, but the specimen. *This must affect also the dying of those who escaped the procedure* (355; my translation; italics added).[8]

Philosophers are faced with a new *aporia.* It arises from the necessity to listen to the silence of the *Muselmann.*

Notes

1. *The German Dictatorship* (New York: Praeger, 1969), esp. ch. VIII.
2. *The Foot of Pride* (Boston: Beacon Press, 1950), p. 211.
3. Gitta Sereny, *Into that Darkness* (London: Andre Deutsch, 1974), p. 101.
4. Cited by Joachim C. Fest. *Hitler* (New York: Vintage, 1975), p. 212.
5. Hitler, *Mein Kampf,* Ralph Manheim, tr. (Boston: Houghton Mifflin, 1943), pp. 325, 365.

6. Cited by Herbert Luethy, "Der Fuehrer," N. Podhoretz, ed., in *The Commentary Reader* (New York: Atheneum, 1966), p. 64.

7. *Survival in Auschwitz*, S. Woolf, tr. (New York: Orion, 1959), p. 82, italics added.

8. *Negative Dialektik* (Frankfurt: Suhrkamp, 1975).

14 *The "World" of the Holocaust*

World War II decided at least one thing: it destroyed the world of the Holocaust. We use the word "world" advisedly. Auschwitz and Treblinka were a world, with a structure of their own, a logic of their own, a horizon of their own, even a language of their own; but they were unlike any world ever dreamt of in Heidegger's[1] or any other philosophy.

· · · · ·

In due course we must consider the victims, their suffering, their resistance, their identity. For the present, let us be silent of them and consider the technicians, administrators, rulers and philosophers.

Lest unauthentic refuge be sought in the most obvious place, it must be stressed from the start that the sadists, perverts, madmen—the kind that may be found anywhere and at any time—were least in significance. (They were probably least in number as well: only so many of them can be enlisted by even the most sedulous organizers.) More significant were the ordinary men and women who performed their new, extraordinary jobs in much the same manner in which they had once performed—and would soon again perform—their ordinary jobs. However, most significant of all—indeed, setting the tone—were the idealists: these were much like other idealists, except that their ideals were torture and murder. (They did not just "use" torture, but "worshiped" it.) On their part, these idealists were subdivided into those who practiced the ideals and those who provided the theory. And the theory and practice, in the last analysis, had their "reality" and "law" in the Führer himself.[2]

Of the last-named two groups, the practitioners and the philosophers, one

Reprinted, with changes, from *To Mend the World* (New York: Schocken Books, 1982), 181–89, by permission of the publisher.

should give examples. Rudolf Hoess was brought up in the Black Forest, which he loved. His great, life-long ambition was to return to the soil and till it. He was good to his wife and his children. He was dedicated to his *Volk* and thus abominated Julius Streicher's "pornographic anti-Semitism that was harmful to German women and children." Yet this man was commandant of Auschwitz. In all likelihood, he was the greatest torturer and mass murderer in history.

To Kommandant Hoess the Führer himself was law. That law left some small room for doubt as to the fate to be meted out to the "enemies of the state" that were within his jurisdiction. In the case of Jews there was no room for doubt. To be a Jew was in *itself* a capital crime: such was the essence of Hoess's "serious"—as contrasted with Streicher's "pornographic"—anti-Semitism.[3]

Hoess practiced this law. The Führer's philosophers furnished the necessary theory. Once the University of Jena had been home, successively, to Fichte, Schelling, and Hegel . . . Now it was home to Professor Johann von Leers, the author of learned arguments to the effect that states harboring Jews were harboring the plague, and that the Reich had the moral duty and, by the principle of hot pursuit, the legal right to conquer such countries, if only in order to wipe the plague out.[4]

Such was the theory. It was so well in tune with practice that practitioners such as Kommandant Hoess—by his own voluntary confession—could be both deeply moved by the innocent play of Gypsy children—considered "non-Aryan" by one school of Nazi thought, though considered "Aryan" by another—and yet cold-bloodedly plot their murder.[5] And the theory and the practice had both their ultimate source in the Führer himself. As early as in September 1919, Hitler had written:

> Antisemitism arising out of purely emotional causes finds its ultimate expression in pogroms. Rational antisemitism must be directed toward a methodical legal struggle. . . . The final aim must be the deliberate removal [*Entfernung*] of the Jews as a whole.[6]

Only a few years later the sentiments of this letter became the core of the "program" of a party—its core, if not its sole unambiguous content. By 1935 the "legal struggle" had become a legislation distinguishing between "non-Aryan" guilt and "Aryan" innocence. And in the end the "final aim"—"the deliberate *Entfernung* of the Jews as a whole"—became the "Final Solution."[7]

The roles of Führer, philosopher and practitioner were remarkably united in the person of Reichsführer Heinrich Himmler. It is therefore necessary for us to consider him. On a noted occasion Himmler addressed his idealistic subordinates as follows:

> I want to make reference before you here, in complete frankness, to a really grave matter. Among ourselves, this once, it shall be uttered quite frankly; but in public we will never speak of it. Just as we did not hesitate on June 30, 1934 to do our duty as ordered, to stand up against the wall comrades who had transgressed, and shoot them, so we have never talked about this and never will. It was the tact which, I am glad to say, is a matter of course to us that made us never discuss it among ourselves, never talk about it. Each of us shuddered, and yet each one knew that he would do it again if it were ordered and if it were necessary. I am referring to the evacuation of

the Jews, to the annihilation of the Jewish people. This is one of those things that are easily said. "The Jewish people is going to be annihilated," says every party member. "Sure, it's in our program, elimination of the Jews, annihilation—we'll take care of it." And then they all come trudging, eighty million worthy Germans, and each has his one decent Jew. Sure, the others are swine, but this one is an A–1 Jew. Of all those who talk this way, no one has seen it happen, not one has been through it. Most of you know what it means to see a hundred corpses lie side by side, or five hundred, or a thousand. To have endured this and—excepting cases of human weakness—to have remained decent, that is what has made us hard. In our history, this is an unwritten and never-to-be-written page of glory.[8]

Himmler, as is well known, was himself not hard enough; on a visit to Auschwitz he was sick to his stomach. Not so well known is that on another visit

he stopped beside the burning pit and waited for a pair of gloves. Then he put on the gloves, picked one of the dead bodies off the pile, and threw it into the fire. "Thank God," he cried with a loud voice. "At last I too have burned a Jew with my own hands."[9]

We must take Himmler's speech—one of several—as an authoritative document. (Hence we have cited it at some length.) The leading Nazi spirits were not perverts or opportunists or even ordinary jobholders but rather extraordinary idealists, i.e., criminals with a good conscience and a pure heart. This is one lesson of Himmler's speech, already known to us but now authoritatively confirmed. The other, however, is new and more important still, for it concerns not the Holocaust alone but rather the Führer's Reich as a whole. Most of the eighty million Germans, Himmler states, fell short of sufficient loyalty to the Führer's law; yet they all subscribed to it. This is, of course, a gross lie on Himmler's part, a crude Nazi joke and an insult to countless decent Germans, never converted to "Aryan" ideology. Alas, no lie but rather a brute fact is that the eighty million, the countless decent ones included, obeyed the Führer's law and owed life itself to this compliance. By the laws of every other world, a person is punished for *doing*, i.e., the breaking of the laws. By the "Aryan" laws of the Führer's world, "non-Aryans" were "punished" for *being*, i.e., their accidental ancestors. By the laws of every other world—in theory if never wholly in practice—a person is presumed innocent until proven guilty. By the laws of the Führer's world, *all* persons were suspect of "non-Aryan" criminality unless they proved, or were prepared to prove, their "Aryan" innocence. Hence the awesome fact is *that all* giving *such proof, prepared to give it, or even simply surviving on the presumption of "Aryan" descent—i.e., no less than all the eighty million Germans as well as many in Nazi-occupied Europe—are implicated, however remotely, indirectly, and innocently, in the crime crying to heaven in the screams of the children of Auschwitz and in the no less terrible silence of the* Muselmänner. *Only those defying the* Führer's *law (and in so doing risking or forfeiting lives) are wholly exempt.* One searches all history in vain for a parallel to this German tragedy.

We use the term "tragedy" advisedly. One must emphasize that *subjectively* many or most Germans were innocent—all those who knew nothing or could do nothing. Yet it is just to these that the term "tragedy" applies. (To apply it to the criminals is a mistake.) Indeed, the more one has reason to insist on subjective innocence the more starkly comes into view the contradiction between it and objective implication—survival on the presumption of an "Aryan" innocence that implies "non-Aryan" guilt. Deliberately, insidiously, diabolically, the laws of the Third Reich drew, spiderlike, the *whole* German people into a web, the core of which was the Holocaust. And the gulf created and legislated since 1933 was between German (and, subsequently European) Jewry as a whole and—with exceptions noted—the *entire* German people and much of Nazi-occupied Europe. No wonder the mind shrinks from this scandalous fact. No wonder the Holocaust is widely viewed as an accident—for historians a footnote—in the history of Germany, Europe, the world.

To disprove this last-named view one need go no further than the dynamics of Nazism itself, i.e., to consider how, as the inner logic of the Führer's law and reality unfolded, the Third Reich took its terrible historical course. The Nazi Empire had not one but two aims that brooked no compromise. One was the annihilation of the Jewish people. The other—this in behalf of social Darwinist "principles" freely mixed with dreams, ambitions, and myths harking back to Kaiser Wilhelm II, to some German romantics, to Frederick the Great, and to Kaiser Barbarossa— was the conquest of *Lebensraum* and of lesser races by the master race, all this with an ultimate (if vague) view to world conquest. (The secret code name for the war on Russia was "Operation Barbarossa"; the public slogan since 1933 had been "today Germany—tomorrow the world.") All this, however, was when the Third Reich was at the height of its power. At the time of the apocalypse, only the first of these aims proved itself to be absolute. As for the second—this still in behalf of social Darwinist principles, though Barbarossa was by then forgotten—the German people were now being handed over for destruction cynically and even enthusiastically—and of all "races," to the once-despised Slavs. Thus the *sole absolute* article of faith that remained was expressed in the burning of Jewish children. That otherwise this was a "revolution of nihilism" was expressed in a *Führerbefehl* in the doomed Berlin bunker. Hitler ordered the flooding of the Berlin subways, the hiding place of men, women, and children. This would not stop the Russian armies. However, it would drown German children.

Such was the essence of Nazism as revealed in the end. Such, revealed in part, had been its essence all along. As early as 1936, Julius Streicher was quoted in print as follows:

Who fights the Jew fights the devil!
Who masters the devil conquers heaven![10]

Streicher no more than echoed the Führer himself who earlier still had written: "In defending myself against the Jew, I fight for the work of God."[11] The distinction between "pornographic" and "serious" or "idealistic" Nazi anti-Semitism dissolves. *In extremis* they became in fact, as in essence they were all along, one and the same.[12]

Such was the *Welt* (or *Unwelt*)—its inner core the Holocaust, its outer expression the Nazi Reich as a whole—in which the German tragic contradiction between subjective innocence and objective implication-by-dint-of-"Aryan"-survival assumed its unheard of, unprecedented reality. Once the German philosopher Schelling had written deeply, compellingly about innocent guilt in Greek tragedy—a mere conceit of poets.[13] One asks: Where is the philosopher—he ought to be, *can only* be German—to face a German tragedy which is no mere poetic conceit and which no poet could ever have conceived?

Notes

1. [The following account is part of an encounter between the Holocaust and the philosophy of Martin Heidegger (see introduction to Part 3)—*Ed.*]

2. This brief synopsis is indebted to the work of Holocaust historians such as Yehuda Bauer and Raul Hilberg. Their work uncovers a reality rarely perceived by general historians who, if they do not dismiss the Holocaust in a footnote, resort with amazing regularity to metaphors such as "racist madness," as if they, rather than explain anything, did not themselves stand in need of explanation. See also *To Mend the World*, p. 231n.

3. Rudolf Hoess, *Commandant of Auschwitz* (London: Pan Books, 1961), p. 145 and passim.

4. *Die Verbrechernatur der Juden* (Berlin, 1944), p. 8. On the Nazi concept of Jews as bacilli, see Erich Goldhagen, "Weltanschauung und Endlösung," *Vierteljahreshefte für Zeitgeschichte* (1976), p. 379. In a letter to me Professor Goldhagen stresses that whereas of course the bacilli idea was common among Nazis, von Leers had the unusual distinction of not bothering to veil his call for mass murder in euphemistic language. Goldhagen also informs me that after the war von Leers, his Nazi ardor undiminished, launched the first neo-Nazi journal in Argentina where he had fled. Later he went to Egypt and under an assumed Arabic name wrote anti-Zionist pamphlets for the Information Ministry, until his death in 1967. His widow (who shared his views) returned to Germany, where she embarrassed neo-Nazis by defending Hitler's "extermination" of the Jews openly, instead of classifying it among his "mistakes."

5. Hoess, *Commandant of Auschwitz*, p. 41. See also *To Mend the World*, p. 242n.

6. This letter is cited in nearly all Hitler biographies.

7. Exactly when and how the Final Solution was decided on is for historians to determine. For our part we assert only this much, that the extremes in the historians' debate are both absurd: that Hitler planned the Final Solution from the start, so that the whole process was ultimately the execution of but one man's plan; and that, since Hitler's Reich was a "totalitarian anarchy" composed of conflicting "fiefdoms," the "road" was so "crooked" as to reach Auschwitz only by accident. (See also *Jewish Return*, p. 68ff.) Clearly, the genocidal impulse was in the "movement" from the start, but it also took decisions on the road for it to be accelerated and intensified.

8. This speech of Himmler's, given on October 4, 1943, is quite rightly cited in many books dealing with the subject. See, e.g., Lucy Dawidowicz, *A Holocaust Reader* (New York: Behrman, 1976), pp. 120ff.

9. Dov Shilansky, *Musulman* (Tel Aviv: Menora, 1962), p. 123. For Nazi *Einsatzgruppen* to wear gloves when dealing with Jews was not unusual; see Goldhagen, "Weltanschauung und Endlösung," p. 586.

10. *The Yellow Spot: The Extermination of the Jews in Germany* (London: Gollancz, 1936), p. 47. The very title of this book refutes those who, years later, still claimed that they did not know and could not guess. In his moving (but unheeded) introduction the Bishop of Durham confessed—in 1936!—that in the records of persecution, many and sombre as they are, he could not find "anything quite equivalent to the persecution of the Jews which now proceeds in Germany" (p.6).

11. *Mein Kampf*, tr. Ralph Manheim (Boston: Houghton Mifflin, 1943), p. 65.

12. This completes our first account of the Holocaust world, with the focus on the criminals. It will be followed in Chapter IV, section 8 by a deeper account, in which the focus is on the victims. For the language employed in both these accounts, see *To Mend the World*, chapter I, section 8.

13. See *Werke*, IV, pp. 650ff. Also my article, "Schelling's Philosophy of the Literary Arts," *Philosophical Quarterly*, 1954, pp. 310ff.

15 *The Logic of Destruction*

It is not necessary to assume that the Nazi logic of destruction,[1] like Athene from the head of Zeus, leapt fully-armed from some Nazi bureaucratic mind. (Indeed, this assumption is farfetched.) It is more reasonable to assume a progress in which design and chance gradually—from the Nazi point of view, by good fortune or a stroke of genius—reached a sort of synthesis. We have elsewhere described the Sachsenhausen of 1938 (midway in the process) as "groundwork for Auschwitz,"[2] and will here briefly return to one aspect of this theme. Labor at Sachsenhausen had three components. One was meaningful work—tiles and uniforms for the Reich. The second was meaningless work—carrying sand from spot A to spot B one day, back the next day from spot B to spot A, always on the double. Both these aspects had an obvious purpose—the one, needed products, the other, torture of the prisoners—and were, so to speak, innocuous: they were open and above board. Each had many precedents—the one in economic history, the other in the history of torture—and left guards and prisoners in no doubt as to their role. All this was untrue of the third aspect of labor in Sachsenhausen: yet it was this that was the sole original aspect and also the most important. This was *meaningless labor endowed with a fictitious meaning.* Thus the daily march to and from the tile factory (a) had to be orderly, (b) was so organized as to produce inevitable chaos, and (c) was also so arranged that in the midst of chaos the fiction of order was maintained. The procedure was simple. Yet the principle was new and, in its implications, enormous and all-shattering. The two obvious purposes—the production of tiles and uniforms, and the torture of the prisoners—were synthesized into a whole, indeed, a world. And in this synthesis a new, eerie reality was given for all occupants of this world—on the one hand, the Kommandant and his henchmen,

Reprinted, with changes, from *To Mend the World*, (New York: Schocken Books, 1982), 206–15, by permission of the publisher.

145

on the other, the victims—to an old, time-honored, once-decent Prussian principle. The principle was: *Ordnung muss sein.* One considers the synthesis of the old and the new principles and already seems to visualize human beings marched to gas chambers by the sound of military music, greeted by the legend *Arbeit Macht Frei.*

Such was the labor aspect of the Nazi logic of destruction, while it was still taking shape. The complete shape of that logic was well described by Jean Améry as follows:

> In relation to the prisoner the SS was applying a logic of destruction that operated just as consistently as the logic of the preservation of life operated in the outside world. You always had to be cleanly shaven, but it was strictly forbidden to possess a razor or scissors, and you went to the barber only once every two weeks. On threat of punishment no button could be missing on the striped inmate suit, but if you lost one at work, which was inevitable, there was practically no chance of replacing it. You had to be strong, but were systematically weakened. Upon entrance into the camp everything was taken from you, but then you were derided by the robbers because you owned nothing. . . . The intellectual revolted [against this logic] in the impotence of mere thought. In the beginning he subscribed to the rebellious wisdom of folly that that which ought not to be cannot be. However, this was only the beginning. The rejection of the SS logic, the rebellious murmuring of incantations such as "but this is not possible" did not last long.[3]

That this was quite literally a logic of *destruction*—not one of mere petty chicanery—is corroborated by Filip Müller, "the only man who saw the Jewish people die and lived to tell what he saw."[4] Müller writes:

> Among the many slogans adorning the walls of our block [in Auschwitz] there was one which . . . warned us that "one louse may be your death." This was no exaggeration either, for a louse might infect its host with typhus, a disease which in Auschwitz spelled certain death. Alternatively, any louse discovered during a shirt check might have grave consequences in question. The reason for this could be found in the strange logic of what was known as Auschwitz justice. It argued that any prisoner on whom a louse was found after a delousing order had been issued, had obviously failed or, worse still, refused to obey orders and must therefore be severely punished. To be lousy in Auschwitz was a serious crime and liable to cost a man his life. That water came out of the taps only on special occasions or that we prisoners had neither soap nor towel was something in which nobody was interested.[5]

The last sentence in this passage should not be taken too literally. Some people—not necessarily everyone—were very much interested in the absence of soap and towels, and in the scarcity of water, and in the fictitious concern for the health of prisoners soon to be murdered.

But does even "destruction" exhaust this "logic"? The Gulag has rightly been called a "destructive labor camp."[6] The SS logic of destruction aimed at their victims' *self*-destruction as well. This found no clearer or more systematic expression than what is called—this too rightly—"excremental assault."[7] Again we ask how the system originated; and again we hazard the guess that in the origins—say, some time in 1933 or 1934—chance and design were intermingled. On the one hand, the prisoners must keep clean, which is to say that they must relieve themselves at places set aside for the purpose. But on the other hand, they cannot just wander off from work or roll call at any time of their own choosing. Both rules are innocuous in the sense defined above, and could be supported by the old Prussian principle already cited—that *Ordnung muss sein.* All innocuousness vanished, however, when sometime, somewhere, some bright architect of torture discovered—from the Nazi point of view, by good fortune or a stroke of genius— that while the two rules are not *intrinsically* in conflict, they can be *made to be so* quite easily, for the simple reason that "death . . . [is] planted in a need which . . . [cannot], like other needs, be repressed or delayed or passively endured, [for] the needs of the bowels are absolute."[8] A survivor writes:

> Imagine what it would be like to be forbidden to go to the toilet; imagine also that you were suffering from an increasingly severe dysentery, caused and aggravated by a diet of cabbage soup as well as by the constant cold. Naturally, you would try to go anyway. Sometimes you might succeed. But your absences would be noticed and you would be beaten, knocked down and trampled on. By now, you would know what the risks were, but urgency would oblige you to repeat the attempt, cost what it may. . . . I soon learned to deal with the dysentery by tying strings around the lower end of my drawers.[9]

Clearly, excremental assault was designed to produce in the victim a "self-disgust" to the point of wanting death or even committing suicide. And this— nothing less—was the essential goal. The Nazi logic of destruction was aimed, ultimately, at the victims' *self*-destruction.

One must ask why the Nazi logic took this further, unsurpassable step. The question must be pondered carefully. But no matter how hard one ponders it, any answer can only come to this: if Bolshevism can seek nothing higher from the "class"-enemy than a conversion, accompanied by confession to never-committed crimes, then Nazism can seek nothing higher from the "non-Aryan" "race"-enemy than self-destruction, preceded by self-transformation into the loathsome creature which, according to Nazi doctrine, he has been since birth. This answer may seem wrong, for the Nazi logic of destruction destroyed millions who were by no means loathsome since birth, among them not only political enemies but also members of "inferior races." (Women of Slavic origin *could* be chosen for the breeding policies of the master race.) Yet no other answer is intelligible. We are therefore forced to view "Aryans" subjected, say, to excremental assault, as being as it were, honorary Jews, and we do so in full knowledge of the fact that "a conquered Europe passed before the *Kommandant* at the [Auschwitz] gate, on their way to and from work: Polish, French, Russian, Yugoslav, Dutch, Belgian, Greek."[10]

That the Nazi logic of destruction aimed at Jewish self-destruction may be learned from no less an authority than the Führer himself. Hitler once remarked that the only decent Jew he ever heard of was the Viennese writer Otto Weininger who, desperately wanting but unable to be an "Aryan," committed suicide at the age of twenty-three in a fit of self-loathing. Much the same idea, transposed into Nazi humor, was expressed by Josef Goebbels when the *Anschluss* produced a rash of Jewish suicides in Vienna.

There is talk of mass Jewish suicide in Vienna. It is not true. The number of suicides remains the same. The difference is that whereas Germans committed suicide before, it is now Jews. We cannot provide every Viennese Jew with a special policeman to protect him from committing suicide.[11]

From the Nazi point of view, the ideal "solution" of the "Jewish problem" was wholesale Jewish suicide, but only if preceded and motivated by Jewish self-loathing, or wholesale Jewish self-loathing, but only if it was extreme enough to lead to Jewish suicide. This idea, to be sure, was not universally shared—not, for example, by those "SD intellectuals" who "wanted to be regarded as 'decent' " and merely wished to "solve the so-called Jewish problem in a cold, rational manner."[12] However, its acceptance was wide enough to set the tone for the world of Auschwitz and to dominate its logic.

This is not to deny that even in the highest SS circles there was room for some strange, not to say weird, exceptions. Rumor had it at the time that none other than Reinhard Heydrich had a "non-Aryan" ancestor. Refutations were produced, yet the rumor persisted. (It is believed by some to this day.)[13] After Heydrich's assassination by Czech patriots, Himmler delivered himself of the following:

He had overcome the Jew in himself by purely intellectual means and had swung over to the other side. He was convinced that the Jewish elements in his blood were damnable; he hated the blood which played him so false. The *Führer* could really have picked no better man than Heydrich for the campaign against the Jews. For them he was without mercy or pity.

For the rest it will interest you to know that Heydrich was a very good violinist. He once played a serenade in my honor; it was really excellent—a pity he did not do more in this field.[14]

The opportunity to "overcome the Jew in himself" was given to the chief architect of the Final Solution. It was not given to his victims.

Hitler's ideal "solution" of the "Jewish problem" was hampered less by insufficient zeal on the part of his operators than by recalcitrance on the part of his Jewish victims. Jews sick with self-hatred rarely reached the point of suicide. Jews committing suicide did so far less frequently out of self-loathing than out of despair or self-respect.[15] Most serious of all, so long as they were still able to choose at all, they chose life much rather than death, and loathed (or despised) their persecutors rather than themselves. From the Nazi point of view, this was one obstacle to the ideal goal. Still more serious was another: Jewish babies, like all babies, are incapable of either self-loathing or suicide. In their case, the ideal Nazi "solution" of the "Jewish problem" was impossible. There were not many adult Weiningers. Baby Weiningers do not exist.

If Jews would not commit suicide in self-loathing, then driving them into death was, from the Nazi point of view, the next best thing. Perhaps it was even the best thing. For, as Jean Améry has written, "There was a Germany that drove Jews and political opponents into death, since it believed itself capable of self-realization only in this manner.[16] (Would not widespread Jewish suicide frustrate this form of self-realization?) These are two ways of looking at the matter. It is hard to say which is more adequate.

In any case, one characteristic action of the Holocaust world was the most painful possible murder of Jewish babies, conducted, whenever possible, in the hearing or sight of their mothers. The reader will remember—how could he forget—the testimony of a Polish guard at the Nuremberg trials.[17] [It is easy to] cast doubt on the witness's opinion that the children were thrown into the flames alive for reasons of economy alone. That this hypothesis is false is proved by the testimony of a Ravensbrück survivor. She reports:

> In 1942 the medical service of the Revier were required to perform abortions on all pregnant women. If a child happened to born alive, it would be smothered or drowned in a bucket *in front of the mother*. Given a newborn child's natural resistance to drowning, a *baby's agony might last for twenty or thirty minutes.*[18]

The italics are ours. They are not by the eye-witness author. Perhaps a survivor of Auschwitz or Ravensbrück no longer knows what, and what not, to italicize.

Such, in the case of Jewish babies and their mothers, was the Nazi "solution" of the "Jewish problem" that approximated most closely the ideal or even expressed it perfectly. With adults there was greater variety, as well as much room for ingenuity. To follow one line of thought, if one could not make Jews destroy themselves one could, perhaps, make them destroy each other. By making some Jews rule over others one could achieve this aim equally by using the base and the noble. Base Jewish rulers would destroy the Jews ruled by them, so as to save themselves. Noble Jews would sacrifice some Jews they ruled so as to save others. Neither type of Jewish ruler, of course, would himself be spared. The base would not long survive their victims. The noble, in addition, would not wish to survive them, for—so they thought—their own souls were already destroyed. Was there ever a nobler and more tragic Jewish ruler than Adam Czerniakow, who "stood at the helm" of the Warsaw Ghetto and "died with his people"?[19]

This was an indirect method of making Jews—collectively if not individually—destroy themselves, and it called for much ingenuity. But there were also direct methods, some of which required no ingenuity at all, and of these—since all men must defecate—excremental assault was probably the most universally effective. (Other worlds have dreamt of making men equal in possessions, rights, dignity, holiness: the Auschwitz world sought to reduce its victims to the equality of the bowels.) The action most revelatory of the Gulag world is assault-by-psychiatry on dissidents, on the grounds that critics of the already-existing, perfect society can only be insane. The action most revelatory of the Holocaust world was excremental assault on Jews—and, as we have seen, all honorary Jews sucked into the system—on the ground that, before dying, they must be *made* into the self-loathing vermin that, according to Nazi thought, they *are*. Hence Treblinka Kommandant Franz Stangl lied when he said that the purpose of all the humiliation and cruelty was to make killing easier on the nerves of the operators. ("It is easier to kill a dog than a man, easier still to kill a rat or frog, and no problem at all to kill insects.")[20] At best he spoke a half-truth. Is shooting a person—quickly, cleanly—harder on the nerves than conducting the slow, methodical process by which a person is reduced to a dog, a rat, an insect—or, if to none of these, to a human being who is already dead while he is still alive? Beyond doubt this living death was not a means to death only, but also an end in itself. The most characteristic success of the Gulag world is one new man—the former dissident who voluntarily undergoes psychiatric treatment on the grounds that his erstwhile dissent was ipso facto insanity. The most characteristic success of the Holocaust world—other than the screams and gasps of the children and the agony of their mothers—is another new man: the *Muselmann* who is already dead while still alive. . . . And since the screams and gasps of Jewish children are no different from those of other children, we must conclude that the *Muselmann*—"one hesitates to call him living, and hesitates to call his death death"—is the most notable, if indeed not the sole, truly original contribution of the Third Reich to civilization. He is the true *novum* of the New Order.[21]

Notes

1. A phrase coined by Jean Améry.

2. *Jewish Return*, chapter 5.

3. Améry, pp. 10–11.

4. Yehuda Bauer, in Filip Müller, *Auschwitz Inferno* (London: Routledge and Kegan Paul, 1979), p. xi.

5. Ibid., pp. 6ff.

6. By Aleksandr I. Solzhenitsyn.

7. The apt title of chapter 3 in Terrence Des Pres, *The Survivor* (New York: Oxford University Press, 1976). That chapter, and indeed Des Pres's entire book, should be read in conjunction with the present section.

8. Ibid., p. 55.

9. Micheline Maurel, *An Ordinary Camp*, tr. Margaret S. Summers (New York: Simon and Schuster, 1958), pp. 38 ff., quoted by Des Pres, *The Survivor*, pp. 55ff.

10. Lewinska, p. 71. In an essay dated July 1979, unpublished but widely circulated, John Murray Cuddihy asks why such as myself consider the Holocaust unique, proceeds to state the "obvious first answer" that it "*was* unique," but manages to ignore this answer in the whole rest of his essay, in favor of a largely irrelevant mixture of liberal-Christian apologetics and sociological ruminations. Had he stayed with his own "first answer," he would have had to notice that, with the sole possible exception of Gypsies, only Jews were condemned by Nazi doctrine to "removal" (*Entfernung*) *solely because they were.* And he might also then have understood that my previous description (*Jewish Return*, p. 93) of non-Jewish "innocent victims" as "quasi-Jews," reflects not a placing of them into some lesser "residual category" but rather the fact that they too—as if they were Jews—were murdered simply because they *were*.

11. Quoted by Arthur D. Morse, *While Six Million Died* (New York: Random House, 1967), pp. 204ff.

12. See Heinz Höhne, *The Order of the Death's Head* (London: Pan, 1969), pp. 301ff. I have already criticized Höhne for failing to ask whether the "cold, rational manner" in which the "problem" was "solved" at Auschwitz does not make the "decent" "SD intellectuals" more deadly than the Streicher-type "fanatics" (see *Jewish Return*, pp. 69ff.). In any case, as is recognized by historians more reflective than Höhne, without the cooperation of the "decent" ones the aim wanted by the "fanatics" would have been unattainable.

13. For the decisive refutation, see Jacob Robinson, *And the Crooked Shall Be Made Straight* (Philadelphia: Jewish Publication Society, 1965), pp. 145ff. The story is still accepted by Joachim C. Fest, *The Face of the Third Reich* (New York: Penguin, 1979), p. 163.

14. Cited from Kersten's *Memoirs* by Fest, *The Face of the Third Reich*, p. 165. Kersten was Himmler's masseur and confidant.

15. An instance in which despair and self-respect were combined is reported from Mauthausen. Eugen Kogon writes: "The second day after their arrival the Jews were shunted into the quarry. They were not allowed to use the steps to the bottom of the pit: they had to slide down the loose stones at the side and . . . many died or were severely injured. The survivors then had to shoulder hods, and two prisoners were compelled to load each Jew with an excessively heavy rock. The Jews then had to run up the steps. In some instances the rocks immediately rolled downhill, crushing the feet of those be-

hind. Many of the Jews were driven to despair the very first day and committed suicide by jumping into the pit. On the third day the S.S. opened the so-called 'Death Gate' and with a fearful barrage of blows drove the Jews across the guard line, the guards on the watchtowers shooting them down in heaps with their machine-guns. The next day the Jews no longer jumped into the pit individually. They joined hands and one man would pull nine or twelve of his comrades over the lip into a gruesome death." *The Theory and Practice of Hell* (New York: Berkeley, 1964, p. 180).

This passage recalls nothing so much as the opening words of a prayer probably composed during the Crusade of 1096 for the Jewish victims of Mayence and Worms: "May the Merciful Father who dwells on high in His infinite mercy remember those saintly, upright and blameless souls . . . who gave their lives for the sanctification of the divine Name. They were lovely and amiable in their life, and were not parted in their death. . . ."

16. Améry, p. 11. I have altered the Rosenfeld translation slightly.

17. See *To Mend the World*, p. 131. The Polish guard's testimony should now be quoted more fully, as follows:

"*Witness:* Women carrying children were always sent with them to the crematorium. The children were then torn from their parents outside the crematorium and sent to the gas chambers separately. When the extermination of the Jews in the gas chambers was at its height, orders were issued that the children were to be thrown into the crematorium furnaces, or into the pit near the crematorium, without being gassed first.

"*Smirnov* (Russian prosecutor): How am I to understand this? Did they throw them into the fire alive, or did they kill them first?

"*Witness:* They threw them in alive.

"*Smirnov:* Why did they do this?

"*Witness:* It is very difficult to say. We don't know whether they wanted to economize on gas, or if it was because there was not enough room in the gas chambers."

18. Germaine Tillion, *Ravensbrück* (New York: Anchor, 1975), p. 77.

19. Raul Hilberg sent to this family a copy of *The Warsaw Diary of Adam Czerniakow*, ed. Raul Hilberg, Stanislaw Staron, Josef Kermisz (New York: Stein and Day, 1979). This he inscribed as follows: "For Emil and Rose Fackenheim—this incomparable log from one who stood at the helm and died with his people."

20. A remark of Hannah Arendt's quoted by Des Pres, *The Survivor*, p. 61. Gitta Sereny asked Stangl: "If they were going to kill them anyway, what was the point of all the humiliation, why the cruelty?" Stangl replied: "To condition those who actually had to carry out the policies; to make it possible for them to do what they did." Sereny comments: "And this, I believe, was true" (Gitta Sereny, *Into That Darkness* [London: Andre Deutsch, 1974], p. 101). Despite certain weaknesses that may be guessed from the last-cited comment, Sereny's interviews of Stangl are of the greatest importance. Like Hoess's autobiography, they must be read to be believed. And even then they remain past belief.

21. This concludes my second, and more difficult, attempt to write in the language of "restrained outrage" (see *To Mend the World*, chapter I, section 8, and p. 188).

16 *The Evil of the Leaders*

Let us begin by considering the actual torturers and murderers and take both them and their victims as "conditioned." ("It is easier to kill a dog than a man, easier yet to kill a rat or frog, and no problem at all to kill insects.")[1] But then we *resist* our having-taken-them-thus as a *having-been* taken, as an amoral indulgence and an intellectual weakness, with the spectre not far away of a yielding to the lure of the evil kingdom: the victims, including the *Muselmänner* and to say nothing of the babies, are *not* and *never became* insects; and *not a single one* of the torturers and murderers was *simply* "conditioned" to view or treat them as such.

We consider next, Kommandant Hoess, the immediate conditioner. No person in his senses, of course, will take him as he portrays himself in that unbelievable autobiography of his which we have already cited, for he is a criminal and a liar who shows no signs of repentance. However, we *do* take him on *some* things as he takes himself. After all, we do and must see the system as dynamic, ever-escalating, all-absorbing, overwhelming. Also, we do and must see the Kommandant himself as a brutal soldier-type, to be sure, but not as a raving sadist or maniac but rather well within the bounds of human normalcy. Hence we will wish to take his word to the effect that his last truly free act was the voluntary joining of the "ranks of the active SS," and that thereafter there "was no returning." Hence, too, we will wish to take him—the one who directly gives the orders and is at hand to see the results—as being "not indifferent to human suffering." Having taken both, we are then led to see the strange—nay, unique—spectacle of Hoess watching the torture and the murders as though not he but someone else had ordered them, and of the Kommandant commiserating, not with his victims but rather with his own tender self that is compelled to watch such scenes.[2] We see the spec-

Reprinted, with changes, from *To Mend the World* (New York: Schocken Books, 1982), 241–47 by permission of the publisher.

tacle, and end up understanding it, if understand it we can, as a strange case of "schizophrenia."[3] We *take* all this, and then *resist* our having taken it thus as a snare and a horrifying temptation. It is *not true* that there was "no returning" for Hoess. Like other, less highly placed ones, Hoess was at *all* times free to volunteer for the Russian front: he *chose not to use* that freedom.[4] He was not sick with schizophrenia; his condition was self-induced, hence not shizophrenia at all. Doubtless there is a sense in which one can speak of all of Nazi Germany as suffering from a universal split consciousness, and say that this condition made possible the committing and condoning of heinous crimes with a well-conditioned conscience. But in speaking in this manner we must not fail to notice that "conditioned conscience" is a moral and intellectual scandal. As for such as Kommandant Hoess, they were the *producers* of the split in question, as much as its products. Who produced it if not such as he?

In answer to this question we turn from Hoess, the immediate conditioner, to more remote conditioners such as Eichmann and Himmler—more remote, and hence better able to avoid watching the results of their orders. The one is a model bureaucrat who admits quite readily to the desk murder of millions that conforms to regulations, but at the same time denies hotly (and quite possibly truthfully) the charge of having killed just a single Jew personally—an action that he would presumably consider highly irregular. The other is an ideologue who supervises it all, makes speeches boasting about it all, but who cannot stand the sight when he witnesses it. Thus we take Eichmann and Himmler as removed from the flesh-and-blood torture and murder by the abstractions, respectively, of bureaucracy and ideology. But then we remember—we must *force ourselves* to remember, for the thought slips away—Eichmann's smirk in Jerusalem and Himmler's gloves at Auschwitz, and we catch ourselves as being, as it were, on the brink of philosophical blasphemy—the dissipation of an unspeakable evil into the product of a faceless, impersonal, possibly even "value-free" (though ideologically-inspired) technological apparatus that is the work of everyone and no one. . . . We *must* resist it. But can we do more?

We can do at least one thing more, namely, consider the ultimate author of the Final Solution. In the case of Hitler we find that while the "doctrine" is always both clear and public there is nothing but a "striking silence" about the ultimate "consequences" of the doctrine: indeed, "not a single concrete reference of his to the practice of annihilation has come down to us." Thus we are inclined to take a noted historian's "guess" as to the "motives" of the Führer's "silence about the central concern of his life," listed by him as composed of a "characteristic mania for secrecy, a remnant of bourgeois morality [and] the desire to keep what was happening abstract and not weaken his own passion by letting him see what it led to."[5] We take this guess, and indeed take it as natural, . . . Yet we must then resist our having-taken it, for it pushes us in the direction of the ultimate absurdity. Formerly our thought, following conventional wisdom, was driven toward the view that only one was responsible, that all the others, ultimately considered, were cogs in the wheel. Now that at length we reach this one, are we to point back to all the others as responsible for the "consequences," while this one is guilty of nothing more than the "doctrine"—a nineteenth-century platitude until it was acted on?[6] Or, more precisely, that having given the "abstract" *Führerbefehl*, he withdrew from the scene and the responsibility? In its search of the *doers* of the evil deed, is our thought to point from the lower to the higher and highest in the order of command, only in order to lapse, once having reached the highest, into the vast absurdity of pointing back to the lower and lowest? (Are we to end up with the unknown soldier who was an SS torturer and murderer, and with him alone?) *Is the evil—the doers are inseparable from the deeds, and the deeds are inseparable from the doers—to be located wherever thought is not?*

The most extreme outcome of such a way of thinking—or rather, of *not* thinking that which is most of all in need of being thought—is the thesis that the Holocaust never happened at all. This, of course, is a Nazi or neo-Nazi thesis which is not respectable. (It should be mentioned, however, that at this time of writing there are learned professors who advance this thesis, and that others defend them in the name of academic freedom.) However, quite respectable, it seems—or in any case neither Nazi nor neo-Nazi—is the thesis that while the *Endlösung* doubtless happened, *nobody really wanted it*, that it was "what the Germans call a *Verlegenheitslösung*—the way out of an awkward dilemma." True, Hitler ordered the wholesale persecution, deportation, ghettoization of the Jewish people. That he did not order their wholesale murder is argued by the respectable work under consideration not only from the absence of conclusive documentary evidence but also—an argument given much greater weight by the author—from the fact that, if ones studies Hitler with some empathy and through the testimonies of those who knew him, followed him, admired, or even loved him, then the Führer emerges as a figure not lacking in humanity. (If one studied them in the same manner one would presumably reach a similar conclusion about Himmler and Heydrich, Eichmann and Hoess.) Then why did *anybody* do it? David Irving, the author of the massive, two-volume work under review, writes as follows:

> Hitler had unquestionably decreed that Europe's Jews were to be "swept back" to the east. . . . But the SS authorities, Gauleiters and regional commissars and governors in "the east" proved wholly unequal to the problems caused by this uprooting in midwar. The Jews were brought by the trainload to ghettos already overcrowded and underprovisioned.[7]

It seems that if a bureaucrat has sleepless nights because he cannot house and feed masses of men, women, and children entrusted to his care, then the best *Lösung* of the problem (and an end to the sleepless nights) is wholesale murder. Such is the absurd outcome of *not* thinking what is above all in need of being thought.

It is present in a "revisionism" that has come to be widespread. Above we showed that the Holocaust was the climax of the sole firm commitment—the "removal" of the Jews—in what was otherwise a revolution of nihilism. The passage of time has produced a total perversion of the truth, to the effect that the Holocaust was some sort of *Betriebsunfall* ("factory accident") and that Hitler was nothing worse than a conventional (if "extreme") nationalist politician—at least until, plagued by gastric troubles, a maxillary sinus needing irrigation, and a quack physician who gave him poison instead of medicine, he lost his grip. Such is the perverse revisionism that has been produced by the passage of time. The passage of time alone, of course, would never have produced it, were it not for the inherent difficulty—and widespread unwillingness—to think the unthinkable.

That even minds wholly immune to perversity may lapse into locating the evil where thought is not, is illustrated by an incident that occurred during the Nuremberg Trials. (Many other illustrations could be given.) With Hitler dead, Goering was Nazi number one, and Captain G.M. Gilbert, a U.S. Army psychologist, interviewed him and all the other big Nazi criminals almost every day while the proceedings were under way. In these interviews, Goering proved that he had not been Nazi number two for nothing, by the jovial bluster with which he managed to give tit for tat on such charges as waging aggressive warfare and committing war crimes. Only with the Holocaust was this impossible, but this subject Goering adroitly avoided. One day this could not be done, for a witness had testified how the children were thrown into the crematorium alive. Goering responded by denying all knowledge. He said: "You know how it is even in a battalion—a battalion commander doesn't know anything that goes on in the line. The higher you stand, the less you see of what is going on below." Goering's response no longer surprises us. Hoess had blamed the tortures, if not the murders, on those below him—and was himself the immediate conditioner who watched the results. Goering blamed the whole crime on those beneath him—and was himself the man who had charged Heydrich with the Final Solution. In both cases the "schizophrenia," if any, was self-induced, and is, in this exploration, no longer remarkable. What *is* remarkable is the reaction of Gilbert who reports the incident. The American captain was a shrewd, tough-minded, high-minded interviewer. He was well-equipped to understand Goering's kind of "schizophrenia" or (to put it bluntly) to recognize a liar when he heard one. Yet though he criticizes Goering's "explanation" he nevertheless accepts it. He writes: "I could hardly have thought of a more damning argument against the military hierarchy, but Goering, in his militaristic perversion, thought he had given a reasonable explanation."[8] Such is the fate of a thought that lapses into not thinking or, which is the same thing, that locates the evil that must be thought where thought is not.

This fate—in its high-minded version, to say nothing of its perverted, low-minded version—can be avoided only by a thought that is determined *to place itself and the evil to be thought, as it were, into the same space.* Yet, since the evil systematically eludes it, thought can abide by this determination only indirectly, i.e., by means of a pursuit radical enough so as to move circularly and thus to grasp the evil *as a whole.* But just what is this grasp? We have already insisted that it is not a comprehension. It is, rather, at once a *surprised acceptance and a horrified resistance.* It is a horrified surprise and, since the thought that is *in* this surprise is forced to accept what is yet in all eternity unacceptable, *thought is required to become "ecstatic," such as to point beyond resistance within its own native sphere, to a resistance that is beyond the sphere of thought altogether, and in the sphere of life.* Kant's moral will would not be moral at all if, instead of willing-to-act, it withdrew into the enjoyment of its own purity. Resistance-in-thought to the Holocaust would degenerate into academic self-satisfaction unless it climaxed in calling for, praying for, working for, resistance in life.

Notes

1. See *To Mend the World,* p. 214n.
2. Hoess writes: "On one occasion two small children were so absorbed in some game that they quite refused to let their mother tear them away from it. Even the Jews of the Special Detach-

ment were reluctant to pick the children up. The imploring look in the eyes of the mother who certainly knew what was happening, is something I shall never forget. The people were already in the gas-chamber and becoming restive, and I had to act. Everyone was looking at me. I nodded to the junior non-commissioned officer on duty and he picked up the screaming, struggling children in his arms and carried them into the gas-chamber, accompanied by their mother who was weeping in the most heart-rending fashion. My pity was so great that I longed to vanish from the scene: yet I might not show the slightest trace of emotion. I had to see everything. I had to watch hour after hour . . ."(*Commandant of Auschwitz*, pp. 172 ff; see also pp. 66, 72, 86). Martin Broszat comments: "His psychological egocentricity enabled Hoess to transform a vicious murder of defenseless children into a tragedy for the murderer" (*Kommandant in Auschwitz*, ed. Martin Broszat [Stuttgart: Deutsche Verlags-Anstalt, 1958], p.18).

3. Fest, *The Face of the Third Reich*, pp. 425, 427; Broszat, *Kommandant in Auschwitz*, p. 17. Broszat writes: "Hoess is an extreme case of the universal split consciousness that made it possible for countless human beings in Nazi Germany to serve the regime of Hitler and Himmler with a feeling of selfless devotion and undisturbed consciousness, even when it was no longer possible to ignore its criminal character" (p. 18).

4. Otto Friedrich writes: "Dr. Ella Lingens, a prisoner, recalled at the Frankfurt trial that there was one island of peace—at the [Auschwitz] Babice subcamp, because of an officer named Flacke. 'How he did it I don't know,' she testified. 'His camp was clean and the food also.' The Frankfurt judge, who had heard endless protestations that orders had to be obeyed, was amazed. " 'Do you wish to say,' he asked, "that everyone could decide for himself to be either good or evil at Auschwitz?' " 'That is exactly what I wish to say,' she answered" ("The Kingdom of Auschwitz," *Toronto Globe and Mail*, October 2, 1981, p. 10).

5. Joachim D. Fest, *Hitler* (New York: Vintage, 1975), p. 681.

6. After having shown that Hitler's "ideas," far from original, had by 1914 "become the common-places of radical anti-Semitic and pan-German journalism and cafe-talk in every city in Central Europe," the historian Alan Bullock goes on: "Hitler's originality lay not in his ideas, but in the terrifyingly literal way in which he set to work to translate fantasy into reality, and his unequalled grasp of the means to do this" (cited in *Encounters*, p. 193). See also *To Mend the World*, p. 296n.

7. David Irving, *Hitler's War* (New York: Viking, 1977), p. xivff.

8. G. M. Gilbert, *Nuremberg Diary* (New York: Signet, 1947). p. 163.

THE EXPOSURE TO AUSCHWITZ AND THE 614TH COMMANDMENT

17 *The 614th Commandment*

Our topic has two presuppositions which, I take it, we are not going to question but will simply take for granted. First, there is a unique and unprecedented crisis in this period of Jewish history which needs to be faced by all Jews, from the Orthodox at one extreme to the secularists at the other. (Thus we are not going to discuss the various forms of Judaism and Jewishness as though nothing had happened.) Second, whatever our response to the present crisis, it will be, in any case, a stubborn persistence in our Jewishness, not an attempt to abandon it or escape from it. (Thus we shall leave dialogues with Jews who do not want to be Jews for another day.)

How shall we understand the crisis of this period in Jewish history? We shall, I believe, be misled if we think in the style of the social sciences which try to grasp the particular in terms of the universal. We shall then, at best, understand the present Jewish crisis only in terms of the universal Western or human crisis, thus failing to grasp its uniqueness; at worst we shall abuse such an understanding as a means of escaping into the condition of contemporary-man-in-general. Instead of relying on the sociological mind, we must rely on the historical mind, which moves from the particular to the universal. But the historical mind, too, has its limitations. Thus no contemporary Jewish historian at the time of the destruction of the First or the Second Temple could have fully understood the world-historical significance of that event, if only because, in the midst of the crisis, he was not yet on the other side of it. We, too, are in the midst of the contemporary crisis, and hence unable fully to understand it. As for our attitude toward the future, this cannot be one of understanding or prediction, but only one of commitment and, possibly, faith.

Reprinted from *The Jewish Return into History* (New York: Schocken Books, 1978), 19–24, by permission of the publisher.

157

How shall we achieve such fragmentary understanding of our present crisis as is possible while we are still in the midst of it? A crisis as yet unended can only be understood in terms of contradictions as yet unresolved. Jewish existence today is permeated by three main contradictions:

1. The American Jew of today is a "universalist," if only because he has come closer to the full achievement of equal status in society than any other Jew in the history of the Diaspora; yet this development coincides with the resurrection of Jewish "particularism" in the rebirth of a Jewish nation.

2. The Jew of today is committed to modern "secularism," as the source of his emancipation; yet his future survival as Jew depends on past religious resources. Hence even the most Orthodox Jew of today is a secularist insofar as, and to the extent that, he participates in the political and social processes of society. And even the most secularist Jew is religious insofar as, and to the extent that, he must fall back on the religious past in his struggle for a Jewish future.

3. Finally—and this is by far the most radical contradiction, and one which threatens to engulf the other two—the Jew in two of the three main present centers of Jewry, America and Israel, is at home in the modern world, for he has found a freedom and autonomy impossible in the premodern world. Yet he is but twenty-five years removed from a catastrophe unequaled in all of Jewish history—a catastrophe that in its distinctive characterizations is modern in nature.

These are the three main contradictions. Merely to state them is to show how false it would be for us to see our present Jewish crisis as nothing more than an illustration of the general Western or human crisis. I will add to the general point nothing more than the mere listing of two specific examples. First, we may have a problem with "secularity," like our Christian neighbors. But our problem is not theirs, if only because for us—who have "celebrated" the secular city since the French Revolution—the time for such celebrating is past since the Holocaust. Second, while we have our problems with academically inspired atheism and agnosticism, they are central at best only for Jews who want to be men-in-general. For the authentic Jew who faces up to his singled-out Jewish condition—even for the authentic agnostic or atheistic Jew—a merely academically inspired doubt in God must seem sophomoric when he, after Auschwitz, must grapple with despair.

We must, then, take care lest we move perversely in responding to our present crisis. We must first face up and respond to our Jewish singled-out condition. Only thus and then can we hope to enter authentically into an understanding of and relation with other manifestations of a present crisis which is doubtless universal.

In groping for authentic responses to our present Jewish crisis, we do well to begin with responses which have already occurred. I believe that there are two such responses: first, a commitment to Jewish survival; and second, a commitment to Jewish unity.

I confess I used to be highly critical of Jewish philosophies which seemed to advocate no more than survival for survival's sake. I have changed my mind. I now believe that, in this present, unbelievable age, even a mere collective commitment to Jewish group-survival for its own sake is a momentous response, with the greatest implications. I am convinced that future historians will understand it, not, as our present detractors would have it, as the tribal response-mechanism of a fossil, but rather as a profound, albeit as yet fragmentary, act of faith, in an age of crisis to which the response might well have been either flight in total disarray or complete despair.

The second response we have already found is a commitment to Jewish unity. This, to be sure, is incomplete and must probably remain incomplete. Yet it is nonetheless real. Thus, the American Council for Judaism is an anachronism, as is, I venture to say, an Israeli nationalism which would cut off all ties with the Diaspora. No less anachronistic is a Jewish secularism so blind in its worship of the modern secular world as wholly to spurn the religious resources of the Jewish past; likewise, an Orthodoxy so untouched by the modern secular world as to have remained in a premodern ghetto.

Such, then, are the responses to the present crisis in Jewish history which we have already found in principle, however inadequately in practice. And their implications are even now altogether momentous. Whether aware of what we have decided or not, we have made the collective decision to endure the contradictions of present Jewish existence. We have collectively rejected the option, either of "checking out" of Jewish existence altogether or of so avoiding the present contradictions as to shatter Jewish existence into fragments.

But the question now is whether we can go beyond so fragmentary a commitment. In the present situation, this question becomes: can we confront the Holocaust, and yet not despair? Not accidentally has it taken twenty years for us to face this question, and it is not certain that we can face it yet. The contradiction is too staggering, and every authentic escape is barred. *For we are forbidden to turn present and future life into death, as the price of remembering death at Auschwitz. And we are equally forbidden to affirm present and future life, at the price of forgetting Auschwitz.*

We have lived in this contradiction for twenty years without being able to face it. Unless I am mistaken, we are now beginning to face it, however fragmentarily and inconclusively. And from this beginning confrontation there emerges what I will boldly term a 614th commandment: *the authentic Jew of today is forbidden to hand Hitler yet another, posthumous victory.* (This formulation is terribly inadequate, yet I am forced to use it until one more adequate is found. First, although no anti-Orthodox implication is intended, as though the 613 commandments stood necessarily in need of change, we must face the fact that something radically new has happened. Second, although the commandment should be positive rather than negative, we must face the fact that Hitler did win at least one victory—the murder of six million Jews. Third, although the very name of Hitler should be erased rather than remembered, we cannot disguise the uniqueness of his evil under a comfortable generality, such as persecution-in-general, tyranny-in-general, or even the demonic-in-general.)

I think the authentic Jew of today is beginning to hear the 614th commandment. And he hears it whether, as agnostic, he hears no more, or whether, as believer, he hears the voice of the *metzaveh* (the commander) in the *mitzvah* (the commandment). Moreover, it may well be the case that the authentic Jewish agnostic and the authentic Jewish believer are closer today than at any previous time.

To be sure, the agnostic hears no more than the *mitzvah*. Yet if he is Jewishly authentic, he cannot but face the fragmentariness of his hearing. He cannot, like agnostics and atheists all around him, regard this *mitzvah* as the product of self-sufficient human reason, realizing itself in an ever-advancing history of autonomous human enlightenment. The 614th commandment must be, to him, an abrupt and absolute *given*, revealed in the midst of total catastrophe.

On the other hand, the believer, who bears the voice of the *metzaveh* in the *mitzvah*, can hardly hear anything more than the *mitzvah*. The reasons that made Martin Buber speak of an eclipse of God are still compelling. And if, nevertheless, a bond between Israel and the God of Israel can be experienced in the abyss, this can hardly be more than the *mitzvah* itself.

The implications of even so slender a bond are momentous. If the 614th commandment is binding upon the authentic Jew, then we are, first, commanded to survive as Jews, lest the Jewish people perish. We are commanded, second, to remember in our very guts and bones the martyrs of the Holocaust, lest their memory perish. We are forbidden, thirdly, to deny or despair of God, however much we may have to contend with him or with belief in him, lest Judaism perish. We are forbidden, finally, to despair of the world as the place which is to become the kingdom of God, lest we help make it a meaningless place in which God is dead or irrelevant and everything is permitted. To abandon any of these imperatives, in response to Hitler's victory at Auschwitz, would be to hand him yet other, posthumous victories.

How can we possibly obey these imperatives? To do so requires the endurance of intolerable contradictions. Such endurance cannot but bespeak an as yet unutterable faith. If we are capable of this endurance, then the faith implicit in it may well be of historic consequence. At least twice before—at the time of the destruction of the First and of the Second Temples—Jewish endurance in the midst of catastrophe helped transform the world. We cannot know the future, if only because the present is without precedent. But this ignorance on our part can have no effect on our present action. The uncertainty of what will be may not shake our certainty of what we must do.

18 *Jewish Faith and the Holocaust: A Fragment*

I

Within the past two centuries, three events have shaken and are still shaking Jewish religious existence—the Emancipation and its aftereffects, the Nazi Holocaust, and the rise of the first Jewish state in two thousand years—and of these, two have occurred in our own generation. From the point of view of Jewish religious existence, as from so many other points of view, the Holocaust is the most shattering. Doubtless the Emancipation and all its works have posed and continue to pose powerful challenges, with which Jewish thought has been wrestling all along—scientific agnosticism, secularism, assimilation, and the like. The Emancipation presents, however, a challenge *ab extra*, from without, and for all its well-demonstrated power to weaken and undermine Jewish religious existence, I have long been convinced that the challenge can be met, religiously and intellectually. The state of Israel, by contrast, is a challenge *ab intra*, from within—at least to much that Jewish existence has been throughout two millennia. But this challenge is positive—the fact that in one sense (if not in many others) a long exile has ended. That it represents a positive challenge was revealed during and immediately after the Six Day War, when biblical (i.e., preexilic) language suddenly came to life.

The Holocaust, too, challenges Jewish faith from within, but the negativity of its challenge is total, without light or relief. After the events associated with the name of Auschwitz, everything is shaken, nothing is safe.

To avoid Auschwitz, or to act as though it had never occurred, would be blasphemous. Yet how face it and be faithful to its victims? No precedent exists either within Jewish history or outside it. Even when a Jewish religious thinker barely begins to face Auschwitz, he perceives the possibility of a desperate choice between the faith of a millennial Jewish past, which has so far persisted through

Reprinted, with changes, from *The Jewish Return into History* (New York: Schocken Books, 1978), 25–32, by permission of the publisher.

every trial, and faithfulness to the victims of the present. But at the edge of this abyss there must be a great pause, a lengthy silence, and an endurance.

II

Men shun the scandal of the particularity of Auschwitz. Germans link it with Dresden; American liberals, with Hiroshima. Christians deplore antisemitism-in-general, while Communists erect monuments to victims-of-Fascism-in-general, depriving the dead of Auschwitz of their Jewish identity even in death. Rather than face Auschwitz, men everywhere seek refuge in generalities, comfortable precisely because they are generalities. And such is the extent to which reality is shunned that no cries of protest are heard even when in the world community's own forum obscene comparisons are made between Israeli soldiers and Nazi murderers.

The Gentile world shuns Auschwitz because of the terror of Auschwitz—and because of real or imagined implication in the guilt for Auschwitz. But Jews shun Auschwitz as well. Only after many years did significant Jewish responses begin to appear. Little of real significance is being or can be said even now. Perhaps there should still be silence. It is certain, however, that the voices, now beginning to be heard, will grow ever louder and more numerous. For Jews now know that they must ever after remember Auschwitz, and be its witnesses to the world. Not to be a witness would be a betrayal. In the murder camps the victims often rebelled with no other hope than that one of them might escape to tell the tale. For Jews now to refrain from telling the tale would be unthinkable. Jewish faith still recalls the Exodus, Sinai, the two destructions of the Temple. A Judaism that survived at the price of ignoring Auschwitz would not deserve to survive.

It is because the world shrinks so fully from the truth that once a Jew begins to speak at all he must say the most obvious. Must he say that the death of a Jewish child at Auschwitz is no more lamentable than the death of a German child at Dresden? He must say it. And in saying it, he must also refuse to dissolve Auschwitz into suffering-in-general, even though he is almost sure to be considered a Jewish particularist who cares about Jews but not about mankind. Must he distinguish between the mass-killing at Hiroshima and that at Auschwitz? At the risk of being thought a sacrilegious quibbler, he must, with endless patience, forever repeat that Eichmann was moved by no such "rational" objective as victory when he diverted trains needed for military purposes in order to dispatch Jews to their death. He must add that there was no "irrational" objective either. Torquemada burned bodies in order to save souls. Eichmann sought to destroy both bodies and souls. Where else and at what other time have executioners ever separated those to be murdered now from those to be murdered later to the strain of Viennese waltzes? Where else has human skin ever been made into lampshades, and human body-fat into soap—not by isolated perverts but under the direction of ordinary bureaucrats? Auschwitz is a unique descent into hell. It is an unprecedented celebration of evil. It is evil for evil's sake.

A Jew must bear witness to this truth. Nor may he conceal the fact that Jews in their particularity were the singled-out victims. Of course, they were by no means the sole victims. And a Jew would infinitely prefer to think that to the Nazis, Jews were merely a species of the genus "inferior race." This indeed was the theme of Allied wartime propaganda, and it is still perpetuated by liberals, Communists, and guilt-ridden Christian theologians. Indeed, "liberal"-minded Jews themselves perpetuate it. The superficial reason is that this view of Auschwitz unites victims of all races and creeds: it is "brotherly" propaganda. Under the surface, however, there broods at least in Jewish if not in some Gentile minds an idea horrible beyond all description. Would even Nazis have singled out Jews for such a terrible fate unless Jews had done *something* to bring it upon themselves? Most of the blame attaches to the murderers: must not at least some measure of blame attach to the victims as well? Such are the wounds that Nazism has inflicted on some Jewish minds. And such is the extent to which Nazism has defiled the world that, while it should have destroyed every vestige of antisemitism in every Gentile mind on earth, Auschwitz has, in some Gentile minds, actually increased it.[1]

These wounds and this defilement can be confronted only with the truth. And the ineluctable truth is that Jews at Auschwitz were not a species of the genus "inferior race," but rather the prototype by which "inferior race" was defined. Not until the Nazi revolution had become an anti-Jewish revolution did it begin to succeed as a movement; and when all its other works came crashing down only one of its goals remained: the murder of Jews.[2] This is the scandal that requires, of Germans, a ruthless examination of their whole history; of Christians, a pitiless reckoning with the history of Christian antisemitism; of the whole world, an inquiry into the grounds of its indifference for twelve long years. Resort to theories of suffering-in-general or persecution-in-general permits such investigations to be evaded.

Yet even where the quest for explanations is genuine there is not, and never will be, an adequate explanation. Auschwitz is the scandal of evil for evil's sake, an eruption of demonism without analogy; and the singling-out of Jews, ultimately, is an unparalleled expression of what the rabbis call groundless hate. This is the rock on which throughout eternity all rational explanations will crash and break apart.

How can a Jew respond to thus having been singled out, and to being singled out even now whenever he tries to bear witness? Resisting rational explanations, Auschwitz will forever resist religious explanations as well. Attempts to find rational causes succeed, at least up to a point, and the search for the religious, ideological, social, and economic factors leading to Auschwitz must be relentlessly pressed. In contrast, the search for a purpose in Auschwitz is foredoomed to total failure. Not that good men in their despair have not made the attempt. Good Orthodox Jews have resorted to the ancient "for our sins we are punished," but this recourse, unacceptable already to Job, is in this case all the more impossible. A good Christian theologian sees the purpose of Auschwitz as a divine reminder of the sufferings of Christ, but this testifies to a moving sense of desperation—and to an incredible lapse of theological judgment. A good Jewish secularist will connect the Holocaust with the rise of the state of Israel, but while to see a causal connection here is possible and necessary, to see a purpose is intolerable. A total and uncompromising sweep must be made of these and other explanations, all designed to give purpose to Auschwitz. No purpose, religious or non-religious, will ever be found in Auschwitz. The very attempt to find one is blasphemous.

Yet it is of the utmost importance to recognize that seeking a purpose is one thing, but seeking a response quite another. The first is wholly out of the question. The second is inescapable. Even after two decades any sort of adequate response may as yet transcend the power of any Jew. But his faith, his destiny, his very survival will depend on whether, in the end, he will be able to respond.

How can a Jew begin to seek a response? Looking for precedents, he finds none either in Jewish or in non-Jewish history. Jewish (like Christian) martyrs have died for their faith, certain that God needs martyrs. Job suffered despite his faith, able to protest within the sphere of faith. Black Christians have died for their race, unshaken in a faith which was not at issue. The one million Jewish children murdered in the Nazi Holocaust died neither because of their faith, nor in spite of their faith, nor for reasons unrelated to faith. They were murdered because of the faith of their great-grandparents. Had these great-grandparents abandoned their Jewish faith, and failed to bring up Jewish children, then their fourth-generation descendants might have been among the Nazi executioners, but not among their Jewish victims. Like Abraham of old, European Jews some time in the mid-nineteenth century offered a human sacrifice, by the mere minimal commitment to the Jewish faith of bringing up Jewish children. But unlike Abraham they did not know what they were doing, and there was no reprieve. This is the brute fact which makes all comparisons odious or irrelevant. This is what makes Jewish religious existence today unique, without support from analogies anywhere in the past. This is the scandal of the particularity of Auschwitz which, once confronted by Jewish faith, threatens total despair.

I confess that it took me twenty years until I was able to look at this scandal, but when at length I did, I made what to me was, and still is, a momentous discovery: that while religious thinkers were vainly struggling for a response to Auschwitz, Jews throughout the world—rich and poor, learned and ignorant, religious and nonreligious—had to some degree been responding all along. For twelve long years Jews had been exposed to a murderous hate which was as groundless as it was implacable. For twelve long years the world had been lukewarm or indifferent, unconcerned over the prospect of a world without Jews. For twelve long years the whole world had conspired to make Jews wish to cease to be Jews wherever, whenever, and in whatever way they could. Yet to this unprecedented invitation to group suicide, Jews responded with an unexpected will to live—with, under the circumstances, an incredible commitment to Jewish group survival.

In ordinary times, a commitment of this kind may be a mere mixture of nostalgia and vague loyalties not far removed from tribalism; and, unable to face Auschwitz, I had myself long viewed it as such, placing little value on a Jewish survival which was, or seemed to be, only survival for survival's sake. I was wrong, and even the shallowest Jewish survivalist philosophy of the postwar period was right by comparison. For in the age of Auschwitz a Jewish commitment to Jewish survival is in itself a monumental act of faithfulness, as well as a monumental, albeit as yet fragmentary, act of faith. Even to do no more than remain a Jew after Auschwitz is to confront the demons of Auschwitz in all their guises, and to bear witness against them. It is to believe that these demons cannot, will not, and must not prevail, and to stake on that belief one's own life and the lives of one's children, and of one's children's children. To be a Jew after Auschwitz is to have wrested hope—for the Jew and for the world—from the abyss of total despair. In the words of a speaker at a recent gathering of Bergen-Belsen survivors, the Jew after Auschwitz has a second *Shema Yisrael:* no second Auschwitz, no second Bergen-Belsen, no second Buchenwald—anywhere in the world, for anyone in the world!

What accounts for this commitment to Jewish existence when there might have been, and by every rule of human logic should have been, a terrified and demoralized flight from Jewish existence? Why, since Auschwitz, have all previous distinctions among Jews—between religious and secularist, Orthodox and liberal—diminished in importance, to be replaced by a new major distinction between Jews committed to Jewish survival, willing to be singled out and counted, and Jews in flight, who rationalize this flight as a rise to humanity-in-general? In my view, nothing less will do than to say that a commanding Voice speaks from Auschwitz, and that there are Jews who hear it and Jews who stop their ears.

The ultimate question is: where was God at Auschwitz? For years I sought refuge in Buber's image of an eclipse of God. This image, still meaningful in other respects, no longer seems to me applicable to Auschwitz. Most assuredly no *redeeming* Voice is heard from Auschwitz, or ever will be heard. However, a *commanding* Voice is being heard, and has, however faintly, been heard from the start. Religious Jews hear it, and they identify its source. Secularist Jews also hear it, even though perforce they leave it unidentified. At Auschwitz, Jews came face to face with absolute evil. They were and still are singled out by it, but in the midst of it they hear an absolute commandment: *Jews are forbidden to grant posthumous victories to Hitler.* They are commanded to survive as Jews, lest the Jewish people perish. They are commanded to remember the victims of Auschwitz, lest their memory perish. They are forbidden to despair of man and his world, and to escape into either cynicism or otherworldliness, lest they cooperate in delivering the world over to the forces of Auschwitz. Finally, they are forbidden to despair of the God of Israel, lest Judaism perish. A secularist Jew cannot make himself believe by a mere act of will, nor can he be commanded to do so; yet he can perform the commandment of Auschwitz. And a religious Jew who has stayed with his God may be forced into new, possibly revolutionary, relationships with him. One possibility, however, is wholly unthinkable. A Jew may not respond to Hitler's attempt to destroy Judaism by himself cooperating in its destruction. In ancient times, the unthinkable Jewish sin was idolatry. Today, it is to respond to Hitler by doing his work.

In the Midrash, God is, even in time of unrelieved tragedy, only "seemingly" powerless, for the Messiah is still expected. In Elie Wiesel's *Night*, God hangs on the gallows, and for the hero of Wiesel's *The Gates of the Forest*, a Messiah who is able to come, and yet at Auschwitz failed to come, is not to be conceived. Yet this same hero asserts that precisely because it is too late we are commanded to hope. He also says the Kaddish, "that solemn affirmation, filled with grandeur and serenity, by which man returns to God His crown and His scepter." But how a Jew after Auschwitz can return these to God is not yet known. Nor is it yet known how God can receive them.

· · · · ·

IV

On another public occasion, in March 1967, I asked the following question: Would we [like Job] be able to say that the question of Auschwitz will be answered in any sense whatever in case the eclipse of God were ended and He appeared to us? An impossible and intolerable question.[3] Less than three months later this purely hypothetical question had become actual, when at Jerusalem the threat of total annihilation gave way to sudden salvation, atheists spoke of miracles, and hardboiled Western reporters resorted to biblical images.

The question *is* impossible and intolerable. Even Job's question is not answered by God's presence, and to him children are restored. The children of Auschwitz will not be restored, and the question of Auschwitz will not be answered by a saving divine presence.

And yet, is a Jew after Auschwitz permitted to despair of salvation because of Auschwitz? Is it permitted him to cast out all hope and all joy? But on the other side, can there be any hope and any joy, purchased at the price of forgetting? Any one of these responses would be further victories handed to Hitler, and are thus impossible.

It was into precisely this impossible and intolerable contradiction that believing Jews were placed by the events at Jerusalem in May and June 1967. Those events cast into clear relief the whole as yet unassimilated fact of an embattled, endangered, but nevertheless free Jewish state, emerging from ashes and catastrophe. Solely because of the connection of the events of May and June with Auschwitz did a military victory (rarely applauded in Judaism, and never for its own sake) acquire an inescapable religious dimension.

In this context, let me quote from a letter I recently received from Professor Harold Fisch of Bar-Ilan University in Israel:

> May I report to you a conversation I had last summer with a colleague, a psychologist, who had served during the war as an artillery officer in Sinai. I asked him how he accounted for the remarkable heroism of the quite ordinary soldier of the line, for, as you may know, exemplary heroism was the normal thing at that time; mere carrying out of duty was the exception. Where, I asked him, was the psychological spring? To my surprise, he answered that what deeply motivated each and every soldier was the memory of the Holocaust, and the feeling that *above all this must never happen again*. There had been an ominous similarity between the statements of Arab leaders, their radio, and newspapers, and the remembered threats of the Nazis: we had entered into a *Shoah* (holocaust) psychosis, all around us enemies threatening us with extermination and having both the means and the will to carry out their threat. As the ring closed in and help seemed far, one noticed one's neighbors who had been in Auschwitz and Bergen-Belsen going about white-faced. It was all too obvious what was the source of their dread. The years in between had momentarily fallen away, and they were back in that veritable nightmare world. The dark night of the soul was upon us. *And it was the commandment which the Lord of history had, so to speak, pronounced at Auschwitz which saved us.* [Italics added.] I told my friend that I could not entirely accept his explanation because I knew that a majority of the soldiers had no personal or family recollections of the European Holocaust: they had come from North Africa or Yemen, or even the neighboring Arab countries where at the time such horrors were unknown. How could they feel the force of the analogy as could the survivors of Buchenwald? He told me that the intervening twenty years had brought it about that the Holocaust had become a collective experience pressing consciously and unconsciously on the minds of all, even the young, for whom Jewish history in the Diaspora had come to an end with the beginnings of Israeli independence.

It is solely because of this connection of the events of May and June with Auschwitz that a Jew must both tremble and rejoice. He must tremble lest he permit any light after Auschwitz to relieve the darkness of Auschwitz. He must rejoice, lest he add to the darkness of Auschwitz. Rejoicing after Auschwitz and because of Auschwitz, the Jew must be a Jew, *Am Yisrael Chai* ("the people Israel, alive"), a witness to the world, preparing a way for God.

Notes

1. Witness the recent Polish propaganda campaign—tantamount to a rewriting of Holocaust history—in which it was suggested that the Jews had cooperated with the Nazis in their own destruction. Since I wrote these words, the idea of a Nazi-Zionist axis has become standard Soviet propaganda.

2. See, e.g., George L. Mosse, *The Crisis of German Ideology* (New York: Universal Library, 1964), especially chap. 17.

3. [See *Judaism*, vol. 16, no. 3, Summer Issue 1967, p. 296, for the text of the discussion following the address reprinted in the previous selection.—*Ed.*]

19 *The Commanding Voice of Auschwitz*

Mid-nineteenth-century European Jews did not know the effect of their action upon their remote descendents when they remained faithful to Judaism and raised Jewish children. What if they had known? Could they then have remained faithful? Should they? And what of us who know, when we consider the possibility of a second Auschwitz three generations hence. (Which would we rather have our great-grandchildren be—victims, or bystanders and executioners?) Yet for us to cease to be Jews (and to cease to bring up Jewish children) would be to abandon our millennial post as witnesses to the God of history.

In view of such terrifying questions which arise, it is not strange that until a few years ago Jewish theological thought has observed a nearly total silence on the subject of the holocaust. A recent questionnaire does not even include it among the questions, and few of the respondents refer to it in their replies.[1] Is this nothing but cowardice? Such is the view of a "radical" Jewish theologian, who asserts that "the facts are in," that the traditional theological "options" are clear-cut, obvious, and "will not magically increase with the passing of time," and that the conclusion is certain: the Midrashic framework is shattered forever by Auschwitz; the God of history is dead.[2]

But might it not be a well-justified fear and trembling, and a crushing sense of the most awesome responsibility to four thousand years of Jewish faith, which has kept Jewish theological thought, like Job, in a state of silence, and which makes us refuse to rush in where angels fear to tread, now that speech has become inevitable? The critic, who rightly states that it "remains emotionally impossible for most Jews to deal . . . with the trauma of Auschwitz," is quick to attribute the silence of others to a defence mechanism which makes them deny that Auschwitz ever happened.[3] What assures him of his own capacities to deal with the trauma—or stills his fear that some other mechanism may cause him to utter words which should never have been spoken? We need not go beyond his jarring expression "the facts are in." Will all the facts ever be in? And what, in this case, are the facts apart from the interpretation? The statistics? The novelist Manès Sperber, himself a survivor, writes:

> *Even if all the firmament were made of parchment, all the trees were pens, all the seas ink, and even if all the inhabitants of the earth were scribes, and they wrote day and night—they would never succeed in describing the grandeur and the splendour of the Creator of the universe.*
> Fifty years separate me from the child who learned to recite these opening lines of a long Aramaic poem that had been transmitted, with an unalterable oral commentary accompanying it, from generation to generation. I come back to the resonance of these phrases whenever I bring myself, once again, to the realization that we will never succeed in making the *hurban*—the Jewish catastrophe of our time—understood to those who will live after us. The innumerable documents that we owe to the indefatigable bureaucracy of the exterminators, the many narratives by witnesses who miraculously escaped, the diaries, chronicles and records—all these millions of words remind me that "even if all the firmament. . . ."[4]

Clearly the long theological silence was necessary. Silence would, perhaps, be best even now, were it not for the fact that among the people the flood-gates are broken, and that for this reason alone the time of theological silence is irretrievably past.

Even to begin to speak is to question radically some time-honored Midrashic doctrines; and, of these, one is immediately shattered. As we have seen, even the ancient rabbis were forced to suspend the Biblical "for our sins are we punished," perhaps not in response to the destruction of the Temple by Titus, but in response to the paganization of Jerusalem by Hadrian.[5] We too may at most only suspend the Biblical doctrine, if only because we, no more than the rabbis, dare either to deny our own sinfulness or to disconnect it from history. Yet, suspend it we must. For however we twist and turn this doctrine in response to Auschwitz, it becomes a religious absurdity and even a sacrilege. Are "sin" and "retribution" to be given an individual connotation? What a sacrilegious thought when among the Nazis' victims were more than one million children! Are we to give them a collective connotation? What an appalling idea when it was not our Western, agnostic, faithless, and rich but rather the poorest, most pious, and most faithful Jewish communities which were most grievously stricken! As in our torment we turn, as an ultimate resort, to the traditional doctrine that all Israelites of all generations are responsible for each other, we are still totally aghast, for not a single one of the six million died because they had failed to keep the divine-Jewish covenant: they all died because their great-grandparents *had* kept it, if only to the minimum extent of raising Jewish children. Here is the point where we reach radical religious absurdity. Here is the rock on which the "for our sins are we punished" suffers total shipwreck.

Did Jews at Auschwitz die, then, because of the sins of others? The fact, to be sure, is obvious enough, and evidence continues to mount that these others were by no means confined to the Nazi murderers.[6] What is in question, however, is whether a religious meaning can be found in this fact—whether we, like count-less generations before us, can have recourse to the thought of martyrdom.

We have already made reference to Abraham's sacrifice of Isaac. The Midrash (which, like the Bible itself, abhors human sacrifice) transfigures the story into one of martyrdom. Isaac was not a child but rather a grown-up man of thirty-seven years, and he was no unwilling sacrifice but rather a willing martyr—for *Kiddush Hashem*, the sanctification of the divine Name. This Midrashic interpre-tation continued to be alive in the Jewish religious consciousness, and during the crusades it sustained countless martyrs.[7]

Can it sustain the Jewish religious consciousness after Auschwitz?[8] When the crusading mobs fell upon the Jews of the Rhenish cities of Worms and Mayence (1096 C.E.) they left them, in theory if not in practice, with the choice between death and conversion, thus enabling them to choose martyrdom. At Auschwitz, however, there was no choice; the young and the old, the faithful and the faithless were slaughtered without discrimination. Can there be martyrdom where there is no choice?

Yet we protest against a negative answer, for we protest against allowing Hitler to dictate the terms of our religious life. If not martyrdom, there can be a faithful-ness resembling it, when a man has no choice between life and death but only be-tween faith and despair.

But could and did Jews at Auschwitz choose faithfulness unto death? There ev-ery effort was made to destroy faith where faith had existed. Torquemada de-stroyed bodies in order to save souls. Eichmann sought to destroy souls before he destroyed bodies. Throughout the ages pious Jews have died saying the *Shema Yisrael*—"Hear, O Israel, the Lord our God, the Lord is One" (Deut. 6:4). The Nazi murder machine was systematically designed to stifle this *Shema Yisrael* on Jew-ish lips before it murdered Jews themselves. Auschwitz was the supreme, most diabolical attempt ever made to murder martyrdom itself and, failing that, to de-prive all death, martyrdom included, of its dignity.

Hitler and Eichmann have won their victories. A museum in an Israeli kibbutz of death-camp survivors[9] demonstrates that, given the power, determination, ma-chinery, and diabolical cunning, it is possible to murder a nation of heroes. It would, alas, be possible to show that, given these instruments, it is possible to de-grade and dehumanize a community of saints. A good Christian suggests that per-haps Auschwitz was a divine reminder of the sufferings of Christ.[10] Should he not ask instead whether his Master himself, had He been present at Auschwitz, could have resisted degradation and dehumanization? What are the sufferings of the Cross compared to those of a mother whose child is slaughtered to the sound of laughter or the strains of a Viennese waltz? This question may sound sacrilegious to Christian ears. Yet we dare not shirk it, for we—Christian as well as Jew—must ask: at Auschwitz, did the grave win the victory after all, or, worse than the grave, did the devil himself win?

Yet we still insist, and this with certain knowledge, that pious Jews *did* die in faithfulness, their faith untouched and unsullied by all the sadism and the horror.[11] Even so, however, Jewish if not Christian[12] exaltation of martyrdom is radically shaken—perhaps forever. The Midrashic Abraham remonstrates with God after the trial is over, for he demands to know its purpose; and he is told that the idolatrous nations, not God Himself, had stood in need of his testimony.[13] The martyrs of Worms and Mayence remembered this Midrash when they saw their children slaughtered before their very eyes, or, worse, themselves laid hands upon them; yet even they must surely have asked themselves whether murder and idolatry had diminished since the times of Abraham, and whether any purpose was served by further Jewish martyrdom. After Auschwitz, however, ours is a far worse question. One would dearly like to believe that the shock of the holocaust has made impossible a second holocaust anywhere. Is the grim truth not rather that a second holocaust has been made more likely, not less likely, by the fact of the first? For there are few signs anywhere of that radical repentance which alone could rid the world of Hitler's shadow.

If this is indeed the grim truth, is not, after Auschwitz, any Jewish willingness to suffer martyrdom, instead of an inspiration to potential saints, much rather an encouragement to potential criminals? After Auschwitz, is not even the saintliest Jew driven to the inexorable conclusion that he owes the moral obligation to the antisemites of the world not to encourage them by his own powerlessness? Such, at any rate, is the view of a novelist, himself a survivor, who asserts that the Warsaw Ghetto uprising and the Eichmann trial have brought to an end "the millennial epoch of the Jews' sanctifying God and themselves by their submitting to a violent death."[14]

We turn next to Midrashim of protest. There is a kind of faith which will accept all things and renounce every protest. There is also a kind of protest which has despaired of faith. In Judaism there has always been protest which *stays within* the sphere of faith. Abraham remonstrates with God. So do Jeremiah and Job. So does, in modern times, the Hasidic Rabbi Levi Yitzḥak of Berdiczev. He once interrupted the sacred Yom Kippur service in order to protest that, whereas kings of flesh and blood protected their peoples, Israel was unprotected by her King in heaven. Yet having made his protest, he recited the Kaddish, which begins with these words: "Extolled and hallowed be the name of God throughout the world. . . ."

Can Jewish protest today remain within the sphere of faith? Jeremiah protests against the prosperity of the wicked; we protest against the slaughter of the innocent. To Job children were restored; that the children of Auschwitz will be restored is a belief which we dare not abuse for the purpose of finding comfort. Job protests on his own behalf, and within the sphere of faith; we protest on behalf of others, and above all on behalf of those who would not or could not be or stay within the sphere of Jewish faith and yet were murdered on account of it. In faithfulness to the victims we must refuse comfort; and in faithfulness to Judaism we must refuse to disconnect God from the holocaust. Thus, in our case, protest threatens to escalate into a totally destructive conflict between the faith of the past and faithfulness to the present.

As we shrink from this conflict we seek refuge in Midrashim of divine powerlessness. However, here too we seem threatened with ruin. In the Midrash the fear of God still exists among the nations, and Israel survives, albeit powerless and scattered among the nations. In Nazi Europe, however, the fear of God was dead, and Jews were hunted without mercy or scruple. In the Midrash, God goes into exile with His people and returns with them; from Auschwitz there was no return. Hence, whereas in the Midrash God is only "as it were" powerless, in *Night*, Wiesel sees Him in the face of a child hanging on the gallows.

One day when we came back from work, we saw three gallows rearing up in the assembly place, three black crows. Roll Call. SS all around us, machine guns trained: the traditional ceremony. Three victims in chains—and one of them, the little servant, the sad-eyed angel.

The SS seemed more preoccupied, more disturbed than usual. To hang a young boy in front of thousands of spectators was no light matter. The head of the camp read the verdict. All eyes were on the child. He was lividly pale, almost calm, biting his lips. The gallows threw its shadow over him. . . .

The three victims mounted together onto the chairs.

The three necks were placed at the same moment within the nooses.

"Long live liberty!" cried the two adults.

But the child was silent.

"Where is God? Where is He?" someone behind me asked.

At a sign from the head of the camp, the three chairs tipped over. . . .

I heard a voice within me answer . . . :

"Where is He? Here He is—He is hanging on this gallows. . . ."[15]

To stake all on divine powerlessness today, therefore, would be to take it both radically and literally. God suffers literal and radical powerlessness, i.e., actual death; and any resurrected divine power will be manifest, not so much within history as beyond it. A Jew, in short, would have to become a Christian. But never in the two thousand years of Jewish-Christian confrontation has it been less possible for a Jew to abandon either his Jewishness or his Judaism and embrace Christianity.

Jewish faith thus seems to find no refuge in Midrashim of divine powerlessness, none in otherworldliness, none in the redeeming power of martyrdom, and most of all none in the view that Auschwitz is punishment for the sins of Israel. Unless the God of history is to be abandoned, only a prayer remains, addressed to divine Power, but spoken softly lest it be heard.

One refuge is still unexplored. Rabbi Akiba once taught that God, as it were powerless, shares Israel's exile. It will be recalled that Rabbi Eliezer responded differently to the destruction of the second Temple and the paganization of Jerusalem. The gates of prayer were closed, and only those of tears were still open. Israel was separated from her Father in heaven as by a wall of iron. God was no longer present in history. Was God absent at Auschwitz? Is He in eclipse even now? May pious Jews pray as loudly as they like, because God cannot or does not hear?

We have seen that Buber's image of the eclipse of God can sustain Jewish faith in its confrontation with modern secularism.[16] It now appears, however, that this image fails to sustain us in our confrontation with the Nazi holocaust. Why could Rabbi Eliezer continue to pray when the gates of prayer were closed? Because the divine Presence remained the object of hope, and because for this reason the root experiences of the past could continue to be reenacted. For the hero of Wiesel's *The Gates of the Forest*, however, a Messiah who can come, and yet at Auschwitz did not come, has become an impossibility,[17] and this impossibility, were it to be and remain total and absolute,[18] would be of devastating consequence. A divine eclipse which were *total* in the present would cut off both past and future. The pious Jew during the Passover Seder has always reenacted the salvation at the Red Sea. The event always remained real for him because He who once had saved was saving still.[19] And this latter affirmation could continue to be made, even in times of catastrophe, because the divine salvation remained present in the form of hope. What if our present is without hope? The unprecedented catastrophe of the holocaust now discloses for us that the eclipse of God remains a religious possibility within Judaism *only if it is not total.* If *all present* access to the God of history is *wholly* lost, the God of history is Himself lost.[20]

With this conclusion we have come face to face with the horrifying possibility mentioned at the beginning—that Hitler has succeeded in murdering, not only one third of the Jewish people, but the Jewish faith as well. Only one response may seem to remain—the cry of total despair—"there is no judgment and no judge."

But this conclusion has been reached long ago by the Jewish secularist, albeit for totally different reasons and to a totally different effect.

Jewish secularism has been a possibility ever since the Age of Enlightenment, and its vitality has been confirmed in our time in the most dramatic possible way by the foundation of a secular Jewish state. Today we must ask whether secularism may not be now the common fate of all Jews who persist in their Jewishness. However, we shall find that, if the death camps threaten the Jewish faith, they threaten no less any secularism which would take its place. All religious faith is in crisis in our time. A Jew who confronts Auschwitz and reaffirms his Jewishness discovers that every form of modern secularism is equally in crisis.

We have previously considered[21] the rational grounds for secularism. We must now inquire into the grounds of its attractiveness for modern Jews. The secularism which we have termed subjectivist reductionism dissipates all gods, destroys all meaning except what is humanly created, and deprives Jewish existence of its millennial distinctiveness. Why should Jews *want* to—rather than be *rationally compelled* to—accept such a creed?

Subjectivist reductionism has a general attraction. To the pious a life without Absolutes may be meaningless and goalless. To the secularist such a life is one of liberty. To the believer the divine Presence exalts as it gives life a focus. To the secularist it seems to tyrannize, for it stifles life's natural pluralism for him. The life of faith is abnormal, and the dissipation of faith ushers in human normalcy. Such is the creed of the secular city.[22]

If for modern Jews this creed has always had a special attraction, it is because of the vision of "normalcy" which is part of it. The modern Jew has become modern by virtue of the Emancipation, and the Emancipation has been a process of "normalization." Its Gentile donors may have often had in mind the end of the Jewish people,[23] its Jewish recipients wished to normalize the Jewish people even when they were determined to perpetuate it; and, after many centuries of religious discrimination and persecution, this is not surprising.

Nor in view of these many centuries is it surprising that "Jewish normalcy" has often been not *one limited* goal but rather *the ultimate* goal. This is true of many "religious" Jews when they categorize themselves as Jewish by "denomination" and British, French, or American by "nationality." It is more true of "secularist" Jews proper when they define themselves as a "nationality" like all others. Most of all it is true of those Zionist Jews who, when they embark on the most abnormal enterprise of restoring a nation after two thousand years, are committed to the goal of becoming a nation like all others. The assimilationist has wished all along to solve the so-called "Jewish problem" by dissolving Jewish existence; the secularist, by depriving it of its millennial distinctiveness.

We cannot guess what might have happened to this modern Jewish secularist or quasi-secularist drive for normalcy had the Nazi holocaust never occurred. We must face the fact, however, that had normalcy remained the all-overriding goal, the Jewish response to the holocaust should have been the exact opposite of the one which actually was and is being given. For twelve long years Jews had been singled out by a hate which was as groundless as it was implacable. For twelve long years a power had held sway in the heart of Europe to which the death of every Jewish man, woman, and child was the one and only unshakable principle. For twelve long years the world had failed to oppose this principle with an equally unshakable principle of its own. Any Jew, then or now, making normalcy his supreme goal should have been, and still should be, in flight from this singled-out condition in total disarray. In fact, however, secularist no less than religious Jews have responded with a reaffirmation of their Jewish existence such as no social scientist would have predicted even if the holocaust had never occurred. Jewish theology still does not know how to respond to Auschwitz. Jews themselves—rich and poor, learned and ignorant, believer and secularist—have responded in some measure all along.

No doubt social scientists have their ready explanations. Persecution stiffens resistance. Humiliation causes pride in half-remembered loyalties. The ancient rabbis themselves suggest that Israel thrives on persecution. Such are the normal explanations, and in normal times they may well be right.

The times, however, are not normal times. A Jew at Auschwitz was not a specimen of the class "victim of prejudice" or even "victim of genocide." He was *singled out* by a demonic power which sought his death *absolutely*, i.e., as an end in itself. For a Jew today merely to affirm his Jewish existence is to accept his singled-out condition; it is to oppose the demons of Auschwitz: and it is to oppose them in the only way in which they can be opposed—with an *absolute* opposition. Moreover, it is to stake on that absolute opposition nothing less than his life and the lives of his children and the lives of his children's children.

The holocaust has thus placed the Jewish secularist into a position for which secularism has no precedent within or without Jewish existence. As a secularist, he views the modern world as a desacralized world from which all gods have vanished. As a Jewish secularist he knows that the devil, if not God, is alive. As a secularist he has relativized all former absolutes. As a Jewish secularist he opposes the demons of Auschwitz absolutely by his mere commitment to Jewish survival. Thus a radical contradiction has appeared in Jewish secularist existence in our time. As secularist the Jewish secularist seeks Jewish normalcy; as Jewish secularist he fragments this normalcy by accepting his singled-out Jewish condition. As secularist, he reduces all absolute to relative affirmations; as Jewish secularist he opposes absolutely the demons of death with his own Jewish life. Throughout the ages the religious Jew was a witness to God. After Auschwitz even the most secularist of Jews bears witness, by the mere affirmation of his Jewishness, against the devil.[24]

The Jewish secularist cannot escape this contradiction; or rather, he could escape it only if he either pretended that the Nazi holocaust had never occurred or else fled from his Jewishness. Will Herberg has therefore rightly asserted that Jewish secularism has become illogical in our time—that, by the logic of his position, the Jewish secularist should abandon his Jewishness.[25] Herberg has failed to notice, however, a truth of far greater consequence which the Jewish secularist himself recognizes: the devil confounds our logic.

Still, not all Jewish secularism falls into immediate contradiction. We have seen that, beside a secularism which dissolves all religious absolutes, there is a secularism which internalizes and transforms these absolutes.[26] Hence a Jewish secularism is conceivable which opposes the demons of Auschwitz absolutely—but in behalf of "free," autonomous, post-religious humanity.

A Jewish secularism of this kind was always problematic. Either the ancient religious absolutes remained absolute in the process of internalization; but then they were universals such as Reason or Progress, and Jewish existence had become accidental. Or else they remained particularized enough to sustain Jewish existence in its particularity; but then they would become idolatrous unless they lost their absoluteness. Jewish romantics and pragmatists both perceived that any specifically "Jewish genius" could be but one instrument in an orchestra requiring many others, and that any Jewish loyalty to Jewish "peoplehood" required by such a genius could exist only within a "pluralistic" scheme in which many loyalties made their respective claims, and in which none was absolute. The God of Judaism—who was and remained other-than-man—could both be Himself universal and single out the Jewish people. The internalized God of secularism could only be either universal (and then not single out at all) or else particular (and then not single out absolutely).

After Auschwitz both alternatives, always problematic within Jewish existence, are fragmented. Jewish opposition to the demons of Auschwitz cannot be understood in terms of humanly created ideals. Those of Reason fail, for Reason is too innocent of demonic evil to fathom the scandal of the particularity of Auschwitz, and too abstractly universal to do justice to the singled-out Jewish condition. The ideals of Progress fail, for Progress makes of Auschwitz at best a throwback into tribalism and at worst a dialectically justified necessity. Least adequate are any ideals which might be furnished by a specifically Jewish genius, for Jewish survival after Auschwitz is not one relative ideal among others but rather an imperative which brooks no compromise. In short, within the context of Jewish existence the secularism which we have termed subjectivist reductionism is breached by *absolute* Jewish opposition to the demons of Auschwitz; and the secularism which we have seen exemplified in Nietzscheanism and left-wing Hegelianism is breached because internalized absolutes either cannot single out or else cannot remain absolute. Jewish opposition to Auschwitz cannot be grasped in terms of humanly created ideals but only as an *imposed commandment*. And the Jewish secularist, no less than the believer, is *absolutely singled out* by a Voice as truly *other* than man-made ideals—an imperative as truly *given*—as was the Voice of Sinai.

According to the Midrash, God wished to give the Torah immediately upon the Exodus from Egypt, but had to postpone the gift until Israel was united.[27] Today, the distinction between religious and secularist Jews is superseded by that between unauthentic Jews who flee from their Jewishness and authentic Jews who affirm it. This latter group includes religious and secularist Jews. These are united by a commanding Voice which speaks from Auschwitz.

The Commanding Voice of Auschwitz

What does the Voice of Auschwitz command?

> Jews are forbidden to hand Hitler posthumous victories. They are commanded to survive as Jews, lest the Jewish people perish. They are commanded to remember the victims of Auschwitz lest their memory perish. They are forbidden to despair of man and his world, and to escape into either cynicism or otherworldliness, lest they cooperate in delivering the world over to the forces of Auschwitz. Finally, they are forbidden to despair of the God of Israel, lest Judaism perish. A secularist Jew cannot make himself believe by a mere act of will, nor can he be commanded to do so. . . . And a religious Jew who has stayed with his God may be forced into new, possibly revolutionary relationships with Him. One possibility, however, is wholly unthinkable. A Jew may not respond to Hitler's attempt to destroy Judaism by himself cooperating in its destruction. In ancient times, the unthinkable Jewish sin was idolatry. Today, it is to respond to Hitler by doing his work.[28]

Elie Wiesel has compared the holocaust with Sinai in revelatory significance—and expressed the fear that we are not listening. We shrink from this daring comparison—but even more from not listening. We shrink from any claim to have heard—but even more from a false refuge, in an endless agnosticism, from a Voice speaking to us. I was able to make the above, fragmentary statement (which I have already previously made and here merely quote) only because it no more than articulates what is being heard by Jews the world over—rich and poor, learned and ignorant, believing and secularist. I cannot go beyond this earlier statement but only expand it.

1. The First Fragment

In the murder camps the unarmed, decimated, emaciated survivors often rallied their feeble remaining resources for a final, desperate attempt at revolt. The revolt was hopeless. There was no hope but one. One might escape. Why must one escape? To tell the tale. Why must the tale be told when evidence was already at hand that the world would not listen?[29] Because not to tell the tale, when it might be told, was unthinkable. The Nazis were not satisfied with mere murder. Before murdering Jews, they were trying to reduce them to numbers; after murdering them, they were dumping their corpses into nameless ditches or making them into soap. They were making as sure as was possible to wipe out every trace of memory. Millions would be as though they had never been. But to the pitiful and glorious desperadoes of Warsaw, Treblinka, and Auschwitz, who would soon themselves be as though they had never been, not to rescue for memory what could be rescued was unthinkable because it was sacrilege.[30]

It will remain a sacrilege ever after. Today, suggestions come from every side to the effect that the past had best be forgotten, or at least remain unmentioned, or at least be coupled with the greatest and most thoughtless speed with other, but quite different, human tragedies. Sometimes these suggestions come from Jews rationalizing their flight from the Nazi holocaust. More often they come from non-Jews, who rationalize their own flight, or even maintain, affrontingly enough, that unless Jews universalize the holocaust, thus robbing the Jews of Auschwitz of their Jewish identity, they are guilty of disregard for humanity.[31] But for a Jew hearing the commanding Voice of Auschwitz the duty to remember and to tell the tale, is not negotiable. It is holy. The religious Jew still possesses this word. The secularist Jew is commanded to restore it. A secular holiness, as it were, has forced itself into his vocabulary.

2. The Second Fragment

Jewish survival, were it even for no more than survival's sake, is a holy duty as well. The murderers of Auschwitz cut off Jews from humanity and denied them the right to existence; yet in being denied that right, Jews represented all humanity. Jews after Auschwitz represent all humanity when they affirm their Jewishness and deny the Nazi denial. They would fail if they affirmed the mere *right* to their Jewishness, participating, as it were, in an obscene debate between others who deny the right of Jews to exist and Jews who affirm it.[32] Nor would they deny the Nazi denial if they affirmed merely their humanity-in-general, permitting an antisemitic split between their humanity and their Jewishness, or, worse, agreeing to vanish as Jews in one way, in response to Hitler's attempt to make them vanish in another. The commanding Voice of Auschwitz singles Jews out; Jewish survival is a commandment which brooks no compromise. It was this Voice which was heard by the Jews of Israel in May and June 1967 when they refused to lie down and be slaughtered.[33]

Yet such is the extent of Hitler's posthumous victories that Jews, commanded to survive as Jews, are widely denied even the right. More precisely—for overt antisemitism is not popular in the post-holocaust world—they are granted the right only on certain conditions. Russians, Poles, Indians, and Arabs have a natural right to exist; Jews must earn that right. Other states must refrain from wars of aggression; the State of Israel is an "aggressor" even if it fights for its life. Peoples unscarred by Auschwitz ought to protest when any evil resembling Auschwitz is in sight, such as the black ghettoes or Vietnam. The Jewish survivors of Auschwitz have no right to survive unless they engage in such protests. Other peoples may include secularists and believers. Jews must be divided into bad secularists or Zionists, and good—albeit anachronistic—saints who stay on the cross.

The commanding Voice of Auschwitz bids Jews reject all such views as a monumental affront. It bids them reject as no longer tolerable every version—Christian or leftist, Gentile or Jewish—of the view that the Jewish people is an anachronism, when it is the elements of the world perpetrating and permitting Auschwitz, not its survivors, that are anachronistic. A Jew is commanded to descend from the cross and, in so doing, not only to reiterate his ancient rejection of an ancient Christian view but also to suspend the time-honored Jewish exaltation of martyrdom. For after Auschwitz, Jewish life is more sacred then Jewish death, were it even for the sanctification of the divine Name. The left-wing secularist Israeli journalist Amos Kenan writes: "After the death camps, we are left only one supreme value: existence."[34]

3. The Third Fragment

But such as Kenan, being committed and unrepentant lovers of the downtrodden, accept other supreme values as well, and will suspend these only when Jewish existence itself is threatened or denied. Kenan has a universal vision of peace, justice, and brotherhood. He loves the poor of Cuba and hates death in Vietnam. In these and other commitments such left-wing secularists share the ancient Jewish religious, messianically inspired refusal to embrace either pagan cynicism (which despairs of the world and accepts the *status quo*) or Christian or pseudo-Christian otherworldliness (which despairs of the world and flees from it). The commanding Voice of Auschwitz bids Jews, religious and secularist, not to abandon the world to the forces of Auschwitz, but rather to continue to work and hope for it. Two possibilities are equally ruled out: to despair of the world on account of Auschwitz, abandoning the age-old Jewish identification with poor and persecuted humanity; and to abuse such identification as a means of flight from Jewish destiny. It is precisely *because* of the uniqueness of Auschwitz, and *in* his Jewish particularity, that a Jew must be at one with humanity. For it is precisely because Auschwitz has made the world a desperate place that a Jew is forbidden to despair of it.[35] The hero of Wiesel's *The Gates of the Forest* asserts that it is too late for the Messiah—and that for exactly this reason we are commanded to hope.[36]

4. The Fourth Fragment

The Voice of Auschwitz commands the religious Jew after Auschwitz to continue to wrestle with his God in however revolutionary ways; and it forbids the secularist Jew (who has already, and on other grounds, lost Him) to use Auschwitz as an additional weapon wherewith to deny Him.

The ways of the religious Jew are revolutionary, for there is no previous Jewish protest against divine Power like his protest. Continuing to hear the Voice of Sinai as he hears the Voice of Auschwitz, his citing of God against God may have to assume extremes which dwarf those of Abraham, Jeremiah, Job, Rabbi Levi Yitzḥak. (You have abandoned the covenant? We shall not abandon it! You no longer want Jews to survive? We shall survive, as better, more faithful, more pious Jews! You have destroyed all grounds for hope? We shall obey the commandment to hope which You Yourself have given!) Nor is there any previous Jewish compassion with divine powerlessness like the compassion required by such a powerlessness. (The fear of God is dead among the nations? We shall keep it alive and be its witnesses! The times are too late for the coming of the Messiah? We shall persist without hope and recreate hope—and, as it were, divine Power—by our persistence!) For the religious Jew, who remains within the Midrashic framework, the Voice of Auschwitz manifests a divine Presence which, as it were, is shorn of all except commanding Power. *This* Power, however, is inescapable.

No less inescapable is this Power for the secularist Jew who has all along been outside the Midrashic framework and this despite the fact that the Voice of Auschwitz does not enable him to return into that framework. He cannot return; but neither may he turn the Voice of Auschwitz against that of Sinai. For he may not cut off his secular present from the religious past: the Voice of Auschwitz commands preservation of that past. Nor may he widen the chasm between himself and the religious Jew: the Voice of Auschwitz commands Jewish unity.

As religious and secularist Jews are united in kinship with all the victims of Auschwitz and against all the executioners, they face a many-sided mystery and find a simple certainty. As regards the minds and souls of the victims of Auschwitz, God's presence to them is a many-sided mystery which will never be exhausted either by subsequent committed believers or by subsequent committed unbelievers, and least of all by subsequent neutral theorists—psychological, sociological, philosophical, theological—who spin out their theories immune to love and hate, submission and rage, faith and despair. As regards the murderers of Auschwitz, however, there was no mystery, for they denied, mocked, murdered the God of Israel six million times—and together with Him four thousand years of Jewish faith. For a Jew after Auschwitz, only one thing is certain: he may not side with the murderers and do what they have left undone. The religious Jew who has heard the Voice of Sinai must continue to listen as he hears the commanding Voice of Auschwitz. And the secularist Jew, who has all along lost Sinai and now hears the Voice of Auschwitz, cannot abuse that Voice as a means to destroy four thousand years of Jewish believing testimony. The rabbis assert that the first temple was destroyed because of idolatry. Jews may not destroy the Temple which is the tears of Auschwitz by doing, wittingly or unwittingly, Hitler's work.

5. The Clash Between the Fragments

Such is the commanding Voice of Auschwitz as it is increasingly being heard by Jews of this generation. But how can it be obeyed? Each of the four fragments described—and they are mere fragments, and the description has been poor and inadequate—is by itself overwhelming. Taken together, they seem unbearable. For there are clashes between them which tear us apart.

How can the religious Jew be faithful to both the faith of the past and the victims of the present? We have already asked this question, but are now further from an answer than before. For a reconciliation by means of willing martyrdom is ruled out by the duty to Jewish survival, and a reconciliation by means of refuge in otherworldly mysticism is ruled out by the duty to hold fast to the world and to continue to hope and work for it. God, world and Israel are in so total a conflict when they meet at Auschwitz as to seem to leave religious Jews confronting that conflict with nothing but a prayer addressed to God, yet spoken softly lest it be heard: in short, with madness.

But the conflict is no less unbearable for the secularist Jew. To be sure, the space once occupied by God is void for him or else occupied by a question mark. Only three of the four fragments effectively remain. Yet the conflict which remains tears him asunder.

Søren Kierkegaard's "knight of faith" was obliged to retrace the road which led Abraham to Mount Moriah, where Isaac's sacrifice was to take place.[37] A Jew today is obliged to retrace the road which led his brethren to Auschwitz. It is a road of pain and mourning, of humiliation, guilt, and despair. To retrace it is living death. How suffer this death *and also* choose Jewish life which, like all life, must include joy, laughter, and childlike innocence? How reconcile *such* a remembrance with life itself? How dare a Jewish parent crush his child's innocence with the knowledge that his uncle or grandfather was denied life because of his Jewishness? And how dare he *not* burden him with this knowledge? The conflict is inescapable, for we may neither forget the past for the sake of present life, nor destroy present life by a mourning without relief—and there is no relief.

Nor is this all. The first two fragments above clash with each other: each clashes with the third as well. No Jewish secularist today may continue to hope and work for mankind as though Auschwitz had never happened, falling back on secularist beliefs of yesterday that man is good, progress real, and brotherhood inevitable. Yet neither may he, on account of Auschwitz, despair of human brotherhood and cease to hope and work for it. How face Auschwitz and not despair? How hope and work, and not act as though Auschwitz had never occurred? Yet to forget and to despair are both forbidden.

Perhaps reconciliation would be possible if the Jewish secularist of today, like the Trotskys and Rosa Luxemburgs of yesterday, could sacrifice Jewish existence on the altar of future humanity. (Is this in the minds of "progressive" Jews when they protest against war in Vietnam but refuse to protest against Polish antisemitism? Or in the minds of what Kenan calls the "good people" of the world when they demand that Israel hand over weapons to those sworn to destroy her?) This sacrifice, however, is forbidden, and the altar is false. The left-wing Israeli secularist Kenan may accept all sorts of advice from his progressive friends, but not that he allow himself to be shot for the good of humanity. Perhaps he has listened for a moment even to this advice, for he hates a gun in his hand. Perhaps he has even wished for a second he could accept it, feeling, like many of his pious ancestors, that it is better to be killed than to kill. Yet he firmly rejects such advice, for he is *commanded* to reject it; rather than be shot, he will shoot first when there is no third alternative. But he will shoot with tears in his eyes. He writes:

> Why weren't the June 4 borders peace borders on the fourth of June, but will only become so now? Why weren't the UN Partition Plan borders of 1947 peace borders then, but will become so now? Why should I return his gun to the bandit as a reward for having failed to kill me?
> I want peace peace peace peace, peace peace peace.
> I am ready to give everything back in exchange for peace.
> And I shall give nothing back without peace.
> I am ready to solve the refugee problem. I am ready to accept an independent Palestinian state. I am ready to sit and talk. About everything, all at the same time. Direct talks, indirect talks, all this is immaterial. But peace.
> Until you agree to have peace, I shall give back nothing. And if you force me to become a conqueror, I shall become a conqueror. And if you force me to become an oppressor, I shall become an oppressor. And if you force me into the same camp with all the forces of darkness in the world, there I shall be.[38]

Kenan's article ends:

> ... if I survive ..., without a god but without prophets either, my life will have no sense whatever. I shall have nothing else to do but walk on the banks of streams, or on the top of the rocks, watch the wonders of nature, and console myself with the words of Ecclesiastes, the wisest of men: For the light is sweet, and it is good for the eyes to see the sun.[39]

The conclusion, then, is inescapable. Secularist Jewish existence after Auschwitz is threatened with a madness no less extreme than that which produces a prayer addressed to God, yet spoken softly lest it be heard.

The Voice of Auschwitz commands Jews not to go mad. It commands them to accept their singled out condition, face up to its contradictions, and endure them. Moreover, it gives the power of endurance, the power of sanity. The Jew of today can endure because he must endure, and he must endure because he is commanded to endure.

We ask: whence has come our strength to endure even these twenty-five years—not to flee or disintegrate but rather to stay, however feebly, at our solitary post, to affirm, however weakly, our Jewishness, and to bear witness, if only by this affirmation, against the forces of hell itself? The question produces abiding wonder. It is at a commanding Voice without which we, like the Psalmist (Ps. 119:92), would have perished in our affliction.

Notes

1. See "The State of Jewish Belief: A Symposium," *Commentary* (August 1966), pp. 71–160; reprinted as *The Condition of Jewish Belief* (New York: Macmillan, 1966).

2. See R. L. Rubenstein, "Homeland and Holocaust," *The Religious Situation 1968* (Boston: Beacon, 1968), p. 110.

3. *Op. cit.*, p. 57

4. *. . . than a Tear in the Sea* (Bergen Belsen Memorial Press, 1967), p. vii.

5. See above, pp. 26 ff.

6. See most recently A. D. Morse, *While Six Million Died* (New York: Random House, 1967).

7. For this Midrash and its medieval use see Shalom Spiegel, *The Last Trial* (New York: Pantheon, 1967). Spiegel shows the element of protest among the medieval chroniclers which is prominent above all because, while Isaac had been reprieved, no reprieve had occurred for the many Isaacs during the Crusades.

8. We say "after" and not "at" Auschwitz because any opinion as to what was or was not religiously possible at Auschwitz itself is ultimately permissible, if for anyone, only for an actual survivor.

9. *Kibbutz Lohamay Ha-getoat.*

10. In "Jewish Faith and the Holocaust" (*Commentary*, 1968), I have already characterized this attempt to find a purpose in Auschwitz as reflecting "a moving sense of desperation, and an incredible lapse of theological judgment." Since the passage I criticize was part of a sermon which was not published but only mimeographed and privately distributed, I feel obliged to withhold the name of the well-known author.

11. Secularist Jews, too, died with Jewish faithfulness; but we are not presently concerned with Jewish secularism.

12. See note 13.

13. This contrasts with Søren Kierkegaard's *Fear and Trembling*, in which God needs to have Abraham's testimony and Abraham needs to give it. Whether Christian (like Jewish) resort to martyrdom is decisively affected by Auschwitz depends on whether worldly effectiveness, however remote or improbable, is part of its meaning, Kierkegaard to the contrary notwithstanding.

14. Manès Sperber, *op. cit.*, p. xiv. I am constrained to quote this remarkable passage in full:

Genocide, whatever its extent, never succeeds completely. That perpetrated by the Nazis failed more than any other, because it provided the main reasons for the creation of the State of Israel. Encouraged by the way Hitler had practiced genocide without encountering resistance, the Arabs surged in upon the nascent Israeli nation to exterminate it and make themselves its immediate heirs. The military and political leaders of the Arab states, along with Foreign Minister Bevin and his advisers in the Colonial Office, did not understand that the *millennial epoch* of the Jews' sanctifying of God and themselves by their submitting to violent death *had just come to an end with the Warsaw Ghetto uprising.* With this conclusive experience of European Jewry there also came to an end the illusion that they could count on other men to defend them. The Arab armies were cut to pieces and thrown beyond the borders by men who, in going to battle with no thought of retreat, meant also to avenge a people murdered and not buried, whose brothers, sons or nephews they were. They meant to teach the world that the long hunting season was over forever, and that one could no longer kill Jews easily or with impunity. To be sure, the soldiers of this new Hebrew army, Zionists for the most part, were fighting for the land that their labor had redeemed, for the villages, towns and kibbutzim that they had brought into being out of nothingness, and for the lives of all of them. But they were fighting above all—particularly since 1945 and beyond the spring of 1948—to deliver their people from a degradation that threatened to encourage exterminators, their sons and their grandsons, as well as their innumerable silent accomplices the world over.

For the greatest boon that can be brought to peoples tempted by aggressive anti-Semitism is to make the crime that it inspires dangerous for the instigators and executors themselves. Between 1933 and 1945, the whole world provided Hitler—who moved only step-by-step at first—with proof that he could undertake anything he pleased against the Jews, with nothing to fear but verbal protestations never followed up with the slightest reprisal. This is why the abduction of Eichmann by agents of the State of Israel and his trial in Jerusalem are events of *major significance* (pp. xiii–xiv).

The less than ten pages of which this passage is part were written in 1964; Sperber states that it took him weeks to write them, "every time escaping anew from the shadows of a past whose memory threatens the present" (p. xvi).

15. Elie Wiesel, *Night* (New York: Pyramid Books, 1961), p. 78.

16. See *God's Presence in History*, pp. 49, 61.

17. *The Gates of the Forest* (New York: Holt, Rinehart and Winston, 1966), p. 225.

18. For Wiesel on this question, see *God's Presence in History*, p. 88.

19. See *God's Presence in History*, chapter 1, note 13.

20. Buber himself sees this with the utmost clarity. See the weighty passage quoted at the end of chapter II, *God's Presence in History*.

21. In *God's Presence in History*, chapter II.

22. To have caught the mood of this creed is the greatest accomplishment of Harvey Cox's *The Secular City* (New York: Macmillan, 1965).

23. Kant expected the "euthanasia" of Judaism. His intentions at the time were benevolent; but today the very phrase sounds obscene.

24. For my interpretation of Nazism as the supreme and unsurpassable modern idolatry, see "Idolatry as a Modern Religious Possibility," *The Religious Situation 1968* (Boston: Beacon, 1968), pp. 254–87 (reprinted as chapter IV of *Encounters between Judaism and Modern Philosophy*).

25. In a public address by the author.

26. See *God's Presence in History*, pp. 49ff.

27. *Midrash Tanhuma*, ed. Buber (Wilma, 1885), Yitro, 37b.

28. Once again I quote from the article cited in note 10.

29. See especially Elie Wiesel, "A Plea for the Dead," *Legends of Our Time* (Holt, Rinehart and Winston, 1968), pp. 174–97.

30. See especially Yuri Suhl, *They Fought Back* (New York: Crown, 1967).

31. Wiesel is dismayed to discover that some critics of Nelly Sachs's poetry try to minimize its Jewishness and contrast a "universal vision" with a merely Jewish one. He comments:

> Her greatness lies in her Jewishness, and this makes it belong to all mankind. It is perhaps only natural that there are those who try to remove her, if not to estrange her, from us. But this will never happen. She has many Jewish melodies left to sing. . . . What disturbs me is that strangers have stolen them. ("Conversation With Nelly Sachs," *Jewish Heritage* [Spring 1968], p. 33.)

32. In recent years some North American TV stations and university groups have seen fit to furnish American Nazis and German neo-Nazis with a forum, and even invited Jews to debate with them, apparently utterly oblivious to the obscenity of such invitations.

33. See a letter by Professor Harold Fisch of Bar Ilan University quoted in the article cited in note 10, and also note 14.

34. "A letter to All Good People—To Fidel Castro, Sartre, Russell and All the Rest," *Midstream*, October 1968 (This article originally appeared first in *Yediot Aharonot* and was republished in *The New Statesman*). Here and in the following, I single out this article, not only because of its excellence, but also (a fact doubtless largely accounting for this excellence) because its author is a left-wing

secularist (who cannot and will not abandon his universalistic ideals) and an Israeli (who cannot and will not condone collective Jewish suicide).

35. I distinguish with the utmost sharpness between (a) the view that because of Auschwitz the justification of Jewish existence depends on Jews behaving like superhuman saints toward all other peoples ever after and (b) the view that because of Auschwitz Jews are obligated to (i) Jewish survival as an end which, less than ever, needs any justification (ii) work for oppressed and suffering humanity everywhere. I accept the second view, and (as will be seen) the inevitably painful conflicts that go with it. The first view is totally unacceptable.

36. Elie Wiesel, *The Gates of the Forest* (New York: Holt, Rinehart and Winston, 1966), 225.

37. See *Fear and Trembling* (Garden City, N.Y.: Anchor, 1954).

38. *Op. cit.,* p. 35.

39. *Op. cit.,* p. 36.

RESISTANCE AND
TIKKUN OLAM

20   Tikkun Olam

With this monumental conclusion [that resistance during the Holocaust was a way of being and is now, for our thought, an ontological category] what may be called a necessary excursus, extending over the last two sections of the present exploration, has come to a climax and an end. Prior to these sections we reached an impasse with the question whether perhaps *no* thought can be where the Holocaust is; whether perhaps *all* thought is "paralyzed" vis-à-vis that event; and whether perhaps paralysis at this catastrophic point calls into question significant post-Holocaust thought everywhere. The two sections that followed were an excursus in that that question was suspended; and the excursus was necessary because only the astounding fact that *existence* was not wholly paralyzed *during* the Holocaust *itself* could give our thought any hope of breaking the impasse. Now that the astounding fact has been confronted, contemplated, explored, the suspended question returns; and there arises for future thought—the focus of our concern is Jewish thought, but also involved are philosophical and, to a lesser extent, Christian thought—an imperative that brooks no compromise. *Authentic thought was actual during the Holocaust among resisting victims; therefore such thought must be possible for us after the event: and, being possible, it is mandatory. Moreover, their resisting thought pointed to and helped make possible a re-sisting life; our post-Holocaust thought, however authentic in other respects, would still lapse into unauthenticity if it remained in an academically self-enclosed circle—if it failed to point to, and help make possible, a post-Holocaust life.*

But can this imperative be obeyed? Only through a new departure with the help of a new category. In this whole work we have been engaged in thinking—

Reprinted, with changes, from *To Mend the World* (New York: Schocken Books, 1982), 249–55, by permission of the publisher.

philosophical, Jewish, and within proper limits, Christian. When it was "old" thinking it required access to Eternity. When it was "new" thinking it still required historical continuity. (This is obvious in the case of Jewish and Christian thinking, with their need for access to the Scriptures. In the case of philosophical thinking it was demonstrated for us by Heidegger, for his earlier thinking needs "recovery" of "tradition," and his later must "think more primally still what was originally thought.") Our own thinking in this book, recover as it did the past, itself presupposed a continuity between present and past. Yet our question now is whether the continuity indispensable for thought is still available. This question first appeared when our own thought, surprised and horrified by the Holocaust, could only resist but not comprehend it.

The continuity is broken, and thought, if it is not itself to be and remain broken, requires a new departure and a new category. Only thus can the imperative that brooks no compromise be obeyed. Historical continuity is shattered because "at Auschwitz not only man died, but also the idea of man"; because our "estrangement from God" has become so "cruel" that, even if He were to speak to us, we have no way of understanding how to "recognize" Him.[1] We need a new departure and a new category because the Holocaust is not a "relapse into barbarism," a "phase in an historical dialectic," a radical-but-merely-"parochial" catastrophe. It is a total rupture.

Rupture, *Teshuva*, and *Tikkun Olam*

> How has the Lord covered the daughter of Zion with a cloud in His anger, and cast down from heaven to earth the beauty of Israel. . . . The Lord has swallowed up without pity all the habitations of Jacob. . . . He has profaned the kingdom and its princes. . . . The Lord was like an enemy. He has swallowed up Israel. . . . He has increased in the daughter of Yehuda mourning and lamentation. (Lam. 2:1, 2, 5)

A

This passage from Lamentations takes us closer to total rupture than any passage in all philosophy. (Nietzsche or Sartre or Heidegger might find, mixed with mourning, exhilaration in the solitariness caused by an absent God, or a freedom caused by a God that has died. There is no exhilaration but only terror in a God present still—but become an enemy.) It takes us closer, too, than any passage in all Christianity. For a Christian, Good Friday is always before Easter, which is why even Kierkegaard, though horrified by the fall of Jerusalem, has the edifying thought of being *with* God in his knowledge of being always wrong over against Him. The Jewish author of Lamentations has no such certainty. He exists in an unredeemed world, in possession only of the promise of redemption. And since, unlike the Christian, he belongs not to a spiritual but rather a flesh-and-blood people, it is always possible—"so changeable are human affairs"[2]—that this promise is falsified by history, that a destruction so total might occur that no remnant is left. Then why is Lamentations in the Jewish Bible?

The commitment to include the book in the biblical canon is much the same that ordained its liturgical use. (Both are part of rabbinic or "normative" Judaism.)

The way of its use on the ninth of Av demonstrates with great clarity just how close the rabbinic mind comes to the very brink of rupture—and that it is, nevertheless, able to withdraw. Lamentations ends with a stark question that remains unanswered: "Hast Thou utterly rejected us? Art Thou angry with us beyond measure?" (Lam. 5:22). However, after the liturgical reading of this verse, the second-to-last verse is repeated: "Turn us unto Thee, O Lord, and we shall be turned. Renew our days as of old" (Lam. 5:21). Here is the oldest, deepest life-and-death commitment of the Jewish people in its career in history. Even in extremity there still is a divine turning to the human, and a human being-turned by the Divine; and in the prayer itself there is a human turning to the Divine, even as it is being turned. This dialectic of turning and being-turned is the stance of the ninth of Av toward all past catastrophe. It is the stance toward future catastrophe as well. A remnant has always turned and returned. One always will. It is this remnant that stands between the threat of rupture and rupture itself.

B

But will a remnant *always* return? Will there always *be* a remnant? Or does normative Judaism behave like Kierkegaard's bourgeois Christianity, for which the catastrophic destruction of Jerusalem becomes ever dimmer with the passage of time? Astonishingly, as the centuries wore on, the catastrophe of 70 C.E. became ever more vivid in the Jewish mind. In the Midrash we read:

> When the Holy One, blessed be He, remembers His children who dwell in misery among the nations, He sheds two tears into the sea, and the sound is heard from one end of the earth to the other. It is an earthquake.[3]

One imagines an earthquake, and thinks of floods, fires, collapsing houses. But what one thinks of above all is a rupture of the earth.

Another Midrash has the following:

> The night is divided into three watches, and in each watch sits the Holy One, blessed be He, and roars like a lion: "Woe unto Me that I have destroyed My house and burned My temple and sent My children into exile among the nations."[4]

The Midrash just cited belongs to the third century. Not until the eleventh century did it come to be reflected in ritual. If Rachel's children are in exile, are they not *His* children as well as hers? Shall He not weep with her and on account of her? And if He weeps at midnight, shall not *we* wake at this appointed time and weep with Him and for Him? And if these two laments—His and ours—reflect a rupture, shall not the divine-human *community* of waking and weeping be a *Tikkun*—a mending of what is broken? Thus with the rite of *Tikkun Hatzot*—the "midnight mending"—both a rupture and a mending of it takes shape before our eyes. The rite begins, and must begin, with *Tikkun Rachel*—the weeping for the children in exile—and goes on to *Tikkun Lea*—a rejoicing in the anticipated redemption. But it *can* go on only because *Tikkun Rachel* is *already* a *Tikkun*. It is an at-oneness of God and men because "men bewail not their own afflictions, but the one affliction that really counts in the world, the exile of the *Shekhina*."[5]

C

A "mending" takes place. But is there a real rupture? Normative Judaism shrinks from that assertion. Historical catastrophe is real. So is the divine involvement in it. However, the Midrash does not presume to penetrate the divine nature but is rather a human, metaphorical way of speaking. God only "as it were" weeps or roars like a lion. The Midrashic symbolism does not claim to have an ontological reference.

No such restraint is shown by kabbalistic Judaism in search of a truth beyond the Midrashic symbols. In its own symbolism, "a reality becomes transparent." "The vessels are broken." "The Shekhina is in exile." God Himself is in a state of *Tzimtzum*—a "retreat from the world"—without which the very being of the world would be impossible. These and similar symbols go in their reference beyond rupture in history, to a rupture of cosmic dimensions that involves no less than the "life and action" of Divinity itself.

It is not easy to say whether the kabbalistic impulse goes so far as to assert, at the price of "verging on the blasphemous," a rupture in the very "substance" of Divinity. Even so, the radical problematic in the logic of *Tikkun* comes clearly to light. The "exile of the Shekhina" and the "fracture of the vessels" refers to cosmic, as well as historical realities: it is *that* rupture that our Tikkun is to mend. But how is this possible when *we ourselves* share in the cosmic condition of brokenness? Yet just in response to this problematic the kabbalistic *Tikkun* shows its profoundest energy. It is precisely if the rupture, or the threat of it, is total, that all powers must be summoned for a mending. If the threat is to man, there is need to invoke divine as well as human power. If the threat is to God—the "exile" is "an element in God Himself"—then human power must aid the divine. And if this can be said without blasphemy, it is because the human aid is *itself* aided by the Divine. "The impulse below calls forth an impulse above."[6]

Such was the way in which, in the greatest catastrophes experienced and indeed conceivable prior to the Holocaust, the age-old Jewish dialectic of *Teshuva* was both transformed and preserved.

D

After 586 B.C.E., and again after 70 C.E., the children of Rachel went into exile: at Ravensbrück and Auschwitz, they were drowned in buckets and thrown into the flames. For centuries the kabbalists practiced their *Tikkun*, their "impulse below"—"Torah, prayer and *mitzvot*"—calling forth an "impulse from above": in the Holocaust their bodies, their souls and their *Tikkun* were all indiscriminately murdered. *No Tikkun* is possible of *that* rupture, ever after.

But the impossible *Tikkun* is also necessary. Then and there, many doubtless thought of their "Torah, prayer and *mitzvot*" quite consciously in terms of a *Tikkun*. Others, when engaged in the act of *kiddush ha-hayyim,* doubtless did not. Yet we on our part must think of *all* such acts of *kiddush ha-hayyim* as a *Tikkun*. Does it or does it not matter whether or not Pelagia Lewinska lived or died or, had she died, whether she died with dignity? Is the world different or the same because the Buchenwald Hasidim decided to buy the *tefillin*, and found in them an elixir of life? Or because the Warsaw Ghetto fighters fought? A Tikkun, *here and now, is mandatory for a Tikkun, then and there, was actual.* It is true that because a *Tikkun* of *that* rupture is impossible we cannot live, after the Holocaust, as men and women have lived before. However, if the impossible *Tikkun* were not also necessary, and hence possible, we could not live at all.

This impossible necessity must have been in the mind of Rabbi Yissachar Shlomo Teichthal, a leading Hasid of the Munkacher Rebbe, when he composed his *Em Ha-Banim Smeha* [The mother of the children is happy]. Teichthal wrote his book in the Budapest of 1943, and saw it published in 1944, just three months before the Nazis occupied the city. The rabbi was soon sent to Auschwitz and murdered.

In his book Teichthal wrote the following:

> Now if we shall rise and ascend to Zion we can yet bring about a *Tikkun* of the souls of the people Israel who were murdered as martyrs since it is on their account that we are stimulated to return to our ancestral inheritance. . . . *Thus we bring about their rebirth* [italics added].[7]

The author of this statement, a religious Zionist, was surely ignorant of the worst. However, what he knew was enough to destroy any notion of the Holocaust as a providential means to even the noblest Zionist ends: a state; a state blessed with justice at home and peace abroad; a state home to all persecuted if not all Jews. The attempt to justify the Holocaust as an evil means to any good however glorious would be blasphemous—and is impossible.

But Rabbi Teichthal's statement leaves us in no doubt that its author was innocent of blasphemy. The *Tikkun* he envisaged was not a good requiring and thus retroactively justifying the evil that it was to mend. Rather was it—both "the impulse below" and the "impulse above"—of a wholly different order. The return would not be of some esoteric mystics to an esoteric place in the land; it would be of the *whole* people to the *whole* Land. Israel's exile would come to an *absolute end.* So would the exile of the nations, of the cosmos, of the Godhead itself. The *Muselmänner* would live and be whole. The drowned and burned children of Rachel would be resurrected. And at that time—the End of *all* Time—all the unspeakable anguish would be remembered no more.[8] Such was the divine-human *Tikkun* that was envisaged by Rabbi Teichthal in his desperate ecstasy. After *that* rupture no less a *Tikkun* would be adequate.

Notes

1. Elie Wiesel, *Legends of Our Time* (New York: Avon, 1968), p. 230; Buber cited in To *Mend the World,* chapter IV, section 7.

2. This allusion to Spinoza—see To *Mend the World,* chapter II, p. 57—seems most fitting at this point.

3. Bab. Talmud, Berakhot 59a.

4. Bab. Talmud, Berakhot 3a. Any rabbinic reference to children in exile would at once call to mind Jer. 31:15ff.—the passage in which Rachel weeps for her exiled children and receives the promise of their return.

5. Gershom Sholem, *On the Kabbalah and Its Symbolism* (New York: Shocken, 1965), pp. 146 ff.

6. Gershom Scholem, *Major Trends in Jewish Mysticism* (New York: Schocken, 1965), pp. 27, 260ff., 232ff., and *passim.* Like every other writer on the Kabbalah, I am greatly indebted to Scholem's

work, all the more so because, in my case, a concern with the Kabbalah assumed real seriousness only with the present work.

7. Cited by Schindler, "Responses of Hasidic Leaders and Hasidim during the Holocaust," pp. 100 ff.

8. Scholem writes: "A young German recently wrote to me expressing the hope that Jews, when thinking of Germany, might keep in mind the words of Isaiah: 'Remember ye not the former things, neither consider the things of old.' I do not know whether the messianic age will bestow forgetfulness upon the Jews. It is a delicate point of theology. But for us, who must live without illusions in an age without a Messiah, such a hope demands the impossible . . ." (*On Jews and Judaism in Crisis* [New York: Schocken, 1976], pp. 91ff.)

21 *Jewish Existence after the Holocaust*

A

What is a Jew? Who is a Jew? These questions have troubled Jews, ever since the Emancipation rendered problematic all the old answers—those of Gentiles and those given by Jews themselves. Today, however, these same old questions, when asked by Jews, bespeak a hidden dread. It is true that the old post-Emancipation answers are still with us: a "religious denomination," a "nationality," a "nation like other nations," or, currently most fashionably in North American, an "ethnic group." Also, the much older Halakhic answer—"a child born of a Jewish mother or a convert to Judaism"—has gained a new lease on life; and, whether it is admitted or not, this is very largely thanks to the existence of the State of Israel. Finally, the fact of Israel itself, a modern state in the modern world, has shaken and confused all the old answers, i.e., the old post-Emancipation ones and the still older Halakhic ones, lending the question of Jewish identity a new kind of urgency. (The state exists. It *is* a state. It has problems that brook no postponement.) All this is true. Not true, however, is that all the above definitions, whether taken separately or together, today either exhaust the depth of the question or even so much as touch a dimension that is now in it. As for conferences on Jewish identity conducted in such terms alone, in these the hidden dread is shut out.

A Jew today is one who, except for an historical accident—Hitler's loss of the war—would have either been murdered or never been born. One makes this statement at a conference on Jewish identity. There is an awkward silence. And then the conference proceeds as if nothing had happened.

Yet the truth of the statement is undeniable. To be sure, the heroism and sacrifices of millions of men and women made the Nazi defeat no mere accident. But victory was not inevitable. Thus without as brief a diversion as the Yugoslav cam-

Reprinted, with changes, from *To Mend the World* (New York: Schocken Books, 1982), 294–302, 308–13, by permission of the publisher.

paign Russia might have been conquered. Thus, too, Hitler might have won the war had he not attacked Russia at all when he did—a gratuitous, suicidal lapse into a two-front war that is surrounded by mystery to this day.

No mystery, however, surrounds the condition of a world following a Nazi victory—the "New Order," as it already was called, or the "Free New Order," as in due course it might have been called. (As it was, the Auschwitz gate already bore the legend *Arbeit macht Frei.*) Such are the names and the propaganda. The reality would have resembled a vast, worldwide concentration camp, ruled by a *Herrenvolk* assisted by dupes, opportunists, and scoundrels, and served by nations conditioned to slavery. We say "worldwide," although a few semi-independent satellite states, modelled, perhaps, after Vichy France, might have been tolerated at the fringes. Of these the United States would surely have been the most prominent.

Such is the outer shape of a worldwide Nazi "New Order." Its inner essence would have been a murder camp for Jews, for without Jews to degrade, torture, and "exterminate," the rulers could have spiritually conditioned neither themselves to mastery nor the world to slavery. (Had Julius Streicher not said: "Who fights the Jew, fights the devil; who masters the devil, conquers heaven"?) However, with all, or almost all, Jews long murdered, the New Order would have had to invent ever-new Jews for the necessary treatment. (Had not Hitler himself once remarked that, if there were no Jews, it would be necessary to invent them?) Or alternatively, in case such an inventing were impossible—who except *real* Jews are the devil?—one would have had to maintain the fiction that Jews long dead were still alive, a mortal threat to the world.[1] (Had not Goebbels declared in the Berlin *Sportpalast* that Jews alone of all peoples had not suffered in the war but only profited from it—this in 1944, when most Jews of Europe were dead?) We speak advisedly of *all*, or almost all, Jews being dead. A worldwide Nazi New Order that permits semi-independent satellite states at its fringes is conceivable; Jews permitted refuge in them are not. (Had not Professor Johann von Leers argued that, by the principle of hot pursuit, the Third Reich had the legal right and the moral duty to invade surrounding countries, for the purpose of "exterminating" the "Jewish vermin"?) And if nevertheless only *almost* all Jews were dead, if a *few* still survived, this would be due to the help of some Gentiles whose ingenuity, endurance, and righteousness will always pass understanding.

Such would be our world today if, by ill fortune, Hitler had won the war. But by good fortune he lost the war; then why, for the sake of a future Jewish identity, conjure up the spectre of his victory? The answer is simple. One survivor, a poet, rightly laments that, except for a few missing persons, the world has not changed. Another, this one a philosopher, charges just as rightly that the world refuses to change, that it views the reminding presence of such as himself as a malfunctioning of the machinery. Long before either Jewish plaint—long before the *Ereignis* itself—the Christian Sören Kierkegaard had spelled out the abstract principle— that a single catastrophic event of monumental import is enough to call all things into question ever after.[2] We have cited such witnesses against others. As we now turn to our native realm of Jewish self-understanding, we can do no other than cite them against ourselves.

Even to do so only tentatively—preliminarily, as it were by way of experiment—is to discover, quite independently from all the previous complicated reflections and simply by looking at the facts, that to minimize, ignore, "overcome," "go beyond" the dark past for the sake of a happy and healthy future Jewish self-understanding is impossible. Empirically, to be sure, all this *is* possible: the phenomenon exists on every side. But morally, religiously, philosophically, humanly it is an impossibility. Shall we trust in God because we—though not they—were spared? Shall we trust in man because here and now—though not then and there—he bears traces of humanity? Shall we trust in ourselves—that we, unlike them, would resist being made into *Muselmänner*, the living dead, with the divine spark within us destroyed?

We can do none of these things; they are all insults, one hopes unwitting, to the dead. And behind these unintended insults lies the attempt to repress the hidden dread, to deny the rupture that is a fact. Above we asserted that philosophy and Christian theology can each find its respective salvation not by avoiding the great rupture, but only by confronting it. We must now turn this assertion against ourselves.

B

The move from non-Jewish to Jewish post-Holocaust thought is not a step but a veritable leap. This is so by dint of a single fact the implications of which brook no evasion. "Aryan" victims of the Third Reich, though robbed, enslaved, subjected to humiliation, torture, and murder, were not *singled out* unless they chose to *single themselves* out; Jews, in contrast, were *being* singled out *without choice of their own.* We have already considered this difference as it was manifest during the Holocaust itself. We must now consider its implications for today.

There are two such implications. First, whereas much of the post-Holocaust world is ruptured, the post-Holocaust *Jewish* world is *doubly* ruptured, divorced by an abyss not only from its own past tradition but also—except for such as Huber and Lichtenberg who, even then, bridged the gulf from the non-Jewish side—from the Gentile world. Second, whereas post-Holocaust philosophical and Christian thought finds a *Tikkun* in such as Huber and Lichtenberg, post-Holocaust Jewish thought finds itself situated after a world which spared no effort to make a *Jewish* Huber or Lichtenberg systematically impossible. For "Aryans," "crime," then as always, was a *doing*, so that in their case the Nazi tyranny, like other tyrannies, *created* the possibilities of heroism and martyrdom. For "non-Aryans," however, the crime was *being itself*, so that in *their* case—a *novum* in history, all previous tyrannies included—every effort was made to *destroy* the very possibility of both heroism and marytrdom, to make all such choosing, actions, and suffering into an irrelevancy and a joke, if indeed not altogether impossible.[3] The Jewish thinker considers the choiceless children; their helpless mothers; and finally—the achievement most revelatory of the essence of the whole Nazi world—the *Muselmänner*, these latter once free persons, and then dead while still alive: and he is filled not only with human grief but also with a metaphysical, religious, theological terror. Ever since Abraham, the Jewish people were singled out, for life unto themselves, and for a blessing unto the nations. And again and again throughout a long history, this people, however weary, responded to this singling-out act with the most profound freedom. . . . Ever since 1933, this people was singled out for death, and no effort or ingenuity was spared to make it into a curse to all those befriending it, while at the same time robbing it of the most elementary, most animal fredom. (No freedom is either more elementary or more animal than to relieve the bowels at the time of need.) The Reich had a research institute on the "Jewish question." Its work included serious, scholarly, professorial studies. These can have had no higher aim than to discover the deepest roots of Jewish existence and, after four thousand years of uninterrupted life, destroy them. The Jewish thinker is forced to ask: Was the effort successful?[4]

C

It is unthinkable that the twofold rupture should win out. It is unthinkable that the age-old fidelity of the religious Jews, having persisted through countless persecutions and against impossible odds—Yehuda Halevi expressed it best[5]—should be destroyed forever. It is unthinkable that the far less ancient, no less noble fidelity of the secular Jew—he holds fast, not to God, but to the "divine spark in man"—should be smashed beyond repair. It is unthinkable that the gulf between Jews and Gentiles, created and legislated since 1933, should be unbridgeable from the Jewish side so that the few but heroic, saintly attempts to bridge it from the Gentile side—we shall never forget such as Lichtenberg and Huber—should come to naught. It is this unthinkability that caused in my own mind, on first confronting it, the perception of a "614th commandment," or a "commanding Voice of Auschwitz," forbidding the post-Holocaust Jew to give Hitler posthumous victories. (This is the only statement of mine that ever widely caught on, articulating, as one reviewer aptly put it, "the sentiments . . . of Jewish shoe salesmen, accountants, policemen, cab-drivers, secretaries."[6]

But we must now face the fact—and here my thinking is forced to move decisively beyond the earlier perception just mentioned—that the unthinkable has been real in our time, hence has ceased to be unthinkable; and that therefore the "614th commandment" or "commanding Voice of Auschwitz" may well be a moral and religious necessity, but also, and at the same time, an ontological impossibility. In his time, as sober a thinker as Immanuel Kant could argue that since moral freedom, while undemonstrable, is at any rate also irrefutable, we all *can* do that which we *ought* to do. On our part and in our time, we need but visualize ourselves as victims of the Nazi logic of destruction in order to see this brave doctrine dissolve into the desperate cry, "I cannot be obligated to do what I no longer can do!" Indeed, such may well have been the last silent cry of many, just before, made into the living dead, they were no longer capable of crying even in silence.[7] Nor are we rescued in this extremity by the Jewish symbol of *Tikkun* in any of its pre-Holocaust uses, even when, as in the most radical of them, a rupture is admitted and confronted. We have seen that during the Holocaust the Nazi logic of destruction murdered kabbalistic no less than nonkabbalistic Jews—and their *Tikkun* with them. A would-be kabbalistic *Tikkun* of *our own* post-Holocaust rupture would inevitably be a flight from *that* rupture, and hence from our post-Holocaust situation as a whole, into an eternity that could only be spurious.

We are thus driven back to insights gained earlier in the present work:[8] the moral necessity of the "614th commandment" or "commanding Voice of Auschwitz" must be "rootless and groundless" (*bodenlos*) unless it is an "ontological" possibility; and it *can* be such a possibility only if it rests on an "ontic" reality.

With this conclusion all our Jewish thinking and seeking either comes to a dead halt or else finds a *novum* that gives it a new point of departure.

D

The Tikkun *which for the post-Holocaust Jew is a moral neccessity is a possibility because during the Holocaust itself a Jewish* Tikkun *was already actual.* This simple but enormous, nay, world-historical truth is the rock on which rests any authentic Jewish future, and any authentic future Jewish identity. (As is gradually emerging, it is also the pivotal point of the developing argument of this whole work.) We have already seen that the singled-out Jewish resistance *in extremis* to the singling-out assault in its own extremity is ontologically ultimate.[9] As we now turn from the Jewish past to a prospective Jewish future we perceive that this ontological Ultimate—a *novum* of inexhaustible wonder, just as the Holocaust itself is a *novum* of inexhaustible horror—is the sole basis, now and henceforth, of a Jewish existence, whether religious or secular, that is not permanently sick with the fear that, were it then and there rather than here and now, *everything*—God and man, commandments and promises, hopes and fears, joys and sorrows, life itself, and even a human way of dying—would be *indiscriminately* prey to the Nazi logic of destruction. The witnesses cited earlier all crowd back into the mind. We recall those we named. We also think of many we did not name and, above all, of the countless ones whose memory can only be nameless. As we ponder—ever reponder—their testimony, we freely concede that we, or others before us, may have romanticized it. We also concede that, yielding to all sorts of delusions, they may have done much romanticizing themselves. (Both errors are human.) But such concessions reveal only the more clearly that the astounding fact is not that many succumbed to the Nazi logic of destruction but rather that there were *some* who did *not* succumb. Indeed, even one would suffice to warrant a unique astonishment—and deny the evil logic its total victory.

We have reached this conclusion before. Our task now is to consider its implications for an authentic Jewish future. Above we repudiated the belief—an outworn idealism then, a case of humanistic twaddle now—that there is a core of human goodness that is indestructible. Now we must repudiate the belief—an outworn theology then, a case of Jewish twaddle now—that there is a Jewish substance—an *inyan elohi*, as it were[10]—that cannot be destroyed. Rather than in any such terms, the Jewish resistance to the singling-out Holocaust assault must be thought of as a life-and-death, day-and-night struggle, forever threatened with collapse and in fear of it, and saved from actual collapse—if at all—only by acts the source of whose strength will never cease to be astonishing. Their resistance, in short, was the *Tikkun* of a rupture. *This* Tikkun *is the* ultimate *ground of our own*.

· · · · ·

G

What is a Jew? Who is a Jew? After *this* catastrophe, what is a Jew's relation to the Jewish past? We resume our original question as we turn from one rupture in post-Holocaust Jewish existence—of the bond with the Gentile world—to the other—of the bond with his own past history, past tradition, past God.

After all previous catastrophes ever since biblical times, a Jew could understand himself as part of a holy remnant. Not that the generation itself was holy, a presumptuous view, and one devoid of any real meaning. The generation was rather *heir* to holy ones—not to the many who had fallen away but rather to the few that, whether in life or the death of martyrdom, had stayed in fidelity at their singled-out Jewish post. Was there ever a self-definition by a flesh-and-blood people that staked so much—staked *all*—on fidelity? It is the deepest definition of Jewish identity in all Jewish history.

It cannot, however, be the self-definition of this Jewish generation for, except for an accident, we, the Jews of today, would either have been murdered or never born. *We are not a holy remnant. We are an accidental remnant.* However we may wish to evade the grim fact, this is the core definition of Jewish identity today.

The result is that we, on our part, cannot consider ourselves heir to the few alone. (For the religious among us, the martyrs and their prayers; for the secularists, the heroes and their battles.) We are obliged to consider ourselves heir to the *whole* murdered people. We think of those made into *Muselmänner* by dint of neither virtue nor vice but some "banal incident." We think of the children; their mothers; of the countless saints, sinners, and ordinary folk who, unsuspecting to the end, were gassed in the twinkling of an eye. And what reaches us is nothing so much as *the cry of an innocence that shakes heaven and earth; that can never be stilled; that overwhelms our hopes, our prayers, our thought.* Maimonides is said to have ruled that any Jew murdered for no reason other than being a Jew is to be considered holy. Folk tradition, already existing, cites Maimonides to this effect and views *all* the Jewish victims of the Holocaust as *kedoshim*—as holy ones. Only in this and no other sense are we, the accidental remnant, also a holy remnant. *In this sense, however, our holiness is ineluctable and brooks no honest escape or refusal.*

This circumstance places us into a hermeneutical situation that, after all that has been said about a post-Holocaust *Tikkun,* is new and unique still. Indeed, the dilemma in which we are placed is so extreme, so unprecedented, so full of anguish as to seem to tear us in two; and as to cause us to wonder whether, at the decisive point where all comes to a head, a post-Holocaust *Tikkun* of any kind is not seen, after all, to be impossible.

The dilemma is as follows. If (as we must) we hold fast to the children, the mothers, the *Muselmänner,* to the whole murdered people and its innocence, then we must surely despair of any possible *Tikkun;* but then we neglect or ignore the few and select—those with the opportunity to resist, the will and strength to resist, deriving the will and strength we know not whence—whose *Tikkun* (as we have seen) precedes and makes mandatory our own. And if (as also we must) we hold fast to just these select and their *Tikkun,* then *our Tikkun,* made possible by *theirs,* neglects and ignores all those who performed no heroic or saintly deeds such as to merit holiness and who yet, murdered as they were in utter innocence, must be considered holy. Not accidentally, "Holocaust theology" has been moving toward two extremes—a "God-is-dead" kind of despair, and a faith for which, having been "with God in hell," either nothing has happened or all is mended.[11] However, post-Holocaust thought—it includes theological concerns but is not confined to them—must dwell, however painful and precariously, between the extremes, and seek a *Tikkun* as it endures the tension.

The *Tikkun* emerging from this tension is composed of three elements: (a) a recovery of Jewish tradition, . . . (b) a recovery in the quite different sense of recuperation from an illness; and (c) a fragmentariness attaching to these two recoveries that makes them both ever-incomplete and ever-laden with risk. Without a recovered Jewish tradition—for the religious Jew, the Word of God; for the secular Jew, the word of man and his "divine spark"—there is no Jewish future. Without a recuperation from the illness, the tradition (and hence the Jewish future) must either flee from the Holocaust or be destroyed by it. And without the stern acceptance of both the fragmentariness and the risk, in both aspects of the recovery, *our* Jewish *Tikkun* lapses into unauthenticity by letting *theirs*, having "done its job," lapse into the irrelevant past.

To hold fast to the last of these three elements is hardest but also most essential. Once Schelling and Hegel spoke scathingly about theological contemporaries who were momentarily awakened from their dogmatic slumber by the Kantian philosophy but soon used that philosophy as a soporific: every old dogma, bar none, could become a "postulate of practical reason." Jewish thought today is in a similar danger. We remember the Holocaust; we are inspired by the martyrdom and the resistance: and then the inspiration quickly degenerates into this, that every dogma, religious or secular, is restored as if nothing had happened. However, the unredeemed anguish of Auschwitz must be ever-present *with* us, even as it is past *for* us. *Yom Ha-Shoah cannot now, or ever after, be assimilated to the ninth of Av.*

The attempt, to be sure, is widely made; but it is impossible. The age-old day of mourning is for catastrophes that are punishment for Jewish sins, vicarious atonement for the sins of others, or in any case meaningful, if inscrutable, divine decrees. The new day of mourning cannot be so understood, for it is for the children, the mothers, the *Muselmänner*—the whole murdered people in its utter innocence. Nor has the *Yom Ha-Shoah* ceremonial any such content, for it commemorates not Jewish sin but innocent Jewish suffering; not sins of others vicariously atoned but such as are incapable of atonement; not an inscrutable decree to be borne with patience but one resisted then, and to be resisted ever after. As for attempts to find a ninth-of-Av-meaning in the Holocaust—punishment for the sins of Zionism; or of anti-Zionism; or a moral stimulus to the world—their very perversity confirms a conclusion reached earlier in the present work: *Galut* Judaism, albeit most assuredly not *Galut* itself, has come to an end.[12]

Even so the attempt to assimilate *Yom Ha-Shoah* to the ninth of Av must be viewed with a certain sympathy. The cycle of the Jewish liturgical year—Rosenzweig described it sublimely—is an experience anticipating redemption. The ninth of Av, though a note of discord, fits into this cycle: but does *Yom Ha-Shoah*? The ninth of Av does not touch the Yom Kippur—the Jewish "experience" of the "end" not through "dying" but living.[13] *Yom Ha-Shoah* cannot but touch it; indeed it threatens to overwhelm the Yom Kippur. Martin Buber has asked his post-Holocaust Jewish question—not whether one can still "believe" in God but whether one can still "speak" to Him.[14] Can the Jew still speak to God on Yom Kippur? If not how can he speak to Him at all? The Jewish fear of *Yom*

Ha-Shoah—the wish to assimilate it to the ninth of Av—is a fear, in behalf not only of *Galut* Judaism but also of Judaism itself.

"Judaism and the Holocaust" must be the last, climactic question not only of the present exploration but also of this whole work.[15] Meanwhile we ask what ways of Jewish *Tikkun* there could be even if the climactic question had to be indefinitely suspended. These ways are many; their scope is universal. (The task is *Tikkun Olam*, to mend the world.) Yet they would all become insubstantial without one *Tikkun* that is a collective, particular Jewish response to history. This *Tikkun* may be said to have begun when the first Jewish "DP" gave a radical response to what he had experienced. Non-Jewish DPs, displaced though they were, had a home to which to return. This Jewish DP did not—and even so was barred by bayonets and laws from the land that had been home once, and that Jewish labor was making into home once again. Understandably, many of his comrades accepted these facts with a shrug of centuries, and waited for someone's charity that would give them the blessings of refuge, peace, and oblivion. (They waited in camps, often the very places of their suffering—and for years.) This Jewish DP took his destiny in his own hands, disregarded the legal niceties of a world that still classified him as Pole or German, still without Jewish rights, and made his way to the one place where there would be neither peace nor oblivion but which would be, without ifs and buts, home.

The *Tikkun* that is Israel is fragmentary. This fact need not be stressed, for it is reported almost daily in the newspapers. The power of the State is small, as is the State itself. It can offer a home to captive Jews but cannot force captors to set them free. Limited abroad, it is limited at home as well. It cannot prevent strife. It cannot even guarantee its Jewish citizens a culture or a strong Jewish identity. *Galut* Judaism may have ended; but there is no end to *Galut* itself, inside as well as outside the State of Israel.

If the *Tikkun* is fragmentary, the whole enterprise is laden with risk. (This too the papers report assiduously.) Within, *Yerida*—emigration of Israelis—threatens to rival or overtake *Aliyah,* the Ingathering. Without, for all the talk of a comprehensive peace, implacable enemies remain; and while enemies elsewhere seek to destroy a regime, or at most conquer a state, *these* enemies seek destruction of a state—and renewed exile for its Jewish inhabitants.

What then is the *Tikkun?* It is Israel itself. It is a state founded, maintained, defended by a people who—so it was once thought—had lost the arts of statecraft and self-defense forever. It is the replanting and reforestation of a land that—so it once seemed—was unredeemable swamps and desert. It is a people gathered from all four corners of the earth on a territory with—so the experts once said—not room enough left to swing a cat. It is a living language that—so even friends once feared—was dead beyond revival. It is a City rebuilt that—so once the consensus of mankind had it—was destined to remain holy ruins. And it is in and through all this, on behalf of the accidental remnant, after unprecedented death, a unique celebration of life.

It is true—so fragmentary and precarious is the great *Tikkun*—that many want no share of it, deny it, distort it, slander it. But slanders and denials have no power over those who are astonished—ever again astonished—by the fact that in this of all ages the Jewish people have returned—*have been* returned?—to Jerusalem.

Their strength, when failing, is renewed by the faith that despite all, because of all, the "impulse from below" will call forth an "impulse from above."

Notes

1. Hitler's remark is reported by Hermann Rauschning and is integrated into the latter's "revolution of nihilism" thesis. In an attempt to refute that thesis Eberhard Jäckel's *Hitlers Weltanschauung* (Tübingen: Wunderlich, 1969) starts out by asserting that Hitler was no nihilist but rather had a coherent, if evil, *Weltanschauung* composed of "principles." The book ends up, however, with the unwitting demonstration that with Hitler all except Jew-hatred was compromisable, and that what is grandiloquently called Hitler's "coherent *Weltanschauung*"—indeed, no less than a "thought system" with "theoretical foundations"—amounts only to this, that the nineteenth-century anti-Semitic slogan "the Jews are our misfortune" is made into a cosmic principle. In *Mein Kampf* Hitler himself writes: "If, with the help of the Marxist creed, the Jew is victorious over the other peoples of the world, his crown will be the funeral wreath of humanity and this planet will, as it did thousands [second edition: millions] of years ago, move through the ether devoid of men . . ." (p. 60).

2. See *To Mend the World*, pp. 134 ff., 189, 278.

3. See further, *Jewish Return*, chapter 15.

4. With this question we are forced to go beyond Buber's stance toward the Holocaust; see *To Mend the World*, chapter IV, section 7. This is not to say, however, that it ceases to be relevant, or that there may not be ways of recovering it.

5. In the *Kuzari* he asserts that the great Jewish virtue is not saintliness or humility but rather fidelity, and implies that this belongs not to some but to the whole people. Jews could "escape degradation by a word spoken lightly" (IV, pp. 22, 23). Only because they stay in fidelity at their singled-out Jewish posts do they exist as Jews at all.

6. *Jewish Return*, chapters 2, 3, 8; *God's Presence*, chapter 3; David Singer in *Commentary* (Oct. 1978), p. 83.

7. The careful reader will notice that, compared to my *Encounters* (in which all of ch. II is taken up with the Kantian "ought"), the role of Kantianism has diminished in the present work. This is so because of considerations which reach their climax in the present section.

8. See *To Mend the World*, chapter IV, section 4.

9. See *To Mend the World*, chapter IV, sections 8 and 9.

10. An allusion to Yehuda Halevi's *Kuzari, II*, pp. 34ff. Halevi attempts to establish the continuity of the Divine-Jewish covenant through the dubious doctrine of a "divine content" planted hereditarily into the Jewish people. That he does not embrace racism is proved by the fact that the whole work is addressed to a would-be convert. Nor is any respectable modern Jewish thinker a racist. However, not a few have affirmed an absolutely indestructible Jewish tradition—religious, moral, or, more vaguely, cultural.

11. The most influential expression of the first extreme is Richard Rubenstein's *After Auschwitz* (Indianapolis and New York: Bobbs-Merrill, 1966). A poignant expression of the second is Eliezer Berkowitz, *With God in Hell* (New York: Sanhedrin, 1979). As is clear from his *Faith after the Holocaust* (New York: Ktav, 1973), Berkowitz does not assert either that nothing has happened or all is mended. He does, however, affirm a *faith* for which this is true, i.e., one which, though deeply shaken by the Holocaust, is not altered in consequence.

12. See *To Mend the World*, chapter II, section 4.

13. See *Der Stern der Erlösung* (Frankfurt: Kauffmann, 1921), 493; *The Star of Redemption*, trans. William W. Hallo (New York: Holt, Rinehart and Winston, 1971), 393; *To Mend the World*, chapter II, section 3.

14. See *To Mend the World*, chapter IV, section 7.

15. See *To Mend the World*, chapter V.

4

Post-Holocaust
Jewish Thought

Introduction

Fittingly the concluding selection in Part 4 is the final chapter of *To Mend the World*, and fittingly too, that book ends with a Midrash: " 'You are My witnesses, says the Lord'—that is, if you are My witnesses, I am God, and if you are not My witnesses, I am, as it were, not God."[1] As Fackenheim notes, this Midrash on Psalm 123:1 has always been a favorite of his. But although he had cited it long ago, in 1952 ("Self-Realization and the Search for God," reprinted above), the changes in his own thinking have led to a significant change in its meaning for him. In the early paper, the Midrash is quoted as one among many[2] that exhibit the mutuality and paradoxical character of the Divine-human encounter, of faith itself. Even though infinite, the Divine Presence somehow depends upon human receptivity. In *To Mend the World*, after the exposure to Auschwitz and the derivation of the imperative to mend Judaism and the world, Fackenheim can say: "whether or not the world today realizes it, it cannot do without Jews—the accidental remnant that, heir to the holy ones, is itself bidden to be holy. Neither, in our time, can God Himself."[3] The change is dramatic; the role of human receptivity is particularized and made radical. Today even God, the possibility of His Presence and any remaining confidence in Him, depends upon Jewish fidelity. In a post-Holocast world, the Jewish people is *even* God's last hope.

Themes already embedded in the new exegesis of this Midrash run through all of Fackenheim's later work—responsibility and necessity, opposition to Jewish powerlessness, Jewish militancy and self-reliance, and an authentic recovery of Bible, Midrash, indeed of the rich diversity of the Jewish past. The selections in this chapter are intended to exhibit these themes and to do so in a way that shows the systematic interconnectedness of Fackenheim's "post-Holocaust" Jewish thought.

The proper place to initiate Jewish *tikkun* is a recovery of the classic texts of Judaism within the context of a post-Holocaust world. Such a task should extend not only to Midrash and Bible but also to Jewish philosophical texts, liturgy, Halachic writings, poetry, and so on. Obliquely certain liturgical issues are addressed in our final selection (*TMW*, chapter V), and we have chosen not to include any of Fackenheim's discussions of Jewish thinkers.[4] Properly we begin with a recovery of Midrash and an attempt to understand the Midrashic world, for it precedes Fackenheim's confrontation with the Bible both chronologically and systematically. Other selections might have been chosen, ones that more explicitly reflect the impact of the Holocaust on Fackenheim's understanding of Midrash in general and on his particular readings.[5] But the first chapter of *God's Presence in History* has special virtues. It contains his most developed "theory" of Midrash to date and of the place of Midrash within Jewish tradition as the object of recovery. In the chapter he introduces and explores the influential categories of "root experience" and "epoch-making event," and he shows how Midrash is the written expression of the paradoxical character of such events and their re-enactment. In addition, although he does not yet read with "suspicion"[6] the Midrashim of trust and salvation, he does attend to the Midrashic response to catastrophe, a theme that recurs in chapter 3 of *God's Presence in History* (see above) when he turns to assessing the adequacy of such a response as it confronts Auschwitz.

The article on reading the Bible, an attempt to rethink Martin Buber's classic paper[7] in a post-Holocaust context, advocates a non-spiritualized return to the realism of the Biblical text. At the same time, it explores how a jointly Jewish and Christian hermeneutics of the Bible might be possible. This latter theme sets the stage for the following pair of readings that deal with Jewish-Christian relations after the Holocaust and in the age of a "new Jerusalem." In 1967, Fackenheim wrote that "the Nazi Holocaust has brought Jews and Christians closer together—and set them farther apart."[8] In a sense his frequent attempts to understand Christian responsibility for the Holocaust, Christian heroism, and the vagaries of the Church's response to its own history, to the question of Jewish survival, and especially to the survival and vitality of the state of Israel—is all an attempt to understand this dialectic of coming together and separation.

To isolate the discussion of antisemitism from that of Christianity and Judaism is artificial but appropriate all the same. The task for the Church—no monolith to be sure—is to recognize its role, to examine itself, to oppose all tendencies to the hatred of Jews, and to acknowledge its obligation to Jewish survival. Fackenheim's discussion of antisemitism, its character and its development, is related to these themes but, as one might expect, extends far beyond them. For Fackenheim deals too with non-Christian antisemitism, with the shortcomings of the "liberal democrat" as the Jew's "feeble protector," and with the ways that anti-Jewishness now masquerades as anti-Zionism.

But one can hardly appreciate either Fackenheim's most recent discussions of Jewish-Christian relations or why he is so enraged about contemporary versions of anti-Zionism if one does not understand how he sees Israel's historic role, and the latter crucially depends upon the relation between Israel and the Holocaust. The understanding of Israel and its role in Jewish existence today has preoccupied Fackenheim since the late 1960s and his first visit to the state. The results are a profound rethinking of Zionism and the place of Israel in a post-Holocaust world, a rethinking that faces honestly the problems that plague the state and her people and at the same time never forgets the mandate, theoretically urgent and existentially real, to appreciate both the religious and secular dimensions of Israeli existence. Just as Rosenzweig provides us with an heroic portrait of the Jew as *baal teshuvah* (penitent), so—in a sense—has Fackenheim most recently begun to sketch a portrait of the paradigmatic Jew as *oleh* (immigrant to Israel).

In the years that separate this new endeavor from 1967, Fackenheim has wrestled with the problems of comprehending the theoretical role of Israel as a paradigmatic post-Holocaust expression of Jewish militancy. The primary result of these struggles is the conviction that since the Holocaust was made possible in part by Jewish powerlessness and a millennial hatred of Jews, the state of Israel, the paradigmatic Jewish expression of opposition to this "unholy combination," is now a moral necessity. "The world is somewhat less dark today because after the Holocaust there arose a state of Israel."[10] But why is this expression of opposition "paradigmatic," and why is it "Jewish?" The answer to these questions already comes in an early effort to expose the Hegelian system to the radical evil of Auschwitz and the rebirth of a Jewish political presence in history—both occurrences that Hegel's philosophy rules out as impossible.

> The Holocaust Kingdom murdered religious and secular Jews alike. . . . Only by virtue of a radical "secular" self-reliance that acts as though the God who once saved could save no more can even the most "religious" survivor hold fast either to the Sinaitic past or to the Messianic future. And only by virtue of a radical "religious" memory and hope can even the most "secularist" survivor rally either the courage or the motivation to decide to remain a Jew, when every natural impulse tempts him to seek forgetfulness and even bare safety elsewhere. . . . This commingling of religiosity and secularity has found historical embodiment in the rebirth of a Jewish State . . . . After the Holocaust, the Israeli nation has become collectively what the survivor is individually.[11]

This statement reveals a central theme of Fackenheim's understanding of Israel and her role in a post-Holocaust world. It also expresses a central feature of all post-Holocaust Jewish authenticity, that it is both secular and religious, both realistic and self-reliant on the one hand, and filled with a precarious awe and hopefulness on the other.

This hopefulness and this realism compel Jewish existence beyond a concern with its own survival. The diversity of themes already surveyed indicates why treating Fackenheim as narrowly parochial is to misunderstand him. Indeed, from an early stage it was clear that the moral dimension of Judaism, its concern with "widows and orphans,"[12] has continually been at the core of Fackenheim's conception of Jewish responsibility. Although published in his early period, "Religious Responsibility for the Social Order" reflects this attitude, as does the presence of certain themes in his later writings. These include the prominant role played in *To Mend the World* by the Nazi "creation" of the *Musselman*, the living dead, as a radical affront to our sense of human dignity and to human existence itself. In the writings of 1967–68 Fackenheim articulates Jewish moral obligation this way: "[Jews] are forbidden to despair of man and his world, and to escape into either cynicism or otherworldliness, lest they cooperate in delivering the world over to the forces of Auschwitz."[13] This sentiment, that our conception of humanity must be recovered and our commitment to human dignity reaffirmed, is prominant in both the selections reprinted below and throughout Fackenheim's recent writings.[14]

It is a well-worn path that leads from a discussion of Jewish ethics to God, but it is a path that Fackenheim does not take. Recall that for him the secular agnostic Jew, if authentic, at least hears the *mitzvah* and that the religious believing

Jew "hardly" hears more. For Fackenheim, the imposed commandment and its interpretations are there, God or no God. The hearing of the Voice is a further step beyond and one that may be difficult, nay impossible for most to take. For much of Jewish history, intimacy with God, the weighty sense of His Presence, these were the beginnings of Jewish self-understanding. Today, after Auschwitz, the Presence of God is the last matter to be discussed, that deepest, most transcendent and yet most difficult, feature of the Jewish past to be recovered and affirmed. Buber's question is still Fackenheim's, although now set in a much more developed setting: "How is a life with God still possible in a time in which there is an Auschwitz? . . . One can still 'believe' in a God who allowed those things to happen, but *how can one still speak to Him? Can one still hear His word?* . . . Can one still call on Him? Dare we recommend to the survivors of Auschwitz, the Job of the gas chambers: 'Call on Him, for He is kind, for His mercy endureth forever?' "[15]

The line of thinking developed in "Jewish Faith and the Holocaust" and chapter 3 of *God's Presence in History* arrived prematurely at the Divine Commanding Presence. There is a good deal of uncertainty about this Presence in these writings, but there nonetheless seems to be a leap—of courage if not of faith. For the non-believing Jew such a Presence is never acknowledged, although Fackenheim sometimes leaves the point unclear. In the *Judaism* Symposium he says that the "agnostic hears no more than the *mitzvah.* . . . The 614th commandment must be, to him an abrupt and absolute *given*, revealed in the midst of total catastrophe" and not the result of some humanly created or natural ideals.[16] But later he will say that "the secular Jew . . . by the sheer act of remaining a Jew, submits to a commanding Voice heard from Auschwitz that bids him testify *that some gods are false.*"[17] The generous reading must surely be that even the religious Jew cannot be so glib about the Divine Presence that commands but does not save. Surely the secular Jew—no matter how uncompromising his response—hears no Voice.

But even if Fackenheim is sure about the limitations of secular Jewish existence, what—since 1967–68—has he come to think about the authentic response of the 'religious' Jew? First, it is undeniable that Fackenheim still is committed to the continued possibility of revelation and to the concept of revelation inspired by Buber and Rosenzweig.[18] The real problem lies elsewhere. It is not the possibility of God's Presence that is at issue but rather its actuality and beyond that—or perhaps antecedent to that—the character of Jewish believing openness today. Is the latter a trusting expectation? Or a diffident chiding? Or both? At one level, these questions are answered in the final pages of *To Mend the World* (reprinted here) and in the course of Fackenheim's reflections on Wiesel's struggles with God.[19] At another, the questions are not yet answered in Fackenheim's writings there or anywhere. They hide in the suggestive recognition that the resisting victims of Auschwitz "felt under orders to live" and then in Nietzsche's enigmatic utterance, quoted by Buber and a favorite of Fackenheim's, "you take, and you do not ask who it is that gives."[20] For Buber, one never knows who the giver is but one does know that there is a giver; for Fackenheim, writing today, even that is too much to say. One thing is certain, that even the measured thoughts that once led to the Divine Commanding Presence may have been too facile, as is the hasty dismissal—urged by others—of the God of history, a victim of hard reality torturing a thought that is too easy, too malleable, too yielding.[21]

It is appropriate to end our remarks here, without a false decisiveness. At the same time, however, we should recall one feature of Fackenheim's interpretation of the Midrash quoted at the end of *To Mend the World*, that in a post-Holocaust world the nature and role of God in human affairs and Jewish history are not simply given to us. The Divine Presence as a present reality depends on the witness of the Jewish people and on the continued fidelity of Jews. In the best of worlds, perhaps the ideal image is that of God as *oleh* (immigrant), to Israel and the world.

Note on Readings

We have had to be very selective in this chapter, since there is so much more available in articles and books than could be reasonably collected into a single volume. In each case we have chosen readings that are both centrally important to a certain theme and show the development of Fackenheim's thinking. The footnotes to this introduction indicate readings that might usefully supplement our own. Among the most important, I think, are: "Demythologizing and Remythologizing in Jewish Experience: Reflections Inspired by Hegel's Philosophy" (*The Jewish Return into History*, ch. 9), which shows an interesting recovery of Midrash and contains a helpful, brief summary of Fackenheim's reading of Hegel; "Israel and the Diaspora: Political Contingencies and Moral Necessities; or, The Shofar of Rabbi Yitzhak Finkler of Piotrkov" (*The Jewish Return into History*, ch. 13); and "Concerning Authentic and Inauthentic Responses to the Holocaust," *Holocaust and Genocide Studies* 1, 1 (1986), 101–20. For those interested in the way that an authentic appreciation of the Jewish situation might influence the way that great Jewish thinkers are recovered, see the papers on Cohen and Buber, mentioned in the footnotes to this introduction.

Notes

1. *TMW*, 331.
2. See "Self-Realization and the Search for God," *QPF*, 39; *GPH*, 23; "Demythologizing and Remythologizing in Jewish Experience," 121.
3. *TMW*, 330.
4. Among his most excellent discussions are "Hermann Cohen—After Fifty Years," *Leo Baeck Lecture*; "Martin Buber: Universal and Jewish Aspects of the I-Thou Philosophy," *Midstream* (1974); *TMW*, chapter 2, 58–91, on Rosenzweig.
5. See "On the Life, Death, and Transfiguration of Martyrdom: Remythologizing in Jewish Experience," *The Jewish Return into History*, ch. 9 (reprinted here); "The Human Condition after Auschwitz," *JRH*, ch.7.
6. The phrase "hermeneutics of suspicion" is Ricoeur's.
7. "The Man of Today and the Jewish Bible," reprinted in Martin Buber, *On the Bible*, 1–13.
8. *JRH*, 32.
9. The terms are Jean-Paul Sartre's in the famous second chapter of *Anti-Semite and Jew* (New York: Schocken Books, 1948). In addition to the two selections reprinted here, see "Jewish 'Ethnicity' in 'Mature Democratic Societies': Ideology and Reality," *JRH*, ch. 11.
10. *JRH*, 198; see also "Israel and the Diaspora," *JRH*, ch. 13, passim, and "The Holocaust and the State of Israel," especially 284.
11. *EJM*, 167.
12. Fackenheim has admitted that the views expressed in the early article are still ones he

holds; they will be expressed in the post-Holocaust context in a forthcoming book on Judaism that includes a chapter on Jewish ethics. In addition, see *EJM*, ch. 2.

13. *GPH*, 84, quoted from "Jewish Faith and the Holocaust," *JRH*, 32.

14. See especially "On the Life, Death, and Transfiguration of Martyrdom"; cf. *TMW*, 201–47; *JRH*, chs. 1, 7.

15. Martin Buber, "The Dialogue Between Heaven and Earth," reprinted in *On Judaism* (originally delivered in 1951); quoted and discussed in *TMW*, 196–97.

16. *JRH*, 23; cf. *GPH*, 83.

17. *EJM*, 167; the point is even more difficult at *GPH*, 83.

18. *TMW*, 7.

19. "Midrashic Existence after the Holocaust," *JRH*, 261–72.

20. Martin Buber, "The Man of Today and the Jewish Bible," in *On the Bible*, ed. N. Glatzer (New York: Schocken Books, 1968), 10; and in Buber's *I and Thou*, trans. Walter Kaufman (New York: Scribners, 1970), 158; originally from Friedrich Nietzsche, *Ecce Homo*, ed. Walter Kaufman (New York: Vintage Books, 1967), 300.

21. See, for the best example, Richard Rubenstein, *After Auschwitz* (New York: Bobbs-Merrill, 1966).

RECOVERING MIDRASH
AND THE BIBLE

22 *The Structure of Jewish Experience*

Introduction

"The heavens were opened," writes the prophet Ezekiel in his opening chapter, "and I saw visions of God" (Ezek. 1:1). These may be common words in certain types of mystical literature which affirm visions of Divinity freely and easily. In the context of the Hebrew Bible (which shrinks from such visions in awe and terror) they are rare and bold. It is therefore not surprising that the chapter which follows these opening words is full of all-but-unintelligible mysteries. According to rabbinic tradition there is not, with the possible exception of Genesis, chapter 1 (which deals with *Ma'assey Bereshith*—"the Works of the Beginning"), any other chapter in the whole Bible which can match in depth and mysteriousness Ezekiel, chapter 1, which deals with *Ma'assey Merkavah* ("the Works of the Wheel")—nothing less than the nature of Divinity itself. No wonder the rabbis considered it dangerous for all except the most pious and learned to try to fathom the secrets of that chapter.

Yet the same tradition which holds this view also seems deliberately and dramatically to contradict it. In a well-known Midrash it is asserted that what Ezekiel once saw in heaven was far less than what all of Israel once saw on earth. Ezekiel, and indeed all the other prophets, did not see God but only visions and similes of God; they were like men who perceive a king of flesh and blood surrounded by servants of flesh and blood, and who are forced to ask, "which one is the king?" In the sharpest possible contrast, the Israelites at the Red Sea had no need to ask which one was the King: "As soon as they saw Him, they recognized Him, and they all opened their mouths and said, 'This is my God, and I will glo-

Reprinted, with changes, from *God's Presence in History: Jewish Affirmations and Philosophical Reflections* (New York: New York University Press, 1970), 3–4, 8–30. Copyright © 1970 by New York University, reprinted by permission of the publisher.

rify Him' " (Exod. 15:2). Even the lowliest maidservant at the Red Sea saw what Isaiah, Ezekiel, and all the other prophets never saw.[1]

The Midrash just cited and paraphrased deals with the subject of this discourse—God's presence in history. This subject is dealt with in countless passages in Jewish and Christian literature. The cited Midrash has special significance, however, because it affirms God's presence in history in full awareness of the fact that the affirmation is strange, extraordinary, or even paradoxical. The God of Israel is no mythological deity which mingles freely with men in history. He is beyond man—so infinitely beyond human reach that an opening of the heavens themselves is required if He is to become humanly accessible. Few are the men to whom such an opening was ever granted, and the reports of these few are so obscure as to be unintelligible to nearly all others. So infinitely is the Divine above the human! Nevertheless, the Midrash insists that not messengers, not angels, not intermediaries, but God Himself acts in human history—and He was unmistakably present to a whole people at least once.

. . . . .

Root Experiences

It would be incongruous for us to reject, as misleading, any beginning with abstract notions of history-in-general, and yet ourselves begin with Jewish history-in-general. We must rather begin with particular events within the history of the Jewish faith, or, more precisely, with epoch-making events.

Even this term is not yet precise or radical enough. In its millennial career the Jewish faith has passed through many epoch-making events, such as the end of prophecy and the destruction of the first Temple, the Maccabean revolt, the destruction of the second Temple, and the expulsion from Spain. These events each made a new claim upon the Jewish faith and, indeed, would not be epoch-making if it were otherwise. They did not, however, produce a new faith. What occurred instead was a confrontation in which the old faith was tested in the light of contemporary experience. Jewish history abounds with such confrontations between past and present. At least until the rise of the modern world, these have all one common characteristic. The strain of confrontation may often have come near a breaking point, yet present experience, however new, unanticipated, and epoch-making, never destroyed the past faith. Its claims upon the present survived. But—and this is crucial—this past faith had not come from nowhere but had *itself* originated in historical events. These historical events, therefore, are *more* than epoch-making. In the context of Judaism, we shall refer to them as *root experiences.*[2]

What, considered abstractly, are the characteristics of a root experience in Judaism? What are the conditions without which a past event cannot continue to make a present claim—the claim that God is present in history? According to Rabbi Eliezer, the author of the Midrash quoted at the beginning of this chapter, the maidservants at the Red Sea saw what even Ezekiel did not see. This means, on the one hand, that Rabbi Eliezer himself does *not* see and, on the other hand, that he *knows* that the maidservants *saw,* and he does not. If he himself saw, he would not defer to their vision—his own being superior or equal to theirs and in any case a present standard by which to measure the past. If he did not know that they had seen, their past vision would be of no present relevance and, indeed, would be wholly inaccessible. Only because of this dialectical relation between present and past can a past experience legislate to the present. *This is the first condition of a root experience in Judaism.*

By itself, however, this condition (as yet far from fully intelligible)[3] is far from sufficient as well. According to our Midrash, this condition would apply to Ezekiel's vision as much as to the maidservants' at the Red Sea. Yet Ezekiel's vision is not a root experience in Judaism. It is the experience of an isolated individual and may legislate to isolated individuals after him—those few to whom the heavens are accessible. At the Red Sea, however, the whole people saw, the lowly maidservants included, and what occurred before their eyes was not an opening of heaven but a transformation of earth—an historic event affecting decisively all future Jewish generations. These future generations, on their part, do not, like the maidservants at the Red Sea, see the presence of God. But to this day they recall twice daily in their prayers the natural-historical event through which that presence was once manifest, and the Passover Seder is wholly dedicated to it. Indeed, according to some rabbis, so profoundly legislating is this past event to future times that it will continue to be remembered even in the Messianic days.[4] *Its public, historical character is the* second *condition of a root experience in Judaism.*

Still missing is a third condition, and this will turn out to be the crucial one. The vision of the maidservants at the Red Sea may be analyzed into two components. First, they experienced impending disaster at the hands of the pursuing Egyptian army and then salvation through the division of the Red Sea; that is, they experienced a natural-historical event. But they also experienced the presence of God. Subsequent generations, on their part, recollect the natural-historical event, but they do not see what the maidservants saw. Both points are not in question in the Midrashic account. What is in question is whether, and if so how, *subsequent generations have access to the vision of the maidservants—to the presence of God.*

If they have no such access, then the event at the Red Sea cannot be a root experience in Judaism. A skeptic would in any case deny that the natural-historical event even happened, or else view it as a mere fortunate coincidence. What matters here is that even a believer would have little cause for remembering it. For the "miracle" remembered would be for him, not a past event of divine Presence, but merely one particular effect of a general—and remote—divine Cause. And, if his concern were with the general divine Cause, no particular effect would stand out in importance; and, if it were with particular effects, it should be with *present* effects, not with the dimly remembered past. In connection with a discussion of the religious relevance of history, Hegel somewhere wryly quotes a proverb to the effect that with the passage of time the past loses its truth. If later generations of Jewish believers have no access whatever to the vision of the maidservants, this proverb would be applicable to the event at the Red Sea.

Such proverbs cease to apply, however, if the past vision of the maidservants is somehow still presently accessible; for in that case a divine Presence, manifest in and through the past natural-historical event, could not fail to legislate to future generations. (This is true at least if, as the Midrash states, the Divinity manifest is not a finite, tribal deity but the universal "Creator of the World." The past presence of such a God can continue to legislate even in the Messianic days.) *This accessibility of past to present is the* third *and final characteristic of a root experience in Judaism.*

This characteristic is clearly if implicitly asserted by Jewish tradition. Thus the pious Jew remembering the Exodus and the salvation at the Red Sea does not call to mind events now dead and gone. He reenacts these events *as a present reality:* only thus is he assured that the past saving God saves still,[5] and that He will finally bring ultimate salvation. We have already stressed that Rabbi Eliezer knows that the maidservants saw the divine Presence at the Red Sea; we must now add that *he could not have this knowledge unless he had somehow himself access to their vision.*

But how shall we understand this access when Rabbi Eliezer—and the pious Jew during the Passover Seder—does not see what the maidservants saw? Indeed, how shall we understand the original event itself—a divine Presence which is manifest *in* and *through* a natural-historical event, not in the heavens beyond it?

An understanding is given in a remarkable passage in Martin Buber's *Moses*— one so remarkable and relevant to our purpose that we shall return to it again and again throughout this book. Buber writes:

> What is decisive with respect to the inner history of Mankind . . . is that the children of Israel understood this as an act of their God, as a "miracle"; which does not mean that they interpreted it as a miracle, but that they experienced it as such, that as such they perceived it. . . .
>
> The concept of miracle which is permissible from the historical approach can be defined at its starting point as an abiding astonishment. The . . . religious person . . . abides in that wonder; no knowledge, no cognition, can weaken his astonishment. Any causal explanation only deepens the wonder for him. The great turning-points in religious history are based on the fact that again and ever again an individual and a group attached to him wonder and keep on wondering; at a natural phenomenon, at an historical event, or at both together; always at something which intervenes fatefully in the life of this individual and this group. They sense and experience it as a wonder. This, to be sure, is only the starting-point of the historical concept of wonder, but it cannot be explained away. Miracle is not something "supernatural" or "superhistorical," but an incident, an event which can be fully included in the objective, scientific nexus of nature and history; the vital meaning of which, however, for the person to whom it occurs, destroys the security of the whole nexus of knowledge for him, and explodes the fixity of the fields of experience named "Nature" and "History.". . .
>
> We may ascribe what gives rise to our astonishment to a specific power. . . . For the performance of the miracle a particular magical spirit, a special demon, a special idol is called into being. It is an idol just because it is special. But this is not what historical consideration means by miracle. For where a doer is restricted by other doers, the current system of cause and effect is replaced by another. . . . *The real miracle means that in the astonishing experience of the event the current system of cause and effect becomes, as it were, transparent and permits a glimpse of the sphere in which a sole power, not restricted by any other, is at work.*[6]

Buber's modern terms may be applied to the ancient Midrash in every particular. First, they remove a false understanding. Second, they make sense of a divine Presence manifest in and through a natural-historical event. Third, they explain how Rabbi Eliezer, while unable to see what the maidservants saw, nevertheless has access to their experience. Let us consider these three points in turn.

Those present at the Red Sea do not *infer* their God from the natural-historical event in an attempt to *explain* that event. A god of this kind would not be "Creator of the world" or "sole Power" but only a "magical spirit." He would not be "immediately recognized" but at most would be a probable hypothesis. And he would not be present but, rather, necessarily absent. As for the abiding astonishment, this would be dissipated by the explanation. This much would be true even of the original witnesses at the Red Sea. As for subsequent believers (who already possess this or some other explanation), they would not be astonished at all. And the past would be a dead past without present relevance. So much for the first point. What of the second?

The "sole Power" is immediately present at the Red Sea, in and through *the natural-historical event* for *the abiding astonishment of the witnesses.* All three terms introduced by Buber are needed, and they are intelligible only in their relation. (a) Except for the immediate presence of the sole Power the natural-historical event would not be a miracle but rather a strange incident in need of explanation; and the astonishment would only be curiosity or, in any case, not abide, for it would vanish when the explanation is given. (b) Except for the abiding astonishment, the sole Power would not be present or, in any case, not be *known* to be present; and the miracle would, once again, be a mere incident to be explained. (c) Except for the natural-historical event, the sole Power, if present at all, would either be present in the heavens beyond history, or else dissolve all historical particularity by its presence within it; and the abiding astonishment would be equally historically vacuous. But the salvation at the Red Sea is not historically vacuous. It has "intervene[d] fatefully" in the history, if not of all mankind, certainly of Israel.

To come to the third point, how then is Rabbi Eliezer (and the pious Jew during the Passover Seder) related to the maidservants at the Red Sea? *In reenacting the natural-historical event, he reenacts the abiding astonishment as well, and makes it his own.* Hence the "sole Power" present then is present still. Hence memory turns into faith and hope. Hence the event at the Red Sea is recalled now and will continue to be recalled even in the Messianic days. Thus the reenacted past legislates to present and future. Thus, in Judaism, it is a root experience.

Saving and Commanding Divine Presence

We have thus far used one particular root experience in Judaism in an attempt to elicit the characteristics of all such experiences. We must now turn, however briefly, to one other such experience—the commanding Presence at Sinai. Not only is every attempt to understand Judaism without Sinai impossible, it is also the case that, except for a commanding Presence, any divine Presence in history remains, for Jewish experience, at best fragmentary.

The divine Presence thus far considered is a saving Presence. Salvation is not here, however, what it might be in a different religious context. It occurs *within* history, not in an Eternity beyond it, nor for a soul divorced from it, nor as an apocalyptic or Messianic event which consummates history. It therefore points necessarily to *human action.* In the Biblical account Moses cries unto God, but is told to bid his people go forward (Exod. 14:15). The Midrash dwells on this thought and affirms that no salvation would have occurred had Israel shrunk in fear from walking through the divided sea.[7] And it exalts one Naḥshon Ben Amminadab who, in the midst of universal hesitation, was first to jump into the waves.[8] *A commanding Voice is heard even as the saving event is seen; and salvation itself is not complete until the Voice is heeded.*

The astonishment abides as the commanding Voice is heard: this becomes clear when that Voice comes on the scene in its own right to legislate to future generations—in the root experience of Sinai. The structure of that experience is reflected in the following Midrash:

> Rabbi Azaryiah and Rabbi Aḥa in the name of Rabbi Yoḥanan said: When the Israelites heard at Sinai the word "I" [i.e., the first word of the ten commandments], their souls left them, as it says, "If we hear the voice . . . any more, then we shall die" (Deut. 5:22). . . . The Word then returned to the Holy One, blessed be He and said: "Sovereign of the Universe, Thou art full of life, and Thy law is full of life, and Thou has sent me to the dead, for they are all dead." Thereupon the Holy One, blessed be He, sweetened [i.e., softened] the Word for them. . . .[9]

The Midrash affirms that at Sinai, as at the Red Sea, the whole people saw what Ezekiel and the other prophets never saw.[10] Yet because the divine Presence is here a *commanding* Presence, the astonishment has a different structure. A commandment effected by a distant divine Cause would be divine only by virtue of its external sanction and inspire no abiding astonishment. If the astonishment abides, it is because Divinity is *present in* the commandment. Because it is a *commanding* rather than a saving Presence, however, the abiding astonishment turns into deadly terror. Indeed, such a Presence is, in the first instance, nothing short of paradoxical. For, being *commanding*, it *addresses human freedom.* And being *sole Power*, it *destroys* that freedom because it is only human. Yet the freedom destroyed is also required.

Hence the divine commanding Presence can be divine, commanding, and present only if it is *doubly* present; and the human astonishment must be a *double* astonishment. As *sole* Power, the divine commanding Presence *destroys* human freedom; as *gracious* Power, it *restores* that freedom, and indeed *exalts* it, for human freedom is made part of a covenant with Divinity itself. And the human astonishment, which is *terror* at a Presence at once divine and commanding, turns into a *second* astonishment, which is *joy*, at a Grace which restores and exalts human freedom by its commanding Presence.[11]

According to the Midrash all generations of Israel were present at Sinai, and the Torah is given whenever a man receives it.[12] A man can receive it only if he reenacts the double astonishment. If he remains frozen in stark terror, he cannot observe the commandments at all. And, if he evades that terror, he may observe the commandments, but he has lost the divine commanding Presence. Only by reenacting both the terror and the joy can he participate in a life of the commandments which lives before the sole Power and yet is human.

Dialectical Contradictions

But threats arise to the reenactment of the root-experiences of Judaism from two main quarters. One quarter is history itself. Since the reenactment does not occur in an historical vacuum, each historical present, or at any rate each epoch-making historical present, makes its own demands over against the past and its reenactment; and, since each epoch-making present must be taken seriously in its own right, it is not possible to anticipate the outcome. (Threats of this kind will occupy us during the remainder of this book.) Another type of threat, however, may be dealt with at once, for it is general, unchanging, and abstractable from history. This is the threat posed by reflective, philosophical thought.

The root experience itself is an immediacy, and so is its reenactment by subsequent believers. It is the potential object, however, of *philosophical reflection;* and the moment such reflection occurs it reveals the root experience to be shot through with at least three all-pervasive, dialectical contradictions.

The first of these is between divine transcendence and divine involvement. The "sole Power" present at the Red Sea and Mount Sinai manifests a *transcendent* God, for involvement would limit His Power; it manifests an *involved* God as well if only because it *is* a Presence. As will be seen, this contradiction exists even in the case of the saving Presence. In the case of the commanding Presence it is unmistakable.

This contradiction is logically first, but no more significant than the other two—respectively, between divine Power and human freedom, and between divine involvement with history and the evil which exists within it.

Divinity would not contradict human freedom if it were either present but finite, or infinite but absent—confined, so to speak, to heaven and leaving to man the undisputed control of earth. An infinite divine Presence, in contrast, is a present sole Power, which "explodes the fixity of nature and history," rendering "transparent" the causal nexus constituting both; and this negates the self and its freedom.

At the same time, the divine Presence *requires* the self and its freedom in the very moment of its presence. There is no abiding astonishment unless men exist who can be astonished; moreover, the divine Presence—saving as well as commanding—remains incomplete unless human astonishment terminates in action. Conceivably Ezekiel's selfhood dissolved in the moment in which the heavens were opened. This is impossible when, as at the Red Sea, salvation occurs to a flesh-and-blood people; or when, as at Sinai, the divine Presence gives commandments over for human performance.

The third contradiction arises because a God revealed as sole Power in *one* moment of history is revealed, in that very moment, as the God of *all* history.[13] Above we have rejected, as alien to the dynamic of the Jewish faith, all abstract doctrines concerning God-in-general, Providence-in-general, or man-in-general, which are only accidentally "applied" to the historical particular. It now emerges, however, that universality is implicit *in* the particular. A God present in *one* historical moment would not be "sole Power" if He were *confined to* that moment. He who fought at the Red Sea on Israel's behalf would not be "Creator of the World" if, having once fought, He could fight no more. Nor could the event of His presence be subsequently reenacted. But, if the God present in one moment of history is the God of all history, He is in conflict with the evil which is within it.

This must be listed as a third contradiction over and above that between divine Power and human freedom, if only because not all evil in history is attributable to human sin; and, still more decisively, because sin cannot be viewed as an act of freedom which, real from a human standpoint, is, from the standpoint of divine Providence, either an unreal shadow or an instrument to its purposes. These views are ruled out by the root experiences of Judaism—by the fact that the divine Presence occurs *within* history, not as its consummation or transfiguration. Salvation at the Red Sea is real only because the prior threat of catastrophe is real; as will be seen, it is incomplete even when it occurs; and—to put it mildly—when in subsequent ages this root experience is reenacted salvation is not always a present reality. Similarly, the freedom to reject the divine commanding Presence at Sinai exists at the very moment of presence, and this Presence cannot, as it were, play games with itself when it allows that possibility; moreover—again to put it mildly—subsequent generations of Israelites have not always matched the faithfulness of the generation of Sinai.

Such are the contradictions in the root experiences of Judaism insofar as they concern our present purpose. Philosophical reflection, on becoming aware of these contradictions, is tempted to remove them, and to do so by means of a retroactive *destruction of the root experiences themselves.* At this point, however, Jewish theological thought exhibits a stubbornness which, soon adopted and rarely if ever abandoned, may be viewed as its defining characteristic. Negatively, this stubbornness consists of resisting all forms of thought which would remove the contradictions of the root experiences of Judaism at the price of destroying them. Positively, it consists of developing logical and literary forms which can preserve the root experiences of Judaism despite their contradictions.

Jewish theological thought resists, first, a God who is sole Power but *without involvement,* withdrawn from history and demanding a like withdrawal from history on the part of His human worshippers. There has always been room for mysticism within Judaism, but never for an otherworldly mysticism which abandons salvation *in* and commandments *for* history, thus retroactively destroying the events at the Red Sea and Sinai.

Jewish theological thought resists, second, a sole Power which *overwhelms* history, allowing no room for either freedom or evil and manifesting itself as *Fate.* To be sure, it may seem at times that "all is in the hands of Heaven except the fear of Heaven." Even at such times, however, the fear of Heaven, far from a "small thing,"[14] is what makes history to the extent to which human freedom then can make it. To embrace fatalism would be retroactively to destroy the freedom manifest at both Sinai and the Red Sea, and thus these root experiences themselves.

Jewish theological thought resists, finally, any notion of a God who is not, after all, "sole Power" or "Creator of the world"—*a god as finite as the idols.* Such a notion, to be sure, is not rejected simply; i.e., at the price of belittling or denying either human freedom or evil. But neither is it simply acceptable. Instead, a dialectical tension develops, and this points to a future in which evil is vanquished by divine Power and human freedom, and in which divine Power and human freedom are reconciled. This future, a necessity for theological thought, is a necessity for immediate experience as well, and indeed rivals in significance the root experiences of the Red Sea and Sinai. It is not, however, itself a root experience, for it is a future anticipated rather than a past reenacted. If nevertheless it is as basic as these root experiences, it is because, without that anticipation, any reenactment of the root experiences of Judaism remains incomplete. Indeed, these experiences themselves remain incomplete. The Messianic faith arose at a relatively late date in Jewish history. As will be seen, it is implicit in Judaism ever since the Exodus.

The Midrashic Framework

Negatively, Jewish theological thought resists the dissipation of the root experiences of Judaism. Positively, it aims at preservation. It succeeds in its aim by becoming Midrashic. In the preceding pages we have already made much use of Midrashic thinking. We must now pause briefly to consider its nature.

Five characteristics will suffice for the present purpose:

(i) Midrashic thinking reflects upon the root experiences of Judaism, and is not confined to their immediate—e.g., liturgical—reenactment.

(ii) For this reason Midrashic, like philosophical, reflection becomes aware of the contradictions in the root experiences of Judaism.

(iii) Unlike philosophical reflection, however, it a priori refuses to destroy these experiences, even as it stands outside and reflects upon them. For it remains inside even as it steps outside them, stubbornly committed to their truth. In the above-discussed two Midrashim, Rabbi Eliezer and Rabbi Yoḥanan both *reflect*, respectively, *upon* the events at the Red Sea and Sinai and *remain* immediately *at* the Red Sea and *before* Sinai.

(iv) Midrashic thought, therefore, cannot resolve the contradictions in the root experiences of Judaism but only express them. This expression (a) is fully conscious of the contradictions expressed; (b) is fully deliberate in leaving them unresolved; (c) for both reasons combined, is consciously fragmentary; and (d) is insistent that this fragmentariness is both ultimate for human thought and yet destined to an ultimate resolution. *Midrashic thought, therefore, is both fragmentary and whole.*

(v) Seeking adequate literary form, the Midrashic content can find it only in story, parable, and metaphor. Were they projected into the modern world, Rabbi Eliezer and Rabbi Yoḥanan might follow our present example and engage in a second-order philosophical reflection designed to explore the ontological and epistemological status of their Midrashim. However, this would not replace their first-order reflection which would remain committed to the *truth* of the root experiences of the Red Sea and Sinai even as it reflected upon them. Unless we shall find cause to judge otherwise,[15] to this day their stance remains normative for the Jewish theologian. Having engaged in a second-order reflection upon Midrash as a whole, he must himself retell the old Midrash—or create a new.[16]

The Logic of Midrashic Stubbornness

We shall illustrate the above abstract contentions by a few concrete examples and confine these to the events at the Red Sea and Sinai.

We begin with a verse in the Biblical song sung at the Red Sea: "YHVH is a man of war, YHVH is His name" (Exod. 15:3). Why, the first of the two Midrashim we shall cite asks, are the seemingly superfluous words "YHVH is His name" added? Lest the idolatrous nations have an excuse for believing in many gods. For at the Red Sea He "appeared . . . as a mighty hero doing battle . . . at Sinai He appeared as an old man full or mercy." The words "YHVH is His name" are added, then, to teach that, while a God manifest *in* history manifests Himself differently according to the exigencies of the historical moment, He is, nevertheless, manifest *in each* moment as the *one* sole Power of *every* moment. "It is He who was in the past and He who will be in the future. It is He who is in this world and He who will be in the world to come. . . ."[17]

But our second Midrash shows that this universal revelation at the Red Sea would be wholly pointless if, in the case of the idolatrous nations, it fell on wholly deaf ears. However, it did not fall on deaf ears. All the nations joined in the words "Who is like unto Thee, O Lord, among the gods" (Exod. 15:11)?

> As soon as the nations of the world saw that Pharaoh and his hosts perished in the Red Sea and that the kingdom of the Egyptians came to an end, and that judgments were executed upon their idols, they all renounced their idols, and opened their mouths and, confessing God, said: "Who is like unto Thee, O Lord, among the gods?" You also find that in the future likewise the nations of the world will renounce their idols.[18]

The universality of the sole Power manifest in a unique saving event demands a correspondingly universal human *recognition* of its universality, thus inspiring the poetic truth of the universal abolition of idolatry. We have cited two Midrashim: they must be taken together.

But if taken together they reveal a contradiction. This appears even in the first Midrash taken by itself: a God who, by Himself, was, is, and shall be, yet must be present *differently* if His presence is to be *within* history. A contradiction is more evident in the second Midrash taken by itself: the nations forsake idolatry only poetically, and even then only for a moment, a fact which makes a Messianic reference necessary. The contradiction is altogether inescapable when the two Midrashim are taken together. The God who is Lord of history was, is, and shall be sovereign as sole Power. Yet, even in a supreme (albeit pre-Messianic) manifestation of His power, He stands in need of human glorification; and the fact that this glorification is momentarily given by all the nations reveals more poignantly the paradox of a subsequent relapse into idolatry by the nations, Israel herself included. Confronting this contradiction and commenting upon the verse "I will glorify Him" (Exod. 15:7), Rabbi Yishmael asks: "Is it possible for a man of flesh and blood to add to the glory of His Creator?"[19]

Rabbi Yishmael's question is radical. If the event of divine saving Presence is complete without glorifying human recognition, then man, his abiding astonishment included, has lost all significance for the Divine; and the Divine is sole Power, either because It is indifferent to history or because It overwhelms history. And if human glorification is required, then even a saving divine Presence—not to speak of a commanding Presence—is incomplete without it. No wonder Rabbi Shim'on Bar Yoḥai seeks to avoid the dilemma when he comments on the same Biblical verse as follows: "When I praise God, He is lovely; and when I do not praise Him, He is, so to speak, lovely in Himself."[20]

Rabbi Shim'on's answer does not, however, escape from the dilemma. How can human praise add to the divine glory and yet human failure to give praise not diminish it? Other rabbis (and Shim'on Bar Yoḥai himself in a different context) admit that human failure to give praise, so to speak, weakens the Power on high.[21]

Rabbi Yishmael himself answers his own question as follows: " 'I will glorify Him' means: I shall be beautiful before Him in obeying the commandments."[22] This answer, however, only serves to reproduce the dilemma in a still more ultimate form. A saving divine Presence may require only human recognition; a commanding divine Presence requires human action. The saving Presence may conceivably (if only momentarily) overwhelm human freedom. The commanding Presence cannot do likewise without becoming an intrinsic impossibility. Hence, as the Midrashic writers turn from the first to the second, they are forced to face up to an unmitigated paradox: " 'Ye are My witnesses, saith the Lord, and I am God' (Isa. 43:12). That is, when ye are My witnesses, I am God, and when ye are not My witnesses, I am, as it were, not God."[23] "When the Israelites do God's will, they add to the power of God on high. When the Israelites do not do God's will, they, as it were, weaken the great power of God."[24]

Taking all the cited Midrashim together, we find that the contradictions between divine transcendence and divine involvement and between divine Power and human freedom are not resolved but only expressed; and, indeed, that the expression could not be more frank, open, and conscious.

However, the Midrash holds fast to the *truth* of these contradictory affirmations even as it expresses their contradictoriness. In rabbinic theology, the term "as it were" (*k'b'yakhol*) is a fully developed technical term, signifying, on the one hand, that the affirmation in question is not literally true but only a human way of speaking; and, on the other hand, that it is a truth nonetheless which cannot be humanly transcended. The rabbinic thinker both *reflects upon* his relation to God and yet *stands directly before* Him, and his theology is consciously and stubbornly fragmentary.

But this does not exhaust the stubbornness of rabbinic thought. Conceivably one might speculate that the contradictions between divine transcendence and divine involvement and between divine Power and human freedom, all too real from the standpoint of man, are nevertheless transcended from the standpoint of God. And such speculation might (as, for example, in Kant)[25] take the form of a mere experiment of thought, or (as notably in Hegel)[26] that of a bold, actual ascent of thought to Divinity. In either case speculation might entertain the idea that history in the sight of God is other than history in human experience. For man, history is shot through with sin and suffering, only rarely lit up by the divine Presence; for God, it is transparent in the light of divine Power, and all darkness consists of insubstantial shadows. What is grimly real for human experience is, in the ultimate perspective, a cosmic game.[27]

Rabbinic thought stubbornly rejects a God playing such games and stubbornly holds fast to the reality of human history—even in the sight of God. To do otherwise would be, in the final analysis, to be unfaithful to the root experiences of Judaism—to a God present *in* history. How could Divinity be actually present as commanding unless obedience and disobedience made a real, ultimate difference? How could even a saving Divinity be actually present if the human perception of salvation were a matter of irrelevance?

All problems and dilemmas might resolve themselves if the saving divine Presence transfigured history. The divine saving Presence at the Red Sea, however, *occurs in* history and does *not* end or transfigure it. A much-quoted Midrash relates that when the ministering angels beheld the destruction of the Egyptians at the Red Sea they wanted to break out into song. God, however, reproved them, saying, "My children lie drowned in the Red Sea, and you would sing?"[28] This Midrash is much-quoted, for it encourages moralistic sermons concerning a God endowed with universal benevolence. The real content of the Midrash, however, is otherwise. *Even in the supreme but pre-Messianic moment of His saving presence God cannot save Israelites without killing Egyptians.* Thus the infinite joy of the moment—a moment in which even the maidservants saw what no prophet saw—is mingled with sorrow, and the sorrow is infinite because the joy is infinite. Thus the root experience in Judaism is fragmentary and points to a future consummation because of its fragmentariness. Thus God and man in Judaism pay each their price for the stubbornness with which they hold fast to actual—not "spiritual"—history.

The Divine Presence and Catastrophe

But one may hold fast to history and yet do so not very seriously. Seriousness is tested in self-exposure to crisis situations. Rabbinic faith and thought were uniquely tested when, in 70 C.E., the Temple was destroyed by Titus, and still more so when, after the Bar Kochba revolt, Hadrian transformed Jerusalem into a pagan city (135 C.E.). Rarely in all the subsequent centuries was there to be a comparable clash between the root experiences of Judaism and present historical realities, and the well-nigh inescapable temptation of the times was to flee from history into either gnostic individualism or apocalyptic otherworldliness. The rabbis, however, remained *within* the Midrashic framework, and indeed, responded to the radical crisis with the most profound thought ever produced within that framework. This was because they both faced the present with unyielding realism and held fast to the root experiences of Judaism with unyielding stubbornness.[29]

Never before had the conflict between past and present been so radical. It is true that the God of past history, revealed as the God of all history at the Red Sea and Sinai, could often seem to be in conflict with present history. But one obvious response to this apparent conflict had always been to view suffering as deserved punishment, and in the earlier books of the Bible—notably Judges—this response had seemed totally adequate. To be sure, this was no longer so in the later books of the Bible. But the Book of Job questions this response only on behalf of the individual; and while the prophet Jeremiah protests against the prosperity of the wicked (Jer. 12:1) he is also able to view the destruction of the first Temple as a divinely willed punishment and the tyrant Nebukadnezzar as the rod of God's anger and His instrument (Jer. 25:9, 27:6, 43:10).

No rabbi described Titus as God's instrument. No rabbi understood the paganization of Jerusalem as an event which was divinely willed. To quote N. N. Glatzer, the rabbis

> could still understand a *destroyed* Jerusalem in terms of a divine plan for history, not, however, a *pagan* Jerusalem. Only because of despair of the realization of the kingdom of God on earth did the protest against Rome in the form of an armed national insurrection come to include the Tannaitic rabbis, who had hitherto not required that form, guided as they had been by the idea of a divine plan. Only thus can one understand the fact that Rabbi Akiba, who had hitherto shown great . . . patience vis-à-vis Rome, was now gripped by the national impatience and agreed with Bar Kochba. . . .[30]

It is true that in their catastrophic present the rabbis did not fail to explore and deepen already familiar lines of response. Thus the second destruction of the Temple, like the first, was viewed as a case of deserved punishment; and the punishment then, as before, became bearable because repentance would end the exile even as sin had caused it. And yet, the vast Roman Empire was absurdly out of proportion to the sins of a handful of Jews; and to the repentance of that handful, ludicrously world-historical consequences had to be ascribed. Taken by itself and made absolute, then, this response was totally inadequate; it was bound to produce the view that God had destroyed His sanctuary without adequate cause, and that He was now distant and uncaring. "The concept of sin was insufficient to explain the course of events."[31]

Another long familiar response, too, if taken by itself and made absolute, was bound to lead to despair. In catastrophe the Psalmist had lamented that there was now a hiding of the divine Face and yet could hope that God's presence would again be manifest. The rabbis too spoke of a divine self-concealment. But was this enough? And was there any imminent hope? Not the second as far as one could anticipate. Not the first if the brute present realities were the evidence. According to Rabbi Shim'on Ben Gamliel, to write of the sufferings of the time was beyond all human power.[32] Rabbi Akiba, more full of hope than any other rabbi after the Temple had been destroyed,[33] was cruelly put to death by the tyrant Rufus after the Bar Kochba revolt. Was this how God "judged the righteous through the wicked"?[34] No wonder Rabbi Eleazar lamented that, ever since the destruction of the Temple, the gates of prayer were closed, and only those of tears were still open.[35] In earlier Jewish experiences the divine self-concealment had only been partial and temporary. Now it seemed otherwise. Now Rabbi Eleazar was forced to say: "Since the day of the destruction of the Temple, a wall of iron separates Israel from her Father in heaven."[36]

Had the rabbis staked all on the response of a divine self-concealment they would have lost the divine Presence in history in the time of Hadrian. Neither the past saving Presence nor the past commanding Presence could have continued to be reenacted. The past saving Presence would have been overwhelmed by the present catastrophe. Even the past commanding Presence would have vanished; there would have remained only obedience to commandments performed in God's absence. This being the case, what hope for a Messianic divine Presence could have remained in an age of *so total* a divine self-concealment?

In this extreme crisis the rabbis struck out boldly in a new direction. Far from being unconcerned or concealed, God, so to speak, cried out every night in bitter lament, as with a lion's voice.[37] Rather than judge the righteous through the wicked, He, as it were, lamented His own decision; in causing His Temple to be destroyed and His people to be exiled, either He could not act otherwise or had grievously erred.[38] Here as elsewhere Rabbi Akiba is bolder than any other rabbinic theologian:

> Were it not expressly written in Scripture, it would be impossible to say it. Israel said to God, "Thou hast redeemed Thyself," as though one could conceive such a thing. Likewise, you find that whithersoever Israel was exiled, the Shekhinah, as it were, went into exile with them. When they went into exile to Egypt, the Shekhinah went

into exile with them, as it is said, "I exiled Myself unto the house of thy fathers when they were in Egypt" (I Sam 2:27). When they were exiled to Babylon, the Shekhinah went into exile with them, as it is said, "For your sake I ordered Myself to go to Babylon" (Isa. 43:14). When they were exiled to Elam, the Shekhinah went into exile with them, as it is said, "I will set My throne in Elam" (Jer. 49:38). When they were exiled to Edom, the Shekhinah went into exile with them, as it is said, "Who is this that cometh from Edom . . ." (Isa. 63:1). And when they return in the future, the Shekhinah, as it were, will return with them, as it is said: "That then the Lord thy God will return with thy captivity" (Deut. 30:3). Note that it does not say, "The Lord will bring back" (veheshib), but it says, "He will return" (ve-shab).[39]

What an altogether breath-taking turn of thought! The thought is breath-taking, for it is as if Rabbi Akiba had looked ahead to an exile unequalled in length and depth of misery and then taken the only turn of thought which could have saved Jewish faith during that millennial trial. The Jew would be in exile, but not cut off from the divine Presence. He could still hold fast to history, for the God who had been present in history once was present in it still and would in the end bring total redemption. Thus for nearly two millennia the Jew—mocked, slandered, persecuted, homeless—held fast to the God of history with a faith which, if not in principle unshakeable,[40] remained in fact unshaken.

But Rabbi Akiba's turn of thought raises one all-important question. A God in exile still commands, for He continues to be present. His presence still comforts, for it holds out hope for a future salvation as His past saving acts are remembered. But where, we must ask, is the "sole Power" or the "Creator of the world"?

As if in reply to this question, Rabbi Joshua ben Levi taught a century after Rabbi Akiba:

> The men of the Great Assembly are given this title because they restored God's crown to its former state. For Moses had said, "the great, powerful and awe-inspiring God." Then came Jeremiah and said, "The Gentiles are destroying His Temple: where then is the fear of Him?" Hence he omitted[41] the adjective "awe-inspiring." Then came Daniel and said, "The Gentiles are enslaving His children: where then is His power?" Hence he omitted[42] the adjective "powerful." Then, however, came the men of the Great Assembly and said: "On the contrary, this is His power, that He controls His anger and is long-suffering to evil-doers; and this is His fear—how could one nation exist among the nations of the world without the fear of the Holy One, blessed be He?"
>
> Why did these sages alter what Moses had ordained? Rabbi Eleazer replied: "They knew of the Holy One, blessed be He, that He is truthful, and would say nothing untrue about Him."[43]

We conclude, then, that the rabbis remained true to the catastrophic historical present, even as they remained faithful to the saving and commanding past. They remained stubborn witnesses to the nations that all history both stands in need of redemption and is destined to receive it.

Notes

1. *Mekilta de-Rabbi Ishmael*, ed. J. Z. Lauterbach (Philadelphia: The Jewish Publication Society of America [1933], 1949), II, 24 ff. (Subsequently cited as *Mek.*)
2. For this concept I am indebted to Irving Greenberg's concept of "orienting-experience" (see

GPH, Preface). I here prefer the term "root experience" because I wish to analyze the intrinsic characteristics of the experience before considering its historical efficacy. It would be desirable to find a word uniting both connotations, but I have not been able to find such a word.

3. See *GPH*, pp. 13 ff.

4. *Mek*, I, 135 ff. The passage refers to the commemoration of the Exodus as a whole.

5. In the Passover Haggadah we find the following statement:

> It was not one only who rose against us to annihilate us, but in every generation there are those who rise against us to annihilate us. But the Holy One, blessed be He, saves us from their hand.

It is only a small exaggeration for me to say that whether, and if so how, the contemporary religious Jew can still include this sentence in the Passover Seder liturgy is the paramount question behind my entire investigation in this book.

6. Martin Buber, *Moses* (New York: Harper Torchbooks, 1958 [London: East and West Library]), pp. 75–77. (Italics added.)

7. See *Mek*, I, 216:

> Rabbi Eliezer says, The Holy One, blessed be He, said to Moses: "Moses, My children are in distress. The sea forms a bar and the enemy pursues. Yet you stand and say long prayers! Why do you cry unto Me?" Rabbi Eliezer was wont to say, there is a time to be brief in prayer, and a time to be lengthy.

8. *Mek*, I, 237.

9. *Midrash Rabbah*, Song of Songs, V 16 §3, trans. Maurice Simon (London: Soncino Press, 1961), pp. 252ff.

10. *Mek*, II, 212.

11. On this subject, see further my *Quest for Past and Future*, ch. 14 [see above, Part 2, Chapter 5].

12. See, e.g., *Midrash Tanḥumah*, Yitro.

13. On this point, see Buber's treatment of "moment gods," *Between Man and Man* (Boston: Beacon Press, 1955), p. 15.

14. *Bab. Talmud*, Tractate Berakhoth 33b. Rabbi Hanina, the author of this statement, adds that "God has in His storehouse nothing but the fear of heaven."

15. See *GPH*, chapter II.

16. See *GPH*, chapter III.

17. *Mek*, II, 31ff.

18. *Mek*, II, 59ff.

19. *Mek*, II, 25.

20. *Sifre Deut.*, Berakhah § 346.

21. Ibid.; *Sifre Deut.*, Ha'azinu § 319.

22. *Mek*, II, 25.

23. *Midrash Rabbah*, Psalms, on Ps. 123:1.

24. *Midrash Rabbah*, Lamentations, on Lam. 1:6.

25. See his *Critique of Judgment*, § 76.

26. See my *The Religious Dimension in Hegel's Thought* (Bloomington: Indiana University Press, 1968), especially chs. 5 and 6.

27. Hegel rejects and possibly is able to avoid this conclusion. But if he can avoid it it is because his rise in thought to Divinity is a Christian or post-Christian possibility.

28. *Bab. Talmud*, Tractate Megillah 10b.

29. This is comprehensively expounded and documented by N. N. Glatzer, *Untersuchungen zur Geschichtslehre der Tannaiten* (Berlin: Schocken, 1933). The present section of this chapter is greatly indebted to Glatzer's masterful work.

30. Ibid., p. 5.

31. Ibid., p. 106.

32. *Bab. Talmud*, Tractate Shabbath 13b.

33. Once four rabbis—Gamliel, Eleazar Ben Azaryah, Joshua, and Akiba—walked by the ruins

of the Temple. Suddenly they saw a fox emerging from the place which had once been the Holy of Holies. The others wept. Akiba, however, laughed, for he saw this event as confirming a prophecy of doom and was thus strengthened in his faith in another prophecy which promised redemption (*Midrash Rabbah*, Lamentations, III:18).

34. *Midrash Rabbah*, Lamentations, III:17.

35. *Bab. Talmud*, Tractate Berakhoth 32b.

36. Ibid.

37. *Bab. Talmud*, Tractate Berakhoth 3a.

38. Ibid.

39. *Mek*, I, 114 ff. See Lauterbach's notes which make it clear that the Scriptural proof-texts must be given a special interpretation in order to bear out Rabbi Akiba's Midrash.

40. See GPH, chapters II and III.

41. In Jer. 32: 16 ff.

42. In Dan. ch. 9.

43. *Bab. Talmud*, Tractate Yoma 69b.

23 New Hearts and the Old Covenant: On Some Possibilities of a Fraternal Jewish-Christian Reading of the Jewish Bible Today

1

In 1936 Martin Buber published a classic essay, "The Man of Today and the Jewish Bible."[1] In this he made some assertions which we should like here to use as hermeneutical principles. First, the Jewish Bible, though composed of many books, is nevertheless *one* Book because of its "basic theme," the "encounter of a people with the Nameless One." Second, generation after generation must wrestle with this book, although they do not by any means always do so in a spirit of "obedience" and a "willingness to listen," but often with "annoyance" and even "outrage." Third, decay takes place only when, as with modern man, all sense of commitment to the Book has vanished. We wish to follow these assertions, here used as guiding principles, with only three qualifications necessitated by the events that have occurred since the essay was written. First, we look at the world of today, and find that we can no longer speak of "modern man" but rather, in this context, only of modern Jews and Christians. Second, shortly after Buber's essay was written, an unprecedented event threatened and widely succeeded in dividing Jew and Christian, by murdering the one and tempting the other to become a bystander, accomplice or even active participant in the crime. Third, this event has created a new moral and religious necessity to do everything possible to bridge the ancient gulf between the two alienated brothers. But any such attempt depends in large measure on the ability of Jews and Christians to read the Book together.

Reprinted from *The Divine Helmsman: Studies on God's Control of Human Events*, eds. James J. Crenshaw and Samuel Sandmel (New York: Ktav Publishing, 1980), 191–205. Copyright © 1980 by Ktav Publishing, reprinted by arrangement with the author and publisher.

2

In this essay we shall not consider the One Book but only one chapter of one book of the One Book and, moreover, shall confine ourselves still further to only two passages which, in the JPS version, read as follows:

> Thus saith the Lord:
> A voice is heard in Ramah,
> Lamentation and bitter weeping,
> Rachel weeping for her children;
> She refuseth to be comforted for her children,
> Because they are not.

> Thus saith the Lord:
> Refrain thy voice from weeping,
> And thine eyes from tears;
> For thy work shall be rewarded, saith the Lord;
> And they shall come back from the land of the enemy.
> And there is hope for thy future, saith the Lord;
> And thy children shall return to their own border.
> (Jeremiah 31:15–17)

> Behold, the days come, saith the Lord, that I will make
> a new covenant with the house of Israel, and with the house of Judah;
> not according to the covenant that I made with their fathers in the
> day that I took them
> by the hand to bring them out of the land of Egypt;
> forasmuch as they broke My covenant, although I was a
> lord over them, saith the Lord. But this is the cove-
> nant that I will make with the house of Israel after
> those days, saith the Lord, I will put My Law into
> their inward parts, and in their hearts will I write
> it; and I will be their God, and they shall be My
> people; and they shall teach no more every man his
> neighbour, and every man his brother, saying: 'Know
> the Lord'; for they shall all know Me, from the least
> of them, unto the greatest of them, saith the Lord;
> for I will forgive their iniquity, and their sin will
> I remember no more.
> (Jeremiah 31:31–34)

The importance of the second above passage for the Christian reader is obvious: the very name 'New Testament' derives from it (See Heb. 8:8 ff.; 10:16–17). Since the importance of the first above passage for the Jewish reader is not so obvious, we shall furnish an illustration. A third century Midrash reads as follows:

> The night is divided into three watches, and in each watch sits the Holy One, blessed be He, and roars like a lion: 'Woe unto Me who have destroyed My house and burned My temple and sent My children into exile among the Gentiles!' (Bab. Talmud, Berakhot 3a)

God Himself, as it were, weeps for His children. He weeps not for symbolic children in a symbolic exile but rather for actual children in an actual exile. He weeps as would a flesh-and-blood father or mother. He weeps as Rachel does.

Gershom Scholem has noted that it took nearly a thousand years for this Midrash to find liturgical expression.[2] If God wakes up at midnight, shall *we* not wake with Him? And if He weeps for us and our children, shall we too not weep, not so much with Him as *for* Him?[3] And shall this divine-human community of waking and weeping not be the turning point, the beginning of the redemption? *Tikkun Hatzot*—the liturgical "midnight watch"—was thus divided into two parts. To be sure, the second—*Tikkun Leah*—consists of prayers expressing the hope for redemption. These prayers, however, would be fleshless, bloodless and vapid unless they were preceded by *Tikkun Rachel*—the mourning for the flesh-and-blood children in exile, suffering and unredeemed. This writer has heard of one man in his own city who observes *Tikkun Hatzot* to this day.

Must Jews and Christians, then, give different weight to the two Jeremiah passages which are our text? Perhaps this is inevitable. But let it be remembered that the two passages—part of the same chapter!—belong to the one Book. Neither passage may be denigrated, belittled, overlooked.

The most obvious way of reaching this hermeneutical goal lies in objective scholarship, opposed as it is to all bias. The Biblical scholar may be dubious about Buber's "One Book" thesis. He is committed, however, to a "value-free" stance in which no part of the Book is denigrated—or exalted—at the expense of others. Hence a venture in Biblical scholarship can be shared by participants who are Jews, Christians and those who are neither.

Let us test this commitment to a value-free stance with an example. The Anchor Bible is a respected work of Biblical scholarship. Its contributors include Christians and Jews. Its translations are accompanied by a maximum of philological notes and—presumably because of a suspicion of value judgments—by a minimum of interpretive comments. Yet John Bright, the author of the Jeremiah volume, writes as follows about Jer. 31:31 ff.:

> This passage represents . . . the high point of his theology. It is certainly one of the profoundest and most moving passages in the entire Bible.[4]

Of the Rachel passage Bright has nothing to say.

Whether or not assertions concerning "high points in theology" are value judgments is too large and deep a question for this brief essay and will therefore be dealt with only marginally below. But there is surely little doubt on the score about judgments concerning "profundity." And all doubt vanishes when a text is described as "most moving." We ask: most moving *for whom?* We might answer our question by resorting to a complicated philosophical discourse. However, far more telling in the present context is the simple and indisputable fact that, at least ever since the institution of *Tikkun Hatzot*, at least all Jews observing the rite have been moved far more deeply by the Rachel passage; and they have surely found themselves unable to pass on to the "new covenant" passage *except through* the Rachel passage. And what was true through the ages of a small group of observant Jews is true today of all Jews who remember—how can they forget?—what happened to the children of Rachel at Auschwitz and Ravensbrück.

3

Remarks by scholars about "moving passages" and "high points in theology" could be dismissed as mere lapses from the standards of value-free objectivity. Yet it is not merely the frequency of such "lapses" in the writings of Biblical scholars that gives us pause and raises questions, vis-à-vis the One Book, about the nature of objectivity itself. For one thing, no scholar, however committed to impartial justice to all parts of the One Book, can give equal attention to every segment within it: selectivity is inevitable. For another—and this is more serious still—, the scholar's task extends beyond such external matters as dating the texts to an attempt to understand them, and it is a notorious and possibly inevitable fact that one scholar's understanding differs from another. Thirdly, to these difficulties which apply to all texts must be added the difficulty concerning *this* text: the scholar, if he is Jewish or Christian, is heir to a tradition which regards it as revealed. (One might say in passing that a scholar who *qua* scholar denied the revealed status of this Book would surely be as little objective as one who *qua* scholar affirmed it, and that it is by no means obvious that this Book's claim to revealed status can even be suspended by resort to purely objective standards.) These difficulties cause the possibility to come into view that a truly *objective* selectivity from the texts and understanding of them, as well as an equally objective stance toward one's own tradition, cannot be found in the texts *alone*—confronted, as it were, nakedly—, but must lie at least in part in objective *standards brought to* the texts.

Let us test this view of scholarly objectivity by summarizing and comparing two interpretations of Jer. 31:31 ff., both of which, consciously or unconsciously, express and illustrate it.

> *Interpretation A:*
> This passage is the "climax" of Jeremiah's prophecies of salvation, for the new covenant is not a mere renewal of the old. Its essence lies in the "transformation" of the "duty to obey" the "covenantal law" as the "expression of an alien will" into a "need to obey felt by the heart itself," with the result that the law loses its "heterogeneous character."[5]

> *Interpretation B:*
> This passage represents the resolution of a "tension" between the "moral demand that sets limits to the working of God" and the "religious demand that subjects all to divine control." The "eschatological" resolution will render man "incapable of sinning."[6]

We make four observations:

(a) Neither interpreter *finds* his categories *in* the text, which does not know of an "alien" will or a "heterogeneous" law any more than of a "tension" between a "moral" and a "religious" demand. Consciously or unconsciously, these categories are *brought to* the text.

(b) The categories used by both interpreters are recognizably Kantian.

(c) Despite this fact, the two interpretations not only differ; if pressed, they are incompatible. For the first interpreter the new covenant *may* become (if it is not *already*) a *reality*, so that the old covenant may become (if it is not already) *de facto* superseded. (If further proof of this is needed, this first interpreter supplies it in full.)[7] For the second interpreter, the new covenant is an *ideal* which as such can be approximated but *never* be real, so that the old covenant as a *reality* is not and *cannot be* superseded.

(d) The author of the first interpretation is a Christian, that of the second, a Jew.

These four observations, taken together, pose a question. Shall we argue that the two interpreters have arrived at their respective categories on purely objective-philosophical grounds, so that it is only by dint of a happy coincidence, as it were, that the conclusions reached by them conform to their respective religious commitments? Or shall we argue that happy coincidences such as these are past reasonable belief, that on the contrary the choice of categories of interpretation is somehow dependent on a prior religious commitment? To be sure, it would be wayward to accuse serious scholars of what might be called philosophically-disguised propaganda—the deliberate use (or abuse) of whatever philosophical categories fit a predetermined religious case. But it is not wayward to suggest that there is at work, in both these cases and possibly inevitably, a pre-reflective understanding of the text which, to put it cautiously, somehow enters into the choice of interpretative categories once reflection comes on the scene. If such is our answer to the question, it follows that the highest degree of self-critical acumen, and hence possible objectivity, is reached only once the pre-reflective understanding of the text—in the one case Christian, in the other, Jewish—is brought to full self-consciousness.

Such is in fact part and parcel of the most sophisticated contemporary hermeneutical theory.[8] This latter argues that the modern interpreter cannot stand either above or over against history but is as much immersed in *his* history as is the text itself in *its own*. It pursues this doctrine ruthlessly with the insistence that the highest objectivity attainable for the interpreter is the rise above his own "bias" in the recognition of it, and that he can reach none higher. This radicalism has one virtue that excels all others: it induces humility toward interpreters of different ages and other traditions. Above all, it induces humility toward the text itself.

4

This sophisticated modern theory has a certain resemblance to much pre-modern, pre-critical, "old-fashioned" hermeneutical theory, both Christian and Jewish. Thus much Christian thought holds that a sacred text, to be understood, must be read in the spirit in which it was written, and that is the Holy Spirit at work in the history of the church (See e.g. Thomas À Kempis). On its part, much traditional Jewish teaching has it that "everything is in the Torah" (*Pirke Abot* V 25), that this is found when the Torah that is "written" is read in the light of the Torah that is "oral," and that this latter is alive in an unbroken tradition of learned and pious interpreters. However, whatever the persisting merits of this "old-fashioned" hermeneutics—and they are considerable—it is clear at once that it cannot lead to the Jewish-Christian dialogue which, as was hinted at the outset, is a contemporary imperative. To return to our texts, there is no need for examples or proofs to show that for the "old-fashioned" Christian hermeneutic the "new covenant" of Jer 31:31 ff. is a present, at least in principle accomplished fact in the Church of the Christ, that the spiritual children of Rachel have returned from their spiritual exile, and that their mother has long since heeded the divine bidding to refrain from weeping and tears. As for her physical children in their physical exile, they are at best an embarrassment and at worst an anachromism.[9]

Less obvious is the case of the "old-fashioned" Jewish hermeneutics if only because, unlike the Christian, it is required to take both texts on their own terms and not from a purportedly higher point of view. Rashi (1040–1105), the most popular of medieval Jewish commentators, simply omits any comment on Jer 31:31 ff. *ad locum*, although he does comment briefly—and innocuously—on the passage elsewhere.[10] Kimchi (1160?–1235?), one of the most sophisticated, does offer a comment which, however, includes the following sentence:

> He [i.e., Jeremiah] does not say that they will all be equal in wisdom, for *this is not possible* . . . ,but to "know Him" means to fear Him and follow in His ways. (Italics added)

Kimchi's words are as telling as Rashi's silence. Both contain a hidden apologetic, and this is anti-Christian. This element is present even when (as e.g. in one Midrash) a new covenant superseding the old is openly acknowledged—but firmly projected into the world-to-come.[11]

On the "old-fashioned" basis, then—or at least on it alone—, it is clearly impossible for Jews and Christians to read our texts together. The revealed authorities which inspire their respective reading are incompatible and mutually exclusive. There can be no "dialogue."

5

A "modern" hermeneutic is more promising for three main reasons. First, it must accept the methods of modern scholarship and can quarrel with specific results on no extraneous grounds and for no ulterior motives. Second, it cannot base a religious commitment—if such there is—on a revealed authority but must, on the contrary, view any acceptance of a revelation and its authority as resting on a logically prior religious commitment.[12] Third, it must bring to the fullest possible critical consciousness a "bias" on the interpreter's own part which is by no means confined to his unconscious or pre-conscious bond with a religious tradition (to say nothing of a free, fully-conscious religious commitment listed separately as our second point), but rather encompasses the full length and breadth of his historical situatedness as a whole. (With the last-named factor we resume contact with the contemporary hermeneutics to which reference has already been made.) It is obvious that, each in its own way, all three factors encourage what Franz Rosenzweig terms an "unfanatical" dialogical openness.

Of the first above factor nothing more need be said in the present context. Concerning the second and the third, the most thought-provoking question is which is the more fundamental in our time. At one time, much theologizing would lay most of the emphasis on the second if it did not ignore the third altogether. The events of our time, however, have caused our historical situatedness to loom so large as to render suspect any faith-commitment which is divorced from it. Indeed, even prior to these events hard-headed critics (of which Marxists are only the most vocal, and far from the most profound) have always viewed all commitments made in an historical vacuum with a well-warranted skepticism.

We may illustrate the need for such skepticism by considering two recent interpretations of our texts by two respected scholars. In a work published in 1963 Samuel Sandmel understands Jer 31:31 ff. as pointing to a "transition from the old Hebrew religion to Judaism." The "old Hebrew religion"—the covenant shared by a flesh-and-blood people in a land and a state—did in fact end, and "was inexorably bound to end in doom" when "the Babylonians had invaded and captured and destroyed." For the "Judaism" to follow—a "new worship" based on "inner conviction" and for that reason possible "outside Palestine"—"exile" was "no longer . . . a climactic catastrophe" but merely a "significant incident."[13] Such is this Jewish author's view of the new covenant. Of Rachel and her children he has nothing to say.

A good deal is said on this latter subject by S. R. Hopper, the "expositor" of the Book of Jeremiah in the respected *Interpreter's Bible*. However, the exile of the children, hardly mentioned, becomes at once transformed into "the abyss of emptiness within." And throughout the entire ensuing discourse it seems legitimate to resort to Yeats, Hölderlin, Francis Thompson and Heidegger for significant symbols of exile and return from exile. Only one thing seems totally ruled out: a confrontation with *non*-symbolic, *actual* exile, and the promise of a physical return from it. Thus it comes as no surprise that, whereas Sandmel's account of Jer 31:31 ff. spiritualizes the flesh-and-blood people, Hopper's account does away with it. (Indeed, having recourse to Heidegger, he does not hesitate to suggest that the old covenant was not with God but only with a "god"—and that this god is "passing.") Jer 31:31 ff. is the "gospel before the Gospel," superseded once the Gospel itself comes on the scene.[14] In short, Sandmel spiritualizes the flesh-and-blood children of Rachel. Hopper spiritualizes them away.

That both these expositions are shot through with commitments to a faith is surely obvious, and would be admitted by both at least in a moment of encounter. However, their conflict in faith would seem less significant than the bias which they share: both fail to confront Rachel's children in their actual exile, and neither brings to consciousness the bias which produces this failure. At one time any Marxist critic might have disposed of the faith of both writers as part of the ideological superstructure of a bourgeois existence that dwells in safety. However, such a criticism, in any case shallow and less than fair, has shown itself in our time as shot through with exactly the same bias as the would-be objects of its criticism. For no Marxist thinker that this writer knows of has as yet shown signs— any more than these two works, both written many years after it happened—of having confronted what was done to the utterly non-symbolic, physical children of Rachel during the Nazi Holocaust.

6

According to a reliable witness at the Nuremberg trials, this is what took place at Auschwitz in the summer of 1944:

> *Witness:* . . . women carrying children were [always] sent with them to the crematorium. The children were then torn from their parents outside the crematorium and

sent to the gas chambers separately. When the extermination of the Jews in the gas chambers was at its height, orders were issued that children were to be thrown straight into the crematorium furnaces, or into the pit near the crematorium, without being gassed first.

Smirnov (Soviet prosecutor): How am I to understand this? Did they throw them in the fire alive, or did they kill them first?

Witness: They threw them in alive. Their screams could be heard at the camp. It is difficult to say how many children were destroyed in this way.

Smirnov: Why did they do this?

Witness: It's very difficult to say. We don't know whether they wanted to economize on gas, or if it was because there was not enough room in the gas chambers.[15]

This is a report about Rachel's children. A Ravensbrück witness supplies the missing report about Rachel herself:

> In 1942, the medical services of the Revier were required to perform abortions on all pregnant women. If a child happened to be born alive, it would be smothered or drowned in a bucket, in front of the mother. Given a new-born child's natural resistance to drowning, a baby's agony might last for twenty or thirty minutes. . . .[16]

It is not possible for Rachel today to refrain her voice from weeping, or her eyes from tears. It is not possible for God's prophet or God himself today to bid her do so or, if doing this bidding, to be obeyed. Jews today cannot obey such a bidding. Neither can Christians. For, as Irving Greenberg has written,

> Judaism and Christianity do not merely tell of God's love for man, but stand or fall on their fundamental claim that the human being is . . . of ultimate and absolute value. ("He who saves one life is as if he saved the whole world"—Bab. Talmud, Sanhedrin 37a; "God so loved the world that He gave His only begotten son"—John 3:16.) It is the contradiction of this intrinsic value and the reality of human suffering that validates the absolute centrality and necessity of redemption, of the Messianic hope . . . The Holocaust poses the most radical counter-testimony to both Judaism and Christianity . . . The cruelty and the killing raise the question whether even those who believe after such an event dare talk about God who loves and cares without making a mockery of those who suffered.[17]

Christians today cannot pass over or beyond Rachel's tears. That Jews cannot do so has already found liturgical expression. It took a thousand years for the Midrash in which God weeps for His exiled children to find liturgical expression. One generation after Auschwitz and Ravensbrück there already exists a portion in a Yom Kippur liturgy which begins with Jer 31:14—Rachel weeping and refusing to be comforted—and climaxes with the question: "How can Your presence abide in a world where murder rules?"[18]

7

Then how can either Jewish or Christian readers proceed from the "Rachel" passage to the "new covenant" passage, the one in hope, the other with a faith in an (at least in principle) accomplished fact? It is tempting to overlook, belittle, denigrate this text, but this is not possible. Indeed, a new necessity exists for Jews and Christians to read it together. However, an "ugly, broad ditch" has erupted between the weeping Rachel and the good news of the new heart, and we "cannot get across" it, "however often and however earnestly . . . [we may try] to take the leap." Lessing (whose celebrated statement we quote) had in mind nothing more serious than a theological problem.[19] ("How can the acceptance of contingent historical truths be the source of my eternal salvation?") For this reason, he could hope for a theological solution which would "help him over" his ditch. *Our* ditch has erupted, however, not because of a theological "problem" but because of a human predicament without precedent. A theological "solution" of *this* predicament could consist only of some such assertion as that the burning and drowning children were a necessary part of the old covenant, or—"a reminder of the sufferings of the Christ"[20]—reenacted and overcome in the new. But such assertions are not "solutions" of a "problem" but rather a "mockery of those who suffered." What may or may not have been once a "high point in theology" has become a human impossibility.

Our ugly, broad ditch, then, remains. And we, who are at one side of it and must attempt to, yet cannot, reach the other have reached the point at which, as Buber said a generation ago, we must continue to occupy ourselves with the text but can no longer do so in "obedience," or a "willingness to listen," but only with "annoyance" and even "outrage."

8

It would be both thoughtless and un-Biblical to be annoyed-in-general or outraged-in-general. Instead, we are required to focus all attention on the unique scandal that, today, haunts us and gives us no peace. In this century (but prior to the kingdom of darkness) a great Christian thinker, Rudolf Otto, was able to write that even Job himself finds peace. This occurs when at length he surrenders to the numinous divine Presence, and so complete is the peace that when finally children are restored to him they are a mere "extra payment thrown in after quittance has already been rendered."[21] In the previous century Sören Kierkegaard, a still greater (and far more Biblical) Christian thinker had considered this "payment" neither "extra" nor indeed a "payment" but had rather perceived it as an essential gift of divine grace, so that, if Job is "blessed," this is solely because he has "received everything double."[22] Otto writes as he does because he considers the Christ as the "solution" of "that most mystical of all problems of the old covenant, the problem of the guiltless suffering of the righteous."

> The thirty-eighth chapter of Job is the prophecy of Golgotha. But on Golgotha the solution of the problem, already adumbrated in Job, is repeated and surpassed.[23]

On his part, Kierkegaard writes as he does because he is not concerned with "problems" to be "solved" (as they are for Otto) in a process of religious "evolution" but rather with a human predicament which is not just Job's but his own as well. Hence he writes:

Did Job lose his case? Yes, eternally: for he can appeal to no higher court than that which judged him. Did Job gain his case? Yes, eternally . . . for the fact that he loses his case *before God*.[24]

But does Job receive *everything* double? A. S. Peake notices that "while his possessions are doubled, it is a fine trait that the number of children is the same as before"—a fine trait at least "for us" who believe that "no lost child can be replaced."[25] It seems that even Kierkegaard (who speaks of Job's restored gifts indiscriminately as "everything"), though more Biblical than Otto, is not Biblical enough.

But then, is the Bible itself, as it were, Biblical enough? Joseph and Benjamin are irreplaceable children of Rachel. Other irreplaceable children in the Bible include Isaac, Jacob, Rebeccah, Leah and Rachel herself. Isaac is Abraham's "son," his "only son," whom he "loves." (Gen. 22:2) But what is true of such as these is not true, so it seems, of the children of Job. What of children such as these? Writing in Budapest in 1943, Rabbi Yissachar Shlomo Teichthal, a leading Hasid of the Munkacher Rebbe, had the boldness to write the following words:

> Now if we shall rise and ascend to Zion, we can yet reconstruct the souls of the people Israel who were murdered sanctifying the divine Name since, owing to their sacrifice, we were stimulated to return to our ancestral inheritance . . . Thus *we bring about their rebirth* . . . (Italics added)[26]

Like Job, Rabbi Teichthal did not seek an illegitimate refuge from his present anguish in the hereafter. But unlike Job he was exposed to so unprecedented an extremity that he could not (like Job according to Otto) carry out a mystical surrender; nor (like Job according to Kierkegaard) find himself blessed by receiving what Job had received. Presumably he did not or could not know of the children of Auschwitz and Ravensbrück. But what he did know was enough. And his knowledge forced him into the desperate faith that the return from exile of the children who had survived would restore to life the countless and nameless ones who had been brutally murdered. But whereas the return came to pass, this desperate faith—the hope for the End and the determination to help bring it about—did not.

Our "annoyance" with and "outrage" at the text—the stern refusal of Rachel to be comforted—is focused, then, on one single fact. This fact haunts, or ought to haunt, the religious consciousness of Jews and Christians alike. To Job sons and daughters are restored; but they are not the same sons and daughters. Children of Rachel have returned from exile; but they are not the same children.[27]

9. Postscript

Simha Holzberg is an orthodox Jew and a Hasid. He fought in the Warsaw Ghetto Uprising. He survived, made his way to Israel, and prospered. Holzberg, in short, was fortunate. But he was also haunted and without peace, rushing from school to school, kibbutz to kibbutz, synagogue to synagogue, always urging Jews to do more, to mourn more deeply, to remember more profoundly. It was not enough. It could not have been enough. Then came the Six Day War, and with it its widows and orphans. Then he made the deepest commitment of his life. He became the adoptive father of orphans, vowing to care for them until they were married.

Holzberg has remained a man of anguish. The great Wound is not healed nor can it be healed. The unprecedented extremity is not "overcome" or reduced to a "problem" about to be "solved" or already solved. However, this Israeli Jew has ceased to be haunted and has even found a measure of peace. When last heard of by this writer, he was already the adoptive grandfather of more than a hundred grandchildren.

Notes

1. *Werke* (Heidelberg: Lambert Schneider, 1964), vol. 2, 849 ff.

2. *On the Kabbalah and Its Symbolism* (New York: Schocken, 1965), 146.

3. See ibid. 149: "In observing . . . [*Tikkun Rachel*], men 'participate in the suffering of the *Shekhinah*' and bewail not their own afflictions, but the one affliction that really counts in the world, namely, the exile of the *Shekhinah*."

4. John Bright, *Jeremiah* (New York: Doubleday, 1965) 287. See also the amazingly similar comments in the *Cambridge Bible Commentary:* E. W. Nicholson gives only factual material about the Rachel passage but writes of Jer 31:31 ff. as follows: "This short passage is one of the most important in the Book of Jeremiah. Indeed it represents one of the deepest insights in the entire prophetic literature in the Old Testament" (*Jeremiah 26–52* [Cambridge University Press] 70).

5. Arthur Weiser, *Das Buch des Propheten Jeremiah* (Göttingen: Vandenhoeck & Ruprecht, 1952) 293 ff.

6. Yehezkel Kaufmann, *The Religion of Israel* (Chicago: University of Chicago Press, 1960) 75.

7. Weiser's commentary on Jer 31:31 concludes as follows: "According to Luke 22:20 and 1 Cor 11:25 Jesus, in instituting holy communion, understands Jeremiah's promise of the new covenant as fulfilled in his own person . . ."

8. We have in mind especially, though not exclusively, the work of H. G. Gadamer.

9. See e.g. Calvin on Jer 31:31 ff.: "He says that the covenant which he will make will not be such as he had made with their fathers. Here he clearly distinguishes the new covenant from the Law. The contrast ought to be borne in mind; for no one of the Jews thought it possible that God would add anything better to the Law. For though they regarded the Law almost as nothing, yet we know that hypocrites pretended with great ardour of zeal that they were so devoted to the Law that they thought that heaven and earth could sooner be blended together than any change should be made in the Law . . ." (*Commentaries on the Prophet Jeremiah and Lamentations* [Edinburgh, 1854] 128).

10. On Lev. 26:9 Rashi writes: ". . . and will establish My covenant with you": a new covenant not like the first covenant which you broke, but a new covenant which will not be broken, as it is written in Jer 31:31 ff . . ."

11. See e.g. *Tanh.B.*, Yitro 38b: "God said to Israel, 'On this day I have given you the Law, and individuals toil at it, but in the world to come I will teach it to all Israel, and they will not forget it.' "

12. See my treatment of this issue elsewhere, e.g. *Quest for Past and Future* (Boston: Beacon, 1970), ch. 8.

13. Samuel Sandmel, *The Hebrew Scriptures* (New York: Knopf, 1963) 147 ff.

14. *The Interpreter's Bible* (New York-Nashville: Abingdon, 1956) vol. 5, 1031 ff.

15. Quoted by Irving Greenberg, "Cloud of Smoke, Pillar of Fire: Judaism, Christianity, and Modernity after the Holocaust" in *Auschwitz: Beginning of a New Era*, E. Fleischner, ed. (New York: Ktav, 1977) 9 ff.

16. G. Tillion, *Ravensbrück* (New York: Anchor, 1975) 77.

17. Greenberg, ibid. 9–11.

18. *Gate of Repentance* (London: Union of Liberal and Progressive Synagogues, 1973) 297 ff.

19. *Lessing's Theological Writings*, H. Chalmers, ed. (London: Adam and Charles Black, 1956) 51–56.

20. Common charity prevents me from naming the Christian theologian who made this statement.

21. Rudolf Otto, *The Idea of the Holy* (Oxford University Press, 1950) 77 ff.

22. S. Kierkegaard, *Repetition* (Princeton University Press, 1946) 132.

23. Otto, ibid., 172 ff.

24. Kierkegaard, ibid. 133

25. A. S. Peake, *Job* (Edinburgh: T. C. & E. Clark, 1904) 346. The "fine trait" perceived by Peake is not perceived by the *Anchor Bible* commentator and translator who—alone, it seems, and on dubious philological evidence—renders Job 42:13 "He had twice (?) seven sons and three daughters" and proceeds to comment: "In any case, the number of daughters remains the same. A larger number of girls would have been a burden rather than a boon . . . The pagan Arabs used to bury unwanted daughters at birth for fear that the family would be impoverished by feeding them or later disgraced by their conduct . . ." (M. H. Pope, *Job* [New York: Doubleday, 1965] 289, 291) Why the behavior of some pagan Arabs should be the key to the understanding of a crucial Biblical passage Pope does not say. We should mention that Rashi, *ad loc.* too—one may perhaps say disappointingly—asserts that the number of Job's sons is doubled. However, he at least spares us comparisons between Job and "pagan Arabs."

26. Quoted by P. Schindler, *Responses of Hassidic Leaders and Hassidim during the Holocaust in Europe, 1939–45* (Ann Arbor: University Microfilms, 1972) 102 ff.

27. Astoundingly, the nineteenth century "Malbim" *ad locum* (Meir Loeb Ben Yechiel Michael) attributes to the rabbis the view that Job is given back the *same* children. He relies on the seventeenth century commentator Shmuel Edels (the "MaHa RShA") who in turn bases himself upon Bab. Talmud Baba Bathra f.15ff. However, this Talmudic passage gives no stronger encouragement to this interpretation than the failure to include among its citations from the Book of Job the passage (1:19) in which the death of Job's children is reported.

JEWISH-CHRISTIAN DIALOGUE

24 *Jews and Christians after Auschwitz*

The Nazi Holocaust has brought Jews and Christians closer together—and set them further apart. The first truth is comforting and obvious. The second is painful, complex, and obscure, but perhaps in the end more necessary to confront. The gulf between Jews and Christians that Hitler succeeded in creating can be bridged only if it is recognized. But to bridge it is of incalculable importance for the future of both Judaism and Christianity.

Since an objective grasp of this issue is almost impossible, I had better state my views in terms of my own subjective development. Twenty years ago I believed that what once separated Jew and Christian was now dwarfed by what united them—namely their opposition to Nazism. I was of course not unaware of phenomena like the Nazi "German-Christian" church, or of the fact that respectable and indeed outstanding theologians were part of it. But so far as my native Germany was concerned, it was not the Christian Nazis who mattered to me; it was rather the Christian anti-Nazis, however small their number—not the "German-Christian" but rather the German confessional church. And what mattered theologically was thinkers like Barth and Tillich, able to recognize Nazi idolatry and to fight it courageously and unequivocally. To this day I still revere Kierkegaard, the first Christian thinker to perceive the nature and extent of modern idolatry, who would surely have been put into a concentration camp had he lived and written in Nazi Germany. To this day I am supported in my Judaism by the faithfulness of Christians to their Christianity. And when a new generation of Christian theologians arises to proclaim the death of God I feel, as a Jew, abandoned and betrayed.

The ancient rabbis recognized "righteous Gentiles" as being equal to the high priest in the sight of God; but they had no real acquaintance with Christianity

Reprinted, with changes, from "Jewish Faith and the Holocaust," in *The Jewish Return into History* (New York: Schocken Books, 1978), 32–40, by permission of the publisher.

and, of course, none with Islam. Medieval Jewish thinkers recognized Christianity and Mohammedanism as valid monotheistic religions, and considering the state of medieval Jewish-Christian and Jewish-Moslem relations, it is surprising that they did. But since the experience of Nazism and of Christian opposition to Nazism (which goes back to my adolescence), I have been convinced that there is now a need for Jewish recognition that the Christian (and the Mohammedan) not only affirms the One God but also stands in a living relation to him. Where to go from here I cannot say. I never could accept Rosenzweig's famous "double covenant" doctrine, according to which all except Jews (who are already "with the Father") need the Son in order to find him. How can a modern Jew pray for the conversion of the whole non-Jewish world to Christianity when even premodern Jews could pay homage to Moslem monotheism? Rosenzweig's doctrine seems altogether outmoded at a time when Christians themselves are beginning to replace missionary efforts with interreligious dialogue, and I wonder whether even for Rosenzweig this doctrine was more than a stage in his self-emancipation from modern paganism.

Thus, though I very much feel the need for a Jewish doctrine of Christianity, I am left without one and must for the time being rest content only with openness to Jewish-Christian dialogue. As regards the prospect of such dialogue, I confess that I have over the years become less optimistic in the hope that the long age of Christian triumphalism over Judaism is truly being superseded by an age of Jewish-Christian dialogue. In view of recent Christian developments, such as ecclesiastical declarations deploring antisemitism and absolving Jews of the charge of deicide, this may seem a strange, and even perverse, personal opinion. Yet I think that recent events have shown it to be realistic.

To most impartial observers it has always been a plain fact that, ever since the Age of Enlightenment, it was secularists who spearheaded the struggle for Jewish emancipation; organized Christian forces sometimes accepted emancipation, often opposed it, but rarely if ever led the fight. This fact, plain to so many, I myself failed to see (or refused to accept) until quite recently. I saw the distinction between the new Nazi and the old Christian antisemitism, but could not bear to admit a relation between them. In the grim years of Nazism and immediately thereafter, I found it humanly impossible to see enemies on every side. Twenty-five years later, however, it is necessary to confront yet another painful truth.

I will confine myself to two examples, both concerning German Christians opposed to Nazism. In 1933, many Jews then in Germany, myself included, made a veritable saint of Cardinal Faulhaber, crediting him with opposing both Nazism and Nazi antisemitism. This image remained with me for many years. I had read the Cardinal's relevant sermons, but had somehow not noticed what they said. Not until about three years ago, when I came upon Guenter Lewy's masterful *The Catholic Church and Nazi Germany*, did I realize that Faulhaber had confined his defense to the Jews of the Old Testament, and had gone out of his way to make clear that he was not defending his Jewish contemporaries. To quote Lewy:

> We must distinguish, he told the faithful, between the people of Israel before the death of Christ, who were vehicles of divine revelation, and the Jews after the death of Christ, who have become restless wanderers over the earth. But even the Jewish people of ancient times could not justly claim credit for the wisdom of the Old Testa-

ment. So unique were these laws that one was bound to say: "People of Israel, this did not grow in your own garden of your own planting. This condemnation of usurious land-grabbing, this war against the oppression of the farmer by debt, this prohibition of usury, is not the product of your spirit."[1]

Rarely has the Christian belief in the revealed character of the Hebrew Bible been put to so perverse a use.

My second example is even more painful, for it involves none other than the universally beloved Dietrich Bonhoeffer, brave anti-Nazi Christian witness and martyr to his cause. Even now I find it hard to believe that he should have confined his attack on Nazi Aryan legislation to its application to converted Jews; and I find it even harder to believe that these words were written by Bonhoeffer in Nazi Germany in response to Nazi antisemitism:

> Now the measures of the state toward Judaism in addition stand in quite special context for the church. The church of Christ has never lost sight of the thought that the "chosen people," who nailed the redeemer of the world to the cross, must bear the curse for its action through a long history of suffering.[2]

Rather than comment myself, I prefer to cite the comment of the American Christian theologian, J. Coert Rylaarsdam:

> We all think of Dietrich Bonhoeffer as a good Christian, even a martyr, perhaps. With great courage he insisted on "the crown rights of the Redeemer" within his own church. Moreover, he insisted that Jews who had converted to Christianity were entitled to the same rights in the church as other Christians, a position by no means unanimously held in the church of Hitler's Germany. Nevertheless, standing in the Christian tradition of the curse, Bonhoeffer did not hesitate to appeal to it to rationalize Hitler's program for Jews faithful to their own faith.[3]

To keep the record straight, one must add that the passages in question were written in 1933 (when, according to his friend Eberhard Bethge, Bonhoeffer still suffered from "lack of reality-relatedness"), that his opposition to Nazism became more complete as it came to assume secular-political expression, and, indeed, that he took personal risks to save Jewish lives. Even so, I know of no evidence yet (though I would dearly love to hear of any) to the effect that Bonhoeffer ever totally repudiated the Christian "tradition of the curse." From the very beginning he opposed the encroachment of racism upon the church and spoke up for Jews converted to Christianity. By 1940 he charged that the church "was silent when she should have cried out because the blood of the innocent was crying aloud to heaven . . . she is guilty of the deaths of the weakest and most defenseless brothers of Jesus Christ." But during the most grievous Jewish martyrdom in all of history, did he ever repudiate a millennial Christian tradition, and seek a bond (even if only in his own mind) with "Jews faithful to their own faith," because, and not in spite of, their faithfulness? How different would Bonhoeffer's struggle have been if he had repudiated the "Christian tradition of the curse" from the start! How different would Jewish fate have been in our time had his whole church repudiated it!

In America, to be sure, it has always been different, and the churches of the

1960s differ everywhere from those of the 1940s, there being historic changes in the making in Christian attitudes toward Jews. The question is, however, whether American differences are not mainly due to the effect of secular democracy, and also whether the changes in Christian attitudes toward Jews possess the radicalism which, after Auschwitz, is a categorical imperative. Here again, only ruthless truthfulness can save the future of Jewish-Christian dialogue. And the truth, as I am now forced to see it, is that the organized Christian forces will find it easiest to drop the ancient charge of deicide, harder to recognize roots of anti-semitism in the New Testament, and hardest of all to face up to the fact that Jews and Judaism are both still alive. Confronted with the awkward fact of Jewish survival after the advent of Christianity, theologians have looked upon Judiasm as a fossil, an anachronism, a shadow. It is not easy to reverse a doctrine which has persisted for two millennia (assuming not only religious, but also, as in Toynbee, secular, and, as in Marx, anti-religious forms), and to recognize that both Jews and Judaism have maintained an unbroken existence throughout the entire Christian era. But how can a Jew, however he may strain his ears, hear God speak to the Christian church, if even after Auschwitz this ancient calumny is not at length totally and categorically rejected? And how, he wonders, can a Christian enter into dialogue with a Jew unless he recognizes that the person across the table is no shadow but alive?

These questions became traumatically vivid for any Jew committed to Jewish-Christian dialogue during the momentous events of May and June 1967, when the state of Israel, the most incontestable proof that the Jewish people still lives, was threatened with destruction. The secular Western press understood well enough that Israel was fighting for her life. Yet only a handful of Christian spokesmen showed the same understanding. Why should Christian spokesmen have remained neutral as between Israel's claim to the right to live and Arab claims to the right to destroy her—if not because of old, unconscious, theologically-inspired doubts as to whether the "fossil" Israel did indeed have the right to live? Why has there always been much Christian concern for Arab refugees from Israel, but none whatever for Jewish refugees from Arab countries—if not because of old, no longer consciously remembered ecclesiastical doctrines to the effect that Jews (unlike Arabs) must be kept landless, and therefore rightless? Why were ecclesiastical authorities untroubled by two decades of Moslem control of the Christian holy places (and of Arab desecration of Jewish holy places), and yet now so deeply distressed by Jewish control?

But a still more ultimate question is raised by the events of 1967. For two long weeks in May the worldwide Jewish community perceived the specter of a second Jewish Holocaust in a single generation. For two weeks it listened to the same words emanating from Cairo and Damascus which had once emanated from Berlin, largely composed, one may be sure, by pupils of Joseph Goebbels. For two weeks it longed for Christian words of apprehension and concern. But whereas some such words came from secular sources, from the churches there was little but silence.[4] Once again, Jews were alone. This fact, transcending as it does all politics, is a trauma for Jews regardless of political persuasion—non-Zionists and even anti-Zionists as well as Zionists. Moreover, it stands between Jews and Christians even now, for when Jews ask why there was no moral Christian outcry against a second Auschwitz they are still widely misunderstood, as demanding of Christians that they side politically with Israel against the Arab states.

Any Jew pondering this ultimate question must surely reject the idea that the Christian churches abandoned Jews knowingly to a second Holocaust. What, then, was revealed by the Christian silence in the spring of 1967? Not, I believe, an old Christian antisemitism, but rather a new Jewish-Christian problem—the fearful truth that Hitler, against his will bringing Jews and Christians closer, also had his will in setting them further apart.

A Jew at Auschwitz was murdered because he was a Jew; a Christian was murdered only if he was a saint: but there are few saints among either Jews or Christians. Hitler gave a new and perverse reality to the ancient Jewish doctrine that anyone born a Jew is a Jew. He also gave a new and perverse reality to the ancient Christian doctrine that one becomes a Christian only through an act of voluntary commitment—and, with diabolical cunning as well as terror, he led Christians into temptation. Hitler tried to create an abyss between Jews and Christians; he succeeded; and—this is the horror—he continues to enjoy posthumous successes. The Jew after Auschwitz exists with the knowledge of abandonment; the Christian cannot bear to face his responsibility for this abandonment. He knows that, as a Christian, he should voluntarily have gone to Auschwitz, where his own Master would have been dragged, voluntarily or involuntarily, and he is wracked by a sense of guilt the deeper the less he has cause to feel it. Hence the Christian failure to face Auschwitz. Hence Christian recourse to innocuous generalities. Hence, too, Christian silence in May 1967. If in May 1967 the Christian community did not cry out against a second Auschwitz, it was not because of its indifference to the words emanating from Cairo and Damascus, but rather because it did not hear them. It failed to recognize the danger of a second Holocaust because it has yet to recognize the fact of the first.

To bridge the Jewish-Christian gulf which Hitler has succeeded in creating is a task of incalculable importance, and at a Jewish-Christian colloquium prior to the events of May 1967 I attempted a hesitant step in that direction. I said there that if every Christian in Hitler's Europe had followed the example of the King of Denmark and decided to put on the yellow star, there would today be neither confusion nor despair in the church, nor talk of the death of God. I said with every emphasis at my command that, as a Jew after Auschwitz, I did not and could not speak as a judge, but only as a witness. To remove every trace of ambiguity or doubt I stated not politely, but quite truthfully, that I had been sixteen years of age when Hitler came to power, and had not known then, any more than I knew now, whether I would have become a Nazi had I been born a Gentile. Yet a leading Christian thinker, himself a lifelong anti-Nazi, mistook my statement for a case of Jewish triumphalism. So wide still is the gulf between Jews and Christians that Hitler opened decades ago. So close are we to handing him further, posthumous victories.

Notes

1. Guenter Lewy, *The Catholic Church and Nazi Germany* (New York: McGraw-Hill, 1964), p. 276.

2. Dietrich Bonhoeffer, *No Rusty Swords* (London: Fontana, 1970), p. 222. See also *Jewish Return*, pp. 74–75.

3. J. Coert Rylaarsdam, "The Disavowal of the Curse: A New Beginning?," *Dialogue*, Summer 1967, p. 192.

4. See A. Roy and Alice L. Eckardt, "Again, Silence in the Churches," *The Christian Century*, July 26 and August 2, 1967.

25 *Letters on Bonhoeffer*

I

February 1979

Dear Dr. Bethge:

I wish to tell you an incident which occurred in connection with my study of your masterful Bonhoeffer biography. My report will end with a question: I wonder if you can answer it? If so, your answer may well be of great importance for many people.

As soon as I obtained your book I decided to do what I always do with books that I wish to study quietly and with concentration, to read it in bed before going to sleep at the end of day. In this respect your book posed a certain difficulty: it is rather heavy. Hence I openly confess that, especially since it was so absorbing and I always went on reading more than I intended, on not a few occasions the book slipped out my hands and I fell asleep.

One night I sat up suddenly, and all tiredness had vanished. You write about the seven-point-memorandum that Bonhoeffer and some of his friends sent to Hitler—privately, as a letter of protest. They waited for an answer, naively, one must say. And then two of them, Werner Koch and Ernst Tillich, sent the memorandum to the press abroad, thereby transforming a heroic but surely futile gesture into an enormous political act. Whereupon the two were arrested by the Gestapo and sent to the concentration camp of Sachsenhausen.

Why did I sit up suddenly? After the Krystallnacht of November 1938 I myself was sent to Sachsenhausen and put into the same block as Tillich. Until my release three months later I saw him frequently and talked with him. He was a great

Translated by Emil Fackenheim from *Wie Eine Flaschenpost: Oekumenische Briefe und Bietraege fuer Eberhard Bethge* (Munich: Chr. Kaiser, 1979), 331–32 and *Konsequenzen: Dietrich Bonhoeffers Kirchenverstaendis Heute*, eds. Ernst Feil and Ilse Toedt (Munich: Chr. Kaiser, 1980), 1972–73.

source of strength for me, and possibly I, too, gave him a little comfort, for in our Jewish block there were only three Christians, and we had quite a few theological discussions. One of the others, Hans Ehrenberg, was depressed on Christmas eve since there were no Christians there to hear his Good News. Hence I, together with my fellow rabbinic students, asked him to share it with us, and that's what he did.

Naturally one subject of conversation with Tillich was more momentous than any other. We knew why *we* were in Sachsenhausen; but why was Tillich? (Ehrenberg was a "non-Aryan.") To this important question he answered that he had distributed some anti-Nazi pamphlets. And until I read your book I did not know the truth! He could not tell us. According to your book all the signatories of the memorandum were accused by *Gauleiter* Holz of high treason. Had Tillich told one and all what he had done the Nazis would surely have murdered him. Thus it happened that I understood only thirty years later that I was present when a historic event unfolded.

Now my question. I consider Bonhoeffer's conversion from a theological opponent with "insufficient reality-relatedness" (to use your term) to political plotter on Hitler's life a historic event, the consequences of which for a possible German as well as Christian future (including that of Jewish-Christian relations) are as yet far from sufficiently considered. Here you could be helpful in answering this question if you can: when Koch and Tillich were incarcerated for transforming a non-political gesture into a political act—how did this affect the others and in particular Bonhoeffer? Did it contribute to his theopolitical development? If so, how?

In asking this question I recall that Christmas eve in Sachsenhausen. I no longer remember what Ehrenberg said. But I remember very well our feelings that night. To this day I can say that never before or since has it seemed so right and meaningful to me that Christians and Jews should worship together.

II

1. I remember a passage in Bonhoeffer in which he accuses the church of having abandoned the Jews, "the most defenseless brothers of Jesus". . . . This says something about Bonhoeffer *the man* in his attitude toward Jews.

2. More important for the future is Bonhoeffer *the theologian*. I have heard Christians say that Bonhoeffer the man was better than Bonhoeffer the theologian; that is, that *theologically* he fought only in behalf of "non-Aryan" Christians. If he went beyond that, I for my part would wish to stress that. Moreover, it would be of inestimable importance for Christian theology. My own formulation would be this, that Germans can no longer speak evangelically to Jews.

3. If Bonhoeffer in fact said some such thing, one must ask exactly what he meant. Did he mean no more than this, that under certain existential conditions an evangelizing address to Jews is impossible? Or that the Holocaust was an epoch-making event that has altered Jewish-Christian relations ever after? Or that the Holocaust has only revealed what from the start was a Christian aberration. . .?
(From a query addressed to the English section of the Bonhoeffer Society, in the spring of 1979)

III

Rosenzweig wrote, for the first time, a Jewish hermeneutic of Christianity that recognized Christianity for Christians from a Jewish point of view. My purpose is to venture, within an overall work on Jewish existence after the Holocaust, a Jewish hermeneutic of Christianity after the Holocaust, naturally only as a brief sketch of fundamentals. This will assume that the Holocaust was an elemental event for Christianity also, but that the needed Christian hermeneutic can only be done by Christians themselves. (From a letter to Eberhard Bethge dated June 29, 1979.)

26 Concerning Post-Holocaust Christianity

A

Was the generation then living more wicked than the foregoing generations? . . . Was the whole nation corrupt, was there none righteous in Jerusalem, not a single one who could check God's wrath? . . . No, its destruction was determined; in vain the besieged city looked in anguish for a way out, the army of the enemy crushed it in its mighty embrace, and heaven remained shut and sent forth no angel except the angel of death. . . . Shall then the righteous suffer with the unrighteous?

What answer should me make? Should we say, "There now have elapsed now nearly two thousand years since those days; such a horror the world never saw before and never will again see; we thank God that we live in peace and security, that the scream of anguish from those days reaches us only very faintly. . . ."

Can anything be imagined more cowardly and disconsolate than such talk? *Is then the inexplicable explained by saying that it has occurred only once in the world? Or is not this explicable, that it did occur? And has not this, the fact that it did occur, the power to make everything inexplicable, even the most explicable of events?* [My italics.][1]

. . . Like philosophy, Christianity is ruptured by the Holocaust and stands in need of a *Tikkun*. Even in his own time Kierkegaard—surely the greatest, boldest, most uncompromising modern Christian thinker—gave an uncharacteristically lame answer to his own bold question: Man is always wrong over against God, and this thought "edifies." A lame response to the destruction of Jerusalem in 70 C.E., vis-à-vis the Holocaust, is it not blasphemous toward man and without glorification of God? Were the children wrong over against God? Their mothers? The *Muselmänner*? Are *we* wrong if we weep, protest, accuse on their behalf? Can any

Reprinted, with changes, from *To Mend the World* (New York: Schocken Books, 1982), 278–94, by permission of the publisher.

conceivable relation to God *edify* us as we hear those screams and gasps, and that no less terrible silence? Surely the Christian Good News that God saves in the Christ is itself broken by this news.

We must stress at the outset that the following is not a post-Holocaust resumption of the ancient Jewish-Christian debate concerning redemption. This debate, in any case proved to be fruitless by the experience of two millennia, could well degenerate into obscenity if it became involved in the comparison of sufferings, and if the Holocaust itself became a theological debating point. Rather than resume that debate, or any other Jewish-Christian debate, we shall attempt to enter into the Christian self-understanding, with a view to helping it confront the Holocaust. This is to serve the wider purpose of renewing—*of mending*—Jewish-Christian dialogue.

We speak advisedly of a renewal and a mending. We began this work with Franz Rosenzweig, who found himself standing both within and above Judaism, and able, for the first time in the history of Jewish thought, to give recognition to the Christian covenant from a Jewish point of view. Later we discovered the need for a post-Constantinian, post-Hegelian dialogical openness in which, from a Jewish point of view, dialogue with Christianity—though the future is open—is of central significance for a modern confrontation with revelation, this latter essential to both. Now that we have placed ourselves firmly within the stern limits of our post-Holocaust situation, these exalted aspirations are all unreal in comparison with the arduous task of narrowing the abyss between "Aryans" and "non-Aryans"—i.e., most Christians and all Jews—created and legislated in 1933, and made into an overwhelming reality with the rule of the Antichrist in Christian Europe. And that this was "only once" and "long ago" would be "cowardly and disconsolate talk" even if one glance at the newspapers—for instance, the report of a session of the United Nations—did not prove that the talk is false. One fervently prays that the Holocaust is over, and that it could have happened "only once." But anti-Semitism in the USSR, Nazis at large in Argentina, a declining Jewish birthrate and the isolation of Israel are all part of the sobering evidence that its aftereffects are still here.

B

No Christian *Tikkun* is possible unless the rupture is recognized. With few exceptions, Christian theologians avoid this recognition. Some argue that this "horror" "occurred only once" and "long ago"—not, to be sure, two thousand years, but at any rate well over thirty. Others argue that it was *not* just once, that today there are other "Holocausts" so that, lest attention be diverted from these new ones, the "old" one is best assimilated to the others if not forgotten.[2] We do not of course deny that the horrors of the present age—hunger in Africa, torture in the Gulag and, at this moment of writing, what some Cambodians do to others—require a deep moral concern by Jews and Christians alike. In some cases, a theological concern is required as well. But these concerns become flawed the moment they are abused to avoid the unique scandal that Auschwitz constitutes for Christianity. And since current Christian theology, not lacking in boldness, is not afraid of scandals, we must suspect a deep, unacknowledged Christian trauma.

We shall attempt to reach this trauma with three questions in an ascending order of theological gravity. Even the first seems traumatic enough, for Christians though asked the question, have mostly ignored it.[3] *Where would Jesus of Nazareth have been in Nazi-occupied Europe?* If he was who he is said to have been, he would have gone to Auschwitz or Treblinka voluntarily even if, as Nazi-Christian doctrine asserts,[4] he had been an "Aryan." If not going voluntarily, he would have been dragged into a cattle car involuntarily, for he was not an "Aryan" but a Jew. A Jesus that goes voluntarily reveals the scarcity of his disciples in the great time of testing—that saints, those Christian included, were few. A Jesus dragged off involuntarily reveals the still more terrible truth that, without Jew-hatred in Christianity itself, Auschwitz, in the heart of Christian Europe, would have been impossible.

Here more is at stake than the need to acknowledge sin. Christians have always known how to acknowledge sin, including the sin of crucifying the Christ all over again. However, the crucifixion of Christ-in-general is one thing; quite another is the crucifixion-in-particular of six million human beings, among them the helpless children, their weeping mothers, and the silent *Muselmänner*.[5] To be sure, only the actual jobholders and tone-setting idealists knew the exact project and carried it out. But Christian theologians need no instruction in the guilt of complicity; and the complicity, in this case, included giving "only" lip service to the "Aryan" Gospel, passing by on the other side, not wanting to know what was suspected by everyone, and keeping silent when "the Jews are our brothers" or "we are all Jews" would have been the redemptive Word. Dietrich Bonhoeffer has charged that "the church has not raised her voice on behalf of the victims and has not found ways to hasten to their aid; . . . she is guilty of the deaths of the weakest and most defenseless brothers of Jesus Christ."[6] Nearly half a century later, what need one add to this charge, made by a great Christian thinker and martyr during the Holocaust, except a simple but devastating question: Why has the Christian theological response, in this nearly half a century, been so feeble, and so superficial? Why has it been even ambiguous?

The answer can be sought only in a deep, unadmitted, religious and theological trauma. Toward non-Christian worlds—especially toward the so-called Third World—Christians are currently seeking to replace their former missionary stance with one of "outreach." This change, rightly seen as required, is considered to be bold, radical, risky, for it threatens, or seems to threaten, the universality of the Christian claim to Truth. Yet this boldness, radicalism and risk all pale in comparison with those involved in the other required Christian change—repentance of supersessionism vis-à-vis Judaism and the Jewish people. The first change requires a new openness toward worlds hitherto unknown or unrecognized; the second, no less than a revolution in attitude toward a world—that of Judaism—known all along but explicitly denied recognition. Moreover, since negating-of-Judaism has generally been part and parcel of the Christian affirmation itself—it originates in the Christian Scriptures—Christian dialogue with Jews and Judaism, if seriously engaged in, is no mere species of the genus Christian-dialogue-in-general with non-Christians-in-general. It involves on the part of the Christian thinker no less radical an enterprise than (to fall back on a Heideggerian conception) the "destructive recovery" of the *whole* Christian "tradition"—an enterprise whose outcome and consequences are unforeseeable.

So radical is the risk. The demand to run it, of course, has existed ever since the age *post Hegel mortuum* has made Christian Constantinianism into an anachronism. In the age of Auschwitz, however, the demand not only has a new existential urgency. It is also the case that a theology that heeds the demand finds itself permeated with a new, unprecedented religious trauma. Without doubt an abyss yawns between Christian supersessionism and Auschwitz: the Holocaust world sought the death of Jewish bodies and souls, whereas to Christian faith human life, and hence Jewish life, is sacred, so that even at their worst—e.g., in the Inquisition—Christians burned Jewish bodies so as to save Jewish souls. Even so, the terrible fact is that there is a thread that spans the abyss. In seeking to Christianize Indians or Chinese, Christians never sought to make an end to Indians or Chinese. Just this was—and is—involved in the attempt to make the "old" Israel over into part of the "new."[7] And since the *very existence* of Jews—believing Jews, unbelieving Jews, agnostic Jews but in any case human beings who have not ceased to be Jews—is a stumbling block to supersessionist Christian theology, the Christian theologian J. Coert Rylaarsdam gave expression, hyperbolic to be sure, to a religious if not a literal truth when he wrote that Christians generally have recognized only two good Jews, a dead Jew and a Christian.[8] The thread that spans the abyss, then, is the idea that, strictly speaking, Jews—and no one but Jews—should not exist at all.

The Christian thinker prepared to face this trauma in the sphere of religious life comes, when persisting in his task, on yet another trauma—this in the sphere of theological thought. He must ask: What can be the weight and inner truth of his own theological thinking, conducted in the safety of Western seminaries now, when it pits itself against the cowardice, inner falsehood and downright depravity of Christian life and thought then and there—when there was a cost to discipleship? Hitler, Himmler, and Eichmann, baptized Christians all, were never threatened with excommunication; neither were the ordinary murderers. Vatican protests, on the rare occasions when they occurred, by the confession of their own authors did not spring "from a false sense of compassion." (Compassion, when extended to Jews, was considered false.)[9] And while the heroic Protestant Confessional Church did fight on behalf of "non-Aryan" Christians it abandoned the Jews.[10] At stake in this melancholy litany is not only the "mere Christendom" of Christian sinners, among them the confused, the opportunists, and co-opted establishments. For the Christian thinker, it is also, and more significantly and painfully, the Christianity of Christian saints—and their theology more than their personal lives. (Indeed, the Christian failure vis-à-vis Nazi Jew-hatred would have been impossible without a history of Jew-hatred on the part of Christian saints, among them St. Chrysostom, St. Augustine, St. Thomas, and Martin Luther.)[11] Then how can the Christian thinker trust the Holy Spirit to speak to his own thought now, when on Jews and Judaism it failed to speak, or spoke at best ambiguously, through the whole Christian tradition—and when, at the time of supreme testing, the Christian catastrophe was all but complete? The theological trust— one can say nothing else—is ruptured. And the question is: Can there be a *Tikkun?*

Karl Barth, the last great Christian supersessionist thinker—and one if anyone in his dark time surely in many ways guided by the Holy Spirit—still thought theologically *about* Jews.[12] A Christian thinker repenting of supersessionism can surely think theologically about Jews only *with* Jews—and seek the Holy Spirit only *between* himself and his Jewish partners in dialogue. How can he hope for its presence? An abyss was created and legislated since 1933 between "Aryans" (i.e., most Christians) and "non-Aryans" (i.e., all Jews). No dialogue between Jews and Christians is possible today unless it aims at narrowing if not closing that abyss. No narrowing is possible unless the abyss is first of all recognized. And all recognition must disclose that Jews and Christians come to this dialogue with different priorities.

For Christians, the first priority may be theological self-understanding. For Jews it is, and after Auschwitz must be, simple safety for their children. In pursuit of this goal, Jews seek—are *morally required* to seek—independence of other people's charity. They therefore seek safety—are morally required to seek it—through the existence of a Jewish state. Except among the theologically or humanly perverse, Zionism—the commitment to the safety and genuine sovereignty of the State of Israel—is not negotiable. Nor can it be weakened or obscured in dialogue with Christians.

But Zionism, as just defined, must after Auschwitz be a Christian commitment as well. No less than Jews themselves, Christians must wish Jewish existence to be liberated from dependence on charity. On behalf of their partners in dialogue, they must wish independence from charity-in-general. On behalf of their own Christianity, they must wish it from Christian charity-in-particular. The post-Holocaust Christian must repent of the Christian sin of supersessionism. One asks: How can he *trust* in his own repentance—that it is both genuine and complete? There is only one answer: If he supports firmly and unequivocally the Jewish search for independence not only from the power of its enemies but also from that of Christian friends. Without Zionism—Christian as well as Jewish—the Holy Spirit cannot dwell between Jews and Christians in dialogue.

The Holocaust is a trauma today for Christian-Jewish relations: Is it a trauma also for Christianity quite apart from those relations? With this question we turn from the first to the second question raised by the Holocaust for the Christian faith. In the Christ God is said to have taken upon Himself in advance *all possible* suffering, and vicariously to have atoned in advance for *all possible* sin. But we have already seen that in the Holocaust "more was real than is possible." The Holocaust was a *world* of evil—an *Unwelt* or antiworld—that was previously unthought and unthinkable. It ruptures philosophical thought. It also ruptures—though this was only marginally our subject—art and literature. Are not then Christian thought and faith ruptured as well? Where is the sting of *that* death removed? Where is *that* sin vicariously atoned?

Up to a point, a response to these questions may be said to be given in a "leftward" move of contemporary Christian thought that, at the risk of the Easter paling in comparison to the Good Friday, hears the Christian Good News as a promise and a beginning rather than as an accomplished fact. (Thus a connection of sorts may exist between such phenomena as "liberation theology" and "political theology," and the trauma, otherwise unacknowledged, of the Holocaust.) If a connection there is, then the most apt illustration of this leftward move in Christian theology was given by Philip Maury with an episode about World War II. Maury was in the French resistance. There had been years of hiding, of resisting, of betrayals—and of the ever-present fear that it would all be in vain. Then, at the risk of both their lives, a friend telephoned him with the Good News that the Allies had landed; and he, Maury, proceeded to spread the news at the risk of his and other lives. Darkness was still holding sway. But there now was a light so *all*-sustaining that to see it, and help others see it, was worth the risk of life. It is a compelling parable.

Compelling too, however, is that the parable points to its own limitations. The sustaining life was *itself* limited. So far as the children, the mothers, the *Muselmänner* were concerned, the Allies had landed too late. What is worse, they had failed to bomb the Auschwitz railways while there was time. *Has the Good Friday, then, overwhelmed the Easter? Is the Good News of the Overcoming itself overcome?*

This is our second question. We move to the third, most traumatic of all; this arises if we transport Christian faith and thought into the Holocaust world itself. One would wish to ask about the children, unable to choose, and hence unfree to choose martyrdom; but Jesus of Nazareth was not a child. One would wish to ask, too, about the mothers wanting to die in their children's stead but denied this choice; but Jesus of Nazareth was not a parent.[13] He was a free person and is said by Christians to have been *the* free person. Surely all Christian doctrine centers on this freedom. Yet just this freedom gives rise to a traumatic question. At Auschwitz, other free persons were reduced to *Muselmänner*, to the living dead. This is a *novum* in human history and an unprecedented scandal. We ask: *Could Jesus of Nazareth have been made into a* Muselmann?

Liberal Christian theology (for which Jesus is human, nothing but human) cannot dismiss this possibility without a gratuitous, posthumous insult to every person who in fact did become a *Muselmann*. We have already cited a great text on this subject. We must re-cite it now, more fully even than before:

> On their entry into the camp, through basic incapacity, or through some banal incident, they are overcome before they can adapt themselves; they are beaten by time, they do not begin to learn German, to disentangle the infernal knot of laws and prohibitions until their body is already in decay, and nothing can save them from the selections or from death by exhaustion. Their life is short, but their number is endless; they, the *Muselmänner*, the drowned, form the backbone of the camp, an anonymous mass, continually renewed and always identical, of non-men who march and labour in silence, the divine spark dead within them, already too empty really to suffer. One hesitates to call them living: one hesitates to call their death death, in the face of which they have no fear, as they are too tired to understand.[14]

Was Jesus free of "basic incapacities," i.e., not human after all? Or a lucky one that was spared "misfortune" and "banal incidents"?

Liberal Christian theology cannot evade the *Muselmann*. Its orthodox (or neo-orthodox) counterpart is forced into new, desperate forms of age-old Christian theological dilemmas. If the incarnate Son of God was as fully human as all humanity, then the trinitarian Christian, like the liberal Christian and lest he heap a posthumous insult on all actual *Muselmänner*, must acknowledge the possibility of an incarnate *Muselmann*. And if the incarnate Son of God *remains* divine in spirit and power even in his incarnate state in Auschwitz, then, to be sure, the "divine spark" within him remains untouched, for it is untouchable. However, this very untouchability cruelly mocks all who were *not* untouchable—equally those who were destroyed and those who remained undestroyed only by dint of a desperate, day-and-night, life-and-death struggle. We have already asked whether at Auschwitz the Christian Good News of the Overcoming is not itself overcome. Only one question, for Christianity, is grimmer still: Whether, with both alternatives open to trinitarian thought, the once-Good News does not become a savage joke. In the first case—an incarnate Son of God fully human and made into a *Muselmann*—do not the Nazis laugh their kind of laughter at the victims, the Father, the Son, the Good News itself? ("Where is your God now?") In the second case—a Son of God incarnate and untouchable, hence detached by a gulf from the victims—do not Father and Son, as it were, join in the Nazi laughter? For whereas the process endured by the victims is grimly real, the trinitarian process is only a divine play. With this alternative, the conclusion, long suspected but suspended in the preceding, can no longer be postponed or avoided. However the Christian theologian seeks to understand the Good News that is his heritage, it is ruptured by the Holocaust. One ponders this awesome fact and is shaken.

The one who is shaken need not himself be a Christian. He may also be a Jew. As such he is far removed from Christian Trinitarianism. He may even suspect it of being mixed with paganism if not idolatry. Even so, he need by no means be indifferent. And if he ever had but a single true Christian friend—a true Christian and a true friend—indifference is impossible. This Christian was his friend. When the law made friendship with a Jew into an "Aryan" crime, *this* Christian—unlike too many others to remember—remained his friend, and risked his life. In this he felt guided and instructed by the Holy Spirit. A Jew must ask: Can this feeling have been a mere sham and a delusion?[15]

C

With this question in mind, we now approach a unique, unprecedented Christian prayer. The place, appropriately enough, was Berlin, the capital of the Third Reich. The date was November 10, 1938, the day of *Kristallnacht*. This too was appropriate, for this day revealed to the whole world that the Nazi persecution of the Jewish people would stop at nothing. (Jewish stores were plundered in broad daylight. Synagogues burned all over Germany. Jewish males vanished one did not know, but could guess, where.) On that day, anyone walking the streets of Berlin saw.[16] Few did anything. *Domprobst* [Prior] Bernhard Lichtenberg of the Hedwigskirche walked, saw, and did just one thing. He went back to his church and prayed publicly "on behalf of the Jews and the poor concentration camp prisoners." And he continued to recite his public prayer every day until, on October 23, 1941, he was at length arrested.[17]

Not until May 22, 1942 was Lichtenberg brought to trial. (Here, too, there was a trial.) He was found guilty under a variety of paragraphs of law. As for clemency, he was denied it on the grounds that he "had shown no signs of repentance or of a change of attitude" during the six months of his imprisonment. Thereupon the *Domprobst* asked for permission to speak and said the following:

> *Herr Staatsanwalt*, the many paragraphs which you read to me—these do not interest me in the slightest. However, the last point you made—[and here, according to an eyewitness, his voice suddenly became clearer and stronger]—to the effect that I have

not changed and would speak and act exactly as before, that, *Herr Staatsanwalt,* is completely accurate.

The presiding judge then asked Lichtenberg how he came to pray on behalf of the Jews. Lichtenberg replied:

> This question I can answer quite precisely. It happened in November 1938, when the store windows were smashed and the synagogues burned. . . . When I saw this destruction, with the police looking on doing nothing, I was scandalized by all this vandalism and asked myself what, if such things were possible in an ordered state, could still bring help.

Then, emphasizing every word, he concluded:

> Then I told myself that only one thing could still help, namely, prayer. That night I prayed for the first time as follows: "Now let us pray for the persecuted 'non-Aryan' Christians and Jews."[18]

When, soon thereafter, Lichtenberg died, an anonymous non-Catholic who had been in prison with him walked over to a Catholic after the funeral and said: "Today they buried a saint."

We do not know how the venerable old priest expected his prayer to help. We *do* know how it *did* help. The twelve years of the Third Reich were a unique devil's *kairos* in the history of the Christian church. They were also, potentially, a unique *kairos* of God, in that even a silent, secret Christian prayer on behalf of Jews, whenever it was sincerely spoken, had a redemptive effect on the Christian soul. So long as it was on behalf *of Jews*—not merely mankind-in-general or "all-oppressed-in-general" or even "Semites-in-general,"[19] such a prayer went far toward closing the abyss that had been created and legislated between "Aryan" Christians and such as the Buchenwald Hasidim. (They too believed that prayer helps and were helped.) Indeed, it went far toward narrowing the far older gulf created and legislated by the laos of the "new" covenant against the people of the "old."

But the full and unique nature of the divine *kairos,* in the midst of the diabolical *kairos,* was disclosed by the fact that Lichtenberg's prayer was *public rather than merely private,* and that even so it did not resort to evasions or circumlocutions. Nor was his choice of words thoughtless or a passing whim. In prison he decided that he would join the Berlin Jews after his release. They had been deported to the Lodz Ghetto, were in need of pastoral care, and he would be a *Judenseelsorger.* (He was taken to Dachau instead and died on the way.) When visited in prison by his bishop, Lichtenberg told him of his plan, wondering what the Holy Father would think of it. Had he lived to the end of the war and learned all, he would have been dismayed, though surely unwavering. For what at great risk and finally the cost of his life was done by Lichtenberg every day for nearly three years—pray for Jews *in public* and *by name*—was not done even once by the Vicar of the Christ in the safety of the Vatican. Excuses and explanations have been given. They will continue to be given. Some may have a certain pragmatic validity. None will ever obscure the pragmatic and transpragmatic truth that had masses of Christians, Protestant and Catholic, within and without Nazi-occupied Europe, prayed sincerely, publicly, and *by name* for the maligned, hounded, martyred Jews of Nazi Europe, their prayers would have moved more than mountains: *they would have caused the collapse of the kingdom of the Antichrist, the inner core of which was the Holocaust world.* Nazism originated as a system of words. To the end it continued to require and rest on a system of words. And the key-word in the whole vocabulary was "Jew," used as a hissing and a by-word, and unutterable except with a sense of ineffable horror. Never in the bimillennial history of the Church was there a greater *kairos* for changing the world with the Word. Never were the gates of Christian prayer more open, the Holy Spirit at once more clearly present and more vulnerable. *And never was a* kairos *more betrayed, the Holy Spirit more wounded, than when the Word was not spoken, and instead there was a dead, murderous silence.*[20]

Lichtenberg's prayer, then, is an abiding indictment of the silence of the churches. As such it "helps" in that it discloses a rupture in Christianity and ipso facto inspires a search for a *Tikkun*. This, however, is the negative aspect of its "help" alone. Lichtenberg's prayer is *itself* a *Tikkun:* this is the positive aspect of the help given by it.

One may doubt whether this *Tikkun* can be recognized, let alone explicated by a theology that understands itself as a thought deducing truths from the revealed, authoritatively interpreted Scriptures. (Such a thought, resting as it does on authority, is open to no threats and no surprises.) This, however, is a form of the "fanatical," "old" thinking which we have long seen reason to abandon in favor of the "unfanatical" "new" thinking. Theology, within the "new" thinking, may be defined as "astonished response, articulated in thought," and within Christianity the central astonishment is the wonder of its Good News. But after the Holocaust, there can be no radical wonder that is not threatened by radical horror; and it is therefore not surprising that most Christian theology today, to protect the wonder, ignores that horror, minimizes it, flattens it out into a universalized horror that is at everything and nothing. But there is no salvation in such theologizing: to flatten out the horror is to flatten out the wonder as well. Only through self-exposure to the horror can Christian faith and thought preserve their integrity—and hope to be astonished anew by its old Good News. In our time, this old-new News is not that all is well, that nothing has happened, that now as before it is Good Friday after Easter.[21] It is rather that in a world in which *nothing* was well, *all* was happening, a terrible new Good Friday was every day overwhelming the old Easter, *Lichtenberg's prayer was actual, and, therefore, possible.* The Good News is in the prayer itself, and in the Holy Spirit that dwells in it. This *Tikkun* is the *Boden* on which Christian theology can undertake the "destructive recovery" of the Christian Scriptures, of the Christian tradition, of the Christian faith. It is the rock on which Christian faith can rebuild the broken church.

D

This is the limit of our reflections. They are, as was said at the outset, the reflections not of a Christian or crypto- or quasi-Christian, but those of a Jew.[22] As was also said at the outset (but must be repeated), there could be no thought of using (or, which in this case is the same thing, abusing) the Holocaust for any kind of Jewish-Christian debate, one about redemption included. Irving Greenberg has written that Judaism and Christianity are equally religions of redemption, and that the Holocaust is the radical "countertestimony" to both.[23] The most fitting beginning of an attempt to narrow, and eventually close, the gap between Jew and Christian, made into an abyss since 1933 but existing through the centuries, is for the alienated brothers to share in a sorrow that is unique to our time, and belongs to all humanity in our time. Of this Primo Levi has written:

> If I could enclose all the evil of our time in one image, I would choose this image which is familiar to me: an emaciated man, with head dropped and shoulders curved, on whose face and in whose eyes not a trace of thought is to be seen.[24]

Notes

1. S. Kierkegaard, *Either/Or* (New York: Anchor, 1959), II, pp. 344ff. See *To Mend the World,* chapter III, section 11.

2. *Auschwitz: Beginning of a New Era?,* ed. Eva Fleischner (New York: Ktav, 1977) is a Jewish-Christian dialogue that attempts to focus on the Holocaust without diversions or evasions. Yet its editor included a piece—except for a few poems, the last, i.e., climactic contribution!—which in effect undermines the whole effort. In this piece Auschwitz is flattened out into a case of atrocity-in-general. (Others are Dresden, Vietnam, and Hiroshima.) Further, it is reduced to a parochially Western European atrocity, and for this reason to be left behind in the advance to a less parochial stage of history. The piece climaxes in the call for a "correction" of the whole concept of Jewish-Christian dialogue. Such dialogue, on the one hand, is to be broadened by the inclusion of Muslims and, on the other, to be narrowed in that only "Oriental and non-Zionist Jews" are to be admitted. The author of the article, Gabriel Habib, seems unaware of the fact that most "Oriental Jews," having fled to Israel from Arab and Muslim persecution, are vigorous Zionists—for excellent reasons.

3. I have already raised the first of these questions in *Jewish Return,* chapter 4. The second and third I have not raised previously.

4. Once, in a Jerusalem lecture, I employed the term "Nazi Christian." Afterward a visiting Christian stormed forward to protest that "Nazi-Christian" is a contradiction in terms. I could only agree—and add that, at least for twelve years, the conceptually impossible had been empirically factual.

5. See Franklin H. Littell, *The Crucifixion of the Jews* (New York: Harper and Row, 1975).

6. *Ethics* (New York: Macmillan, 1965), p. 114. On Bonhoeffer, see further below.

7. "Jews-For-Jesus" is clearly a post-Holocaust phenomenon in that an old impetus of Jewish flight-into-Christianity is combined with a new reluctance to abandon the post-Holocaust Jewish remnant. However, the "movement" combines the uncombinable: unless its members propose in perpetuity to marry only other Jews-for-Jesus, their distant offspring may conceivably be for Jesus, but they will not be Jews.

8. Cited in *Jewish Return,* pp. 36, 156.

9. See *Eichmann in Jerusalem,* p. 200. The Papal Nuncio used this phrase when he explained, or rather excused, the Vatican's intervention with Admiral Horthy in behalf of Hungarian Jews. Arendt comments that the phrase "is likely to be a lasting monument to what the continued dealings with, and the desire to compromise with, the men who preached the gospel of 'ruthless toughness' had done to the mentality of the highest dignitaries of the Church."

10. See *The German Church Struggle and the Holocaust,* eds. Franklin H. Littell and Hubert G. Locke (Detroit: Wayne State University Press, 1974).

11. See Rosemary Ruether, *Faith and Fratricide* (New York: Seabury Press, 1974).

12. Barth made a few attempts to speak with Jews toward the end of his life—when, so far as his *Church Dogmatics* is concerned, it was too late.

13. In the light of the Holocaust, a renewed future Christian emphasis on the person of Mary seems a distinct possibility.

14. Primo Levi, *Survival in Auschwitz,* tran. Stuart Wolf (New York: Orion Press, 1959), p. 82. See *To Mend the World,* pp. 99, 131.

15. I write these words in memory of Adolph Lörcher. Lörcher, a German patriot and a Christian, was my high school teacher at the *Stadtgymnasium* in the German city of Halle, until my graduation in 1935. In addition to Greek he taught religion, and while Jews were exempt I attended his classes voluntarily, for with Lörcher teaching Christianity was inseparable from attacking Nazism—at a time when other teachers no longer wanted (or dared) to speak. After my graduation we stayed in touch at his insistence, and in 1938 he wrote to a friend abroad in my behalf, thereby risking his life. After my release from Sachsenhausen in February 1939 I no longer visited my remaining "Aryan" friends before leaving Germany: I had no wish to endanger them. Lörcher phoned to say that he would never forgive me if I did not visit him. When visit him I did, he had in readiness two copies of Martin Buber's *Kingship of God*, one to give to me and the other to keep for himself. I have my copy to this day. It bears Lörcher's inscription: *dyoin thateron*—"one of two."

16. I was among those walking the streets of Berlin on that day. On the fashionable Kurfürstendamm I saw the windows of elegant stores broken, and well-dressed people step in to help themselves. In another street a piano, thrown out of a Jewish window, was lying on the sidewalk. People stood around watching. A solid citizen walked over, touched a key, and produced a sound. (It seemed like mutilating a corpse.) The citizen laughed. "The Jew still can play!" he exclaimed.

17. See *Das Dritte Reich und die Juden*, ed. Leon Poliakov and Josef Wulf, 2nd ed. (Berlin: Verlags GMBH, 1955), pp. 432–37.

18. In the context Lichtenberg had to use the Nazi term "non-Aryan." But this in no way suggests that he agreed with any part of Nazi doctrine.

19. Pius XII on occasion spoke up on behalf of "the oppressed." His predecessor, Pius XI, is justly praised for going further, with his famous statement that spiritually Christians are Semites. Even so he still only opposed one code word with another. He did not unmask and oppose the Jew-hatred disguised in "anti-Semitism" by publicly declaring Christian love of Jews.

20. Beata Klarsfeld has said: "If only the Pope had come to Berlin in 1933 and told the Nazis *'Ich bin ein Jud,'* millions might have been spared. Instead, it was a Catholic President [John F. Kennedy] who told the Communists he was a Berliner" (reported by William Stevenson, *The Borman Brotherhood* [New York: Harcourt Brace Jovanovitch, 1973], p. 238).

21. An allusion to the teaching of Karl Barth, see *To Mend the World*, p. 133.

22. They would have been quite impossible, however, without the comradeship and friendship of Christians that have accompanied me all my life. I have already mentioned Adolph Lörcher. I must also mention Ernst Tillich, an inspiring comrade during my three months in Sachsenhausen. (We Jews were there because of our "race." He was there from choice—a Christian foe of Nazism.) Finally I must mention Alice Eckardt, Roy Eckardt, and Franklin Littell who, in long years of friendship and shared labor, have taught me that for a Jew to be "soft on Christians" would be no act of help or love but rather a betrayal.

In addition to personal Christian friends, I must also mention some Christian thinkers. In a letter to me dated April 20, 1979, Eberhard Bethge writes that Dietrich Bonhoeffer "belongs to those making possible a [Christian] theology [after the Holocaust]," and this despite the fact that "to expect such a theology from him is impossible." I agree with this assessment. Next, the unique figure of Reinhold Niebuhr is surely foremost among the pioneers—and sorely missed today. Further, some presently perceive the task and are at work on it. Johann Baptist Metz has written that Auschwitz was "the apotheosis of evil"; that anyone wanting to "comprehend" it has "comprehended nothing"; that a Christian theodicy in this sphere is "blasphemy"; that Christians, still unready to listen to Jews, must at last do so, instead of "offering dialogue to victims"; and that all this is a theological as well as a human necessity, since "by Auschwitz everything is to be measured" ("Ökumene nach Auschwitz," in *Gott nach Auschwitz* [Freiburg: Herder, 1979], pp. 121–44). Finally, I must mention two Christian thinkers who, each in his own way, have prepared the way for a post-Holocaust Christianity: Franklin Littell, by initially single-handedly placing the Holocaust on the Christian agenda, and Roy Eckardt, by penetrating into theological realms as yet unapproached, so far as I can see, by any other Christian thinker.

23. See Irving Greenberg, as cited in *To Mend the World*, chapter I, section 4.

24. Levi, *Survival in Auschwitz*, p. 81.

27 *Post-Holocaust Anti-Jewishness, Jewish Identity, and the Centrality of Israel: An Essay in the Philosophy of History*

I

The prefix "post" in the title of this essay may have two meanings. One signifies a merely temporal relation, so that any event after 1945 is "post-Holocaust." The other is historical in a pregnant rather than a merely trivial sense. An event succeeds another historically if the first somehow enters into its substance; if it is different from what it would have been if the first had never happened. Thus, much history is merely temporal. More importantly, historical events in the deeper sense are always of unpredictable import while they happen and even long thereafter. Only when they are assimilated by the historical consciousness of succeeding generations are they capable of transforming the future, and thus become historical in the deeper sense.

At least some current anti-Jewish attitudes are post-Holocaust in the historical sense. This is shown by the very terminology that is forced upon us. Prior to the Holocaust, many antisemites would protest—rightly so—their friendship for some Jews, and thus were called—rightly so—"decent" antisemites. After the Holocaust, virtually all antisemites go to any length to deny, always to others (and often to themselves as well) that they *are* antisemites. The word "antisemitism," itself a nineteenth-century code word for anti-Jewishness, has become unusable for anyone seriously concerned to identify and comprehend post-Holocaust anti-Jewish attitudes.[1]

Only a few anti-Jewish attitudes may seem post-Holocaust in the historical sense. Moreover, these seem bound to diminish still further as the dread event passes from "experience" into "history."[2] However, the possibility is worthy of consideration that on both scores the exact opposite is the case. Not all forms of anti-Jewishness that look unrelated to the Holocaust are in fact unrelated to it.

Reprinted from *The Jewish Return into History* (New York: Schocken Books, 1978), 210–33, by permission of the publisher.

255

And while the Holocaust doubtless is passing from experience into history, it is only beginning to be absorbed by the historical consciousness—the consciousness both of those living in history and those writing about it.[3]

No one presently alive can answer the question raised by the relation between the Holocaust and the historical consciousness. We must at least pause, however, to ponder its momentousness. Will the Holocaust ultimately be forgotten or—perhaps this is the more precise way of putting it—be consciously and unconsciously expunged from the mind? Or will it, on the contrary, increasingly permeate both the lives of civilizations and the consciousness of its writers, philosophers and historians? In that case, the event may well assume a world-historical significance.

The question just raised is one for the future. In contrast, whether or not all forms of anti-Jewishness that look unrelated to the Holocaust are in fact unrelated to it is a question for the present. It may even now be illustrated by examples such as these:

1. Germans of the new generation protest rightly that they are not guilty. This does not alter the fact that *any* form of anti-Jewishness displayed by present and future Germans is historically post-Holocaust, for the slate of *no* people's history—that of Germans included—can be wiped clean. Unless they opt out of German history, i.e., emigrate, young Germans are burdened with the past and responsible for the future.

2. Soviet Russia and other iron curtain countries actually try to wipe the slate clean, sparing no effort to make the Holocaust either a nonevent or a non-Jewish event. (There either are no memorials, or they are to the "victims of fascism.") This crime against the truth is enough to make all anti-Jewishness in these countries historically post-Holocaust.

3. The Arab world protests that the sins of Christian Europe have been visited on its Palestinian segment. This protest is in bad faith when—to mention no others—it excises two facts from the record. One is the active participation of Haj Amin al-Husseini, Grand Mufti of Jerusalem, in Hitler's murder of Jewish children. The other is the link between Auschwitz and the war on the newly born Jewish state waged by five Arab armies. This attempt at politicide was encouraged by Hitler's practice of genocide with almost total impunity. And, of course, the victim in both cases—in the one case, actual, in the other, intended—was the same people.

To be fair, one may wish to doubt whether the third case of anti-Jewishness given is historically post-Holocaust, or even a case of anti-Jewishness at all; and in this spirit one may wish to consider the two excised events—the activities of the Grand Mufti during World War II and the Arab invasions in the 1948 war—as rightly excised, i.e., not as facts which, themselves shaped by the Holocaust, continued to shape subsequent history, but rather as random facts of the dead past. One's doubts are removed, however, by the present Arab propaganda system (assiduously assisted by the Communist) when it declares Israelis the new Nazis, Palestinian Arabs the new Jews, Arab refugees victims of a "holocaust," Zionism a form of racism and, by some mathematical tour de force, the Arab "victims" of "Zionism," in American terms, equivalent to six million.[4] It is impossible to view this system as innocent, i.e., as truly ignorant of what happened a generation ago. One can only view it as an attempt to wipe out the holocaust as a Jewish event, indeed, to appropriate it as an Arab one, rewriting Israeli history as being a "Final Solution of the Arab Problem."

That none of these forms of historically post-Holocaust anti-Jewishness can be equated with the unsurpassable Nazi kind goes without saying. (It requires saying only because of the widespread dismissal of *all* Jewish explorations of *any* post-Holocaust manifestation of anti-Jewishness as products, either of a complex about the dread event, or of attempts to exploit it. This extraordinary dismissal is itself in need of a scrutiny that cannot be attempted here.) However, they are all unable to claim or recapture the "decency" of pre-Holocaust antisemitism. Only two decent Gentile relationships toward the Jewish people remain. The one is that of being truly and genuinely innocent of the fact that one generation ago the Nazi regime first persecuted and then murdered the Jewish people, while at the same time the rest of the world first shut its gates to Jews fleeing for their lives and then failed to bomb the railways to Auschwitz. (This "antisemitism" is a fossil, a relic from earlier, more innocent times. Its own innocence may be barbaric, but it is an innocence all the same.) The other Gentile relationship to the Jewish people either always was free of anti-Jewish animus or else, in response to the catastrophe, is trying desperately to rid itself of it. In contrast, all historically post-Holocaust forms of anti-Jewishness are posthumous victories for Hitler and witting or unwitting continuations of his work.

II

These consequences follow from the fact of Nazism. No historical fact is ever decisive proof of anything. However, being the unsurpassable form of anti-Jewishness, Nazism comes as close as possible to proving that *no* form of anti-Jewishness is ever caused by Jewish behavior. This is not to say that it does not matter what Jews do. It matters greatly, both in and for itself and in response to manifestations of anti-Jewishness. In causal terms, however, *all* forms of anti-Jewishness are strains of a Gentile disease. This might have been recognized when in nineteenth-century Europe right-wing antisemites hated "the Jews" because they were revolutionaries, while left-wing antisemites criticized them because they were capitalists, and when universalist liberals and particularistic nationalists complained, respectively, that "the Jews" mixed too little and too much with Gentile society. Occasionally anti-Jewishness was in fact recognized as a Gentile disease. Lessing did so in the eighteenth century.[5] In the twentieth century, the late, great Reinhold Niebuhr wrote: "When a minority group is hated for its virtues as well as its vices, and when its vices are hated not so much because they are vices as because they bear the stamp of uniqueness, we are obviously dealing with a collective psychology that is not easily altered by a little more enlightenment."[6] These words were written in 1942, before the worst was known. Now that it *is* known anyone responding by word or deed with the proverb "where there is smoke there is fire" is not a diagnostician of anti-Jewishness and its causes but himself a victim of the disease. This fact is in no way altered by assurances to the effect that the smoke is out of all proportion to any possible fire.

Like all theses about history, the present one requires qualifications:

1. An exposed social situation, whether of their own choosing (such as reli-

gious separatism) or of the world's making (such as spatial or social ghettoization) makes "the Jews" convenient scapegoats on which knaves and fools can blame the current ills of society. This theory is fashionable among the enlightened of all ages, Gentile and Jewish. It turns the mind to a rational cure—the healing of the true ills in question. More important still, it denies the disease itself the sort of uniqueness that is forever anathema to the enlightened. However, by itself the "scapegoat theory of antisemitism" explains neither the tenacity of anti-Jewishness nor the variety of its forms, to say nothing of why other groups, no less exposed, were made into scapegoats rarely, differently, or not at all.[7]

2. "The Jews" can in fact show behavior that may seem to cause anti-Jewish attitudes. Jewish usury in the Middle Ages is a case in point. However, the fact that even then (to paraphrase Niebuhr) Jews were hated for the virtues as well as their vices would in itself suffice to overthrow this theory. Add that Jews were driven into usury by state and church policies *already* anti-Jewish in inspiration and purpose, and the Jewish "vice" in question emerges, not as the cause of anti-Jewishness, but rather as an effect of self-fulfilling anti-Jewish prophecies.[8] Never was the principle behind such prophecies expressed with such cynical openness as when Goebbels announced a policy of robbing Jews of their livelihood, thus driving them into crime, and then punishing them as a criminal group.

3. The above are cases of victimization. These must be distinguished from authentic actions. The most clearly authentic case of a collective Jewish action in recent history is the founding of the state of Israel. Obviously there could be no anti-Zionism without Zionism, and no Israel without Zionism. Somewhat less obviously, anti-Zionism may "spill over" into anti-Jewishness. Hence, it may seem that here is at least one bona fide case in which Jewish behavior can actually *cause* anti-Jewish attitudes where none existed.

However, even so drastic a Jewish action can at most only reinforce existing anti-Jewish attitudes. It cannot create them. In the "first world," why are Jews criticized for their "passivity" in Nazi Europe and for their "aggressiveness" and "intransigence" in Israel—often in the same quarters? Why do those praising Algerians and Vietnamese when they fight for liberty blame Israelis when they fight for life itself? In the "second world," why is "acquisition of territory through conquest" legitimate for large and safe nations—the Baltic countries by Soviet Russia, Tibet by Red China—but illegitimate for a small and beleaguered nation, and of all small countries, only for that of the Jews? In the "third world," why was an exchange of populations possible between India and Pakistan but remains inconceivable to this day between Arabs and Israelis? That Palestinian Arabs should have become hostile to the "invaders" is understandable, and perhaps natural or even inevitable. But one wonders whether, had these "invaders" not been Jews, their hostility—to say nothing of that of the Arab world—would have remained implacable. Indeed, except in the context of Muslim and post-Muslim Arab anti-Jewish attitudes, Arab policies toward Israel would appear to be unintelligible.[9]

Moreover, while in some quarters aggravating the disease of anti-Jewishness, we may ask whether in other quarters the fact of Israel has not helped alleviate or even cure it. Since we cannot replay history, we cannot answer this question. However, we should be faint-hearted if we did not at least raise it. Anti-Jewish attitudes in North American and some other Western countries have, in our age, reached their lowest ebb since pre-Christian times. Doubtless this is because the

Holocaust has generated thought and contrition among Gentiles, and thought and militancy among Jews. However, except for Israel would anyone truly remember? Except for this unique witness, would either Jews or Gentiles understand the radical fact that Jews *need* not be tolerees when they are not victims; and, having understood, would they seek to cure the Gentile world of the disease, the Jewish people of its effects?

III

If anti-Jewishness is a Gentile disease we must ask, especially in view of the durability of the phenomenon, why it should forever be necessary to restate this truth. One answer, applying to a variety of "group prejudices," will be readily accepted. However, this answer must be supplemented by a second, applicable to anti-Jewishness alone.

We use the word "prejudice" in quotation marks, for a disorder far deeper than obtuseness to "the facts" is involved in such relations as between racist and his victim or between colonizer and colonized. Nor can "enlightenment" by itself cure it. The oppressor, first, believes it to be true that the oppressed is inferior. Second, he acts out his belief so as to make it true. Third, his success is complete only when the oppressed accepts his own inferiority and the truth of his oppressor's belief. In that case, there is a harmony of sorts in the relation—the ultimate reason why it can last. In the eyes of neither oppressor nor oppressed is the oppression "real" oppression. Each knows—and has—his place.

This insight, first stated by Hegel and developed, in ways sound or not so sound, by such thinkers as Marx, Kojève, Sartre, and Fanon, is today widely accepted wherever serious attempts are made to end (rather than merely to alleviate) such social ills as racism and colonialism. And the slogan "Zionism is the liberation movement of the Jewish people" illustrates the belief that the social disease of anti-Jewishness and its cure are wholly parallel to these others.

However, even the relation between "antisemite" and self-hating Jew is not wholly parallel, and not all Jews are self-hating. The self-hating Jew hates his Jewishness, while the antisemite considers his Jew-hatred to be both caused and justified by the other's Jewishness. On his part, the Jew who is not self-hating hates not his Jewishness but rather his condition of exile which distorts his Jewishness, and he seeks to liberate his Jewishness from exile, not himself from his Jewishness. As for the antisemite, he hates (as we have already stressed) Jewish virtues as well as Jewish vices. And if and when forced to justify his hatred of *these* he emerges as hating the Jew, not for being or doing this or that; the doing of this or that is hated precisely when and because it is done by a Jew. He hates the Jew for being at all.

As we have seen, there can be a relation of false harmony between colonizer and colonized, or between racist and his victim. As for the antisemite, he is (as Sartre has rightly said) a criminal who seeks the Jew's death.[10] The Jew's place in *such* a relation would have to be not to exist at all—or to commit suicide. In fairness to all "decent" oppressors, racist and colonizer as well as antisemite, one must add that there are both degrees of hostility and ways of disguising it from others and, above all, from oneself. And in fairness to the "decent" antisemites of pre-Holocaust times, one must further add that the group-death of the Jewish people could be achieved in two ways—genocide or radical assimilation. As decent a thinker as Kant could assert that the "euthanasia" of the Jewish people was desirable for Jews and Gentiles alike. That this particular expression sounds singularly unfortunate two centuries later is hardly his fault.

If racism, colonialism, and anti-Jewishness were wholly parallel phenomena, one would expect opponents of the first two to be firm supporters of the state of Israel, however critical of this or that policy of an Israeli government. This, of course, is not so. In one kind of quarter, the Jewish state is hated because its Jews are no one's victims or tolerees; in quarters of another kind, because it willfully considers itself Jewish. (In 1944, Sartre wrote that "the antisemite reproaches the Jew with being Jewish; the democrat reproaches him with willfully considering himself a Jew."[11]) That fascist and Communist United Nations representatives should have joined hands to denounce Zionism as a form of racism will always remain incredible. It would have been impossible if there were not two ways of destroying Jewish existence—one, by destroying the existence, the other, by destroying the Jewishness.

What elements, then, in addition to racism and colonialism, enter into anti-Jewishness—its unique persistence, mutability and nature? The first two factors may seem to be accounted for in terms of Diaspora history, a history longer and more varied than those, say, of black slavery in America and European colonialism in Africa. But this answer only raises the further questions of why the Jewish Diaspora was accompanied by antagonism (which is not true of all diasporas), and why even radical changes (such as that from the premodern to the modern world) did not, as was in fact hoped, end the antagonism but merely changed its nature, rationalizations and self-definitions.

We are driven, then, to pursue further the insight articulated by Reinhold Niebuhr. Had Jews been hated only by the virtuous for their vices (such as "usury" in the Middle Ages or "lack of refinement" at the time of Mendelssohn), anti-Jewishness should have ended with the disappearance either of the "vices" or the standards which considered them so. Had they been hated only for their virtues by the vicious, anti-Jewishness should at no time have had the social and spiritual respectability that has made it so uniquely powerful, lasting, and deadly. *It is the anti-Jewishness of the saints (in secular terms: the idealists), far more than that of the sinners, which characterizes the uniqueness of the disease.*

This conclusion disposes of a theory of anti-Jewishness long fashionable among traditional Jews and now also existing in a secularist form. There is *Sin'ah* (Jew hatred) because of Sinai, a Jewish tradition affirms. Jews are hated, claims its secularist counterpart, because they brought respect for human life into the world. This theory fails to explain why Jews are hated for their vices by Gentile fellow sinners. Far more seriously, it fails to account for the startling fact of saintly hatred, the more so when its object includes Jewish virtues. We are here speaking of people of love, grace, and humility, who care for the poor, the widows, and the strangers within their gates, and who would lay down their lives to save another; people whose own lives declare the sacredness of human life, their oneness with all human suffering, their refusal to justify evil, violence, and even a single tear. Yet there is the one exception, the hatred of "the Jews." Why should religious saints hate rather than love Jews on account of Sinai? Why should secular idealists hate rather than love them for having brought respect for human life into the world? In failing to answer these questions the theory implies that anti-Jewishness is incurable so long as there are Jews, when in fact (as we shall see) we must view it as obdurate but not beyond a cure. And, in failing to ask these questions, it fails to confront anti-Jewishness in the aspect that lends it its unique power, and among those who, once confronted, might be best able to cure themselves. We are referring, of course, to the anti-Jewishness of the saints and idealists.

Anti-Jewishness has its effective origins in Christianity and reflects these origins to this day. This thesis, like our earlier one, must be qualified and in this case (lest it be misunderstood) before it is even expounded.

1. Anti-Jewish attitudes predate Christianity in pagan antiquity. However, the "saints" of the Greco-Roman world could and did recognize Jewish virtues. Thus, the philosopher Theophrastus "recoiled" from Jewish animal sacrifices, yet admired Jews as "philosophers by race."[12] Christianity not only perpetuated but also transformed pre-Christian anti-Jewish attitudes, and the transformation was crucial.

2. Anti-Jewish attitudes postdate Christianity in modern secularism, i.e., pseudo-Christian right-wing nationalism, anti-Christian left-wing liberalism and radicalism and, most important, the Nazi idolatry which aimed at the destruction of Christianity as a goal second in importance only to that of the Jewish people.

However, the modern nationalist pseudo-Christianity would have been impossible without actual Christianity. The modern liberal-leftist aim to make "the Jews"—and no one but the Jews—into men-in-general is a transformation of the Christian opposition to Jews-in-particular. And the Nazi murder camps were the apocalyptic nemesis of an anti-Jewishness that has persisted, at times dormantly, at times violently, among Christian saints through the centuries. At its bravest and most authentic, organized German Christianity resisted the Nazi onslaught on the Jewish people only because it was in reality an attack on Jesus Christ.[13] One can imagine Theophrastus consenting to attacks on the Jewish sacrifice of animals. But one cannot imagine him defending the "philosophers by race" on grounds no more forceful than that what was really attacked was philosophy.

3. *Not all Christians are or ever have been afflicted by the disease of anti-Jewishness.* In view of the content of the thesis, this qualification is crucial. However, while its truth would seem obvious its significance is complex, obscure, and possibly even beyond the powers of anyone's present comprehension.

In the present context, it must suffice to reject a false view of its significance. The distinction between the anti-Jewishness of "mere Christendom" and a "true Christianity" free of all hatred (and hence necessarily free of Jew-hatred) is obviously apologetic. That it is false as well is shown sufficiently by the fact of anti-Jewish saints, among them St. Chrysostom, St. Augustine, and Luther. That this fact of saintly Christian anti-Jewishness is significant beyond its Christian limits is indicated by the presence, in all post-Christian forms of the phenomenon, of anti-Jewish idealists. Thus, nineteenth-century secularist antisemitism—right-wing, left-wing, and liberal—all included secular saints, i.e., enemies and critics of "the Jews" inspired not by low passions but by high ideals. Had the target of these saints been only Jewish vices, real or imagined (as they often pretended, both to others and themselves), that target would not have been "the Jews." Yet while the Jewish defense organizations of those times kept stressing precisely that point, their labors were quite in vain.

Nazism escalated the logic of anti-Jewishness to its unsurpassable extreme. Jewish virtue and vice were irrelevant. Jewish birth was in itself a crime deserving torture and death. The most shocking fact about the most shocking Nazi crime, however, is that it was, in essence, an "idealistic" enterprise—the work not of petty scoundrels or vicious sadists but of men and women sacrificing all to the "Final Solution."[14]

Indeed, so shocking is this fact as to have rendered all historically post-Holocaust anti-Jewishness on the part of religious or secular saints seemingly impossible. It is all the more startling—and depressing evidence to the tenacity and mutability of the anti-Jewish virus—that the impossibility is only seeming; that saintly anti-Jewishness has not ended but rather developed a wholly new strain which, for the first time in history, goes to any length to deny that "the Jews" are its target. Pre-Nazi "decent" antisemites would salve their consciences by citing "exceptions" even while attacking "the Jews." Nazism did away with the exceptions.[15] Post-Nazi saintly anti-Jewishness shrinks from this horror so radically as to attack only those Jews who are not "true" Jews.

From this stance there is only one step to the identification of "false" Jews with "Zionists," a step all the easier the more undefined the "Zionism." That this new distinction between "true" and "false" Jews is but the old disease in yet another form is obvious once one discovers who belongs in these two groups. The "false" Jewish Zionists include, first, *all* Israelis, right and left, religious and secularist, "hawks" and "doves," so long as they refuse to submit to politicide. They include, second, *all* Jews *anywhere* so long as they refuse to abandon the state of Israel to politicide. As for the "true" Jews, they reduce themselves to two kinds: those dissolving their Jewish identity for the sake of mankind; and those prepared—one generation after Hitler—to entrust their Jewish destiny to the mercies of the world. This new strain of the ancient anti-Jewishness finds its climax when the one calling the "false" Jews back to their "true" Jewishness claims himself to be—symbolically to be sure—the "true" Jew.[16]

The inquiry into the uniqueness of the disease of anti-Jewishness, its nature, tenacity, and mutability, thus refocuses itself into an inquiry into the hatred of Jewish virtues by Gentile religious saints and idealists. There are stirrings within the Christian community, few as yet to be sure, but compelling by their courage and relentlessness, of an attempt to discover the primal roots of the dread plague within the Christian tradition itself. "The antisemitism in the New Testament" is no longer an uncommon phrase, although it still awaits a thorough exploration. For our purpose it suffices to indicate the profound ambiguity of the Books themselves which, on the one hand, affirm God's promise to keep his people Israel and yet, on the other, deny that very peoplehood: only "the faithful," but not all of Israel is Israel; and, read back into the "Old Testament," these faithful reduce themselves to but a few isolated individuals. The flesh-and-blood people is lost. Thus it is no wonder that for centuries the church considered herself as either the "true" Israel opposed to one always "false," or else as the "new" Israel opposed to one long dead.

Some Christians go even further. Is Jew-hatred built into the Christian Gospel itself? Is it part of the *kerygma* itself so that only the most radical attempt to identify the evil and transform the teaching can save the Good News?

Whatever the answer to these radical questions, the hatred of Jewish virtues by

Gentile religious saints and secularist idealists may be said to have found its first systematic expression in the Patristic *anti-Judaeos* literature. Here the Jews are guilty *both* for obeying "the law" *and* disobeying it; of "legalistically" observing the Sabbath *and* giving to God only one day out of seven; and their wickedness is *both* imputable as though it were willed *and* incurable as though it were hereditary.[17] Add to this page from the "dark ages" the fact that Luther rewrote just that page even while writing a crucial page of modern history,[18] and it is no longer altogether obscure why nineteenth-century European nationalist idealists considered even patriotic Jews suspect because they *were* Jews; why their no less idealistic internationalist opponents considered even radical Jews suspect so long as they *considered themselves* Jews; why during the apocalypse German Nazis treated Jewish birth as a crime, not despite but because of their idealism; and why today high-minded post-Holocaust rightists and leftists unite to deny the legitimacy of the state of Israel—the one because this state is composed of and governed by Jews, the other because it is composed of and governed by people who wilfully consider themselves Jews.[19]

What remains still obscure in all these forms of saintly anti-Jewishness is its relentlessness and centrality in the respective schemes of things. What drove some Church Fathers into the radically un-Christian assertion that even baptism cannot redeem "the Jews"? What caused Eichmann's priorities when he redirected trains from the Russian front to Auschwitz?

In the nineteenth century, Bruno Bauer, ex-Protestant-theologian, left-wing atheist, and anti-Jewish archideologue, asserted the following. Not the Christian "daughter" is guilty for wishing to get rid of the Jewish "mother." The Jewish "mother" is guilty for wanting to live. The Jewish "mother" *had* to die if the Christian "daughter" and her secularist offspring were to live.[20] This piece of imagery diagnoses brilliantly, if unwittingly, the Gentile disease of anti-Jewishness, its nature, tenacity, and mutability. Why do some saints and idealists, Christian and post-Christian, consider, in Jews and Jews alone, those characteristics as vices that anywhere else they would consider as virtues? Why is, to them, the viciousness of Jewish virtue both unredeemable and central in the scheme of things? In Bauer's imagery, because the mere survival of the "mother" threatens the "daughter's" very life. Otherwise put, because *for these saints and idealists their self-affirmation is inseparable from the negation of "the Jew."* On this point, the noblest saints afflicted by the disease are at one with the most depraved sinners. Julius Streicher wrote: "Who fights the Jew fights the devil. Who masters the devil conquers Heaven."[21]

But Bauer's imagery also shows—this still more unwittingly—that the disease of anti-Jewishness is neither inevitable nor incurable. The mother-daughter relationship need not be antagonistic, to say nothing of taking the form of a life-and-death struggle. Minimally, the two can part company when the daughter has reached maturity. Maximally, each can find strength and joy in the otherness of the other.

IV

Why do anti-Jewish attitudes exist outside the Christian world? Almost no part of the globe is wholly outside Christian or post-Christian influence. Moreover, the Streicher-inspired cartoons prevalent in the pre-1967 Arab Press and the Arab translations of European antisemitic tracts are evidence of the ease with which even the most depraved strains of the anti-Jewish virus can be exported. However, unless these exports found a native response their effect would surely be marginal. In the Arab world this is not so. A segment of Palestinian Arabs has opposed, to a self-destructive extreme, any form of Jewish state in their neighborhood. The most moderate of current Arab statesmen has described the small Jewish island in an Arab ocean as a "dagger" in the heart of his own far larger and more populous country. Indeed, Arab nationalism as a whole has a component so inextricably bound up with the negation of the "Zionist entity" as to cause wonder whether, were this negative end ever achieved, Arab nationalism—or at least its pan-Arab variety—would not disintegrate.

One need not go far afield in order to recognize that Islam, the second "daughter" of the Jewish "mother," too, has fallen prey to the disease of anti-Jewishness, and has done so on her own, quite apart from any influence of her "sister."[22] The ways are in some respects different, in others the same. The main difference: the Christian anti-Jewishness and its derivatives negate Jewish existence; the Muslim anti-Jewishness and its derivatives negate only Jewish equality, especially when it finds a political expression. The main resemblance: both forms of hostility include saints and idealists among their subjects and Jewish virtues among their objects.

The main cause of the difference is obvious enough: Christianity originated on Jewish soil, in the midst of a flesh-and-blood, still semi-autonomous, Jewish nation. When Islam originated, Jews had already been in exile for centuries and were, so far as the new religion was concerned, not a flesh-and-blood people but only a religious sect. In view of the vastness of this difference, the resemblance is all the more depressing: despite the "mother's" shadowy existence, the younger "daughter" found herself threatened by any sign of life shown by her, and is today shocked to the marrow by the "mother's" miraculous new youth. It is fortunate, however, that Muslim and post-Muslim-secular-Arab anti-Jewishness is neither universal nor inevitable. In this case, too, antagonism is not the only possible mother-daughter relation.

V

The cure of the Gentile disease of anti-Jewishness can only be the task of the patients. The two "daughters" of the Jewish "mother" and their respective offspring can be healed by no one but themselves. However, the Jewish "mother" can assist in two interrelated ways. One is to remove herself, so far as she is able, from the reach of the other's power. (Of this more will be said below.) The other is to cure herself insofar as she has been infected by the daughters' disease, i.e., to break the circle in which the oppressor has made himself into a just accuser and the victim has confessed his guilt. The negative task of breaking this circle has as its positive counterpart the search for an authentic identity.

This search must obviously seek an end of all Jewish self-hatred, open or disguised. Less obvious is the need to end or transform a plethora of qualified Jewish self-affirmations, which are unauthentic to the extent to which they have yielded to and internalized a plethora of qualified anti-Jewish negations. The nineteenth-century German (or French or Hungarian) super-patriot of the Mosaic faith; his internationalist contemporary who expressed his Jewishness by dissolving it, thus leading all peoples in the march toward mankind; the open-minded Jew who kept his Jewishness from his son and daughter lest he deprive them of a free identity of their own when "they were old enough to choose": these and other Jewish identities were all unauthentic. Yet they all survive to this day. Others have been added by the events of this century. One is the Jew who forgets the Holocaust as if it were a guilty secret, or as if it were selfish for a Jew to remember it. Another is the "true" Jew who outdoes all other "anti-Zionists" in opposing all the "false" Jewish Zionists. An authentic Jewish identity is possible only if two questions are separated with absolute clarity: (1) How shall a Jew respond to anti-Jewish attitudes and, indeed, what Gentile attitudes can properly be viewed by him as being anti-Jewish? (2) What does, can, shall it mean to be a Jew, today and tomorrow?

This separation by no means marks the end of the contemporary Jewish identity crisis. It would be more correct to say that it only reveals it. For just as there are unauthentic Jewish identities, so there are also authentic identity crises. The emancipation of the search for a Jewish identity from the tyranny of all forms of internalized anti-Jewishness only brings into clear focus the fact that the authentic identity crisis of the contemporary Jew is without precedent. The premodern Jew knew his identity: he was covenanted to the God of Israel. His secularist modern descendant could seek a new Jewish identity by abolishing those "abnormalities" caused by a religious tradition to which he yet owed his very existence. However, the present-day religious Jew no longer can view the Jewish secularist as nothing but an apostate, and the present-day secularist Jew no longer can view the religious Jew as nothing but a dead relic. Each must include the other when defining his own Jewish identity, and while the problem is with us the solution has yet to come. This unprecedented crisis in post-modern Jewish identity is the result of two enormous facts. Of these one is the state of Israel. The other, however, has an enormity forcing us to view it quite by itself: *every Jew alive today would either be dead or be unborn but for a geographical accident.*

This is a *novum* in the human condition, without parallels inside Jewish history or outside it. Philosophers have not yet noticed this *novum*. Jewish thinkers have not done too much better. Its significance for Jewish identity is as yet obscure. Only one thing is clear and devoid of all obscurity: one cannot authentically cope with one's Jewish identity crisis without facing the *novum* in all its starkness and uniqueness. It is said that this is the first time in Jewish history when a Jew can cease to be a Jew without having to become something else, and that therefore the present Jewish identity crisis can authentically be solved by the dissolution of Jewish identity. It is not obvious that the conclusion follows from the premise. A generation ago Franz Rosenzweig knew that he could not authentically become a Christian without first knowing the Judaism he was about to leave. He never left, and subsequently helped write a new page in Jewish history. No Jew today can authentically abandon his Jewish identity without first asking whether in so doing he helps close the book of a history that should be closed, or abandons those who write a new page that cries out to be written; whether he leaves the ranks of pointless past victims or joins the ranks of possible future murderers and bystanders; whether he serves the cause of God and man or betrays it.

VI

It is doubtful whether the Jewish people could cure itself spiritually from its infection by the disease of anti-Jewishness were it not for the fact that one of its parts has removed itself physically from the reach of anti-Jewish power. It has done so by founding the Third Jewish Commonwealth. This event, momentous in Gentile as well as Jewish history (the former minimally to the extent that it has suffered from the disease of anti-Jewishness), has transformed the Jewish condition in two respects which concern our present purpose. Being a small yet independent state, Israel has given a new dimension to the unauthenticity of the Jew who lets his Jewishness be defined by others. And having built the Law of Return into its very substance, Israel has given a new dimension to the unauthenticity of the Jew who is voluntarily a toleree (to say nothing of being a victim) of the societies, theologies, philosophies, and ideologies of others. Thus it has come to pass, as a corresponding fact, that in the search for an authentic Jewish identity Israel is central.

These assertions may seem wayward or downright foolish at a time when the new, post-Holocaust "anti-Zionist" strain of anti-Jewishness has become so worldwide as to have given rise, among certain Jews, to complaints that the Jewish state, meant to solve the Jewish problem, has become the Jewish problem, and that, meant to be a spiritual center, it resembles more closely a beleaguered fortress.

Yet Herzl and Achad Ha-am, though each was wrong in one respect, were right in another. Herzl was wrong in his naive belief that a Jewish state would establish a natural Jewish existence and end the disease of anti-Jewishness; he was more right than he could have known in his belief that the Jewish people must stop tolerating what, since the Holocaust, has become intolerable: Jewish acceptance of the status of victim of those sick with anti-Jewishness, or the status of toleree of the semicured. Not long ago a Zionist leader proposed that Israel become the ward of the world community. Only a few years later it is clear that, so long as the world community is infected with the disease of anti-Jewishness, the guardian is unsuitable and that, if and when the disease vanishes, the guardian will not be necessary. Herzl was more right than many who came after him.

Achad Ha-am too was wrong and right. The Jewish state does not abound with synagogues filled with superior piety or universities of superior excellence. The life style of its citizens is too harried by the petty problems of daily existence and the deep worries about national existence to be of much help to Jewish visitors in search of a Jewish life style of their own. There is more leisure for matters spiritual at the periphery than at the center. The Jewish state is not, or not yet, a spiritual center of world Jewry in this sense. Yet, Achad Ha-am was right in a way he could not have known. Without Israel, the Diaspora's own spirituality would shrivel into mere fideism. Without the Jewish state, Diaspora Judaism, even after the Holocaust, would belittle "mere" Jewish survival unless it served ideals acceptable to others who would let Jews survive, provided they served just those ideals.[23] Without Israel's Law of Return Diaspora Judaism would make Jewish homelessness into a blessing, viewing the bitter fact of persecution as meaningful martyrdom, and the degrading condition of toleree as a chance to turn the other cheek. This would be true of the Judaism of the modern-minded. As for the Orthodox, they would try to rebuild ghetto walls which have crumbled beyond repair.

VII

A modern view of great longevity has it that the Jewish people has survived through the ages only because of the pressures of its enemies. Friends holding this view have always wished an end of the enmity, foes holding it have always wished the end of the Jewish people. Still others, neither friend nor foe or a little of each, wanted an end of both. The pre-Holocaust version of this view extends to both the people and its faith. The post-Holocaust version professes to respect the intrinsic value and vitality of the faith, seeking an end only of the people, and of these only insofar as they insist on *being* a people. Only the "Zionists" and their "entity" are without intrinsic value and vitality, a pseudo-nation bound to dissolve once enemies cease to threaten it. "Zionism" and "antisemitism" belong together, and the first is the product of the second.

This is said to be the rationale of the current policies of Egypt, Israel's most peaceful Arab neighbor state. Peace with Israel is not considered incompatible with seeking her destruction but rather, on the contrary, the surest way to bring it about. An Israel at peace would be destroyed internally by factional strife—between secularists and Orthodox, Europeans and Orientals, rich and poor; she would be externally abandoned on the one hand, by Diaspora Jewry, on the other, by what is left of world conscience.

Jews cannot speak on behalf of world conscience. On their own behalf, however, they should accept this challenge, both the explicit challenge to Israel and the implicit challenge to the whole Jewish people. Let her enemies make peace with the state of Israel! And let the world cure itself of its anti-Jewishness! And let it then be shown by future history whether Jewish rebirth at Jerusalem after Jewish death at Auschwitz was, after all, a mere illusion—the birth a stillbirth— or whether, on the contrary, it was a live birth, with the prospect that the new Jerusalem might grow to be a blessing, matching or possibly even surpassing the old.

In the premodern world Yehudah Halevi wrote: "Jerusalem can be rebuilt only when Israel yearns after it to such an extent that we love even its stones and dust."[24] A post-Holocaust Jew might add: "In loving the stones and dust of Jerusalem, the Jewish people will rebuild itself after its greatest catastrophe; and only in rebuilding itself can it be a light unto the nations."

Notes

1. We shall generally use "antisemitism" in this essay only for pre-Holocaust forms of anti-Jewishness.

2. See Shlomo Avineri's essay in *World Jewry and the State of Israel*.

3. Raul Hilberg's assertion to this effect, made in 1961, is still substantially correct.

4. See Yassir Arafat's address to the United Nations General Assembly in 1974.

5. In Lessing's *Nathan the Wise* a Templar approaches a Christian Patriarch with the hypothetical case of a Jew who had pity on a Christian orphan and raised her in his home. The judgment he

receives is that the Jew must burn at the stake. The troubled Templar's questions—what if he brought her up as a Jewess? What if he did *not* bring her up as a Jewess but simply as a decent person? What if, though the Jew could not save her soul, God in his power can save it?—all receive the same reply: "No matter! The Jew must burn!"

6. Reinhold Niebuhr, *Love and Justice: Selections from the Shorter Writings of Reinhold Niebuhr*, ed., D. B. Robertson (New York: Meridian, 1967), p. 133.

7. In his *Anti-Semite and Jew* (New York: Schocken, 1948) Jean Paul Sartre achieves some deep insights into antisemitism but loses them totally when at one point he lapses into the scapegoat theory. See p. 54.

In a celebrated joke an antisemitic speaker at a meeting shouts "the Jews are our misfortune!" Heckler: "The Jews and the cyclists!" Speaker (puzzled): "Why the cyclists?" Heckler: "Why the Jews?" This joke, a classic illustration of the scapegoat theory, never cured a single antisemite. However, its enlightened tellers have always fondly believed it could.

8. In 1784, Moses Mendelssohn wrote: "We continue to be barred from the arts, the sciences, the useful trades and occupations of mankind . . . while our alleged lack of refinement is used as a pretext for our further oppression. They tie our hands and then reproach us for not using them." *Jerusalem: And Other Jewish Writings*, trans. A. Jospe (New York: Schocken, 1969), p. 146.

9. See *World Jewry and the State*, sec. IV.

10. Sartre, *Anti-Semite and Jew*, p. 49.

11. Ibid., p. 58.

12. See M. Stern, ed., *Greek and Latin Authors on Jews and Judaism*, vol. 1, (Jerusalem: The Israel Academy of Sciences and Humanities, 1974), pp. 8 ff.

13. Theodore A. Gill writes as follows: "And even after it got rolling, the Confessing Church was late in its perceptions. I simply cannot get gooseflesh over the systematic refinement in Barmen's discovery that the attacks on the Jews must be resisted because they were in reality attacks on Jesus Christ. That is not high theology. That is blasphemy, the unwitting blasphemy, I hope, of men playing a dandy hand at doctrine. It was played out to the end, too. In the letter sent around preparing for the Stuttgart confession after the war, was there much about the guilt against the Jews? Was there anything? [There was not. E.L.F.]

We have little to learn from any church or any prophet who cannot recognize murder until it is murder in the cathedral. "What Can America Learn from the Church Struggle?" in *The German Church Struggle and the Holocaust*, F. H. Littell and H. G. Locke, eds. (Detroit: Wayne State University Press, 1974), p. 286.

14. In a secret address to the S.S. given on October 4, 1943, Heinrich Himmler said the following: " 'The Jewish people is going to be annihilated,' says every party member. 'Sure, it's in our program, elimination of the Jews, annihilation—we'll take care of it.' And then they all come trudging, 80 million worthy Germans, and each has his one decent Jew. Sure, the others are swine, but this one is an A-1 Jew. Of all those who talk this way, not one has seen it happen, not one has been through it. Most of you must know what it means to see a hundred corpses lie side by side, or five hundred, or a thousand. To have stuck this out and—excepting the cases of human weakness—to have remained decent, that is what has made us hard. In our history, this is an unwritten and never-to-be-written page of glory" (Lucy Dawidowicz, ed., *A Holocaust Reader* [New York: Behrman, 1976], p. 133).

15. In the Himmler address quoted in the preceding note, the "decent" antisemites of earlier times have become insufficiently idealistic, and the new "decency" of Jew-hatred consists precisely of considering Jewish virtue and vice equally irrelevant to the crime of Jewish birth.

16. A. Roy Eckardt has analyzed this strain of anti-Jewishness as it erupted among certain liberal Christians following the Yom Kippur War, among them Professor Robert Cushman who asserted that decent respect for the opinions of mankind dictated that the price for Israel's existence was too high, and Father Daniel Berrigan who set himself up, before an Arab group, as the true—if symbolic—Jew. ("The Devil and Yom Kippur," *Midstream*, August to September 1974.) However, this strain has been evident at least since the Six Day War when voices from Geneva thought it their duty to remind Jews in Israel of their prophetic heritage. This was after the victory. Earlier, when Israel was threatened, Geneva had shown no signs of concern.

17. To focus attention on the *anti-Judaeos* literature, for purposes of Roman Catholic self-criticism, is one of the great merits of Rosemary Ruether's *Faith and Fratricide* (New York: Seabury Press, 1974), chap. 3.

18. In our context it is worth recalling that the early Luther was decidedly pro-Jewish but

matched or even exceeded his medieval predecessors in anti-Jewish venom in his old age, surely because Jews proved to be no less stubborn in insisting on surviving as Jews vis-à-vis the new form of Christianity as they had been vis-à-vis the old.

19. Here is one reason why liberals and leftists are so easily taken in by the transparently fraudulent idea of a "Palestinian secular democratic state in which Jews, Muslims, and Christians can live together." That Arab propaganda does its best to exploit this liberal-leftist weakness was to be expected.

20. See Bruno Bauer, *The Jewish Problem*, trans. Helen Lederer (Cincinnati: Hebrew Union College, 1958). Bauer writes: "The hostility of the Christian world toward the Jews has been called inexplicable. Is not Judaism the mother of Christianity, the Jewish religion the predecessor of Christianity? Why this hatred of the Christians, this enormous ingratitude of the consequent for the cause, of the daughter for the mother?" (p. 7). He answers his own question as follows: "Not the daughter is ungrateful toward the mother, but the mother does not want to acknowledge her daughter. The daughter has really the higher right, because she represents the true nature of the mother. . . . If one wants to call both sides egotistical, then the daughter is selfish for wanting her own way and progress, and the mother because she wants her own way but no progress" (p. 18). On Bauer, see further my *Encounters between Judaism and Modern Philosophy* (New York: Basic Books, 1973), pp. 142 ff.

21. Quoted in *The Yellow Spot: The Extermination of the Jews in Germany* (London: Gollancz, 1936), p. 47. This book, its title, and its date of publication all refute the accepted view that "it wasn't known and couldn't have been predicted." In fact, its anonymous compilers and the Bishop of Durham (who wrote a moving preface) were voices in the wilderness. Why?

22. See Moshe Ma'oz's essay in *World Jewry and the State of Israel*.

23. A decade ago Milton Himmelfarb exclaimed: "After the Holocaust, let no one call Jewish survival 'mere'!" Now Terrence Des Pres has written *The Survivor* (New York: Oxford University Press, 1976), a profound meditation which questions "a tradition that speaks of 'merely' surviving, as if in itself life were not worth much; as if we felt life is justified only by things which negate it" (p. 5). He finds "the grandeur of death . . . lost in a world of mass murder" (p. 6), and sees a significance both profound and universal in the defiant affirmation of life shown by inmates of the death camps.

24. *Sefer Ha-Kuzari*, part V, sec. 27.

28 *Philosophical Reflections on Antisemitism*

I would like to begin with a personal anecdote dating back some forty years. I was a Reform rabbi in Hamilton, Canada, and by tradition in that city the Reform rabbi is almost automatically chairman of the Public Relations Committee of the Jewish community. One afternoon, in that capacity, I got an urgent phone call from some members of a small Orthodox synagogue. It was a great emergency, they said, and I had to come right over. So I jumped on the bus and went there. There I was told that a terrible catastrophe had occurred, and that I had to write letters to newspapers all over Canada. What had happened? A window had been broken! So I told them not to worry, that some kids had thrown stones, and that they might have done it just as easily at a church. And I went home thinking there were still some Jews who saw an antisemite behind every tree.

I report this anecdote because although in a superficial sense I was right, I now think that in a profound sense these old East European Jews were right and I was wrong. Remember, that was the time when one part of the world was murdering every available Jew while the rest of the world was doing very little about it. It has taken researchers a long time to find out what the government of Canada, our country, was doing—or rather was *not* doing—about saving some Jewish souls. These old Jews, I think, knew the depressing facts in their guts. They had relatives being murdered on the other side, and they were helpless. Compared to that monumental manifestation of antisemitism, the reason for which the kids threw stones and whether they would have been equally likely to throw those stones at a church constituted a very minor point.

So I now repent of my "liberal" folly of forty years ago. I also distance myself from the kind of Jewish intellectuals who place liberal slogans and ideologies be-

Reprinted from *Antisemitism in the Contemporary World*, ed. Michael Curtis (Boulder, Colorado: Westview Press, 1986), 21–38, by permission of the publisher.

tween themselves and the stark particularity of the phenomenon known as anti-semitism. There are those quick conclusions that antisemitism is a "prejudice," and of course one removes prejudice with "enlightenment." Then there is the quick resort to the "scapegoat theory," which never bothers to explain why the scapegoats are always, or for the most part, the Jews. There is a certain mentality among many liberal Jewish intellectuals that is unable to face reality and instead places ideologies between itself and that reality. I have learned to reject such escapist ideologies from ordinary Jewish people, and in particular from survivors—the very people who are often pictured by these intellectuals as "traumatized." Yet the survivors are the ones who know best that we cannot afford to see an anti-semite behind a tree when one isn't there.

I have also learned a lot from some Gentile scholars who, because they are Gentiles, are free of the Jewish hangups I am alluding to. Perhaps foremost among them is the man in whose honor this chapter was originally written. I have never participated in the annual University of Toronto Zionist Symposium when the committee would have dreamt of choosing anyone except Harry Crowe as chairman and when Harry did not bring profound insights to bear on whatever the topic was. I also want to mention—especially because this chapter will involve a great deal of criticism of Christianity—a great Christian thinker, probably the greatest of our time. In the 1940s Reinhold Niebuhr wrote the following: "When a minority group is hated for its virtues as well as its vices, and when its vices are hated, not so much because they are vices, but because they bear the stamp of uniqueness, we are obviously dealing with a collective psychology that is not easily altered by a little more enlightenment."[1] I have pondered this statement many times and concluded that what is needed is philosophical reflection. (I distinguish this sharply from ideology, which is escapist and, in this case, flees into generalities. Philosophy must be anything but escapist.) When there is something unique to wonder at, it is precisely then that philosophy must not resort to generalities but, rather, must stop at the phenomenon in question.

I

To begin with, let me therefore list some peculiarities of antisemitism that would seem to call for philosophical reflection. The first one Niebuhr has already brought to our attention: the peculiarity that Jews are criticized by antisemites for their virtues as well as for their vices. For example, nineteenth-century antisemites claimed to hate Jews because they were a "nation within a nation" (i.e., still had some collective vitality) and a "bloodless shadow" (i.e., because they did not have it). The familiar shout was "Hep! Hep!" which is the abbreviation of a Latin phrase (*Hyroselyma Est Perdita*") meaning "Jerusalem is destroyed." They gloated over that, that Jews were not a nation! The Jews, in other words, must not be a nation like other nations and also must not *not* be a nation like other nations. One feels like saying, "Antisemite, please make up your mind. Which is the virtue and which is the vice? Take your pick, criticize Jews for the vice, but not for the virtue!"

In our own century, a generation ago, Jews were criticized for supposedly flocking like sheep to the slaughter, when others in the same situation might have been praised for the martyrdom with which they faced death without resisting their persecutors when this was futile. Yet today Jews are criticized for being militarists, when others in the same situation would surely be praised for the courage with which they defend themselves against those who want to destroy them. Once again, one would like to say to the antisemite, "Make up your mind. Which is the virtue, which is the vice?" Here, then, is one phenomenon for which I see no counterpart in any other form of "prejudice" or in any of the countless other evils that beset our world. Of course, it is very easy to mention antisemitism and then immediately to talk about other evils, like racism, or the war in Vietnam, or Hiroshima. The typical liberal intellectual or clergyman quickly draws parallels between them and antisemitism! The liberal, as Jean-Paul Sartre has said, is a very busy man, fighting as he does many evils. However, when we talk about antisemitism, let us not talk about other evils—which is not to say, of course, that other evils might not be equally bad or even worse.

The next unique, and perhaps related, characteristic of antisemitism is its extraordinary persistence. Civilizations change, yet antisemitism persists. Again and again, a new world comes into being and it is said that antisemitism was only a "medieval" thing, now past. (Maybe it was just "religious prejudice.") And then, after a while, along comes a Voltaire, and in the new world antisemitism reappears as an antireligious prejudice.

Third, and presumably related to the second characteristic, there seems to be an extraordinary mutability to the phenomenon, such that many would say the various forms are not the same at all. ("Religious" antisemitism, say, has no connection with "racist" antisemitism.) Undoubtedly, there are profound differences. But no one reflecting deeply on the issue can say that the two are not the same phenomenon at all.

Next, I have used the word "prejudice" in quotation marks. Unlike a genuine prejudice, antisemitism does not seem to disappear when knowledge comes on the scene. Let me give two examples, one at the lowest, most horrendous level, the other at the highest and most exalted, if indeed not saintly, level. In 1944, Joseph Goebbels declared in a public speech in the Berlin Sportpalast that in this war all the nations of Europe had suffered, but that there was one people who had not suffered but only profited from the war—the Jews. Of course, Goebbels, if anyone, knew that when he was uttering these words most of the Jews of Europe had already been murdered. This did not stop him from saying what he did with every sign of conviction.

That was the horrendous. Let me turn now to the most exalted. Among recent Christian theologians few have been more saintly, more courageous than Karl Barth. In his *Dogmatics*, Barth described a visit to a synagogue in Prague, the famous Altneuschul. He remarked that when he saw the synagogue surrounded by a cemetery, he realized that Jews were the shadow of a people no longer alive. A few friends and I once had a meeting with Barth, one of the few if not the only Jewish-Christian dialogue in which the great thinker ever participated. One of us, perhaps the most forward of the lot, and in this it was proper to be forward—Steven Schwarzschild—said to Barth: "Professor Barth, did you go inside that synagogue? If you had, you would have seen Jews profoundly alive, Jews studying the Talmud." In retrospect, I wonder whether, had Barth gone inside that synagogue, it would have made any difference. Jews would still have been a shadow. Knowledge apparently does not by itself remove antisemitism, which is why one cannot call it a prejudice. ("Prejudice" is judgment before knowledge.) And one could give a long list of saints as well as sinners, of the experts as well as the ignorant, who were and are antisemites.

All the above aspects of uniqueness pale in comparison to yet another. This climactic one no discussion of antisemitism in our time can ignore. It is clearly present in the unsurpassable form of antisemitism—the Nazi Holocaust. And while one hates to mention any other form of antisemitism in the same breath as Nazism, to say that there is no connection would be absurd. Hence the need for philosophical reflection.

Not many philosophers have given it that. Among those few was Jean-Paul Sartre. And his book, *Anti-Semite and Jew*, deserves serious attention.[2] What he concluded from the facts as he knew them is that antisemitism is not a legitimate opinion, not a prejudice, but, rather, a criminal passion and that it is criminal because its ultimate goal is the death of the Jew. Here a searching philosopher has come to the bottom of things: What else can the real goal be when the enemy of Jews hates their virtues as well as their vices? Their vices as well as their virtues?

Sartre saw this very clearly. What he did not see is where this strange and unique phenomenon comes from, and how it could have arisen at all. The reason Sartre did not see this lies in his failure to consider history. To explain and understand the phenomenon without history is impossible.

II

A profound historian of the Holocaust, Raul Hilberg, early in his monumental work *The Destruction of the European Jews*, wrote a sentence that, when I first read it, shocked me profoundly. It continues to shock me but, pondering it again and again, I now find it necessary to quote it because I think it is true: "The missionaries of Christianity had said in effect 'you have no right to live among us as Jews.' The secular rulers who followed had proclaimed: 'You have no right to live among us.' The German Nazis at last decreed: 'You have no right to live.' "[3] I find this statement shocking yet true for two reasons. First, it asserts the persistence of Jew-hatred, during long centuries when many times it seemed to have virtually disappeared. The Middle Ages were by no means, as far as Jews are concerned, a uniformly black period. There were long periods of Christian-Jewish tolerance, if not friendship. The early vitriolic sermons of, say, Saint John Chrysostom seemed to have been forgotten. This, however, does not alter the shocking fact that during the Crusades Jew-hatred suddenly reappeared as if from underground. Again, before 1933 in Germany, if anyone had suggested to me that there was some connection between contemporary life and medieval church legislation against the Jews I would have laughed. Anyone would have laughed. Yet Hilberg has chilling tables of comparison between medieval-Christian and Nazi-German anti-Jewish legislation.

Persistence, then, is the first fact brought out by Hilberg, and it teaches a fundamental lesson—that it won't do to sweep Jew-hatred under the carpet. I am reminded of my student days some forty years ago, when I studied the writings of St. Thomas Aquinas, with a very beloved teacher at the Toronto Institute of Medieval Studies. One day I came to his office to study St. Thomas and there on his desk was a pamphlet in French entitled "St. Thomas and the Jews." I said that I was interested and asked if I could borrow it. He replied that he didn't want me to see it. I insisted, and he gave it to me. It was written by a Catholic writer from Quebec who was deriving from St. Thomas the available anti-Jewish sentiments for modern application, to the effect that Jews do not deserve equal rights in a democratic but somehow Christian state. I think now that although my teacher had the right moral sensibility, he was wrong in thinking that I should not see the document or, more important, the anti-Jewish passages in Aquinas's work itself. Perhaps what we really should have studied was not St. Thomas's doctrine of analogy but rather how Jews and Christians together can cope with the phenomenon of Christian Jew-hatred that has been between them for so many centuries. No, sweeping the past under the carpet, though no doubt well-intentioned, won't do. That is the first lesson.

The second lesson comes when we consider the second fact implied in Hilberg's statement. If the persistence of antisemitism through the centuries is shocking, then what shall we say of the escalation of it? We have been told by the Catholic theologian Rosemary Ruether that even St. Chrysostom never preached violence against Jews. (After all, the man was a saint.) Yet without those sermons of his, or others like them, the expulsions of Jews in the Middle Ages—surely acts of violence—could not have occurred. One can picture St. Chrysostom actually protesting against these violent acts while having to admit to himself that without his preachings they could not have taken place.

Yet, concerning escalation, the medieval version was dwarfed by the unsurpassable modern one, which did not occur until our own time. Torquemada burnt Jewish bodies in order to save Jewish souls. The Eichmanns of this world did their best to destroy Jewish souls before consigning Jewish bodies to the gas chambers. From this terrible process of escalation we must derive our second lesson. If the first lesson is not to sweep the past evil under the carpet, the second is that nothing less will do than to deescalate the escalation, unless the new escalation is to win the victory. We may think that we live in a modern, postmedieval world, yet it is still a world in which it is widely taken for granted that Jews are supposed to be homeless. That was not so before the medieval expulsions. Shall the post-Holocaust world be one in which the very right of Jews to exist is debatable?

III

I have used Hilberg's thesis, yet there is a most obvious objection to it: What of ancient pagan antisemitism, prior to the Christian variety? There were accusations of antisemitism such as those of Manetho, the Egyptian priest, and of Apion, against whom Josephus wrote. Writers such as these balked at "Jewish exclusiveness." In wider circles, a great deal of anti-Jewishness undoubtedly resulted from the wars that the Jewish people waged in order not to be engulfed by the flood of Hellenism—namely, the Maccabean War, the anti-Roman War ending in the second destruction of Jerusalem, and finally the Bar Kochba War. Reflecting on those early phenomena, I have found myself in the rare position of answering in the affirmative a most crucial question, "Do Jews themselves cause antisemitism?" Yes, maybe in one respect they do! Significantly, this issue was articulated for me by a philosopher, the late Leo Strauss. If there is a people who reject what other nations consider holiest, namely their gods, and scorn them as idols or nothings, then there is bound to be a deep resentment. We hear of ancient

Jews not wanting Roman emperor statues in their temples. That attitude must have caused much resentment.

There is, then, a considerable case to be made for the significance of ancient antisemitism. Yet in weighing this case, I conclude that had the Christian transfiguration of antisemitism not occurred in the ancient world, it would have died with the ancient world. It was, in fact, well on the way to happening. To give an example on the side of the Jews, the bitter opposition to idolatry was becoming milder. Corresponding to this milder attitude on the part of the rabbis, of course, is a demythologization on the part of the Greco-Roman world itself. I will give a few examples of relative Roman tolerance. Hadrian, the most anti-Jewish Roman emperor, went so far as to make Jerusalem into a pagan city and to forbid Jews to live in it; yet four years later, his successor, Emperor Antoninus, revoked the decree. Later in the Roman Empire, Jews were permitted to remain Jews and yet to become Roman citizens. Perhaps one could say that the ancient pagans criticized Jews for their presumed vices but not for their presumed virtues. Theophrastus, the disciple of Aristotle, attacked what he considered the barbaric Jewish institution of animal sacrifices, but he praised Jews for their monotheism—for being, as he put it, "philosophers by race."

Now compare all this to early Christianity. When I say "early Christianity," I confine myself to the Church Fathers. One could make a very large case about the New Testament. But let us assume, for the purposes of this argument, that many of the anti-Jewish elements in the New Testament would not have become effective unless there had been a need to reiterate them in later generations—and this is what happened in the case of the Church Fathers. The Roman Empire, as I have said, admitted Jews to citizenship; it had hardly become "holy" in the fourth century when their citizenship was revoked. More significant still, the expulsion of Jews from Jerusalem under Hadrian lasted only four years; but for more than one Church Father, "circumcision was given by God to the Jews not as a sign of Divine favour, but as a mark of their future reprobation, so that they might be recognized by those presently occupying the city and preventing them from entering it."[4] God Himself, then, presumably wanted the Jews to be expelled from Jerusalem, and the Roman Empire revoked what, in the mind of the Church, was not being revoked by God! One can see here a connection with the nineteenth-century anti-Jewish insult in Germany, "Hep! Hep!" ("Jerusalem is destroyed").

Let me give you a few examples from the Patristic anti-Judaic literature. Rosemary Ruether deserves great credit for having brought this literature out from under the carpet, and in what follows I rely on her entirely. St. Augustine, a thinker I have always cherished, appropriated the Old Testament for Christianity. What does this mean? In the Old Testament itself there are both curses and blessings for Jews. In the Christian appropriation, all the curses go to the Jews, and the blessings to the Christians—a transformation that at once produces two evils: self-righteousness among the Christians and condemnation of the Jews. For St. Chrysostom it was not enough even to appropriate the Old Testament in this manner. For him even the Maccabees become martyrs for Christ's sake. When confronted with such a stance, a Jew might understandably exclaim, "If you must rob us of our Bible, won't you at least leave our post-Biblical heritage alone?" "No," the Church replied; "if you have saints, they belong to us." Here, in essence, is the much-quoted modern antisemitic statement, the significance of which is much deeper than is commonly realized: "Some of my best friends are Jews." This, supposedly a refutation of the charge of antisemitism, is in fact an expression of it. It means that anyone who is a good friend isn't really a Jew. Jews may be saints; the very fact that they are saints makes them an exception, and what that means is that they are not Jews at all. Antisemites who say that some of their best friends are Jews could maintain, theoretically, that 99 percent of all Jews are their friends. But that would still leave the *real* Jews, who are not.

In the following example what I said previously about Jewish vices and virtues really comes clear. The present virtues of the Jews, St. Chrysostom wrote, are worse than their past vices. In the past, as we read in the Old Testament, the Jews perpetually broke the Law, which is why they were reprimanded by God. What are they doing now? Why, they are *keeping* the Law! And that they should keep the Law now is worse than to have broken it in the past. In fact, who are the Jews? They are the ones who forever do what God does not want them to do. For Chrysostom, that is almost the definition of Jews. And from here there is only one step to the statement that the father of the Jews is not Abraham but Cain. This is said by none other than that beloved friend from my student days, St. Augustine. Justin Martyr took up the issue from here in asserting that if their father is Cain, the Jews must be landless. Their city and their land are not only desolate, but now they must remain so forever. Not surprisingly, it is St. Chrysostom with whom the logic of this kind of thought reached the ultimate conclusion: that the Jews are "fit for slaughter." Here we have the roots of the phenomenon described by Sartre, who did not however, get to the roots because he ignored history.

Now, what should we conclude from all this? Obviously the Church Fathers went much further than the New Testament. For example, when it comes to the argument of whether St. Paul was an antisemite, it is always possible to stress that he did not reject his own people forever. There is a qualitative difference involved when the father of the Jews is regarded as Cain rather than Abraham, and when their land is not only desolate now but must stay so forever. How is this to be explained? As Ruether writes, "For the Christianity of the Fathers, Anti-Judaism is not merely a defence against attacks but an intrinsic need of Christian self-affirmation."[5]

IV

So much for the first part of Hilberg's statement. Let me now come to the second, that pertaining to the "secular rulers"—those who, in effect, said to the Jews: "You have no right to live among us." I previously mentioned that even St. Chrysostom never incited to violence. Of course, violence is, potentially at least, in his very words. Moreover, it would be a mistake to generalize that the saints, just because they were saints, never advocated violence. Thus, in the first century when a synagogue in Callinuum was destroyed and the Roman emperor demanded that compensation should be paid to have it rebuilt, St. Ambrose protested strongly and thereby, at least implicitly, endorsed the violence.

Still, there is a quantum leap from words to deeds when the latter are no longer sporadic—from the position "you have no right to live among us as Jews," to the position "you have no right to live among us." This leap occurred when beliefs and words become enacted into law. Law creates a world, and in the new world

Jews have no right to live. Moreover, the escalation creating a new world creates precedents for later times. In this connection one hesitates to mention, but cannot help mentioning, that in 1919 Adolf Hitler wrote a notorious letter in which he said that pogroms were not enough. They were emotional, unsystematic, and therefore ineffective. Needed was "the removal of the Jews as a whole," and this required the action of law. Hitler did not specify at that time what kind of "removal" he had in mind—whether it was medieval or modern. Still, the medieval precedent was there.

What sort of world is created by the law? In this case, it was a world in which antisemitism was a self-fulfilling prophecy. Jews were supposed to be landless, so the law had to make them landless, by prohibiting them from owning it. Jews were supposed to be cursed, so the law had to make them cursed. Jews were supposed to suffer, so the law had to make them suffer. This sort of logic led to the medieval expulsions, and thus the Jews were no longer at home in the lands of their domicile; yet they also could not return to their own land for it had been devastated, and Jerusalem, too, had been destroyed, so they became "eternal wanderers." (Ahasuerus, the Jew as restless wanderer, is a legend not of Jewish making but, rather, one of Christian making.)

This, then, is the world produced by medieval Christian law, and once it has been produced it tends to seem right and natural. It has been taken for natural even though, of course, it is historical. And, unless the whole escalation is deescalated, the precedent will persist and continue to exert its power. To quote from my recent *To Mend the World:*

> [In 1933] Martin Buber was forced to write to the Nazi Christian theologian Gerhard Kittel as follows: "Authentic Jewry, you say, remains faithful to the symbol of the restless and homeless alien who wanders the earth. Judaism does not know such a symbol. The wandering Jew is a figure in Christian legend, not a Jewish figure." Kittel had invoked the image of the wandering Jew, not only to justify the Nazi reversal of the emancipation of German Jews, but also to argue that "authentic" Jews (and needless to say, Christians) were religiously required to accept it. Close to forty years later Father Daniel Berrigan asserted that in Israel "the wandering Jew became the settler Jew . . . [and] the slave became master and created slaves." Just as Kittel had no need to investigate whether German Jews had behaved like a "foreign people," so Berrigan had no need to find out whether kibbutzniks were "settlers" and Israel in general "masters" who "created slaves." In both cases the "eternal wanderer" stereotype was quite enough.[6]

The stereotype has power over the nice people as well as the nasty ones. Ours is a grim age in which there are many groups and vast numbers of refugees. All of them together do not attract the attention of the Palestinian Arabs alone. Why is this so? Correspondingly, why doesn't anybody ever stop to consider that more than half of the Jewish population of Israel consists of Jewish refugees from Arab countries? Why is this so? Are all those guilty of one or both of these errors to be called antisemites? No, but they are heirs to the medieval world. That there are Jewish refugees is a fact of life accepted as natural even by those who do not like it. That the Jewish self-liberation in the former Palestine should, unhappily, have created refugees who are not Jewish is unnatural even in the eyes of many who endorse the collective Jewish self-liberation. As the saying goes, it doesn't make news when a dog bites a man, but it does make news when a man bites a dog. The difference, of course, is that the proverbial man-dog case is based on nature but there is nothing natural about the other case. It is a case of history having regrettably become second nature.

V

I now come to Hilberg's third point—a concept that boggles the mind. As the Nazi policy represents the unprecedented with which we still are struggling, and as we are not very close to understanding it, I can only try my best to explain.

In the beginning was the word—the code word *antisemitism*. Somebody concocted that code word way back in the nineteenth century, but it does not matter who it was.[7] What really matters is that it caught on. (It is still being used, in fact.) As the nineteenth century was a scientific age in which many people no longer believed in Christ, it became difficult to call Jews "Christ-killers." Hence it became necessary to find a new—and, if possible, scientific-sounding—word to rationalize the old hatred. The word found was *antisemitism*.

James Parkes has argued for many years that we shouldn't spell *antisemitism* with a hyphen because that suggests there is something called *semitism* that the *anti* is against. But of course there is no such thing as semitism, nor has antisemitism ever been directed against the Arabs.[8]

In nineteenth-century Germany, there were three kinds of antisemite: the right-wing antisemites, for whom the Jews were all revolutionaries; the left-wing antisemites, for whom the Jews were all money-bags and capitalists; and the liberal antisemites, who didn't actually hate Jews but did disapprove of them. Given that two kinds of liberals existed in Germany at the time, there were two reasons for disapproval. The internationalist liberals disapproved of Jews because they were too clannish and did not take part in the concerns of mankind. The nationalist liberals, who were more typically German, complained that the Jews were not clannish enough, that they mixed with German culture.

Now that was an extraordinary situation. Jews couldn't be both all Marxists and capitalists, too clannish and not clannish enough. And one should have thought that these contradictory accusations would cancel each other out. That is what the Jewish defense organizations of those days believed, which is why they proposed to refute these accusations—an activity that proved totally useless. These organizations believed in what one might call the logic of God—a logic in the service of the truth. What they did not realize is that there is also a logic of the devil. The latter serves the lie, and tries to preserve the hatred that lies underneath by creating from the lie a consistent system. That, in this case, was quite a job—but the *Protocols of the Elders of Zion*, that notorious forgery, caught on like wildfire nevertheless. Even the *London Times* thought for a while there was something to the *Protocols*.[9] And Henry Ford peddled the book in the United States.[10] Why, according to the *Protocols*, the Jews only pretend to be revolutionaries concerned with the poor or, alternatively, to be interested only in money. They only pretend to love German culture. It's all part of a secret Jewish plot to dominate the world.

Here you see what has been happening all along. When an escalation takes place, the hatred is not only preserved; it is escalated and transfigured. Great as their Jew-hatred was, the Church Fathers would have said that there was one way in which a Jew could save himself, and that was by accepting redemption in Christ. But what would be said within the modern plot theory when a Jew became a Christian and joined a church? Why, now they are infiltrating the Church! So the hatred itself becomes transformed and escalated.

Now, from the standpoint of the "devil," there is still one stage left if the hatred is to become ultimate and unsurpassable. This I recognized one day in a flash, when the Canadian Broadcasting Corporation (which at one time loved to include Nazis in its shows as they were good for the ratings) featured Norman Lincoln Rockwell. The American Nazi maintained that "Hitler never murdered all the Jews, only Jewish traitors!" And the fellow who interviewed him did not have the wit or gumption to ask: "What about the children?" Children, even Jewish ones, are not plotters or traitors. So from the standpoint of the "devil," if the hatred was to reach the ultimate, one had to produce an equation without precedent and equal anywhere in human history: *For Jews and for Jews only, existence itself is a crime, punishable by torture and death.* That is what happened in the Nazi regime; on the one hand, Jews were "vermin" to be "exterminated" and, on the other hand, devils to be tortured. Nazi antisemitism is improperly called racism—a great evil, of course, but an evil different from antisemitism. Racism holds that there are lower races who, nevertheless, are still human. For Nazis, Jews are not of the human race at all, as neither vermin nor devils are human.

The Nazis often did not understand this equation themselves. There was one fearful moment in an interview with Franz Stangl, the commandant of Treblinka. The interviewer asked this question: "If they were going to murder them anyway, what was the purpose of those terrible tortures that preceded the murders?" Stangl replied to the effect that the Nazis had tried to condition the murderers to the terrible deeds they had to do. But this does not make any sense at all. Which would have been easier on the stomachs of all those Nazi murderers—to kill people with clean rifle or machine gun shots? Or to go through endless processes of torture? Generals Patton and Eisenhower witnessed some of the evidence when they entered the concentration camp at Ohrdruf. Patton became sick, and Eisenhower said, "I want every American unit not actually in the front lines to see this place. We are told that the American soldier does not know what he is fighting for. At least he will know what he is fighting against." He added that the American mind cannot understand this. He should have said "the human mind." And yet it happened.[11]

I must discuss this terrible escalation once more, this time not from the standpoint of the Jewish victims but from that of the German people themselves. Those nineteenth-century right-wing antisemites, however absurd their belief that the German Jews who loved German culture actually wanted to destroy it, at least loved German culture themselves. In turn, the left-wing antisemites, however absurd their belief that the Jews were all in league with Rothschild, were at least concerned with the poor.

But what, one must ask, was the positive counterpart to the Nazi murder of the Jews? Superficially it seems that there was such a counterpart: "Today we have Germany, tomorrow the world." This slogan was shouted from the house tops. But when one asks what the Nazis were going to do with the world once they had it, no answer is available. Hermann Rauschning called the Nazi revolution a "revolution of nihilism." And except for one matter he was right. At the height of the Nazi regime, however, it looked as if there were two points: murder of Jews and domination of the world. These two points were no longer true, however, at the time of the apocalypse. In the Berlin bunker, Hitler and Goebbels, the only true Nazis left in the last days of the war, expressed ghoulish satisfaction at what they thought was the imminent demise not of their enemies, to say nothing of the Jews, but of the German people themselves. And there were two significant last acts that Hitler performed. One was a last will and testament spouting once more a murderous hatred of Jews. The other was an order, no longer obeyed, to flood the Berlin subways in a last attempt to stop the Russian armies. Visualize the apocalyptic scene: Berlin was surrounded by the Russian armies. Bombs were falling from the skies. And German civilians were hiding in the subways. The officer given the order said to Hitler: "But *mein Führer*, if we flood those subways, we shall drown German men, women and children!" And Hitler, that great lover of German children, replied, "Let them drown!" Of all the world's empires, the German Nazi Empire was the only one that left not a single positive accomplishment in its wake—for which reason we cannot entirely blame the German people when they act as if those twelve years that were equal to a thousand never happened at all. There is just one lasting monument, and that one is a negative. It is the presence of an absence—6 million murdered Jews.

VI

After all this there was a moment of great repose when the death camps were revealed and many, myself included, were prepared to declare that this was the end of antisemitism everywhere—that it was the ultimate revelation of an evil that had haunted Europe and much of the rest of the world for far too long a time. And in that moment of repose occurred some glorious achievements. In that moment the State of Israel was declared by the United Nations. (Now that organization is rightly called by the Christian theologian Roy Eckardt "the effective world centre of antisemitism.") Then there was also a deep soul-searching in the churches in an attempt to remove, to root out, the "teaching of contempt" (as it was called) for the Jewish people—an effort culminating, perhaps, in Vatican II, (the council, convened by Pope John XXIII [1962–1965], that repudiated the idea of collective Jewish guilt for the crucifixion and stressed the spiritual bond between Catholics and Jews). Then there was an acceptance of the Jewish collective right to a state of their own, not only by the West but by the East as well. If one reads Gromyko's UN speech of May 14, 1947, supporting partition of the area of Palestine and the creation of a Jewish state (which took place at the time of the vote in behalf of a Jewish state), one can hardly believe it.

The repose was soon destroyed. It was destroyed, or beginning to be destroyed, in the three weeks preceding the Six-Day War, when the same sort of words emanated from Cairo, Amman, and Damascus that had once emanated from Berlin and Vienna. The man who said at that time, "Kill the Jews wherever you find them, kill them with your nails and with your teeth"—that was King Hussein of Jordan. Another moderate, Faisal of Saudi Arabia, said in 1971 that Jews had strayed from the Law of Moses, killed Jesus, and were cursed by God through the

Prophets forever. Yet another, Anwar Sadat, maintained as early as 1955 that "our war against the Jews is an old battle which Mohammed began. It is our duty to fight the Jews, in the name of Allah and in the name of our religion. It is our duty to finish the war which we have begun." (One wonders what "finishing it" would mean.) That same statesman declared in 1972 that Israel must be returned to the humiliation and wretchedness that was established in the Koran, and that Jews are a nation of liars, and traitors, a people born for deeds of treachery.[12] Jews reading such words can only conclude that just as one "daughter religion" of Judaism—Christianity—has found it difficult to tolerate her "mother," so, to put it mildly, did the other (namely, Islam).

This hostile rhetoric is one kind of thing that destroyed repose for Jews in those three weeks preceding the Six-Day War. Another was the silence in the churches. Some Jewish people had been in dialogue with Christians for a long time; for me personally, the dialogue began in the concentration camp of Sachsenhausen in 1938 with a few Christians who were there for much nobler reasons than such as I. Yet now, when there seemed to be the threat of a second Holocaust, there was a silence in the churches. All these years we had talked theology—and there was silence now because the subject that concerned us was "politics."

This experience of silence prompted me to think up a parable. Two friends walk in a forest, engaged in friendly conversation. Suddenly, one falls into a swamp and shouts "Help!" But the other cannot hear him. Well, since all great parables must have at least two versions, here is the second: The one falls into the swamp, and the other hears him but asks, "What is the matter? We had such a nice conversation, so why are you changing the subject?" That was my parable in 1967. Since then, with the resurgence of the old antisemitism and the appearance of a new, I changed the parable. The one falling into the swamp shouts: "Help—and watch out, my friend! You too may fall into a swamp—and the swamp will be the same." After the Holocaust, any new antisemitism tolerated within Christianity may destroy what is left of the reality of the religion of love.

This year I wonder whether the parable might have to be changed again—whether, perhaps, the other hears his friend but falls into the swamp all the same and, in his attempt to get out, accidentally—or perhaps not so accidentally—steps on his friend and shoves him down deeper. That possibility occurred to me when I read with shock of the pope's granting of an interview with Yasser Arafat. This is a subject to which I shall have to return in a few moments.

Meanwhile, I must first face the logically and morally impossible fact of a post-Holocaust antisemitism. Surely such a thing is impossible following the ultimate revelation of antisemitism given to the whole world! Of course, here and there may be those who have never heard of the Holocaust or else have truly forgotten it. Can post-Holocaust antisemitism exist when antisemites themselves invoke the Holocaust and turn it against the Jewish people? How is such a thing possible? The conclusion to which I am driven is this: that there has been a resurrection of the devil's logic. In effect, the present right-wing version of the devil's logic states that Hitler never murdered any Jews—and that he should have finished the job.

So much for the devil's new logic on the extreme right. We now turn to the extreme left. If for the right, Hitler never murdered any Jews, for the left he murdered, yes, not Jews but his victims were human beings-in-general. Hence Jews today are thought by some to be guilty of parochialism if they so much as mention the Jewish identity of the Jewish victims, if indeed not guilty of a racism that sets the Jewish above all the other "victims of fascism."

Five years ago, my wife and I went to visit refuseniks in the Soviet Union. When we arrived in Riga, a refusenik urged us to visit Salaspils, a nearby concentration camp site, but after that to go as well to Rumbula, a camp where, as was not the case at Salaspils, only Jews were murdered. So we went to Salaspils, a tremendous memorial site where no expenditure has been spared to keep memory alive. (Not the slightest evidence remained, however, that any Jews were murdered there.) We stayed on at Salaspils for such a long time that the head of the place noticed us and asked us to sign the visitor's book. So we opened the book, and the first statement was a very moving one in Hungarian, saying that the world must see to it that such terrible things can never happen again. We then opened the next page and saw a long statement in Arabic, with a translation in English attached, to the effect that "We too have suffered, at the hands of the Israeli Nazis, and mourn for those who suffered at the hands of the German Nazis." I wrote in response, "Let no one pervert, for whatever cause, what happened here."

We then asked our tourist guide to stop at Rumbula, a totally neglected place. We got out of the car, looked at the miserable stone, and asked our guide to translate for us. And this is what it said: "To the memory of concentration camp inmates, political prisoners, etc." Jews are the "etc."

Soon after that, in Minsk, we stood before the only memorial (so far as I know) in the whole Soviet Union in which Jews are mentioned, which says in Yiddish: "In memory of the 3,000 Jews murdered here, by the greatest enemies of all mankind." Rather universalistic, yes? But not universalistic enough for Stalin, for it is in Yiddish and it mentions Jews. So the man who put it up was sent to Siberia. Throughout the Soviet Union the memory of Hitler's Jewish victims is systematically suppressed! Thus they are murdered a second time. But then, all this is no different from what happened on the University of Toronto campus in the autumn of 1982 with the emergence of the Trotskyite slogan "Lebanon is the Holocaust, and Beirut the Warsaw Ghetto." This is stealing the Holocaust, for whatever the sufferings and evils in Lebanon, they bear no resemblance to the Holocaust. And the theft can only have one purpose: to do on the left what the neo-Nazis are doing on the right. For the right, the Holocaust never happened, yet the job should be finished. For the left, it happened, yes, but it did not happen to the Jews; rather, it happened to humans-in-general or, perhaps more precisely, to all mankind except Jews.

But what about the people who really matter to the Jewish people and the fight against antisemitism—their friends the liberals? Perhaps we should have guessed all along that this liberal friendship wouldn't always be easy, either, given that in the 1950s Arnold Toynbee compared what the Israelis supposedly were doing to the Palestinian Arabs with what the Nazis had done to the Jews. The same thing happened in Montreal, and the public debate that ensued between Toynbee and the then Israeli Ambassador Yaacov Herzog is available in print as well as on two long-playing records.[13] There, one may hear Toynbee saying twice: "What the Nazis did to Jews was nothing peculiar." Here we have a supposedly great historian who is blotting out the uniqueness of the Holocaust—the murder trains, the gas chambers, the poisonous propaganda leading up to it, to say nothing of its background in Christian Jew-hatred. In 1974, too, Yasser Arafat appeared before the United Nations and committed a systematic theft of the Holocaust; but it was hardly noticed: "If you want to understand it in your terms" [of course, he was addressing the liberal Western democracies, not the Arabs], "the number of Palestinian victims at the hands of the Israeli fascists . . . would be 6,000,000." Nobody can understand the mathematics or should attempt to do so, for the purpose is clear enough. This statement was a bare-faced theft of the Holocaust and a rape of the Western conscience, for of course everyone is familiar with the figure 6,000,000.

So we come to the recent news out of Lebanon that there were supposedly 600,000 homeless Lebanese in the recent war. How many casualties were there? Sixty thousand (*Barrie Examiner*). How many PLO prisoners were there in places in Israel that "could only be called concentration camps"? Six thousand (*Edmonton Sun*). The *Sun* apparently knows what a concentration camp is. It is impossible to consider the number 6 in these cases as incidental. And this is confirmed when one reads that maybe the number in the Nazi Holocaust was only 60,000, that maybe somebody added "00" at the end. And the obscenity of it all reached a climax when, in supposedly respectable magazines, the PLO in Beirut was compared to the Warsaw Ghetto uprising. Of course, unlike the PLO, the Jews in Warsaw had not murdered children; and unlike the Jews in Warsaw, the PLO could get out of Beirut and did get out, with great applause by the world. But this difference in behavior failed to stop the journalists not only from making the comparison but also, in one case, from adding that the Israelis were obtuse to the "irony" of it all.

What is the upshot of these somber recent developments? Despite all protestations to the contrary, the post-Holocaust transfiguration of antisemitism is "anti-Zionism." A qualitative change has once again occurred, of course, but it is the same reality. For pre-Holocaust antisemites, Jews, and Jews only, have no right to exist—or, at any rate, their right to exist is debatable. For post-Holocaust antisemites the Jewish state, and that state alone, has no right to exist—or, at any rate, in its case alone the right to exist is debatable. In a way, the most shocking phenomenon of all concerns those people who forever keep repeating that Israel has a right to exist, and who in saying this legitimate those who say the opposite or act on it. What would anyone think of a person who got up and said "Canada has a right to exist!" Or Ghana?

This is why, in the minds of Jewish people, the pope's recent meeting with Yasser Arafat was a shocking episode and one, indeed, that may have caused a severe setback in Catholic-Jewish relations. For if in this meeting the pope asked Arafat to abrogate the PLO's Palestinian National Covenant (which clearly calls for Israel's destruction through "armed struggle"), the media did not report it. Would the pope meet with the IRA? Yet the IRA does not seek to destroy Britain.

In my view, one element of that meeting was worse even than the meeting itself. The pope used the occasion to express, once again, the Vatican's wish for the internationalization of Jerusalem. That, of course, may seem a humane, universalistic gesture. However, after 2,000 years of Christian antisemitism, much of it institutionalized, one must ask a few tough questions. The late King Saud of Saudi Arabia lamented that he could not worship in the al-Aksa Mosque because Jerusalem was in Jewish hands; yet he never bothered to go there even once in the nineteen years that it remained in Muslim hands. This is only one striking piece of evidence indicating that Muslim anti-Jewishness is not dead, that it is Jewish Jerusalem that must be negated. So I must ask this question: Why, in the nineteen years that Jerusalem was in Jordanian hands, did the Vatican never once call for the internationalization of Jerusalem?

The Christian theologian Krister Stendahl of Harvard University has noted that in the view of Muslims and Christians Jerusalem has holy sites, but that for Jews Jerusalem itself is holy. That is why the present rebuilding of Jewish Jerusalem is of religious as well as secular significance—almost 2,000 years after the Jewish Jerusalem was destroyed. Yet this is the time that the Vatican chooses to call for the internationalization of Jerusalem—surely a fact requiring the deepest soul-searching on the part of many Christians.

The matter goes beyond ecclesiastical establishments, however. Reporters are keenly interested in all sorts of Arab opinions. Regarding Israelis they seem most interested in critics of the Begin government. But they must begin to ask what Israelis themselves think about Jerusalem. In a recent poll, half the Israeli population was in favor of territorial accommodation in return for peace. On the subject of Jerusalem, the opinions were almost unanimous that the city must remain both united and Jewish.

VII

This brings me to my conclusion, which necessarily concerns not the phenomenon of antisemitism but rather the response to it by Jews themselves. Again and again the sickness of antisemitism, though often thought dead, acquires a new lease on life. How should Jews respond to this depressing fact? Perhaps the medieval philosopher-poet Yehuda Halevi put it best. Living at a time, he says, in which Christians and Muslims are fighting each other, dragging Jews down to doom, he was nevertheless able to write a glowing account of Judaism. In this account, a pagan king who has studied philosophy, Christianity, Islam, and Judaism and finally converts to Judaism asks this deep question of a rabbi: Has he correctly observed that Christians and Muslims are superior in saintliness to Jews? The former have monks and saints, but Jews do not even have monasteries. The rabbi agrees but stresses that the great Jewish virtue is different. It is fidelity. How easy would it be for Jews to escape persecution by converting to Islam or Christianity! Yet only because of fidelity do they still exist at all. Fidelity, therefore, is the virtue of the Jewish people *as a whole*, not just that of the saints or prophets among them. Without fidelity they would have ceased to be.

The focus of this fidelity today is Jerusalem. As Yehuda Halevi once wrote, "Jerusalem will not be redeemed, until Jews yearn for her very dust and stones."

Jews who walk the streets of Jerusalem today are filled with the pain of 2,000 years, but also with a sense of wonder and a great rejoicing. They must surely recall the words of *Lamentations*, which describe from the Jewish side what from the anti-Jewish side is meant by the cry, "Hep! Hep!"—namely, "How solitary doeth the city sit that was full of people." If they look around, they would see Jews from Western countries as well as Muslim and Arab countries—Jews from as far away as India and China. They would be filled with a profound astonishment, as if to say: "The city that sat solitary yesterday, that was ruins even if holy ruins—how full of people it is now!" "Hep! Hep!"—the deepest Jewish response to this in our time is Jewish Jerusalem rebuilt. It is today the most profound expression of the Jewish faith that the long but not incurable disease of Jew-hatred will one day come to an end.

Notes

1. D. B. Robertson, ed., *Love and Justice: Selection from the Shorter Writings of Reinhold Niebuhr* (Cleveland: World Publishing Co., 1967), p. 133.

2. Jean-Paul Sartre, *Anti-Semite and Jew* (New York: Schocken, 1948).

3. Raul Hilberg, *The Destruction of the European Jews* (Chicago: Quadrangle, 1978), pp. 3ff.

4. Rosemary Ruether, *Faith and Fratricide* (New York: Seabury, 1979), p. 147.

5. Ibid., p. 181.

6. Emil L. Fackenheim, *To Mend the World* (New York: Schocken, 1982), p. 93.

7. A rabble-rouser by the name of Wilhelm Marr made the word prominent, but he may not have been the first to use it.

8. See the related discussion in Fackenheim, *To Mend the World*, p. 214.

9. Ralph Lord Roy, *Apostles of Discord* (Boston: Beacon Press, 1953).

10. Albert Lee, *Henry Ford and the Jews* (New York: Stein & Day, 1980).

11. Quoted and discussed in Fackenheim, *To Mend the World*, pp. 202ff.

12. See M. Moaz, "Anti-Jewishness in Official Arab Literature and Communications," in M. Davis, ed., *World Jewry and the State of Israel* (New York: Arno Press, 1977), pp. 33ff.

13. CBS Records, CP 13–14. See also Yaacov Herzog, *A People That Dwells Alone* (London: Weidenfeld Nicolson, 1975), pp. 21–47.

FOUR

ISRAEL: RELIGIOUS PURPOSE AND SECULAR SELF-RELIANCE

29 *The Holocaust and the State of Israel: Their Relation*

I. Hope

> Our Father in Heaven, the Rock of Israel and her Redeemer, bless Thou the state of Israel, the beginning of the dawn of our redemption. . . .

This prayer by the Israeli Chief Rabbinate does not hesitate to describe the state of Israel as "the beginning of the dawn of the redemption" of the Jewish people. That the official rabbinate of Israel should formulate such a prayer is in itself surprising: what is positively astonishing, however, is its wide acceptance by Jews everywhere. Religious Jews inside and outside Israel recite it in the synagogue, and secularist Israelis, who neither frequent synagogues nor recite prayers, recite *this* prayer, as it were, not with their lips but with their lives.

Messianic expectations by religious Jews are not new or unusual: neither is the association of these with the ingathering of the exiles in a restored Jewish commonwealth. More than merely unusual, however, if not altogether without precedent, is the linking of these, even by fervent believers, with a historical event *already clearly and unequivocally present.* No matter how cautiously interpreted, the messianic future cannot be shorn of an element of absoluteness, whereas the historical present is inexorably ambiguous in essence and precarious in its very existence. The state of Israel is not exempt from the condition of historicity. Hence a prayer which links this present state with the messianic future reflects a boldness that the ancient sages of the Gentiles might well have considered tantamount to *hubris,* or tempting the gods.

The rabbis of ancient Israel would have doubts of their own. Unlike the gods, their God is Lord of history. Moreover, he has given promises, the reliance on which is not *hubris* but rather fidelity. But *when* will the time be ripe for "the

Reprinted from *The Jewish Return into History* (New York: Schocken Books, 1978), 273–86, by permission of the publisher.

End?" And *how*—if at all—can one detect the signs? These questions receive only reluctant and conflicting answers from the rabbis. To be sure, they *must* link history with its messianic fulfillment, but prudently shrink from extending this linking to *particular* events *already present*. Thus the rabbis too understand, no less well than the sages of the Gentiles, that—this side of its messianic transfiguration—all history is precarious.

For this reason rabbinic imagery picturing the messianic days as gradually unfolding is inevitably at odds with its opposite, which views "the End" as ushered in by catastrophe. At one extreme, it is imagined that all foreign domination over Israel will cease *before* the coming of the Son of David, and that the "mountains will grow branches and bear fruit" for its returning inhabitants (TB Sanh. 98a). At the other, the End is pictured as preceded by impoverishment in the land, and indeed by a terror in Jerusalem so extreme that her gates will all be equal—not one will furnish escape (TB Sanh. 98a). The one projection can be furnished with a proof-text (Ezek. 36:8) which makes it the "clearest sign" of the End. But so can the other (Zech. 8:10, also Ps. 119:165). These and similar conflicting projections cannot but produce in all (or most) rabbis the insight that they are mere speculations—that all attempts to link the precarious present with the absolute future are themselves precarious and cannot be otherwise.

This condition cannot be transcended even when a sober appraisal of actual history brings about a near-consensus among the rabbis. Under the influence of idealism, some modern Jewish thinkers were to conceive of messianism as a mere ideal which, on the one hand, could only be approached and not reached and, on the other, was *being* approached in a linear or dialectical progression *already present*. Such notions are foreign to rabbinic realism, to which the messianic days are more than a mere ideal and which, at the same time, can see no clear messianic direction in past or present. Recognizing catastrophe as a persisting possibility, this realism creates the imagery of a pre-messianic travail—the "birth-pangs of the Messiah"—as an all but normative check on all gradualist or sentimental utopianism. Yet even so normative an image can bring about no firm link between the absolute future and historical events already present. Thus, in the midst of catastrophe, the pessimistic Rabbi Hillel can despair of messianism altogether, holding that King Hezekiah has already been the promised Messiah, and that none other is to be expected (TB Sanh. 99a). On his part, Rabbi Johanan cannot go beyond the admonition that "when you see an age in which suffering pours like a stream, then hope for him" (TB Sanh. 98a). But hope is not a certainty, and suffering, however harrowing, is not a proof. Thus the link between the forever precarious historical present and the messianic future is itself forever precarious, a fact poignantly expressed in Midrashim in which the Israelites plead with God to make an end of the painful historical alternation between exile and redemption, and bring the final redemption.

Yet unless the messianic future is to become ever elusive and thus irrelevant, its linking with a *possible* present, however precarious, is indispensable and, with its risks paradigmatically shown by Rabbi Akiba's support of the Bar Kokhba rebellion, this too becomes normative for the Jewish religious consciousness—and remains so, through the ages. Thus at one extreme the mystical Nahmanides (1194–1270) does not hesitate to rob empirical history of its intrinsic precariousness by means of the suspect ancient device of "calculating the End," maintaining that the rabbinic strictures against the practice no longer apply when the End is so near.[1] (This view is to be reiterated by more than one rabbi during the Nazi Holocaust, with increasing conviction by those surviving to see the birth of the state of Israel.)[2] Yet he *stays with* empirical history when he sees messianic (albeit negative) *evidence* in the fact that, while many Gentile nations have succeeded in destroying the land, not one has succeeded in rebuilding it (Ramban to Lev. 26:32). At the other extreme the sober Maimonides (1135–1204) assimilates the messianic future to the historical present, sufficiently so as to reaffirm a rabbinic view that "the sole difference between the present and the messianic days is delivery from servitude to foreign powers" (TB Sanh. 91b). At the same time, he must ascribe an *absolute* perfection to future men (Jews and Gentiles alike) to be able to assert that the kingdom of the Son of David, unlike David's own, will be destroyed neither by sin within nor by aggression from without. He does not resolve but only expresses this tension by echoing the rabbinic saying that those be "blasted who reckon out the end" (TB Sanh. 97b).[3]

In view of this inherent and inevitable tension between contingent historical present and absolute messianic future in the Jewish religious consciousness, it is not surprising that the modern world should have produced a deep and widespread desire or need to get rid of that tension. This is done covertly when the absolute future is projected into an irrelevant infinity, and overtly when it is abandoned altogether. The result is a "normalization" which occurs when Jewish existence is classified without remainder in available categories, such as "religious denomination" or "ethnic subculture" and, above all, of course, when there is total assimilation.

The modern Zionist movement originally appears on the scene as another normalization effort and, indeed, at one extreme one so radical as total assimilation is at the other. No Jewish self-classification as "religious denomination" or "ethnic subculture" can ever be quite successful, not the one because one is born a Jew, not the other because one is somehow obliged to remain one, and various identity-crises reflect these difficulties. In contrast, Zionism characteristically seems to come on the scene with the aim of making Jews "a nation like any other nation," just as, at the opposite extreme, assimilationism aims at dissolving Jews *into* other nations. Thus Jewish "normalization" seems complete only at the extremes.

However, as Zionism unfolds in thought and action, it gradually emerges that the messianic future, ignored or even repudiated, lives on within it, changed or unchanged, as the hidden inspiration without which the movement cannot survive. To be sure, Herzl's "If you will it, it is no dream" is a strikingly secularist appeal, exalting as it does the will above all else: it may even be understood as an anti-religious protest. Yet the goal aimed at by this will is so radically at odds with all the "natural" trends of modern history as to require a mainspring far deeper and more original than the imitation of the varieties of nineteenth-century European nationalism, and one more positive and radical than escape into "normalcy" from what was then known as antisemitism. To this day this deeper inspiration has found little articulation in Zionist *thought*. Yet had it not existed throughout Zionist *life*—from the days of the early settlers through the Yom Kippur War—Herzl's dream would either not have become real at all or else not have stayed real for long. No other twentieth-century "liberation movement" has had to contend with all (or any) of these problems: the reuniting of a people rent apart by vast culture gaps of centuries; the reviving of an ancient language; the recreation, virtually overnight, of self-government and self-defense in a people robbed of these arts for two millennia; to say nothing of defending a young state for a whole generation against overwhelming odds, and on a territory virtually indefensible. Only a will in touch with an absolute dimension could have come anywhere near solving these problems; and even those acting on this will may well be astonished by its accomplishments. Hence it has come to pass that the categories "religious" and "secularist" (whatever their undiminished validity in other contexts) have been radically shaken by the Zionist reality, a fact that has produced strange bedfellows. On one side, ultra-religious Jews waiting for God's Messiah and secularist Jews wanting neither God nor Messiah are united in hostility to the will that animates the Zionist reality, obtuse to its meaning. On the other side, religious Zionists do not count on miracles, while secularist Zionists have been known to be astonished. These two are united as well, if not when things appear normal, at any rate in those extreme moments when all appearances fall away and only truth remains.

IIa. Catastrophe

The Holocaust is unique in history, and therefore in Jewish history. Previously, genocide has been a means to such human (if evil) ends as power, greed, an extreme of nationalist or imperialist self-assertion, and at times this means may even have become, demonically, an end *beside* these others. In the Holocaust Kingdom genocide showed itself gradually to be *the sole ultimate end* to which all else—power, greed, and even "Aryan" self-assertion—were sacrificed, for "Aryan" had no other clear meaning than "not-non-Aryan." And since the Nazis were not antisemites because they were "racists" but rather racists because they were antisemites, the "non-Aryan" was, paradigmatically, the Jew. Thus the event belongs to Jewish and world history alike.

Nor is "genocide" adequate to describe the Holocaust Kingdom. Torquemada burned Jewish bodies to save Jewish souls. Eichmann created a system which, by torturing with terror and hope, by assailing all human dignity and self-respect, was designed to destroy the souls of all available Jewish men, women, and children before consigning their bodies to the gas chambers. The Holocaust Kingdom was a celebration of degradation as much as of death, and of death as much as of degradation. The celebrants willingly or even enthusiastically descended into hell themselves, even as they created hell for their victims. As for the world—it tolerated the criminals and abandoned the innocents. Thus the Holocaust is not only a unique event: it is epoch-making. The world, just as the Jewish world, can never again be the same.

The event therefore resists explanation—the historical kind that seeks causes, and the theological kind that seeks meaning and purpose. More precisely, the better the mind succeeds with the necessary task of explaining what can be explained, the more it is shattered by its ultimate failure. What holds true of the Holocaust holds true also of its connection with the state of Israel. Here, too, the explaining mind suffers ultimate failure. *Yet it is necessary, not only to perceive a bond between the two events but also so to act as to make it unbreakable.*

Historians see a causal connection between the Holocaust and the foundation of the state of Israel. The reasoning is as follows. Had it not been for the European Jewish catastrophe, all the centuries of religious longing for Zion, all the decades of secularist Zionist activity, together with all such external encouragement as given by the Balfour Declaration, would have produced no more than a Palestinian ghetto. This might have been a community with impressive internal achievements but, rather than a "national home" for homeless Jews, it would have been itself at the mercy of some alien government of dubious benevolence. Only the Holocaust produced a desperate determination in the survivors and those identified with them, outside and especially within the *Yishuv*, ended vacillation in the Zionist leadership as to the wisdom of seeking political self-determination, and produced a moment of respite from political cynicism in the international community, long enough to give legal sanction to a Jewish state. Even so "the UN resolution of 1947 came at the last possible moment."[4]

This reasoning is plausible; no more so, however, than its exact opposite. Why were the survivors not desperate to stay away from Palestine rather than reach it—the one place on earth which would tie them inescapably to a Jewish destiny? (After what that destiny had been to them, the desire to hide or flee from their Jewishness would have been "natural.") Why did the Zionist leadership rise from vacillation to resoluteness rather than simply disintegrate? (Confronted by absolute enemies, it was at the mercy of its friends.) As for the world's respite from political cynicism, this was neither of long duration nor unambiguous while it lasted. Ernest Bevin and his Colonial Office were rendered more—not less—intransigent to Zionist pressures by the catastrophic loss of lives and power which the Jewish people had just suffered. And the five Arab armies that "surged in upon the nascent Israeli nation to exterminate it and make themselves its immediate heirs" were "encouraged by the way Hitler had practiced genocide without encountering resistance."[5] Thus while, as previously argued, the state of Israel after the Holocaust may be viewed as a near necessity, yet we now see that it may be viewed, with equal justice, as a near impossibility. Historical explanation falls short in this manner because all human responses to the Holocaust are ultimately incalculable.

If historical explanations (seeking merely causes) remain precarious, theological explanations (seeking nothing less than meaning and purpose) collapse altogether, not because they are theological but because they are explanations. They fail whether they *find* a purpose, such as punishment for sin, or merely *assert* a purpose without finding it, such as a divine will, purposive yet inscrutable. This theological failure is by no means overcome if the Holocaust is considered as a means, inscrutable but necessary, to no less an end than the "dawn of redemption," of which in turn the state of Israel is viewed as the necessary "beginning." No meaning or purpose will ever be found in the event, and one does not glorify God by associating his will with it. Indeed, the very attempt is a sacrilege. (I have elsewhere argued that Jewish thought at its deepest level, especially vis-à-vis catastrophe, does not express itself in explanatory systems but rather in conflicting Midrashim, the goal of which is not how to explain God but how to live with him. Radicalizing the midrashic approach, I have also argued that to find a meaning in the Holocaust is impossible, but to seek a response is inescapable.)[6]

What then must be said of such as Rabbi Israel Shapiro of the city of Grodzisk who told his Jews at Treblinka that *these* were at last the *real* birth-pangs of the

Messiah, that they all were blessed to have merited the honor of being the sacri-fices, and that their ashes would serve to purify all Israel?[7]

First, this response must be revered *as a response;* however—in equal rever-ence for all the innocent millions, the children included, who had neither the abil-ity, nor the opportunity, nor the desire, to be willing martyrs—it must be *rid to-tally of every appearance of being an explanation.* Did God *want* Auschwitz? Even the ancient rabbis sometimes seem to view the messianic birth-pangs not as a means used by a purposive (if inscrutable) divine will, but rather as, so to speak, a cosmic catastrophe which must occur before divine power and mercy can find their redemptive manifestation.

Second, Rabbi Shapiro's extreme of pious hope must be juxtaposed by opposites no less pious and no less to be revered. The pious men of a *shtibl* in the Lodz Ghetto spent a whole day fasting, praying, reciting psalms, and then, having opened the holy ark, convoked a solemn *din Torah,* and forbade God to punish his people any further. (Elsewhere God was put on trial—and found guilty.)[8] And in the Warsaw Ghetto a handful of Jews, ragged, alone, poorly armed, carried out the first uprising against the Holocaust Kingdom in all of Europe. The rabbis showed religious piety when, rather than excuse God or curse him, they cited his own promises against him. The fighters showed secular piety when, rather than surren-der to the Satanic Kingdom, they took up arms against it. The common element in these two responses was not hope but rather despair. To the rabbis who found him guilty, the God who had broken his promises in the Holocaust could no longer be trusted to keep *any* promise, the messianic included. And precisely when hope had come to an end the fighters took to arms—in a rebellion that had no hope of succeeding.

With this conclusion, every explanatory connection between the Holocaust and the state of Israel has broken down, the causal historical kind in part, the te-leological religious kind entirely, and even the hope connecting the one event with the other competes with despair. Yet, as we have said, it is necessary not only to perceive a bond between the two events but also so to connect them as to make the bond unbreakable. Such a bond is *possible* because to seek a *cause* or a *meaning* is one thing, to give a *response* is another. And it is necessary because the heart of every *authentic* response to the Holocaust—religious and secularist, Jewish and non-Jewish—is a commitment to the autonomy and security of the state of Israel.

IIb. Response

The Chronicler Yosef Gottfarstein reports:

> The Jews of Kelmé, Lithuania, were already standing beside the pits which they had been forced to dig for themselves—standing ready to be slain for the Sanctification of the Name. Their spiritual leader, Rabbi Daniel, asked the German officer in com-mand of the operation to allow him to say some parting words to his flock, and the latter agreed, but ordered Rabbi Daniel to be brief. Speaking serenely, slowly, as though he were delivering one of his regular Sabbath sermons in the synagogue, Rabbi Daniel used his last minutes on earth to encourage his flock to perform Kid-dush Hashem in the proper manner. Suddenly the German officer cut in and shouted

at the rabbi to finish so that he could get on with the shooting. Still speaking calmly, the rabbi concluded as follows: "My dear Jews! The moment has come for us to perform the precept of Kiddush Hashem of which we have spoken, to perform it in fact! I beg one thing of you: don't get excited and confused; accept this judgment calmly and in a worthy manner!"

Then he turned to the German officer and said: "I have finished. You may begin."

Gottfarstein continues:

> . . . At Kedainiai the Jews were already inside the pit, waiting to be murdered by the Germans, when suddenly a butcher leaped out of the pit, pounced on the German officer in command, and sank his teeth into the officer's throat, holding on till the latter died.
>
> When Rabbi Shapiro, the last Rabbi of Kovno, was asked which of these two acts he thought was more praiseworthy, he said: There is no doubt that Rabbi Daniel's final message to his flock concerning the importance of the precept of Kiddush Hashem was most fitting. But that Jew who sank his teeth into the German's throat also performed the precept in letter and in spirit, because the precept includes the aspect of action. "I am sure that if the opportunity had presented itself, Rabbi Daniel would also have been capable of doing what the butcher did," Rabbi Shapiro added.[9]

"I have finished. You may begin." We search all history for a more radical contrast between pure, holy goodness and a radical evil utterly and eternally beyond all redemption. The German officer saw what he saw. He heard what he heard. So did his men. How then could even one go on with the shooting? Yet they all did.

This unredeemable evil must have been in Rabbi Shapiro's mind when he did not hesitate to rank a simple, presumably ignorant, and perhaps not very pious butcher with a saintly rabbi learned in the ways of the Torah and earnestly obeying its commandments. For us who come after, the resistance as faith and dignity of Rabbi Daniel and his flock, the *kiddush ha-Shem* of the butcher, and the judgment concerning these two forms of testimony made by Rabbi Shapiro of Kovno, itself a form of testimony, are nothing less than a dual revelation: a holy dignity-in-degradation, a heroic war against Satanic death—each a resistance to the climax of a millennial, unholy combination of hatred of Jews with Jewish powerlessness which we are bidden to end forever.

To listen to this revelation is inevitably to be turned from the rabbi who had only his faith and the butcher who had only his teeth to the Warsaw Ghetto fighters in their ragged dignity and with their wretched arms. Of the second day of the uprising one of the leaders, Itzhak Cukierman (Zukerman) reports:

> . . . By following guerrilla warfare theory, we saved lives, added to our supply of arms and, most important, proved to ourselves that the German was but flesh and blood, as any man.
>
> And prior to this we had not been aware of this amazing truth! If one lone German appeared in the Ghetto the Jews would flee *en masse*, as would Poles on the Aryan side. . . .
>
> The Germans were not psychologically prepared for the change that had come over the Jewish community and the Jewish fighters. They were seized with panic.[10]

Amazingly, the Holocaust Kingdom was breached. At least in principle, the millennial unholy combination was broken.

This fact recreated in Zuckerman hope in the midst of despair: "We knew that Israel would continue to live, and that for the sake of all Jews everywhere and for Jewish existence and dignity—even for future generations—only one thing would do: Revolt!"[11]

Another leader of the uprising, Mordecai Anielewicz, was to perish in the flames of the Ghetto. Yet in his last letter he wrote: "My life's aspiration is fulfilled. The Jewish self-defense has arisen. Blissful and chosen is my fate to be among the first Jewish fighters in the Ghetto." "Blissful" and "chosen" are almost exactly the words used by Rabbi Israel Shapiro of the city of Grodzisk as he led his flock to the crematoria of Treblinka, sure that their ashes would hasten the coming of the Messiah.

But *was* Jewish destiny so much as touched by the handfuls of desperate men and women in the ghettos and camps? And is it *true in any sense whatever* that the millennial, unholy combination of hatred of Jews and Jewish powerlessness has been so much as breached? Rabbi Shapiro was unable to sustain his faith in God without also clinging to the "aspect of action" in *kiddush ha-Shem*, as performed by the butcher. The fighters were unable to persist in their fight without staking their faith on future Jewish generations. Was not, in both cases, the faith groundless and hollow, overwhelmed by despair?

Mordecai Anielewicz died in May 1943. Named after him, kibbutz Yad Mordekhai was founded in the same year. Five years after Mordecai's death, almost to the day, a small band of members of the kibbutz bearing his name held off a well-equipped Egyptian army for five long days—days in which the defense of Tel Aviv could be prepared, days crucial for the survival of the Jewish state. The Warsaw Ghetto fighters had not, after all, been mistaken.

Their hope, however, had not been a rational one, much less a calculated prediction. It had been a blessed self-fulfilling prophecy, for the heroism and self-sacrifice of the prophets had been the indispensable element without which the prophecy could not have been fulfilled. The battle for Yad Mordekhai began in the streets of Warsaw. To this day the justly larger-than-life statue of Mordecai Anielewicz dominates the kibbutz named after him, reminding the forgetful and teaching the thoughtless that what links Rabbi Daniel, the butcher, the two Rabbis Shapiro, and the Ghetto fighters with Yad Mordekhai is neither a causal necessity nor a divine miracle, if these are thought of as divorced from human believing and acting. It is a fervent believing, turned by despair from patient waiting into heroic acting. It is an acting which through despair has recovered faith.

Behind the statue stands the shattered water tower of the kibbutz, a mute reminder that even after its climax the combination of hatred of Jews and Jewish powerlessness has not come to an end. However, the shattered tower is dwarfed by the statue, and is at its back. The statue faces what Mordecai longed for and never despaired of—green fields, crops, trees, birds, flowers, Israel.

> Our Father in Heaven, the Rock of Israel and her Redeemer, bless Thou the state of Israel, the beginning of the dawn of our redemption. Shield her with the wings of Thy love, and spread over her the tabernacle of Thy peace. . . . "

Notes

1. J. Lipschitz, ed., *Sefer Ha-Geulah* (London, 1909), especially pp. 3–16, 29.

2. See e.g., M. M. Kasher, ed., *Haggadat Pesah Arzi-Yisraelit* (New York: American Biblical Encyclopedia Society, 1950), pp. 132 ff.

3. Maimonides, Yad, *Hilkhot Melakhim*, 5:11–12.

4. Walter Laqueur, *A History of Zionism* (London: Weidenfeld & Nicolson, 1972; New York: Schocken, 1976), p. 593.

5. M. Sperber, . . . *Than a Tear in the Sea* (New York: Bergen-Belsen Memorial Press, 1967), p. XIV.

6. Emil Fackenheim, *Quest for Past and Future* (Bloomington: Indiana University Press, 1968; Boston: Beacon, 1970), chap. 1; and *God's Presence in History* (New York: New York University Press, 1970; New York: Harper Torchbook, 1973), chaps. 1 and 3.

7. Cited in Kasher, *Haggadat*, p. 137.

8. *Ani Ma'amin* (Jerusalem: Mosad Ha-Rav Kook, 1965), p. 206.

9. "Kiddush Hashem over the Ages and Its Uniqueness in the Holocaust Period" in *Jewish Resistance during the Holocaust* (Jerusalem: Yad Vashem, 1971), p. 473.

10. Meyer Barkai, tr. and ed., *The Fighting Ghettos* (New York: Tower, 1962), pp. 26 ff.

11. Ibid., p. 30.

30 Diaspora and Nation: The Contemporary Situation

In Jewish history there are eternal themes, those which never seem to change. There are also ephemeral themes, those which change so swiftly that one must be glued to radio and newspaper to keep abreast. The theme "Diaspora and Nation," it would seem, would be mislocated in either class. For us to treat it as eternal would be to dismiss the unique demands of "the contemporary situation." To view it in terms of the latest headlines would toss us from crisis to crisis, unable to meet these demands or even to understand them. They can be responded to only if our contemporary situation is viewed in an historical perspective.

But how can we, of this Jewish generation, attain such a perspective when we are *in fact* being tossed from one crisis to another? We can do so only by seeking an Archimedean point, as it were, beyond the turbulence of the events; that is, by focussing attention on events that have constituted our epoch—events that are epoch-making. Of course—so we must add with the necessary sobriety—such events are *themselves in history*. A *truly* Archimedean point *beyond* history is not attainable. Hence, to fathom what may be said a millennium or even a century from now about both our epoch and our attempts to grapple with it may be desirable, almost above all things, but it is beyond our power.

What events, so far as the theme "Diaspora and Nation" is concerned, constitute our epoch? One event stands out above all others; none other even approaches it. This is the proclamation on May 14, 1948, of a Jewish state after nearly two millennia of Jewish statelessness. Doubtless there is much continuity between the before and the after. Yet a new page in the history of our theme was opened on that day. That this is so is proved in the most objective manner imaginable by the *nova* in Jewish history since that event. To be sure, these *nova* have become so commonplace for us that they *no longer seem new*. Yet this fact is itself

Reprinted from *Forum: On the Jewish People, Zionism and Israel* 50 (Winter 1983–84).

pregnant with significance when it is remembered that prior to May 14, 1948, not one of them either was, or could have been, predicted.

It behooves us to grasp these *nova as nova*. Only thus, instead of merely *being in* our contemporary situation, can we *grasp* it and *respond to* it. Only thus can we gain, in the stormy times in which we are destined to live, what we stand most in need of: historical perspective.

1. The First Novum: The Success of the Ingathering

The first *novum* is the success of the Ingathering. In our day-to-day occupation with problems and crises, we tend to focus all attention on the failures. (*Yerida* is the great one. Conflicts between Sefardim and Ashkenazim are not small.) These are seen in perspective, however, only against a success so monumental as to be quite literally without equal anywhere. Prior to the advent of statehood, enemies and even fearful friends judged that *Eretz Yisrael* had already reached its "absorptive capacity," with not enough room left to "swing a cat." This judgement seemed sober at the time; yet it has been decisively refuted. In procuring that refutation, Zionism has fulfilled its most indispensable promise—a home for homeless Jews. No aspect of the Zionist dream is more essential. None, in our time, has been more desperately urgent.

The fulfilled promise includes not only the provision of physical space. It also includes the provision of social and economic space. In the newspapers we read of failures that make "Project Renewal" necessary, as well as of other failures for which no remedial project is as yet in sight. These failures, too, are seen in proper perspective only against the background of a more profound success. Jews dispersed in all four corners of the earth have been gathered in—and have become, once again, one nation.

This success of the Ingathering—physical, economic, and social—would have turned into catastrophe if the state that did the Ingathering had not conjoined with it yet another success, that of self-defense against foes bent on its annihilation. Once enemies and even fearful friends predicted that a Jewish state, if it *per mirabile* came into being, would be indefensible and soon destroyed. Yet thus far at least, the Jewish State has warded off all assailants. To be sure, to judge by today's syndicated pundits, there is no wonder and no *novum* here, for it is but a case of a well-armed, well-trained Western outpost pitted against ill-armed, ill-trained, hopeless "Third World" natives. But one need only re-read the syndicated pundits of yesterday in order to realize that the Jewish State's self-defense, too, is a *novum*, part of the larger *novum* of the successful Ingathering.

This latter has yet another aspect, the achievement of legitimacy. In the contemporary world it is becoming increasingly difficult to fathom what constitutes the legitimacy of a state. But no matter what standard one may wish to employ— international endorsement for the state, prior even to its coming into existence; historic rights; the democratically expressed will of its inhabitants; the affirmation of this will through the investment of capital, labor and blood; and, last but not least, the need of an oppressed people, rivalling if not surpassing in desperation the need of any liberation movement—one may doubt whether any state currently existing is more profoundly legitimate.

Such has been the success of the Ingathering that, except at the lunatic fringes,

Jewish anti-Zionism is dead. Not long ago such anti-Zionism enjoyed considerable respectability. Prior to the great Ingathering, one could be a "good Jew" and be hostile to Zionism. After the Ingathering, the consensus of "good" Jews supports the Jewish State, and even lukewarm Jews pay lip service.

This, then, is the first *novum* in our contemporary situation, relating to the theme "Diaspora and Nation." The *facts*, of course, are familiar. We know them, have absorbed them, take them for granted. We are even bored. Yet not until we see them—ever again re-see them—as a *novum* have we achieved the proper historical perspective. And to have achieved *that* is to be—ever again to be—amazed.

2. The Second Novum: The Failure of Western Aliya

This amazement brings to light a second *novum* in our contemporary situation—the failure of Western *Aliya*. If the coming into being of a Jewish state in our time were a trivial event—one that, having happened in one generation, had no deep or lasting effect on the next—there would be no reason to be surprised that Jews in London, New York or Toronto give no thought to moving to that state, simply because it has offered a home to a homeless cousin or aunt. The birth of Israel, however, has not been a trivial event. It is the most enormous, and certainly the most drastic, collective Jewish achievement in nearly two millennia. It has become an event around which all Jews orient their lives, including those indifferent to their Jewish identity. Even Jews hostile to Israel stand more erect on account of its existence. Moreover, coming as it did on the heels of the greatest catastrophe in all of Jewish history, Israel's rebirth cannot but have religious, or quasi-religious, redemptive connotations even for the most secular of Jews.

Then why did good Western Jews—proud Jews, dedicated Jews, Jews committed to carrying forward the Jewish heritage from past to future—not come by the hundreds of thousands, so as to have a direct share in the great enterprise? Future generations will surely find this puzzling. It is a failure that may well come to haunt us all.

The failure of *Aliya* from the Western democracies ought to cause fundamental concern even now. Zionism and the Jewish state stand or fall with the keeping of what we have characterized as the most essential promise, the giving of a home to homeless Jews. But can either Zionism or the Jewish State stand without the *Aliya* of Jews who need no home—the *Olim* who come not from necessity but from choice?

Although the failure of *Aliya* from the free democracies of the West may bring to mind what can be called the "fleshpots-of-Egypt syndrome," this is not a helpful conceptualization. It is true that this syndrome has always been with us; it is with us now. But it is unhelpful to cite it when we think of good and dedicated Jews who wish to be where their hearts are, and yet are not in Israel. We insult such Jews when we pin the "fleshpots-of-Egypt" label on them. We also arouse their disbelief, for so far as Jews in the Western liberal democracies are concerned, the West is not Egypt.

What becomes apparent here is that the early modern, if not the premodern, Jew in *Galut* had *two* visions of emancipation: a liberal state as well as a Jewish State. To be sure, in the subsequent course of history these two visions came into conflict, but it now emerges that they are also intertwined. For us today, to either negate or deprecate the Jewish State in favor of the liberal state, or the liberal state in favor of the Jewish state, is self-destructive. In addition, we can not appraise fairly the large *novum* under consideration—the failure of *Aliya* from the West— unless we also take note of a smaller *novum* that is part of it. There exists today a Jew who is fully at home in Britain or Canada or the United States; who wholly identifies with the security and welfare of the State of Israel; who does not cringe under the impact of charges of dual loyalty, but on the contrary glories in them; and who holds these convictions despite the fact that *Aliya* has not entered his mind. It is senseless to try to make this Jew over into a homeless Jew, or to attempt to frighten him with the spectre of anti-Semitism in what is home to him. *Olim* from the West will come, if come they will, not by leaving their old homes behind but by bringing them along. And they will come, if at all—this is a subject to which we shall have to return—not because of fear but only because of love.

3. The Third Novum: The Transmutation of Anti-Semitism

We now turn to the third *novum* in our contemporary situation since May 14, 1948—the shocking and depressing fact that the advent of the Jewish State did not end anti-Semitism or even move it to the periphery; on the contrary, the Jewish State has become the focus of its assault. "Anti-Zionism" has found a worldwide forum in, of all places, the United Nations—the organization founded by the victors over Nazism; and, much though it is denied in nearly all anti-Zionist quarters, anti-Zionism *is* anti-Semitism. In its long and depressing history, Jew-hatred has had a number of transmutations. ("Anti-Semitism" itself is one of them.) Of these, "anti-Zionism" is the most recent.

This is as unexpected as it is shocking. That a Jewish state would end anti-Semitism is, of course, part and parcel of classical Zionist theory. In the years immediately following the second World War—when the world shrank, or seemed to shrink, from the horrors of the Holocaust, and with it from anti-Semitism—it was the hope and expectation of us all. Three decades later Zionist theory and practice must both face the fact that, if the liberal state has failed in its promise to end anti-Semitism, so has the Jewish State. In both cases, so it seems in retrospect, this particular promise was the product of an age more naive in its expectations concerning man and his world than our own. Modern enlightenment, rather than end the bimillennial, groundless hatred of the Jewish People, has merely produced more sophisticated—"enlightened"—disguises and rationalizations of it.

This is not the place to consider the shocking reemergence of so-called "classical" anti-Semitism in the Soviet Union and some of its satellites; beyond our scope too is an Arab hostility to Israel which, in its persistent, total refusal to accept the Jewish State on any terms whatsoever, is surely of an order different from the negative passions aroused by normal political conflicts. Our sole object here is the new anti-Semitism that *is* anti-Zionism, i.e., to show that anti-Zionism, 1980's-style, is not merely accidentally tinged with anti-Semitism in this or that case but is rather anti-Semitic in its essence. The anti-Zionism of our age is the latest incarnation of the anti-Jewish idea.

Just what that idea is was shown in a masterful account of the 1940's, in Jean Paul Sartre's *Anti-Semite and Jew.* Anti-Semitism, for Sartre, is a criminal passion, the object of which, in the last analysis, is the death of the Jew. It is therefore neither an "opinion" to be debated, nor even a "prejudice" to be refuted. And if it is, nevertheless, treated as an opinion to be debated, or a prejudice to be refuted, then those on *both* sides become infected with the poison of anti-Semitism. In asserting that "Jews have the right to exist," the "philo-Semite," to be sure, *opposes* the anti-Semite, but he also legitimates him at the same time. Who would ever dream of going about saying that Englishmen or Frenchmen have the right to exist? Even in the case of Armenians or North American Indians such a statement would sound odd, for their genocidal enemies acted on the principle that there were too many of them, not on the principle that their crime was to exist at all.

The old "pro-Semitic" anti-Semite who implies that the Jew's right to exist is debatable has largely disappeared. Now that there is a Jewish state, however, his place has been taken by a "pro-Zionist" anti-Semite who implies that the Jewish State's right to exist is debatable. Who would ever dream of going about saying that England or France has a right to exist—or even Poland, Iran or Uganda? Yet, in the case of the Jewish state, the statement is commonplace. *Anti-Semitism, old style, seeks Jewish genocide; new style, it seeks Jewish politicide; and in both cases the poison infects not only those who pursue that goal but also those who, though opposing it, debate and thereby legitimate it.*

The debate exists in large part because, with the possible exception of Egypt, Israel's Arab neighbors deny her right to exist to this day. (So, needless to say, does the P.L.O.) This, however, is far from the whole story. When in 1939 Hitler denied Czechoslovakia's right to exist, Britain and France, despite their earlier craven betrayal at Munich, decreed that war must be declared. Ever since Israel's birth in 1948, however, with the Arab states uncompromisingly seeking her destruction, the Western democracies all too often seek to mediate "even-handedly" between Israel's right to exist and the Arab "right" to destroy her; in every instance (which comes to much the same thing) they pretend to find Arab "moderation" where none exists. And when the odious Zionism-is-racism resolution was voted on in the United Nations, the friends of Israel did vote against it to be sure. However, *no one walked out.* Thus that organization—which, we repeat, was once founded by the victors over Nazism—has become contaminated by anti-Semitism, infecting not only those members who instigated the resolution, voted for it, or abstained, but infecting the whole body. Today, as Roy Eckardt has put it, it is in effect the world center of anti-Semitism.

Whence comes the anti-Semitic passion, i.e., the denial of the right to exist itself, which for two millennia was directed at the Jewish person, and is now directed at the Jewish State? How can one explain it except in terms of a long tradition, no longer really remembered but for all that still potent, according to which, in the case of Jews and no one else, their existence itself is enough cause to delay the redemption, and a world-made-*judenrein* enough to hasten it. In 1936 Julius Streicher was on record to the effect that to fight the Jews was to fight the devil, and that to fight the devil was to save the world. Shortly after the Yom Kippur War, an American clergyman went on record to the effect that Israel might have to die for the peace of the world.

That these ideas are not without political consequences is reflected at present in the compulsive search, even on the part of Israel's friends, for a "comprehensive settlement" of the Arab-Israeli conflict. Does anyone look for this kind of settlement in Poland? Northern Ireland? Central America? South Africa? Afghanistan? Vietnam? Berlin? At one time, the last-named "problem" seemed most likely to ignite World War III. Yet precisely a prudent shrinking from "solutions" on all sides has thus far averted the danger. What effect can the demand for a comprehensive settlement of the "Israeli" problem have except to encourage Israel's most intransigent enemies? (The P.L.O. National Covenant, now as before, calls for the Jewish State's destruction. Jordan and Saudi Arabia, now as before, are the only states in the world that are on principle *judenrein*.) The world's willingness to make over the Arab problem; the intransigent refusal to accept Israel—into "the Palestinian problem;" an "intransigent" Israel's unwillingness to make "concessions" threatening her very survival—can mean, at worst, that mental reservations still remain, even among Israel's friends, about her right to exist as a sovereign state. Even at best it means that the world is tired of the new "Jewish problem," much as, not so long ago, it was of the old.

4. The Fourth Novum: The Collective Jewish Confrontation with the Holocaust

The only decent response by the world to this new form of anti-Semitism is auto-emancipation. The primary response by the Jewish People must be to strengthen the State of Israel and to express the determination that, while Israel needs friends like all states, she must be no one's ward. This response is being reinforced in our time by yet a fourth and final *novum* in our situation to which attention must be drawn—the collective Jewish confrontation with the Holocaust.

The catastrophe, of course, was being confronted all along by the victims, the survivors, their relatives and friends and, last but not least, by all those engaged in rescue. It was not being confronted, however, by the Jewish People collectively. In view of the traumatic nature of the event, it could not have been. By the same token, the event should have become even dimmer with the passage of time, but this, surprisingly, has not come to pass. Indeed, just the opposite has occurred: the Holocaust is becoming increasingly part of the collective Jewish consciousness. This too is a *novum* that could not have been predicted on May 14, 1948.

As a result, there is already a collective response that may be said to approximate normativeness. *The Holocaust was the climactic event, surpassable only in quantity but not in quality, of a bimillennial, unholy togetherness of groundless Jew-hatred and Jewish powerlessness. Following this event, Jews find themselves morally obliged, on their own behalf as well as that of the world, to break this togetherness. And since not they but only others can do away with the hatred, they must, so far as possible, do away with the powerlessness.*

As we saw above, a result of the success of the Ingathering is that support of the State of Israel is part and parcel of the Jewish consensus. Now we must go a step further. *If there were no Jewish State in existence today, it would be morally and spiritually necessary, for religious and secular Jews alike, to establish it.* Such is the consensus of *amcha*, the people, concerning the future destiny not only of Jews *but also of Judaism.*

The consensus is of *amcha*, and does not necessarily include the professors. Thus one professor, on the theological right, will argue that there is no difference between the six million and one child dying of cancer, that the two are religiously equally acceptable or unacceptable. Another, this one on the theological left, will argue that there is no difference between Auschwitz and Hiroshima, that the trauma, while real, belongs not to Jews-in-particular but to mankind-in-general. But the people perceives that something radical *has* happened to Jews-in-particular and that, in consequence, a radical alteration in the Jewish condition is necessary. After every previous catastrophe, the survivors could understand themselves to be a holy remnant. Some had perished; others had fallen away; they, the survivors, existed because still others had not previously fallen away. They were heir to a holiness which they were bidden to perpetuate. We, however, are not a holy remnant but an accidental remnant—survivors not by dint of Jewish fidelity but by dint of geography. How can we bridge the rupture between past and present? The people's consensus, often inarticulate yet altogether firm, is this: a Jewish State is central to a future Judaism as well as to future Jews.

What is at stake is once again obscured by professorial ideological predilections. The power of the Jewish State, we are informed, is small, while at the same time the Diaspora is not altogether powerless. Hence, whereas Israel is one Jewish center, it is only one among others. And while a Jewish State makes some difference to the condition of Jews, it makes no difference at all to that of Judaism.

Yet the following truth is gradually coming to consciousness. *Ever since the last epoch-making catastrophe—the destruction of the Temple in 70 C.E.—Jews have lived by Galut-Judaism; ever since our epoch-making catastrophe—the Holocaust—Galut-Judaism, if most decidedly not Galut itself, is coming to an end.*

What is Galut-Judaism? It is the faith by which the Jew, while lamenting the exile, is able to bear it in patience and confidence; he can bear it, for it is meaningful. Whether it is punishment for Jewish sins, vicarious atonement for the sins of others, or simply endowed with inscrutable meaning known only to God, it can be borne with fortitude and with an unshakable faith.

We should be deeply ungrateful if we failed to cherish Galut-Judaism and its countless expressions of endurance, courage and saintliness. I remember a painting from childhood in which bearded old Jews flee from a pogrom. They are terrified, but not so terrified as to leave everything behind. They do not carry (as anti-Semites would doubtless have it) bags of gold; they carry Torah scrolls. The painting says it crudely, for it is no great work of art. The poet Heine said the same thing with his consummate artistry: the Torah, for millennia, was the Jew's portable fatherland. The secret behind its role is fathomed in a *Midrash* in which Rabbi Akiba declares that whenever Israel went into exile the *Shekhina*, the spirit of God, went with them. In this way the Jewish People survived, unbroken, in exile after exile; whenever a *minyan* of ten men gathered in some miserable hovel, the hovel was not, after all, miserable, for they would read and be spoken to, not merely by words written on parchment but also, through the words, by the Presence of God.

Still another *Midrash* captures the very essence of Galut-Judaism. When the Temple was destroyed and Israel went into exile, God exacted three oaths, one from the Gentiles and two from the Jews. The Gentiles were made to swear that they would not excessively oppress the Jews, now dispersed among them, helpless and impotent. The Jews were made to swear, first, that they would not resist the

Gentiles' oppression and, second, that they would not "climb the walls" i.e., try to return by force to Jerusalem before the time was ripe. Within Galut-Judaism, then, the Jew waits patiently for the End, *secure in the knowledge that some Jews—if not he—will live to see it.*

But the same *Midrash* that captures the essence of Galut-Judaism also explains why it has come to an end in our time. In our age the Gentiles *did* oppress the Jews excessively; one need only think of Auschwitz. And since the Gentiles broke their oath, the Jews, on their part, are free of theirs.

It is necessary to go still a crucial step further. Post-Holocaust Jews, we have seen, are not a holy remnant. They are an accidental remnant. Moreover, they know that what did happen once can happen again—and next time there may be no accidents. *Jewish survival, then, once received as a gift and relied on as a gift, can be relied on no more, and what once was a gift has become a duty.* Hence the post-Holocaust Jew is not only *permitted* to resist those that oppress him; he is *required.* He is not merely *allowed* to climb the walls of Jerusalem; to do so is a *mitzva.* Two new oaths have taken the place of the old.

To many of the pious, all this is anathema. Doubtless this is largely due to the wish, understandable enough, to see the Torah, a portable fatherland for so long, as a fatherland still. But alas, the Torah, though beloved still, no longer serves the protective role of a fatherland. This painful fact found horrendous expression in a small town in Poland in September 1939. The chronicler Shim'on Huberband reports how the Nazis swooped down on the town, grabbed a young rabbi, wrapped him in a Torah Scroll, poured gasoline on both and set them on fire. And, so Huberband concludes his report, "the holy man and the holy book were burned together."

A new page must be opened in the history, not only of Jews, but also of Judaism. And the first and most essential act to be recorded is the Jewish return to the fatherland—to the "old" Land made "new."

5. The Flight Into Unauthenticity in the Diaspora

We have spoken of a Jewish consensus. A critic will quickly point out that this consensus is not a statistical finding or empirical generalization, but is rather shot through with "value judgements." So was our assertion concerning the "end" of Galut-Judaism. Indeed, even our account of the four *nova* in the contemporary situation, straining for objectivity though it did, was not free of value judgements, for the term *novum,* as employed by us, implies not only newness but also significance. The late Will Herberg once spoke of the Holocaust and the State of Israel as mere "novelties" that were of no account to Jewish destiny, for the latter was unchanging and unchangeable between Sinai and Messianic days. If this is so, then the *nova* listed by us are mere episodes; and Galut-Judaism is identical with Judaism.

Views of this sort have come to enjoy considerable popularity in the Diaspora ever since the Yom Kippur War. While the war was still on, a Toronto father tried to dissuade his son from going to Israel to fight. It was his Jewish duty, he argued, to stay in Canada, for in case Israel, God forbid, were to go down, he and his kind would be needed to rebuild a Jewish future. This Jew was not just expressing a father's natural fear for his son's life. He was also hedging his bets on behalf of Judaism—and relapsing into Galut-Judaism.

Not long afterward, a distinguished rabbi declared in a public lecture that he was no longer certain that Israel would survive, but that he *was* certain that the Jewish People would survive. (He failed to explain what, after the Holocaust, justified the latter certainty.) He too was hedging his bets. He too relapsed into Galut-Judaism.

The question still is, of course, whether a return to Galut-Judaism *is* a relapse. The *Midrash* concerning the climbing of the walls, we have said, grasps the essence of Galut-Judaism. We must now face the fact that it can be given (and in our time is being given) an application quite different from ours. It is not the Gentiles who first broke their oath, leaving the Jews free of theirs. It is rather the Jews who initiated the process. The great sin is the Zionists' climbing of the walls. It is this sin that smashed a well-balanced bimillennial Galut existence, precarious and yet secure, in which Jews, Gentiles and God all had their appointed roles. And it is as a consequence of this Jewish breaking of the oaths that the Gentiles were freed of theirs. Thus God Himself gave the Nazis free reign.

This interpretation is logically possible. Religiously, morally, humanly, however, it is an impossibility. We think of the victims, saints and sinners alike; of the children; of ourselves who have survived, not because our parents were faithful but because they emigrated from Europe; and we think of the young rabbi and how he died. And we are forced to conclude that one does not honor God's name by associating His will with the Holocaust. Though we may all at times wish to retain it or return to it, Galut-Judaism has become a spiritual impossibility, for it involves blasphemy toward God and Man. The return to it is a lapse from our intellectual tasks, into unauthenticity.

With this conclusion, we have no choice but to reject a lapse backward, and instead to press forward. Few Jews in our time need to be told that, unlike the existence of other states, that of Israel continues to be precarious. One learns this from the newspapers almost daily. This knowledge, however, can only serve to strengthen our resolve. Shortly after the founding of the state, the Chief Rabbinate declared it to be "the beginning of the growth of the redemption" of the Jewish People. The declaration, wisely enough, was quite agnostic as to what would come after "the beginning." But it was wiser still in declaring that the beginning itself—the existence of the Jewish State—was for the profoundest religious reasons, not negotiable.

6. Thoughts Concerning Aliya

For the Diaspora Jew of our time, the clearest, most unambiguous way of "pressing forward" is to "go upward," i.e., to make *Aliya*. Above we said that the Jewish State stands or falls in its provision for the *Aliya* of necessity but that, in the long run, it cannot stand as a *Jewish* state without the *Aliya* of freedom—Jews who come not out of fear but out of love. We return to this theme now, the most important in our whole inquiry. What dedicated Jew would not wish to have been with Rabbi Yochanan Ben Zakkai or Rabbi Akiba who, when all hung in the balance, opened a new page in the history of Judaism? Then what dedicated Jew cannot wish to be with the Israelis, in an age when once again all hangs in the balance, and a brave attempt is being made to open another new page? Why then do we lack a superabundance of *Olim* who are moved not by necessity, nor by mere guilt or duty, but rather because they cannot bear to stay away?

Is the cause the present worldwide slander of Zionism and the isolation of Israel? Dedicated Jews—a "people that dwells apart"—though never loving isolation, have also never overly feared it. Nor have they shrunk from hardships, sacrifices, the tearing up of roots. Perhaps a potent cause is the lack of an adequate philosophy. Despite many failures, Zionist life in our time, so we have argued from the start, has been the story of a monumental success. Zionist thought, in contrast, has lagged far behind. The Jewish condition has been altered in the eventful decades behind us. What is still lacking is an adequate Jewish self-consciousness.

Perhaps we can learn a lesson here from the period of Galut-Judaism, when the Torah was the Jews' portable fatherland. It was the fatherland of the whole Jewish People, yet not every Jew did or could devote his life to it. Some know of the Torah and of those studying it only from hearsay. Others studied its words and also observed them, while the focus of their lives was yet elsewhere. And again others advanced the study of the Torah by supporting those who did nothing but study it. If, nevertheless, the Torah was the fatherland of the *whole* Jewish People, it was because the *Talmid Hakham* served as model, and a Jew who had chosen to be otherwise had chosen at most second best. The *Talmid Hakham* stood for the whole. And from his total commitment, love of Torah emanated to all.

In our time, the *Oleh* ought to serve a similar role. Even among those dedicated to *Aliya*, some simply cannot go. Others simply will not go. And others still have a personal scale of priorities in which *Aliya* occupies less than the highest rank. All this is natural, as in the times when the Torah was the Jew's fatherland, but not all gave their very lives to it. What is not natural is that personal conflicts, shot through with unacknowledged guilt, result in a false consciousness that rationalize away the guilt. A legitimate decision against *Aliya* is illegitimately made into ideology. A personal order of priorities in which *Aliya* is sacrificed to a medical career is blown up into a philosophy of Judaism in which the urgent need of the present hour—massive *Aliya* from the West before it is too late—is dissolved into an abstract commitment to the brotherhood of man, to the duty-to-men-in-general, and the duty-to-heal-in-particular. Perhaps it is thus that a Zionism has arisen in the Diaspora in which *Aliya* has no place, and that a love for Jerusalem that may be dormant in many a Jewish heart remains merely dormant, turning into "To Jerusalem and Back."

If so, what is needed, perhaps above all things, is a new Jewish self-understanding in the Diaspora in which the *Oleh* occupies the place once occupied by the *Talmid Hakham*. Just as then, when not everyone devoted his life to Torah, so today not everyone can make *Aliya*. Nor is either the one or the other to be expected. (One is a Jew by birth, not by subscription to an idea, whether it be Torah study or immigration to Israel.) What the Jew-by-birth in our time *can* do, however, is to recognize that, just as one kind of Jew—the Torah student—once set the unifying standard for all Jews, so the standard is set today by another kind—the *Oleh*. Though thoroughly at home in his country of birth, the *Oleh* makes *Aliya* because of love. If this recognition is achieved, then the great Jewish success of our time—the Ingathering—can be participated in even by those remaining in the Diaspora who have no direct share in it.

In the age in which the Ingathering is already an accomplished fact, a question arises that bids fair to dominate the Jewish future. The *Oleh* "goes up" to the Land: what does he do upon arrival? For the *Oleh* of necessity, liberation from oppression or homelessness may be ascent enough. But for the *Oleh*-of-freedom, must we say that the end of the ascent is "mere" "normalcy"?

To this question the present writer, himself still partly in the Diaspora, can venture only a fragment of an answer. Moreover, the answer perforce will be the work of future generations, and it will be expressed far less in their words than in their lives. Still, a fragment of an answer may be suggested. Throughout the generations, a Jew regarded himself as though he personally had gone forth from Egypt; perhaps, throughout generations to come, future Israeli Jews must regard themselves as though they personally had made *Aliya*. The Ingathering; the leaving behind of the past and taking it up into the present; the new relation to the old Land, to the old Book, to the old God; all this cannot ever be a process over and done with, but must rather be one which is ever-incomplete and ever-new. To those for whom it is ever-new, the whole Zionist enterprise will reveal itself as filled with a fundamental wonder, not only at what is yet to be but also at what already is.

Epilogue

Once, during a long, hot wearying bus ride from Galilee to Jerusalem, the landscape—trees upon trees—at first seemed to do nothing to relieve the weariness. Gradually I began to imagine the country-side as it must have been a century ago, and a teaching of Nachmanides came to my mind. The medieval mystic asked the ancient question of when the redemption would arrive, and of how one could recognize the signs. There had been so many false signs and so many false Messiahs! At length he judged that there was only one sign that could be trusted. Many nations had conquered and devastated the Land, but none had rebuilt it. When you see trees growing in the Land, Nachmanides concluded, then you may gather hope.

I saw the trees of Galilee, and was astonished.

FIVE

THE IDEA OF
HUMANITY
AFTER AUSCHWITZ

31 *Religious Responsibility for the Social Order:* A Jewish View

The following article was part of a Protestant-Catholic-Jewish dialogue, held at the annual board meeting of the National Conference of Christians and Jews in Washington D. C., on November 20, 1961. The other participants were Prof. J. Pelikan and Father G. Weigel, S.J. I have found the topic not only most important but also—if seriously tackled, and tackled in a brief statement—difficult and full of snares. Among the snares which I sought to avoid and expose are: (a) the mistaking of the separation of church and state for a dualism which makes religion other-worldly, and society, either amoral or else morally concerned in a way which does not only not need religious inspiration but positively rejects it; (b) the belief (found in the various forms of "Biblicism," on the one hand, natural law positions, on the other) that it is the business of religion to offer moral doctrines which are specific and concrete, and yet timelessly valid; (c) the opposite belief that, precisely because religion cannot offer such doctrines, it must confine itself to innocuous generalities, thus leaving the big decisions concerning war and peace, the implementation of social justice etc., entirely in the hands of religiously and morally neutral "experts."

I

If there is a single religious affirmation which, first coming with Judaism into the world, has remained basic to Jewish belief until today, it is that the God on high loves widows and orphans below; and that He commands men, from on high, to do His will in the social order below. Elsewhere, too, men have had an

Reprinted from *Quest for Past and Future* (Bloomington: Indiana University Press, 1968), 188–94.

awareness of the Divine, and a sense of responsibility in the social realm. It was the distinctive contribution of the Hebrew prophets to proclaim that the two cannot be rent apart; that men ought to treat each other as created in the image of a God who challenges them to this task.

II

It is in the light of this basic affirmation that I must seek to answer the question concerning religious responsibility for the social order. And I must begin by opposing all attempts to tear asunder what the prophetic affirmation joins together; that is, on the one hand, a secularism which bids religion mind its business, of which responsibility for the social order is to be no part, and, on the other hand, an otherworldly religion which, accepting this advice, disclaims all responsibility for the social order. Forms of such divorce have existed in all ages. That they may exist in one and the same person has been terribly illustrated in our own time—by those Germans who thought it possible to be Nazis and Christians at once.

I must stress that opposing divorce between the religious and the social realm is by no means equivalent to rejecting the separation between church and state, of which more below. I must stress, too, that secularist social morality has often put to shame a social morality supposedly religiously inspired; that those rejecting or suspending belief in God have often done His will toward men more perfectly than those professing belief in Him. And this fact must give us pause. Even so, one may question whether secularist morality can, for long, treat men as created in the image of a God in Whom it does not believe; whether it can forever resist the temptation to reduce man, from an end in himself, to a mere means, thus degenerating either into a merely relativistic morality, or else—and worse—into one resting on pseudo-absolutes, such as the interests of a deified class, nation or state.

The dangers of divorce between the religious and the social may seem remote to North Americans, who tend to be practical in religion and religiously-inspired in their social morality; and indeed, for the worst examples of divorce we must surely look elsewhere. Still, we are by no means exempt from danger. For a religious civilization such as ours invites a secularism assuming a pseudo-religious garb; and hence religion, meant to be openness to the divine imperative, may become a device for avoiding it. Thus, for example, those who begin by responding to the divine imperative with a dedication to freedom and democracy, may end up deifying their dedication; and to the extent to which they in fact do so their actual dedication—as well as what it is dedicated to—is perverted. Of this danger, there are ominous indications in our time.

III

So much for the divorce between the religious and the social, which the prophetic imperative bids us oppose. What of their relation, which that imperative bids us affirm? This question, unlike the former, is fraught with great difficulty. And its essential cause is that, while the prophetic imperative is divine the social world in which it is to find realization is human; and the human world has characteristics which render complex, not only any attempt to *realize* the prophetic imperative, but even any attempt—such as the present—merely to *state* it, in terms concrete enough to be applicable. Three characteristics must here be noted.

(1) All social organization involves power. But power is amoral before it can be made moral, and presumably it always retains aspects of amorality or even immorality. This fact confronts those who would heed the prophetic imperative with a dilemma. They may either forswear all use of power, in order to remain true to the prophetic imperative. But then they condemn their own efforts to ineffectiveness, at least beyond the most private relations and in the social order as a whole; and thus they contribute either to total anarchy or else—more likely—to an amoral order based on naked power. Yet most forms of social order are better than anarchy, and a partly moralized order, better than one not moralized at all. Alternatively, they may seek power, for the sake of the prophetic imperative which demands realization. But then they must recognize that they become compromised in its use; and their religious motivation is no protection against such compromise. Indeed, experience shows that power wielded in the name of God is subject to special perversions.

This is why those who are organized by commitment to the prophetic imperative cannot, on the one hand, escape their responsibility of moralizing power, while on the other hand they must resist all temptations to make a bid for direct power, confining themselves to indirect methods of pressure-by-exhortation. Here lies perhaps the deepest justification for the American principle of the separation of state and church.

(2) What must be the content of such exhortation? May religion advocate specific measures in the name of God, leaving to the state and society the task of their enactment? Here I come upon a second complexity of the human condition, which makes such a neat arrangement impossible. This is that concrete moral ends are, in the actual human situation, in conflict both with other ends and with the means required to enact them. I cannot think of a single moral and religious end, concrete enough to be directly applicable, and yet valid without exception. Thus believing all human life to be sacred I believe all wars to be evil; and yet I must admit that some wars had justly to be fought. But the concept of "just war" does not supply me with universally applicable criteria. Again, though believing in the Biblical injunction to be fruitful and multiply I cannot deduce from this belief the universal wrongness of artificial birth control. For I must measure the Biblical injunction against the dangers of overpopulation and mass-starvation. In short, I find myself unable to subscribe to what has been called the natural law, supplying us with a knowledge of right and wrong sufficiently concrete to be directly applicable, and yet valid regardless of time and circumstances.

(3) Must religion, then, confine itself to the affirmation of abstract principles, leaving to other forces not merely the task of enactment but also that of specific application? Is religion confined to affirming in general the sacredness of life and liberty, and the evil of exploitation, but barred from taking a specific stand as to when life may be taken and liberty curtailed; and as to what constitutes a just minimum wage? Here we come upon this further characteristic of the human condition, that the moral and religious conscience of a society is manifest, not in an abstract affirmation of liberty or condemnation of exploitation, but in what it protests against, as constituting a case of curtailed liberty, or a case of exploitation.

Relevancy lies in the particular. As for the general, this is apt to be invoked not only by the indifferent but even by the enemy; peace has been invoked by the mongers of war, freedom and democracy, by their worst foes. This tendency to hypocrisy is evident throughout human history. But, as George Orwell has shown with such depressing persuasiveness, not until the Twentieth Century have men made it into a system.

Another neat arrangement of the respective responsibilities of religion and society for the social order has thus collapsed. A religion which confines itself to general principles condemns itself to ineffectiveness and innocuousness. The Hebrew prophets, in contrast, were neither innocuous nor ineffective. And this was because they asserted the will of God, not in terms of abstract general principles, but in and for the here and now.

IV

In the light of these reflections, how, then, can I link, positively and concretely, prophetic religion to its responsibilities for the social order? The link is found, I think, not in rules or principles but in a believing attitude.

This believing attitude must, first, stubbornly insist that the will of God is to be done in the social world of man, and that we are responsible for our share in it. It must resist the temptation, born of the frustations of all ages and especially of our own, of escaping into dualism, whether into a divine world above, unconcerned with man, or into a human world below, unconcerned with God and hence not really human.

This believing attitude must, secondly, face up to the will of God, not in general, or for some other place and time, but here and now. There is no situation which is morally and religiously neutral. There is no power-struggle, however necessarily Machiavellian, which is not at the same time a situation in which the prophetic imperative speaks to us. And even the thunder of nuclear tests must not be allowed to drown its voice.

Thirdly, the prophetic imperative, being divine, must be taken with radical seriousness, not given mere half-hearted and niggardly concessions. It is one thing to be forced to compromise in the struggle against war, oppression, discrimination and poverty, and to accept such compromises temporarily and with an aching heart. It is another thing entirely to mistake what are at best incomplete achievements finally and self-righteously, as if they were perfect. This believing attitude can never forget that so long as the divine image is violated even in one single human being, the Kingdom of God on earth is incomplete.

Fourthly, this believing attitude knows that while the prophetic imperative is divine even our best efforts to respond to it are only human. And this is true not only of our organized forms of acting but also of our organized forms of belief, doctrine and preaching. Society and religion, even at their best, are under the judgment of God.

Finally and most importantly, this believing attitude knows that while we have our responsible share in the doing of God's will in the social world of man, the fate of that world is not in our hands alone. Throughout the ages, those committed to the prophetic imperative have always been threatened by despair, when faced with the discrepancy between what ought to be and what is. This danger assumes unheard-of proportions in a world confronted with possibilities of total destruction. Today, more than ever, one can heed the prophetic imperative with any kind of confidence only if one heeds it with an ultimate confidence; with the confidence in a God who, while bidding us to work in His world, is also its absolute Sovereign.

32 On the Life, Death, and Transfiguration of Martyrdom: The Jewish Testimony to the Divine Image in Our Time

I

The colloquy of which this paper is part is doubly fashionable. Western religion, long self-enclosed, has now opened itself in all directions and to every influence. Western philosophy, having said little to a world wanting to hear much in its but recent tough-minded analytic extreme, is now swinging to an extreme so tender-minded as to define its critical function loosely when it defines it at all. The spirit of the age is thus well reflected in a meeting in which Christianity, Judaism, Islam, Hinduism, and Confucianism are all represented and in which, to judge by the titles, philosophy is as much an expression of religion as its critic.

But fashion is one thing, seriousness another. It is no accident that Western philosophy began with demythologizing the gods and that, even at a time when the man-made gods were replaced by the man-creating God, philosophy insisted on guarding its *lumen naturale* against incursions by an acknowledged *lumen supernaturale*. Nor is it an accident that the religions represented in this colloquy showed toward each other, for most of their history, an attitude of hostility, indifference, or at best of a tolerance not unmixed with condescension.

Can it be otherwise? Can philosophy let go of its critical function without self-betrayal? Can a religious witness believe himself to stand related to the Divine and yet let the truth of that relation be called into question by alternative or even conflicting religious testimonies? One thus wonders whether the current, superficially admirable looseness in philosophy does not hide a loss of direction, and whether the superficially no less admirable "dialogical" openness in religion is not an attempt to compensate for a lack of conviction. The last-named possibility was well expressed by a wit who defined ecumenism as the belief that anyone's religion is better than one's own.

Much of the current openness in religion and philosophy reflects a mere failure

Reprinted, with changes, from *The Jewish Return into History* (New York: Schocken Books, 1978), 234–51, by permission of the publisher.

of nerve. At a deeper level, however, it responds to a historical necessity. The increasing, worldwide interdependence of civilizations, their religions included; a universal, steadily increasing secularization, accompanied by a rise of this-worldly expectations; and, perhaps above all, an accelerated pace accompanying all these manifestations of contemporary life, together with vast, mostly technologically induced promises and threats: these are just the most obvious facts necessitating looseness in philosophy and openness in religion. And the authentic question arising may be stated in the form of a dilemma. In response to the challenge of the age, religious and philosophical traditions may strive to dissolve their respective identities into a larger, possibly worldwide whole: but the universalism thus arrived at could only be a flattened-out syncretism. Alternatively, and in an attempt to preserve their identities, they may strive to withdraw from living contacts already actual into themselves: but the shell of such a particularism could only be frozen and sterile. The dilemma is between two forms of lifelessness, and the question is whether we can escape it.

II. Post-Hegelian Perspectives

This dilemma was anticipated and confronted with unequaled profundity by the thought of Hegel. And, although it will appear that our own stance cannot be Hegel's own, we do well to begin with some relevant Hegelian theses:[1]

1. Philosophical thought is not divorced from but rather *rooted in* human existence. It *arises* from existential situations in order, partly or wholly, to rise above them.

2. Existence itself has an irreducible religious dimension. Marx, Freud, and others were to embrace a religious reductionism. This was repudiated and refuted by Hegel in advance. Religious truth must be understood as it understands itself before philosophy can rise to its conceptualization. Marxists and Freudians demythologize. Hegel transmythologizes. And unlike them he does not destroy religious truth but rather preserves it.

3. Committed to these principles, Hegel is faced with the very dilemma which we have already stated. Either the religious truth preserved by philosophical conceptualization is a "universal" religion of "mankind," whether culled from existing religious sources or wholly constructed by philosophy; but then it is a lifeless syncretism or construction, and philosophy does not preserve religious truth but rather helps destroy it. Or the religion conceptualized and preserved is one particular living religion: but then the philosophy which preserves its truth is guilty of parochialism and, moreover, finds its nemesis in other philosophies which conceptualize and preserve other, no less living, religions. Confronting the dilemma head-on, Hegel seeks to meet it with the crucial notion of *mediation*. Mediating philosophic thought must, first, do justice to every religion in *its own*, unique, self-understanding. It must, second, rise partly or wholly *above* this self-understanding. And it will, third, *prove* the success of this rise if and when, partly or wholly, it mediates the conflict or divergence between one religion and some or all others.

4. Mediation is thus needed *among* religions. At least in the modern world, it is also needed *between* the religious sphere of life as a whole and an independent secular sphere of life. For it is the characteristic of the modern world that secular

life, manifest in such forms as science and technology and, above all, in the social and political sphere, has emancipated itself from premodern religious authority. In the view of countless thinkers after Hegel, this fact has made all religion an anachronism. Hegel himself rejects and refutes this view in advance with his own mediation between religion and secularity, whose result is that modern religion stands in need of secular expression lest it lapse into a worldless pietism; and that modern secularity stands in need of religious inspiration lest it lapse into either spiritual chaos or spiritless fragmentation.

5. In theory, a religion may emerge from Hegel's mediating justice in one of three ways:

(a) Its truth may be preserved, encompassed, and hence superseded by a higher religion. In that case, the religion survives, if survive it does, only as an anachronism.

(b) Its truth may remain unencompassed by another. In that case, it depends for its authentic survival only on its own vitality and power of rejuvenation.

(c) Its truth may be a *novum* in history, relative to hitherto existing religious and/or secular forms of life, and responding to a *novum* in history itself. In that case, it necessitates a reappraisal of existing realities which may be worldwide in scope. And, if the *novum* is radical, the necessary reappraisal encompasses philosophy itself.

6. These three possibilities exist in theory. In practice they have reduced themselves to two in Hegel's own age. For Protestant Christianity is the "absolute" or all-encompassing religious truth, and between it and secular modernity there has come into being a mediation that is, in principle at least, all-encompassing and thus unsurpassable. Hence, first, no religious *novum* is either possible or necessary. Hence, second, all existing religions that continue to exist side by side Protestant Christianity are, radically considered, anachronisms. Hence, finally, an absolute or all-encompassing mediation has become possible in the sphere of philosophical thought. The philosophy that has achieved this mediation is Hegel's own.

The above suffices not only as a summary of Hegel's thought but also as a proof why, on our part, we cannot be Hegelians but at most only post-Hegelians. For the sixth above thesis we non-Protestants are bound to reject as an expression of nineteenth-century Protestant-European imperialism. Moreover, most if not all contemporary Protestants would join us in rejecting it and indeed exceed us in vehemence. Finally, it is safe to say that Hegel himself would not be a Hegelian today.[2]

We say "post"- rather than "non"- or "anti-Hegelian" because Hegel's was not a thoughtless imperialism. Like Marx and others after him and on account of him, he foresaw that modern-secular European "freedom" would be of world-historical significance, and held that this secular emancipation *from* religion has been made possible by a religious emancipation *in* religion which had found in Protestantism its most effective if not sole expression. Unlike these heirs of his, he foresaw (as we have already stressed) that modern-secular freedom would degenerate into spiritual chaos or spiritless fragmentation unless it continued to be religiously nourished. Thus Hegel's European-Protestant imperialism is not a historically contingent aberration. It is a historically necessary experiment that failed.

It failed for three fundamental reasons:

1. While doing justice to non-Protestant religions to an astounding degree, Hegel does less than the full justice required by his own philosophy.

2. While anticipating the threat of fragmentation posed by "the Understanding," Hegel did not and could not anticipate that at least in one of its forms—technology—this threat would escalate into one to man's very humanity and, indeed, to his survival.

3. While allowing for relative evil, Hegel's philosophy cannot recognize absolute evil. In the religious realm, there is only relative idolatry which bears unwitting witness to a higher religious truth. In the political realm, even the worst state is better than no state at all, for it serves life and leads to a higher life. There is no room in Hegel's philosophy for an idolatry that revels in the defilement of everything human and blasphemes against everything divine; nor for an anti-society whose factories are geared to but one ultimate produce, and that is death. Leaving room for no absolute evil anywhere, his thought leaves room for it, least of all, in the Christian Europe of modern times. Yet precisely this was the space and time of Auschwitz and Buchenwald.[3]

The failure of Hegel's experiment transforms his remaining theses as follows:

1. Philosophic thought, having foundered in its attempt to achieve a transhistorical absoluteness, is cast back into history and becomes a historically situated reflection which (to use Kierkegaard's expression) points to a religious immediacy after reflection.

2. Religious immediacy, being *after* reflection, is forced to recognize *its own* historical situatedness. This imposes upon it a threefold obligation: the need to prove its own continued vitality and relevance; the need to meet the challenge of a *novum* if history produces a *novum*; and the need to be open to the challenge and testimony of other forms of religious immediacy. (This dialogical openness replaces Hegel's mediation.) However, especially in the age of Auschwitz, it is evident that this openness would degenerate if it were indiscriminate. It must be rendered discriminating by the power to oppose absolute evil.

III. The Jewish Testimony to the Divine Image

In the light of these criteria we shall now expound, first, a traditional Jewish religious testimony and then a contemporary *novum* concerning it. We shall confine ourselves to a single commitment, as made by one crucial witness at a crucial moment in Jewish history. The witness is Rabbi Akiba. His testimony is as follows:

> Beloved is man, for he was created in the image of God; but it was by a special love that it was made known to him that he was created in the image of God, as it is said, "For in the image of God made He man." [Gen. 9:6][4]

One is tempted to dismiss this affirmation as a high-sounding platitude so universalistic as to be discoverable anywhere and nowhere, committing an author to everything and nothing and thus costing him nothing. One is stopped short by the fact that this particular author died a martyr's death at the behest of Rome, the then citadel of universalism.

If taken seriously, Akiba's testimony raises an exegetical question. The rabbi cites a book. Like all books, it is a particular book. It is a—*the*—Jewish book.

Could it be, then, that, its universalistic words notwithstanding, the scope of this testimony is confined to those who know the citation because they possess the book, that is, to Jews?

This "particularistic" exegesis is ruled out, however, not only by the context of the statement[5] but further by a well-known debate between Akiba and Rabbi Shim'on Ben Azzai. The task in this debate is to find a passage in the Jewish book which contains its greatest principle. Akiba cites "Thou shalt love thy neighbor as thyself" (Lev. 19:18). Ben Azzai cites "This is the book of the generations of man" (Gen. 5:1). Ben Azzai does not wish to contradict Akiba, a close friend recognized by him as the greater man.[6] The debate is not an argument but rather a conjoining of two mutually inseparable principles. This exegesis is nicely confirmed by the fact that the debate exists in a second version in which the order of the two cited texts is reversed.[7]

The conjoining of the two principles has a twofold significance. First, the ethical commitment—love of neighbor—is mere sentimentality without the corresponding ontological commitment—the divine image in man—just as this particular ontological commitment remains empty if not fraudulent without an ethics, and just *this particular* ethics. Second, because of the content of this ethics and this ontology, there must be a conjunction of the metaphysically most radical universalism with the existentially most radical particularism. In *The Fathers according to Rabbi Nathan* we read:

> He who sustains one soul is accounted by Scripture as though he had sustained a whole world . . . and he who destroys one soul is accounted by Scriptures as though he had destroyed a whole world. . . . For thus we find of Cain who killed his brother Abel as it is said, *The voice of thy brother's blood crieth unto Me* (Gen. 4:10): though he shed the blood of one, it is said *damin* ("bloods") in the plural. Which teaches that the blood of Abel's children and the children's children and all his descendents to the end of all generations destined to come forth from him—all of them stood crying out before the Holy One, blessed be He.
>
> Thus thou dost learn that one man's life is equal to all the work of Creation.[8]

The author of this statement is not Akiba but an unknown contemporary or near-contemporary. It is certain, however, that Akiba, like him, embraces a universalism so radical in metaphysical scope as to trace the divine image to Adam, and a particularism so radical in existential seriousness as to regard the life of even a single man as equivalent to the whole world.

Our exegetical question is thus answered. This answer, however, in turn gives rise to a question that is not merely exegetical but rather religious and philosophical. Does Akiba's ontology of the divine image in man refer to an unsullied human essence? Then why does this essence contrast so starkly with man's historical existence? Or is man's essence wholly manifest in and inseparable from his historical existence? Then what remains intact of the divine image—and of the God who created it? These questions are faced with unyielding sternness in a rabbinic debate reported in the Talmud as follows:

> The schools of Hillel and Shammai disputed two and a half years whether it would have been better if man had or had not been created. Finally they agreed that it would

have been better had he not been created, but since he has been created, let him investigate his past doings, and let him examine what he is about to do.[9]

The debate reported in this text may have taken place before 70 C.E., when the Jerusalem Temple was destroyed by the Romans. Its conclusion makes its occurrence after the catastrophe more likely. Regardless of the scholarly question of dating the debate, however, much could have been said by the Hillelites, even after 70 C.E., in support of the view that it was better for man to be created, on the grounds of the divine image in man. And much could have been said by the Shammai'ites, even before the catastrophe, in support of the view that it would have been better for man not to have been created, on the basis of historical evidence. However, *nothing* could be and was said by *either* school, before or even after the event, to lend support to the view that this was not, after all, a divinely created world, and that hence man was not, after all, created in the divine image. Indeed, this view is explicitly defied with the demand that concludes the debate, to the effect that, even in a world giving every evidence against the goodness of being, man must *act* according to the divine image which he *is*. Such a demand, however, is possible only because the *knowledge* of man as the divine image remains accessible even at a time when the *reality* seems all but vanished. It remains accessible, if nowhere else, in the Jewish book.

In 70 C.E. Titus destroyed the Jewish state but permitted the study and teaching of the Jewish book. In 135 C.E. (after the collapse of the Bar Kokhba revolt) Hadrian went further. He forbade the study and teaching of the Jewish book on pain of death. The act of Titus had made inescapable, for the schools of Hillel and Shammai, the question whether for man, the divine image, it was better to be or not to be. The more radical act of Hadrian now raised for Rabbi Akiba the still more radical prospect of a time in which the very question could no longer be debated. After 70 C.E., the knowledge of the divine image remained even if the reality seemed all but vanished. After 135 C.E., Akiba had to reckon with the possibility of the destruction of the Jewish book, and hence the vanishing of the knowledge.

Akiba's response to this extreme situation—the most extreme in Jewish experience prior to the Nazi Holocaust—was astonishingly simple. The Jewish book teaches that man is created in the image of God. Reality shows that not every man *knows* that he is created in the image of God. It is therefore a Jewish duty to bear witness to this knowledge. This duty does not vanish at a time when the teaching of the Jewish book is forbidden. On the contrary, it then becomes most inescapable. If the penalty is death, then this risk must be taken. And if death comes as the result of defying the prohibition it assumes the form of martyrdom, the extreme act of testimony.

Akiba died pronouncing words from the forbidden book, "Hear, O Israel, the Lord our God, the Lord is One." It is significant that ever since Akiba's martyr's death, countless Jews have died many kinds of death with the same words on their lips. It is also significant that Rufus, the Roman officer in charge of Akiba's execution, made no attempt to silence him. On the contrary, he listened, and was astonished.[10]

IV. The Novum in Contemporary Jewish Existence

The Roman Empire was ignorant of the divine image. Heir to a bimillennial tradition, which included the Jewish book, the Nazi empire did not share this ignorance but rather repudiated the knowledge—consciously, deliberately, thoroughly. In its ignorance the Roman Empire violated the divine image, sometimes slightly, sometimes catastrophically, but always haphazardly. In its repudiation of the knowledge, the Nazi empire was neither haphazard nor content to violate the divine image. It sought to destroy the reality of the divine image so systematically as to make its rejection of the knowledge of it into a self-fulfilling prophecy. This empire was therefore a *novum* in human history; and the evidence around us—the cheapness of life, the banality of death, the ideological glorification of murder—shows that, for all its short duration, this *novum* was no mere episode.

Aiming at the destruction of the divine image of all peoples, the Nazi Empire focused its effort on one particular people. It asserted itself as "Aryan." Yet it could find no definition of "Aryan" other than "not-non-Aryan," and the "non-Aryan" was legally defined as a—full, half, quarter—Jew.[11] And the process which began with a definition making its victim rightless climaxed in an acted-out legal philosophy which defined the victim's very existence as a crime punishable by torture and death.[12]

If the Nazi empire was a *novum* in human history, this law was a *novum* in legal history. All periods of human history have had their share of lawless violence. All societies have had their share of unjust laws, not a few of them criminal. All law hitherto, however, defined crime as an *action*, something someone *did*. When, in the case of one group of persons, Nazi law defined *mere existence* as a capital crime, the society governed by it showed itself to be more than merely criminal vis-à-vis its victims, but rather an anti-society vis-à-vis the human race. In the view of Akiba and his friends, he who destroyed one soul had been as though he destroyed the whole world. In making *being* alive a *putative* crime for "non-Aryans," Nazi law sought to implicate all "Aryans" in its domain in an *actual* crime, by the mere act—accomplished by the proof of one's "Aryan" ancestry—of *staying* alive.

In this manner the Nazi rejection of the knowledge of the divine image was translated into law. The law itself came closest to the self-fulfilling prophecy aimed at in the murder camp. The murder camp was not an accidental by-product of the Nazi empire. It was its pure essence.

The divine image in man *can* be destroyed. No more threatening proof to this effect can be found than the so-called *Muselmann* in the Nazi death camp. A survivor writes:

> On their entry into the camp, through basic incapacity, or by misfortune, or through some banal incident, they are overcome before they can adapt themselves; they are beaten by time, they do not begin to learn German, to disentangle the infernal knot of laws and prohibitions until their body is already in decay, and nothing can save them from selections or death by exhaustion. Their life is short, but their number is endless; they, the *Muselmaenner*, the drowned, form the backbone of the camp, an anonymous mass, continuously renewed and always identical, of non-men who march and labor in silence, the divine spark dead within them, already too empty to

really suffer. One hesitates to call them living; one hesitates to call their death death.[13]

A recent writer comments:

> This is the empirical instance of death-in-life. No more awful thing can be said of the concentration camps than that countless men and women were murdered in spirit as the means of killing them in body.[14]

The *Muselmaenner* are a new way of human being in history, the living dead. What shall we say of those implicated in the production of this way of being—propagandists, paragraph-experts, paper-pushers as well as those actually giving the orders and wielding the clubs—except that in murdering the "divine spark" in others they also killed it in themselves?

The murder camp did not succeed in destroying the divine image in all its victims. Akiba had died with words of the Jewish book on his lips. Countless nameless Akibas cited these same words at the time of death in the murder camps. Yet we cannot record this unprecedented spiritual triumph without at the same time recording an unprecedented spiritual tragedy. In making the teaching of the Jewish book a capital crime, Hadrian had created the possibility of martyrdom for Jewish believers. In making Jewish existence a capital crime, Hitler murdered Jewish martyrdom itself. When Akiba died with the words of the Jewish book on his lips, Rufus had listened in astonishment. When the nameless Akibas in the Nazi empire did likewise, the countless nameless Eichmanns reacted, either not at all, or with a new species of humor. Nor was this response without its logic. In the Roman Empire a martyr had *chosen* death. Since the Nazi empire destroyed this choice, a victim's retreat to the remaining choice—the manner of his death—was, in the eyes of all the murderers and most of the bystanders, either a triviality or an occasion for laughter. Humor has been defined as the experience that the small incongruities of life are not serious, and faith, as the commitment to the proposition that the large incongruities of life are not ultimate.[15] Since the Nazi empire spared no effort to make death itself banal, even the most sublime expression of faith—in this case, the manner of dying—reduced itself, in the context of that empire, to a small incongruity, that is, a case of the comical.

Yet believers will cry out that the testimony of the nameless Akibas, unheard on earth, is heard in heaven. Unbelievers will cry out that this proof of humanity will forever inspire humanity, even among persons without religious faith. Both will unite in the protest that the context of the Nazi empire is not *our* context, and must not be.

Both protests are powerful. Jointly they are irresistible. Yet they would lose all their power unless they face up to the question posed by the Nazi empire. This empire succeeded in destroying the divine image in some. It also succeeded in destroying an ancient way of testifying to the divine image in others. After this double success, carefully planned and executed, how can one witness to the divine image in man and hope to be believed? How can one believe one's own testimony? This question, in any case inescapable, is all the more so because the conditions that have given rise to it are not gone. The Nazi death camp is destroyed. The Soviet "Destructive Labor" camp[16] remains. Moreover, outside the Soviet empire the Nazi camp enjoys an afterlife of sorts. Death, forced into banality in the death camps, widely remains banal. And martyr and hero in behalf of a cause have given way to the terrorist whose glamor lies not in his ends but rather in his indiscriminate means.

The question is raised by the Nazi murder camp. An answer can come only *from* the murder camps—not from the philosopher reflecting on evil-in-general or the preacher inveighing against it but only from the testimony of the survivor. A recent book by that title[17] has three special credentials. The work of a non-Jewish author, the book disposes of the view that the Nazi empire is not in fact a *novum* in history but only viewed as such by traumatized Jewish writers. Encompassing the Soviet "Destructive Labor" camp as well as the Nazi death camp, it also disposes of the view that the *novum* was an episode, now dead and gone. Most important, the book does not psychoanalyze or otherwise explain the survivor. It exposes itself to his testimony.

This testimony—unprecedented in human history and a revolutionary challenge to religion and philosophy—may be summed up as follows. In an anti-society geared to torture and death, mere living is not "mere." When law defines existence itself as a crime, illegality becomes sacred. When a system makes surrender to death the norm, survival becomes a heroic act of resistance. When every effort is made to reduce dying to a banality, life does not need to be sanctified. It already *is* holy.

This summary remains an empty shell without the actual testimony of the survivors: those who actually survived the Nazi empire to tell the tale; but also the far more numerous others who survived, not the camps, but only *in* the camps—a year, a month, or even a single day beyond imaginable human endurance—and whose story is told by others. And the story of most can never be told

The weight of their collective testimony forces us to revolutionize our questions. One asks: why did many become *Muselmaenner*, the living dead? The true question is: why were there some who did *not* succumb to living death, and the answer is that they rallied a will-to-live no one knew existed. One asks: why were many reduced to what philosophers are wont to call the "state of nature," a war of each against all, with friend betraying friend, parent set against child and child against parent, all for a crust of bread? The true question is why not all succumbed to this state, and the answer is that, in a world that was no mere jungle but rather hell itself, some found an astounding need—indeed, an imperative and a law—to help others as much as to be helped by them. The contemplation of the murder camp as a system produces the most astonishing reversal of all. In an age in which men and women are programmed for all sorts of purposes, one takes for granted that the Nazi death camp, the supreme programming system of all, succeeded in programming its victims, and then wonders how men and women could be programmed into cooperating in their own destruction. The astounding fact is that the *recognition* of the system *as such* lent the intended victim his supreme power for resisting it. One survivor writes:

> At the outset the living places, the ditches, the mud, the piles of excrement behind the blocks, had appalled me with their horrible filth. . . . And then I saw the light! I saw that it was not a question of disorder of lack of organization but that, on the contrary, a very thoroughly considered conscious idea was in the back of the camp's exis-

319   On Martyrdom

tence. They had condemned us to die in our own filth, to drown in mud, in our own excrement. They wished to abase us, to destroy our human dignity . . ., to fill us with horror and contempt toward ourselves and our fellows. . . . But from the instant when I grasped the motivating principle . . . it was as if I had been awakened from a dream. . . . *I felt under orders to live.* . . . And if I did die in Auschwitz, it would be as a human being, I would hold on to my dignity. I was not going to become the contemptible, disgusting brute my enemy wished me to be. . . . And a terrible struggle began which went on day and night.[18]

These answers, given not with words, but with lives lived beyond all limits of endurance hitherto known or imagined, are a testimony whose significance, to be contemplated by thinkers and poets present and yet unborn, is universal.

As for the Jewish people after the Holocaust, they are singled out by this testimony by dint of a simple, yet enormous and still all-but-unfathomable fact: but for an accident of geography, every Jew alive today would either have been murdered, or never been born, or be a survivor.

It is not possible for the post-Holocaust Jew to ignore or leap over this fact in an attempt to reenact or rejuvenate Rabbi Akiba's tradition, believing and behaving as though nothing had happened. More precisely, he can ignore or leap over the fact only by blaspheming against those who did or could not resist, and against those who could and did resist—a day, a year, or even by dint of good fortune until the enemy was destroyed. Prior to the Nazi empire, a Jew, in order to possess the Jewish book, had to view himself as though he had personally stood at Sinai. After the Nazi empire, a Jew is able to keep the Jewish book only if he views himself as though he had personally been present at Auschwitz or Buchenwald as well; and whether he then will still wish or be able to keep the book cannot be known in advance. Would he have been a *Muselmann?* Or have summoned the will to live? Would he have survived in a state of war against his fellow victims, or in alliance with them? By losing his human dignity or by finding it? He will never know. And he is required to re-enact *all* these possibilities and make them his own. Only then can he hope to emerge from reenactment without lapsing, either into a cheap faith in the divine image in man (a blasphemous honor to the Nazi criminals and a blasphemous insult to their victims, the living dead) or into a cheap despair (a disregard no less blasphemous of all resistance fighters everywhere, not least of those whose resistance took the form of survival in the murder camps). To new prisoners on their first night in Sachsenhausen, a survivor spoke these words: "I have not told you of our experiences to harrow you, but to strengthen you. . . . Now you may decide if you are justified in despairing."[19]

A Jew cannot take upon himself the age-old task of testifying to the divine image in man without believing his own testimony. In our time, however, he cannot authentically believe in this testimony without exposing himself *both* to the fact that the image of God was destroyed, *and* to the fact that the unsurpassable attempt to destroy it was successfully resisted, supremely so, by the survivor. *Hence the wish to bear witness turns into a commandment, the commandment to restore the diving image to the limits of his power.* And the prime witness to the knowledge that the destroyed image *can* be restored is not one who, like Akiba in his situation, is prepared to die for the knowledge. It is a new witness: the survivor, determined to *live and be human* in a world where murder was law and degradation holy; whose testimony consisted, with every breath, of restoring the divine image in himself even as it was ceaselessly being destroyed. A Bergen-Belsen survivor has said: "In my happier days I used to remark on the aptitude of the saying, 'When in life we are in the midst of death.' I have since learned that it is more apt to say, 'When in death we are in the midst of life.' "[20]

Notes

1. The theses here merely asserted are developed in my *The Religious Dimension in Hegel's Thought* (Bloomington: Indiana University Press, 1968; Boston: Beacon Press, 1970).

2. See my "Would Hegel Today Be a Hegelian?" *Dialogue*, IX, pp. 222–26.

3. The three reasons here merely stated are argued for in chap. 3 of my *Encounters between Judaism and Modern Philosophy* (New York: Basic Books, 1973). The chapter is entitled "Moses and the Hegelians."

4. *Pirke Abot* III, 18.

5. The particularistic exegesis would make a redundancy of the saying of Akiba which immediately follows. This reads: "Beloved are Israel, for they were called children of the All-Present; but it was by a special love that it was made known to them that they were called children of the All-Present, as it is said. 'Ye are children unto the Lord your God' " (Deut. 14:1).

6. On hearing a dispute concerning marital law in which Akiba espoused successfully the principle of a widow's human rights, Ben Azzai exclaimed, "Alas, that I did not have Akiba for a teacher!" (*Babyl. Talmud, Nedarim* 74b).

7. For the two versions, see *Sifra* 98b and *Genesis Rabba, Bereshit,* XXIV, 7.

8. *The Fathers according to Rabbi Nathan,* trans. J. Goldin (New Haven: Yale University Press, 1955; New York: Schocken, 1974), pp. 125–26.

9. *Babylonian Talmud, Erubim* 13b.

10. L. Finkelstein writes: "The popular story tells that the Romans killed him by tearing his flesh from his living body. As he lay in unspeakable agony, he suddenly noticed the first streaks of dawn breaking over the eastern hills. It was the hour when the Law requires each Jew to pronounce the *Shema.* Oblivious to his surroundings, Akiba intoned in a loud, steady voice, the forbidden words of his faith. 'Hear, O Israel, the Lord our God, the Lord is One. And thou shalt love the Lord thy God with all thine heart, and with all thy soul, and with all thy might.'

"Rufus, the Roman general, who superintended the horrible execution, cried out: 'Are you a wizard or are you utterly insensible to pain?' 'I am neither,' replied the martyr, 'but all my life I have been waiting for the moment when I might truly fulfil this commandment. I have always loved the Lord with all my might, and with all my heart; now I know that I love him with all my life.' And, repeating the verse again, he died as he reached the words, 'The Lord is one' " (*Akiba: Scholar, Saint, and Martyr* [New York: Atheneum, 1970], pp. 276–77.)

11. In commenting on the 1935 Nuremberg laws, Raul Hilberg writes: "It is to be noted that while heretofore the population had been divided only into 'Aryans' and 'non-Aryans,' there were now two kinds of non-Aryans: Jews and so-called *Mischlinge.* Half-Jews who did not belong to the Jewish religion or who were not married to a Jewish person on September 15, 1935, were to be called *Mischlinge* of the first degree. One-quarter Jews became *Mischlinge* of the second degree. The fate of the *Mischlinge* was never settled to the complete satisfaction of the Nazi party, and they were the subject of considerable discussion during the 'final solution' conferences of 1941 and 1942 (*Documents of Destruction,* ed. R. Hilberg [New York: Quadrangle, 1971], pp. 18–19.

12. In a book entitled *The Criminal Nature of the Jews,* published in 1944, Johannes von Leers asserted that since the Jews were not only a pseudo-people but also a race of born criminals, a nation had not only the right to kill the Jews living in its midst, but also the right, deriving from the juridical doctrine of hot pursuit, of seizing the Jews of its neighbors and exterminating them. Indeed, a nation harboring Jews was as criminally culpable as someone failing to take measures against cholera bacilli. (See the account by Erich Goldhagen, "Pragmatism, Function, and Belief in Nazi Anti-Semitism," *Midstream,* December 1972, p. 60.) Von Leers was Professor of History at the University of Jena.

Raul Hilberg's magisterial *The Destruction of the European Jews* (New York: Quadrangle, 1961), ends its concluding "Reflections" with this sentence: "When in the early days of 1933 the first civil servant wrote the first definition of an 'non-Aryan' into a civil service ordinance, the fate of European Jewry was sealed," p. 669.

13. Primo Levi, *Survival in Auschwitz* (New York: Collier Books, 1961), p. 82. Cited by Terrence Des Pres, *The Survivor* (New York: Oxford University Press, 1976), p. 89.

14. Des Pres, ibid., p. 88.

15. By Reinhold Niebuhr, probably in part under the inspiration of Kierkegaard.

16. Aptly so called by A. I. Solzhenitsyn.

17. See note 13. The following section is deeply indebted to this profound work.

18. P. Lewinska, *Twenty Months in Auschwitz* (New York: Lyle Stuart, 1968), pp. 41 ff., 50. Cited by Des Pres, *The Survivor*, pp. 62 ff. (Italics added.)

19. Cited by Des Pres, ibid., p. 209, as the concluding sentence of his book.

20. Quoted by Des Pres, ibid., p. 96. It is apt that this, as well as the preceding quotation—the conclusion of this article—should be anonymous.

33   *Philosophy, the Holocaust, and Human Dignity*

B

A philosophical *Tikkun* is possible *after* the Holocaust because a philosophical *Tikkun already* took place, however fragmentarily, during the Holocaust itself. What the greatest German philosopher of the age [Martin Heidegger] failed to achieve in decades after the *Ereignis*, was accomplished, at least in principle, by an obscure German professor of philosophy in the midst of the *Ereignis* itself. (Here and in the following we do not mean that *this* one was the *only* one; we *do* mean that even a single case, provided it was *genuine*, is a *novum* that alters everything.)

It is obviously necessary to explain and defend this assertion. Above we made mention, in the context inevitably all-too-briefly, of the German resistance. There was no purer resistance to the Nazi regime than the handful of Munich students who called themselves the "White Rose." They knew that their action—distributing anti-Nazi pamphlets at the late date of 1943—was almost sure to be futile. They knew, too, that they were almost certain to be caught and put to death. They knew it: yet they did it. And they were caught and brutally, legally, murdered.[1]

Appropriately enough, the court decreeing their murders was a *Volksgericht*, the most assiduous of all institutions administering the Führer's law. Just as appropriately, the presiding judge was Doktor Roland Freisler, most assiduous among the Führer's officers of law. No less fitting, however, were the person and the ideas of the spokesman and mentor of the accused. Kurt Huber was a professor of philosophy. His posthumous papers contain a "Final Statement of the Accused," which in substance, if not in actual words, was delivered before the court. In this, Huber said that he had acted out of responsibility for all Germany; that

Reprinted, with changes, from *To Mend the World* (New York: Schocken Books, 1982), 317–331, by permission of the publisher.

his action was not illegal but rather an attempt to restore legality; that this was so because there were unwritten as well as written laws; and that although he was set by the court at the level of the lowest criminals, he would be vindicated by History. Huber's "Final Statement" ends as follows:

> *Und handeln sollst Du so, als hinge*
> *Von Dir und Deinem Tun allein*
> *Das Schicksal ab der deutschen Dinge,*
> *Und die Verantwortung wär dein.*

> And act thou shalt as though
> The destiny of all things German
> Depended on you and your lonely acting,
> And the responsibility were yours.[2]

The words are J. G. Fichte's. So is the philosophical teaching. Kant had ascribed a moral mission to all mankind. Fichte, his disciple, singled out the Germans for a special mission. The master, Kant, had seen the essence of a moral action not in its intended or actual consequences, but rather in the will that motivated it. Fichte, the one-time apprentice, considered an action morally impure if the agent thought of consequences at all. These two Fichtean doctrines, both un-Kantian, are dubious in the extreme. Each had a baneful effect in German history that needs no rehearsing here, for it is well known and obvious. Yet both had a moment of truth when Kurt Huber invoked them before the Munich *Volksgericht* on April 19, 1943, just before he and his fellow-conspirators were put to death. It was a truth and a moment never reached by the greatest philosopher of the age, during a lengthy, distinguished and on the whole quite peaceful and undisturbed career.

We do not, of course, mean to set above the thought of Heidegger that of Huber or, rather, the old-fashioned, Kantian-Fichtean idealism that he espoused. Earlier in this work, when we summarized the course of modern philosophy on the road to *Being and Time*, the name of Fichte was barely mentioned. Now that his name most emphatically is mentioned, it is with the express reservation that his philosophy, or what of it is relevant in this context, had, perhaps, but a single moment of truth. (It had, in any case, only one *great* and *historic* such moment.) The import of Huber lies in his deed more than in this thought; in his thought insofar as it first motivated and then articulated the deed; and in both together by virtue of the unique place, time, and circumstances in which the deed was done and the thought expressed.

As regards the deed by itself, Huber, of course, was not unique. There were, first, the student members of the White Rose. Then there were others in other places who were not students, knew neither of philosophy nor of unwritten laws but who, nevertheless, defied the evil written laws out of an ordinary decency. What marks Huber off from the others is that he invoked philosophy in behalf of his action. However, the invoked philosophy—so we have said—was old-fashioned. Indeed, it is not too much to say that it was outlandish at any time, and that in Huber's time—and in ours—it was and is long out-of-date.

This last assertion needs no proof in the case of Fichte, who taught that all history was in necessary progress toward reason and moral freedom.[3] (Thus the moral agent could afford to ignore consequences; History-writ-Large would take care of them.) Proof is needed, however, in the case of Kant, for the concerned Kantian teaching, the categorical imperative, has been an inspiration from Kant's own time to our own, and not only to philosophers but also to ordinary folk.

What was soon to be at stake with this Kantian teaching is intimated by two contemporary philosophies, the Heideggerian and the Sartrean. Neither of them is old-fashioned nor out-of-date. Both, to this day, are rightly regarded as being among the great achievements of this century. A categorical imperative of sorts may be extracted from both Heidegger and Sartre. (Briefly: "be authentic!") It is, however, formalized to a totally un-Kantian extreme, with the result that Heidegger's thought, though not compelling his 1933 surrender to Nazism, was unable to prevent it; and that Sartre, though resisting Nazism, could find no adequate grounds for doing so in his philosophy. To Sartre—if not to Heidegger—this was a source of philosophical anguish. And philosophers today, were they not forgetful of that time of philosophical testing, might find cause in this failure for uneasiness about philosophy itself in our age.[4]

Still, philosophical powerlessness, as here displayed, is as old as Nietzsche's wrestling with nihilism, and is neither new nor unique to that time of testing. And a long distance exists between these intimations, coming from a time before the worst was known, and the philosophical horror that grips us when the worst is known and philosophically confronted. As friends of the categorical imperative, we are inspired by what Huber said in 1943 before the Munich *Volksgericht*, in support of what he had done. (He cited Fichte but referred to Kant as well.) Then what shall we think of what Adolf Eichmann said before the 1961 Jerusalem court, in support of what *he* had done? He too invoked the categorical imperative—and was not altogether mistaken. There is only one thing we *can* think: we must rethink Kant's *own* teaching, and consider its contemporary fate.

Let us summarize Kant's categorical imperative as succinctly as possible. (1) It is morally necessary to do duty for duty's sake. (2) It is morally necessary so to act that the "maxim" of one's acting could become, through one's will, universal law. (3) It is morally necessary to treat humanity, whether in one's own person or in that of another, never as a means only, always as an end as well. No lengthier summary than these three principles is necessary; none terser is possible. How did Eichmann stand related to them?

There is no doubt that he obeyed the first Kantian principle: he was a dutiful idealistic mass-murderer, not merely a sadistic or opportunistic one. In this exploration, we have come in many contexts upon the Nazi idealist, from the Führer down to the unknown SS criminal with a pure heart. Now, however, the context is philosophy itself, and the horror of this idealist is philosophical.

The horror is increased by the fact that Eichmann obeyed the second Kantian principle as well. For there is no doubt that the "maxim" of his acting was to make through his own will the Führer's will into universal law. His idea of law was, of course, quite different from the Kantian. However, we cannot take philosophical refuge in this difference; the horror pursues us into the place of refuge itself.

What is the difference between the two ideas? Kant's universal law *is* law and universal only if it respects no persons and treats all as equals. (Thus *no* man has the right to lie, since *not all* men can have it.) Eichmann's universal law discriminates between "Aryans" and "non-Aryans," between "master-" and "slave-races," and, above all, is itself subject to arbitrary suspension at the Führer's whim. (Thus the "master-race" has the right to lie, and even the duty. And the Führer is beyond truth and falsehood, just as he is beyond good and evil.)[5] This is the difference between the two ideas of universal law. It is easy for us to know which to love and which to abominate. However, the philosophical question is: *Just where is it written that all are equal? that the law must respect no persons?*[6]

This question was asked by a young Jewish philosopher in 1935 as he sat in a Viennese coffee house, studying in a newspaper the Nuremberg laws which had just been promulgated. Jean Améry was no old-fashioned Kantian but close in philosophical outlook to Sartre. Also, he was a realistic observer of the then-dominant realities, not only in Germany but also beyond. Hence he put the philosophical question in the following terms: The Hitler regime is accepted as legitimate by the German people; it is accepted as legitimate by the world as well; then what substance is there to appeals against the laws enacted by this regime to a higher, unwritten, law which views all as equal, all as persons? There is no substance, he grimly replied to his own question. Such appeals are insubstantial gestures. And such as he himself were objects of a "death sentence," "corpses on vacation." Still alive only by accident, as a Jew he had the "sole duty to disappear from the face of the earth."[7]

Three years later, following the *Anschluss*, Eichmann came to Vienna, in pursuit of the maxim of making the Führer's will into universal law.

Adolf Eichmann thus obeyed the first two principles of Kant's categorical imperative if, to be sure, in a fashion Kant never dreamt of. The same cannot be said of the third principle, for this—also in a fashion never dreamt of by Kant and indeed inconceivable prior to the event itself—was defied by Eichmann and his like, not only at Auschwitz, but throughout the length and breadth of the Third Reich. That human personality is an end in itself is the heart and soul of Kant's categorical imperative. As for the Third Reich, *its* heart and soul was the aim to destroy just this principle—by no means only in the case of Jews, "inferior races," and enemies of the Reich, but also, and perhaps above all, in the case of the "master race" itself. From the start the great dream was to stamp out personality as the *Volk* marched in unison at the Führer's behest; and the dream was not destroyed when, at the time of the apocalypse, it turned into a nightmare. For philosophy, the grim fact is this: Kant's own principle is not immune to this unheard of, unprecedented, unique assault.

Concerning Kant's own principle, the respected scholar H. J. Paton writes:

> As Kant well knows, men are not saints. Nevertheless—and this is a fundamental conviction of Kant—a good will is present in every man, however much it may be overlaid by selfishness, and however little it may be manifested in action. Because of this he is still entitled to respect and is not to be treated as a mere instrument or a mere thing. As a being capable of moral action, a man, however degraded, has still an infinite potential value; and his freedom to work out his own salvation in his own way must not be restricted except insofar as it impinges on the like freedom of others. We shall never understand Kant aright unless we see him as the apostle of human freedom and the champion of the common man.[8]

Doubtless Paton is correct. Doubtless Kant's "treat all as persons, as endowed with dignity!" rests on the belief that *real, empirical* humans *are* persons, endowed with dignity. Many take Kant as doing no more than express his own personal convictions, whether or not these are due to his Christian upbringing. Taken as a serious philosophical doctrine, his philosophical *Idea* of Humanity *must* have, and according to Kant *does* have, a matrix or *Boden* in *actual* humanity. Kant, in short, *believes* in humanity: *but is that belief warranted?* Perhaps it was so in Kant's time. Arguably it was once warranted at *any* time if only because, while undemonstrable, this belief was at least also irrefutable. (Who can refute a "good will" in the "common man" which is admittedly "overlaid with selfishness" and hence "not manifest in action"?) But is this belief warranted in the age of Auschwitz? Then and there, one kind of common man—the *Muselmann*—was made into a uniquely uncommon victim, while the other, the manufacturer of the victim, was made—*let himself* be made—into a uniquely uncommon criminal. And "uniquely uncommon" in both cases was this, that personality was destroyed. It is true that Kant's belief in humanity could at no time be verified. However, not until the advent of the Holocaust world was this belief *refuted*, for here the *reality* that is object of the belief was *itself systematically annihilated.* That this was possible is the awful legacy of Auschwitz to all humanity. The awful legacy for philosophy is that the annihilation of human personality robs the Idea of Humanity of its indispensable basis. And thus it could come to pass that Kant's categorical imperative, with its heart and soul destroyed, was invoked by its most dedicated enemies. Kant had formulated his imperative in behalf of human dignity. The Eichmanns of the Third Reich invoked it in behalf of a destruction of that dignity so total that, were the dream to come true, no remnant would be left. No more terrible illustration can be found of Elie Wiesel's dictum that at Auschwitz not only man died; that the Idea of Man died as well.[9]

C

Then what did the philosophy professor Kurt Huber think he was doing when he invoked an old-fashioned philosophy before the Munich *Volksgericht?* More precisely—since the term "old-fashioned" suggests that he did not quite *know* what he was doing—*what was he doing?* (This, as will be seen, is in any case the central question.) We cannot say that he proved in his own person that goodness is part of a human "substance" and hence indestructible. (If so, why were there so few? Why not a great army of professors, poets, priests, philosophers?) The "good in man" *can* be destroyed. It *was* being destroyed, and by no means only among those exposed to the Nazi logic of destruction. Then did the "good" in *this* "man" escape *actual* destruction only through an accidental circumstance? But Huber did not belong to the aristocratic, still privileged and shielded officer class. He was no part of a conspiratorial group whose members strengthened each other's resolve. He was not, personally, a man of superhuman courage. In fact, he and the other members of the "White Rose" were rather ordinary. The students had grown up and been indoctrinated in the Third Reich, and some had been soldiers on the Russian front. Huber himself still made a distinction, long robbed of moral validity, between serving the Third Reich and serving in its armed forces.[10] Then what made Huber do it?

In a different context, we would have to ask this question about all those "righteous Gentiles," few in number and mostly ordinary folk, who had no more reason for defying the Nazi regime than the millions that went along, and yet did defy it.[11] Here we must ask it about Huber, for he invoked a philosophical Idea in support of his action. Shall we say that the Idea *caused* his action, made it *necessary?* This would have been Fichte's view, in his own Age of Progress. In *our own* century—part of the age of progress no more—Hermann Cohen could still cling to this view prior to World War I. (To the orthodox Jewish objection that unlike the existing God of tradition, the God of Cohen's philosophy, the *Idea* of God, had no power, Cohen still replied that *only* the Idea has power.) However, this could not be Huber's view during World War II and after ten years of Nazi rule. In Huber's time, the Idea—of God, of Man, of God and Man—was weak. It was ignored when it was not actually scorned, and among the scorners were professors of philosophy. As for unwritten law deriving from the Idea, this was ignored by all except the victims of the written law, and their appeals to it were futile gestures. Huber himself had sought not to restore this or that law but legality itself.

Did the Idea, then, have *no* power over his action? But then his words before the Munich *Volksgericht* were, at worst, the words of a liar and a charlatan; even at best, his declared reason for acting was a mere rationalization. From such a view of Huber's trial—the most significant trial for philosophy since that of Socrates—there is but one step to the view that the reasons for philosophical beliefs or actions are *always* other than those given; that—except when it is engaged in scholastic debates of no relevance to human life—*all* philosophical reason is mere rationalization. However, we have seen long ago that "the high" must be understood in its own terms, not "in the light of the low"—and earlier still that there are situations of great moment in which common sense and common decency both dictate that a person's behavior be understood exactly as he understood it himself.[12]

What we *must* say, then, is the following. If Huber, in contemplating the great but fearful deed, was irresolute—and what reflective man would not have been?— then it was the Idea that strengthened his resolve. And if the Idea was weak— abandoned, betrayed, assailed, and mocked on all sides—then it was just this weakness that so intensified his resolve as to make him act (if act he must) without regard to consequences, and—except only for a few comrades—alone. Thus he *gave* strength to the Idea even as, in turn, he *was given* strength *by* it. This dialectic bears a remarkable resemblance to the dialectic of *Teshuva* and also, once self-exposure to the threat of rupture made it come into view, the kabbalistic dialectic of *Tikkun*.[13]

Huber's action *was* a *Tikkun*. He was old-fashioned enough to invoke the unwritten law as if, dwelling in a Platonic heaven, it were always accessible when in fact his own present was so divorced from it that only a *Tikkun* could *make* it accessible. However, his action *was itself* the required *Tikkun*. In obeying the unwritten law he *restored* that law—it must be written *somewhere*—*by writing it into his own heart*. In acting in behalf of Kant's Idea of Humanity, he *mended* that Idea—it was broken—for he recreated the matrix or *Boden* of it in *actual* humanity, even if only in his own person. Such was Huber's *Tikkun* of philosophy, in the age of its most catastrophic rupture.

This *Tikkun*, then and there, created the possibility and necessity of a post-Holocaust philosophy, here and now. This cannot consist of a return to Huber's— or any other—old-fashioned philosophy. Rather must it bring the *Tikkun*, performed by Huber in behalf of an old-fashioned philosophy, to a post-Holocaust philosophical consciousness. The Idea of Man can be—has been—destroyed, for humanity can be—has been—destroyed. But because humanity itself *has been* mended—*in* some men and women *by* some men and women—the Idea of Man *can* be mended. In the foregoing, we have come upon two *nova* of our age, a rupture and a *Tikkun*. Now we have come upon these same two *nova*, in the form that makes a post-Holocaust philosophy both necessary and possible.

Notes

1. See Inge Scholl, *Students Against Tyranny* (Middletown, Conn.: Weslyan University Press, 1970).

2. Ibid., pp. 63 ff. (The translation of Fichte's poem is mine.)

3. Fichte identified God as the "moral order of the world"—an ideal progressively shaping the real world.

4. Hans Jonas writes: "When in 1945 I reentered vanquished Germany as a member of the Jewish Brigade in the British army, I had to decide whom of my former teachers in philosophy I could in good conscience visit, and whom not. It turned out that the 'no' fell on my main teacher . . . who by the criteria which then had to govern my choice had failed the human test of the time; whereas the 'yes' included the much lesser figure of a rather narrow traditionalist Kantian persuasion, who meant little to me philosophically but of whose record in those dark years I heard admirable things. When I did visit him and congratulated him on the courage of his principled stand, he said a memorable thing: 'Jonas,' he said, 'I tell you this: without Kant's teaching I couldn't have done it.' " ("Contemporary Problems in Ethics from a Jewish Perspective," in *Judaism and Ethics*, ed. Daniel Silver [New York: Ktav, 1970], p. 31). Jonas's main teacher was Heidegger.

5. Arendt reports that, when one of the judges, indignant at Eichmann's invocation of Kant in connection with his crimes, decided to question him, the latter "to the surprise of everyone . . . came up with an approximately correct definition of the categorical imperative." In this context she also quotes Hans Frank's Nazi updating of Kant's doctrine: "Act in such a way that the *Führer*, if he knew your action, would approve of it" (*Eichmann in Jerusalem*, p. 136).

6. In his *Freedom and Reason* (New York: Oxford University Press, 1970, ch. 9) R. M. Hare stages an imaginary debate between two philosophers, a liberal and a Nazi, concerning the "extermination" of Jews. First eliminated in the debate are the opportunists and sadists among the Nazis who act merely from inclination. Next eliminated are those principled but not principled enough. When at length the liberal is confronted with a Nazi principled enough voluntarily to go to Auschwitz when he is discovered to be himself "non-Aryan," the liberal, to be sure, can abominate the Nazi principles, but he can do no more.

7. Améry, pp. 85–86.

8. *The Categorical Imperative* (Chicago: University of Chicago Press, 1948), p. 171.

9. *Legends of Our Time*, p. 230.

10. Since Hitler's attack on the Soviet Union regular German army units were systematically implicated in SS crimes.

11. In traditional Jewish thought "righteous Gentiles" are those who, obeying the laws given to Noah, "have a share in the world-to-come" and are "priests of God." In the Holocaust world this term acquired a new, deeper meaning, as yet unfathomed by Jewish—or any other—thought, since in that world even ordinary decency, when shown to Jews, was little short of miraculous.

12. See *To Mend the World*, chapter IV.

13. See *To Mend the World*, chapter IV.

SECTION SIX

GOD AND JEWISH EXISTENCE AFTER THE HOLOCAUST

34 *Midrashic Existence after the Holocaust*

How does one religious Jew respond to Planet Auschwitz, a place of limitless crimes and limitless suffering, surpassing hell?

> Never shall I forget that night, the first night in camp, which has turned my life into one long night, seven times cursed and seven times sealed. Never shall I forget that smoke. Never shall I forget the little faces of the children, whose bodies I saw turned into wreaths of smoke beneath the silent blue sky.

Pious Jews always dreamed of a time when "wickedness" would "vanish like smoke."[1] Now a wickedness never dreamed of snatched their symbol, turned it into a weapon of terrifying literalness and used it to murder their little ones and their prayers. Hence Elie Wiesel continues the above passage—there is none greater or more relentless in his writings—with these words:

> Never shall I forget those flames which consumed my faith forever.[2]

How can a Jew say anything religious thereafter?[3]

The religious Word may be in flight from the world into the soul within or to heaven above, or even from this world altogether into a world-to-come; a Jew, however, even when he is sorely tempted, cannot flee from the world, for he belongs to a flesh-and-blood people—*a people with children*. Again, the Word may despair of the world and yet stay with it; but then surely the despair is of God as well, and the Word is no longer religious. The religious Word, then, seems no longer possible within Jewish existence. Yet, prior to Buchenwald, some Jews

Reprinted, with changes, from *The Jewish Return into History* (New York: Schocken Books, 1978), 261–72, by permission of the publisher.

have always found it possible to hold fast to God, hold fast to the world, and affirm a bond between them with their lips and, indeed, with their very lives. The most authentic Word expressing this bond is Midrash, and a life witnessing to it may be called midrashic existence.

To affirm a bond between God and the world is always problematical. Midrash, however, is aware of this fact. Radically considered, a bond between a God who is truly God and a world which is truly world may well be considered as not merely problematical but nothing short of paradoxical. On its part, however, Midrash does not shrink from paradox, but confronts it and yet in the very act of confrontation reaffirms the bond.

This stance requires closer inspection. Philosophical reflection may find it necessary to choose between a God who is divine only if he is omnibenevolent and omnipotent, and a world which is truly world only because it contains elements contradicting these divine attributes, namely, evil and human freedom. Midrash recognizes the tension yet refuses to choose. Thus when the Israelites do God's will they, as it were, strengthen his power, and when they fail to do his will they, as it were, weaken it. Thus, too, redemption will come when men have become good enough to make the Messiah's coming possible, or wicked enough to make it necessary. It would be wayward to regard such Midrashim as insufficiently demythologized fragments of "philosophizing," the first groping for a "finite God-concept" which would at one blow "solve" the "problems" of evil and freedom, the second struggling with two conflicting "views of history," the one "progressive," the other "catastrophic." Midrash cannot embrace a "progressive view" of history, for this would dispense with the need for the acting of God; nor a "catastrophic view," for this would destroy the significance of the acting of man. Nor can Midrash accept a "finite God concept" but must rather sweep aside all God-concepts so as to confront God himself—a God absolute yet "as it were" (k'b'yachol) finite in the mutual confrontation. The term k'b'yachol alone—a full-blown technical term in midrashic thought—suffices to show that Midrash does not "grope" for "concepts" in order to "solve problems" and dissolve paradox. The midrashic Word is story. It *remains* story because it both points to and articulates a life *lived with* problems and paradox—the problems and paradox of a divine-human relation. This life is midrashic existence.

Midrashic existence acts as though all depended on man and prays as though all depended on God. It considers itself worth nothing so that it can only wait for redemption; and worth everything so that a single pure deed or prayer may have redemptive power. It holds all these aspects together because it knows itself to stand in a mutual, covenantal relation—mutual even though the partners are radically unequal, for the one is man and the other is God. Climactically, midrashic existence endures the strain between these extremes without palliatives or relief. It cannot seek refuge from the real in a "spiritual" world, for it is the existence, not of souls, monks, sectarian individuals, but rather of a flesh-and-blood people—*a people with children.* Thus it is not surprising that during the trimillennial history of the Jewish people individuals and whole groups should always have failed to endure this tension. The truly astounding fact is much rather that endurance of the tension has been continuous; that prior to the Holocaust it has never been broken.[4]

Does this endurance extend over Planet Auschwitz? One cannot answer this question lightly. For one dare not ignore or belittle the fact that countless and nameless Jews persisted even then in acting as though all depended on them, and in praying as though all depended on God—all this as if nothing had changed. Nor dare we ignore the fact that everything *had* changed. The Midrash sees Israel, as it were, augment or diminish God's power. Elie Wiesel's most famous Midrash sees God hang on the gallows of a dying child,[5] despite prayers of saints meant to augment his power and because of acts of criminals meant to destroy it. The Midrash sees the Messiah come when men are either wholly righteous or wholly wicked. On Planet Auschwitz the Messiah failed to come even though both conditions were fulfilled. The "judges," "law-enforcers," and "ordinary employees" were wholly wicked, for the anti-world which they ruled, administered, and ran was wholly wicked. The "punished criminals" were wholly righteous for, as a statement wrongly attributed to Maimonides rightly says, a Jew murdered for no reason other than his Jewishness must be viewed as if he were a saint.[6] Hence the protagonist of *The Gates of the Forest* asserts that it is too late for the coming of the Messiah—that a Messiah who can come, but at Auschwitz did not come, has lost his meaning.[7]

Midrash is meant for every kind of imperfect world. It was not meant for Planet Auschwitz, the anti-world.

Mad Midrash

What then makes Elie Wiesel's work possible? No matter what its content—Israel, Russian Jews, Hasidism, the Bible—the Holocaust is always part of the hidden agenda. And no matter what its form—eyewitness reports, essays, a cantata, a play, to say nothing of the novels—it always has recognizable midrashic elements. The first is not accidental, for Wiesel cannot relate himself to *any* Jewish reality before and indeed after the Holocaust as though the dread event had not happened. The second is not accidental, for Wiesel cannot respond to the event by rejecting or fleeing from Jewish past and future—both informed by the hallowed tradition—but only by affirming both, and the most authentic and unmistakable verbal expression of this affirmation is Midrash. Indeed, precisely this togetherness of a relentless self-exposure to the Holocaust and a Jewishness steeped in tradition has given Wiesel the stature of a teacher. Yet the question "what makes his work possible?" is necessary, for it is just this togetherness that seems impossible.

This impossible togetherness produces the unprecedented phenomenon of mad Midrash. Moshe the mad *Shammash* appears on the very first page of *Night*, and no matter what guises he assumes in subsequent works he never disappears. At times he is only behind the scene. At other times his presence is manifest even though he is not the speaker. (Thus, the God who hangs on the gallows of the dying boy may seem close and assimilable to the Christ. But there is no suggestion of the death of God let alone of his resurrection: this God is part not of the Christian message but of a mad Jewish Midrash. Again, the outburst, "It is too late for the coming of the Messiah!" may seem close and assimilable to a tragic humanism. It becomes a mad Midrash through the sequel "precisely for this reason we are commanded to hope.")[8] The madness of mad Moshe is most unmistakable when he speaks with his own voice. This he does when he enters a small synagogue in Nazi-occupied Europe, listens for a while to the worshipers, and warns them not to pray so loud lest God hear them; lest He notice that some Jews are still alive in Nazi Europe.[9]

What is this madness?

Not insanity, if "insanity" is "flight from reality." It is just because it dare not flee from *its* reality that this Midrash is mad. This madness is obliged—condemned?—to be sane.

Not "irrationality," if this is ignorance or lack of discernment. There is, to be sure, a rationality of a lesser sort which one displays by discerning the ways of one's world, by going about in it, going along with it. But just a rationality of this sort shows its own ultimate irrationality when it goes along a road descending into hell and beyond. After all is over, such a rationality can only plead that it "did not know." Midrashic madness, in contrast, *knows*, in some cases has known all along. Its discernment is informed by a Truth transcending the world of which it is a victim. Irrational by the standards of lesser rationalities, its rationality is ultimate.

Midrashic madness, third, is not mysticism, if "mysticism" is a rise to a divine ecstasy in which innocence and guilt, joy and anguish, good and evil are all indiscriminately transcended. Midrash must hold fast to the world; mad Midrash cannot but hold fast to *its* world, the anti-world.

How then can it retain this stance and *remain* Midrash, that is, hold fast to God as well as its world? Only by dint of an absolute protest against the anti-world and its God—as it were, an anti-God over against mad Moshe, a God mad with him, or a God torn between these extremes. This protest is serious only if it turns into a determination to *restore* the world. To be sure, the world-to-be-restored will be, as it always has been, an imperfect world. But although tarnished by a thousand blemishes it is neither part of nor heir to the anti-world. On the contrary, the attempt to restore it strikes at the very core of the anti-world, thus aiming at its absolute overthrow. Thus, the mad midrashic Word turns into a *Kaddish* for all the victims of the anti-world, "that solemn affirmation full of grandeur and serenity, by which man returns to God His crown and sceptre."[10]

Mad Midrash and Post-Holocaust Jewish Praxis

Midrashic madness is not insanity, not irrationality, not a flight from the world into mysticism. These negations must forever be reenacted if midrashic madness is to preserve its integrity. Still a fourth negation is necessary, however, but this is in a class by itself. The negations made hitherto oppose threats and temptations from without. The negation to be made now opposes a threat arising from within the sphere of midrashic madness itself. This threat is its last temptation.

The midrashic Word was seen to point to, and be the linguistic expression of, midrashic existence. For this relation between Word and existence, however, midrashic madness can have no counterpart. Midrashic existence is lived in and with an imperfect (albeit ever perfectible) world. The existence to which mad Midrash points, the anti-world, cannot be lived in and with but only opposed. To be sure, as we have seen, this opposition is already built into midrashic madness itself. Yet, no longer having an existential counterpart, the Word is tempted to withdraw into inwardness, expand this inwardness into a self-contained quasi-existence, and thus descend from literature into aestheticizing.[11] Already theo-political in its own right, mad Midrash must overcome this last temptation by pointing beyond the theological Word to a praxis whose politics forever questions all theology even as it remains itself theologically questioned. Thus, a clear road leads from *Night* to the *Jews of Silence*—a road understood only if its ultimate goal is not characters divorced from all else in a book but also a people outside and beyond the book: a people which (in no small measure thanks to *this* book) has ceased to be silent. A road too—though this one not so clear—leads from the final *Kaddish* for Leib the Lion in *The Gates of the Forest* to the final argument with Gad the Israeli officer in *A Beggar in Jerusalem*. Leib has fought against, but been killed by, the Holocaust Kingdom when it murdered his people. Gad is killed only after having helped save the state which is the heir of the murdered people. The *Kaddish* for Leib can do no more than restore to God a crown and scepter which have little power and majesty so long as the world remains unrestored. Gad helps restore the world—or at any rate, what after the anti-world has become its indispensable center—when he helps save the Jewish state, the heir of the annihilated Jews, from being itself annihilated.

This act on Gad's part is preceded by an argument with the protagonist. This latter knows (to paraphrase his words) that the world has not changed, that they would let it happen again, that Jews are still expendable and that, what with superiority of arms and men on the side of an implacable enemy, to expect victory—or, which is the same thing, survival—is irrational. (Although, as we have said at the very outset, the existence of the Jewish state, after what has happened, is sacred, it is not, to put it mildly, secure.) Gad in no way challenges these facts. Yet he affirms that "the national funeral" of the Jewish state "will not take place. Not now, not ever." He admits the protagonist's murmured protest that a faith such as this borders on madness yet insists that not madness but only death is to be feared and, indeed, that death can be driven away, some wars be won, by invoking madness.[12]

Gad wins this argument even though, as an individual, he is killed in the war "shortly thereafter." For midrashic madness points to *an existence in which the madness is transfigured*. Midrashic madness is the Word spoken in the anti-world which ought not to be but is. The existence it points to acts to restore a world which ought to be but is not, committed to the faith that what ought to be must and will be, and this is *its* madness. After Planet Auschwitz, there can be no health without *this* madness, no joy, no life. Without this madness a Jew cannot do—with God or without him—what a Voice from Sinai bids him do: choose life.

Epilogue

Almost a century ago Friedrich Nietzsche—not the wisest of Germans, but the one best equipped to understand madness—let a madman appear on the scene, crying that God is dead, that God stays dead, that men are his murderers, but that despite this fact the deed has not yet come to their ears.[13] Somewhat later he let Zarathustra—a sage beyond madness—prognosticate two possibilities. The one hoped for—his "last will"—was:

Dead are all gods . . ., now let the superman live.[14] The dreaded possibility was the "last man":

> Alas, the time is coming when man will no longer give birth to a star. Alas, the time of the most despicable man is coming who can no longer despise himself. . . . A little

poison now and then: it makes for pleasant dreams. And much poison in the end, for it makes for a pleasant death. . . . One still works, for work entertains. But one takes care lest the pastime cause fatigue . . .

No shepherd and one flock. Each wants the same, is the same. He who feels differently enters the madhouse of his own accord.[15]

But Nietzsche's wisdom was not wise enough. A century after, the Nietzschean madness—mad because God is dead—is joined by a madness that is mad because he is alive.[16] And both are joined (surpassed?) by a new maturity which, amusedly or wearily but in either case condescendingly, dismisses the whole question.

This new maturity fancies itself as representing Nietzsche's prophesied superman. Yet in fact the notion of a superman fit to take the place vacated by God has become a sad joke. For Planet Auschwitz murdered, along with men, women, and children, the idea of Man itself. And from Gulag and all the other heirs of Auschwitz resounds the daily cry: "Man is dead. Man stays dead!"

Thus of Nietzsche's three prognostications only the third has been borne out, and even this fails us in the end. It is not hard to recognize Nietzsche's "last man" in features of contemporary life, among them gray uniformity, computerized pleasure, an inability to create and an unwillingness to sacrifice. But behind such characteristics of decadence lurk far more ominous dangers. There is callous indifference to murder abroad and on the streets at home. There is an infatuation with death and perversity. And pleasure seeks escape from boredom, not just (as Nietzsche naively imagined) in a poison making sweet dreams but in quite a different poison which produces an ever-accelerating search for ever-new depravities. The specter of the Holocaust is quite unmistakably behind these phenomena. And it was only to be expected that sooner or later someone would make Auschwitz into a joke.[17]

In the beginning was the universe, and with it came man, the animal capable of laughter. He laughed at small incongruities—a man slipping on a banana skin—but stopped laughing when the incongruity became large—if the man broke his neck. Then came the Holocaust universe, and with it the S.S. man. He laughed only at large incongruities—the smashing of a non-Aryan baby's skull. Now the post-Holocaust universe has arrived, and it has produced a species of post-Holocaust man, Aryan and non-Aryan alike, who laughs at all the incongruities once considered large—the crimes of the murderers, the anguish of the victims, and above all his own previous "unliberated" inability to laugh at either.[18] Man becomes human through his capacity to laugh. With *this* laughter his self-destruction is complete.

Or so it would be if the new maturity had really heard what it laughs at. However, though it wearily fancies itself as having heard everything it has as yet understood nothing. The deed is done, but it has not yet come to men's ears. If a few feel differently, it is because their ears have heard, if indeed they are not survivors who have seen with their own eyes. These few will *not* enter the madhouse of their own accord. Never! They *must* not enter the madhouse. The post-Holocaust universe is in need of them. It needs them if man is to become, not a superman replacing God, or a "last man" replacing man. It needs them if he is to become, after what has happened, once again human.

Yes, it *is* necessary for us who are not survivors to become heirs of their witness in this world and beyond.

Notes

1. Consider the following prayer in the traditional High Holiday service: "May the righteous see and rejoice, the upright exult, and the godly thrill with delight. Iniquity shall shut its mouth, wickedness shall vanish like smoke, when Thou wilt abolish the rule of tyranny on earth."

2. Elie Wiesel, *Night* (New York: Avon, 1972), p. 44.

3. This question will dominate the remainder of this essay. Except for the Epilogue, the essay does not consider possibilities which may exist outside Jewish existence or, within Jewish existence, for religious Jews who never committed themselves to words such as those just quoted, or for those who, having done so, remained silent thereafter, or for those who exist outside the sphere of Jewish religiosity.

4. The above view of Midrash is summarized in a rather doctrinaire fashion because I have stated and defended it in many places over the years; see my *Quest for Past and Future* (Bloomington: Indiana University Press, 1968; Boston: Beacon, 1970), *passim*, and especially *God's Presence in History* (New York: New York University Press, 1970; New York: Harper Torchbook, 1973), chap. 1.

5. Wiesel, *Night*, pp. 75 ff.

6. The above two judgments are made with a view to guilt and innocence in the context of social structures. The issue "individual vs. collective guilt (or innocence)" becomes spurious and indeed evasive when it is abused to ignore these structures and their moral implications.

7. Elie Wiesel, *The Gates of the Forest* (New York: Holt, Rinehart & Winston, 1966), p. 225.

8. Ibid.

9. See my *God's Presence in History*, chap. 3.

10. Wiesel, *The Gates of the Forest*, p. 225.

11. Perhaps the foremost aim of Kierkegaard's literary production is to wrestle with this last temptation. Still more instructive is Hegel's critique (in his *Phenomenology*), of the "beautiful soul's" withdrawal into inwardness, for in Hegel's account it is unambiguous that the withdrawal is from political action, and that its unadmitted purpose is to avoid the necessity of dirtying its hands.

12. Elie Wiesel, *A Beggar in Jerusalem* (New York: Random House, 1970), pp. 61 ff.

13. *The Gay Science*, # 125.

14. *Zarathustra*, end of pt. I. While significantly the earlier passage speaks of the death of God, the present one asserts the death of "all gods." Hegel—who preceded Nietzsche in both assertions—let the death of all gods happen in the Roman pantheon, with the consequence that the event did not encompass God, while asserting the death of God within the Christian realm, where it was followed by a resurrection. Hegel was unable to place Jewish existence within either of these contexts.

15. *Zarathustra*, pt. I, sec. 5

16. See my *God's Presence in History*, chap. 3. The reader who wonders why this writer's second set of reflections on the work of Elie Wiesel, like his first, implicates thoughts by Nietzsche may be assured that this is not accidental. In both cases there is a shared anguish—in the first, concerning the fate of God, in the second, concerning the fate of man. And in both cases there is a need to confront Nietzsche's post-Protestant view of the anguish with a Jewish view—a need which after the Holocaust brooks no compromise.

17. See Konrad Kellen, "Seven Beauties: Auschwitz—The Ultimate Joke?" *Midstream*, October 1976, pp. 59–66. This brilliant essay is a review not only of Lina Wertmüller's movie *Seven Beauties*, but also of the reception it has received by the critics. Kellen writes: "Wertmüller uses the agony of Auschwitz not just as backdrop for some depraved and ridiculous sexual fantasy, but as a joke. This is something new, surpassing in intellectual and moral depravity all that "entertainers" have done so far. Even the Nazis did not treat the extermination camps as a joke. On visiting Auschwitz, Heinrich Himmler, inhuman though he was, became ill; but not Wertmüller or her giggling, guffawing audiences throughout the Western civilized world." (p. 59)

18. Kellen's article gives numerous examples of critics, Jewish as well as non-Jewish, who found (or pretended to have found) the Wertmüller Auschwitz-as-fun "liberating." Why liberating? Because, Kellen replies, the people in question never rejected Nazism viscerally, as a "blemish on the entire human race." One need hardly add that this answer only begins a much-needed enquiry into this kind of "liberation."

35 Teshuva *Today*

1. The Problematics of *Teshuva* in Our Time

The explorations of this work may all be said to have concerned a single theme—*Teshuva* for the Jewish people in our time. We first came upon that theme with Franz Rosenzweig, the Jew who became a *Ba'al Teshuva* virtually at the portals of the Christian Church—and the greatest Jewish thinker since Spinoza.[1] The theme appeared next with Spinoza himself, the first great modern Jewish man-in-general who would be required today by his own principles to return, not to be sure to the old Jewish God, but to his old-new people in their old-new land.[2] The theme appeared again with Hegelianism, the modern way of thought that preserves and supersedes rather than rejects or abandons the past, and that therefore may seem least in need of any turning or returning; and that yet in our time must repent of its Constantinianism, nowhere more clearly so than vis-à-vis Jews and Judaism.[3] From these forms of *Teshuva*, all at best peripheral to Jewish history (but not to modernity), we were finally led to its Jewish core, and this, appropriately enough, not until our own thought was self-immersed in history.[4] Yet just this self-immersion helped disclose also most fully the problematics of *Teshuva* in our time. Even in other times *Teshuva* was problematic whenever catastrophe produced (or seemed to produce) a rupture in history, so that *Teshuva* had to assume the form of *Tikkun* if the rupture was to be mended. The problematics have become radical, inescapable in our time, with a rupture so complete that any *Tikkun* can at best be only fragmentary. Hence our climactic question remains yet to be asked: *Can* Teshuva *after the Holocaust be the same as before? Is it possible at all?*

Teshuva is at the core of all Jewish existence. Enemies (and sometimes also du-

Reprinted, with changes, from *To Mend the World* (New York: Schocken Books, 1982), 317–31, by permission of the publisher.

337

bious friends) have invented and perpetuated the myth of the Jew as Ahasverus, that ancient restless wanderer who only seeks—but cannot find—a peaceful death. If the real Jewish people, while often without peace, were rarely without vibrant life, it is because of the ever-renewing, ever-rejuvenating power of *Teshuva*. A castigating Jeremiah conjures up the affection of Israel's youth, when she followed after God in the wilderness, a land not sown (Jer. 2:2)—a useless exercise unless youthfulness can be recovered. Lamentations—according to tradition, the work of the same prophet—confronts radical catastrophe with *Teshuva:* it is the sole alternative to despair. And just this vision of the "old-new," as found in its ancient-religious context, inspired Theodor Herzl, in his modern-secular context, when he conceived of a return of the old-new people to its old-new land. (Even so, his vision was not visionary enough. The old language he considered dead is renewed.)[5]

Yet *Teshuva*, occurring in history, was also always threatened *by* history, never more so than when pagan experience seemed to be the simple truth—when the past seemed lost beyond recovery. Is not Jeremiah's vision of the desert one of a past that never was? Is not the culminating cry of Lamentations—"Turn us, O Lord, unto Thee, and we shall be turned; renew our days as of old" (5:21)—either a fruitless hankering after a dead past, or else a present reconstruction of the past in the present's own image? As for Herzl's project, is it not either an anachronistic, romantic attempt to revive the old, or else a modern nationalism that, like others, puts a mythical past to present uses? Doubts such as these have existed at all times. They have increased in modern, more historically-conscious times. And they can be stilled only if *Teshuva*, though ever-situated in history, is at the same time endowed with a transcendent dimension. Hence, the quest for *Teshuva* in our time must be so expanded as to include transcendence for our time.

The preceding explorations have furthered this latter quest—and come to a halt. In Rosenzweig and Spinoza we came upon two antithetical commitments to transcendence—both no less than to eternity—but found both ruptured in our time: the one because the eternal people, witness to the eternal Truth, have barely survived; the other because a radical evil then impossible—"contrary to human nature"—has become actual. Thus our first exploration reached an impasse.

A coming to a halt occurred also in our second exploration. In a post-Hegelian encounter with Hegel we came upon a variety of commitments to transcendence (whether or not to eternity),[6] and were left in a state of dialogical openness, in point of fact to some of these commitments, potentially to them all. However, this openness too was ruptured—by a world of radical evil that (being radical) has a transcendent dimension of its own, and that yet (being evil) demands not dialogical openness but, on the contrary, an opposition uncomprising and complete.

In these two explorations, a commitment to transcendence was not in principle called into question. As we proceeded from these two to the third exploration, we saw no reason for dwelling on an external-reductionist kind of criticism that in the last analysis presupposes what it claims to prove.[7] But we did see every reason for exploring an internal criticism, i.e., a stance that takes with total, non-reductionist seriousness the traditional commitment to transcendence; that takes with total, non-escapist seriousness man's historically situated finitude; and that brings these two commitments of its own to bear on each other. In pursuit of such a criticism we made two crucial discoveries. First, the thinking most rigorously self-exposed to history, the Heideggerian, is in principle unable to confront *that* history—the Holocaust. Second, in our second attempt to confront it we came not only upon a rupture of history but also a *Tikkun* of it. That *Tikkun*, like every previous case of *Tikkun*, is a form of *Teshuva* in response to extremity. However—this is crucial—it differs from every previous case in that it is in principle fragmentary. The Holocaust is a *caesura*, not only for the historian, the poet, the philosopher. It is a *caesura* also for the Jewish faith. Hence we must redefine our quest for *Teshuva* yet again, to read as follows: What is the fate of eternity in our time?

2. Rosenzweig after Heidegger

With this paradoxical question we resume a theme long suspended but not forgotten. Franz Rosenzweig's "new thinking" is situated in history, yet reaches eternity—a "Jewish vigil of the Day of Redemption." Hence we tested it through another "new thinking"—the Heideggerian. (This latter, *remaining* as it does situated in historical finitude, recognizes a Jewish vigil of the Day of Redemption as little as it does the Christian's "Rebirth" or the philosopher's "Platonic Sun.")[8] As it has turned out, however, in this process the testing philosophy was being tested as well, and the overall result is ironical. Rosenzweig died prior to the advent of the Nazi regime; Heidegger survived it long enough to have all the leisure necessary to ponder it. Rosenzweig's thought, though situated in history, rises above it, and hence also above the evil that is part of it; Heidegger's thought in both its earlier and later periods remains in history, unable to rise above it. *Yet it is Heidegger's thought that cannot confront the Holocaust; and it is Rosenzweig's thought that—had the thinker lived long enough—would have found a confrontation with the* Ereignis *inescapable.*

The confrontation would have been necessary because of Rosenzweig's "absolute empiricism." The *Star of Redemption* requires empirical confirmation at many points, the crucial ones being the apex of Judaism (its highest experience) and the matrix of Judaism (the existence of Jews). As Rosenzweig sees it, the passage of time has done nothing to shake either apex or matrix. However, had he lived through the passage of *our* time, he would have seen both "confirmations" shaken.

Our quest seeks eternity in our time. Rosenzweig's own quest finds, in the Yom Kippur, an eternity-in-*any*-time, for in the highest Jewish experience a "love strong as death" breaks the "scythe of the grim reaper," carries the worshipper "beyond the grave while still alive," and thus reveals an "absolute transcendence" for all humanity.[9] We shall not, at this late stage, subject this teaching to a reductionist criticism. (To do so would be incongruous, out of keeping with the most basic commitments of this whole work and, indeed, would retroactively destroy its significance.) What we must and shall do is ask whether Rosenzweig's eternity-in-time is accessible in *our* time. That Eternity, being in time, requires a witness, and this latter cannot testify without an eternity of his own. The witness—the Jewish people—exists in time, but rises above it in his highest experience, the apex of Judaism. If it *can* so rise—if the apex of Judaism is possible—it is because the matrix of Judaism—the existence of the Jewish people—is taken for granted. A contracting logic may decimate the Jewish people through pogroms, apostasies, and other ravages of Jewish history. But that even a remnant should be destroyed—it is a holy remnant—is, or very nearly is—impossible.

But the nearly impossible has in our time become almost actual. The holy remnant has become an accidental remnant, and the question is whether this threat to the matrix of Judaism can leave its apex unaffected. For a last time therefore our quest must be redefined. We first inquired about *Teshuva* in our time. This led to a quest for transcendence, and this latter in turn to a quest for the fate of eternity in our time. For Jewish thought after the Holocaust, these questions all find their focus and concentration in a single one on which the future of Judaism depends. *After the Holocaust, can the Yom Kippur be what it was before? Is it still possible at all?*

3. Yom Kippur after the Holocaust

Once at Auschwitz a group of girls on forced labor decided, so far as possible, to observe Yom Kippur. Prayer, of course, was out of the question; but fasting, they thought, was not. So they applied to their SS supervisor for permission to fast, and for a lighter work load for that day for which, they hastened to assure her, they would compensate on other days. Furious, the woman denied both requests, imposed overtime work in honor of the holiday, and threatened that anyone lagging in work on account of the fast would be sent to the crematorium without delay. Undeterred, the girls worked and fasted through the long day, exhilarated by the thought of Jews the world over sharing in it. When the day was done, they tasted their piece of black bread, and their "satisfaction was full." Yet this "story" of their "victory" ended with a "bitter disappointment." They had miscalculated. They had fasted on the wrong day.[10]

Was a love strong as death *not* present on that day? Were these girls *not* beyond the grave while still alive? Did an absolute transcendence *not* become real in the midst of that time and on behalf of all humanity? Heaven forbid that we should say any such thing! If the prayer that was in that fast was not heard, then no prayer on any Yom Kippur ever was heard, or could be heard. If this human love had no response in a divine love, then every Good News about divine love anywhere is a sham and a mockery. In this book we have made no attempt to demonstrate the commitment to transcendence, whether within Judaism or without it. (Only the "old" philosophical "thinking" seeks proofs, while its theological counterpart seeks infallible authorities.) At the same time, we have found not a single reason—philosophical, religious, moral, to say nothing of reasons psychological or sociological—for rejecting that commitment. *We see no reason now.*

But Yom Kippur *after* Auschwitz cannot be what *at* Auschwitz it still was. *Their* Yom Kippur necessitates a change in *our own.* This is a change to be approached cautiously and with care, for much—to the religious Jew all—is at stake in it. We must therefore search, so far as possible, for a precedent.

When the Syrians attacked on the Sabbath, the Maccabees were faced with a dilemma. They could defend themselves: but then they, the defenders of the Torah, would themselves violate it. Or they could let themselves be slain, but in so doing would not defend the Torah: a Judaism without Jews is impossible. The dilemma was insoluble.

But it was also unacceptable. And since the Torah—its Giver is divine—has infinite resources, the dilemma must, after all, be capable of a solution. To "violate" the Torah in order to protect it was not a violation but rather an interpretation. And since the Torah, the Word of God, could not be interpreted by the mere word of man, the interpretation itself could not be merely-human. Thus, in due course, there emerged, alongside the "written Torah," the "oral Torah" of rabbinic Judaism. In this manner the Sabbath was changed, and saved in being changed. In this manner a new page was opened in Maccabean times, in the history not only of Jews but also of Judaism.[11]

This is our precedent. But it helps us only up to a point. The Sabbath-attacks of the Syrians had a pragmatic purpose—to catch the Jews defenseless. No such purpose was in the Nazi mind when—a favorite practice—deportations and selections were conducted on the holy days of Judaism. (The Jews were defenseless on those days. But they were also defenseless on all other days.) The true Nazi purpose was expressed best by Dr. Josef Mengele. It was the Auschwitz doctor's task to separate those to be murdered at once from those to be made to work now and murdered at a future date. Dr. Mengele was fond of performing his task on Yom Kippur. He was familiar with enough Jewish theology to know that on Yom Kippur God judges who will live and who will die. To cite his own boast, it would be he, Dr. Josef Mengele and not God, that would judge what Jews were to live and what to die.

Dr. Mengele was no mere new Antiochus or Titus or even Hadrian. The Syrians sought no more than the destruction of the Jewish state. The same is true of the Romans under Titus. Even Hadrian attacked Judaism only because it seemed—and was—a political threat. This was until Hadrian. But after Hadrian Judaism ceased to be a political threat. A *Galut* Judaism arose that relied only on God; that expected from the world only Jewish survival; and that, persisting in the first and obtaining the second, culminated in the Yom Kippur experience. It was this Judaism that, along with the Jewish people, such as Dr. Mengele sought to exterminate.

Whether or not Dr. Mengele's Yom Kippur selections destroyed *their* Yom Kippur is a question that resurrects the deepest, most painful tensions that have beset our post-Holocaust Jewish thought. (We cannot forget the girls at Auschwitz who observed Yom Kippur. And we equally cannot forget those victims, innocent all, for whom Nazi terror destroyed it.)[12] The result is that *their* Yom Kippur must *alter ours.* For we cannot resort to the "cowardly and disconsolate talk" that it happened only once, that it is improbable or impossible for it to recur, and that in any case the Yom Kippur's transcendence-of-time dissolves into irrelevance *that* time. An *absolute* transcendence of time is not attainable in *our* time. *For to return the throne of judgment usurped by Dr. Mengele back to God has become a Jewish necessity, and the necessity does not exist beside the Yom Kippur experience but is part of it.*[13] And since this returning would be an impotent gesture without a Jewish state, we are forced to conclude that *if in our time there were no State of Israel, it would be religious necessity, with or without the help of God, to create it. Without such a state, the end of* Galut *Judaism would also be the end of Judaism.* Our generation has opened—has been required to open—a new page in the history, not only of Jews but also of Judaism.

This opening of a new page in the history of Judaism found a deeply symbolic expression on the first day of the Yom Kippur War. The surprise attack forced Israeli soldiers to rush helter-skelter from streets, homes, synagogues, to trucks, cars, any vehicle at all that would take them speedily to their units. It was then and there that some old men somewhere in Jerusalem interrupted their prayers, rushed into the streets and tore out pages from their prayer books in order to give them to the departing soldiers. These pious men did not hesitate to mutilate their holy books. On their part, religious and secularist soldiers alike did not hesitate to accept the gift. On that Yom Kippur, some fought so that others could pray; and some prayed so that others could fight. Both statements are true. But only both together, on *that* Yom Kippur, expressed the full truth. The full truth, however, includes secular Jews. Hence we must ask: What can Yom Kippur be for secularist Jews?

4. The Message of Beit Ha-Tefutsot

In Tel Aviv there is a museum that does not have its like anywhere. Beit Ha-Tefutsot, "the House of the Diaspora," houses no rare, expensive relics but is content with mere replicas. It is intended not for the delight of the connoisseur or the advancement of the scholar but rather for the instruction of a whole people—one that needs the instruction if it is to survive. The museum tells the story of this people in its own land but—so its very name indicates—says far more about its story in other lands. And the lands are so many and so far apart that the Ingathering, when at last it occurred, was from all four corners of the earth. At one time in its history, Zionist thought simply rejected all the stories in all these lands. The mere existence of a "House of the Diaspora" in an Israeli museum proves that Zionist thought in our time seeks to take up the old into the new. To do so, however, is to take up old diversities, and among these none is either more ultimate or more significant than that between religious and secular. Because of its ultimacy, the diversity between these extremes forever threatens to become an out-and-out conflict. Because of its significance, nothing is more essential than a mediation of just that conflict. On such a mediation a Jewish future—the page of history already opened—depends.

Beit Ha-Tefutsot contains a section devoted to the liturgical life of the Jewish people, and, in keeping with the whole spirit of the museum, this section cannot avoid making a commitment. One walks down a hall and sees depicted, on one side, the chief festivals of the Jewish *Heilsgeschichte*—Pesach, Shavuot, and Succot. On the other side are the "Days of Martyrdom and Resistance," among them Purim, Hanukkah, and the ninth of Av—but also *Yom Ha-Shoah* and *Yom Ha-Atzmaut.*

The commitment that is in this portrayal alters Jewish tradition in two respects. First, it raises to a level of equality "secular" Jewish festivals that tradition had made into "minor" ones, and moreover, made over into religious ones: thus it addresses itself to the *whole* Jewish people. Second, in including *Yom Ha-Shoah* and *Yom Ha-Atzmaut* it carries Jewish liturgical life forward into present reality. As a result of these two changes, the visitor has in mind two questions as he walks down the hall, toward the place assigned to the Yom Kippur. Can the whole Jewish people share in the Yom Kippur? And can the Yom Kippur itself fail to be overwhelmed by *Yom Ha-Shoah?* As he reaches the place he finds this Talmudic quotation:

> The gates of prayer are sometimes closed.
> But the gates of *Teshuva* are always open.[14]

Thus, in our search for the meaning of *Teshuva* for the Jewish people in our time, we have come full circle.

5. The Sharing of *Teshuva* after the Holocaust

We have not returned, however, without lessons learned on the way, so that our original question may now be further specified as follows. How are the gates of *Teshuva* open on Yom Kippur today? What is a *Teshuva* shared by the whole people, despite the differences that divide them? And can, perhaps, the walking through these open gates help reopen those other gates—the gates of prayer that are closed?

These questions, of course, are all concerned with God, the ultimate (if largely hidden) Subject of all our preceding explorations. The subject was not hidden without good cause. Ever since, in the modern world, the shibboleth of revelation has divided Jews into religious and secularist, theology, the beginning with God, has served to widen rather than narrow the fateful gap. Ever since the Holocaust, it divides religious Jews as well. (Martin Buber—no theologian—has raised the question of whether today a Jew can still speak to God. Theologians are apt to answer the question, or at any rate to supply new, divisive "concepts of God" that are to make it answerable.)[15] A deep and much-quoted saying in the Zohar asserts as valid for all times, that God, Torah, and Israel are at one.[16] Perhaps, in ancient times, when the Jewish people were alone against idolatry, the true and all-uniting beginning was with God. In our time, this beginning deepens the divisions *within* Israel, and hence also those *between* Israel, Torah, and God.

A Halakhic beginning with "Torah" is no more promising. It is true that a commitment to a shared Jewish future involves a recovery of the Jewish past, and hence of Torah. However, a beginning with Torah—in place of a recovery of it—rules out from the start possibilities of sharing, for to the religious Jew, Torah is the Word of God, and to his secular brother, the word of man. Perhaps in medieval times, when the Jewish people in exile were tempted to apostasy by Islam and Christianity, they were a people only by virtue of the Torah.[17] In our time, this beginning, too, widens divisions within Israel, and hence also between Israel, Torah, and God.

We are therefore at length led to the third term in the mystical triad of the Zohar—a beginning with Israel. How can the *whole* Jewish people share in *Teshuva* on Yom Kippur in our time? The religious Jew, now as always, spends the day in the synagogue, praying and reading the Torah. The secular Jew, whether inside or outside the synagogue,[18] can at any rate read the Torah—the Book of the *whole* Jewish people. It is true that the two ways of reading are not one shared activity. Indeed, if each is performed within a self-enclosed world—the one, a system of religious certainties, the other, a system of anti-religious ones—the two ways of reading may exacerbate the potential for conflict. However, what may in our time break through all systems of certainties is an *overwhelming— and shared—astonishment.*

It is an age-old truth that just as Israel has kept the Torah so the Torah has kept

Israel. This old truth has become manifest in our time in a new form. The Torah itself asks whether this ever happened, that God took one nation from the midst of another (Deut. 4:34). In our time we must ask whether this ever happened that, after two millennia, a people was returned to its language, its state, its land. *Without a Book—this Book—this return could not possibly have taken place.* This is the shared astonishment behind all religio-secular diversities. This is the shared experience that makes possible a bond between all Israel and Torah. These are the gates of *Teshuva* open to the whole Jewish people today.

If gates of *Teshuva* are open for *every* Jew, are gates of prayer open for *any* Jew? In the *Mahzor*, the High Holy Day Prayer Book, we read:

> Now, Lord our God, put Thy awe upon all whom Thou has made, Thy dread upon all whom Thou hast created. Let Thy works revere Thee, let all Thy creatures worship Thee. May they all blend into one brotherhood to do Thy will with a perfect heart. For we know, our God, that Thine is the dominion, power and might. Thou are revered above all Thou hast created.[19]

Never was this prayer as necessary as after a world in which the power was Dr. Mengele's—and never as inaccessible. It is necessary because the prayed-for Messiah is necessary. It is inaccessible because a Messiah that can come yet at Auschwitz did not come, is himself inaccessible.[20]

The worshiper that reads on comes upon *Ele Ezkera*—a martyrology. With Bar Kochba defeated, Hadrian forbade the practice of Judaism on pain of death. Ten rabbis defied the edict, were caught, and tortured to death by Roman soldiers. Then the angels in heaven cried, "Is this the Torah, and this its reward?" And a voice from heaven replied: "If I hear another word, I will turn the world into water!" The voice went on: "This is My decree: accept it, all you who love the Torah!"[21]

The Jew at prayer today reads these words. And considering that Rabbi Akiba, Rabbi Ishmael and others had all chosen to be martyrs, had died as martyrs, he can accept the decree that came from heaven; for God needs martyrs. He can accept it for *that* time: but he cannot accept it for *our* time. For the children, the mothers, and the *Muselmänner* had *not* chosen to be martyrs, had *not* died as martyrs: and that God needs *that* death is unacceptable. Hence even the most devout Jew at prayer today must ask, on the holiest day of Judaism: why is the world today not water? He must ask the question. But he cannot answer it.

For this reason the Jew at prayer today is gripped by the most radical of all human questions. Why does anything exist at all? Why is there not rather Nothing? In philosophy, this question is asked in abstract, sweeping generality.[22] For the Jew at prayer on Yom Kippur today, it arises in singling-out particularity. Why does anything—Man, World, God—*still* exist *now*—and not water? Why does *he himself* still exist—an accidental remnant? And where, if not even *he* were left, would be the witness to the divine Judgment? Where the divine Judgment? As his prayer is informed by these questions, it is transformed. It becomes a gift whereby is returned to God "His crown and His scepter."[23] And in this returning—a Messianic moment, a Messianic fragment—Israel, Torah, and God are one.

An eternity so momentary, so fragmentary, so precarious cannot but give rise to the most profound metaphysical, theological, religious disquiet. One—anyone—wants to "overcome" it, "transcend" it, "go beyond" it. Thus some will seek to separate the witness-to-Judgment from the Judgment itself and, as did former generations, project this latter into the world-to-come. But if a Messianic future is inaccessible so is an otherworldly eternity: we must *stay with* our singled-out, this-worldly anguish, and cannot escape from it. On their part, others may wish to raise "Israel" to the same preworldly, post-worldly universality the Jewish tradition already ascribes to "God" and "Torah."[24] But, heir to the *kedoshim*, to the "holy ones," the flesh-and-blood Israel cannot rise, or wish to rise, above a heritage that is itself holy. To "overcome," "transcend" or "go beyond" our fragmented, momentary, precarious eternity is impossible.

There is yet another attempt to avoid the disquiet, and this, of all attempts, is both the most understandable and least possible. The Jewish people has persevered at a singled-out post through the centuries. All too understandably, this people today may be tired of the post; leaving the task of witnessing to others, it may create the prospect of a world without Jews. This, of course, is not a new prospect. Throughout history many have predicted such a world. Not a few have wanted it. A generation ago, an unprecedented attempt was made to make an end to Jews, and some in this generation regret that it failed of complete success. However, whether or not the world today realizes it, it cannot do without Jews—the accidental remnant that, heir to the holy ones, is itself bidden to be holy. Neither, in our time, can God Himself. An ancient Midrash addresses itself to the world as follows:

> They have said: "Come, let us cut them off from being a nation, that the name of Israel may be remembered no more." (Ps. 83:5) Their enemies said: "As long as the nation of Israel abides, God will be named the God of Israel. But if Israel is uprooted, whose God will He be named?"[25]

Another Midrash addressed Israel itself:

> "You are My witnesses, says the Lord"—that is, if you are My witnesses, I am God, and if you are not My witnesses, I am, as it were, not God."[26]

Notes

1. See *To Mend the World*, chapter II, section 3.
2. Ibid., chapter II, section 4.
3. Ibid., chapter II, section 10.
4. Ibid., chapter IV, section 10.
5. In *The Jewish State* (London: Zionist Organization, 1936), Herzl writes: "We cannot, after all, converse with one another in Hebrew. Which of us knows enough Hebrew to ask for a railway ticket in that language? It cannot be done" (p. 134).
6. The case of left-wing Hegelianism is sufficient proof that the two are not necessarily identical. This is corroborated by the case of Heidegger which does not appear until the third exploration.
7. In the present book, empiricist reductionism, having been dealt with in chapter 1 of *Encounters*, has no longer been an issue. In contrast, a dialectical reductionism, even after chapter 3 of *Encounters*, still required and received treatment in chapter III of the present work. See also *Presence*, ch. 2.
8. See *To Mend the World*, chapter IV, section 10.
9. Ibid., chapter II, section 3.
10. See Moshe Prager, *Sparks of Glory* (New York: Shengold, 1974) pp. 70 ff.

11. On this subject, see further *Encounters*, pp. 106 ff.

12. In this and the following it is necessary to hold fast to the stance-between-the-extremes set forth in *To Mend the World* chapter IV, section 14F.

13. Presumably the custom of Israel Bond appeals during the Yom Kippur service originated pragmatically, in the need to reach large numbers in a receptive mood. Its implicit religious meaning, over and above the pragmatic, became fully explicit on one Yom Kippur—the first day of the Yom Kippur war.

14. *Midrash Deut. Rabba*, 2.12.

15. A currently fashionable Jewish theological resort is to the Whiteheadian God who can only inspire and not save. It is doubtful whether to this God there can be any kind of Jewish speech. (What remains of the Psalms when addressed to a God that cannot save? Or that can save only if "salvation" is so spiritualized as to be cut off from questions of life and death?) More doubtful still is, if Jewish speech to this God there is and can be, whether this God can survive the Holocaust, for that catastophe casts into doubt the divine power to inspire as well as that of saving.

16. A popular summary probably based on Zohar V73b and/or 93a.

17. A dictum attributed to Saadia Gaon (882–942).

18. In Israel, it is a custom for secular Jews to attend synagogue on Yom Kippur.

19. This prayer is part of High Holy Day services on Rosh Ha-Shana as well as Yom Kippur.

20. In Elie Wiesel's *Gates of the Forest* the protagonist concludes that it is too late for the coming of the Messiah, and that it is necessary to manage without him (New York: Holt, Rinehart and Winston, 1966), p. 225.

21. This prayer is found in the Yom Kippur Mussaf liturgy only: to recite *these* things more than once during the Jewish liturgical year would be impossible. One may well ask: How is it possible to recite them even once?

22. Greek philosophers did not ask this question at all. Among moderns, it was raised (under the influence, remotely but unmistakably, of the Jewish-Christian doctrine of creation) by Leibniz, Schelling, and Heidegger, with increasing radicalism. Leibniz's answer is a conventional recourse to God. Schelling too resorts to God, but can reach Him only through a leap. For Heidegger the question is no longer answerable, and its significance now lies in being asked.

23. Wiesel, *Gates of the Forest*, p. 225.

24. Traditional Jewish teaching contains a doctrine of a preworldly Torah. The world was created through the Torah which is itself uncreated.

25. *Midrash Psalms*, on Ps. 83:5.

26. Midrash Psalms, on Ps. 123:1. I first cited this Midrash nearly thirty years ago (see *Quest*, p. 39). The careful reader will notice that its significance has changed for me in these many years—with an immense burden now falling on the "as it were."

5

Autobiographical Reflections

36 *Reminiscences: From Germany to Canada*

Growing up in Germany

I know that you were born in 1916 in Halle, Germany. What kind of place was that?

Halle was an old industrial city with about 200,000 people. It had an old university. A Jewish community had lived there for a thousand years. George Frederick Handel came from Halle, but so did Reinhard Heydrich, one of the most horrible of the Nazis. There are so many absurdities. My father's best friend lived in the same house as Heydrich. And Heydrich, however evil he was, protected this man during Krystallnacht. Later, Heydrich was assassinated by Czech patriots, and as a result, my father's friend had no one to protect him.

How many were in your family?

I was the middle of three brothers. My father was a lawyer, probably the best known lawyer in town. He was an excellent orator, and to the extent that I have any talent in that area, I got it from him. He was dramatic in the courtroom, and his specialty was criminal law.

That's interesting, because you've been a kind of theological prosecutor yourself. What about your mother?

My mother was descended from a line of rabbis. There was a family tradition that we were descended from the Rambam, but I'm inclined to doubt it.

You never know. On the other hand, I have the impression that every Jewish family in Europe had some such tradition. What about your father's side?

Reprinted, with changes, from "An Interview with Emil Fackenheim," by William Novack in *New Traditions* 3 (Summer, 1986).

349

His lineage was very different. One of his ancestors was one of the first Jewish soldiers in the Thirty Years' War.

Did you grow up in a Reform Jewish household?

Not really. We were Liberal Jews, but that isn't the same as Reform Judaism, American style, which had no real following in Germany. There were two American-style Reform congregations, one in Berlin and one in Hamburg, but we considered them assimilationists.

What we had was like Conservative Judaism—but with an organ. That may sound funny, but in a Liberal synagogue in Berlin, an organ made sense, in part because of the German-Jewish composers, notably Lewandowski. Did you know that even Franz Rosenzweig once wanted to bring the music of Bach into the synagogue? And nobody ever accused *him* of being an assimilationist. It's just that we all believed in this symbiosis of German and Jewish culture. Nobody has ever done justice to the ordinary German Jews who believed in all sincerity that it was possible to be an upright Jew and a German at the same time.

We in North America operate under a similar premise—unless you think it's an illusion.

No, it was different for us because Germany has always been very ideological. You couldn't be a German and a Zionist at the same time. It wasn't like America, with a weak sense of nationalism and a strong sense of religious pluralism. We had bitter fights between Zionists and non-Zionists. When the Nazis came to power, I was the leader of the non-Zionist youth group, the Organization of German-Jewish youth. By the way, the leader of the Zionist youth group now lives in Chicago, while I live in Jerusalem.

Of course, to put it mildly, the German Jews underestimated German antisemitism, and I could tell you many tragic stories. Once, when I was lecturing at Cornell, I noticed a woman who looked vaguely familiar. She came over to talk to me, and it turned out that she was the best friend of the girlfriend of my youth. "I can't help hating my father," she told me. Now her father was a lovely, wonderful person. He was a good Jew, and also a German nationalist. He could never believe that the Germans would harm the Jews. His family shared that belief, and they were all murdered. She was the only survivor. But nobody could have predicted this terrible expression of antisemitism.

When (Gershom) Scholem was a young man, and wanted to study Judaism in an intense way, he had to break with his family. That obviously wasn't the case with you. But was your family actually supportive of your Jewish interests?

Fully. My grandparents both kept kosher, although we didn't. On the other hand, we certainly didn't eat *chazer* (pork) either. We went to synagogue fairly regularly on Friday night, and we ate at my grandmother's for Shabbat.

Did you know early on that you wanted to be a rabbi?

I never decided to be a rabbi. I just wanted to become a knowledgeable Jew, because as a young man my criticism of the Jewish community was that although people were dedicated, most of them didn't know very much.

For example, I had only two hours a week of Jewish education, although in those two hours I learned a great deal. In my bar mitzvah lessons I argued with the rabbi about Spinoza. He used to tell me that Christianity and Islam were the daughter religions of Judaism. I kept wondering why the daughters were often so nasty to the mother.

In those days, I was naively convinced that Judaism had all the answers. I still think so, incidentally. Well, maybe not all the answers.

You studied at a Liberal Rabbinical seminary in Berlin. How would you describe its orientation? Was it anything like Hebrew Union College?

Not quite, because a very funny phenomenon arose in nineteenth-century Germany: *Wissenschaft,* the scientific study of Judaism. The Seminary was called the *Hochschule für die Wissenschaft des Judentums* and it had been founded by Abraham Geiger in the nineteenth century. Theoretically, the most Orthodox and the most agnostic could both study there, although Geiger had the idea that the scholarly study of Judaism automatically refutes Orthodoxy and shows the need for Liberalism. Of course this is far from the case. Abba Eban made the same blunder in his TV show; he should never have brought in all the stuff about Biblical criticism. It didn't belong.

In some ways the seminary was a frustrating place for me. I studied Jewish philosophy, for example, but all I learned were the facts about past Jewish philosophy. I wanted to know if it was *true.*

I understand that Leo Baeck was your Midrash teacher.

He was an awe-inspiring man, but he didn't give me the philosophical answers I was looking for. His answers were always aesthetic.

What about Talmud?

I could never follow the legal intricacies, but I got the spirit of what moves the Talmud and the Midrash.

You have been citing midrashic texts for years, long before Midrash started enjoying its current renaissance. Is that because of Leo Baeck?

He gave me a handful of midrashim that impressed me deeply. But just to tell midrashim can be very cheap; Baeck forced me to think on my own, as did Buber. In the first chapter of *God's Presence in History,* I talk about one particular midrashic statement that's always been important to me. There's a Biblical verse, "I am God and you are My witnesses." The Midrash elaborates: "If you're my witnesses, then I'll be God. But if you're not my witnesses, then *k'vyachol* (as it were) I am not your God."

I remember in Toronto you would frequently mention the famous midrash of the Israelites celebrating at the Red Sea. God rebukes the angels: "How can you rejoice when my children are drowning?" It was a powerful midrash, and you cite a number of other powerful midrashim in your writing.

I don't pretend to be a Midrash scholar. I feel like Rosenzweig, who studied with men who knew far more about Judaism than he did. And yet he had the chutzpah to believe he had something to teach them. There's a long tradition of philosophers dealing with Bible and Midrash.

When did you leave the Seminary?

Krystallnacht, November 10, 1938. I arrived at the *Hochschule* with a friend of mine on that day, and we found the doors were locked. In the next street we saw a piano which had been thrown out of a window. We walked up and down Kurfuerstendamm, which was like the Fifth Avenue of Berlin.

Going for that walk was a stupid thing to do, right?

Oh yes. But when you're young, you're naive. My brother was also in Berlin, and that evening we got together to decide what to do. Was this happening just in Berlin, or all over Germany? We phoned my mother, and she was in hysterics because they had come for my father. I went home to Halle—it was about seventy miles—to be with her. I figured that the safest place was where the Gestapo had already been. But they had tapped the wires, and at ten the next morning they came for me and took me to Sachsenhausen, a concentration camp.

You've written that Sachsenhausen was a kind of training ground for Auschwitz.

I wrote that thirty years later. Bettelheim was in the same sort of camp, but what he wrote about it was completely wrong and insults the survivors. The Nazis could reduce *anyone* to a *Muselmann*, a living corpse. And yet Bettelheim claims that you could resist them if only you were sufficiently "autonomous." Nonsense!

I notice that you tend to downplay Sachsenhausen, especially in terms of Auschwitz. But it was still pretty bad, wasn't it?

It was terrible! It was absolutely terrible. We had a conscious strategy for survival. We fooled ourselves deliberately. My friends and I said: "All right, we'll give them a week. We can stand anything for a week." Back in 1939, they were releasing people every day. Then we'd give them another two weeks, and so on.

All of this time we were doing terrible hard labor. And we were underfed. But the worst part was the cold, and I still have frostbite to this day. I also developed digestive troubles, because you couldn't relieve yourself when you had to. It took a long time to get over this. They would come in the middle of the night and make us do exercises, jumping on the beds. The beds would get dirty and we'd have to clean them up, but there was no way to clean them up.

It reminds me of Egypt, of having to make bricks out of straw. It's strange how these things repeat.

These things have deep roots. Many of the Nazis had a knowledge of the Bible. And there is a long tradition in Germany, going back to Luther, of denigrating or even slandering the "Old Testament."

At any rate, after a while they released fewer and fewer. If you could prove you could leave the country, they'd let you out. In many cases, the relatives back home would bribe the Gestapo, but in my town the Gestapo was unbribable, which is why I was one of the last to get out, in February of 1939, after three months. Of the original five or six thousand, there were only about 300 left.

The night before I was released, two terrible things happened. First, I heard somebody vomit, and I woke up to find that he had vomited on my jacket. In Sachsenhausen that was very serious. I couldn't leave the mess on my jacket, but to wash it I had to go out in the cold in a wet jacket and risk getting pneumonia.

The other thing was that for the first time, that night, a terrible thought entered my mind: maybe there's a core remnant that will *never* be released. And that was when my morale began to falter. The next morning, three people were released, and I was one of them.

A Kind of Freedom

One of my friends was never released, and miraculously, he survived the whole war. When the Russians came, he stole a bicycle and not trusting anyone in Germany, he rode all across to France. You can imagine what condition he must have been in. How did he manage to survive all those years without hope? People who now study the Holocaust rarely ask that question. Or how were the Warsaw Ghetto fighters able to fight without hope? It blows my mind.

Where did you go when you were released?

Just before *Krystallnacht*, my friends and I realized that we would not be able to finish our studies, and that we had to get out as quickly as possible—assuming it still *was* possible. So at random we wrote ten letters to ten American universities applying for scholarships. Nine didn't answer, but Harvard did. To make a long story short, through Harvard I ended up with a scholarship to the University of Aberdeen in Scotland.

What was uppermost in my mind was to continue my career as a Jewish philosopher. That motivation saved my sanity.

The Gestapo had said that if I wasn't out of the country in six weeks, they'd put me back in the concentration camp and never let me out. And I knew they were speaking the truth.

Within a few weeks I got a visa to go to a refugee camp in England. The British were bad in Palestine, but they were decent at home, and they let in 90,000 Jewish refugees in the nine months before the war. I could have gone to this camp and tried to get from there to Aberdeen to pursue my studies. But I was afraid to be stuck there. It would have been the end of my studies.

But at least you would have been in England!

But at that point, you might say that my Jewish studies were more important than my life. This was the one time during that period that I was an agent rather than a victim. I figured that as long as the Gestapo knew I would leave, they'd give me an extension if I asked for it. I went to them and said: "Look, here's proof that I can leave. But I can't go right away. The Jewish community waits until there are a few together, and then we leave in a group." I just made that up. I gambled that they wouldn't check it, and I was right.

A week later, I got my visa for Scotland and *whoosh*—off I went.

And your family perished?

No, a cousin of mine found some lovely people in Glasgow who were willing to guarantee their livelihood. My father got a visa, but unlike myself, he had property. In August, 1939, I got a call from him. "All our remaining property is in Hamburg. It will take another six weeks to clear it. Do I have six weeks?"

I had to make the decision, so I went to the Aberdeen office of Lloyd's of London, and I asked them: "would you insure property presently in Hamburg?" And the official said: "We wouldn't touch it with a ten foot pole." I phoned my father and said, "Come right away." They got out on the last plane before the war. My poor brother didn't get out, and he died.

When the Nazis invaded Holland, a Scottish policeman came for me. "I'm sorry sir," he said, "but you'll have to come along for a few days." He gave me an hour to pack, and I packed forty books. I was studying Greek philosophy at the time.

"But sir," he said, "you don't need all these books. It's only for a few days." I'll never forget my answer, which was a real classic. I told him: "Look, you know your business and I know mine!"

Unfortunately, I was right. The internment lasted a year and a half. After a few weeks, some of us were sent to Australia and others, including me, were sent to Canada. I was soon released on paper, but there was still a problem because I hadn't immigrated to Canada. I ended up in an internment camp in Sherbrooke, Quebec.

They treated us as prisoners of war. They lied to us and said there would be no barbed wire. But there was, and we went on a hunger strike. After two days, I had my first meeting with a Canadian official, a major from Ottawa. He was a fat guy, and he climbed on the table and said: "Most of you are Jews, aren't you? Nevertheless, you have to keep clean." And then he started telling us how to keep clean!

"If you play ball with us," he said, "we'll play ball with you." We promptly called him Major Balls.

In the evening, a soldier came in and said to me and a friend, a fellow rabbi: "The major wants to speak with you."

"What's all this nonsense about a hunger strike?" the major asked. "I've never heard such nonsense in all my life."

I replied: "We have no complaints about the food. The living conditions are not ideal, but we're not complaining. But we do object to the barbed wire. We want to be recognized as the first victims of the people you're now fighting." And then I added, maybe foolishly, "Some of us have been in concentration camps."

He said: "Oh, you've been in a camp before? Then you know how to behave in the presence of an officer. Kindly stand at attention." That was my first impression of Canada.

So you were the leader of the prisoners?
Together with my friend, Henry Fischel. We were the rabbis, and the other Jews were our congregation. We had services and a Torah.

Did you have any contact with Canadian Jews?
They were permitted in on a few occasions, and they provided us with matzah for Pesach. The Jews in the camp identified as either religious or non-religious, and I had to serve as the policeman. Only the religious ones got matzah and other Pesach goodies. I remember catching one of the "religious" ones eating bacon on a piece of matzah. We also had a camp university, and this was the first time I taught philosophy.

So your time was your own?
There were chores everybody had to do. And if you wanted to earn money— thirty cents a day—you could do work. In order to keep physically fit, I volunteered to go outside the camp to chop down trees.

You were a lumberjack?! That reminds me of the old Myron Cohen joke about a little Jewish man who applies for a job as a lumberjack. They're very skeptical, but when he shows them what he can do, they're astounded. "Where did you learn to chop like that?" they ask him.

"I spent a couple of years in the Sahara Forest," he answers.

"You must mean the Sahara Desert," they say.

"Sure," replies the man, "now it's a desert!"

(You have my permission to delete that joke from the printed version.)

I'll leave it in, for I wasn't a very good lumberjack. I think I broke more axe-handles than trees!

How did you end up at the University of Toronto?

When I was released, I went to Toronto, where a family from Vienna sponsored me. I had already been accepted at the University of Toronto, so I went there and told the head of the department, Professor G. S. Brett, that because of my rabbinical degree, the University of Aberdeen had accepted me as a graduate student. He said, "If it's good enough for them, it's good enough for us. But let's stop talking about this foolishness." We started in on Aristotle, and I felt like I had never left home. That was my second "first" experience of Canada, and I never forgot it. Over the years, I received many offers from other institutions. But until I was ready to make aliyah, I really had no desire to leave the University of Toronto.

I know that during this time you were also leading a congregation in Hamilton, Ontario. It's hard to imagine that you'd be happy in that role.

It wasn't too bad. I'm glad I had that experience, because it helped me develop some common sense and love *amcha*. Actually, I first learned to love *amcha* in Sachsenhausen. Whether or not they knew anything about Judaism, here were people thrown into a terrible situation and on the whole they behaved like human beings. This is why Terrence Des Pres' book, *The Survivor*, meant so much to me. It took a goy to express clearly how ordinary Jews behaved decently.

The Hamilton congregation was Reform?

Yes. I was there from 1943 to 1948. After a few years I realized it wasn't for me. I tried adult education, but nobody really wanted it. My greatest satisfaction was with the children. I also learned a lot about public relations, because I was the chairman of the public relations committee of the Jewish community of Hamilton. They always put Reform rabbis in this job, because they can talk to the goyim.

Many people believe that in theological terms, Auschwitz is not so much a Jewish problem as a Christian one.

Exactly.

And are Christians dealing with it?

To some extent, yes. I recently went back to Germany at the invitation of Christians. I began my first speech by saying: "This is my first speech on German soil in 45 years. The last one was as a student rabbi on Yom Kippur 1938, in the Baden-Baden synagogue just before the Nazis burned it down."

When I finished, Martin Stoehr, a Protestant theologian, made the following statement: "In the nearly two thousand years that we have co-existed with Jews, we Christians have never once listened to them. We just preached to them. Then why do we want to listen to Jews now? Not because of our Christian faith, but because one third of the Jewish people was murdered."

Still, this must have been a very difficult invitation to accept.

It was. At one point, I had to get on a train in Germany with two bags. I missed a step and almost fell under the train. I was thinking of all those other trains. Then, in one of the discussions, I developed a tremendous antipathy for this one man, a Catholic. I just hated his guts even though he was saying nice things. Then it hit me: he spoke in the same dialect as Goebbels, because he came from the same district. When I realized that, my hatred for him stopped.

All those echoes. . . .

Yes, it's very difficult. And it's all so mixed up. There are good Germans, like Stoehr. Later, I learned that he heads a committee that sends about twenty German theological students to Israel each year. And I have ended up teaching them at their own institution in Jerusalem. I never dreamed that one of the things aliyah would mean was teaching German Christians in Jerusalem.

37 *Return to Berlin: An Epitaph for German Judaism*

1. I was released from the concentration camp of Sachsenhausen on February 8, 1939. Together with thousands of other German Jews I had been arrested and imprisoned there following the so-called Kristallnacht of November 9, 1938. Returning home, I wondered: should I contact my few remaining German friends before leaving the country? Better not, I decided, for I might endanger them; and if they wished they could contact *me*. Actually, by then only one friend from my high school days was left, and he did not contact me. So I never saw him again, for, though an anti-Nazi to the end of his life, he was killed on the Russian front, fighting Hitler's war.

I *was* contacted by my former high school Greek teacher. (I had completed high school in my native city of Halle in 1935 but, at his insistence, had remained regularly in touch with him while a rabbinical student in Berlin.) He telephoned me and said: "Fackenheim, if you will not come to visit me I shall never forgive you." So of course I went. He had ready two copies, properly inscribed, of Martin Buber's *Koenigtum Gottes*, one for himself to keep, the other for me to take. (This is a custom among classical scholars when friends part. I took my copy and have it to this day.) Then he said: "In all these years I have kept telling you, 'Do not leave, this Nazi disease will pass.' Now you must leave. But you must promise me to return. Germany will be destroyed, and we shall need you to help rebuild her." I thought for a moment and replied: "Dr. Loercher, I have never disagreed with you before. Indeed, two or three years ago I might have agreed to come back. But after what has happened now I know that the Jewish people will need me more. I agree that Germany will be destroyed. But the rebuilding will have to be done by others."

Reprinted, with permission, from *Moment*, Vol. 10, no. 4 (April, 1985): 55–59.

357

2. I reported this conversation in October 1983, when I gave my first address on German soil in 45 years, adding that my last such address had been on Yom Kippur 1938, in the Baden-Baden synagogue just before they burned it down. The 1983 address was in the *Papst Johannes Haus* in Krefeld, to a group of Christians. In response to mine, I heard an address by the Protestant theologian Martin Stoehr, containing some of the greatest, most relentlessly probing words I have ever heard from a Christian. He began as follows: "In the nearly two thousand years that we have co-existed with Jews, we Christians have never once listened to them, and in this respect our Christian faith has not helped us. They why do we want to listen to Jews now? Not because of our Christian faith, but because one third of the Jewish people was murdered." Then followed a ruthlessly honest account of anti-Semitism in Christendom, tolerated if not encouraged throughout Christian history, its theology included. Stoehr ended as follows: "We Christians have to begin at the very beginning, with the first two questions of the Bible: 'Where are you, man?' and 'Where is your brother?' "

Stoehr's words filled me with love, but also with sadness. Even to so great a Christian as Dietrich Bonhoeffer it does not seem to have occurred to meet with, let alone listen to, his fellow-Berliner, the great Rabbi Leo Baeck. Now that some Christians in Germany are willing, or indeed eager, to listen to Jews, what Jews are left to speak to them? Of a once-great, thousand-year-old community, only a small, accidental remnant. A few days before my Krefeld meeting I had by chance heard a learned radio lecture on the subject of atheism. Vaguely annoyed because the "good guys"—i.e. the religious—seemed to be all Christians and the "bad" atheist Jews like Marx and Freud, I was happily surprised at the ending, a retelling of a Chassidic story. But I was sad at the same time. The lecturer may have studied Chassidism, the mystical Jewish movement that was founded in the 18th century in Eastern Europe and survives vigorously to this day, or perhaps he had at least read earnestly some of Martin Buber's writings on the subject, but it was obvious that he had never discussed Chassidism with a knowledgeable Jew, presumably for lack of opportunity. He retold the story correctly—but he mispronounced the word "Chassidism."

After my own Krefeld address was finished, an old man came up to me and said: "You have listened to your old teacher after all! You have returned to help us to rebuild Germany!" I embraced him in turn and replied: "Yes, I have come back. And if you want me to I'll come back again. But only to visit. I am going to live in Jerusalem."

3. I repeated the story of my Greek teacher when in November 1984 I returned to Germany, this time to address a Jewish audience. It was my first time in Berlin since I had left from Tempelhof Airport on May 12, 1939. I had learned much on my visit to Germany a year earlier. But (as will emerge in the course of this telling), only after my return to Berlin do I understand (or think I understand) why in all these years I have found it so hard to revisit Germany.

I was a student at the Berlin Liberal rabbinical seminary, the famed *Hochschule fuer die Wissenschaft des Judentums*, from 1935 to 1938. In the week I began my studies my father was arrested for six weeks by the Gestapo. My studies ended, abruptly, with the Kristallnacht, concentration camp and flight from Germany. In the years between 1935 and 1938, Berlin, or more precisely Jewish Berlin and more specifically still the *Hochschule,* was at once the most absurd and the most appropriate place for the study of Judaism. The most absurd for the reason that made a cousin of mine ask me, "How can you study at a time like this?" (I replied: "It is true we are sitting on a powder keg, but we must be calm and bold enough to smoke a cigar while sitting on it.") Most appropriate because never before and rarely since has there been a place where the meaning of Judaism for our time was so intensely studied and reflected on. And on Shabbat we would attend the crowded synagogue services, inspired by both the music and sermons of Leo Baeck and Max Wiener, Joachim Prinz and Manfred Swarsensky. In these brief years, Judaism in Germany underwent an extraordinary renaissance to which far too little attention has been paid by historians or by anyone else.

All this, of course, came to an abrupt, total, brutal end when on the night of November 9, 1938, synagogues were burning all over Germany, Jewish property was smashed and stolen, and Jewish men vanished one knew not (but could guess) where. On the day after that night—I was not arrested until the next day—a friend and I, foolishly enough, but sure that this was a day for the history books and had to be experienced, walked up and down the famous Kurfuerstendamm. (It was, and continues to be, the Fifth Avenue of Berlin.) There we saw what in a way was the worst spectacle of all: not stormtroopers but rather respectable citizens, fashionably dressed, stepping over all that broken glass into Jewish store windows, and helping themselves to shoes, dresses and the like.

And now, my first return to Berlin! I had asked my hosts for a volunteer, an owner of a car, willing to spend an afternoon taking me around. A very engaging, interesting young Jewish Berliner was glad to oblige. I recognized the street signs but very little else. What else had I expected? What with an absence of 45 years, painful but repressed memories and, last but not least, fierce air raids that had destroyed so much, why should I remember, or find, the streets or houses in which I had once lived? So much has had to be rebuilt! But has *Germany* been rebuilt, or is she being rebuilt, in the sense meant by my old teacher? Among the Berlin street names that I recognized were those of poets and philosophers, Kantstrasse, Schellingstrasse, Lessingstrasse and so on; and I kept wondering, what other capital (or former capital) gives so much honor in its street names to poets and philosophers? But is anything but the street names left, or being rebuilt? In a theological discussion during my 1983 visit no one other than I seemed to refer to Kant or Hegel.

In a way, the question was answered at the climax of my Berlin tour: the Wall. Why doesn't anyone report what that awful, awesome place is really like? Why are there no adequate pictures? Perhaps I have missed the stories and pictures. Or perhaps one must be there and see it for oneself. For my companion—hardly a German, but decidedly a Berliner, his father born in Berlin, so, too, after the war and the camps, he—the Potsdamer Platz was the most awesome sight. (It is what Times Square is, or used to be, for New Yorkers.) Once it was a glittering center of activity. Now, on "our" side, it is a place for sightseers. There are stands, specially built for the purpose, on which visitors can climb up the steps and look across; and there is ample room for the tourist buses that always seem to be there, as well as for booths where pop and souvenirs are sold. And when one climbs up the steps one sees, on "their" side, a desolation and a dreariness that are difficult to imagine. (A mental note: communism equals dreariness, an equation my wife and I had already arrived at when, during a visit with refuseniks some years earlier, we walked the streets of several cities in the Soviet Union. And it is confirmed whenever one switches on the radio and listens to "their" news, or what they call news.) There is a vast empty space separating East Berlin from the Wall, so that at least here no one would even attempt to climb the Wall: He would be gunned down before getting near it. Hundreds of black birds were sitting in the empty space. "What birds are these?" I asked of my companion. I didn't know, and neither did he. But they've just *got* to be ravens, I thought. A medieval legend I was taught at school has it that Emperor Barbarossa sits inside the Kyffhaeuser mountain, his red beard growing ever longer, waiting for *der Tag* when he can reappear, recreate in a new form the glory that once was the Holy Roman Empire of the German Nation, and thus realize German destiny; but so long as the ravens still fly around the mountain, the time has not yet arrived. It was considered to have arrived when Nazi Germany launched its invasion of Russia—not coincidentally code-named Operation Barbarossa. Now *der Tag* has come and gone, and the ravens—and Russian communism—are in what was once the heart of Germany.

The heart of Germany, however, only much later than the Middle Ages. For my companion the Potsdamer Platz may have been the most awesome sight; for me, never a Berliner but once—eternities ago, it seems—a German, the most awesome sight was the other chief place for sightseers, the *Reichstag*, dilapidated and, aptly enough, a museum, on "our" side. (The dedication above the entrance says "*Dem Deutschen Volke*—For the German People." Now, a student of linguistics tells me, words such as *Volk* are avoided by sensitive Germans.) The *Brandenburger Tor*, once the pride of Prussia, is on the other side, and between the two is that Wall, to climb which is to risk death. (On the day I arrived a youth had succeeded in getting across the Wall. They had shot but missed, and he had only broken his leg when jumping down. He was in the hospital, showered by West Berliners with flowers and candy.) Bismarck, I thought, must turn over in his grave.

But (far more important to me than Bismarck) so must Hegel. At the height of his career teaching at the newly-founded Berlin University, Hegel had attempted to develop a political philosophy in which might is synthesized with right. Suspicious of German nationalism (and especially of the romantic kind that longed for a revival of the Middle Ages), Hegel had aimed at nothing larger than Prussia. And just how well his suspicions were founded was proved in the First World War, instigated by poor disciples and heirs of Bismarck, and no disciples at all of Hegel. After that war came the Weimar Republic—right without might, or as the late Leo Strauss put it, "the sorry spectacle of justice without the sword, or justice unable to use the sword." And the Weimar Republic was in turn succeeded by a regime that was the most deliberate, most systematic, most horrendous destruction of right by might in all of human history. It was also—to quote Strauss again—"the only German regime—the only regime ever anywhere—which had no other clear principle than murderous hatred of Jews, for 'Aryan' had no clear meaning other than 'non-Jewish.' " (The Japanese, after all, were honorary Aryans.)

I looked at the dreariness beyond the Wall and then more closely at the Wall itself. It is full of graffiti, some of the John-loves-Jane variety, some, more apt, denouncing communist oppression and demanding the removal of the Wall. What would be the most apt legend of all, however, was nowhere in sight. I heard it in my mind's ear all the while, as I had once heard it so often spoken aloud by Nazi *Sprechchoere*: "*Wir danken unserem Fuehrer*"—"We thank our Fuehrer."

With these words in my head, a talmudic saying comes back as well: If only the Gentiles understood, they would mourn the destruction of the Temple more than the Jews. If only the Germans understood, they would feel an unprecedented closeness to, and identification with, the Jewish people, for the same Third Reich—whose 12 years were equal to a thousand—that murdered one third of the Jewish people also destroyed Germany. Is Germany being rebuilt? *Can* she be rebuilt? These are questions for others to worry over. There was a time when the poet Heinrich Heine (who was a great Jew and also a great German) was unable to sleep when during the night he would think about Germany. But, as Leo Baeck, my midrash professor during my *Hochschule* days, recognized as early as 1933, the one-thousand-year-old history of German Jews has come to an end.

4. My Berlin tour had taken place on a Friday afternoon. In the evening I attended Shabbat services at a synagogue in my own tradition, the only Liberal synagogue in Berlin, located on Pestalozzistrasse. One Liberal synagogue in all of Berlin! At one time, if any city deserved the name of the Jerusalem of Western Europe, it was Berlin. Certainly it was the Jerusalem of Liberal Judaism, and no building expressed this with greater magnificence than the famous Fasanenstrasse-Synagogue, festively inaugurated in 1912 in the presence of prominent government officials. (The Army and indeed even the Kaiser himself were represented.) Of that synagogue, burnt down like all the others, only the front portal remains. Behind it lies the new, modest Jewish community center. It is good that the portal was left standing.

Nothing but a small plate indicates to the passer-by on Pestalozzistrasse that here there is a synagogue. Like many Berlin buildings, it is located behind an inner court. (So is the Orthodox synagogue on Joachimstalerstrasse which I attended the next morning. I understand that only one of the few synagogues remaining in Berlin is visible as such from the street. Is this accidental?) After having been body-searched thoroughly by two armed policemen, I enter the synagogue for Friday night services. A stark sign reminds those entering of the six million—as indeed does everything in this building. It is not as bad as I feared, is my first reaction as I enter: a hundred or so worshipers. (A hundred Liberal Jews attending Friday night services in all of Berlin! At one time it was thousands.) Only later do I learn from the rabbi that about 30 of those attending are visiting Gentiles. Also, 10 or 20 must have been visitors from abroad, such as I.

There is a story about the visiting Gentiles. The group wishing to attend was three times as large, but they were asked to come some at a time, lest the visitors outnumber the worshipers, and the worship cease to be a service and become an exhibition or display. I later heard a similar story in Stuttgart.

The service begins, and from the first sound of the organ I am deeply moved. I do not apologize. In Jerusalem today an organ is out of place in a synagogue. In a Liberal synagogue of Berlin it is not. It is true that the instrument was borrowed from the church, and that as such it comes into the category of *chukkat hagoy*—Gentile custom—that is viewed with suspicion when imported into Judaism. What in German Liberal Judaism gave the organ Jewish legitimacy was the music of German-Jewish synagogue composers of whom Lewandowski was the greatest. And let it be remembered that even Franz Rosenzweig (whom no one can accuse of craven assimilation or lack of Jewish identity) once wanted to bring Bach's music into the synagogue.

I continue to be moved as the service continues, but little by little my mood changes. I try to join in the singing of the choir, but it seems that no one else does. I have a *siddur* in front of me; few others have the prayerbook before them. As I walk out I realize that the mood of worship I felt at the beginning has been replaced by nostalgia, and that I have participated in a memorial concert rather than in a service.

Also on the way out I notice a sign on the wall. (In the Moscow synagogue, too, there is a sign on the wall, referring to the Jewish people as the "children of Aaron," lest, if referred to as "children of Israel," they be suspected of a connection with that imperialist-fascist-militaristic entity, the State of Israel.) The Berlin sign just *had* to be a line from one of the two most famous songs emerging from the Holocaust. And it could not be, "Never say you walk the last road," the song of the Vilna Ghetto resistance fighters, for then the synagogue would have to be not in Berlin but in Israel. The sign reads: "I believe with perfect faith in the coming of the Messiah, and although he tarry, I will wait daily for his coming." Surely it is only in the hope of redemption that a Jew can pray in the Berlin of today at all! But how can he wait for the Messiah, in, of all places, post-Holocaust Berlin? Or, is it "how much longer?" Maimonides, the author of the statement, must have had many Jewish catastrophes in mind when, judiciously enough, he included the words "although he tarry." But the possibility of a Holocaust surely never entered his mind.

Next morning I attend services at the Orthodox synagogue. Much better, is my first impression. More people. Real *davvening*, real prayer. Reading the Torah. And if there is a good deal of talking, especially during the Torah reading, I for one am not offended, though when I was a young purist I used to be. (The habit of talking during the service is an old one.) Why shouldn't there be some talking? The synagogue is a meeting place also, and for all I know the one time in the week that these Berlin Jews meet is on Shabbat in *shul*.

I feel quite at home until, having been called up to hold the Torah, I stand right next to the rabbi while he recites the prayer for the State of Israel. The text is before him, and I read it with him, except that he omits the phrase that refers to the State of Israel as "the first flowering of our redemption." Of course, I know that the phrase is controversial and omitted in many synagogues. But omit it in Berlin?! The very last place on earth where it ought to be omitted, and I have yet to meet a Jew in Berlin—or, for that matter, in Germany—who could bear to live in Germany were it not for the strength derived from the knowledge that there is—as, alas, then there was not—a Jewish state.

Later during the service I am accosted by an old Jew. "Where are you from?" "Jerusalem, but I lived here as a student over 40 years ago." "How do you find it?" "Very sad." "It could have been worse." The exchange is ended and, shocked, I wonder what on earth the old man could have meant. Just this, I suppose: that there might not even be a *minyan*.

After the service, a *kiddush* and a meal, during which the rabbi makes a speech, bragging that a rabbi is visiting us from Haifa, and that he would come to the only authentic—i.e. Orthodox—service and not to the Liberal one. In post-Holocaust Berlin, most offensive, I feel. And the Haifa rabbi should have suspended his Orthodox scruples in this place and attended services at the Liberal synagogue also.

But then it all becomes clear—the rabbi's omission during the prayer for the State of Israel, the old man's comment, and the behavior of the two rabbis at the *kiddush*. If in the Liberal synagogue one cannot forget for a moment one's time and place, everything in the Orthodox synagogue is marked by a total absence of a knowledge of both. In short, a few synagogues continue to exist in what once was the Jerusalem of Western Europe. But the synagogue in which there still is real worship is not really in Berlin at all, for it could be anywhere; and in the synagogue which is permeated with a deep knowledge of its time and place, worship has turned into mourning and memory.

And so I understood: the Third Reich, which murdered most of the Jews of Europe, also destroyed a spiritual reality to which I was deeply attached from childhood on, and which lasted from Moses Mendelssohn to Leo Baeck. It destroyed German Judaism.

5. Because of the larger, vaster tragedy of European Jewry as a whole, the very special tragedy of the German Jews—they were murdered, so to speak, by the people with whom they went to school—has found insufficient attention. And to the extent that any German Jews have been noticed, it is largely the assimilated Jews, intellectuals alienated from Judaism (whether, as in former days, they were denounced for assimilating or, as currently in many quarters, they are objects of a posthumous celebration). Yet to be appreciated are the ordinary Jewish citizens—my own parents among them—who were able to reconcile a genuine, upright commitment to Judaism with a no less genuine participation in the social and cultural German reality around them.

It is true, as the late Gershom Scholem kept stressing, that the so-called German-Jewish symbiosis was always unreal on the part of the Germans. On the part of the Jews it was real enough. And it bore rich intellectual and spiritual fruit in such figures as the neo-Orthodox Samson Raphael Hirsch and the liberal Abraham Geiger, in the Hegelian Samuel Hirsch and the post-Hegelian Zionist Moses Hess, in the neo-Kantian Hermann Cohen and the post-idealists Martin Buber and Franz Rosenzweig, and, among my own teachers at the *Hochschule*, in unforgettable persons such as Ismar Elbogen and Max Wiener, Eugen Taeubler and Leo Baeck. These men and their work have inspired, and will continue to inspire, Judaism in other lands.

But the fate that has befallen German Judaism itself is illustrated by one of its last great products. In 1925 Buber and Rosenzweig set out to produce a new kind of translation of the Hebrew Bible into German: They set out to make the German language speak Hebrew. But by the time Buber completed the work in 1961—Rosenzweig had died in 1929—the readership addressed no longer existed. There is some reason to believe that the work (and other works that are the heritage of German Judaism) will be studied by Germans: and this may have some bearing on the unanswered question of whether Germany is being rebuilt or can be rebuilt. As for German Judaism, it cannot be rebuilt, and all that remains is an epitaph.

6. My last significant act on this trip to Germany was a visit to the old Jewish cemetery in Frankfurt. Harking back to the 13th century, it was used until the mid-19th, when a new site was found. Even for the mere 15 minutes or so that we meant to stay, my hostess locked the gate from inside. "You never know," she explained.

Inside, nearly half the space is empty. Surely the new cemetery was not established with the old one still half empty: What caused the emptiness? Half the gravestones were overturned: What caused it, the ravages of time or of Nazi vandalism?

Whatever the answers—I had no time to stay and find out—it is good that the old cemetary is left untouched, as a monument to the history of Jews and Judaism in Germany. But how deep, how widespread among the millions who lived through it all is the interest to come and ponder the significance of this place and all it represents? Not very deep, not very widespread, is my impression. But will the interest deepen or widen with the passage of time? I think not.

38 Was Hitler's War Just Another German War? A Post-Mortem on Bitburg

1

"Ich hatt' einen Kameraden, einen bess'ren finds't Du nicht. . . ."—"I once had a comrade, you'll never find one better. . . .": thus begins a dirge that is played by the military band, and sung by those present, whenever a German soldier is buried, and at a ceremony when those fallen in a war are remembered. It never fails to move. It never failed to move me when, well over fifty years ago, I was still a German as well as a Jew. The words of the song go on how the two comrades march in the same step, how a bullet comes flying and who knows whether it is for the one or the other, and how, when the other falls, he, the surviving comrade, cannot even shake the other's hand for the last time, for onward he must march. *Ich hatt' einen Kameraden* was sung at Bitburg.

I too once had a German comrade. We did not exactly do everything together, for he disliked sport. But we bicycled together, explored the countryside together, played music together. Also, we discussed politics, for he was a genuine democrat, one of only two (not counting myself, the only Jew) in my class at high school. His whole family were democrats, and I am convinced that he remained a sincere democrat and anti-Nazi to the end of his life. Yet Jürgen Wenzlau was killed on the Russian front, fighting Hitler's war.

If circumstances got me near the place where my friend lies buried I would be sure to visit his grave. I would mourn Jürgen. Yet if there were a public ceremony commemorating the German World War II dead at Jürgen's cemetery, I would absolutely refuse to attend. So should President Reagan have refused to attend, and—what is far more serious—Chancellor Kohl should never have invited him. All this even if not a single S.S. man were buried at Bitburg.

In a way, the presence of S.S. men's graves at Bitburg was unfortunate, for it

The theme dealt with briefly in this essay is treated at length in *To Mend the World: Foundations of Future Jewish Thought* (New York: Schocken Books, 1982).

clouded the issue. It was one thing for Frenchmen and Germans to join in commemorating the dead on both sides in World War I. But it was another thing entirely to do the same thing about the fallen in World War II. For that was not a war between two sides, "theirs" and "ours." It was a war for the survival of civilization itself. When Generals Eisenhower and Patton came to the murder camp of Ohrdruf, Eisenhower, on seeing what he saw, said that this was beyond the American mind to comprehend. Then he gave orders to the effect that as many G.I.s as possible were to visit that place. He said: "It is said that the American soldier does not understand what he is fighting for. Let him come, see and understand at least what he is fighting against." Have Americans forgotten what they were fighting against? Have Germans forgotten—have they ever learned?—that the total defeat of their armies in World War II was the necessary condition for the survival of civilization, and therefore of German civilization?

In saying what he did and putting it as he did, General—later President—Eisenhower recognized that Ohrdruf and all it stood for, and the war, were not two things separate, but that they were firmly, if possibly obscurely, interrelated. Does the present White House incumbent still recognize this fact? Much more importantly, is it still recognized by the present German head of state? In his country there are thoughtful, conscientious young people who, taking upon themselves the responsibility for a German future, delve deeply into the German past, with a view to discovering how what did happen could have happened. Will Bitburg undermine their efforts, with its implication that, except of course for Auschwitz, Hitler's war was just another German war, and that Auschwitz was an accident, perpetrated by just a few?

That Hitler's war was not just another German war was recognized at the time by Dietrich Bonhoeffer, a great Christian and leading member of the German anti-Nazi Confessional Church. Bonhoeffer was also a German patriot. Hence it was only after much agonizing that he could bring himself to pray for the defeat of his own country, in which Caesar's throne was then occupied by the anti-Christ. (Having joined a plot on Hitler's life and [been] caught and murdered by the Nazis, he died a martyr for his convictions.) The Bonhoeffers, however, were all-too-few. Martin Niemoeller, too, was a great Christian, a leading member of the Confessional Church and a German patriot. For his opposition to Naziism he was imprisoned in the concentration camp of Sachsenhausen. Yet when war broke out, Niemoeller, who had been a submarine commander in World War I, offered his services to the *Führer*. Luckily for him, Hitler turned him down. Otherwise he too, like Jürgen Wenzlau, might have been killed in the war and—which is worse—killed fighting Hitler's war.

2

That the German second world war *was* Hitler's war—that it and Auschwitz are inseparable—is a lesson to be learned from a work written, aptly enough, by a German historian. Karl Dietrich Bracher's *The German Dictatorship* (New York: Praeger, 1970) demonstrates that Nazi Germany was a dual system. The one, the inner core of the whole, was the S.S. state, a tightly organized system wholly dedicated to Nazi aims, among which was the murder of every available Jew. (Auschwitz was among the essential Nazi aims; arguably it was foremost.) The other was the traditional German system: the civil service, the railroads, the schools and universities, the clergy, the army. Quite deliberately, the second system was allowed independent existence to the very end of the war. But it was also increasingly used by the first system—manipulated, penetrated, perverted. (During the war the army, which prided itself on its Prussian-inspired code of honor, became gradually involved in Nazi crimes. I am sure Jürgen Wenzlau never did.) The traditional system remained largely non-Nazi. Here and there it even had anti-Nazi pockets, and there were sporadic acts of resistance. *But since* no *part of the traditional German system ever resisted* radically and systematically *the Nazi use and manipulation of it, it enabled the S.S. state to do what this latter would never have accomplished simply by itself. Had the railway men gone on strike or simply melted away, there would have been no Auschwitz. Had the German army resisted* absolutely—the *Wehrmacht* could have overthrown the Nazi regime as late as in 1938—*there would have been neither Auschwitz nor World War II.*

This is why no non-German head of state should ever again be asked to participate in a ceremony commemorating German soldiers fallen in World War II. It is also why Germans, alone in their commemoration, are faced with a tragedy without precedent. Jürgen Wenzlau, a good man to the end—you'll never find a better comrade!—died fighting for the wrong cause, not only by the standards of "our side" but by any decent standard of all mankind.

3

In a secret speech delivered in 1944 to the S.S. elite, Heinrich Himmler asserted that all the seventy million Germans wished to get rid of the Jews, but that only they, the S.S., had the guts to do it, and to allow for no "decent" Jews who were to be spared. Himmler was correct enough about the S.S. elite. But he grossly slandered countless decent Germans who never accepted the Nazi *Weltanschauung.*

Yet there was an element of truth in Himmler's slander: the whole German people, or nearly all of them, were implicated in the process that led to Auschwitz. In every civilized state a person is innocent until he is proven guilty; in the Nazi state everyone was suspected of "non-Aryan" guilt until he had proved his "Aryan" innocence. In every normal state a person is punished for something he *has done.* In the Nazi state—it was an anti-state—a "non-Aryan" was "punished" by humiliation, torture and death for the "crime" *of existence. Hence everyone within that anti-state proving his "Aryan" "Innocence", prepared to prove it, or even just surviving on the presumption of it, was implicated, however innocently, in the process of abandoning the "non-Aryan" victims to their fate.* Spiderlike, the Nazi *Reich* sought to implicate in its crimes the *entire* German people; and, lamentably enough but by no means unnaturally, it achieved a near-total success. It is true that some Germans escaped the spider's web: those clear-sighted enough to oppose the regime *absolutely,* i.e., in most cases at the cost of their lives. But not many people are that clear-sighted; and few people anywhere are willing to die for their convictions. One ponders the success of the Nazi *Reich*—its twelve years were equal to a thousand—and is aghast. What is before our eyes can only be called a German tragedy, unparalleled anywhere.

Germany once was the land of poets and philosophers. Once the philosopher

Schelling wrote of "innocent guilt" in considering Oedipus, a tragedy merely on the stage, displayed for us who are mere spectators. When will the philosopher arise—he can only be German—who will ponder a tragedy which unfolded on no mere stage, and of which none of us will ever be able to be mere spectators? One must hope that arise he will. For only from a confrontation with the tragedy of the German past can a true German future arise.

39 *Reflections on Aliyah*

In 1970 or thereabouts I happened to give a public lecture at a Canadian university, after which a student, not Jewish, got up and asked: "After having heard you I have a question: Why are you in Canada? Why aren't you in Israel?"

I thought for a moment and replied something like this: "One night in the Berlin of 1937 or 1938, some friends of mine and myself, rabbinical students all, had a long discussion as to where, given the chance, a German Jew committed to Judaism ought to emigrate. At length we concluded that there were only two possibilities. Either we reacted to the momentous events of our time by pursuing the academic study of Judaism, but then we had to head West, for America; or we joined a kibbutz, but then we had to give up all academic aspirations. (About the possibilities of academic study of Judaism in the future Israel we were, as it turned out, unduly pessimistic.) Soon after, I made my choice, ended up in Canada, and did not reconsider until the Six-Day War. (I was at home in Canada, and continue to be so.) Ever since then, however, I have asked myself whether back in the 1930s, I did not make the wrong choice."

It was not so much the Six-Day War itself as the dreadful, crucial three weeks that preceded it. The same words emanated from Radio Cairo, Damascus, and Amman that only so recently had emanated from Berlin and Vienna. The reaction of the world, too, brought the past grimly back to mind. At first there was talk of some 20-odd seafaring nations breaking Colonel Nasser's blockade of the Gulf of Aqaba. The number soon dwindled, until it was reduced to three. And then there were none at all. (The United Nations so-called Peace Force had long departed from the Sinai, at Nasser's bidding, and the churches, once again, were silent.) We stared into the abyss.

Thereafter, of course, came the last-minute, sudden, surprising, miraculous—

Reprinted from *Midstream* (August/September, 1985): 25–28.

or so it felt—salvation; and sudden, last-minute salvation has been a Jewish root-experience ever since the Red Sea, never forgotten, ever again celebrated in prayer and song. However, since the Holocaust, salvation can no longer be counted on. The abyss remained. It remains with us to this day.

Jews in this century have stared at the abyss before. Indeed, it very nearly devoured us all—Hitler, God forbid, might have won the war. Nonetheless, except for the survivors and a few others whose voices were not listened to or not understood, we did not or could not see what we stared at and, more often than not, averted our eyes. Not really seeing what was there, we could tell ourselves (and each other) that, in the eyes of the Jewish faith, the murder of six million Jews was in principle no different from the death of one child; or that the catastrophe resembled all the others that are mourned on the Ninth of Av; or even that, once again, we had been punished for our sins. For my part, I had expressed myself in print to the effect that, whereas empirical, historical events can serve to confirm the Jewish faith—I was thinking of saving events such as those celebrated on Pesach, Hanukkah, and Purim—no empirical, historical events can refute or indeed so much as touch that faith; that out of tragedy and catastrophe Jewish faith always and necessarily emerges triumphant. While I had written, philosophically, about radical-evil-in-general and, theologically, about the demonic-in-general, however, I had not written about the Holocaust-in-particular—the screams of the little children who at Auschwitz were thrown into the fire without first being killed. Not until the threat of a second Jewish Holocaust, this time in Jerusalem, did we fully confront the fact of the first.

Why, except for its magnitude, was the Holocaust not just another Jewish catastrophe, to be classified with the first destruction of the Temple, its second destruction, the expulsion from Spain? And why was the feared (and threatening) second Holocaust more than a repetition of what we had hoped and prayed was intrinsically unrepeatable? Why—an unutterable blasphemy!—would the destruction of Israel be the End?

1. The Holocaust was not just another (albeit gigantic) pogrom from which one could hide until the visitation of the drunken Cossacks had passed. *This* enemy was coldly sober, coldly rational, coldly systematic; except for a lucky few, there was no hiding.

2. The Holocaust was not just another (albeit in quantity and scope unprecedented) expulsion. So long as the Third Reich was satisfied with expelling Jews, there was, except for those fortunate or prescient enough, no place to go. And when the Reich became dissatisfied with mere expulsion, Jews trapped in Nazi-occupied Europe had no escape.

3. The Holocaust was not an assault calling for bribing the enemy or buying him off or appeasing him; *this* enemy was an "idealist" who could not be bribed or bought off, and who remained unappeased until the last available Jew was dead.

4. Finally—and perhaps most devastatingly—the Holocaust did not present itself as demanding the response of martyrdom. When the Roman Emperor Hadrian forbade the practice of Judaism on pain of death, he showed himself to be an enemy of unprecedented ferocity. (He set out as well to make Jerusalem into a pagan city when Titus had been satisfied merely to destroy it as a Jewish one.) But he also created hitherto unheard-of possibilities of martyrdom. And when such as

Rabbi Akiba defied the tyrant, were caught, tortured, and killed, but died with the *Shema* on their lips, they placed into Jewish history an inspiration that reverberated through the ages as Jews gathered, and ever again re-gathered, the courage, the morale, the faith to endure a long night of exile.

On its part, the Nazi empire, far from repeating the Roman folly of creating Jewish martyrs, was on the contrary cunningly designed to murder Jewish martyrdom. Believers and unbelievers, saints and sinners, men, women, children, and even babies in arms were indiscriminately "exterminated"; not even the old and senile were permitted to end their lives in peace. Within the Nazi universe, what mattered was only that Jews existed; as for their beliefs or their deeds, even, and indeed especially, when they were saintly or heroic, they were of no account. (The heroic or saintly behavior of countless nameless Akibas, if it was noticed at all, moved their tormentors and eventual murderers only to laughter.) As for us who come after, of all things unbearable about the Holocaust, the most unbearable, and most necessary to remember and therefore to bear, are not the prayers of the martyrs or the hero's death of the fighters but rather the cry of innocence that comes to us from all those who *did not, or could not, or would not choose* heroism or martyrdom or any of the ways in which men and women throughout the ages have managed to give meaning to suffering and death. The men. The women. The children. Theirs is a cry unlike any other. He who listens can hear it still— and can conceive of no possible future world that will silence it.

This, then, is what began to be revealed in the weeks preceding the Six-Day War, and what has had to be faced by the collective Jewish consciousness ever since. But what was revealed in the threat of a second Jewish Holocaust, this time in Israel? And why was it not only a possible repetition of what we had hoped and prayed was intrinsically unrepeatable? Why would it be, after nearly four millennia of continuous Jewish existence, nothing less than the end?

When Jews like Akiba responded to Hadrian's attack on Judaism with a martyr's death, they set the tone for many centuries of what may be called Galut Judaism, i.e., the ability to bear the sufferings of exile. This ability rests on a threefold knowledge: the sufferings, although harsh, are meaningful; the Messiah, though he hesitates, will eventually arrive; and, since the enemy's assaults have their limits, the Jewish people will live to see the Messianic days. But what of us who come, not after Hadrian, but after Hitler? Are the screams of the children meaningful? Can the coming of a Messiah be counted on when, at the time of the most desperate need, he failed to arrive? And if and when come he does, will the Jewish people live to see him when, except for an accident—Hitler's loss of the war—all Jews living even now would either have been murdered or never been born? Something had to change *radically* if, after *that* catastrophe, the Jewish people had to find the morale, the strength, the will to continue its history: and in the fear for Israel in the weeks prior to the Six-Day War we discovered, in utter amazement, that the change *had already occurred.* No more hiding until the drunkenness of the pogromnik has passed, but the proud and self-confident display of Jewish identity! No more appeasing or bribing of assailants, but resistance, if necessary with the force of arms! No more wandering from exile to exile but, after 2,000 years of exile and Diaspora, a return home!

Whether in a spirit of criticism or simply of bewilderment, Christian friends often say that Israel seems to have become the religion of the Jews in the Diaspora. Something is being noticed here, but it is not understood. What has been happening may be put as follows: When Rabbi Akiba, his predecessors, colleagues, and followers created Galut Judaism, they opened a new page in the history of both Jews and Judaism. The Warsaw Ghetto fighters and, following them, the Israeli army, opened another new page—this too in the history of Judaism as well as of Jews—when, though *Galut* is still grimly real, Galut *Judaism*, the unresisting acceptance of Galut as meaningful, however painful, was coming to an end.

This opening of a new page the world has yet to notice, and even Jews themselves have been slow to recognize it. It is true that Jewish anti-Zionism ended, or very nearly ended, even before the founding of the state—with a whimper. (A new whimper was heard during the war in Lebanon when quite a few Jews, never before publicly identified as Jews, made what Norman Podhoretz has called the "supreme sacrifice" of public Jewish self-identification—in order to attack Israel more effectively.) And ever since the state has existed there has been a broad pro-Israel Jewish consensus. But not until in 1967, when we were gripped by the fear of losing Israel, did we grasp its significance. Indeed, even now we are confused in our grasp; and the strange, extraordinary fact is that *amcha*—ordinary Jewish folk—is clearer and more steadfast in its perceptions than the learned and the clever—professors, intellectuals, theologians, not to mention sundry sophisticated rabbis. In the circles of these one can still hear it said that Hitler was just another mad dictator, without posthumous result after his removal; that Auschwitz, an expression of "man's inhumanity to man," was like Hiroshima, Vietnam, Biafra—anything but itself; or that, like earlier Jewish catastrophes that our sages once found meaningful, the screams of the children at Auschwitz too have a divine meaning. (Some even tell us what the meaning is.) Also heard—and there is a connection here—are arguments as to whether today there is one Jewish center, or two, or three, or none at all. And in one respected, traditional, academic magazine, a professor has argued calmly and in some detail that if, God forbid, Israel were destroyed, Judaism—if not Jews—would go on as if nothing had occurred. All such talk, weird in its abstractness and unreality, contrasts sharply with the clarity and steadfastness of the ordinary Jewish people who, in creating, maintaining, building, supporting the new Jewish state have already done the decisive deed.[1] In those days in the summer of 1967, when this great truth first struck us, it was impossible not to be in awe of what, in this of all times, the Jewish people, collectively, have done, what the thinkers among us have yet to understand. It was, and to this day remains, impossible not to love the Jewish people. It was, and to this day remains, impossible not to love Israel.

Though pro-Zionist since 1933 and pro-Israel since 1948, I had in 1967 never visited Israel, or even seriously considered a visit. In 1968 my wife Rose and I took our first trip. Other visits soon followed, among them a pilgrimage in the company of Bergen-Belsen survivors that took us first to Bergen-Belsen and then to Jerusalem. Then Rose declared that she would not go again without the children, so regular summer visits with Suzy and David followed, which soon earned us the nickname "the commuters." (The visits were for a full two months, and it should here be gratefully recorded that they were supported by Canada Council summer grants. The Council accepted my argument that I could no longer engage in Jewish thought without regular visits to Jerusalem.) And from then on it was only a question of time and external circumstances until, two years ago, the family—Suzy, now aged 22, David, now 19, and Yossi, aged 5, as well as Rose and I—made aliyah.

From the moment we touched ground in Eretz Yisrael that summer of 1968 Rose and I were in love. The crowd awaiting the visitors at the airport—all Israel is a family! The first Hebrew sign at a gas station—a mute testimony to Jewish life as a flesh-and-blood reality, not merely a "spiritual" one! The Galil ablaze with flowers, and the unexpected colors of the desert. An innkeeper in Beersheva, a survivor, who said—it sounded like a prayer of thanksgiving—"I need only bread and water, so long as I am free." And then, of course, the multitude of Jews coming, so it seemed, from all four corners of the earth. People in love discover that the trite love songs that they have known all their lives are true. In that great summer of 1968 Rose and I discovered the same thing about the old, boring Zionist slogans. "The Ingathering of the Dispersed," "The End of the Exile," "Making the Desert Bloom"—these platitudes were nothing but the simple truth, a truth more profound than the profundities of philosophers, to say nothing of the pseudo-dialectical contortions of so many intellectuals.

And then there was Jerusalem. I come from a tradition for which, if Berlin was not exactly Jerusalem neither was Jerusalem itself. Jerusalem, or what was left of it, was simply ruins from the forgotten past, and neither Muslims nor Christians wanted it at that time.[2] Why, then, should Jerusalem have meant something special to a Jew like me?

I know only part of the answer. I cannot explain why, after a few days in Israel in 1968, my heart should have started pounding when at length we approached Jerusalem. Nor can I explain why, when we got to the Wall, I permitted myself to be dressed in tallith and tefillin and, hand on the Wall, photographed. I *can* explain, however, why Rose and I were moved when we came to the hustle and bustle of Rehov Yafo and Rehov Ben Yehuda. (Indeed, when we stop and think, we are still moved by that hustle and bustle and so, we think, should everyone.) "How doth the city sit solitary that was full of people!" Thus begins the Book of Lamentations, thus is the lament of the Ninth of Av. It is the core of all Jewish sorrow. And out of the Jewish sorrow of our time—there is none other like it—there arises a cry of wonder and joy that, too, is like none other: "How is the city full of people that only yesterday, it seems, did sit solitary!" Of all the profound Zionist platitudes surely the one most pregnant with significance for the future of both Jews and Judaism is that which speaks of the rebuilding of Jerusalem.

A few years after our first visit, I undertook teaching a summer course in Jewish philosophy at the Hebrew University. (I wanted to find out what it would be like teaching that subject in Jerusalem.) So, five mornings a week for three weeks I climbed over rocks, dust, and rubble in the new campus that was being built on Mount Scopus and lectured to the noise of drills and hammers. Then one day, a few minutes before the end of the lecture, I came upon the passage in Yehuda Halevi's *Kuzari* in which the rabbi explains to the pagan king he has been instructing that Jerusalem will not be redeemed until Jews yearn for her very stones and dust. For a moment I stopped. I looked at my watch: the hour was up. I looked at my students: here they were: Jews from America and England, Canada, South Af-

373   Reflections on Aliyah

rica, and even Australia! (Years later, among those present was also a Christian missionary who loved Israel, all the way from Japan.) What were they all doing, at this of all times, when 100 or even 50 years ago not one of them would have come? I turned to my listeners and said: "Ladies and gentlemen, you have heard. What are you waiting for? There are plenty of stones. There is plenty of dust." Then I walked out.

It is no longer visits now, short or long, but aliyah. We are in the stage known as "sufferings of the absorption." And we keep hearing the joke about the fellow who, prior to his death, is permitted to visit heaven and hell and choose between them. Finding heaven to be boring and hell a place where there is music and laughter, drinks and song, he naturally chooses hell, only to discover when he gets there for good that the place has been transformed into one of hell-fire, devils with pitchforks, and all the rest. "This is not like the last time at all," the fellow hollers. The reply and punch line: "But last time you were a visitor!"

What is to be said about the "sufferings" of aliyah? For us personally, nothing, except that we seem to be holding our own. Suzy at Hebrew University; David in Zahal (the army); and Yossi as he uses Hebrew, strong language included, in his various encounters in the playground.

But much could be said, and something must be said, about the problems of the Israeli reality that become increasingly real for the one-time visitor as he becomes an oleh. There are the tensions between the religious and the secularist; between Right and Left; between rich and poor; between Israeli Jews and Israeli Arabs. There are the economic woes. Above all, there is the persistent, obdurate, depressing refusal of the Arab world to accept the reality and legitimacy of Israel; and this is accompanied by growing success in hoodwinking the nice people of the world as to the true purpose of the refusal. (The nice people are, now as always, tired of the so-called "Jewish problem.") And what use is it to say that it is really an Arab problem, and that the problem will evaporate once Israel is permitted to live in peace with her neighbors? It is necessary to say this to the world. But what help is it to the new oleh when we can as yet make no prediction as to when or how the "Arab problem" will be solved? This question weighs heavily on Israel—and on a Jew once he has made Israel's destiny his own.

Then what happens when the Zionist slogans, having lost the freshness of the moment of discovery, once again become mere slogans under the impact of reality? Much the same, Rose and I think, as when being-in-love has yielded to marriage. A couple long married may be tired of the old love songs, or even find them irrelevant. Love itself, however, need never grow old; and it was a stroke of genius that made Herzl call his novel *Old-New Land*. In marriage what can and should take the place of being in love is the shared experience of a lifetime. In the case of Israel, and of the bond of the Jewish people with her, it is historical perspective. Zionism is the boldest, bravest, most devout collective enterprise the Jewish people have ever undertaken since, refusing to despair after the destruction of the second Jewish commonwealth, they carried the Torah into a long and arduous exile. Begun in the 19th century, the enterprise reached its climax at the precise moment when, following an unprecedented catastrophe, the normal reactions should have been not courage, faith, and a firm resolve, but rather disintegration and despair. It is not really so surprising that an enterprise so unprecedented should have run up against great obstacles; that Israel, a fact affecting the whole Jewish people, is today, as it were, in a tunnel, with as yet little light visible at the other side. (To go further, we cannot yet even know whether what gives that light is the sun or a destructive fire.) Yet a Jew with the perspective of the last two millennia cannot but consider joining those in the tunnel a privilege for which his ancestors would have envied him. And in gaining entry he will be prepared to work his way through it, prepared to face whatever may wait on the other side.

I cast my mind back to 1970 or thereabouts, to that student at a Canadian university who asked me that question. Surely I am not the first to whom this sort of thing has happened! Indeed, I seem to have read about it somewhere. And then I remember! Somewhere in the final part of Yehuda Halevi's *Kuzari* in which the rabbi instructs the pagan king in the holiness of the Land, and how it is a duty for a Jew to go and live in it. Whereupon the king reprimands the rabbi, to the effect that if he speaks truthfully, he is derelict in his duty in not living in the Land; and the rabbi, having been instructed by the one he has instructed, makes aliyah. It is unlikely that that student, a non-Jew like the king of the Khazars, will read these pages. If by some chance he does, it is not likely that he will remember the incident and his own question. Even so, I wish to express my gratitude to him, giving thanks to one who, having been instructed by me, became himself my instructor.

Notes

1. The enemy, of course, wants to undo it. And those who accept at face value the code language by means of which he disguises his purpose are already spiritually prepared once again to be bystanders.

2. If, in our time, Muslims and Christians want Jerusalem, is it not because "the Jews" now have it? (The late King Saud of Saudi Arabia lamented that he could not worship at the al-Aqsa Mosque because it was Jewish-controlled, but did not visit there once in the 19 years that it was Muslim-controlled.) And are Christians different? In those 19 years the Vatican did not call once for the internationalization of, or international status for, Jerusalem but has been doing so incessantly ever since.

Appendix: Unsere Stellung zur Halacha

Es ist bezeichnend für den heutigen Menschen, der als Aussenstehender an die Religion herantritt, dass er sie nach ihrer *Naturgemässheit* beurteilt und sich entsprechend zu ihr verhält. Ihre Lehren werden auf ihre Anwendbarkeit für die menschliche Gesellschaft geprüft; eine andere Form nur ist es, wenn die Lehren und Bräuche darauf gefragt werden, ob sie den Menschen *ansprechen:* Ob die Einstellung eine rationale oder eine irrationale ist, gemeinsam ist doch dieses, dass die Religion an der *eigenen Natur* des Urteilenden, sei es eines Individuums oder einer Gemeinschaft, gemessen und beurteilt wird.

Hier muss der schwerste Anstoss erregt werden durch die Summe von Bräuchen, die uns als *Halacha* entgegentritt. Um diesen recht zu verstehen, ist es nötig, gegen zwei Versuche, diesen Anstoss zu mildern, den ursprünglichen Anspruch der Halacha zu wahren. Man versucht, die Halacha religionsgeschichtlich zu erklären: Wie in jeder Religion auf einer gewissen Stufe religiöses Brauchtum entstehe, so sei es auch hier. In der von da aus bestimmten Stellungnahme unterscheiden sich radikale und gemässigte Richtung nur graduell: Ob und wie weit diesem Brauchtum auch heute noch ein Sinn zugesprochen wird, etwa zum Guten zu erziehen oder das Weihegefühl des Menschen zu sättigen. Kaum wesentlich verschieden ist der andere Versuch, der die Halacha als Volksbrauch erklärt: Von hier aus wird dann als nationale Forderung die Wiederbelebung dieses Brauchtums gefördert. Beiden gemeinsam ist, dass der Mensch geistige Erzeugnisse seiner Vorfahren *an sich selbst* misst und sie danach beurteilt. Man weiss sich sozusagen "unter sich"; wie in allen Gebieten des Lebens die Menschen heute gewöhnt sind, "unter sich" zu sein, wie sie jede Art von Belehrungen, Rechtsvorschriften sich selbst zu geben gewöhnt sind, so soll es auch hier, bei der Halacha sein: Auch hier findet man etwas vor, was Menschen sich selbst gesagt haben, was Menschen darum an sich selbst messen, über dessen Wert und Verbindlichkeit sie selbst entscheiden.

Was man sich selbst sagt, kann aber nie mehr als Brauch sein; die Halacha tritt uns entgegen als *Gebot*, als Gebot darum *des Anderen.* Und nun wird der Anstoss der von hier kommt recht deutlich. Diese Halacha verlangt, ausgeübt zu werden, und zwar nicht bei einigen feierlichen Anlässen, in einigen Stimmungsaugenblicken, sondern im ganzen täglichen Leben. Aber wo gäbe es heute jemand unter den Menschen, an die wir uns richten, dem der Gott, dessen Gebot die Halacha zu sein beansprucht, im ganzen alltäglichen Leben gegenwärtig wäre! Wo könnte jemand in seinem Alltagsleben es sich ständig *von dem Anderen sagen lassen!* Es würde nicht nur ein unwürdiger, sondern ein auf die Dauer erfolgloser Versuch sein, sich darüber hinwegzutäuschen. Und der andere Anstoss kommt von eben daher. Des Absoluten ist sich der Mensch heute nur in "Grenzsituationen" gegenwärtig. Als Geheimnis, unergründlich, unaussprechbar, jedes Wort, jedes Denken verstummen machend bricht es zuweilen, ungreifbar, unerhellbar am Rande menschlicher Existenz auf; unerhellbar in dem Maße, dass der Mensch es kaum wagt, sich ihm mit den Maßstäben zu nähern, die seine höchsten sind, den sittlichen. Und hier, wo selbst diese Maßstäbe, diese Inhalte zu versagen scheinen, da treten in einem festen System Inhalte, Forderungen an den Menschen heran, die ihm, kleine und kleinste Bräuche, angesichts des Göttlichen scheinbar zwangsläufig als Kleinigkeitskramerei erscheinen müssen.

Zu zwei Fragen also gilt es Stellung zu nehmen:

1. Ist es uns möglich, es uns ständig sagen zu lassen, ständig nicht-nur-natürlich, nicht nur "unter uns" zu sein, oder wird zwangsläufig nicht mehr nichts anderes möglich sein als religiöser, als Volksbrauch, dem ursprünglichen Anspruch der Halacha widersprechend?

2. Wie haben wir uns von hier aus zu den zahllosen einzelnen Gesetzen, Vorschriften der Überlieferung zu verhalten?

Beide Fragen hängen aufs innerste zusammen und können in der Beantwortung nicht so klar wie in der Fragestellung getrennt werden.

In die Schöpfungsordnung, die im wahrsten Sinne *Ordnung* ist, in der es eigentlich nur ein Sein und ein Werden, aber kein *Sollen* gibt, die fraglos und harmonisch *Natur* ist, schlägt bereits früh als ein Dynamisches ein Sollen hinein, als sittliches Sollen unter die Menschen gebracht. Darin scheidet sich Menschsein als Nicht-nur-Natursein von blossem Natursein: es tritt in die Harmonie des gesetzmässigen Wachsens und Vergehens, die Harmonie der Natur ein ständig Unharmonisches, Forderndes, in den natürlichen Ablauf als ein Anderes hineingesetzt. Erst unsere Zeit hat zu Unrecht dieses revolutionär, absolut fordernde Sittliche, jeweils die Harmonie störende, vorwärts treibende, ständig in Frage stellende zu einem Element der Daseinsordnung degradiert, hat aus der Forderung nach letzter Gerechtigkeit die Forderung nach der gesetzmässigen Daseinsordnung der menschlichen Gesellschaft, aus einem Absoluten, das gerade darum den natürlichen Ablauf stören muss, ein Relatives, einen Knecht gerade eines Natురseins, der Gesellschaft gemacht.

Ein Forderndes erfährt Israel am Sinai mit elementarer Gewalt; ein derart Elementares, dass dieses Volk von hier aus die Harmonie, die Nur-Naturhaftigkeit, die Fraglosigkeit völlig verliert. Ob Israel will oder nicht, "der Berg" ist seitdem "über es gestülpt." Eine scheinbare Paradoxie: ein lebendiges Volk, im lebendigen Zusammenhang, in horizontaler wie in vertikaler Richtung, in seinem gleichzeitig Lebenden und den Ahnen und Enkeln, ein lebendiges Volk ist gleichzeitig unnatürlich, unharmonisch, ständig in Frage gestellt.

Dieses Volk hat nun jeweils versucht, der Forderung zu antworten, sie zu verstehen und sie zu erfüllen. Es hat jeweils versucht, *nicht es sich selbst zu sagen, sondern es sich sagen zu lassen.* So steht die Halacha in ihrer heutigen, schriftlich niedergelegten Gestalt vor uns als ein Zeugnis des Bemühens zahlloser Geschlechter, es sich sagen zu lassen, dieses Es, was mit dem Sittlichen des Vor-Sinai nicht restlos aussagbar ist, was überhaupt nicht ausfüllend aussagbar ist. So geschah es, dass man in einem Wollen von metaphysischem Ernste, der elementaren Forderung mit menschlicher Kraft gerecht zu werden, aus dem einfachen Bibelwort gewaltige Gedankengebäude errichtete, Folianten mit zahllosen Vorschriften füllte. Wir stehen staunend vor diesem Werk, vor jener Energie, die im innersten Bewusstsein des menschliche Kraft übersteigenden Gebotes die Intensität gleichsam in die Breite übertrug durch das Bestreben, das menschliche Leben bis ins kleinste dem Gebote zu unterwerfen.

Aber jene Glaubensgewissheit, die es den Alten ermöglichte, genau umschriebene Vorschriften auszuüben und doch dabei zu wissen, dass sie es sich nicht selbst gesagt, sondern es sich hatten sagen lassen, wir können sie nur verstehen. Das ungeheuer Fordernde steht für uns nicht, wie bei den Alten, mitten im Leben, es steht am Rande unserer Existenz, es ist darum für uns dunkler, unaussprechbarer, unerreichbarer, darum auch unausführbarer als für jene. Wir können glauben, dass das Tun, das Leben jener echte Antwort war auf die Forderung vom Sinai her, dass es echte Erfüllung war, dass hier ein echtes Annehmen der Thora geschah, das jeweils erst letzte Erfüllung des Zwanges ist, der den Berg über Israel stülpt; aber wir können nicht glauben, dass jene Vorschriften, die als Niederschlag davon systematisch angeordnet und aufgeschrieben vor uns liegen, klar ausgesprochen und tubar für jedermann, nun das Gesetz wären, das es nur gälte auszuüben. Davor hält uns nicht nur die Erkenntnis zurück, dass hier wirklich, im einzelnen betrachtet vielfach einzelne Volksbräuche, ja zum Teil aus fremden Kulturen übernommene zu finden sind, und dass die Späteren wirklich Vorschriften im Namen der Früheren gaben, an die jene nie gedacht haben, sondern vielmehr das Wissen, das dadurch zum ersten Mal das Unaussprechbare aussprechbar gemacht, das Unendliche verendlicht würde. Der Schulchan Aruch ist für uns die ehrfurchtsvoll betrachtete *Form*, in der die Erfüllung einstmals geschah, in der sie sicherlich weitgehend auch in unseren Tagen geschehen kann, aber er ist nicht das Fordernde, das Unaussprechbare selbst: mit dem geheimnisvollen Gott ist sein Gebot letzthin Geheimnis.

Damit scheinen wir freilich in eine nahezu verzweifelnde Lage zu geraten. Wie soll jeder Einzelne von uns es sich sagen lassen, wenn es ihm nicht gesagt wird? Und wie soll ein Unaussprechbares, Geheimnisvolles von uns doch ausgesprochen und getan, vor allem getan werden? Auf diese beiden Fragen gilt es nun endgültig Antwort zu geben, und von ihnen hängt die Halacha und ihr Schicksal in unseren Taben ab. Der Einzelne als Einzelner ist nicht gemeint, ist nie gemeint worden. Der Anruf vom Sinai geht an den *Klal Israel* in seiner Verbindung der gleichzeitig Lebenden mit der Kette der Geschlechter. Und diese gleichzeitig Lebenden heute haben sicherlich die Glaubens*gewissheit* der Vorfahren verloren, aber sie haben nicht die Glaubens*aufgeschlossenheit* verloren. Die Aufgabe der heutigen Generation ist es, glaubensbereit zu sein, *bereit, das Andere als Forderndes in ihre Mitte einzulassen.* Die Gemeinschaft Israel muss dazu die Verbindung zu den Ahnen aufsuchen, um gleichsam so selbst am Sinai stehen zu können, um so erst wirklich Klal Israel nicht nur in horizontaler sondern in vertikaler Richtung zu sein. Ob unser Tun Antwort sein wird auf das Fordernde, wir können es nicht wissen. Wir können nur bereit sein und aus dieser Bereitschaft gleichsam *fragend zu tun versuchen*. Stellen wir uns in die Kette der Geschlechter ein, so ist dies noch nicht mit Erfüllung identisch; aber es bringt uns ein Stück weiter, dem Sinai näher. Und es wird darum wohl so sein müssen, dass wir im einzelnen mit dem Tun unserer Ahnen anfangen. Wohl wird dies nichts nützen, wenn wir es als "Brauch" "übernehmen", oder wenn wir nur zu klären versuchen, worin ein "moralischer Sinn" liegt, wenn wir es also uns selbst sagen wollen; aber wenn wir an das Vermächtnis unserer Ahnen herantreten mit der Bereitschaft, es uns sagen, uns gebieten zu lassen, das Unendliche in das Endliche, das Geheimnis in das Offenbare, das Übernatürliche in das Natürliche eintreten zu lassen, wenn wir *tun* in Glaubensbereitschaft, so ist getan, was zu tun heute in Israels Macht steht.

Wenn wir so an das Erbgut der Ahnen herantreten, dann wird vielleicht deutlich werden, dass jener alte Glaube, dass Raschi nur auslege was Moses meint in einem tieferen Sinne wahr ist; das beide, dass alle Geschlechter an dem *einen* Sinai stehen, dass zwar jeder das Gebot in einer anderen Form vernimmt, erfüllt, aber dass das Unendliche, das "Wort an Israel" selbst immer das eine, dasselbe ist. Vielleicht können auch wir dieses Wort so vernehmen, vielleicht können wir, aller wissenschaftlichen Durchforschung zum Trotz darum wissen, dass das von uns Vernommene, von uns Erfüllte eben das ist, was Moses in der Thora niederschrieb und was Raschi auslegte.

Dass wir nicht glaubenssicher, nur glaubensbereit sein können, äussert sich zwangsläufig auch darin, dass es uns kaum möglich sein wird, die Halacha als feste Lebensordnung jeweils bereit zu haben. Gewiss, es muss, es soll im ganzen Leben getan werden, aber wir können jene Fraglosigkeit nicht besitzen, die im Grunde hier nie sein darf. Denn ständig in Gottes Gebot stehen heisst ein Leben führen in Natur und doch nicht in Natur, heisst eigentlich im Paradox leben. Doch wir sehen, und es ist wie eine Verheissung an uns, dass unsere Vorfahren es vermochten, gleichwohl hierin zu *leben*, leben, dass doch auch seiner Fraglosigkeit bedarf, leben in doch auch naturhafter Lebendigkeit. Und so nimmt Israel in seinem Aufbruch in Bereitschaft zum Glauben und zum Verwirklichen die Verheissung mit, dass die Verwirklichung des Unendlichen im Endlichen, des Geheimnisvollen im Offenbaren, die doch Israels Aufgabe zu sein scheint, auch ein Leben sein kann, Leben mit der ganzen Sinnfülle, die dieses Urwort der Schöpfung besitzt.

Bibliography of Works by Emil Fackenheim

(Note: The books are listed in chronological order according to the year published.)

Paths to Jewish Belief: A Systematic Introduction. New York: Behrman House, 1960. [*PJB*]

Metaphysics and Historicity. Milwaukee: Marquette University Press, 1961. [*MH*]

Quest for Past and Future: Essays in Jewish Theology. Bloomington: Indiana University Press, 1968. Reprint. Boston: Beacon, 1970. [*QPF*]

The Religious Dimension in Hegel's Thought. Bloomington: Indiana University Press, 1968. Reprint. Boston: Beacon Press, 1970. [*RDH*]

God's Presence in History: Jewish Affirmations and Philosophical Reflections. New York: New York University Press, 1970. Reprint. New York: Harper & Row, 1972. [*GPH*]

Encounters Between Judaism and Modern Philosophy: A Preface to Future Jewish Thought. New York: Basic Books Inc., 1973. Reprint. New York: Schocken Books, 1980. [*EJM*]

The Jewish Return Into History: Reflections in the Age of Auschwitz and a New Jerusalem. New York: Schocken Books, 1978. [*JRH*]

To Mend the World: Foundations of Future Jewish Thought. New York: Schocken Books, 1982. [*TMW*]

Chapters in Books

(Note: Certain articles which have appeared in periodical publications also appear as chapters in books. They are cross-referenced either by number or by using the abbreviations, *EJM, JRH,* and *QPF.* They are listed in chronological order according to the year published.)

1950

1. "Mediaeval Jewish Philosophy." In *A History of Philosophical Systems,* edited by Vergilius T. A. Ferm, 178–84. New York: Philosophical Library, 1950. Reprint. Paterson, N. J.: Littlefield, Adams & Co., 1958. Reprint. Freeport: New York, Books for Libraries Press, 1970.

1959

2. "Jewish Existence and the Living God." In *A People and Its Faith,* edited by A. Rose, 105–18. Toronto: University of Toronto Press, 1959. See nos. 22, 87; *QPF,* ch. 7.

1961

3. "Two Types of Reform: Reflections Occasioned by Hasidism." In *Reform Judaism: A Historical Perspective,* edited by Joseph Blau, 458–80. New York: Ktav, 1973. See no. 99; *QPF,* ch. 11.

1962

4. "A Jewish View." In *Religious Responsibility for the Social Order: A Symposium by Three Theologians,* 12–17. New York: National Conference of Christians and Jews, 1962. Also in *Judaism*

and Ethics, edited by Daniel Jeremy Silver, 243–48. New York: Ktav, 1970. See no. 101; *QPF*, ch. 12.

1963

5. "Conjectural Beginning of Human History." Translated by Lewis W. Beck, Robert E. Anchor, and Emil L. Fackenheim. In Immanuel Kant, *On History*, edited by L. W. Beck, 53–68. Indianapolis: Bobbs-Merrill, Library of Liberal Arts, 1963.

1964

6. "Samuel Hirsch and Hegel, A Study of Hirsch's *Religionsphilosophie der Juden* (1842)." In *Studies in Nineteenth Century Jewish Intellectual History*, edited by A. Altmann, Vol. II, 171–201. Cambridge, Mass.: Harvard University Press, 1964.

1965

7. "Judaism and the Meaning of Life." In *The Meaning of Life in Five Great Religions*, edited by J. A. Irving and R. C. Chalmers, 56–78. Toronto: Ryerson Press, 1965. Reprint. Philadelphia: Westminister Press, 1966. See no. 107; *QPF*, ch. 16.
8. "The Revealed Morality of Judaism and Modern Thought: A Confrontation with Kant." In *Rediscovering Judaism*, edited by A. Wolf, 51–75. Chicago: Quadrangle Books, 1965. Also in *Contemporary Jewish Ethics*, edited by M. M. Kellner, 62–83. New York: Sanhedrin Press, 1978. See *EJM*, ch. 2; *QPF*, ch. 14.

1966

9. "A Jew Looks at Secularist Liberalism and Christianity." In *The Restless Church*, edited by Wm. Kilbourn. Toronto: McClelland and Stewart, 1966. New York: Lippincott, 1966, 86–99. See no. 111; *QPF*, ch. 17.
10. "Apologia for a Confirmation Test." In *Judaism and the School*, edited by J. Pilch and M. Ben Horin, 281–94. New York: Bloch, 1966. See no. 96; *QPF*, ch. 9.
11. "The Dilemma of Liberal Judaism." In *The Commentary Reader*, edited by N. Podhoretz, 438–50. New York: Athenaeum, 1966. See no. 93; *QPF*, ch. 8.
12. "On the Eclipse of God." In *The Star and the Cross*, edited by K. J. Hargrove, 227–38. Milwaukee: Bruce Publishing Co., 1966. Also in *A Modern Introduction to Philosophy*, edited by Paul Edwards and Arthur Pap, 523–33. New York: Free Press, 1973. Translated into Hebrew. See no. 106; *QPF*, ch. 15.

1967

13. Contribution to "The State of Jewish Belief," reprinted in *The Condition of Jewish Belief*, edited by the editors of *Commentary*, 51–59. New York: Macmillian. See no. 112.
14. "On the Self-Exposure of Faith to the Modern Secular World: Philosophical Reflections in the Light of Jewish Experience." In *Religion in America*, edited by Wm. G. McLoughlin and R. N. Bellah, 203–29. Boston: Houghton Mifflin, 1968. See no. 116; *QPF*, ch. 18.
15. "Martin Buber's Concept of Revelation." In *The Philosophy of Martin Buber*, edited by P. A. Schilpp and M. Friedman, 273–96. La Salle, Ill.: Open Court, 1967. Published in German.

1968

16. "Idolatry as a Modern Religious Possibility." In *The Religious Situation*, edited by D. H. Cutler, 254–87. Boston: Beacon Press, 1968. See *EJM*, ch. 4.
17. "On Faith in the Secular World." In *Out of the Whirlwind*, edited by A. H. Friedlander, 493–514. New York: Union of American Hebrew Congregations, 1968.
18. "Man and his World in the Perspective of Judaism." In *New Theology*. Vol. 5, edited by M. E. Marty and D. G. Peerman, 47–61. New York: Macmillan, 1968. See no. 115; *JRH*, ch. 1.

1969

19. "Elijah and the Empiricists." In *The Religious Situation*, edited by Donald Cutler, 841–68. Boston: Beacon Press, 1969. See *EJM*, ch. 2.
20. "Transcendence in Contemporary Culture: Philosophical Reflections and Jewish Testimony." In *Transcendence*, edited by H. W. Richardson and D. R. Cutler, 143–52. Boston: Beacon Press, 1969. See *JRH*, ch. 8.

1970

21. "The Commandment to Hope: A Response to Contemporary Jewish Experience." In *The Future of Hope*, edited by W. H. Capps, 68–91, 93, 99–101, 131–33. Philadelphia: Fortress Press, 1970.

22. "Jewish Existence and the Living God: The Religious Duty of Survival." In *Arguments and Doctrines*, edited by A. A. Cohen, 250–67. New York: Harper & Row, 1970. See no. 87; *QPF*, ch. 7.

23. "Jewish Faith and the Holocaust." In *Philosophy in the Age of Crisis*, edited by E. Kuykendall, 464–82. New York: Harper & Row, 1970. Translated into French and Hebrew. Reprint. *The Ways of Religion*, edited by Roger Eastman, 332–44. San Francisco: Canfield Press, 1970. See no. 119; *JRH*, ch. 3.

24. "Self-Realization and the Search for God: A Critique of Modern Humanism and a Defense of Jewish Supernaturalism." In *Arguments and Doctrines*, edited by A. A. Cohen, 225–49. New York: Harper & Row, 1970. See no. 66; *QPF*, ch. 2.

1971

25. "Demythologizing and Remythologizing in Jewish Experience: Reflections Inspired by Hegel's Philosophy." In *Myth and Philosophy: Proceedings of the American Catholic Philosophical Association*, Vol. 45, 16–27. Washington: The Catholic University of America, 1971. See *JRH*, ch. 9.

1973

26. "Canada: Perspectives." In *The Yom Kippur War—Israel and the Jewish People*, edited by Moshe Davis, 107–23. New York: Arno Press, 1973.

27. "Hegel and Judaism: A Flaw in the Hegelian Mediation." In *The Legacy of Hegel, Proceedings of the Marquette Hegel Symposium*, edited by J. J. O'Malley, K. W. Algozin, H. P. Kainz, and L. C. Rice, 161–85. The Hague: Nijhoff, 1973.

28. "The Human Condition After Auschwitz." In *Understanding Jewish Theology: Classical Issues & Modern Perspectives*, edited by Jacob Neusner, 165–75. New York: Ktav, 1973. See *QPF*, ch. 6.

29. "An Outline of a Modern Jewish Theology." In *Faith and Reason: Essays in Judaism*, edited by R. Gordis and R. Waxman, 211–20. New York: Ktav 1973. Also in *Understanding Jewish Theology: Classical Issues & Modern Perspectives*, edited by J. Neusner, 153–62. New York: Ktav, 1973. See no. 73; *QPF*, ch. 6.

1974

30. "The Holocaust and the State of Israel: Their Relation." In *Jewish Encyclopedia Yearbook*, 369–76. Jerusalem: Keter Press, 1974. Reprint. *Auschwitz: Beginning of a New Era?* edited by Eva Fleischner, 205–15. New York: Ktav-Cathedral-ADL, 1977. See *JRH*, ch. 17.

1975

31. Preface to *We Fight to Survive*, by Esther Sterner. Montreal: Jewish Institute of Higher Research, Vol. 12, 1975, vii–ix.

1977

32. "Post-Holocaust Anti-Jewishness, Jewish Identity, and the Centrality of Israel: An Essay in the Philosophy of History." In *World Jewry and the State of Israel*, edited by Moshe Davis, 11–31. New York: Arno Press, 1977. See *JRH*, ch. 14.

33. "The Voice of Auschwitz." In *Modern Jewish Thought: A Source Reader*, edited by Nahum N. Glatzer, 188–96. New York: Schocken Books, 1977. See *GPH*, ch. 3. Translated into German.

1978

34. "*Holocaust: A Symposium.*" Mimeographed record of a symposium held at Syracuse University in 1966, for limited distribution.

35. "Midrashic Existence After the Holocaust: Reflections Occasioned by the Work of Elie Wiesel." In *Confronting the Holocaust: The Impact of Elie Wiesel*, edited by Alvin H. Rosenfeld and Irving Greenberg, 99–116. Bloomington: Indiana University Press, 1978. See *JRH*, ch. 16.

1979

36. Preface to *The Jewish Emergence from Powerlessness*, by Y. Bauer. Toronto: University of Toronto Press, 1979.

1980

37. "New Hearts and the Old Covenant: On Some Possibilities of a Fraternal Jewish Christian Reading of the Jewish Bible Today." In *The Divine Helmsman*, edited by James L. Crenshaw and Samuel Sandmel, 191–205. New York: Ktav, 1980.

1982

38. *1982 Theology Roundtable: Theodicy: When Bad Things Happen to Good People*, Rabbi Harold Kushner, Dr. Emil Fackenheim, and Rabbi Walter Wurzburger. New York: A Publication of the 92nd Street Y, 1982.

39. "The Renewal of the Zionist Impulse." In *Toward a Zionist Renaissance*, edited by G. Wigoder, 32–39. Jerusalem, 1982. See no. 162.

1984

40. "The Study of Contemporary Jewry." In *Contemporary Jewry: Studies in Honor of Moshe Davis*, edited by G. Wigoder, 247–57. Jerusalem, 1984.

1985

41. "The Holocaust as an Unprecedented Event in History, Philosophy and Theology." In *A Handbook of Jewish Theology*, edited by A. A. Cohen and P. Mendes-Flohr. New York: Scribners. See no. 164.

42. "Immanuel Kant." In *Nineteenth Century Religious Thought in the West*, edited by Ninian Smart, John Clayton, Steven Katz, and Patrick Sherry, Vol. 1, 17–40. Cambridge: Cambridge University Press, 1985.

1986

43. "Philosophical Reflections on Antisemitism." In *Antisemitism in the Contemporary World*, edited by Michael Curtis, 21–38. Boulder and London: Westview Press, 1986.

Articles, Reviews, and Occasional Publications

1941

44. "A Communication on Kierkegaard." *Philosophy* 16 (1941): 334–35.

1943

45. "The Conception of Substance in the Philosophy of the Ikhwan as-Safä (Brethren of Purity)." *Mediaeval Studies* 5 (1943): 115–22.

1945

46. "A Treatise on Love" by Ibn Sina, tran. from the Arabic with introduction and notes by E. Fackenheim, *Mediaeval Studies* 7 (1945): 208–88.

1947

47. "The Possibility of the Universe in al-Farabi, Ibn Sina, and Maimonides." *Proceedings of the American Academy for Jewish Research* 16 (1947): 39–70.

48. Review of *The Politics of Aristotle*, by E. Barker. *Review of Metaphysics* 1 no. 1 (1947): 93–108.

49. Review of *Philo*, by H. A. Wolfson. *Review of Metaphysics* 1 no. 2 (1947): 89–106.

1948

50. "Can We Believe in Judaism Religiously?" *Commentary* 6 (1948): 521–27. See *QPF*, ch. 3.

1949

51. Review of *Judaism: A Way of Life*, by S. Cohon. *Commentary* 8 (1949): 302–4.

1950

52. "The Modern Jew's Path to God." *Commentary* 9 (1950): 450–57.

53. Review of *Being and Some Philosophers*, by E. Gilson. *University of Toronto Quarterly* 19 (1950): 300–1.

54. Review of *The Prophetic Faith*, by Martin Buber. *Commentary* 9 (1950): 393–95.

1951

55. "Al-Farabi, His Life, Times and Thought." *Middle Eastern Affairs*, 2 (1951): 53–59.

56. "Can There Be Judaism without Revelation?" *Commentary* 12 (1951): 563–72. See *QPF*, ch. 4.
57. Review of *The Legacy of Maimonides*, by B. Bokser. *Commentary* 11 (1951): 106–7.

1952

58. Review of *Choose Life, the Biblical Call to Revolt*, by E. Gutkind. *Commentary* 14 (1952): 191–92.
59. A Note on *The Doctrine of Being in the Aristotelian Metaphysics*, by J. Owens. *University of Toronto Quarterly* XXI (1952): 296.
60. Review of *The Great Jewish Books*, edited by S. Caplan and H. Ribalov. *Commentary* 14 (1952): 505–8.
61. "Ibn Sina: The Man and His Work." *Middle Eastern Affairs* 3 (1952): 1–17.
62. "Judaism and the 'Lost' Intellectuals." *The Jewish Forum* (1952): 131–32.
63. Review of *Judaism and Modern Man: An Interpretation of Jewish Religion*, by Will Herberg. *Judaism* 1 (1952): 172–76.
64. Review of *Man Is Not Alone: A Philosophy of Religion*, by A. J. Heschel. *Judaism* 1 (1952): 85–89.
65. "Schelling's Philosophy of Religion." *University of Toronto Quarterly* 22 (1952): 1–17.
66. "Self-Realization and the Search for God: A Critique of Modern Humanism and a Defense of Jewish Supernaturalism." *Judaism* 1 (1952): 291–306. Translated into Hebrew.
67. "Shapers of the Modern Outlook, the Metaphysics of A. N. Whitehead." *The Canadian Forum* 32 (1952): 199–200.

1953

68. Review of *Franz Rosenzweig, His Life and Thought*, by Nachum Glatzer. *Judaism* 2 (1953): 367–72.
69. "Jewish Optimism and the Twentieth Century." *The Reconstructionist* 19 (1953): 22–25.
70. "Needed: A New Theology." *American Judaism* 3 (1953): 4–5.

1954

71. Review of *Israel and Palestine: The History of an Idea*, by Martin Buber. *Jewish Quarterly Review* 45 (1954): 170–74.
72. "Kant and Radical Evil." *University of Toronto Quarterly* 23 (1954): 339–53.
73. "Outline of a Modern Jewish Theology." *Judaism* 3 (1954): 241–50. See no. 28.
74. "Schelling's Conception of a Positive Philosophy." *The Review of Metaphysics* 7 (1954): 563–82. Translated into German.
75. "Schelling's Philosophy of the Literary Arts." *The Philosophical Quarterly* 4 (1954): 310–26.

1955

76. Review of *Conservative Judaism: An American Religious Movement*, by Marshall Sklare. *Historia Judaica* 17 (1955): 143–46.
77. "Judaism and the Idea of Progress." *Judaism* 4 (1955): 124–31. See *QPF*, ch. 5.

1956

78. "The Current Religious Revival: Is it Genuine?" *The Canadian Forum* 35 (1956): 269–70.
79. Review of *End of an Exile*, by J. Parkes. *Conservative Judaism* 10 (1956): pp. 53–54.
80. "How a Philosopher Bought a Car." *The Canadian Forum* 34 (1956): 150–53.
81. "Judaism, Christianity and Reinhold Niebuhr." *Judaism* 5 (1956): 316–24.
82. Review of *Judaism for the Modern Age*, by Robert Gordis. *Christian Century* 73 (1956): 145.
83. Review of *On Jewish Learning* by Franz Rosenzweig. *Judaism* 5 (1956): 277–79.

1957

84. "Kant's Concept of History." *Kantstudien* 48 (1957):381–98.
85. Review of *Lessing's Theological Writings*, translated with introduction by Henry Chadwick. *Canadian Journal of Theology* 3 (1957): 199–200.

1958

86. "Liberalism and Reform Judaism." *CCAR Journal* 21 (1958): 1–7.

1959

87. "Jewish Existence and the Living God." *Commentary* 28 (1959): 128–36. See nos. 2, 22.
88. Review of *Johannes Climacus, or De omnibus dubitandum est*, and *A Sermon*, by Soren Kierke-

gaard, translated with an assessment by T. H. Croxall. *Canadian Journal of Theology* 5 (1959): 281–82.

89. "A New Linguistic Approach to the Philosophy of Religion." *CCAR Journal* 24 (1959): 61–64, 69.

90. "Some Recent 'Rationalistic' Reactions to the New Jewish Theology." *CCAR Journal* 26 (1959): 42–48.

91. "Some Recent Works by and on Martin Buber." *Religious Education* 14 (1959): 413–17.

1960

92. "A Critique of Reconstructionism." *CCAR Journal* 7 (1960): 51–56.

93. "The Dilemma of Liberal Judaism." *Commentary* 30 (1960): 301–10. Also in *Contact* 1 (1961): 25–34. See no. 11.

94. Review of *God in Search of Man*, by A. J. Heschel. *Conservative Judaism* 15 (1960): 50–53.

95. Review of *Hegel: A Re-Examination* by J. N. Findlay. *Philosophical Review* 49 (1960): 544–48.

1961

96. "Apologia for a Confirmation Text." *Commentary* 31 (1961): 401–10. See *QPF*, ch. 9.

97. "More on Reconstructionist Theology." *CCAR Journal* 8 (1961): 39–43.

98. Reply to a letter from J. Agus. Parts 1, 2. *Conservative Judaism* 15 (1961): 42–44, 16: 59–60.

99. "Two Types of Reform: Reflections Occasioned by Hasidism." *Central Conference of American Rabbis Yearbook* 71 (Philadelphia 1961): 208–23. See no. 3.

1962

100. "The God of Israel: Can the Modern Jew Believe in Revelation?" *Proceedings of National Hillel Summer Institute* (Washington 1962): 57–65. Mimeographed.

101. "Religious Responsibility for the Social Order." *CCAR Journal* 9 (1962): 3–6, 21. See no. 4.

102. Reply to a letter from J. Agus. *Conservative Judaism* 17 (1962): 84–86.

103. "Torah: Can the Modern Jew Live by Revelation?" *Proceedings of National Hillel Summer Institute* (Washington, 1962): 66–73. Mimeographed.

1963

104. "Human Freedom and Divine Power: Philosophical Reflections on a Religious Issue." *Judaism* 12 (1963): 338–43. See *QPF*, ch. 13.

105. "Kant and Judaism." *Commentary* 34 (1963): 460–67. See QPF, ch. 14.

1964

106. "On the Eclipse of God." *Commentary* 37 (June 1964): 55–60.

1965

107. "Judaism and the Meaning of Life." *Commentary* 39 (April 1965): 49–55. Translated into Spanish.

108. "Legislation against Hate Literature." *Viewpoints* 1 (1965): 15–17.

109. "Metaphysics, Historicity and Historicism." *The Personalist* 46 (1965): 45–51.

110. Reply to M. Stockhammer. "Responsibility and Freedom." *Judaism* 14 (1965): 237–38.

1966

111. "A Jew Looks at Secularist Liberalism and Christianity." *Cross Currents* 16 (1966): 41–53. See no. 9.

112. Contribution to "The State of Jewish Belief." *Commentary* 42 (August 1966): 87–89. See *QPF*, ch. 19.

113. A commentary delivered at the proceedings of an international seminar, March 23–25, 1966 on "Philosophy and Education: A Synoptic View," written by P. H. Phenix. The article by Phenix was published in *Philosophy and Education*. Toronto: Ontario Institute for Studies in Education, 1967.

1967

114. "Jewish Values in the Post-Holocaust Future: A Symposium." *Judaism* 16 (1967): 269–73, 289–90, 295–96. Also *Congress Bulletin* (March–April 1973): 6–7.

115. "Man and His World in the Perspective of Judaism." *Judaism* 16 (1967): 167–75. See no. 18.

116. "On the Self-Exposure of Faith to the Modern Secular World: Philosophical Reflections in the Light of Jewish Experience." *Daedalus* 96 (1967): 193–219. See no. 14.

117. "Salvation in Judaism." *Anglican Dialogue* V (1967): 4–5. Reprinted in *European Judaism* 2 (1967): 23–24. See *QPF*, ch. 10.

118. "The Transcendence and Historicity of Philosophical Truth." In *Proceedings of the 7th Inter-American Congress of Philosophy*. Proceedings held in Laval, Quebec in 1967. Vol. 1, 77–92.

1968

119. "Jewish Faith and the Holocaust: A Fragment." *Commentary* 46 (August 1968): 30–36. See no. 23.

1969

120. "Hermann Cohen—After Fifty Years." The Leo Baeck Memorial Lecture, New York, 1969.

121. "On Jewish Radicals and Radical Jews." *Hadassah Magazine* 50 (1969): 7–32. Abridged in *Jewish Digest* 15 (1970): 10–14. Translated into Hebrew.

122. "What Price Relevance? An Inter-Generational Dialogue." *Jewish Heritage* 12 (1969): 27–30.

123. "Why I Have Changed My Mind about Christians." *Ferment* 2 (1969): 8–11.

1970

124. Contribution to "The Response Symposium." *Response* (Winter, 1970–71): 31–33. (Contribution untitled.)

125. "Judaic Studies on the College Campus." *United Synagogue Review* 23 (1970): 14–15.

126. "On the Actuality of the Rational and the Rationality of the Actual." *Review of Metaphysics* 23 (1970): 690–98.

127. "The People Israel Lives." *The Christian Century* 87 (1970): 563–68. See *JRH*, ch. 4.

128. "Would Hegel Today Be a Hegelian?" *Dialogue* 9 (1970): 222–26.

1971

129. "Hegel." In *Encyclopedia Judaica*. New York: Macmillan, Vol. 8, (1971): 246–47.

130. "In Praise of Dual Loyalty." *The Chronicle Review* (August 1971): 375–78.

131. "Schelling." In *Encylopedia Judaica*. New York: Macmillan, Vol. 19, (1971): 953–54.

1972

132. *The Human Condition After Auschwitz: A Jewish Testimony a Generation After*. The R. G. Rudolph Lecture in Judaic Studies, Syracuse. In *Congress Bi-Weekly*, (April 28, 1972): 6–10; (May 19, 1972): 5–8. Translated into Hebrew.

1973

133. "The Survival of the Jews." *The Centre Magazine* (Nov–Dec. 1973): 15–28. Original title: "Jewish 'Ethnicity' in 'Mature Democratic Societies,' Ideology and Reality" in *JRH*, ch. 11.

1974

134. "Comment on N. Rotenstreich's *Sublimity and Messianism*." *Human Context* 6 (1974): 503–4.

135. "Martin Buber: Universal and Jewish Aspects of the I-Thou Philosophy." *Midstream* 20 (1974): 46–56.

136. "Mordecai Kaplan, a Critic's Tribute." *Sh'ma* 79 (October 18, 1974).

137. "The Ethics of Jewish Survival." *Masada* 6 (1975): 4–8.

1975

138. *From Bergen-Belsen to Jerusalem: Contemporary Implications of the Holocaust*. Jerusalem: Hebrew University Press, 1975. With responses by Arthur Morse, Piotr Rawicz, Manes Sperber, Alfred Kazin, and a rejoinder by the author. Originally a lecture delivered in Jerusalem, July 1970. Translated into English from the tapescript. See *JRH*, ch. 10.

139. "Israel and the Diaspora: Political Contingencies and Moral Necessities, Or The Shofar of Rabbi Yitzhak of Piotrokov." *The Yaacov Herzog Memorial Lecture* delivered at McGill University, Montreal, November 27, 1974. Jerusalem: Jerusalem Post Press, (1975). See *JRH*, ch. 13.

140. "The Nazi Holocaust as a Persisting Trauma for the non-Jewish Mind." *Journal of the History of Ideas* 36 (1975): 369–76. Translated into Hebrew and French. See *JRH*, ch. 6.

141. "Sachsenhausen 1938: Groundwork for Auschwitz." *Midstream* 21 (1975): 27. See *JRH*, ch. 5.

1976

142. "Aliyah and Lesser Reflections." *Masada* 7 (1976): 4.
143. "The Jewish People Return to History." In *Zionism: The Attack in the United Nations and the Future of the Jewish People*. New York, CJFWF 1976.
144. "The Theo-Political Predicament in the Contemporary West: Reflections in the Light of Jewish Experience." *Religious Education* 71 (1976): 267–78. See *JRH*, ch. 12.

1977

145. "Authentic and Unauthentic Responses to the Holocaust." In *The Solomon Goldman Lectures*, Vol. 1, 65–85. Chicago: Spertus College Press, 1977.
146. "Israel's Survival." *Tradition* 16 (1977): 177–78.
147. "The Jewish People Return to History." *Masada* 8 (1977): 5–9.
148. "On the Life, Death and Transfiguration of Martyrdom: Divine Image in Our Time." *Communio* 4 (1977): 19–35. Translated into Hebrew. See *JRH*, ch. 15.
149. "This Year in Israel." *Weekend Magazine* 27 (1977): 13–16.

1978

150. "Philosophy and Jewish Existence in the Present Age." *Da'at* 1 (1978): 5–28.

1979

151. "Jerusalem 'Above' and Jerusalem 'Below': A Jewish View," *Face to Face* 7 (1979): 32–33.
152. Reply to T. Rockmore. On *The Religious Dimension in Hegel's Thought*. In *Independent Journal of Philosophy* 3 (1979): 60.

1980

153. "What the Holocaust Is Not." *Face to Face* 8 (Winter 1979–80): 8–9.
154. Contribution to Symposium on "Prospects for Zionism in the Eighties." *Midstream* 2 (May 1980): 22–23.

1981

155. "On Yiddish: Some Home Thoughts from Abroad." *Viewpoints* 12, no. 2 (Fall 1981): 47–49.

1982

156. "The Renewal of the Zionist Impulse: 1". *Zionist Ideas* 4 (1982): 5–13.
157. "The Renewal of the Zionist Impulse: 2." *Zionist Ideas* 5 (1982): 17.
158. "The Spectrum of Resistance during the Holocaust: An Essay in Description and Definition." *Modern Judaism* 2 (1982): 113–30.

1983

159. "The Jewish National Identity, pt. 2: Diaspora and Nation: The Contemporary Situation. Symposium." *Forum*, (Winter 1983–84), no. 50:1–11.
160. "The Jewish National Identity, pt. 2: Diaspora and Nation: The Contemporary Situation. Symposium. Response." *Forum*, (Winter 1983–84), no. 50:26–27.
161. "The Renewal of the Zionist Impulse." *Forum*, (Spring 1983), no. 48:17–24.

1985

162. "The Holocaust and Philosophy." *Journal of Philosophy* 82 (October 1985): 505–14.
163. "The Holocaust as an Unprecedented Event in History, Philosophy and Theology." *Da'at* (Summer 1985): 123–27. (In Hebrew.)
164. "Leo Strauss and Modern Judaism." *The Claremont Review of Books* 4 (Winter 1985): 21–23.
165. "Reflections on Aliyah." *Midstream* (August–September 1985): 25–28. Translated into Hebrew.
166. "Return to Berlin: An Epitaph for German Judaism." *Moment* (April 1985): 55–59.

1986

167. "Concerning Authentic and Unauthentic Responses to the Holocaust." *Holocaust and Genocide Studies* 1, no. 1 (1986): 101–20.

Index

Raba, 57n.28
Rachel, 223–33, 233n.4
Rashi, 24, 228, 233n.10
Rauschning, Hermann, 198n.1, 279–80
Ravensbrück, 149, 225, 230
Reagan, Ronald, 365
Red Sea, 207–22
Reichstag, 360
Religious faith, crisis of, 102–10
Remnant, accidental, 195, 201, 301–2, 340, 344–45
Resistance, 117
Response, revelation and, 94–96
Responsibility, 54–55
Revelation, 21–25, 34–36, 62–63, 67, 69–83, 83nn.5, 8, 84nn.14, 23, 85–100, 100nn.3, 26, 101nn.41, 44, 49
Revelation, Noahide, 72
Ricoeur, Paul, 205n.6
Robinson, Jacob, 150n.13
Rockwell, Norman Lincoln, 279
Root experience, 208–20
Rosenzweig, Franz, 34, 35, 59–64, 100n.18, 113, 118n.15, 196, 202, 204, 228, 236, 243, 245, 265, 337–40, 350, 351, 362, 363
Roy, Ralph Lord, 285n.9
Rubenstein, Richard, 126, 181n.2, 198, 206n.21
Ruether, Rosemary, 253n.11, 268n.17, 274, 275–76, 285n.4
Rufus, 316, 318, 321n.10
Rumbula, 282
Russell, Bertrand, 108
Rylaarsdam, J. Coert, 237, 240n.3, 247

Saadia Gaon, 346n.17
Sachs, Nelly, 182n.31
Sachsenhausen, 8, 113, 119–24, 145, 241–42, 281, 320, 352–53, 355, 357, 366
Sadat, Anwar, 281
Salaspils, 282
Salvation, 211–12, 214
Sandmel, Samuel, 229, 233n.13
Sartre, Jean-Paul, 67, 205n.9, 259, 268n.7, 272–73, 276, 285n.2, 298–99, 325, 326
Saud, King of Saudi Arabia, 283, 375n.2
Schechter, Solomon, 57n.6
Schelling, 33, 59, 63–64, 64n.1, 87, 101n.48, 143–44, 144n.13, 196, 343, 368
Schindler, P., 189n.8, 234n.26
Schleiermacher, F. D. E., 45, 56nn.3, 4
Scholem, Gershom, 188nn.5, 6, 189n.8, 225, 350, 363
Scholl, Inge, 329n.1
Schwarzschild, Steven, 272

Science and faith, 91, 103–5
Seder, Passover, 210–11
Sereny, Gitta, 151n.20
70 C.E., destruction of, 186, 218–20, 301, 316
Shammai, 315–16
Shapiro, or Rabbi of Korno, 292–93
Shapiro, Rabbi Israel of Grodzisk, 290–91
Shema, 316, 321n.10, 371
Sherbrooke, Quebec, 354–55
Shim'on Bar Yohai, R., 57, 216n.14
Shim'on Ben Azzai, R., 315, 321n.6
Shim'on Ben Gamliel, R., 219
Shulchan Aruch, 24
Sinai, 23, 70–71, 211–18
Six Day War, 14, 113, 161, 165–67, 177, 232–33, 238–39, 268n.16, 280–81, 369–71
Skepticism, 39–40, 41n.4
Socrates, 328
Solzhenitsyn, A. I. 150n.6, 322n.16
Soviet Union, 256, 282, 318–19, 356–60
Spengler, Oswald, 40n.40
Sperber, Manès, 169, 181–82n.14, 294n.5
Spiegel, Shalom, 181n.7
Spinoza, Baruch, 34, 188n.2, 337–38, 350
S.S., 121–22, 129–33, 134n.11, 366–68
Stangl, Franz, 136–37, 149, 151n.20, 279
Stendahl, Krister, 284
Stern, M., 268n.12
Stoehr, Martin, 355–56, 358
Strauss, Leo, 131, 274, 360
Streicher, Julius, 137, 141, 143, 191, 263, 299
Subjectivist reductionism, 106–10, 173
Suhl, Yuri, 182n.30
Suicide, 147–48
Survivors, 319–21
Swarsensky, Manfred, 359

Talmid Hakham, 304
Terrorists, 319
Teshuvah, 328, 337–45
Theophrastus, 261, 275
Tikkun Hatzut, 186, 225
Tikkun Olam, 15, 116–17, 184–88, 244–45, 328–29, 337–45
Tillich, Ernst, 241–42, 254n.22
Tillion, Germaine, 151n.18, 233n.16
Toronto, Ontario, 355
Toronto, University of, 355
Torture, 145–46
Toynbee, Arnold, 282
Tradition, Biblical and rabbinic, 47–51
Tragic, 52–55
Treblinka, 136–38, 140–44, 290–91

Emil L. Fackenheim was Professor of Philosophy at the University of Toronto. Besides his books on philosophy, he has published many articles and reviews in major philosophical and theological journals. He is currently Fellow of the Institute of Contemporary Jewry at the Hebrew University in Jerusalem and teaches at the Overseas School. He was awarded the Irving and Bertha Neuman Distinguished Scholarship of the International Center for University Teaching of Jewish Civilization for 1985–86.

Michael L. Morgan is Associate Professor of Philosophy and Jewish Studies at Indiana University, Bloomington, Indiana. He has published widely on both ancient Greek and modern Jewish philosophy.

The manuscript was prepared for publication by Irene Bintz and Kathryn Wildfong. The book was designed by Joanne Kinney. The typeface for the text and display is Trump. The book is printed on 60-lb. Glatfelter natural smooth and bound in Joanna Western Mills' Arrestox.

Manufactured in the United States of America.